FORGOTTEN
VICTORY

FIRST CANADIAN ARMY
AND THE CRUEL WINTER OF 1944-45

MARK ZUEHLKE

FORGOTTEN
VICTORY

Douglas & McIntyre

DOUGLAS AND MCINTYRE (2013) LTD.
P.O. Box 219, Madeira Park, BC, V0N 2H0
www.douglas-mcintyre.com

Editing by Kathy Vanderlinden
Cover typesetting by Shed Simas
Typesetting by Diane Robertson
Cover photographs: top: Colin Campbell McDougall, LAC PA–159561
bottom: Michael M. Dean photo, LAC PA–168908
Maps by C. Stuart Daniel/Starshell Maps
Photos used by permission of Library and Archives Canada
Printed on 100% PCW
Printed and bound in Canada

BRITISH COLUMBIA
ARTS COUNCIL
An agency of the Province of British Columbia

Canada Council   Conseil des Arts
for the Arts   du Canada

Douglas and McIntyre (2013) Ltd. acknowledges the support of the Canada Council for
the Arts, which last year invested $157 million to bring the arts to Canadians
throughout the country. We also gratefully acknowledge financial support from the
Government of Canada through the Canada Book Fund and from the Province of
British Columbia through the BC Arts Council and the Book Publishing Tax Credit.

CATALOGUING INFORMATION AVAILABLE FROM
LIBRARY AND ARCHIVES CANADA
ISBN 978-1-77162-041-3 (cloth)
ISBN 978-1-77162-105-2 (paper)
ISBN 978-1-77162-042-0 (ebook)

THE CANADIAN BATTLE SERIES*

———————

Tragedy at Dieppe: Operation Jubilee, August 19, 1942

*Breakout from Juno: First Canadian Army and the Normandy Campaign,
July 4–August 21, 1944*

*On to Victory: The Canadian Liberation of the Netherlands,
March 23–May 5, 1945*

*Operation Husky: The Canadian Invasion of Sicily,
July 10–August 7, 1943*

*Terrible Victory: First Canadian Army and the Scheldt Estuary
Campaign, September 13–November 6, 1944*

Holding Juno: Canada's Heroic Defence of the D-Day Beaches, June 7–12, 1944

Juno Beach: Canada's D-Day Victory, June 6, 1944

The Gothic Line: Canada's Month of Hell in World War II Italy

The Liri Valley: Canada's World War II Breakthrough to Rome

Ortona: Canada's Epic World War II Battle

OTHER MILITARY HISTORY BOOKS BY MARK ZUEHLKE

———————

*The Canadian Military Atlas: Four Centuries of Conflict from
New France to Kosovo* (with C. Stuart Daniel)*

*Brave Battalion: The Remarkable Saga of the 16th Battalion
(Canadian Scottish) in the First World War*

The Gallant Cause: Canadians in the Spanish Civil War, 1936–1939

For Honour's Sake: The War of 1812 and the Brokering of an Uneasy Peace

Ortona Street Fight

Assault on Juno

*Available from Douglas & McIntyre

Keep going, Alf. All they've got is rifles and machine guns.

—*Major Fred Tilston, Essex Scottish Regiment*

The Hochwald left no good memories. It was a horror.

—*Private Charles "Chic" Goodman, South Saskatchewan Regiment*

You really hunker down and pray to God that you come out of it all right, because you can't do anything for anyone.

—*Major C.K. Crummer, Lincoln and Welland Regiment*

When will it all end? The idiocy and the tension, the dying of young men?

—*Lieutenant Donald Albert Pearce, Highland Light Infantry Regiment*

[CONTENTS]

PREFACE

T HE WINTER OF 1944-45 was the worst northwest Europe had experienced in fifty years. For the Allied and German troops facing each other along the European fronts from the North Sea to Switzerland, conducting combat operations was gruelling. Many soldiers who endured that long, cruel winter remembered it as the worst of their lives. Despite the dreadful conditions, the war raged on. In First Canadian Army's sector extending across the breadth of Holland, rivers separated it from the opposing Germans. Later to be known as the Winter on the Maas, this was a time of intense patrolling, of fighting small, nameless skirmishes and the occasional larger action to achieve limited objectives. While soldiers endured, their generals planned. No plan called for First Canadian Army to break through the Germans facing them and liberate Holland by direct assault. Instead, eyes fixed eastward toward Germany's Rhineland on the west bank of that great river. It was here that the final destruction of what remained of Germany's elite divisions would occur. And First Canadian Army would be the destroyer.

On February 8, 1945, Operation Veritable opened the last great Canadian offensive of the war. The battle raged for thirty-one days. Horrendous weather conditions rendered the bloody fighting all the more bitter. When the last shots were fired on March 10, the way was open for the final advances that would carry the Allies to victory. First Canadian Army had won one of the war's most decisive victories.

So it is surprising that the Rhineland Campaign figures little in the national memory of World War II. It has, in fact, been largely forgotten—generally consigned to a couple of short chapters in books surveying the course of Canada's full participation in the war. *Forgotten Victory* is intended to redress this historical oversight.

When I find that little has been written about a battle or campaign, my first thought is that there must be little historical record to draw upon. Inevitably, this proves not to be the case. In various archives, I found thousands of pages of relevant documents—operational plans, reports, personal accounts—an almost overwhelming bounty of riches about the Rhineland Campaign. I was also fortunate to find numerous interviews of veterans involved and to be able to interview several personally. Not as many as in past books. The veterans are passing away at a frightful rate, and for many their memories are not so clear these days.

At the end of the Battle of Midway in the Pacific Theatre of World War II, *Chicago Daily News* reporter Robert Casey wrote: "This was a cataclysm observed by tens of thousands of eyes and yet a spectacle no man saw. Hundreds of men brought back their little bits of it—bits that sometimes fitted together and sometimes didn't—to make the mosaic in which we may one day see the picture of what happened."

The Rhineland Campaign was a similar mosaic—one that involved well over 100,000 Canadian and British soldiers. All retained their individual memories of it. Most of the time, it was possible to take those "little bits" of memory and fit them together, weaving them in with the official documents and other records to accurately render the mosaic. Where conflicts remained, I sought to examine and compare every relevant piece of information to get as close to the truth as possible. Like the other volumes of the Canadian Battle Series, *Forgotten Victory* honours those thousands who left their native land to fight a war that was far away and not of their making.

ACKNOWLEDGEMENTS

WORK ON EACH Canadian Battle Series title brings me into contact with acquaintances new and old who contribute in one form or another. On the veteran front, I was privileged to again interview Charles Goodman about his experiences as a very young soldier in the Rhineland. By phone, I got to know Stuart Johns over the course of several interviews. Although he was not present, Regina Rifles veteran J. Walter Keith gathered material from other veterans and from regimental records that helped greatly with creating a clear account of this regiment's experience in Moyland Wood and other parts of the Rhineland fighting.

Ken MacLeod again shared various transcripts and recordings of the large collection of veteran interviews he has collected over the years.

In Holland, Marco Cillessen spent several days guiding me around the Rhineland battlefield. I would never have found many important locations without his invaluable assistance. He also shared much of his extensive knowledge of the battles.

Also in Holland, my invaluable colleague Johan van Doorn once again contributed a vast number of research files that saved me many hours of scouring archives to duplicate the work he had already completed. Johan's understanding of the operations of the winter of 1944–45, particularly those of the Winter on the Maas, greatly informed this book.

Carol Reid at the Canadian War Museum's archives provided me with several interviews and documents I would otherwise have missed. Staff at the Directorate of Heritage and History, Department of National Defence, were as always helpful and informative. Despite horrendous spending cutbacks at Library and Archives Canada, staff . there were as courteous and willing to assist as always. The University of Victoria Libraries Special Collections now has most of the Military Oral History Collection available in downloadable, digital form, an excellent boon for historians. But the collection also has many other documents that were equally important, and staff there helped me access these.

Research for and writing of this book were greatly assisted by a British Columbia Arts Council grant.

During the course of the writing of this book, the financial stability of my long-term publisher, Douglas & McIntyre Publishers Inc., collapsed and the company teetered on the edge of bankruptcy. Thankfully, a last-minute rescue occurred, and new owners have affirmed their belief in the importance of the Canadian Battle Series to our national collective memory. So we go forward into the future with renewed confidence. My agent, Carolyn Swayze, kept a stalwart hand on the tiller of the business side of my writing career during these troubles.

Once again, Kathy Vanderlinden undertook the challenging job of editing one of these complex titles. And C. Stuart Daniel of Starshell Maps again provided those so-necessary maps.

I can never sufficiently thank my partner, Frances Backhouse, for her unending support for my spending a career bringing the stories of our World War II veterans to life for modern readers. We have tramped countless battlefields together, spent endless hours talking about war and old warriors, and found moments of peace in each other's company.

Map 1

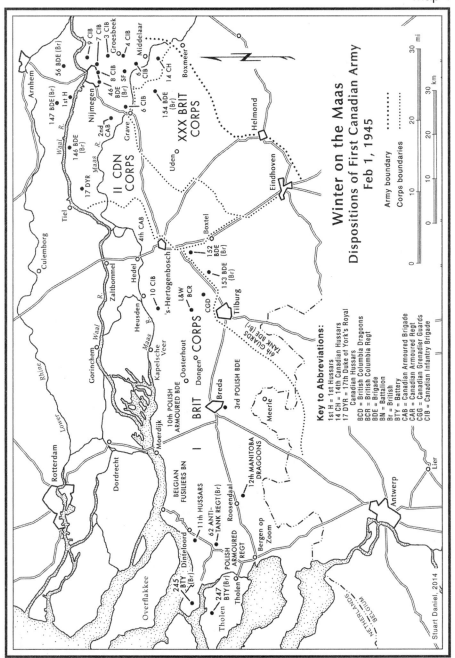

Winter on the Maas
Dispositions of First Canadian Army
Feb 1, 1945

Army boundary ....
Corps boundaries ----------

Key to Abbreviations:
1st H = 1st Hussars
14 CH = 14th Canadian Hussars
17 DYR = 17th Duke of York's Royal
Canadian Hussars
BCD = British Columbia Dragoons
BCR = British Columbia Regt
BDE = Brigade
BN = Battalion
Br = British
BTY = Battery
CAB = Canadian Armoured Brigade
CAR = Canadian Armoured Regt
CGG = Canadian Grenadier Guards
CIB = Canadian Infantry Brigade

Stuart Daniel, 2014

Map 2

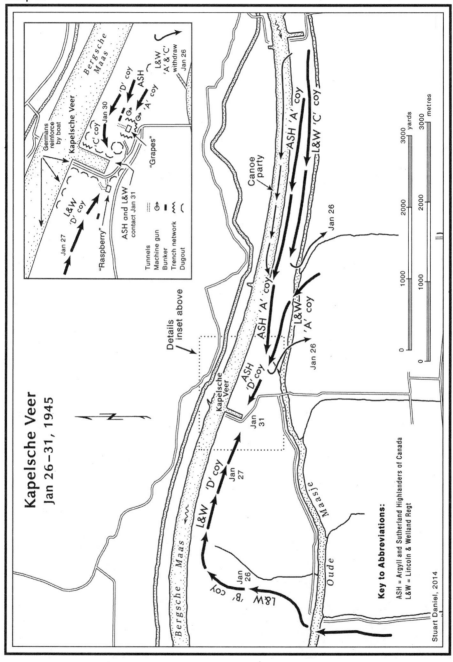

Kapelsche Veer
Jan 26–31, 1945

Key to Abbreviations:

ASH = Argyll and Sutherland Highlanders of Canada
L&W = Lincoln & Welland Regt

Stuart Daniel, 2014

Map 3

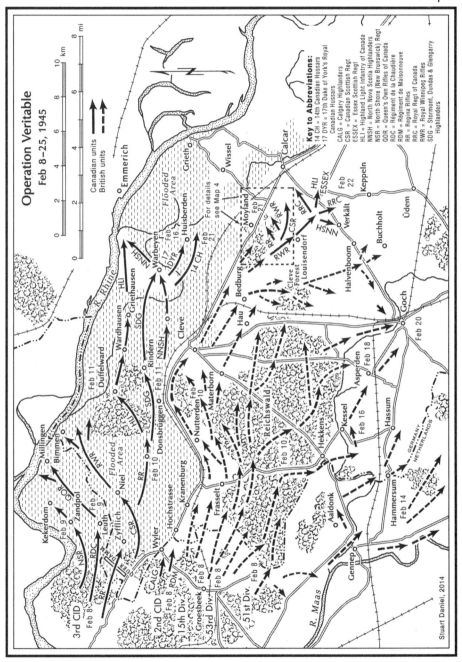

Operation Veritable
Feb 8–25, 1945

Canadian units
British units

Key to Abbreviations:
14 CH = 14th Canadian Hussars
17 DYR = 17th Duke of York's Royal
Canadian Hussars
CALG = Calgary Highlanders
CSR = Canadian Scottish Regt
ESSEX = Essex Scottish Regt
HLI = Highland Light Infantry of Canada
NNSH = North Nova Scotia Highlanders
NSR = North Shore (New Brunswick) Regt
QOR = Queen's Own Rifles of Canada
RDC = Régiment de Maisonneuve
RDM = Regiment de la Chaudière
RR = Regina Rifles
RRC = Royal Regt of Canada
RWR = Royal Winnipeg Rifles
SDG = Stormont, Dundas & Glengarry
Highlanders

Stuart Daniel, 2014

Map 4

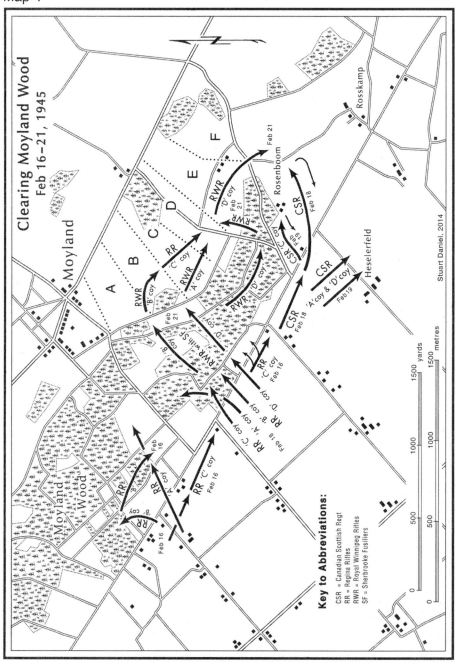

Clearing Moyland Wood
Feb 16–21, 1945

Moyland

Moyland Wood

Rosskamp

Rosenboom

Heselerfeld

Stuart Daniel. 2014

Key to Abbreviations:

CSR = Canadian Scottish Regt
RR = Regina Rifles
RWR = Royal Winnipeg Rifles
SF = Sherbrooke Fusiliers

Map 5

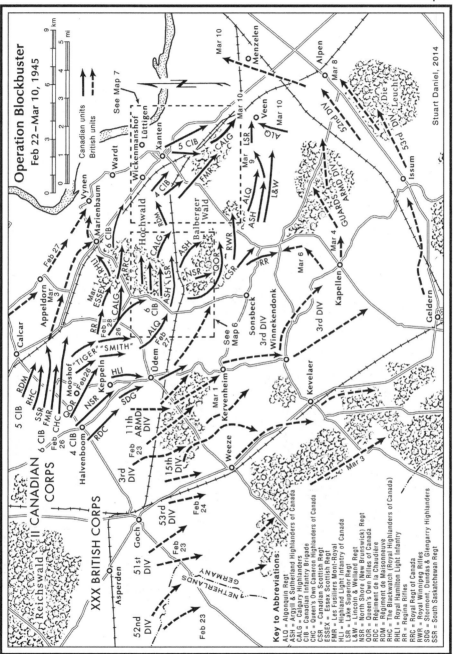

Operation Blockbuster
Feb 22–Mar 10, 1945

Canadian units
British units

Stuart Daniel, 2014

II CANADIAN CORPS

XXX BRITISH CORPS

Key to Abbreviations:
ALQ = Algonquin Regt
ASH = Argyll & Sutherland Highlanders of Canada
CALG = Calgary Highlanders
CIB = Canadian Infantry Brigade
CHC = Queen's Own Cameron Highlanders of Canada
CSR = Canadian Scottish Regt
ESSEX = Essex Scottish Regt
FMR = Les Fusiliers Mont-Royal
HLI = Highland Light Infantry of Canada
L&W = Lincoln & Welland Regt
LSR = Lake Superior Regt
NSR = North Shore (New Brunswick) Regt
QOR = Queen's Own Rifles of Canada
RDC = Régiment de la Chaudière
RDM = Régiment de Maisonneuve
RHC = The Blackwatch (Royal Highlanders of Canada)
RHLI = Royal Hamilton Light Infantry
RR = Regina Rifles
RRC = Royal Regt of Canada
RWR = Royal Winnipeg Rifles
SDG = Stormont, Dundas & Glengarry Highlanders
SSR = South Saskatchewan Regt

Map 6

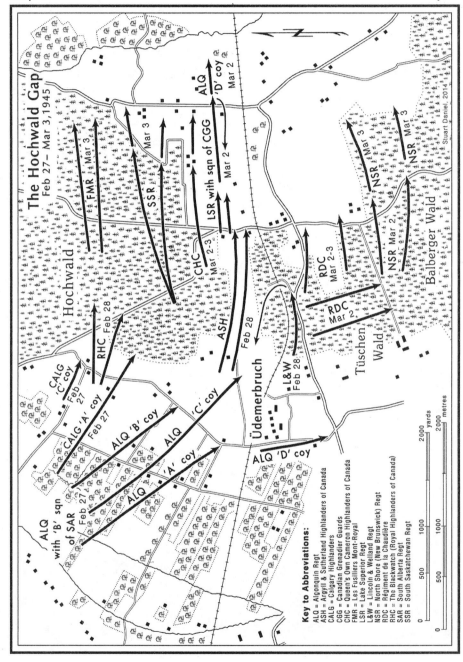

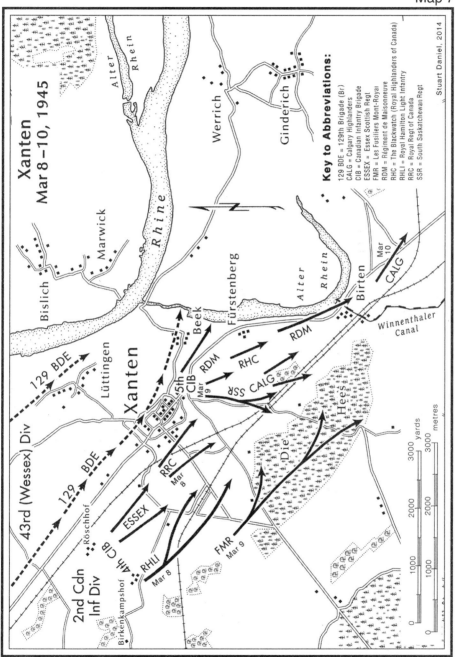

Map 7

Xanten
Mar 8–10, 1945

Stuart Daniel, 2014

Key to Abbreviations:

129 BDE = 129th Brigade (Br)
CALG = Calgary Highlanders
CIB = Canadian Infantry Brigade
ESSEX = Essex Scottish Regt
FMR = Les Fusiliers Mont-Royal
RDM = Régiment de Maisonneuve
RHC = The Blackwatch (Royal Highlanders of Canada)
RHLI = Royal Hamilton Light Infantry
RRC = Royal Regt of Canada
SSR = South Saskatchewan Regt

Ginderich

Werrich

Alter Rhein

Rhein

Alter Rhein

Bislich

Marwick

Rhine

Beek

Fürstenberg

Birten

Mar 10

CALG

Winnenthaler
Canal

Lüttingen

Xanten

129 BDE

129 BDE

43rd (Wessex) Div

Röschhof

CIB RDM

5th
Mar
9

RHC

RDM

SSR CALG

Die Hees

2nd Cdn
Inf Div

4th CIB

RRC
Mar
8

ESSEX

RHLI
Mar 8

FMR
Mar 9

Birkenkampshof

3000 yards

3000 metres

2000

2000 metres

1000

1000

Do the Job

OPERATION MARKET GARDEN was to have won the war. In mid-September 1944, a column of British armoured divisions would barrel boldly up a narrow sixty-four-mile stretch of highway from just south of the Dutch city of Eindhoven to gain Arnhem's bridges and cross the Nederrijn (Lower Rhine). To speed xxx British Corps along, three airborne divisions would drop ahead to seize vital bridges over rivers and canals. The plan was for a "rapid and violent [advance] without regard to what was happening on the flanks." The offensive would end with the industrial Ruhr surrounded and a launch pad provided to overrun the rest of western Germany and bring a final victory.[1]

But things had gone drastically wrong. By nightfall on September 26, nobody on the Allied side of the Nederrijn even knew how many of the ten thousand 1st British Airborne Division soldiers were still alive. They only knew that of the men of 2nd Para, 1st Parachute Brigade, who had parachuted in on September 17 to seize two Arn-hem bridges, only about seven hundred had managed to advance from the landing zones as far as the road bridge. Unforeseen and determined German resistance had trapped the rest of the division inside a quickly shrinking bridgehead centred on the village of Heveadorp, near the outskirts of Oosterbeek and west of Arnhem. Reinforcement attempts—first by the 1st Polish Independent

Parachute Brigade and later by the 4th Battalion (4th Dorsets) of 43rd (Wessex) Infantry Division's Dorsetshire Regiment—had merely left more men trapped across the river.

Hourly, the German stranglehold tightened. Inevitably, those inside the bridgehead must surrender or die fighting. The same fate awaited the paratroopers of the division's 2nd Para, cut off in Arnhem close to the highway bridge. Facing diverse elements of 9th ss Panzer Division and other German units rushed to the scene from Germany, the men of 2nd Para had vainly tried to gain control of the bridge, only to be driven back finally into the city streets. Remnants of the battalion still fought on, but they died for no purpose. Via the bridge, the great Allied column was to have relieved the paratroopers. Had they won the bridge and allowed the column to cross the Nederrijn, Market Garden would have been a stunning success. But by the time the column gained the river, it was far too late and the German grip on the bridge proved too strong to break.

Things had started well on September 17. The U.S. 101st Airborne Division, dropping closest to xxx British Corps, secured the area between Veghel and Zon. At the same time, U.S. 82nd Airborne Division landed between the rivers Maas and Waal—as the Rhine is known in the Netherlands—to seize a crossing at Nijmegen. The 1st British Airborne Division, meanwhile, touched down west of Arnhem and hurried toward the rail and road bridges. When the Germans promptly blew the rail bridge with pre-set explosives, Market Garden's fate hinged on winning the road bridge.

Field Marshal Bernard Law Montgomery's scheme had relied on clockwork timing, but delay piled on delay. By the afternoon of September 19, the British in Arnhem were fighting grimly to sustain a toehold on the Arnhem road bridge against counterattacks by tanks and grenadiers from ss units. The armoured column, meanwhile, had stalled before the Nijmegen road and rail bridges, while American paratroopers and more ss Panzer Division troops slugged it out in a vicious melee. By the morning of September 20, the Americans controlled both bridges, and tanks of the Irish Guards rolled—only to crunch into more heavy German defensive positions. The advance slowed to a snail's pace. Operation Market Garden was in tatters.

Heroic efforts finally established a narrow link to the Nederrijn on September 22. That night, an attempt to ferry Polish paratroopers over the river succeeded in passing across only fifty men aboard an ad hoc flotilla of yellow rubber dinghies before German machine guns zeroed in on the crossing point. Over the next two nights, ferry operations succeeded in adding just five hundred more Poles and British troops to the shrinking bridgehead. The narrow corridor stretching through to Arnhem was itself vulnerable and regularly severed by German attacks from the flanks. On September 26, xxx Corps commander Lieutenant General Brian Horrocks declared the situation hopeless. He ordered that a rescue attempt be made that very night to bring out the troops still trapped across the Nederrijn.[2]

The 43rd (Wessex) Division held the ground facing the river. Lieutenant Colonel Mark Henniker, the division's chief engineer, took responsibility. Two Canadian officers—Major Mike Tucker commanding 23rd Field Company and Major A.W. Jones of 20th Field Company—attended Henniker's first briefing at 1000 hours. Officers commanding the British 553rd and 260th Field Companies were also present. The Canadians were to assist the British engineers and be under their command.[3]

But upon returning to 23rd Field Company's base in Nijmegen, Tucker warned his subordinate officers that in fact it was falling to them to "do the job" with their large motorized stormboats. The inadequately equipped British engineers could at best play a supporting role.[4]

Henniker had offered little intelligence. Nobody knew how many men required rescue, and "only a general idea of the area from which we were to operate could be suggested. It was definitely established that we should use stormboats," Tucker later wrote, "and that we should count only on our own resources for the off-loading and carrying of the stormboats to the launching sites." The slow-talking, fire-plug-shaped Montreal engineer made it his first priority to determine an advanced marshalling area near the river.

Accompanied by reconnaissance officer Lieutenant Russell Kennedy, Tucker drove to Valburg. The roads were typically Dutch—raised high above adjacent flat fields and separated from them by "wide, deep ditches." They were "narrow, with soft shoulders and totally unsuited to heavy military traffic. Entrances to fields [were] also narrow and difficult to negotiate, even in daytime when clear vision may be had." Tucker decided that the village's rail-yard parking lot would suffice for a marshalling area, and a nearby tree-lined side street with "a reasonably wide verge" could "accommodate the bridging vehicles."

On his return to Nijmegen, Tucker got the company rolling. With information on the "scheme...so limited that no plan for the operation could be formed at this time," Tucker wanted his men and equipment in position before nightfall. He reduced the convoy to three jeeps, two wireless-equipped scout cars, two kitchen trucks, and twelve three-ton trucks. Many of the 23rd's 258 men and much equipment remained behind. When the column set out at 1400 hours, a similar formation from 20th Field Company joined it. Also tying in were 10th Canadian Field Park Company trucks carrying the stormboats and one three-ton truck with twelve fitters from this company's Engine and Boat Maintenance Section. There were also two padres in jeeps.

"The column was very carefully controlled," Tucker wrote, since the route was perilous. "The roads were narrow and winding and the corridor held by the troops was a narrow one. Many a vehicle, including a convoy of assault boats intended for [the 4th Dorsets reinforcement effort] the previous night, have missed a turning and... driven straight into the enemy lines to be captured or destroyed." Conditions were rendered more hazardous by incessant rain, which made the roads slippery and severely limited visibility. However, the convoy reached Valburg safely at 1545 hours.[5]

WHILE THE CONVOY was under way, Lieutenant Kennedy and No. 2 Platoon's Lieutenant Bob Tate scoured the river for prospective crossing points. Having just concluded two days' attachment to 43rd Division's 104th Field Company, Kennedy already knew the ground.[6] A good thing, as the 5th Dorsets Battalion troops guarding the river refused to let the men venture beyond the high winter dyke they were using for cover. They warned that the ground beyond was under German observation and any movement drew unwelcome fire. Kennedy and Tate were only allowed to briefly raise their heads above the edge of the dyke for quick glimpses of the river.

Kennedy decided this peekaboo game sufficed to reveal a sobering, even discouraging, reality. Across the water, low-lying hills allowed the Germans to completely dominate the river.[7] The winter dyke, about twenty feet high and with a south bank "sloping to about 45 degrees," stood about a thousand feet from the river.[8] The dyke was not flat on top but concave, with a gentle slope over about two hundred feet to a lower but still steep second berm. About three hundred feet distant stood the summer dyke, which was about half as high and less steep. It also had a concave top. The dykes posed hellish obstacles over which the engineers would have to manhandle stormboats and engines. Between the dykes lay four hundred yards of open ground.[9]

Of the possible crossing points, one adjacent to a large apple orchard south of the winter dyke provided the best cover. The trucks could approach via a muddy lane separated by a ditch from the orchard. If the ditch were then bridged, the trucks could go right up to the dyke.[10] Another point farther west and close to Driel was also identified for use by 20th Field Company.

Kennedy and Tate caught up to Tucker at an Orders Group that Henniker had called for 1700 hours. As they briefed their commander on their findings, Henniker allowed that these were the exact two crossing points his engineers preferred.[11]

The two Canadian companies had thirty-six stormboats available. Normally these boats were loaded on trucks three apiece, which made them difficult to unload quickly and quietly. Consequently, the boats and trucks were to be "loaded tactically." This meant ten trucks each carried one boat and one motor for quick dispersal. Five trucks continued to carry three boats, but the motors were unloaded and stacked six apiece on three other trucks. This resulted in eighteen trucks bearing twenty-five boats and twenty-eight engines. A later 43rd Wessex report claimed that the "remaining boats and engines [were] dumped for lack of transport, though this was NOT the CRE's [Henniker's] intention."[12]

Tucker had no idea of Henniker's intention. He understood that 23rd Field Company was to deploy only fourteen stormboats and seventeen motors.[13] Major Jones, meanwhile, thought his 20th Field Company need provide just eight stormboats. Further written instructions from Henniker read that upon reaching the assembly area, "four boats [were] to be unloaded complete with motors, gear, etc. At this point two boats were to be carried immediately to river bank in time to start ferrying at 2130 hours." The other two boats would be brought up thereafter. As to the remaining four stormboats, no instruction for their use was given. Jones considered the 20th limited to using the first four boats in the rescue attempt.[14]

For 43rd Division's engineers, the plan was becoming increasingly confused. Some reported that the division possessed only sixteen assault boats because of losses suffered the previous night, while others counted thirty-two. Meanwhile, forty German assault boats had surfaced in Nijmegen and were sent to them in two twenty-lot consignments. The first consignment was delivered to 30th Brigade's headquarters, five miles south of the launch sites, at 1815 hours. The second allotment was reportedly going to be brought up after dark, along with four newly found British assault boats. Operating beside the 20th would be 553rd Field Company, Royal Engineers, and the 23rd would work alongside the 260th Field Company. Each British company would muster sixteen assault boats, some German and some their own.[15]

To prevent the Germans from detecting that a rescue was under way, all the division's artillery and machine-gun units along with xxx Corps's medium artillery would unleash a barrage at 2100 hours. As a feint, the division's 129th Infantry Brigade would conduct a diversionary assault crossing near Heteren, three miles downstream. Divisional anti-aircraft guns would also fire tracer rounds across the river at a steady rate to demarcate the flanks of the actual crossing areas and help orient the engineers operating the boats. The first boat crossing was set for 2130 hours.[16] In the 20th's sector, Jones understood he was to deploy two stormboats at that time, and his British counterparts would send across "as many assault boats as available." These would "pick up evacuees and return to the near bank and continue crossing at hourly intervals thereafter." At 0400 hours on the morning of September 26, smoke generators would project a screening cloud that would be maintained until the rescue effort was complete.[17]

What seemed like a fairly developed plan was in fact greatly lacking. Although the two groups of engineers were but 1,500 yards apart and on opposite ends of a gentle convex curve in the river, there was no coordination. There were no wireless links to allow Tucker and Jones to communicate, nor were the British engineers so equipped. The two groups would work in isolation.

Tucker was disturbed by the lack of hard intelligence. Henniker could only say that he "believed that the centre of the bridgehead held by the airborne troops was directly across the river from the site to which we were being directed." There was also still "no indication of the number of troops which we might be required to bring off, but orders were that we should continue until the beach was cleared." Tucker's first boats were to launch at 2140 hours.[18]

Kennedy confessed to an uneasy sense that the generals didn't expect them to "bring out many survivors."[19] Even with Kennedy and Tate's earlier reconnaissance work, Tucker thought it "unlikely we could get up to our site in time." He ordered Tate to rush ahead with a section of No. 2 Platoon to bridge the ditch between the orchard and the lane. Tate's men moved out at 1845. The Engine and Boat Maintenance Section was divided between the two field companies, while the Protestant padre went to 20th Field Company and the Roman Catholic padre stayed with Tucker. This prompted Tucker to jokingly note that the two companies were separated not only logistically but also along religious lines.[20]

The main convoy moved at 1915 hours. It was an "intensely dark" night. Heavy rain was "accompanied by a bitter wind." Tucker welcomed the foul weather. He thought it likely his men would suffer fewer "casualties than...had the night been clear and fine." A man was dropped at each intersection to prevent vehicles from straying. As the convoy drew closer to the river, the Germans must have detected movement. Flares arced into the sky, and artillery began shelling the road. The shots were so inaccurate that they appeared to be fired on pre-set lines rather than at identified targets. One shell landed close enough that a piece of shrapnel struck Sapper J.W. Black in the elbow, temporarily paralyzing his arm but not penetrating flesh or breaking bone. A few minutes later, the supporting artillery and machine-gun barrage started up, and the German fire slackened.

When 20th Field Company's vehicles veered off to proceed to their launching site, three trucks carrying personnel from the 23rd followed. Tucker was unable to send a vehicle to retrieve them. The road was so narrow that even a jeep could not squeeze past the wide, lumbering trucks carrying stormboats. Heading back to find the lost vehicles and men would have to wait until the convoy arrived at the orchard deployment area. Then, just as the convoy closed on the orchard, one boat-carrying truck skidded slightly off the road and became stuck. Extracting it further delayed going back to retrieve the lost group.

It was 2010 hours, with the first boat due to launch in ninety minutes, so Tucker decided to deploy all personnel still with the convoy without maintaining platoon cohesion. Non-commissioned officers cobbled together random groups and set them to various tasks. Tucker decided this ad hoc approach would not detract from the company's efficiency, as "everyone was quick to respond to orders given by the man in charge."

Kennedy oversaw unloading the stormboats and having them carried five hundred yards to the river. Lieutenants Jack Cronyn and James Russell "Russ" Martin laid white tape to mark the route. The establishment of an advance petrol dump and Forward Aid Post fell to Lieutenant Tate. The beach consisted of two small bays, the western one being about twenty yards wide and the eastern one sixty yards. A groin of rock intended to prevent erosion of the summer dyke projected thirty yards into the river between the bays. It was decided to launch the boats in the small bay and use the groin and larger bay as a harbour for the craft. Cronyn was the beach master, and Martin took the first boat to the "far bank to determine the situation there."[21]

BRITISH ENGINEERS GENERALLY disliked stormboats, despite having designed them. Constructed of plywood and weighing about nine hundred pounds, they were six and a half feet wide and twenty feet long. Each boat could carry a jeep, a 6-pound anti-tank gun, or twelve to sixteen soldiers, depending on equipment load. Both bow and stern were square. A narrow bench ran along either side. The boat was powered by a rear-mounted Evinrude fifty-horsepower outboard motor.[22] Lacking a weather cover, these engines were notoriously unreliable in the rain. Because rain had been falling for most of the day and was forecast to continue through the night, Tucker foresaw lots of shorting electrical circuitry and malfunctioning spark plugs. But the Engine and Boat Maintenance men were to quickly repair disabled engines or replace them with spares.

As the 23rd's sappers unloaded the stormboats, the maintenance section tested each engine behind the protective cover of the winter dyke. After the fuel tank was filled with the correct mixture of gas and oil, each motor was mounted on a stormboat. The boat was then carried to the river. Once all boats were away, spare parts and replacement engines were gathered up and carried by the maintenance section to the beach, where an ad hoc repair depot was established.[23]

Getting the boats to the beach proved torturous. About sixteen men tackled each boat, packing them when possible and dragging them as necessary over the rough, muddy ground. The rain had drenched the soil under the grass, so when the men started scaling the dykes, they had scant purchase. They slid backwards, despite trying to gouge out rough steps. The slopes quickly became "a slippery mess which lent no footing whatsoever. Hand ropes were fixed, but even with these the going was extremely difficult."

Descending the dykes proved equally hard. The men carrying the first stormboat lost their footing, and the boat skidded free across the rough ground. When it was launched ten minutes ahead of schedule, at 2130 hours, water gushed through a hole torn in its hull. It was dragged ashore and abandoned.[24]

FIFTEEN HUNDRED YARDS to the east, 20th Field Company had faced a similar trial. The darkness proved impenetrable, and Major Jones had to use a compass as he strung white tape from the unloading area to the beach.[25] Behind him, his men encountered even more obstacles than had 23rd Field Company. Here, a twelve-foot-wide road with a wire fence on either side topped the winter dyke. With machine-gun bullets zipping around him, Sapper Harry Dacker Thicks strode up to the first fence. Lacking wire cutters, he bent each strand with his hands until it finally broke. Having cleared the wire away, he wrenched one of the stout iron posts out of the ground to create a path wide enough for the carrying crews. He then joined the first boat party and helped get it to the river. For his actions, he was awarded a Military Medal.[26]

The beach was under "incessant machine-gun fire from three enemy posts on the far bank directly opposite the site." It seemed the Germans were firing blind along fixed lines, which led Jones and the 553rd Royal Engineers commander to agree not to start the stormboat motors for fear of betraying their position. Flames from a large factory burning at Heveadorp illuminated the beach area with a dull glow that also increased the chances of discovery. Rather than mounting an all-out evacuation effort, they decided to reconnoitre for landing spots on the opposite shore by sending a single assault boat across. Even then, when the British engineering party carrying the boat began to descend the summer dyke to take it to the river, they immediately attracted German fire. But it was wildly inaccurate, most of the bullets flying harmlessly overhead.

British assault boats were foldable, with a wooden bottom and canvas sides held in place by locking struts. They were just under seventeen feet long and five and a half feet wide, and weighed about 350 pounds.[27] Each could carry ten to sixteen men and was normally paddled by a two-man crew. Because of the strong current here, the British engineers deployed six to eight men to paddle each boat.[28]

The single assault boat launched at 2130 hours. Despite the fire spraying the river, it soon gained the other bank. The paddlers found only two 4th Dorset soldiers, whom they brought back to safety. No other personnel remained on the opposite bank, the soldiers said.

Intense German fire and a growing sense of futility slowed the rescue effort here to a sluggish pace. A second assault boat was not launched until 2330 hours. No one was found to rescue. Meanwhile, a platoon section of 4th Dorsets paddled up to the beach aboard an assault boat they had found abandoned on the north bank. They also reported there were no further personnel awaiting evacuation.

The rate of fire striking the beach kept intensifying. Then, at 0100 hours, mortar rounds, which Jones believed were British, saturated the beach. Everybody was driven to cover and remained there for an hour, as one concentration of mortar rounds followed another. When the fire finally lifted, the crew of the first assault boat pushed off again and returned with two stragglers. At 0300 hours, further evacuation efforts here were abandoned.

Thirty minutes later, Jones received orders to send four stormboats upriver fifteen hundred yards to join 23rd Field Company. A mortar round struck the first boat launched and it immediately sank. Although a second boat got away, it quickly came under drenching machine-gun fire, which forced the crew to land and take cover while still only halfway to their destination. When the fire eased, they tried to continue, only to have the motor stall. Giving up, the crew abandoned the boat and waded through hip-deep mud to safety. Dawn was breaking and Jones saw no point in risking further boat crews, as "the enemy had us pinpointed with machine-gun fire and it [was] not likely that either of these boats could have been launched successfully." This evacuation was formally closed by divisional headquarters minutes later. Just forty-eight 4th Dorsets—most escaping on their own—passed through the evacuation point. Given the company's inability to successfully launch any stormboats, Jones declared their use "when in close contact with the enemy" impractical.[29]

THE 23RD FIELD company, meanwhile, was proving Jones wrong. At 2145 hours, Lieutenant Russ Martin and a crew of four sappers launched the 23rd's second boat. Martin, twenty-seven, and Lieutenant Kennedy, a year older, were fast friends. They had both attended Queen's University's engineering program, Martin graduating in 1940 and Kennedy the following year, but hadn't known each other then. They met on October 1, 1941, at a Toronto recruiting centre and were both assigned to engineer training, from which they were posted to the 23rd Field Company.[30]

German artillery, mortar, and machine-gun fire had intensified. Several machine guns fired on fixed lines, bullets sweeping the river and both shorelines. This potentially devastating fire, Major

Tucker saw, consistently snickered harmlessly overhead, but mortar and 88-millimetre artillery fire "fell everywhere." A particular threat came from a mortar sited inside the bridgehead. Eventually, however, it fell silent. Tucker assumed that some paratroopers had "cleaned it up."

As soon as Martin's boat pushed off, darkness swallowed it. A short time later, two sappers reported seeing the boat "break apart and sink as the result of a direct mortar hit." They were less certain when Tucker pressed them, admitting that the "visibility was very bad." Tucker decided he must continue sending boats across the river and hope that some made it.

Martin's stormboat had been missing for about fifty minutes when Corporal James McLachlan helmed the next boat out. Twenty minutes later, another set off with Corporal S.F. Smith and two sappers aboard. McLachlan's boat should have returned by then and Tucker's hopes were ebbing fast. Then it emerged from the darkness. The boat was crammed with wounded soldiers. Most were stretcher cases, so their loading had been slow. Roman Catholic Padre Mongeon mustered a stretcher party. Lacking real stretchers, the engineers improvised, using greatcoats and other clothing. All available additional greatcoats and other dry clothing were given to paratroopers "in desperate need of cover from the elements. Caring for all of these casualties proved a great drain on the manpower of the [company] and prevented adequate reliefs for the boat carrying parties and boat crews." Although there was a Royal Army Medical Corps aid post a short distance behind the river, it had only enough staff to provide medical care for the four engineer companies. No thought had been given to aiding injured paratroopers.

The moment his boat was unloaded, McLachlan set off again. He and his crew would make fifteen crossings. Hereafter, a new boat was launched every twenty minutes, until by 0330 hours all fourteen boats save the one holed earlier were afloat.

Smith, meanwhile, had taken a full load of paratroopers aboard, and during the return crossing, a mortar round falling close by capsized it. A non-swimmer, Smith used his greatcoat as a quasi lifejacket and floated to the south bank. Four paratroopers also reached safety. The other passengers and two sappers were presumed drowned.

Through the early morning hours of September 27, the 23rd's personnel laboured ceaselessly. Other than Martin's boat and the one piloted by Smith, none were sunk on the river. But enemy fire slowly took its toll, and several were so riddled with holes that they had to be abandoned ashore. The same fate befell others damaged by submerged obstacles. Initially, Tucker tried to record the causes of boat losses and to count men rescued, but the rain turned writing paper to pulp. The operation fell into chaos. Boats came and went as fast as possible. Some landed well outside the designated beach sectors. Stalled motors left other boats adrift until they struck the southern bank. The engineers found it ever more difficult to regulate the numbers of men boarding boats. "Men panicked and stormed onto boats, in some cases capsizing them. In many cases they had to be beaten off or threatened with shooting to avoid having the boats swamped," Tucker wrote. "With the approach of dawn this condition became worse. They were so afraid daylight would force us to cease our ferrying before they would be rescued."

Daylight exposed those boats still operating to aimed German fire. The machine guns on the high ground overlooking the bridgehead "rained a murderous hail of bullets...but the downward angle of the fire was much less effective than it would have been had the guns been in position to make more horizontal sweeps." On the south bank, four engineers were wounded. Several snipers on this side of the river were active until some rescued paratroopers formed a fighting squad and "proceeded to liquidate them."[31]

Soon after dawn, the rescue attempt began to run out of steam. Tucker estimated he had just two operational boats left. Kennedy, meanwhile, had walked downstream seeking some sign of his friend Martin's boat and crew. Happening upon an abandoned stormboat, he managed to start its engine. Kennedy motored upstream to the evacuation beach. Lance Corporal H.D. Gillis and Sapper D.J. McCready volunteered to form his crew.

They soon approached a crowd of frantic men. As they piled aboard, Kennedy drew his pistol, but realized he could never fire it. He holstered the gun as the boat sank under their weight. That sobered the paratroopers, who helped the engineers lift the boat out of the water and prepare it for launching. The motor was waterlogged and useless. Taking on a reasonable load, Kennedy promised to return. Using two paddles and some rifle butts, the men paddled for the southern bank. Although carried well downstream, the boat reached safety. Nearby, Kennedy discovered another derelict storm-boat with a functioning motor. His men also found a canvas assault boat, evidently abandoned by 260th Field Company. Kennedy, Gillis, and McCready decided to tie all three boats together. With Kennedy manning the motor and his two-man crew using paddles to keep the boats aligned, they managed to gain the northern bank. It was full daylight, but the paratroopers were patiently waiting in a tidy line. All three boats returned to the south bank fully loaded.

Kennedy wanted to make another run. Gillis said this would be tempting fate for a man like himself, the father of a young child. But McCready agreed, so the two set out with Kennedy's boat towing the other. This time, they were greeted by a desperate rabble, all semblance of order having again evaporated. Kennedy resorted to punching men to prevent them from overwhelming the boats.

The motor stalled as they started back. While Kennedy frantically tried to restart it, paratroopers on McCready's boat cut its tether and began paddling with rifle butts for the other side. Swept helplessly downriver by the current, the boat came into the sights of German machine guns. The men aboard dived overboard and tried to swim to safety. Only four, including Sapper McCready, who suffered a flesh wound, succeeded.

Kennedy finally got his motor running. The packed boat's bow was mere inches above the waterline. Knowing full power would create a wash that would sink them, Kennedy puttered along as if he were on a holiday outing. Bullets kicked up waterspouts alongside, but none struck home. Not far from shore, a sniper round slammed into a man literally jammed under Kennedy's elbow. The paratrooper jerked and went still. Seconds later, the boat touched down and everybody piled out, leaving Kennedy alone with the dead paratrooper. It was 0720 hours. The beach was deserted. Kennedy realized that Tucker had closed the rescue operation. He staggered off the boat, clawed his way up the summer dyke, and stumbled down the other side. A jeep driven by Lieutenant Jack Cronyn drew up. Cronyn offered Kennedy a swig of rum. Knowing he was so exhausted the liquor would knock him right out, Kennedy refused.[32]

Kennedy and McCready's last foray marked the end of the evacuation. Lieutenant Colonel Hennicker had, in fact, ordered Tucker at 0545 hours to shut things down. The 23rd Field Company had carried out approximately 150 crossings, with Tucker estimating average loads of 16 men in each. Some boats had carried significantly more during a crossing and one only 6. Kennedy's last effort likely brought back 125 men. Tucker thought his engineers had rescued some 2,400 to 2,500 men.[33] Henniker put the total number rescued, including Poles and 4th Dorsets, at 2,800.

The close-knit 23rd Field Company had suffered losses, but under the circumstances they were surprisingly light. Martin and his crew were never found, and the two sappers in Corporal Smith's boat were also listed as missing and presumed dead. Five other men suffered wounds. The survivors knew one thing—they had rescued most of those who escaped the Arnhem bridgehead.[34] As the company's war diarist put it, the operation had been "one of which every member of this unit may well be proud."[35] Without them, it would have ended in tragedy.

The evacuation also ended Operation Market Garden. And this closure set in motion a series of events that would lead to First Canadian Army's launching the first major Northwest Europe Allied offensive of 1945, which would be known as the Rhineland Campaign.

PART ONE

WINTER ON THE MAAS

NOVEMBER 9, 1944–FEBRUARY 7, 1945

The Most Important Bit of Ground

<hr/>

HE FAILURE OF Operation Market Garden crushed Allied
dreams of winning the war before Christmas 1944. It also left
them wrong-footed. As one officer on First Canadian Army's staff
observed, Field Marshal Bernard Montgomery's "single-minded pur-
suit of this elusive victory [was] largely instrumental in producing
just the kind of strategic situation that he was most insistent should
always be guarded against, namely getting the Allied forces 'out of
balance.'" In September, virtually every bullet, drop of fuel, tin of
food, and fresh recruit still came to the European mainland via the
Normandy beaches captured on June 6. All this had to then be transported hundreds of miles to the advancing armies.[1]

The Allies desperately needed a large, serviceable port close to
the front lines. Ironically, xxx British Corps had won the best candidate of all—Antwerp, Belgium—on September 4. But this port was
useless until the seventy-five-mile-long Scheldt Estuary, running
from Antwerp to the sea, was under Allied control. Despite the critical need for a major port, however, Montgomery and Supreme
Headquarters, Allied Expeditionary Force (SHAEF) commander
General Dwight D. Eisenhower decided to take a calculated risk and
not immediately try to wrest the Scheldt from German hands. They
would instead gamble on getting over the Rhine and bringing the
war to a quick end in Germany.[2]

As Montgomery shifted British Second Army eastward for Market Garden on September 12, he passed the task of clearing the estuary and securing the ground north of Antwerp to First Canadian Army, but only as its "last priority." His instructions to General Harry Crerar emphasized that this task was only to be embarked upon after the army's current tasks—namely, isolating and capturing the French channel ports of Boulogne, Dunkirk, Calais, and Le Havre—were completed. Each had been transformed into a fortress, with garrisons under orders from Adolf Hitler to hold to the last man. Reducing them had required sieges that left First Canadian Army badly extended and scattered along the length of the French and Belgian coasts. This meant that Crerar had too few troops to both conclude these tasks and simultaneously open the Scheldt Estuary.[3]

Thus the ensuing campaign started sluggishly, with First Canadian Army divisions fed in piecemeal. Clearing the estuary mired the involved Canadian, British, and Polish troops in a costly operation that ran from September 13 to November 6. At approximately 15,000 casualties, victory came at a terrible price. Between October 1 and November 8 alone, First Canadian Army recorded 703 officers and 12,170 other ranks killed, wounded, or missing. Of these, 355 officers and 6,012 other ranks were Canadians.[4] The Germans were badly mauled, losing 41,043 as prisoners. While Allied intelligence staff never determined how many enemy were killed or wounded, one Dutch historian later meticulously combed German records and arrived at 4,079 dead and approximately 16,000 wounded here between September 14 and November 8.[5] After the estuary was cleared of mines, the port was finally opened to Allied freighters on November 28.[6]

By then, First Canadian Army had moved to the river the Dutch called the Maas and the French the Meuse, which flows along a 575-mile course from its headwaters in France on the Langres plateau, through Belgium and Holland, to drain into the North Sea. The Canadians held a long, straggling 140-mile frontage that extended from the Nijmegen Salient to Walcheren Island on the north shore of the Scheldt Estuary. Encompassed within was the southern quarter of Holland and about 20 per cent of its population. These Dutch were delighted by their freedom from German occupation, despite the "extensive damage to property, utilities and services, and an almost complete paralysis of local economy" caused by the fight to liberate them.

Many towns and villages, a Canadian analysis reported, had been severely battered, while the rural area had suffered "widespread destruction of farm buildings, livestock and crops. Far more serious, however, was the almost universal destruction of road and rail bridges, the blocking of canals, and the destruction of or damage to the intricate system of locks. As the retreating enemy had seized all available vehicles, this situation involved the complete disruption of normal transport and internal distributive services. Thus, while food stuffs were dangerously low throughout the zone, the comparative plenty in a few districts could not be made readily available to the more needy. Further, the distribution of the considerable food stocks assembled by the Allied armies against the liberation was similarly impeded, and the daily ration fell from the average of 1,700 calories maintained during the last months of the German occupation to less than 1,000 for the first month of the liberation." Coal, which the Dutch depended on for generating electricity, was also in short supply. This worsened living conditions as winter deepened.

In some areas, dykes had been breached during the fighting. Resultant flooding rendered some areas unlivable, killed masses of livestock, and led to much loss of human life. Hardest hit was Walcheren Island, deliberately flooded by the Allies to cripple its extensive German defences. Eighty per cent of the island was submerged, and the two largest and fortunately unaffected communities there—Middelburg and Vlissing—were almost overwhelmed by refugees. Middelburg's population swelled from 18,000 to 42,000, and Vlissing's grew from 3,000 to 20,000.

"Inadequate nutrition and endemic illnesses—the spreading of which had been facilitated by overcrowding, mass evacuations, and the dislocation of water and sewage systems—had their effect in undermining the health of the two million people in the zone, while the sudden release of emotional strain which followed the liberation had left them exhausted and apathetic." On November 11, First Canadian Army's Civil Affairs unit assumed responsibility for overseeing all civilian administration and relief efforts.[7]

Militarily, the Canadian sector was divided in two, with 1 British Corps, under Lieutenant General John Crocker, responsible for the majority of its length along the lower Maas from Maren, about five miles northeast of 's-Hertogenbosch, westward to the sea. Crocker had "the minimum strength necessary, maintaining a reserve of mobile and armoured troops in suitable positions to deal with any enemy attempts to cross the river." The armoured and mobile reserve was provided by 4th Canadian Armoured and 1st Polish Armoured divisions. This part of the front was expected to remain largely inactive—each side limiting offensive operations to aggressive patrolling and small assaults intended to improve local positions.[8] Facing Crocker's corps was the German Twenty-Fifth Army. Assessments by Oberbefehlshaber (Commander in Chief), West Generalfeldmarschall Gerd von Rundstedt considered its "forces available for the task...extremely scanty." Heeresgruppe H commander Generaloberst Kurt Student and the senior naval officer in Holland, Vizeadmiral Gustav Kleikamp, had wanted to shorten the lines here by abandoning the islands of Schouwen and Overflakkee, which lay south of the mouth of the Maas. The German front would then be entirely anchored behind the river. Hitler had rejected this idea on November 8. Instead, he ordered Von Rundstedt to strengthen the garrisons with "one fully combat-worthy reinforced battalion [supported by] corresponding flak and arty elements for each island."[9] This order only further reduced the combat ability of German forces opposing 1 British Corps.

The lack of German strength along this front suited Crerar because it allowed him to concentrate the bulk of 11 Canadian Corps in defence of a much shorter line. At the centre of this sector, and expected to be more active and contested, lay the pivotal Nijmegen Salient won during Market Garden. It provided "a base from which an attack could be launched against the northern flank of the German battle-line" on the Rhine's west bank. Alternatively, if the Germans withdrew to the river's east bank, "an assault could be made across the Neder Rijn to turn the more formidable obstacle of the Rhine itself."

Crerar understood that the Germans must recognize the salient's strategic importance "for our future purposes. It was a sensitive spot against which he might attack as a riposte to our offensive operations elsewhere, and required to be fully secured, particularly in the stretch between the Maas and the Rhine, and against all forms of attack."[10]

Crerar had only returned to First Canadian Army headquarters on November 7 after a long sick leave. On September 25, he had checked into No. 16 Canadian Hospital in St. Omer complaining of general exhaustion and severe bouts of dysentery. Doctors evacuated him to England to test for blood disorders, possibly anemia.[11] Crerar had consequently missed the Scheldt Estuary Campaign. Instead, Lieutenant General Guy Simonds had moved up from 11 Canadian Corps to command the army.

In the weeks prior to his medical evacuation, Crerar's leadership had been notably sluggish. Always a heavy smoker, he had started chain-smoking. Many headquarters staff felt the army was adrift and Crerar incapable of decisive action. General Staff Colonel George Edwin Beament recalled that at no time before September had the headquarters operated at "such a low ebb...because I think we were lacking in effective leadership."

While not a dynamic leader, Crerar had never previously been indecisive or lethargic. The fifty-five-year-old general had instead a reputation for being methodical, detail oriented, and hard-working. Having ascended the army command chain through a series of staff appointments to the pinnacle of First Canadian Army leadership, Crerar had a penchant for authoring lengthy and extensively detailed operational orders and directives. In Beament's estimation, he also oversaw headquarters planning meetings as if he were a staff college professor leading students in a tactical exercise, where discussion was extensive but results often sketchy.[12] This approach was anathema to Montgomery. For this and other reasons—which ultimately came down to a severe clash of personalities—Montgomery had little respect for Crerar. At various times since the Canadian Army had deployed in Normandy, Montgomery had manoeuvred, unsuccessfully, to have Crerar replaced, by either bringing in a British general or promoting Simonds.

A strict disciplinarian, Simonds possessed a certainty that bordered on egotism. He was Crerar's polar opposite. Tall and lean, with piercing grey-blue eyes, jet-black hair forming a little wave at the temple, and a precisely trimmed moustache, Simonds fit the stereotypical image of a British senior officer. His sentences were clipped and to the point. Born in England but raised in Victoria, British Columbia, Simonds had retained, or deliberately assumed, many British mannerisms and was an unapologetic anglophile. He also enjoyed the confidence of Montgomery, who considered him a worthy protegé.

For his part, Simonds clearly admired Montgomery and even sought to mirror his style of command—right down to wearing a black tanker's beret and dressing in a casual style that did not naturally suit him. This aping of Montgomery irritated Crerar, a stickler for proper dress and adherence to military protocol, and introduced just another element of friction between the two men. But one thing Simonds could never master was Montgomery's easy ability to inspire common soldiers. He was simply too cold and withdrawn. Sharply critical of others, he seemed never to doubt his own ability to see things clearly and make the right decisions. At forty-one, Simonds had had a meteoric rise from the rank of major at war's outbreak to lieutenant general and command of 11 Canadian Corps by January 1944. [13]

Montgomery had thought Crerar's illness a stroke of luck that might enable Simonds to permanently replace him. In early October, he told Canada's National Defence Minister, James Ralston, that Crerar was "adequate but not a ball of fire. Not in the same parish with [Simonds] as Army Commander." He followed up on October 18 with a cable to Chief of the Imperial Staff, General Sir Alan Brooke, suggesting that Canadian Military Headquarters in London should announce that Crerar was temporarily absent "on account of sickness...I do not know what progress Crerar is making but it is highly important that he should NOT repeat NOT return here until he is able to stand up to the rigours of a winter campaign in a damp and cold climate." Montgomery told Brooke he had already suggested that Ralston replace Crerar. "We have much dirty work ahead between now and January and only very hard and tough commanders will stand up to it." He urged Brooke to personally "investigate this matter and advise me as to the real form regarding Crerar's health and stamina."

Montgomery's machinations did not go unnoticed. Crerar responded by having two specialists report on his physical health. They provided a certificate declaring him "perfectly fit to resume his command." Montgomery was gravely disappointed. He was even more frustrated when the Canadian government promoted Crerar to full general on November 16, making him the first Canadian to hold that rank in the field. In another cable to Brooke, he urged that the promotion should clearly not give the impression that it was in "any way for distinguished service in the field...Would make things awkward here if latter meaning was conveyed."[14]

None of this improved Crerar's relationship with either Montgomery or Simonds. Crerar knew the two conspired against him, but he had prevailed, and there was nothing either could do to change that. Simonds reverted to II Canadian Corps command.

Happily for Simonds, Crerar grudgingly recognized his ability. Of his two corps commanders, he would choose Simonds over Crocker for any major operation. Simonds was accordingly given charge of the critical Nijmegen Salient, while Crocker got the longer but largely dormant line to the west.

Born in 1896, Crocker had served as a lieutenant during the Great War, garnering a Military Cross at the Third Battle of Ypres and a Distinguished Service Order in March 1918. The DSO citation stated that his heroism had been worthy of a Victoria Cross. In the inter-war years, he emerged as a key player in the establishment of the Royal Tank Corps and drafting its operational doctrine. Crocker's abilities so impressed Brooke, then commanding 1st Armoured Division, that he selected him for his "general staff officer, one." In April 1940, during the fighting in France, Brooke assigned Crocker command of 3rd Armoured Brigade. After France fell, he was promoted to major general and took the helm of the newly raised 6th Armoured Division. In September 1942, Crocker took command of IX Corps, leading it through the fighting in Tunisia until he was wounded on April 27, 1943. On August 1, Crocker headed up I

Corps—part of Montgomery's Twenty-First Army Group—and played a leading role in Operation Overlord, with the advance from the beaches to capture Caen.[15]

Montgomery tended to meddle in the decision-making process for senior appointments to ensure that they went to men who were part of his inner circle. But he accepted Crocker without apparent question. In the opening weeks of the invasion, the compact nature of the bridgehead in Normandy was such that Crocker oversaw the British–Canadian operations on the invasion's left flank. Not until July 23 did 1 British Corps come under First Canadian Army and Crerar's command. Although Crocker was noted for his mild temperament, the two clashed immediately. First, Crocker had been highly critical of 3rd Canadian Infantry Division's Major General Rod Keller and actively sought to have him sacked. Second, he refused to implement the first operational directive Crerar gave him. Ever ready to bristle at any sign that British officers considered themselves innately superior to Canadians, Crerar flew into a fury. He told Montgomery that Crocker, either for personal reasons or "because of the fact that I am Canadian...resented being placed under my command...[and showed] no tact nor desire to understand my views." He asked Montgomery to swap him for another British corps commander. Montgomery refused, but did give Crocker a mild dressing-down and directed him to be "a loyal subordinate." Thereafter, relations between Crerar and Crocker remained strained, though Crocker followed orders and avoided openly criticizing decisions.[16] At the same time, Crerar consigned Crocker and his corps to the role of supporting 11 Canadian Corps rather than serving as an equal partner. This relationship was reinforced after Crerar resumed command in November 1944. Crocker had meanwhile suffered a personal tragedy when his son, Wilfrid, was killed on October 20 while serving with the 5th Inniskilling Dragoon Guards in Holland. Learning of this while still in England, Crerar had written a sincere note of sympathy.[17] But he was also content to leave Crocker and his corps operating on the sidelines of an inactive front.

IN FACT, CRERAR expected First Canadian Army to pass the rest of 1944 without being "called upon for any large scale operations."

Crocker and Simonds were instead to keep "an eye on possible future requirements" by seizing "any opportunity to improve our present positions vis-a-vis the enemy, if such could be done without marked cost in casualties or material and to keep the enemy anxious, and guessing, concerning our immediate intentions in order that he will retain considerable forces facing" First Canadian Army.[18]

The Scheldt Estuary Campaign had ended with the western Allied armies deployed on a front extending from the Swiss border north through the western foothills of the Vosges mountain range in northeastern France, past the two German-held cities of Metz and Trier, and along the eastern frontiers of Luxembourg and Belgium. From Belgium the line passed through the Dutch provinces of Limburg and North Brabant to the Nijmegen Salient south of Arnhem, then west along the Waal River to the Maas and then the coast at Walcheren Island. This tremendously long line exceeded that of the Great War's western front. The U.S. Sixth Army Group held the most easterly portion, with its First French Army on the right and American Seventh Army to the left. The longer stretch in the centre fell to U.S. Twelfth Army Group with three armies—the Third Army on the right between Nancy and Thionville, First Army in the middle and responsible for the eastern Ardennes, and Ninth Army to the left in the Aachen sector. Twenty-First Army Group held the ground west of this to the sea, with British Second Army on the right and the Canadian Army the left.

Never during the last months of 1944 were operations along this sprawling front static. The Allies, especially the American army groups, pushed forward at various points, while the Germans conducted limited assaults to keep the situation fluid and unpredictable. Neither side could assume that any stretch of line was immune to becoming a flashpoint.

On paper, the Germans had sixty-four divisions organized in three army groups. Heeresgruppe (Army Group) G was responsible for the eastern sector. Its Nineteenth Army and Fifth Panzer Army defended the Vosges mountain region, and First Army held the Saar region in front of the vaunted Siegfried defensive line. Heeresgruppe B held the line west of here to just before the point where the Ruhr River flowed into the Maas at Roermond. It consisted of Seventh

Army, Fifth Panzer Army, Sixth Panzer Army, and Fifteenth Army. West of Roermond to the coast, Heeresgruppe H faced Twenty-First Army Group.[19] It was composed of Twenty-Fifth Army and First Fallschirmjäger (Parachute) Army. The latter controlled the frontage on the eastern flank over to and including the Nijmegen Salient. This salient thrust like a thumb into the German front. Twenty-Fifth Army held the rest of the frontage to the coast.

But despite this apparent show of strength, the Germans were weaker than their order of battle indicated. Generaloberst Kurt Student thought the troops of his Heeresgruppe H "had to be considered, nearly without exception, as severely battered or at least extremely exhausted due to the battles in Belgium and southern Holland." Elements of First Fallschirmjäger Army were exceptions, being in "better condition both in men and materiel." Yet Student admitted to "great anxiety...caused by the makeshift training of the officers and non-commissioned officers. They were mostly without any knowledge of ground combat because they originated from the other components of the German Air Force (Luftwaffe)."[20]

During November, this army group's strength would fall even further as a result of the withdrawal of divisions and much artillery for deployment to more active fronts, as the Germans prepared for a massed offensive in the Ardennes sector. Such withdrawals increased, until late in the month Heeresgruppe H headquarters staff conceded that a "serious defence" of its front was "impossible." Instead, "complete reliance had to be placed upon floods and bad weather to thwart Allied plans."[21] The Germans expected that an overwhelming offensive was imminent, as they believed themselves much outnumbered by the Canadian and British forces. Student admitted later that he "spent some uneasy weeks because of the weakness of the German front and the threatening large-scale attacks by the enemy."[22]

What Student failed to appreciate was that both British Second Army and First Canadian Army were also badly worn down. Crerar was content to give the army time to recover from its heavy losses in the Scheldt Estuary. Montgomery, too, was ready to allow this. But Eisenhower had more ambitious plans for his other six armies. In early November, he started committing them in piecemeal fashion to operations intended to gain control of the Rhine's west bank. First Canadian Army would only support this effort by assuming responsibility for the Nijmegen Salient. This would enable the immediate release of the U.S. 104th Division to Twelfth Army Group and soon thereafter the U.S. 82nd and 101st Airborne Divisions. As well, the British 50th (Northumbrian) Division would be relieved.

Simonds considered the salient "the most important bit of ground along the front of 21 Army Group. Here we hold the only bridge across the main course of the Rhine." He also reiterated Crerar's earlier observation that if the Germans sought to continue holding the west bank of the Rhine, Nijmegen presented the logical place from which to launch an offensive eastward. Should they fall back across the Rhine, Allied control of Nijmegen's bridges would provide a vital crossing of the Maas that could be used to further an advance of little more than ten miles to the Nederrijn at Arnhem. Crossing here would enable the Allies to break the German grip on the Rhine to the immediate east and possibly unhinge their entire defence founded on this river. "The Nijmegen bridge is of greatest importance to us," Simonds declared, "and must be protected against all forms of attack."[23]

THE ALLIED NOVEMBER offensives were designed to reinvigorate operations that had stalled. Not only had Market Garden failed, but prolonged fighting begun on September 14 about five miles southeast of Aachen in what was known as the Hürtgen Forest had also come to naught. The forest, a fifty-square-mile block of tightly spaced fir trees some seventy-five to one hundred feet high, presented a dark and eerie landscape. Dense groundcover combined with rotting logs and thick carpets of soggy needles to conceal a vast array of booby traps and mines. About 120,000 troops had advanced into this nightmarish environment. The ensuing battle proved to be one of the war's fiercest. Casualties soared, with only modest gains won. Uncounted thousands of reinforcements were fed into the battle, many poorly trained and providing little more than cannon fodder. The battle ultimately raged until December 12. Although the forest was won, it came at a cost of 24,000 Americans killed, wounded, missing, or captured. "Another 9,000 succumbed to the misery of the forest itself, the wet and the cold—trench-foot, respiratory diseases, combat fatigue."[24] One American official historian concluded that the battle had been "basically fruitless" and "should have been avoided."[25]

Although the Americans in Hürtgen Forest suffered painfully only to end up far short of the Rhine, other assaults in early November bore fruit. On November 8, General George S. Patton's Third Army advanced steadily to take Metz on the 22nd and by early December to secure bridgeheads across the Saar that included intrusions through the Siegfried Line. All this was achieved at a cost of just under 27,000 casualties. Meanwhile, to the south, Sixth Army Group's Seventh Army had pushed toward Strasbourg on November 13 and entered the city ten days later. Also kicking off on November 8, the French Army succeeded in reaching the Rhine next to the Swiss border by the 20th.[26]

Although these gains were notable, they did not mean much in the grand scheme of things. The Germans still retained a strong grip on the western bank of the Rhine and showed no inclination to be pushed back farther into their homeland. As it became increasingly apparent that a major showdown would be required, eyes turned toward the salient as the best starting point.

[2]

Back to Trench Warfare

THE II CANADIAN corp's move to the Nijmegen Salient started the night of November 8–9 and was not completed until the morning of the 14th. Transporting thousands of troops over distances ranging from 120 to 175 miles posed a major logistical challenge, especially given the limited number of good roads. To reduce congestion, movements were staggered, with 2nd Canadian Infantry Division going first and 3rd Canadian Infantry Division following.

The 2nd Division's three infantry brigades departed on the first night. Mostly quartered in villages and towns immediately south of Antwerp, this division had less distance to travel than the other. The night was "cold and miserable [with] driving sleet," 4th Canadian Infantry Brigade's diarist wrote. Consequently, "it was a very trying trip with the rain and the blackness and there were a number of vehicle casualties mostly caused by drivers falling asleep at the wheel."[1]

Poor road conditions led to accidents and vehicles getting stuck. The division's heavy-weapons support battalion, the Toronto Scottish (MG) Regiment, made the journey without mishap. But its war diarist reported passing many other units' vehicles stranded "after having collided with trees, other vehicles, or...come to grief on the slippery verges."[2] The division's movement schedule called for arrivals between dawn and 0830 hours, but many were hours late. Le Régiment de Maisonneuve, scheduled to arrive at 0820 hours, straggled in at about 1100 hours "on account of the weather conditions and heavy road traffic. The journey [was] surely tiresome for the drivers, with the rain and foggy weather." The regiment disembarked in the small village of Mook, "a very shattered little town..The fighting must have been hard and gives us an idea of the days to come," the regiment's war diarist wrote. "We are getting closer and closer to the FATHERLAND, approximately eight kilometres from the North Western frontier of Germany. We are now on the banks of the Maas River."[3]

For the most part, the division's arrival and entry to the line seemed to have been unobserved by the Germans. The Queen's Own Cameron Highlanders, however, suffered ill luck when the vehicles bearing 'A' Company entered a crossroads on Mook's outskirts just as the Germans ranged in with one of their regular artillery defensive fire missions. Five men were wounded. 'A' Company's misfortunes continued when shelling wounded three more men and killed another as it took over frontage from the British 49th (West Riding) Infantry Division. The company then spent an uneasy early morning being harassed by sniper fire and the occasional grenade chucked into its position. The regiment's other three rifle companies, meanwhile, had suffered no casualties either moving into the salient or taking over assigned front-line positions. There was, however, much griping about the constant light rain and frigid temperatures.[4]

As 2nd Division settled in, 3rd Division mustered. More than three thousand vehicles were required to lift it from resting areas between Antwerp and the ancient Flemish city of Ghent. It was late morning of November 10 when the Stormont, Dundas and Glengarry Highlanders of 9th Brigade were alerted that they were to move from a holding area near Deinze, about six miles southwest of Ghent. Their destination was the Dutch town of Grave, where they would reorganize for deployment to the salient's front lines. Preparations were chaotic. At noon, the Glens were told to be ready by 1500 hours. A few minutes later, the phone rang and a brigade staffer said the Glens must send a guide to "a given point to pick up some DUKWS [amphibious trucks nicknamed ducks]. Another guide was to meet other DUKWS elsewhere at 1730, while yet another guide collected a convoy of TCVS [standard troop-carrying vehicles] at 2300 from a third location." This conversation was still under way when a wireless signal informed them that the move would not begin before 1600 hours. At 1500 hours, the battalion commander, Lieutenant Colonel Roger Rowley, told his companies "to have a meal prepared and devoured by 1630. At 1530 hours we were told we were to move at 1700 hours. No more than [ten] minutes later this was changed to 1800." Nobody could guarantee when the trucks would actually arrive. At 1800, brigade headquarters assured Rowley that all vehicles were en route, so he assembled the battalion. A cold rain fell as the men formed up. They remained in the open, growing increasingly miserable as uniforms became sodden, until the vehicles arrived at 2030 hours. At 2100, the Glens finally set off at the head of the brigade.[5]

The Canadian Scottish Regiment of 7th Brigade spent all of November 10 not sure what was happening. "Yes, we're going. No, we're not," the regiment's war diarist complained. This "continued throughout the afternoon and on into evening. The cold driving rain seemed as though it had come to stay so a miserable night was 'enjoyed' by all." Only at 0900 on November 11 did the regiment depart.

"Each village we passed this morning was crowded with civilians and soldiers solemnly celebrating the anniversary of Nov. 11, 1918. This [was] the first time since [1940] that Armistice Day had been openly declared such in Belgium. Under German occupation it was forbidden to refer to the meaning of Nov. 11." The convoy in which the Can Scots travelled made good time, covering 101 miles and reaching Eindhoven as night fell. The column pressed on. Around midnight, the Can Scots separated from the main convoy and continued along "a soft muddy path that seemed to wander to nowhere." Coming to a farmhouse, the battalion staff announced that this was their new headquarters. The trucks bearing the infantry companies carried on a little farther to a wide field. It was so dark that the men were ordered to sleep in the vehicles until daylight allowed the officers to get their bearings.[6]

The Queen's Own Rifles Regiment of 8th Brigade were still on the move at 0100 on November 12 and driving through "intermittent hail and rain." Every time the column paused, "we were minus a few more vehicles," the regiment's war diarist reported. "At one time we had only four vehicles left in the convoy, but by the time we reached 's-Hertogenbosch we were reinforced by a few more who had taken a wrong road. 'B' Company had quite a time with [a signals] carrier throwing tracks. Finally the carrier ended up on the railway line between Antwerp and Turnhout holding up the train running between these two places for approximately four hours, but with assistance from the engineer and fireman and some passengers finally got it fixed and off the right-of-way." Finally, the main body reached Nijmegen at about 1100 hours, "but we [were] still minus quite a few of our vehicles," the diarist added.[7]

"It was a ride to remember," North Shore (New Brunswick) Regiment's Captain Ned Russell recalled. The regiment left a rest area west of Antwerp for a journey that "took us part of two days...the longest road...convoy I was ever on."[8] No lights were allowed. Vehicles were stretched out nose to tail in long snaking lines. Captain Thomas Bell of the 12th Field Regiment thought it was "a long arduous trip over wet and icy roads."[9] With most of an army involved, the array of vehicles was staggering. Hundreds of canvas-backed trucks and amphibious DUKWs crammed with troops and supplies, equally long lines of special tractors pulling the artillery and their ammunition wagons, tracked Bren carriers, jeeps, long flatbed transports loaded with the steel and wooden beams that engineers used for bridging, ambulances—and all along the line darted motorcycles ridden by dispatch riders and provost personnel trying to keep the convoys orderly and headed along the correct route.

"No one was very happy as traffic snarled and roads jammed and the weather became cooler and tempers shorter," the regimental historian for the North Nova Scotia Highlanders noted.[10] The North Novas had just reached the Belgian–Dutch border when either 4th Canadian Armoured Division or 1st Polish Armoured Division (in the darkness, it was impossible to make out unit markings) sliced through the middle of a 3rd Division convoy. Long columns of Sherman tanks and other vehicles ground slowly across the breach, blocking a portion of the infantry division. When the last of the armoured division finally cleared, Russell realized he was in "the lead vehicle with thousands behind me, and the first part of our convoy now hours ahead of us." He started frantically consulting his maps to keep the convoy on the right track.

Vehicles from other units kept shouldering in. When they turned off toward their destinations, some 3rd Division vehicles often followed blindly in the dark. "Every vehicle in the army seemed to be on the road that night and one just had to keep in place," Lieutenant Blake Oulton of the North Novas observed. Oulton soon realized he was hopelessly lost and had seven of the regiment's trucks lost with him. At dawn, he heard distant guns firing. Stopping to question a priest walking along, Oulton "found I was on the front between Venlo and Maastricht, so turned northward and soon was back on my map." He shortly had to stop again when a British convoy barged in. Oulton was just dozing off in the truck's cab when a motorcyclist stopped alongside. He "asked if I knew where I was going. I assured him that I did. He said: 'I'm cold and wet and hungry and I'm lost.' I replied that I was only hungry and that I was going to Nijmegen." The motorcyclist reported that he had most of Le Régiment de la Chaudière in train and asked if he could follow. At noon this ad hoc column reached the bridge crossing at Grave and found the North Novas and Chaudière battalion commanders impatiently waiting on the other side for their charges. "There were bits of that...convoy straggling in for several days."[11]

Despite the confusion, most units reached assigned positions largely intact. The Regina Rifles, for example, underwent a "long, cold drive northward for about 150 miles...Of the 135 or so vehicles involved in the lift, only one [went] off the road, a tribute to the battalion's drivers and mechanics."[12]

AS THE CONVOYS were driving toward the Nijmegen area, advance parties from the two divisions' brigades and regiments had raced ahead to liaise with the British and American units. Having just taken command of 3rd Division's 8th Brigade on October 29, Brigadier James Alan "Jim" Roberts was anxious to carry out the relief with precision. He had previously commanded 11 Corps's reconnaissance regiment, the 12th Manitoba Dragoon Guards, and this was his first test of brigade leadership. The timetable called for his three regiments to begin relieving the American paratroopers at midnight on the night of November 12–13 and be finished by dawn. Roberts was determined that this exercise should go smoothly and finish on schedule. He therefore allowed lots of time to carry out some advance reconnaissance, arriving at the headquarters of Major General Jim Gavin's 82nd Airborne Division early on the morning of November 11. After stealing an hour for a short rest, a shave, and a wash, Roberts was personally briefed by Gavin before being assigned an American liaison officer to show him the ground.

The two men set out. To avoid attracting the attention of German snipers or artillery- and mortar-spotting teams, they crawled in and out of a long network "of dug-outs, ruined buildings, and a big empty hotel at Berg en Dal, where we entered through the front door and crawled across the ballroom on our bellies, in order to peek out through a huge and still unbroken window onto the slope and flat ground beyond which the Rhine could be clearly seen." Roberts gazed into a shallow valley. On its opposite side lay a German-held state forest—the Reichswald. The brigade was to be responsible for defending a line running from the hamlet of Berg en Dal south to the battered and deserted town of Groesbeek.[13]

Salients were always a mixed blessing. Often, as here, they came about more by chance than design. When Operation Market Garden failed, the Allies were left holding the ground lying agonizingly short of the Arnhem prize. But they controlled only a narrow corridor centred on the series of bridges required to enable the advance toward Arnhem. The ground on either side of this strip remained in German hands. At its southern base, which extended from just north of 's-Hertogenbosch in the west to Mook on the east, it was a respectable width of slightly more than twenty miles, gradually narrowing as it extended northward toward the Nederrijn and looked across to Arnhem. Here at its apex, it was less than two miles wide.

Although the salient was threatened on three sides and all its ground was subject to artillery and mortar bombardment, the Allies never considered abandoning it. This was less because it was ground hard won than because of its potential as a starting point for future operations. The bridges inside the salient provided the necessary links to make such operations viable. At Grave, a strongly constructed, eight-hundred-foot-long road bridge over the Maas had been won intact by U.S. 82nd Airborne Division troops on September 17. Engineers had since erected an adjacent floating bridge to the southeast. A boom slung across next to this bridge provided protection against German attempts to destroy the bridges by floating mines down the river. Even if they succeeded in detonating a mine against the main bridge's piers, a First Canadian Army analysis concluded, the bridge would suffer only "temporary damage." Nothing short of "a very large charge, expertly placed," could collapse it. The bridges were also sufficiently within the salient to be judged mostly secure from the threat of being captured by a German ground assault. A single company from one nearby 2nd Division regiment was deemed sufficient to guard them.[14]

More vulnerable were the bridges over the Waal at Nijmegen. Allied forces had captured both the rail and the two-thousand-foot-long highway bridges. Next to the road bridge, the Allies erected a barge bridge to handle additional traffic. These bridges were vital to the maintenance of the vulnerable apex of the salient—designated the Nijmegen Island. As at Grave, a boom had been installed to prevent floating mine attacks.

Nijmegen Island consisted of the ground between the Waal and the Nederrijn Rivers. Just east of Arnhem, the Rhine River split into these two arms and almost joined again west of the city, so that the ground between loosely resembled an island. It was flat and so low that in certain conditions, only the presence of dykes prevented its complete flooding. Here the U.S. 101st Airborne and British 50th (Northumbrian) Divisions held a badly exposed, mud-soaked frontage under constant surveillance from Germans holding the higher ground around Arnhem. They were slated to be relieved by two British divisions at the end of November, but until then came under 11 Canadian Corps command. Because the Nijmegen bridges and the island were considered vulnerable to German ground assault, their defence was the primary task of 11 Canadian Corps.[15]

Such an assault would most likely come at the salient's east flank from the Reichswald. It was here that an earlier attempt had been undertaken in the middle of October at the direct order of Heeres-gruppe B commander Generalfeldmarschall Walter Model. II Fallschirmjäger Korps commander Generalleutnant Eugen Meindl had stridently resisted the idea, warning that the Allies had been "considerably reinforced" and he lacked artillery sufficient to provide necessary support. Model held firm. To avoid being intercepted by the Allied air cover, Meindl attempted a night attack. Not to his surprise, the assault "became bogged down in the concentrated defensive fire at Groesbeek." Model, who was present at Meindl's headquarters, quickly realized the attack's futility and ordered it broken off at dawn. "The consequences were high casualties of our own and [only] small improvements of our position," Meindl's chief of staff, Oberst Ernst Blauensteiner, later wrote.

Thereafter, the Germans concentrated on defence. "The front was further strengthened and construction of a deeply integrated system of field positions was begun." An "attack between the northern border of the Reichswald and the road Nijmegen–Cleve" was especially feared. "The greatest care was given to the defense of this sector." As October ended, "the good troops had to suffer very much from cold and wet weather. Only a scanty supply of clothing could be reckoned with, overcoats, shelter-halves and…even boots had to be taken away from soldiers not being employed in combat in order to supply the men in the front line with these things."[16]

The German defensive buildup had not gone unnoticed. As early as October 13, 82nd Airborne Division intelligence reports noted that the opposing front had become an "almost continuous line of foxholes." The ground between the German and Allied lines was declared no man's land. As in the Great War, soldiers from either side ventured into it only under cover of darkness.[17]

As the Germans dug in, so did the Allies. Hence, when the Canadians entered the line, they inherited a complex and generally well-developed defensive network. The South Saskatchewan Regiment took over an area just outside the village of Mook during the night of November 9. "The Reichswald forest lay just three-thousand yards distant and the German forward positions were only a thousand yards from our own."[18]

Eighteen-year-old Private Charles "Chic" Goodman of 'B' Company found himself in a slit trench facing the wreckage of a Waco glider used by the airborne division in Market Garden. A number of dead American soldiers were still scattered about it. Because the ground was so exposed to German fire, nobody had attempted to retrieve their bodies. "Gee," Goodman thought, "we're back to trench warfare like my uncle said he had been in."[19]

The weather heightened the illusion of being transported to the earlier war. Each day, the Saskatchewan regimental historian noted, "was most unpleasant with plenty of rain and mud and then deep snow. Even [Bren] carriers were unable to move at times and the wide-tracked 'weasels' were used to carry ammunition and supplies to the forward companies...Movement in the area was impossible except under cover of darkness...Meals were brought up twice daily only. During the day everyone stayed in the few buildings and the slit trenches."[20]

Concerned about his men's well-being to a degree some senior commanders considered a fault, Lieutenant Colonel Vern Stott regularly toured the front lines to assess how they were faring. He thought the Sasks were about "as comfortable as men could be, if you can call it comfortable when the mud comes half way to your knees when you are walking around." The regiment had inherited its forward slit trenches from the American airborne troops, and these had been "dug to hold two men and were covered over to keep out the rain and for the most part they were dry inside."[21]

There was no predictability about the condition of the defensive positions left by the American and British troops. In some areas, the dugouts were large, deep, and well protected by stout roofs often constructed of sheets of plywood and other boards looted from abandoned Groesbeek or other nearby villages. Calgary Highlander Private Frank Holm described a typical slit trench in the salient as "about eight feet long by two feet wide by four feet deep. If possible you covered most of it with a door, planks, branches, or whatever and then shoveled soil over it to a depth of about two feet. There was room for one man to lie full length to sleep while his partner could stand guard at the opening."[22]

The Royal Regiment of Canada's first position was immediately southwest of Groesbeek. "Our role thus far is to be only of a holding nature, keeping an eye open for any moves by the enemy, spotting his positions and harassing his movements. All companies are living below ground. TacHQ [tactical headquarters] is located in a brick building surrounded by earthworks approximately six feet high. The roof, however, is only thin boards with a few branches spread on top as camouflage—quite solid except for a direct hit by anything larger than a 5-centimetre mortar bomb."[23]

Because the salient was so narrow, artillery regiments were often much closer to the front than normal. The 4th Field Regiment found itself assigned "to a rolling bush land area south and east of [Nijmegen] amongst gorse and evergreens just north of the village of Groesbeek...Here the guns were in position 5,000 yards from Germany [and] ready to fire on targets in the enemy's own country for the first time, including the towns and villages at the end of the Siegfried Line and the thick forest known as the Reichswald."

Being so close to Groesbeek, the regiment's gunners immediately set about looting its mostly ruined houses for anything that might make life more comfortable. Although the weather was "cold, wet and foggy," wrote regimental historian Captain George Blackburn, "those at the guns, although in dugouts, were quite comfortable having underground stoves, beds, easy chairs, rugs, etc., from the smashed houses in the area. Everyone slept underground except [Regimental Headquarters] personnel, who had the only building in the district, a large modern one looking like a summer hotel perched on a hill overlooking the gun positions. Work never ended on the dugouts...Most of these underground habitations were shacks built in a hole and covered over with earth. The 14th Battery built an Officers' Mess in this manner which was more comfortable than many Battery messes back in England, and one major built a complete log cabin underground. All dugouts had batteries and electric bulbs, and the 2nd Battery had proper electric lights, the power being brought in off a nearby line."[24]

While the artillery and other support regiments were assigned to areas on a virtually permanent basis, the infantry regiments stayed only for a short time in any one place. Each Canadian division regularly kept two of its brigades in the front lines and the other in reserve. A brigade's time in line averaged two weeks, followed by a week in reserve. Their operational mission was to maintain "aggressive local activity" aimed at dominating no man's land. The terrain largely favoured the Canadians, as Groesbeek stood on a low ridge overlooking the open ground between it and the Reichswald. The no man's land was "open, undulating ground, strewn with the remains of gliders"—some booby-trapped by the Germans, who had also sewn the area with mines. Most of these were Schützenmines— anti-personnel mines with an igniting prong that when stepped on triggered a spring. This caused a canister, loaded with 350 ball bearings or random selections of metal scrap, to jump three feet into the air before exploding.

Each side "enjoyed good observation over the ground west of the Reichswald in daylight; both also made strenuous efforts to establish control over it during darkness," the army's official historian later observed. "There were frequent clashes between German and Canadian patrols, especially in the Groesbeek sector." The Canadians generally mounted four types of patrols. Reconnaissance patrols sought to gain information without getting into a fight and tried to capture prisoners "by stealth." Fighting patrols of normally ten to twelve men, but on occasion numbering an entire platoon, also tried to capture prisoners or gather information, but at times would attempt to destroy a German position. Contact patrols ran almost nightly and were intended to link up with the regiments on either flank to ensure that the front was tied together properly. Standing patrols of up to platoon strength established advance positions in front of a regiment's main defensive line and served to give early warning should the Germans attack. These patrols were prepared to fight, but not die, holding their positions. Instead, they would attempt to hold the Germans for a short time and then withdraw to the security of a now fully alerted main defensive line.[25]

"You could hardly call it fighting," Lieutenant Donald Albert Pearce of the Highland Light Infantry wrote. Each night, the standing patrols went out. Often these set up mere yards from Germans on the same duty. The soldiers watched each other warily, trying to discern intelligence or motives by listening to movements, and before dawn drew back to respective main lines. Throughout the long, dull, miserable nights, however, an almost electrical current of danger lingered—a dread anticipation that the slightest thing might spark a deadly firefight. Dawn was welcomed. The men carefully and quietly emerged from one-man slit trenches stuffed with leaves and twigs that never managed to soak up the icy water that half-filled the space.

Pearce's platoon spent one "bone-freezing" twelve-hour night in slit trenches next to a dyke in the flat ground between a group of villages occupied by the Germans and the slightly higher ground of Wyler that the Canadians held. It was November 22, and to his surprise the Germans failed to send out a patrol. Pearce's men "dangled there...in cold mud...listening for [the German] patrols, whispering to each other through the stiff reeds and grasses, crawling back and forth between [slit trenches]...waiting for the dawn." Pearce felt disappointed, even empty, as if he'd been stood up by a date. Finally, he led the platoon home. They timed their return to coincide with the mists that regularly settled in moments after the false dawn faded. "We always come in just at that time; a few moments earlier there is a cold metal light along the east which silhouettes movement. But if you wait for that to diffuse, and then move silently, you can come in safely through a kind of secondary twilight."

Four days later, Pearce's regiment moved to a new front—within a small pine-forested ravine inside Germany to the south of Groesbeek. The men lived in small caves scoured out of the ravine's slopes. Pearce had a telephone in his cave that connected him with both his company headquarters, a half-mile behind the front, and an artillery forward observer's post about fifteen hundred feet to his front. Like some busybody with a telephone party line back in Canada, Pearce listened in when anybody used the phone. He noticed that those at headquarters and the forward observation officer team communicated in starkly different ways. Headquarters personnel shouted over the phone, seemed always relaxed and confident. Men joked or played cards in the background. The FOO team, hanging out there in no man's land where they literally overlooked German positions, whispered. There "is a catch in their voices; they are tense, worried, their hearts are sometimes beating hard enough to make their voices quiver a little. They try to end conversations with headquarters as soon as possible, and seem to be talking with their heads pulled down between the lapels of their greatcoats. This strange dialogue goes on intermittently all night, one end casually yelling into the phone, the other replying in taut whispers."[26]

Every night, Canadians and Germans prowled no man's land, playing what Essex Scottish Regiment's Captain Fred Tilston described as a "shell game of now it's there and now it isn't." On November 18, the Essex patrols were unable to locate the Germans operating on their front. The following night, however, a 'C' Company patrol led by Lieutenant George Edward Chester was bounced by a German one. The Germans fired several shots, ducked away, and resurfaced in another spot to fire upon Chester's men again. Despite being caught flat-footed, the patrol suffered no casualties.[27]

On November 19, frustrated at failing to capture prisoners with night patrols, the Stormont, Dundas and Glengarry Highlanders started going out by day. Private Ed Scott and Corporal Earl Hannah of 'A' Company set up inside a barn. At about 0545 hours, Scott spotted a man wearing a white camouflage suit like those recently issued to the Canadians. Expecting a contact patrol from the Highland Light Infantry, he called out a challenge the man failed to answer. A second challenge prompted the man to dash for the cover of a nearby hedge. Scott fired his rifle, but missed. Hannah rushed out of the barn and loosed a burst from his Bren gun. Lieutenant J.R. Good quickly turned up to investigate the cause of the shooting. The three men moved warily along the hedge. They found two dead Germans, one an officer, and a wounded man. The tracks of eight more Germans were detected in the snow. The Glens had got their prisoner.[28]

Buildings in no man's land were often used by both sides as observation points, despite most of them having been reduced to ruin by repeated shelling. On the night of November 19–20, the Glens sent a patrol led by Lieutenant Frank Groff to check two buildings. With him were Corporal B. Sauve, a pioneer private carrying a mine detector, and another private. One building was about two

hundred yards out and the other five hundred yards. The patrol easily gained the first building and found it unoccupied. Reaching the
second required crossing a road, which proved to be heavily mined.
Abandoning the road approach, Sauve led the way up a narrow creek
bed. As the men closed on the house, they realized it was hiding not
only a mortar team but also an artillery piece and its crew. Seriously
outgunned, the patrol began to silently withdraw. Suddenly, Sauve
tripped a mine. The explosion ripped off his foot. It also tore out one
of the pioneer's eyes and blinded him in the other. Alerted, the Germans fired into the area, as Groff shouldered the 190-pound Sauve
and staggered under his weight back to the creek. After quickly ban-
daging the corporal's wound, Groff returned to where the blind
pioneer and dazed private remained. Groff guided the two men to
the creek. Telling them to wait there, Groff shoulder-carried Sauve
back to front lines. Although ready to drop from exhaustion, Groff
refused to rest and led a small party back to the creek to evacuate the
two privates. When this group reached safety, Groff collapsed and
was taken to the Regimental Aid Post.[29]

By the beginning of December, the Canadians in the salient had
become considerably more efficient at patrolling. On the night of
December 2, a four-man Royal Hamilton Light Infantry patrol ventured out a short distance southeast of Groesbeek. The Rileys crept
up on three Germans hiding in a haystack and took them prisoner.
German patrol leader Grenadier Franz Bauer was soon spilling his
knowledge of 190th Infanterie-Division's strength, capability, and
positions to Captain J.W. Henley, 2nd Division intelligence officer.
Bauer said his patrol had been sent to "determine at what time the
enemy put out his outposts and in what strength." They had dug
themselves into the haystack and had been observing the ground
facing the Canadian lines for about an hour, he said, when "we were
surprised and taken prisoner by a four-man patrol...Everything happened so fast that in spite of our careful watching and our weapons it
was impossible to defend ourselves.

"It is still a mystery to me how the enemy approached. They stood
before us as if they had come up out of the ground. I must admit that

they were very calm, but nevertheless they must have been very skilled and well-disciplined...otherwise it would have been impossible to surprise us. I...said to my comrades we need not be ashamed of being taken prisoner for we could not keep up with men as skilled and disciplined as those of the Canadian patrol, in spite of the fact we have been soldiering for five years."

Henley added in his written report on Bauer's interrogation, "By any standard our patrol did an excellent job."[30]

Although the Canadians were getting proficient at the deadly task of patrolling, there was a numbing sameness to it that took its toll on morale. Essex Scottish Captain Tilston repeatedly voiced his concerns in the regiment's war diary. "This static type of warfare is not good for Canadians," he noted on November 18. "The troops have been growing more restless daily."[31] He closed the November diary with the observation that the month had been "the easiest" since the regiment had deployed in Normandy, but that it had also been "boring." This led to a sense "that the war would never end—and certainly not until we were asked to adopt a more dynamic role."[32]

[3]

Differences of Opinion

BY LATE FALL of 1944, it was clear that the western Allies needed to do something dynamic, but there was no agreement on what that should entail. After Market Garden, Eisenhower declared that the priority must be to eliminate all German forces west of the Rhine. Yet by mid-November, little had been done to bring that about. On the extreme right of the Allied six-hundred-mile front, the American and French armies of General Jacob L. Devers's Sixth Army Group had bogged down short of the river. In the centre, Lieutenant General Omar N. Bradley's U.S. Twelfth Army Group was mired in costly battles for the Hürtgen Forest. This area had proven to be the western front's most heavily defended sector. On November 16, Bradley attempted to gain renewed momentum in the forest. Despite support from the heaviest tactical bombardment of the war—involving 2,500 American and British bombers unleashing 9,400 tons of high explosive—the Americans gained little ground at great cost in casualties. Bradley's troops ended November still twenty-five miles from the Rhine and facing the Roer River. As the official historian for Twelfth Army Group's Ninth Army noted, "The enemy knowing how the attack must come, had only to block it head-on and inflict the maximum casualties."[1] They had done this well. While the Americans pushed uselessly against the German defences, Montgomery limited Twenty-First Army Group to an attack by British Second Army's xxx Corps alongside Bradley's Ninth Army to cover the American left flank. Like the Americans, this corps suffered heavy casualties for minor gains.[2]

"A lethargy seemed to settle over the American command," wrote the official U.S. army historian Colonel Charles B. MacDonald. "They just kept throwing in one division after another. They seemed to have the feeling, 'Surely one more will do it.' Well, one more didn't do it."[3]

Nobody was more critical of American strategy than Montgomery. As November passed, he became increasingly displeased. On November 28, Eisenhower overnighted at Montgomery's headquarters in Zonhoven, Belgium. Montgomery told Eisenhower his strategy had failed and offered a list of suggestions to rectify the situation. Such was the conversation and Montgomery's delusional tendencies that when the SHAEF commander departed in the morning, he believed his suggestions had been accepted.

Seeking written confirmation of their conversation, Montgomery sent Eisenhower a nine-point summary on November 30. "We have definitely failed to implement the plan contained in the SHAEF directive of 28 October, as amended on later dates. That directive ordered the main effort to be made in the north, to defeat decisively the enemy west of the Rhine, to gain bridgeheads over the Rhine and Ijssel Rivers, and to deploy in strength east of the Rhine preparatory to seizing the Ruhr. We have achieved none of this; and we have no hope of doing so. We have therefore failed; and we have suffered a strategic reverse.

"We now require a new plan," he asserted. "And this time *we must not fail*. In the new plan we must get away from the doctrine of attacking in so many places that nowhere are we strong enough to get decisive results. We must concentrate such strength on the main selected thrust that success will be certain. It is in this respect that we failed badly in present operations."[4]

The desire to concentrate on one objective was a typical Montgomery stratagem and completely at odds with the American approach. The Americans saw that such concentration would require a meticulously developed offensive plan and a slow and deliberate gathering of forces and matériel. Delay would follow delay while

Montgomery tidied everything together. He had, in fact, only initiated the discussion with Eisenhower after concluding that Twenty-First Army Group's front was, in his own words, "tidy."[5]

Montgomery had previously tried to persuade Eisenhower to appoint him senior land force commander, directing operations of all Allied forces in the way he had done during the early phases of the Normandy Campaign. Eisenhower had rebuffed him. His American generals—particularly Bradley and Patton, but also possibly Devers—would surely rebel against serving under any British general, and most certainly Montgomery. It would mean adopting Montgomery's approach, which was anathema to the Americans. "When Montgomery prepared to attack," Bradley said, "he dragged up everything he had for an all-out campaign...We Americans, on the other hand, constantly nibbled away on the key positions of an enemy...constantly kept him knocked off balance."[6]

Montgomery believed this constant nibbling had dissipated Allied strength and brought the front to a stalemate. And he was certain that treating all the army group commanders as equal partners encouraged this dissipation. All he had to do was point to how Patton had developed his so-called Rock Soup attacks to wrest priority on reinforcement and supply away from other American generals. These attacks entailed launching his Third Army into an unauthorized attack on a limited objective. When they got stuck, he then insisted they must be reinforced and the battle expanded to rescue the situation.[7]

Bradley—Patton's direct superior—generally allowed him to get away with this. He did so even when it meant denying vital reinforcements and supplies to General Courtney H. Hodges's beleaguered First Army in the Hürtgen Forest. Bradley considered Patton's actions to be part of the essential nibbling-away process rather than a sly act of insubordination.

Montgomery wanted the Americans, particularly Bradley, to cease and desist probing "here, there and everywhere."[8] All that yielded, he maintained, was a costly butcher's bill while enabling the Germans to continue strengthening their defensive positions.

In the summation of his meeting with Eisenhower, Montgomery noted he had again asked Eisenhower to consider "having a land force commander to work under you and run the land battle for you. But you discarded this idea as being not suitable, and we did not discuss it anymore." Eisenhower, he continued, had then suggested grouping Twenty-First Army and Twelfth Army together under Montgomery. This would subordinate Bradley and Patton to Montgomery. "I said that Bradley and I together are a good team. We worked together in Normandy, under you, and we won a great victory. Things have not been so good since you separated us. I believe to be certain of success you want to bring us together again; and one of us should have the full operational control north of the Ardennes; and if you decide that I should do that work—that is O.K. by me."

Montgomery believed that the dense and large Ardennes Forest provided a logical dividing line for the Allies. "The theatre divides itself naturally into two fronts, one north of the Ardennes and one south of the Ardennes. We want one commander in full operational control north of the Ardennes and one south." While giving lip service to Bradley possibly commanding the northern sector, Montgomery thought the post should naturally be his.

"The above are the main points," the letter concluded. "I am certain there is no time to lose in deciding on the plan for the spring campaign. We can well carry on during the winter; but what is done during winter must all lead up to what is to be done in the spring. Therefore we must decide NOW the big plan for the spring, and work backwards from it." Montgomery proposed that he, Eisenhower, and Bradley meet at Maastricht, the Dutch capital of Limburg province, on either December 6 or 7. "I suggest that we want no-one else at the meeting, except Chiefs of Staff: who must not speak."[9]

"Monty's letter made Ike hot under the collar," Eisenhower's naval aide, U.S. Naval Reserve Captain Harry C. Butcher, wrote. Eisenhower fired back a note saying "that he didn't know what Monty meant by strategic reverse; so far as General Ike was concerned, he realized that we had failed to achieve all that had been hoped, but hopes and plans are based on conditions as we know them or can estimate them when the plans are made." Eisenhower added that "he had no intention of stopping Devers's and Bradley's operations as long as they are clearing up our right flank and giving us...capability of concentration." At the same time, he "did not...plan to push these attacks senselessly." He agreed to Monty's proposed meeting on December 7. Eisenhower "would bring his Chief of Staff [General Walter Bedell Smith] and would not by any means insult him by telling him that he should remain mute at any conference." He urged Montgomery not to "look upon the past performances of this great fighting force as a failure." Despite his irritation, Eisenhower used his usual salutation of "Dear Monty" and ended with the signature "Ike." Correspondence between Eisenhower and Montgomery was always cordial, no matter how close the latter came to being insubordinate in presenting his ideas. Eisenhower was always confident that once orders were issued, Montgomery would do his best to implement them.

Montgomery hastened to make amends with a response on December 2. He was "sorry, indeed, if General Ike thought he had said or implied" that recent Allied performance had constituted failure. He had "never done anything of the sort and had never said anything that could convey that impression." He had merely pointed out that the October 28 directive had not been realized.

Naturally conciliatory, Eisenhower responded that he was "sorry if his letter gave offense and [he] certainly did not want to give an erroneous meaning to Monty's words or to do anything to upset their close relationship."[10]

AS EISENHOWER AND Montgomery were mending bridges on December 2, the relative quiet inside the Nijmegen Salient was shattered at 1300 hours by German artillery loosing "a series of abnormally intensive concentrations." Then, at 1710, teams of German engineers dynamited large gaps in the dykes north of Elst and next to the destroyed Arnhem railway bridge to deliberately flood Nijmegen Island.

Neither action caught 11 Canadian Corps off guard. On November 25, First Canadian Army intelligence staff had intercepted a broadcast by a German commentator predicting that the intense fighting in and around Hürtgen Forest "must hourly be expected to extend into the Nijmegen area." Forces in the salient had been put on alert and "the general atmosphere...in the...salient was tense with the expectancy of impending operations." When the German guns opened up, Canadian and British artillery responded with counter-battery fire. A fierce duel ensued through the night and into the early hours of the following morning.[11]

Although the unusually intense artillery was a concern, the dyke breaching vastly overshadowed it. Nijmegen Island's vulnerability to flooding had long been recognized. The danger had been there even without sabotaged dykes. In 1923, the Nederrijn and Waal had so swelled from winter rains that each reached a height of thirteen metres, overflowed the dykes, and caused a local disaster. If the rivers now rose even to 9.5 metres, resulting flooding might force abandonment of the island. Operation Noah had been designed to address this threat and on November 12 was partially initiated when river levels reached 9.58 metres, with every indication of a continued and rapid rise. The following day, 11 Canadian Corps ordered the civilian population in the eastern area about Elst and Bemmel evacuated. By December 2, some twelve thousand civilians and several thousand head of cattle had been removed. Negotiations with Dutch authorities led to an agreement that between three and four thousand men could remain to "look after stock, property, and crops, and 11 Canadian Corps undertook to transport sufficient labour into the area daily to complete the harvest."[12]

Two British infantry divisions—the 51st (Highland) and 49th (West Riding)—serving under Canadian command defended the island. As more ground flooded and what remained above water turned into sloppy mud, conditions rapidly deteriorated. Soon after the dykes were broken, it became evident that at least some of the island must be abandoned. 11 Canadian Corps Chief of Staff Brigadier Elliot Rodger toured the area on December 4. "The water was spreading slowly and rising into low corners of fields—and in places flowing across roads westward. Civilians (the few who were left) were collecting belongings in farm carts and were collecting herds of cattle and driving them north on small roads to the railway and then east to a collecting area near bridges...Most of the marching troops came off by storm boat and thought *that* at least a good lark."[13]

Rodger not only inspected the flooding but also gathered information on the purpose and extent of a strong attack that 6th

Fallschirmjäger Division had made against the British defenders early that morning. The German thrust had come near the village of Haalderen, about three and a half miles northeast of the Nijmegen bridges. Some initial minor penetrations were gained against the defending Duke of Wellington Regiment. But when the infantry was reinforced by tanks of the Royal Scots Fusiliers, the ground lost was quickly recovered. About 50 Germans were killed and 110 taken prisoner.[14] The attack, corps intelligence staff learned, had been "intended as a cover for an attempt by a special engineer demolition section [raid] against the Nijmegen bridges." The enterprise had entirely failed. A subsequent German investigation blamed the officers for poor leadership, claiming the troops had been inadequately briefed, and an artillery barrage was too late and ineffective. As a result, the engineers never advanced.[15]

Despite the attack's ineffectiveness, corps intelligence staff believed the Germans were going to increase pressure on the salient. A second intercept revealed pleasure over the flooding. "The blowing up of the dykes," it read, "certainly greatly reduced the value of Nijmegen bridgehead as a strategic starting point for an attack. The area between the Waal and Neder Rijn can be used no longer as an assembly area...and a major attack toward the Zuider Zee or Oldenburg has thus become impossible."[16]

First Canadian Army had never considered attacking in the direction of either the shallow North Sea bay off northwest Holland or the West German town. What General Harry Crerar wanted was to clear the Germans out of the eastern part of Nijmegen Island as far as the Pannerdensch Canal. With much of the island now submerged, Operation Siesta—as this attack had been code-named—was shelved.[17]

Montgomery had earlier stressed the importance of Siesta. But during a December 6 visit, his discussions with Crerar focused on a larger and more significant task. First Canadian Army, Montgomery said, "would be called upon to undertake a major offensive operation considerably earlier" than he had originally thought. "It was now the considered conclusion of higher command," Crerar wrote, "that the enemy must be allowed no respite, but rather that he must be denied the time to build up his defences and the size and strength of his tactical and strategical reserves. This meant that neither winter weather, nor bad going conditions, must be allowed to check our offensive operations, no matter what the difficulties and despite discomfort. Secondly, the selective objective for such operations must be of a decisive character. This pointed very definitely to the Ruhr. Thirdly, our operations must be so designed as to force the enemy to engage in mobile warfare in which he would be at a disadvantage owing to the shortage of petrol, mechanical transport and tanks. This requirement indicated the suitability of the area lying between the Rhine and the Meuse. The task required that we should break out from our limited deployment east of Nijmegen (which was clear of the major water obstacles), and then driving south-east and south, with the Meuse on our right and the Rhine on our left, to join up, opposite the Ruhr, with a northerly thrust by the 12th U.S. Army Group then facing Cologne."

To give the Canadian Army sufficient punch, Montgomery offered to add xxx British Corps headquarters and its corps troops, three additional British infantry divisions, one armoured division, four independent tank and armoured brigades, and four army artillery groups to its strength. The xxx Corps commander, Lieutenant General Brian Horrocks, had already developed plans for an identical operation when the Nijmegen Salient had been under his control in October. Consequently, Montgomery and Crerar agreed that it made sense to give xxx Corps "responsibility for launching the attack. Also, in order to avoid congestion and complications in the forward assembly area, the 3rd Canadian Infantry Division, then in position, was to be placed under...Horrocks for the first phase. For, although it was not possible to forecast, with accuracy, the timing, scope and results of this great, and possibly, protracted battle, [Crerar] assumed that the enemy would strongly man, and fight, his several lines of highly organized defences, and it followed, therefore, that the operation, as a whole, would probably divide itself into several phases."

Montgomery thought "all the resources for air support available to the 21st Army Group, including those of Bomber Command and the U.S. Army Air Force, should be made available." General planning and detailed studies were ordered to begin immediately, and Horrocks was to come under Crerar's command on December 13.[18]

THE PLAN MONTGOMERY outlined for Crerar matched what the field marshal was going to advocate the following day, at the December 7 Maastricht conference. Montgomery, Eisenhower, and Bradley convened at 1030 hours. Both Americans had brought their chiefs of staff. Eisenhower was still smarting from Montgomery's implied criticism of recent strategy and achievements. He opened with a summary of events since early September and stated that these "recent operations had been well worthwhile, and were going well."

Montgomery thought "this part of his statement was not very genuine," its intent likely aimed at countering the volley of criticism he knew Montgomery was about to fire. Eisenhower concluded by saying the meeting's purpose was to allow a general airing of views, and he did not anticipate issuing any immediate orders. Those would come later, after he had time to reflect on the discussion. He then invited Montgomery to speak.

Montgomery launched into the same argument presented to Eisenhower verbally and in writing at the end of November. "The only real worthwhile objective on the western front is the Ruhr," he said.[19] Seize this industrial heartland, which provided the "lifeblood" to Germany's military heart, and that vital organ would "cease to beat."[20] The war would then be quickly won—particularly if by spring or early summer the Germans could be drawn into a mobile war. "These two factors are basic and fundamental," Montgomery declared. "It is impossible to argue against them."

So the Ruhr must be the strategic objective, and the main effort must occur in Montgomery's northern sector, because it was "only there that suitable country exists for a mobile campaign." Attacking into Germany elsewhere, he argued, would "produce no results as the country is difficult and very suited for defensive war; to pursue other routes will merely prolong the war...We must be so strong in the north that we can produce decisive results without any possibility of failure."

To gain necessary strength, the U.S. Twelfth Army Group should be entirely shifted north of the Ardennes, with its right flank anchored on the German town of Prüm. Bradley's operations would concentrate on two main axes: Düren in the north toward Cologne, and in the south from Prüm toward Bonn. Montgomery assessed the country within these two axes as good for mobile operations and outside of "existing defence lines and obstacles."

The main Allied operation, however, would entail Montgomery's Twenty-First Army Group launching "a strong offensive from the Nijmegen area, southwards between the rivers, with the object of securing all ground between the Rhine and Meuse as far south as the line Orsoy–Venlo." This would be the only offensive action on his front, and "everything would be put into it." He predicted the offensive would "continue slowly during the winter months." The target date for its launch should be January 1.

Montgomery wanted Bradley's army group strengthened to thirty-five divisions and to have ten of these support his offensive with a northward push to meet the advancing British and Canadian divisions. The Germans on the west bank of the Rhine would be forced to either flee across the river or be crushed between the two advancing forces. With the Rhine's west bank in hand, the Allies could—likely in March—force crossings at points between Nijmegen and Wesel to the south. This would allow the desired mobile operations to cut off the Ruhr valley from the north and slice deep into Germany. Twelfth Army Group would simultaneously cross the Rhine at Bonn and outflank the Ruhr from the south. The U.S. Sixth Army Group, meanwhile, would continue operations in the Saar "as far as its strength and resources will allow."

Montgomery cautioned that it was impossible to predict how operations would develop once the Rhine was crossed. The essential task to concentrate on now was the advance by Twelfth and Twenty-First Army Groups "to battle west of the Rhine." They must "draw in on them all the German strategic reserves and maul them, and then close up to the Rhine."

Again Montgomery insisted that "one commander should be in operations control and direction of all forces north of the Ardennes.

That commander must be either myself or Bradley." Montgomery reiterated that he would "willingly serve under Bradley."[21]

Eisenhower was having none of it. The Ruhr was "merely a geographical objective; our real objective was to kill Germans and it did not matter where we did it."

There "would be more Germans to kill if we went for the Ruhr than anywhere else," Montgomery shot back. "We should also at the same time be gaining objectives toward the capture or isolation of the Ruhr and toward the attainment of the master plan."

Eisenhower conceded that the left wing of Bradley's forces must "be made strong enough to get to the Rhine." But he rejected shifting all of Twelfth Army Group north of Prüm. He wanted to keep the group's right flank strong as well and have it thrust hard toward Kassel in the north and Frankfurt to the south.

He would, however, place Bradley's most northerly army—the Ninth, with its ten divisions—under Montgomery's command for the operation to clear the Rhine's west bank. The southern boundary for Montgomery's thus expanded Twenty-First Army Group would be on the Rhine at about Orsoy, a small village a little south of Wesel and on the northwest corner of the Ruhr valley. Montgomery was to force crossings over the Rhine and outflank the Ruhr from the north.

The left flank of what remained of Twelfth Army Group would "be a containing force, not to cross the Rhine in strength, but to make feints and threats in the Cologne–Bonn area and south of it." There would then be two offensives—Montgomery's to the north and Bradley's in the south aimed at Frankfurt and Kassel.

Eisenhower asked Montgomery what he thought. "I said that we must be clear that we differed, not slightly, *but widely and on fundamental issues,*" Montgomery later wrote. "I said I was quite unable to agree with his plan. If we split our resources, neither thrust would be strong enough to obtain decisive results; this is what he had done in the past, and we were now paying for our mistakes; I hoped we would not do it again."

Currently, they suffered "from a faulty command set-up" that "his plan made...no better. In fact it would make it worse." Bradley would be off in Luxembourg to direct operations toward Frankfurt, but still commanding forces north of the Ardennes. This would result in lapses and delays in clear command of the American forces that remained under Bradley's control. Montgomery pleaded with Eisenhower to give him total command north of the Ardennes and Bradley command of forces south of there. And he again urged Eisenhower to concentrate "all available strength in the north, and [to make] the northern offensive so strong that success was certain."

Unless these two things were done, he believed, "we would not succeed, and...we would arrive at the spring not ready to get on with the business."

Eisenhower bluntly rejected Montgomery's arguments. There would be two strong thrusts and that was that. "In between these two thrusts the plan would be to threaten, and make feints." Montgomery wrote after, "It is clear that, although the present plan has failed, we are still to continue to consider it has not failed and we are to work on it."

After the meeting, Montgomery lamented in a letter to Chief of the Imperial Staff General Sir Alan Brooke that the two-thrust plan "is really rather a tragedy. I think now that if we want the war to end within any reasonable period you will have to get Eisenhower's hand taken off the land battle. I regret to say that in my opinion he just doesn't know what he is doing." He wanted to see Bradley's influence also curbed and even that of Eisenhower's Deputy Supreme Commander, Air Chief Marshal Sir Arthur Tedder. Montgomery alleged that Bradley, abetted by Tedder, had Eisenhower's ear.[22]

Brooke could hardly take any action against Eisenhower—something Montgomery must have realized. When preparing his memoir for publication in 1958, he excised these comments from his copy of the letter.

Montgomery's combativeness during the meeting had, Bradley wrote, "made a very poor impression." He "refused to admit that there was any merit in anybody else's views except his own. Personally I gained the impression that his views as to future operations were largely colored by his desire to command the whole show." Bradley believed Eisenhower had no intention of conceding to this desire or even putting Twelfth Army Group under Montgomery's command.

Bradley told Eisenhower that if he did the unthinkable, "he would of necessity have to relieve me of command, because it would be an indication that I had failed as a separate Army Group Commander."[23]

"And so we really achieved nothing at the Maastricht conference," Montgomery wrote. He found it deeply worrisome that Twelfth Army Group was now "disposed in two main concentrations, each deployed for attack. In between was a gap of some 100 miles, held by [VIII] American Corps of four divisions—under [Major General Troy H.] Middleton."[24]

IN THE MORNING before the Maastricht conference convened, Montgomery had met briefly on the outskirts of Maastricht with Horrocks to advise him of his role in the forthcoming offensive against the west bank of the Rhine. Horrocks said he needed five divisions for the task. Shortly after the conference ended, Montgomery telephoned XXX Corps headquarters and told Horrocks the five divisions were promised and to start "thinking out the operation." At 1820 hours, Montgomery called Crerar. Eisenhower, he said, had agreed that the Americans would take over the southern half of the Twenty-First Army Group front, and that enabled him to add XXX Corps to First Canadian Army's strength. The corps would come in to the right of the Canadians. Responsibility for what was code-named Operation Veritable would definitely fall to First Canadian Army. Crerar would be in overall command, even though Horrocks's XXX Corps would undertake the initial offensive. Montgomery told Crerar to be ready to launch Operation Veritable on January 1. Detailed planning was to begin immediately.

Montgomery may have lost most everything he had fought for at Maastricht, but he would exploit the minor victories. He had won Eisenhower's agreement that the west bank of the Rhine must be cleared. And he had won placement of the U.S. Ninth Army and its ten divisions under his command to help achieve this.[25]

Having recognized that his most northerly army might be given to Montgomery, Bradley had cagily ensured that it would be the Ninth. Having only arrived in Europe on September 5, Ninth Army was the least experienced Allied formation. The XXX Corps had fought alongside it in late November to pinch out a German salient projecting between the British and American forces at the village of Geilenirchen. Eliminating the salient had proved a tough fight.

Horrocks had been surprised to discover that the commanders of the U.S. First and Third Armies demonstrated a "patronizing attitude" toward the soldiers of the Ninth, considering them poorly trained and led. He felt that the Ninth "in this, its first action, had proved that it could fight just as well as, if not better than, some of the so-called veteran U.S. divisions had fought in Normandy." What he felt the Ninth lacked was efficient administration and staff arrangements. These had failed the "extreme gallantry displayed by the raw G.I.s."

Horrocks, usually as close to the front lines as possible, thought the American divisional and corps commanders hung too far back and were largely unknown to the soldiers they commanded. When the battle was joined, they were far to the rear and could little influence its progression. "Oddly enough, the senior officers did not seem to worry much about the welfare of their troops, and regimental *esprit de corps* was largely absent, or at least not obvious."

When Horrocks attended Ninth Army daily headquarters briefings he found them overly protracted and "a complete waste of time—a commodity which is always in short supply in war. In an experienced corps like the one I was privileged to command, ten minutes with my Chief of Staff each morning before setting off to 'smell the battlefield' was quite sufficient."

Despite his criticism of the American command, he considered his relationship with Ninth Army's commander "particularly good."[26] Lieutenant General William H. "Simp" Simpson was a tall, lean Texan of fifty-six years. His nickname came from the fact that he had performed poorly at West Point, reputedly graduating second from the bottom of the class in 1909. But Horrocks found him astute and capable.

Unlike most of his American contemporaries, he did not bristle or complain at being placed under Montgomery's command. Instead, he was mild mannered and rather unassuming despite his towering height, which was emphasized by a clean-shaven head.[27] Montgomery's often overbearing and superior manner did not faze Simpson. He worked with the British in a professional manner and in the spirit of allies serving a common cause. It was a welcome situation that boded well for the forthcoming operation.

A WEEK TO the day following the Maastricht conference, Montgomery's chief of staff, Major General Francis "Freddie" de Guingand, convened a formal planning session for Operation Veritable. The meeting was held at Twenty-First Army Group's headquarters in Zonhoven. First Canadian Army's acting chief of staff, Brigadier George Beament (recently promoted from colonel), and his senior planning staff attended. Detailed planning for Veritable would fall to First Canadian Army, but de Guingand wanted to set out essential details and lines of tactical communication. Veritable, he said, was to be seen "as an essential preliminary to an assault crossing of the Rhine, north of Ruhr." Although it was hoped Veritable could begin on January 1, he recognized that it might have to be "as soon as possible" after that date. It was also believed that the operation might run through to March 1, 1945, since British Second Army would not be conducting any major supporting operations and therefore the entire ball would be carried by First Canadian Army. It was expected that the operation would be completed in time for the assault crossings of the Rhine to begin about March 15. "If Veritable is sticky," de Guingand said, Montgomery might "decide to regroup and order Second Army to assault across the Maas" in support. But he would not make a decision to do so before February 1, and such support would only be possible if the Maas was not in flood.

Having addressed the general details, de Guingand set out specifics of air support, regrouping of corps and divisions to attack and supporting positions, execution of an engineering plan to improve roads and other supply routes (railway beds) as necessary, and development of a cover plan to deceive the Germans into thinking the offensive would fall elsewhere.

There were several major concerns. The Germans might blow the dykes bordering the Rhine to flood much of the proposed battlefield, which could "alter the whole course of the campaign." Another problem revolved around heavy-bombing air support. While RAF Bomber Command and the bombers of U.S. Army Air Force would be on call, the air force representatives present "stressed that the condition of the ground is a vital factor in the effectiveness of heavy bombing. Wet ground renders heavy bombing with instantaneous fuses ineffective." Twenty-First Army Group experts were to "procure research data" covering probable ground conditions and also examine a "special type of flame mixture developed by the U.S. Army which burns better in wet country than in dry."[28]

When Beament and his planners returned to their headquarters in the late afternoon of December 14, the first priority was to issue instructions to implement the cover plan. This was to be carried out by 1 British Corps, which was holding the front running from west of the Nijmegen Salient to the sea. "The 'story,' as one report put it, was to convey to the enemy that U.S. Twelfth Army Group was taking over a sector of Twenty-First Army Group to enable the divisions of xxx British Corps to rest and refit. Political pressure, however, dictated an early attempt to secure the liberation of north Holland and, with that in view, First Canadian Army had received instructions to commence preparations for a crossing of the Maas and the Waal along the axis 's-Hertogenbosch–Utrecht. For this purpose the rested divisions of [xxx] corps, supported by an allied airborne corps, were to be made available to Canadian headquarters."

The "initial large-scale movement of the assault formations" of xxx Corps and four Twenty-First Army Group heavy artillery units through 1 Corps's sector toward the Nijmegen Salient—where the true offensive was to be launched—"could sustain this general conception." To reinforce the ruse, Lieutenant General John Crocker was instructed to "initiate small-scale operations." Principal responsibility for implementing the "deception scheme" was assigned to 4th Canadian Armoured Division under the code name Operation Pounce. Ideally, as information on the operation was leaked to the Germans, it would result in "retention in Holland of forces which might be employed to greater advantage elsewhere."

To facilitate this illusory operation, a simulated airborne landing north of the Waal was planned. Amphibious vehicles and bridging equipment would be concentrated in easily detectable areas between 's-Hertogenbosch and Tilburg. Gun pits would also be dug here to indicate deployment of eight division artillery regiments and two Army Group heavy gun regiments. A bridgehead would be established near Hedel, immediately across the Maas from 's-Hertogenbosch, to ostensibly permit construction of bridges for an advance on the Waal. Pounce was to hit full stride in late December or early January, depending on the date actually fixed for launching Veritable. But 4th Division was to immediately increase patrolling to convince the Germans that something major was afoot.[29]

These patrols were both dangerous and miserable. Reconnaissance and fighting patrols had to navigate the swift current of the Maas in small boats under the cover of darkness. The soldiers then "groped their way across a wintry waste of half-submerged and half-frozen river meadows, and over long stretches of dyke land and drainage ditches." Even the contact patrols on the Canadian side of the river faced the same difficult terrain to establish links with their counterparts on either flank. From December 1 to December 22, 4th Division sent thirty-one patrols over the river. Several succeeded in crossing, "only to be forced back by flooding, wire, machine-gun fire, or flares encountered on the north bank."[30]

On the night of December 14, as part of the deception plan, the Lake Superior Regiment slipped a patrol of two platoons of 'B' Company across the Maas. The patrol was commanded by Lieutenant B. Black. Its object was to penetrate the village of Hoenzadriel and capture prisoners. Accompanying the patrol was a Belgian interpreter, John Saynaeve. Hoenzadriel was about two thousand feet north of the river, which meant a fairly deep penetration. They encountered no barbed-wire barriers, but the danger of mines was always there. In the darkness, the patrol risked becoming lost or separated. "It was a matter of stealth, cunning, caution, and above all concentration," the regiment's historian wrote. "Every moment, every step was vital." Heavy rain had turned the ground to mush and each step caused a squelching sound that the men feared would betray them to German sentries. "The strain upon each man was terrific; and even though he would not admit it, there was not one of the patrol who was not nervous."

Upon entering the village, the patrol discovered two Germans in the basement of the first house they searched and took them prisoner. That met their objective, so Black directed the patrol back toward the river. The "men were just a little elated, perhaps just a little careless, and filled with the desire to hurry. Suddenly one of the men set off a trip flare. At once several German machine guns, firing on fixed line, spattered bullets along the normal paths of entry and exit to the village." Twenty-four-year-old Corporal John William Ewen of Asquith, Saskatchewan, fell dead. It "was then that the men of the patrol became very much afraid." Black ordered them to run for it, but the German prisoners refused. Leaving them behind would betray the patrol's position.[31] Sergeant G. Leary and Saynaeve shot them dead.[32] "It was a brutal decision. The Germans were killed, coldly and deliberately. It was their lives or those of the patrol." Meanwhile, Black managed to call in heavy artillery fire upon the village. The Canadians pressed face down into the muddy, wet ground until the shelling ceased. Many of the houses on the outer edge of the village were aflame as a section of the patrol ventured back to see if they might capture some new prisoners. But the Germans had hurriedly abandoned the place. Collecting Ewen's body, the patrol withdrew to the boats at the river. Next morning, 4th Division's new commander, Major General Chris Vokes—who had just taken over on December 1—visited the Superiors to personally congratulate Lieutenant Black on accomplishing another "successful patrol mission."[33]

[4]

Roll of the Dice

"THE ENEMY IS at present fighting a defensive campaign on all fronts; his situation is such that he cannot stage major offensive operations," Field Marshall Bernard Montgomery wrote to General Harry Crerar in a December 16 Operation Veritable directive. Lacking necessary transport and petrol, he added, the Germans were desperate to prevent the war entering a mobile phase. Their tanks also could no longer compete in mobile battle because the Allies had vastly more tanks and models, including the Sherman Firefly, which was capable of winning one-on-one engagements with both Panthers and Tigers.[1]

Things were so quiet that Montgomery flew to Eindhoven to golf with Dai Rees, a professional golfer now serving as chauffeur to Air Vice-Marshal Harry Broadhurst of 83rd British Tactical Fighter Group. It was on the links with Rees that Montgomery was notified that the Germans had launched an offensive that morning against the thin American line in the Ardennes.

All the Allied commanders were taken by surprise. Having just returned from London, Eisenhower had opted to stay that day at his sumptuous headquarters in the Trianon Palace Hotel, Versailles. He had received a cable from U.S. President Franklin D. Roosevelt announcing that his name was before the Senate for promotion to five-star General of the Armies. "From Lt-Colonel to 5-star General of the Armies in 3 years, 3 months and 16 days!" he confided to his diary. December 16 was a Saturday, and Bradley had come for an overnight visit. The general mood at SHAEF was that this was a quiet weekend to be enjoyed. Eisenhower, his speechwriter Emmet Hughes, chief of staff General Bedell Smith, and Bradley were dealing cards for a round of bridge when they were notified that an attack was under way in the Ardennes. Although the attack fell on his Twelfth Army Group, Bradley decided it was probably little more than a spoiling raid. The bridge game continued. As the night went on, a bottle of champagne was cracked to celebrate Eisenhower's fifth star, and the bridge game ran to five rubbers. The two generals went to bed around midnight.[2]

Bradley had completely misjudged the situation. In the pre-dawn hours of December 16, three German armies comprising thirteen infantry divisions, seven panzer divisions, and two armoured brigades numbering more than 240,000 troops, 700 tanks, and 2,000 guns of all types and calibres hammered down upon 83,000 American troops in five divisions of General Courtney H. Hodges's First Army. This was Hitler's desperate roll of the dice, intended to capture Antwerp and Brussels while simultaneously surrounding and destroying Twenty-First Army Group. It was to be a game changer, seizing the initiative from the western Allies and mauling them so badly that offensive action against Germany would be set back for months. This would allow sufficient time for Hitler to shift divisions from the west to stalemate the Soviet advance in the east. A negotiated peace could then follow.

It was a bold plan—one even its chief planner, Heeresgruppe B commander Generalfeldmarschall Walter Model, knew was unlikely to achieve its main objectives. He believed Antwerp was beyond reach and crushing Twenty-First Army Group a pipe dream. What he banked on was gaining the Meuse in sufficient strength to establish a new front line there before the Americans could bring up reinforcements. This would stop the Allies from driving into Germany's heartland by forcing them instead to push Model's forces back to the border—an undertaking that could require months and thousands of casualties to complete. If the Americans were sufficiently mauled, the negotiated peace might be realized.

The Germans achieved complete surprise across the breadth of the eighty-five-mile Ardennes frontage. At 0530 hours, their guns smothered the American lines under a massive explosive blanket. Divisions of infantrymen suddenly emerged from the mists cloaking the forests and overran the forward defences despite deep snow that hindered movement. Behind the infantry came tanks, totally outnumbering First Army's 242 tanks and 182 self-propelled guns. Against the German artillery, the Americans mustered only 394 guns. The Americans fought bravely, but the onslaught was impossible to contain. Strung out across nearly thirty miles of line, the 28th Infantry Division was overwhelmed by five German divisions. Two exceedingly green regiments of the 106th Division were encircled at Schnee Eifel. Despite holding their ground, the division could do nothing to stop the Germans streaming past on either flank. It was against these two American divisions in the centre that the Germans achieved spectacular initial gains. On the flanks, the Germans met stouter resistance and won little ground.

The heavy artillery barrage inflicted fewer casualties than anticipated. But the shelling cut most of the American communication lines, leaving commanders above brigade level in the dark about their troops. For Americans in the centre, the battle devolved into a number of small, isolated skirmishes. The Germans soon eliminated most of these, but this caused delays, and time was of the essence. The Germans' objectives had to be met before the Allies could respond with organized reinforcement. A particular handicap Model and his planners had failed to appreciate was that their advancing divisions were moving against the "grain of the country," as Lieutenant General Brian Horrocks later noted. Main roads in the Ardennes ran linearly northeast and southwest, with "only second- or third-class roads (in some cases almost tracks) winding...over the rugged, hilly country in between. The Ardennes was easier country to defend than to attack. The vital objectives were therefore the villages or small towns, which contained the road centres and the bridges in the valleys—places like Malmédy, St-Vith, Houffalize, and, in particular, Bastogne."[3]

Throughout the day on December 16, the American commanders remained unsure about the seriousness of the offensive, so their response was hesitant. For months, numerous intelligence indicators had suggested the Germans were planning something big in the Ardennes, but these had either gone unrecognized or been dismissed. On September 25, an Ultra decrypt of a week-old message revealed that all ss units in the west were being withdrawn and assigned to Sixth Panzer Army. Then in early November, Ultra code breakers deciphered the German rail network code. Signals showed that more than four hundred trains were shuttling men and matériel to the Ardennes front. November 23 intercepts noted Luftwaffe squadrons being shifted west and ordered to protect large troop movements into the Eifel area of the Ardennes. On December 7, Ultra advised that Heeresgruppe B was asking for fighter cover for the entire Eifel area and reconnaissance flights to detect crossing points over the Meuse. There were also specific requests for fighter cover to protect rail and truck movements, particularly by Heeresgruppe B's 5th and 6th Panzer Divisions, and 7th Infanterie-Division. On December 12, Ultra observed that all ss units had gone radio silent—standard practice for formations entering the final phase of preparations for an offensive operation.[4]

These Ultra readings should have served as sufficient warning to Eisenhower and Bradley that strong German forces were gathering in front of Twelfth Army Group's most thinly held line. If the Germans were not planning a major offensive, why would the Luftwaffe shift large numbers of fighters within range of the Ardennes when they were needed to defend central Germany's industrial cities from increasingly heavy Allied bomber attacks? Fifth Panzer Division directly faced the centre of the Ardennes front line held by U.S. First Army. Sixth Panzer Division was thought to be lurking farther back to undergo rest and refitting, yet Ultra intercepts indicated that it was mustering. Despite this accumulation of evidence, Ultra analysts did not think it compelling enough to alert the commanders that an offensive was imminent. This was partly because intercepted Enigma transmissions issued by Hitler or senior army commanders, such as Gerd von Rundstedt or Walter Model, had indicated nothing beyond maintaining a strong defensive posture. With so much at stake, the analysts did not want to ring an incorrect and costly alarm.

Lacking proof of an imminent attack, Eisenhower and Bradley decided the Germans were capable only of defensive action. "In so far as they were not firmly warned of the possibility and did not guard against it, the Ultra evidence was misread and misused. Properly understood, it was more than enough to prevent the complete surprise the German offensive achieved, and to prompt a disposition of the Allied forces less calculated to invite disaster than that which actually prevailed on the morning of 16 December," one Ultra historian later wrote.[5]

Besides Ultra, other signs had also pointed to an attack in the Ardennes. On the two nights prior to that of December 15–16, 28th Infantry Division intelligence officers repeatedly warned that their troops were hearing the creaking of the iron-rimmed wheels the Germans used on horse-drawn wagons and the throbbing of engines running in low gear. On December 15, a 106th Division intelligence officer reported sounds of major enemy movement. The same day, a Polish soldier of the 18th Volksgrenadier Division was captured by a 106th patrol. He professed to being glad his war was over because "a large-scale offensive was about to start."[6]

When U.S. First Army intelligence officer Colonel Benjamin Dickson learned that several prisoners were warning on December 14 that an offensive was imminent, he walked over to a situation map and slapped the correct area. "It's the Ardennes," he said. "Nobody paid him much attention," one observer noted. Equally astute, Patton's Third Army intelligence chief, Colonel Oscar Koch, had reached the same conclusion on December 7. When he warned Patton, the general passed the assessment to SHAEF's intelligence head, Major General Kenneth William Dobson Strong. Strong raised the matter with Bradley, who responded that a winter offensive in the Ardennes would "be foolhardy." The Germans, he said, were disposed not for an attack but a "counter-stroke in the event of an Allied breakthrough toward the Rhine in early 1945." Closer to the front, Hodges also initially underestimated the threat to First Army—considering it a strong spoiling attack that he could defeat with the divisions available.[7]

In the early morning hours of December 17, however, Bradley lay awake wondering if the situation was more serious. He decided it was "threatening," but not "yet dangerous or critical." It still seemed like a spoiling attack to draw American divisions from Patton's Third Army away from where it was poised to break into Germany. Thirty-six hours after the attack started, Bradley finally arrived back at Twelfth Army Group headquarters. He was greeted by a message from the commander of 4th Infantry Division. "If you don't get the armor up here quickly, you had better get set to move," the divisional commander warned, as Bradley's headquarters in Luxembourg would be overrun. "Pardon my French," Bradley growled, "but where in hell has this son of a bitch gotten all his strength?" He had figured Hitler all but down for the count. Now, suddenly, German armoured divisions were swarming through the American lines. Belatedly, Bradley admitted they faced a crisis.[8]

UNLIKE BRADLEY AND Eisenhower, Montgomery had immediately grasped the situation. Abandoning his golf game, he rushed back to Twenty-First Army Group's tactical headquarters at Zonhoven. While the American generals installed themselves in luxurious châteaux, Montgomery mostly lived in the field. A small caravan housed his personal office and sleeping quarters. Circled around it was an array of other caravans, specialized vehicles, and large tents. One truck served as a map room. Tents were used for messes. Numerous wireless trucks bristled with antennas. Most of the headquarters staff, including officers, slept under canvas. It all fit Montgomery's ascetic, even monkish, lifestyle. He was a sparing, rather indifferent eater who abstained from alcohol and tobacco.[9] His trademark shabby pullover sweater, sagging corduroy trousers, and black beret not only constituted a deliberately contrived public persona but also suited his nature. He cared not a whit for formal uniforms or how his officers dressed. What mattered was performance.

On December 16, Montgomery decided that Eisenhower's broad-front strategy might prove the Allies' undoing. A quick response to the offensive was critical, so the Americans should immediately abandon the planned U.S. Third Army's offensive in the Saar region and rush those divisions to First Army's aid. Montgomery recalled Horrocks from leave and placed xxx Corps on notice that it might be required to stem the German tide.

Horrocks's xxx Corps had left the front lines on December 13. It was the first time since landing in Normandy that the corps had not been on combat footing. Horrocks had moved his headquarters to Boxtel, a city just south of 's-Hertogenbosch. This positioned him well for the forthcoming Rhineland operation. The corps was close enough to the Nijmegen Salient, from which the offensive would be launched in January. Yet it was equally near 1 British Corps's frontage to support the deception plan that an offensive across the Maas into Holland was imminent. Horrocks had extended generous periods of leave to his troops, to be spent in various nearby Belgian towns and villages. Personally, he accepted a long-standing invitation from the Belgian royal family to visit their Queen Mother at the Royal Palace of Laeken outside Brussels. "With its own golf course and indoor swimming pool, it was the perfect place for a rest, and the clamour of battle seemed miles and miles away," Horrocks later wrote.

His visit there lasted but a day before a senior British Second Army staff officer phoned and tersely reported the German offensive. "Senior U.S. Generals think this is only a holding attack," the officer said, "but that old war horse, Monty, does not like the smell of it at all. He wants you to return tonight and move your Corps, which is the only reserve readily available, to occupy a lay-back position to protect Brussels. Can you return immediately?"

Such a thick fog had settled in that Horrocks could barely see "a yard in front of [his] face," so he opted not to spend the night groping his way back to Boxtel. Instead he called the corps general staff officer, Brigadier C.B. Jones, and instructed him to get the corps mobilized and ready to move at a moment's notice. Jones cut the orders that night, and in the morning Horrocks returned to Boxtel.

Horrocks had been as surprised by the offensive as anybody. He never imagined the Germans, "whom we all regarded as a beaten force, should have been able to concentrate what was obviously a very large contingent opposite the Ardennes, without U.S. Intelligence becoming aware of it." He was deeply disturbed that Eisenhower's "Broad Front policy, with its constant deployment in the line of almost all available forces, inevitably meant a shortage of reserves."[10]

On December 17, Montgomery decided the Americans could likely handle the situation alone. He worried, though, that they would draw divisions away from U.S. Ninth Army to do so. Montgomery signalled SHAEF an outline of how he believed the Americans should respond. In a cable to General Sir Alan Brooke in London that night, Montgomery set out his thoughts. The "proper answer to the enemy offensive is to launch operation VERITABLE as early as possible," he wrote. "But to do this they must draw on their south flank for troops and if they draw on their north flank then VERITABLE will not be able to be launched. If this happens we shall have to admit that we have suffered a bad set-back." The Americans needed to admit that Patton's planned offensive in the Saar was a mistake, cancel it, and shift Third Army divisions to block the German advance.[11]

Eisenhower and Bradley still wanted to believe that the German attack was simply aimed at forcing Patton to halt operations in the Saar. They clung to this delusion until December 18. So their immediate response late on December 16 was only to move two armoured divisions to the Ardennes—the 7th from Ninth Army and the 10th from Third Army. Patton protested his loss—which showed, he acknowledged later, "how little I appreciated the seriousness of the enemy attack on that date." He was not alone, of course. Not until late December 17 did Eisenhower concede that the situation in the Ardennes was sufficiently grave that it was necessary to alert SHAEF's only reserves—the 82nd and 101st Airborne Divisions—and direct their movement from Rheims toward the battlefront.

Tenacious resistance by the embattled First Army divisions had by this time foiled the German plan to gain the Meuse in two days. But the Germans were still advancing, and on December 18, the American position was precarious, especially on the right flank, where Fifth Panzer Army had punched three panzer divisions through a twelve-mile-wide breach and was advancing on Bastogne, a vital crossroads city. Bastogne was a strategic linchpin to control of the southern part of the Ardennes, and the Americans had virtually no troops there. A race ensued, which the Americans narrowly won when 10th Armored Division's Combat Command B—consisting of one tank battalion, one infantry battalion, and supporting artillery—arrived and established blocking positions while the Germans were still five miles distant. Late that night, the 11,000-strong 101st Airborne Division arrived by truck, having driven a hundred miles through the night. However, the Americans in Bastogne were immediately besieged by a larger, stronger force. It seemed doubtful they could hold out.[12]

"ALL THE TALK is of the sudden and massive German counterattack on the American front near the Ardennes," Highland Light Infantry Lieutenant Donald Pearce wrote in his diary on December 19. He was trying to keep warm in a shattered house inside the Nijmegen Salient, having just returned from two days' leave in Brussels. After weeks of dangerous night patrols and the misery of living in half-flooded trenches, Brussels had seemed "a sort of dreamland, made marvellous by deprivation and desire; quite and utterly mysterious."

Pearce and several other officers had spent their nights bar crawling and "buying a drink in each, with each drink caring less and less about the price of the next one." The bars featured "the same inconspicuous music and hypnotizing lights. Carefully groomed girls draw their chairs up beside you, share your bench or climb on your knees, pull you up onto the dance floor, order drinks for both of you, and ask to take you home for 200 francs. They are neat and perfumed and slim; and it begins to look like a good idea."

Everyone in the regiment, he wrote, was "happy the attack didn't come through here. It was certainly expected, and we are a 'thin red line' if there ever was one." Pearce's only understanding of the German offensive derived from BBC broadcasts, and he was heartened to hear that Bastogne and other strongpoints were holding out. "If Jerry had done this, say, two months ago, there would have been reason to fear a real disaster. The resistance he is meeting is evidently much rougher than he bargained on."[13]

Major George Cassidy of 4th Canadian Armoured Division's Algonquin Regiment was better informed than Pearce. The Algonquins, serving under 1 British Corps, held a long frontage along the south bank of the Maas. Dutch underground agents had recently reported a large German buildup, including many paratroops, opposite the Canadian side of the river. Cassidy thought if the German thrust through the Ardennes reached Brussels and Antwerp, Twenty-First Army Group would be cut off from the rest of the Allies and its supply sources. The Germans across the river would then cross it by amphibious assault and attempt to destroy them in detail.

Cassidy realized that the Germans were taking a terrific gamble. But "so had been our Normandy landings and they had succeeded. We would not be wise in merely shrugging off the threat. But we had been all along dangerously thin along the northern flank. The Nijmegen sector, so gallantly fought for and so heavily paid for in September, was still 'out on a limb,' but to relinquish these positions would have nullified our plans for the Rhineland offensive, now obviously to be delayed for some time."[14]

Cassidy made these observations on December 19, the same day Montgomery telephoned General Harry Crerar at 1700 hours and advised "that the enemy's penetration of the First U.S. Army's front was deep and potentially serious. With that in mind, he had decided to make immediate re-dispositions in the [Twenty-First] Army Group in order to secure his right flank. The headquarters of the [xxx] British Corps was to move that night to Hasselt, coming under the command of Lieutenant General Dempsey [British Second Army commander]." Horrocks was to report to Dempsey at once.

The next morning, Montgomery ordered the British 51st (Highland) Infantry Division to move from the Nijmegen Salient to join British Second Army. "This necessitated a reorganization of First Canadian Army's front. To close the gap left by the 51st (Highland) Division and to provide for an Army reserve, I brought the 4th Canadian Armoured Division further east to be concentrated on 21 December in the neighbourhood of Boxtel—effectively removing it from front line defensive duties. Responsibility for the sector previously held by this division was assumed by the [1st Polish Armoured Division] whose former positions were taken over by the [12th Manitoba Dragoon Guards]." This armoured car regiment was left holding a section of line extending twenty-five miles from the headwaters of the Scheldt Estuary to the city of Klundert at the mouth of the Maas. The Canadian Grenadier Guards Armoured Regiment, meanwhile, held the frontage following the estuary to the sea. That tanks and armoured cars were responsible for such long sections of line starkly reflected how thinly First Canadian Army was stretched.

New dispositions set out, Crerar rushed to a conference at 1100 hours with Second Army's Lieutenant General Miles Dempsey and Montgomery at Twenty-First Army Group's tactical headquarters. Montgomery said he felt that on the northern and southern flanks, the German incursion was being contained. In the middle, however, the Germans had gained a deep penetration and "there were no American formations between them and the River Meuse." Montgomery added that "he considered it to be of paramount importance to hold the line of the Meuse and he had already taken steps to secure all crossings and crossing places between Liège and Givet with British armoured troops" under his direct command. Dempsey was to take over that responsibility, and Montgomery instructed him "to secure and cover the crossing of the Meuse from Namur to the east." This line would be secured by Horrocks's xxx Corps, already moving there in accordance with orders from Montgomery.

A few hours earlier, Montgomery announced, Eisenhower had placed those parts of U.S. First Army north of the Ardennes under his command and confirmed his authority over U.S. Ninth Army. Eisenhower was organizing "a counter-stroke against the southern flank of the enemy penetration by Lieutenant General Patton's Third U.S. Army." Montgomery intended to "organize a strategic reserve from U.S. forces in the First and Ninth Armies for a similar operation in the north." But he wanted Dempsey "to be prepared to use the 30th British Corps in a counter-offensive role as far south as Givet. Until the situation clarified and improved, it was his firm intention at all costs to prevent the enemy from crossing the Meuse, in any strength, along this front."

The three generals realized that transferring xxx British Corps away from First Canadian Army potentially threw a wrench into the timing of the Rhineland offensive. But Montgomery said that "if the situation confronting the Allied Armies were to improve materially within the next few days, as seemed possible, and the Second British Army did not become involved in the counteroffensive on the right flank...that it was quite probable that [xxx Corps] would be returned to my command in order that the original plans for First Canadian Army should proceed without loss of time. With that in view the work of improving communications in the Army area, leading to the Nijmegen salient, would be strenuously carried on."

Returning to his headquarters, habitual cigarette smouldering between his fingers, Crerar studied the situation in his methodical manner. He "appreciated the possibility that [it] held further implications for First Canadian Army. The enemy was now staking everything he had on the success of the all-out offensive which he had launched against First U.S. Army. This great operation must soon produce very important results or it would inevitably fail. Such failure would be catastrophic for the enemy. It followed that subsidiary operations against other Allied Armies, no matter how desperate or unpromising they appeared to be, would be undertaken if the distractions they produced in any way served to assist the enemy in his main enterprise." Such operations against his army would likely involve airborne and amphibious assaults across the Maas directed at pushing through North Brabant province to Antwerp. Crerar decided he must keep a close eye on that frontage and be ready to respond instantly to any threats.[15]

PLACING AMERICAN FORCES north of the Ardennes under Montgomery's command had been a difficult decision for Eisenhower. It had actually been two British senior SHAEF officers—Chief of Operations General John Whiteley and Chief of Intelligence Major General Kenneth Strong—who suggested the idea. Whiteley and Strong had agreed this was the only way to provide sound leadership over the American troops cut off from Bradley's southern headquarters. Still, they had hesitated to pose the idea to Eisenhower, fearing it would be perceived as some British conspiracy to increase Montgomery's authority over Allied ground forces. They debated the idea into the late-night hours of December 19.

Shortly after midnight, Strong later wrote, "the news from the front had become so bad that I felt it absolutely essential to inform Bedell Smith about my growing doubts whether the Allies were matching up to the situation. Some German units had penetrated well beyond Bastogne and were getting far too near the Meuse for my liking." He and Whiteley rousted Smith from his bed and Strong pleaded that "Monty be given command at least of the Allied troops north of the penetration." Whiteley added that there had been no communication between Bradley and General Courtney Hodges's First Army headquarters for at least two days. Further, he had received a report indicating that rear area American troops in the north were confused and disorganized. Somebody needed to establish a firm command grip, and only Montgomery was positioned to do this.

Smith was inclined to accept the idea but first wanted Bradley's agreement. When he telephoned Bradley in the early morning hours of December 20, the Twelfth Army Group commander replied that the situation was not serious enough to require a "fundamental change of command." Embarrassed to have even made the suggestion, Smith hung up and angrily turned on the two British officers. He called them sons of bitches and Limey bastards. Between curses, Smith shouted that "whenever there was any real trouble, the British did not appear to trust the Americans to handle it efficiently." The proposal, he declared, "would be completely unacceptable to the Americans." Smith told the two officers he had lost faith in them and they would be relieved in the morning and sent back to Britain.

It was about 0300 hours. All three officers were exhausted. Smith had a famously short fuse that could be ignited at any moment. Whiteley and Strong left, convinced that their careers at SHAEF were at an end. Strong set about preparing his last morning briefing, which he gave at 0900. Smith presided over the briefing, as Eisenhower was working alone in his office. The situation was grim, Strong reported. Sixth Panzer Army had committed at least two new divisions overnight. There were indications that the Germans were transferring divisions from Italy and Russia to reinforce the Ardennes offensive. It appeared the Germans had captured great quantities of fuel that could keep them supplied for several weeks. The fog and resulting poor visibility meant no Allied air support. The embattled troops were fighting not just the enemy but also freezing temperatures and deep snow. German paratroopers wearing American uniforms were reputedly creeping around the rear areas looking to assassinate senior officers. Sixty paratroopers were understood to be closing on Versailles with orders to kill

Eisenhower.

When the briefing ended, Whiteley and Strong walked toward Eisenhower's office to learn their fate. They had not gone far when Smith appeared at Strong's side and took his arm. He told Strong it was now his intention to recommend to Eisenhower that Montgomery take command of the northern sector and attack the German thrust from that direction. Whiteley and Strong were to remain silent. Smith said the proposal would "come much better from an American." Strong had been right, Smith admitted, and what had made him "really mad was that I knew you were right. But my American feelings got the better of me because I also knew of the outcry there would be in the United States about your proposal, if it was put into effect."

At 1000 hours, Smith pitched the proposal to Eisenhower. Surprised that his chief of staff would consider such an idea, but persuaded by his argument, Eisenhower agreed. He immediately called Bradley and broke the news. Everyone in the room could hear Bradley ranting loudly. As Bradley ran out of steam, Eisenhower said quietly, "Well, Brad, those are my orders."

Eisenhower next called Montgomery, at 1030. "He was very excited," Montgomery wrote, "and it was difficult to understand what he was talking about; he roared into the telephone, speaking very fast. The only point I really grasped was that 'it seems to me we now have two fronts' and that I was to assume command of the northern front. This was all I wanted to know. He then went on talking wildly about other things; I could not hear, and said so; at last the line cut out before he had finished."[16]

It was later rumoured that Montgomery had exaggerated the degree of telephone static and used it as an excuse to hang up on Eisenhower. Whatever the truth, Montgomery saw no point in further discussion. The northern front was his to command. That was what mattered. He got to work immediately. From Ultra intercepts and a stream of daily reports from British liaison officers, which he regularly posted throughout the American command chain, Montgomery had an extensive understanding of the dispositions and condition of the forces of both sides engaged in the Ardennes. His first action was the 1100 hours meeting with Crerar and Dempsey to arrange Twenty-First Army Group's response to the German offensive. When that meeting ended, at 1205 hours, Montgomery set off by car to visit U.S. First Army headquarters. He had requested that Ninth Army's Lieutenant General William Simpson meet him and General Courtney Hodges there. A small, fluttering Union Jack was attached to the hood, and the car itself was surrounded by British military police astride motorcycles. A small convoy of other vehicles carried various members of Montgomery's staff. Montgomery was in high spirits. He strode into First Army's headquarters in Verviers at 1330 hours, observed one of his aides-de-camp, "like Christ come to cleanse the temple." Displaying neither humility nor diplomacy, Montgomery's imperious tone struck many of the Americans as conveying "a note of censure."[17]

This impression was correct. Montgomery wrote after his visit that both armies "were in a complete muddle. Bradley had not visited either Army since the attack began; there had been no grip, or tight control, of the battle; the Army Commanders did what they thought best."[18] It was true that neither Hodges nor Simpson had received any direction from Bradley. The only concrete action he had taken regarding the northern sector was to strip Simpson of all but three divisions and assign the rest to Hodges. This gave Hodges a great deal of strength—twenty divisions under command of four corps—but they were spread out across a wide and broken front.

Hodges still nominally commanded the entire Ardennes front, but he could exert no real control over the divisions in the central and southern parts. These divisions were engaged in individual delaying battles that lacked any overall coordination. The new divisions thrown in to restore the broken front arrived randomly and were swept up in new individual battles wherever they contacted the Germans. The fortuitous arrival of 101st Airborne Division at Bastogne had occurred in this manner. The division had come not to defend Bastogne, but rather to reach "an excellent road centre." Also largely by chance, 7th Armored Division had similarly deployed at the important road junction centre of St. Vith. Each divisional commander had then quickly realized that these centres were in danger of being overrun and must be defended.[19] Most of the isolated

American divisions offered fierce and often skillful resistance—a fact acknowledged by the Germans in a message picked up by Ultra. The intercept blamed the German failure to achieve a decisive and quick breakthrough to the Meuse on inadequate bridges, shortages of heavy weapons, and unexpected and strong resistance.[20]

While Montgomery believed only he correctly read German strategy, Hodges and his staff equally recognized Sixth Panzer Army's intention in the northern sector of the Ardennes. It sought to win crossings over the Meuse on either side of Liège and from there to advance to Antwerp. This was confirmed by another Ultra intercept of Luftwaffe instructions that no Meuse bridges on a line running west of Liège to Bastogne be bombed in order to preserve them for German use. Three more Ultra intercepts passed to the senior Allied commanders on December 20 clarified that Sixth Panzer Army was in dire straits. Its 1st ss Panzer Division had run out of fuel and ammunition at Stoumont, a town twenty-six miles southwest of Liège. American armoured units were reportedly closing in on the virtually helpless division.[21]

Montgomery told Hodges and Simpson that he wanted the latter's Ninth Army to assume control of the American sector to the north of the German penetration. The Americans would also form a reserve corps of at least three divisions—the 84th and 75th Infantry Divisions and 3rd Armored Division. This VII Corps would not be committed to battle until it was fully assembled and ready to launch a major counterattack. Montgomery was determined to stop feeding divisions in piecemeal. He believed the period of crisis had passed. It would, he telegraphed London that evening, "take a day or two to get the American front reorganized and in better shape and we may have a few more shocks before that is completed."

Clearly there would still be hard fighting ahead, but Montgomery thought the outcome already decided. British units were in place to defend the vital bridges over the Meuse. He had Horrocks's xxx Corps in position as a reserve that could interdict any German incursion across the river. Only in a truly dire circumstance would he agree to otherwise commit this corps to battle. Montgomery was thinking ahead, determined to keep xxx Corps intact for Operation Veritable. He was confirmed in his earlier estimation that the situation could largely be restored using "American troops already there."[22]

Montgomery's assessment was correct. Although the Germans would continue to batter away and gain some ground, they failed to come close to gaining a crossing over the Meuse. Sixth Panzer Army would continue hammering away with six divisions without any real gain until December 23. Thereafter, they went over to the defence. The German tankers at Stoumont, who never received sufficient fuel or ammunition by desperate air resupply attempts to remain mobile, abandoned their tanks on the 24th. Eight hundred managed to escape back on foot and rejoin the rest of 1st ss Panzer Division.

Fifth Panzer Army, meanwhile, had managed to take St. Vith in fierce fighting on December 21. Montgomery responded by ordering the surrounding defences withdrawn to shorten the American line. Bastogne continued to hold out. The closest the Germans came to the Meuse was when a part of 2nd Panzer Division fought through to the heights of Foye Notre Dame, which lay about three miles from the Dinant bridge crossing. Montgomery already had British 29th Armoured Brigade established in a blocking position in front of the bridge, and the British 53rd (Welsh) Infantry Division stood on the opposite bank. On Christmas Day, a battle group consisting of U.S. 2nd Armored Division and 29th Armoured Brigade eliminated the German detachment. As the British official historian wrote later, *"The German armies got no further. Their advance had come to a feeble end."*[23]

Officially designated the Battle of the Ardennes, but unofficially known as the Battle of the Bulge, the end only came on January 28 when the Germans were pushed back to their December 16 start lines. American casualties tallied 8,497 killed, 46,170 wounded, and 20,905 missing and presumed captured or dead. The British units involved reported 200 dead, 969 wounded, and 239 missing. No definitive German casualty count exists. One German estimate reported total casualties at 81,834, of which 12,652 died. Another put the total at 92,234. The Allies knew they had taken more than 50,000 prisoners. Both sides had lost about 800 tanks and vast amounts of other equipment and supplies. But the Allies could replace this matériel in a couple weeks, something the Germans could never do.[24]

[5]

War Is a Bitch

FIRST CANADIAN ARMY played no role in the Battle of the Ardennes. When the German offensive started, several companies of No. 1 Canadian Forestry Group had been logging and milling timber in sawmills southeast of Namur and at Spa. With the Germans closing on their positions, loggers exchanged saws for rifles and took up defensive positions until they were evacuated. The battle was significant to First Canadian Army, however, because of its effect on the army's future operational role and the potential threat of German attacks to support their main offensive in the Ardennes front lines.[1]

General Harry Crerar had warned his corps commanders on December 23 that an assault against their fronts intended to break through to Antwerp was feasible. "I pointed out that no treachery or trickery would be neglected by the enemy if he considered that it would assist his purpose, and that if other conditions suited, he might select either Christmas Eve or Christmas day or night for offensive action on the assumption that he would thereby gain surprise." His generals were therefore to put their troops on alert and develop plans "to deal vigorously and decisively with any hostile penetration of outpost positions and forward lines of defence and, at the same time, to contain, localize, and mop up any landings of enemy paratroops in the rear areas. They were to organize the defence of all centres of communication, either by troops normally located in such areas, or by forces specially designated for the purpose." Aware that the Germans in the Ardennes were counting on captured American petrol and ammunition to enable their offensive to continue, Crerar said "local reserves of ammunition, petrol, oil, lubricants and supplies" exceeding immediate needs "were to be dumped."[2]

Crerar was responding to a First Canadian Army intelligence summary of December 21 that the Germans were planning to carry out "a large paratroop operation...to disrupt the communications of the armies dependent on Antwerp and Brussels." His intelligence staff said it was "abundantly clear that there are paratroops in German Holland, and that their movements tie in to this design." They predicted that if the Germans in the Ardennes succeeded in crossing the Meuse, paratroop drops behind xxx British Corps could threaten the defence there. Similar landings behind First Canadian Army might cause great chaos to its defence of the Nijmegen Salient and Maas River frontage.

Army intelligence staff expressed alarm over further reports indicating that four parachute divisions were "preparing a large operation on 'North Brabant' or on Brussels, Antwerp and communications lines." The German airfields at Soesterberg, east of Utrecht, and Deelen, immediately north of Arnhem, were to be used for paratroop operations. Other intelligence reported Heeresgruppe H's commander, Generaloberst Kurt Student, holding secret meetings with the paratroop division commanders at Hilversum on December 10. These discussions had been so secret that no regular Wehrmacht officers had been allowed into the building. The intelligence reports also indicated that the Luftwaffe had "at least ninety suitable planes giving a maximum lift of about 1,000 at a time."

Whether the German paratroop attack was launched probably depended on the success of land operations in the Ardennes. If no crossings of the Meuse were won, the airborne attack became "only a possible and NOT a probable operation. But it is being prepared and must be provided against." Crerar fully agreed.[3]

Of major concern were warnings from the Dutch resistance. They had cautioned that German airborne units were specifically planning two operations likely to occur during the night of December 24–25. One involved a drop directly on First Canadian Army headquarters at Tilburg. The other would parachute units behind Kapelsche Veer to destroy the Canadian medium and field artillery regiments stationed there. At the same time that the airborne units would drop, German attacks would be launched across the Maas by potentially three divisions aimed at Breda and then due south to Antwerp. There would also be an amphibious assault by the ten thousand German troops garrisoned on Overflakee and Schouwen against the frontage thinly held by the 12th Manitoba Dragoon Guards Reconnaissance Regiment and supported by five hundred former Dutch resistance fighters.[4]

Crerar took these threats seriously and reorganized the army to meet them. He ordered 4th Canadian Armoured Division, in reserve near Boxtel, moved westward to establish behind the Wilhelmina Canal a secondary defensive line that extended from Breda to Tilburg. The 2nd Canadian Infantry Division's 4th Brigade was slotted into the narrow frontage for which the armoured division had been responsible at Boxtel. He also moved to ensure that 11 Canadian Corps had a reserve in the Nijmegen Salient. Lieutenant General Guy Simonds was instructed to pull 2nd Division, less its 5th Brigade, from the line. The 3rd Canadian Infantry Division, strengthened by the attachment of 5th Brigade, extended its southern flank to fill the gap created by 2nd Division's withdrawal.[5]

On December 22, 4th Division divided its area into sectors and developed plans for defending each of them. Sentries were doubled and all ranks were put on alert to be ready for immediate action. Every man, no matter what his assigned duty, was to carry personal weapons "at all times."[6]

At Crerar's headquarters, the guard battalion, the Royal Montreal Regiment, set about strengthening and organizing defences to ward off an airborne attack.[7]

During his first inspection of the British Columbia Regiment, 4th Division's Major General Chris Vokes warned that they "would very soon be in action." On Christmas Eve, the regiment moved its tanks near the town of Rijen, a few miles from the Maas, and established battle stations not only to defend against a river crossing but to engage paratroopers "expected in the night or early Christmas morning. Everyone," wrote Captain Douglas Harker, "was warned that this would be a fight to the last man and to the last round."[8]

The Canadians were stretched so thin that engineering units were enlisted to send patrols out to watch for German paratroopers and infiltrators wearing Allied uniforms or civilian clothing. All "suspicious characters, whether in uniforms or civilian clothes, are to be detained for questioning and will be held until their identity is established," stated instructions to 2nd Division's engineers. "All ranks will be constantly on the lookout for enemy ruses...Units will seek to confuse the enemy by counter-ruses, such as leaving a decoy jeep (previously immobilized) as a tempting bait [and covering] it from hidden positions nearby...The importance of always safeguarding vehicles is again emphasized. They will be the enemy's first objective...patrols will never leave their vehicles unguarded whilst killing Germans."[9]

The 4th Division's Algonquin Regiment had no sooner established its positions behind the Wilhelmina Canal than patrols were ordered out. Major George Cassidy led one patrol, the troops with him loaded into a jeep. "Christmas Eve was cold, still and clear," he wrote. "Although no snow had fallen in quantity, the ploughed fields crunched under one's steps, while high above hovered the motionless stars, poised and majestic...The hushed world seemed for a moment to have forgotten war, to be wrenching itself back through centuries of sin and cruelty, oppression and tyranny, to the night when the Prince of Peace descended to suffer with mankind.

"But the patrols must go on, even under the cruel irony that it was not the Redeemer that was coming through that ineffable blue-black sky, but the Destroyer on silken wings, as deadly silent as an adder. Tonight would be ideal for his purpose. The flat fields lay open and inviting, the visibility just right. Would he come tonight? Would the next bend in the road reveal a white cluster of shapes in the dull fields? If it did, would we be able to handle the situation? The singing tires of the jeep thrummed through and through with these thoughts, somehow reassuring, as jeeps always were."

Cassidy knew that behind the Algonquin position, First Canadian Army Headquarters was "perilously close to the front, and very vulnerable to a parachute threat...It had to be protected...for if it went, the whole Canadian north flank would collapse. It was a sober picture, and our task was soberly undertaken." When Cassidy's patrol brushed up against the rear area patrols of the Polish division guarding the Maas ahead of them, he found them particularly worried about reports of Germans masquerading as Americans in the Ardennes. They were suspicious of the Algonquins, fingers twitching on triggers. Neither Cassidy nor the Polish officers could communicate easily. He thought it "a matter of even odds whether some dark night we would not find ourselves embroiled in a pitched battle with our allies over the canal."[10]

For his part, Corporal John M. "Pinky" Craig of 4th Division's Argyll and Sutherland Highlanders could hardly believe the "great big area" his anti-tank platoon Bren carrier section was ordered to patrol on Christmas morning. Before setting out, the section was given its turkey. "It was canned turkey...There's two little pieces of turkey in this can and all the rest was dressing...[and] we were given a bottle of English beer." They were to eat dinner in the field. Craig asked his commanding officer how five men were supposed to secure such a large chunk of ground. "Report your position back; where the drop is being made; whether the Germans are dropping; and prepare to fight." Craig snapped back, "What? Did you ever see pictures of those paratroopers coming down? There's thousands of them coming down." The officer cut him off. "That's my order...be prepared to fight."

After the officer left, Craig and his men huddled. "We ain't prepared to do nothing," one man declared. If the Germans showed up, they would get "the heck outta here." Craig agreed, because "what could five guys do against a whole bunch of airborne paratroopers?"

Later, as the day passed and the sky failed to fill with planes loaded full of elite paratroopers, Craig pulled the Bren carrier up next to a farmhouse. He knocked on the door and asked the family inside "if they would mind if we stayed in the house to have our Christmas dinner instead of just eating it out in the carrier or out in the field or something. So we busted everything open and shared it with them, and that's how we had our Christmas dinner." Although they enjoyed sharing the dinner with the family, they grumbled about the skimpy turkey offering and the English beer. Rumour had it the English troops were getting Canadian beer that should have been theirs.[11]

Standing watch on the Maas that Christmas Day, British Columbia Regiment 'C' Squadron commander Major Jim Tedlie munched on a cold turkey leg washed down with beer from a tin mug while seated in the open turret hatch of his Sherman. He stared across the river. All his crew had been well fed a few hours earlier, the Dukes (as the regiment was nicknamed) adhering to Canadian regimental tradition whereby the officers serve the other ranks Christmas dinner before taking their own. Tedlie and the other officers had been just sitting down when the regiment was ordered immediately to the front. Shovelling what they could of their dinner into mess tins, the officers headed for their tanks. Tedlie saw nothing particularly threatening. Off to the flanks, an occasional shell exploded on one side of the river or the other. Sometimes a machine gun loosed off a trail of tracer fire. No mistaking that the war continued, but not too much obvious danger either. Tedlie knew that could change in a heartbeat, so he ensured that the squadron remained alert.[12]

The paratrooper scare ruined many Canadian regiments' plans for Christmas. Planning to rotate squadrons from where they faced the Maas, 4th Division's South Alberta Reconnaissance Regiment had sequestered a large room in a building and set up tables for dinner. Decorations and bunting adorned the tables. Trooper David Marshall later wrote that each soldier "was to get a pint of beer, canned turkey, mashed potatoes, creamed carrots, peas and peaches and a mince tart for dessert. There were also cigarettes, cigars and an orange, a small parcel from the Women's Auxiliary and a diary from the Sally Ann." Marshall was savouring the prospect of dinner, when orders came for the squadron to man its tanks and return to the line.[13]

By Christmas Day, 11 Canadian Corps headquarters staff were beginning to suspect that neither the paratrooper threat nor major offensives across the river would materialize. 11 Canadian Corps's Chief Signals Officer, Brigadier Samuel Findlay "Fin" Clark, led the effort by several senior staff officers, including Chief of Staff Brigadier Elliot Rodger, to pen an appropriate poem for the period. They came up with: "11 Canadian Corps though festive, will / hold tight as hell from Elst to Mill / while pushing piles and grouping guns / will hold the line against the Hun." By midnight, Rodger was able to record in his diary that there "were indications from Army that the flap had passed its climax."[14]

John Morgan Gray, an officer with a nearby Canadian counter-intelligence unit, noted that "the menu [for] Christmas dinner in an old monastery had a picture of Santa Claus in a German helmet swinging down in a parachute and carrying a German Schmeisser sub-machine gun under his arm. As a caption we borrowed a brave sentiment from Henry v: 'And gentlemen in England now abed shall think themselves accursed they were not here.'"[15]

A number of regiments, particularly those in the Nijmegen Salient—considered less at risk of airborne attack than the Maas River line—managed to serve dinners and offer other entertainment for the troops. In general, however, it was all "hastily improvised in strange surroundings," and throughout First Canadian Army a high state of readiness was demanded.[16]

The Highland Light Infantry offered Christmas dinner in a Berg en Dal hotel near their front-line position. Half the regiment was cycled out for dinner on Christmas and the other half attended the following day. Lieutenant Donald Pearce was among those to have his meal on Christmas. "Plenty of rum, turkey, chicken, and pudding have been amassed...I expect to get looped on rum punch," Pearce wrote. On his way back to the front, Pearce stopped to visit the headquarters of the support company with which he had served before being posted to a rifle company. He was plied with more rum and some roast duck. Leaving the headquarters, Pearce realized he had achieved his day's ambition and become, "as I said I would, thoroughly soused." But he also knew he was supposed to be back in charge of his platoon on the front lines by 1630 hours. He was on foot and about halfway there "when a warm drowsiness literally flooded through me, and I lay down beside a mound of frozen straw, a few bundles of it, in an open field, and fell asleep. I woke up a couple hours later. All completely dark. So cold my joints would hardly articulate. The temperature must have been zero, if not below. I imagined myself in hospital in a day or two, a raving madman, delirious with fever and double pneumonia. Haven't even caught cold, damn it," he lamented in his diary.[17]

"How real was the German threat in the Netherlands during the Ardennes offensive?" the Canadian Army's official historian asked later.[18] In December 1944, there was considerable disagreement about whether the intelligence was true. While not dismissing the threat, Simonds had questioned the Germans' ability to execute such operations. But as more German documents were captured and messages decoded, it became apparent that the threat had indeed been real. If the Germans had crossed the Meuse, they would have followed up with crossings of the river in Holland and drops by airborne troops. By New Year's Day, Canadian intelligence staff suspected the operation had been abandoned. Four days later, First Canadian Army's intelligence staff commented, "The evidence...increases and continues to show that the enemy has probably changed his mind about an offensive operation over the lower Maas."[19] The intelligence officers were correct; the danger had passed.

THE ARDENNES OFFENSIVE sparked an intense aerial battle. Initially, neither side could provide air support because of prevailing heavy cloud and fog. By December 17, however, weather conditions had improved. The Allies lashed at the German supply network. Railways, roads, and bridges on routes leading to the Ardennes were bombed. Anything moving by day was subject to attack in what the British official historian described as "one of the most striking demonstrations of Allied air power since the D-Day assault on the Normandy beaches." Six Allied air forces—British Bomber Command, Fighter Command, and Second Tactical Air Force alongside the American Eighth Air Force, Night Air Force, and First Tactical Air Force (Provisional)—participated in operations against the Germans.

During the ten-day period from December 17 to 27, the Luftwaffe desperately tried to gain air superiority over the Ardennes, flying an average of five hundred sorties daily. This was an impressive effort for an air force virtually on its knees. But the Luftwaffe aircraft were overwhelmed by the more than three thousand Allied daily sorties.

The Germans lost seven hundred aircraft in the ten days, compared with just over three hundred Allied planes downed.[20]

To broaden the German aerial response, Hitler had ordered a major v-1 and v-2 assault on Antwerp, seeking to cripple the port and sink Allied ships unloading supplies. The main flight path for the v-1 jet-powered flying bomb passed over the frontage held by 1 British Corps along the Maas River. (The liquid-fuel-powered rocket v-2, with its Mac 1 speed capability and altitude reach of fifty to sixty miles was virtually undetectable until it plunged to earth.) The v-1 was notoriously inaccurate and prone to crashing. Despite a top speed of four hundred miles per hour, it was vulnerable to anti-aircraft fire. When the bombs were detected, First Canadian Army's flak regiments tried to shoot them down. Generally, when one crashed, its one-ton warhead detonated. Consequently, they posed a sporadic hazard to troops and civilians along the regular flight lines.

The Argyll and Sutherland Highlanders were in the middle of one major v-1 flight path on December 26. Two nights before, they had moved to Dorst, a village just east of Breda and about seven miles behind the Maas. Battalion headquarters took over several pubs and adjacent homes for quarters and offices while the line companies spread out among other buildings. Dorst had two advantages missing from their former operational base—running water and electricity. While the regiment's war diarist enthused at length about their new locale in his Christmas Eve entry, he also noted that the Argylls "were now on the direct path the buzz bombs...follow from Holland to Antwerp and many...falling short of their mark, caused heavy blast and much nervousness in the peaceful village."

Christmas Day brought a significant decrease in v-1's aloft. Some Argyll officers suggested the sacred day was responsible "for the sudden reduction in the number of the diabolic weapons." Others concluded that the clear day and good visibility—which would easily reveal launching sites—was partially responsible for the lack of activity. The following day saw "the usual quota of buzz-bombs, one of which, roaring in at a dangerously low altitude, struck a tree near Dorst, causing considerable consternation among the war-weary populace." On December 27, at 1520 hours, "out of a literally clear blue sky, a flying bomb exploded with a deafening roar a mere few hundred yards west of Dorst, luckily missing the highway and striking an uninhabited field. There was considerable glass damage in town, several civilians being injured by flying glass; while none of our troops were hurt."[21]

Lieutenant Douglas S. Cruthers had his platoon headquarters in a house about a hundred yards from where the v-1 exploded. Because the blast was directed forward rather than to all sides, his house was undamaged. But the windows in one nearby all shattered. "Come on, we'd better go over there and see if anybody's hurt," Cruthers yelled. "We ran over to this little house and went inside, and I never saw anything that touched me so much in all my life...Here was this little girl about five, and she'd obviously been standing in the living room. And these little houses aren't that big...And she was just cut to ribbons with flying glass." His first thought was, "You [German] bastards...This poor...defenceless little girl." Then he thought, "God, war is a bitch."[22] In modern warfare, soldiers and civilians alike could die in so many different ways.

On New Year's Day, the Argylls witnessed "a German air attack on the airfield at Gilze," a couple of miles southeast of them. Three enemy planes fell to anti-aircraft fire. But the "few jet-propelled crafts...used...were too fast and thoroughly immune to any fire from the ground."[23]

The Gilze raid was a small part of the "Hangover Raid."[24] Maintaining wireless silence, flying at treetop level to evade radar detection, and following circuitous routes, more than 900 German planes attacked thirteen British and four American tactical airfields. Some Allied aircraft were just taking off to relieve others providing close support to ground forces. Many planes were caught standing in the open, and 150 of these were destroyed. Another 6 were downed in dogfights with German fighters. Forty-six Allied personnel were killed.[25]

Three British airfields—Eindhoven, Heesch, and Evere—were home to Royal Canadian Air Force wings serving as part of RAF Second Tactical Air Force. The No. 39 (Reconnaissance) Wing and No. 143 (Fighter Bomber) Wing at Eindhoven were subjected to a massive strafing attack by a swarm of German aircraft. Surprise was complete. Fourteen No. 143 Wing Typhoons were wrecked. Two of the handful of Typhoons that got airborne were shot down. The German planes circled the airfield, subjecting it to heavy strafing for a further twenty minutes despite fire from three squadrons of RAF anti-aircraft gunners.

Sergeant W.L. Large of No. 143 Wing's 438 Squadron had been standing near a hangar watching Typhoons take off when the German attack started. At first he thought it was a hit-and-run raid, but after a third wave came over and the aircraft began circling to "continue their attacks out of the sun, I figured they were playing for keeps and...hurried back to dispersal where our Bren guns were kept. There I saw [Flight Sergeant C.J.] McGee and we decided to take a whack at everything flying over dispersal. We each took a Bren gun and two boxes of clips and stood outside the dispersal door and waited for any Jerry who came within range...One aircraft coming from the south turned off the runway and made a steep climbing turn about 120 yards away from us at a height of more than forty feet. We both fired, each emptying a magazine at him. We saw strikes down the engine cowling in the direction of the cockpit and saw small pieces fall off."

A burned-out Luftwaffe FW–190 fighter discovered later near the airfield was credited as a kill by Large and McGee.[26] A total of ten German pilots were reported killed or missing after the raid, and six others were captured when they bailed out of damaged planes. Eindhoven suffered heavily. A total of thirty-one aircraft—Canadian and British—were burning or badly shot up. Many buildings were damaged or aflame. Bomb and fuel dumps exploded and burned. Thirteen men, including six Canadians, were dead. Of the many wounded, twenty-four were Canadian.

The Germans had considered the airfield at Evere, just outside Brussels, a prime target because it was among the most heavily utilized bases in western Belgium. Crowded alongside RAF squadrons were those of No. 223 (Canadian) Wing. Damage to the airfield was extensive, and there were many casualties, including one Canadian killed and nine wounded. One of the wounded later died.[27] Damage at Heere, where the five Spitfire fighter squadrons of No. 126 Wing were deployed, was reported as "hardly worth mentioning."[28] The lack of damage was largely due to the Germans apparently not realizing that the airfield existed until one of their squadrons flew directly over it en route to other targets. No. 126 Wing was able to scramble many fighters, and the Spitfires contributed significantly to German losses.

The Hangover Raid was the Luftwaffe's last-gasp attack on the western Allies. Although they attained surprise and inflicted heavy damage on Allied air forces, their losses were heavier than what they meted out. A total of 270 German aircraft were shot down and 40 damaged by anti-aircraft fire or Allied fighters. Aircrew losses totalled 260, including many experienced pilots the Germans "could ill-afford to lose at this stage of the war. They had indeed lost much more than they had gained in this operation," the British Army's official historian convincingly concluded.[29]

AFTER THE HANGOVER Raid ended on the evening of January 1, First Canadian Army entered a week of "little activity on these cold, clear days." Each day there were more indications that the feared offensive against its front along the Maas was "diminishing." Crerar remained wary, however, still convinced that a combined amphibious assault across the river and airborne drops to the rear of his front lines could happen at any time. As a result, "the constant watch was...kept up."[30]

Responsibility for the defence of the islands of Walcheren and North and South Beveland on the Dutch coast had previously rested with an independent command composed of British 4th Commando Brigade, Royal Netherlands Brigade, and several anti-aircraft units. On January 3, Crerar proposed to Montgomery that so long as the threat of German attacks across the Maas remained, this area should be under his command. Montgomery agreed that Crerar should oversee all of Twenty-First Army Group's northern sector. This left him responsible for a 175-mile front.[31]

Crerar decided to temporarily break 4th Canadian Armoured Division into three combat teams. These consisted of an armoured regiment, an infantry regiment, a squadron from the South Alberta Reconnaissance Regiment, and a company from the mobile Lake Superior Regiment. Each was assigned specific areas and ordered to reconnoitre them "down to the lowest level, so that the counter-thrust might be quickly organized."[32]

As indications mounted that what was later dubbed the Christmas Alarm would not develop, Crerar ordered a further reorganization for the week of January 8–15. Retaining its combat team groupings, 4th Canadian Armoured Division would slot into the right flank of 1 British Corps, "leaving the 1st Polish Armoured Division in the centre on a comparatively narrow front, with the 11 Canadian Corps's 12th Manitoba Dragoons armoured reconnaissance regiment left of the Poles. The British 62nd Anti-Tank Regiment faced the sea, and to its left the 4th Commando Brigade guarded Walcheren and South and North Beveland Islands. The 12th Manitoba Dragoons continued to be ably supported by its contingent of about five hundred former Dutch resistance fighters, who acted as infantry and maintained a constant vigil along the banks of the river while the armoured cars prowled.

On January 12, Crerar received the welcome news that the Russians had launched a massive winter offensive. He was soon receiving intelligence reports that "its repercussions would be felt on the enemy situation in the west. Almost immediately I received a report that the 711th Infantry Division, which had been deployed across the Maas during the enemy's recent concentration...had been identified by the Russian General Staff [as having turned up] in Hungary [to face the Soviet Army there]. This was the first time the Germans had found it necessary to withdraw a division away from the west since 6 June, 1944."

Crerar decided his attention could be redirected from the defensive to "rapidly" remounting the offensive against the Rhineland. Doing so would not present serious difficulty. When the Ardennes offensive caused the January 1 start date for this operation to be shelved, Crerar had "made it clear" to his staff that he "considered the operation to be only temporarily postponed, and the necessary preparations had gone on, therefore, without interruption."[33]

Crerar's thinking aligned with that of his senior commanders. On December 31, Eisenhower had outlined a plan for future operations. Its basic purpose was "to destroy enemy forces west of the Rhine, north of the Moselle, and to prepare for crossing the Rhine in force with the *main effort north of the Ruhr.*" All that was required first was the reduction of the Ardennes salient. Once that was accomplished, Twenty-First Army Group "with Ninth U.S. Army under command [would] resume preparations for 'Veritable.'" Eisenhower declared that it was vital the Allies "regain the initiative, and speed and energy are essential."

Montgomery, meanwhile, had again argued by letter on December 29 that unless he was given control of all Allied land forces, future operations could well fail. In a burst of egotism surprising even for Montgomery, he decided Eisenhower was not only sympathetic to this idea but in concurrence. No sooner did Montgomery send off his letter than he was devastated to learn that Eisenhower had just received a cable from General George C. Marshall, Chief of Staff of the U.S. Army, declaring flatly that neither he nor President Roosevelt would countenance a British officer holding operational control over all American troops. Montgomery belatedly decided it was time to "pipe down." On the last day of 1944 he cabled Eisenhower. Montgomery asked him to tear up the letter and reassured him that "you can rely on me one hundred per cent."

Shortly after this *mea culpa,* Eisenhower's outline plan for future operations arrived. It was accompanied by a handwritten letter in which Eisenhower clearly stated that he did not "agree that one Army Group Commander should fight his own battle and give orders to another Army Group Commander. My plan places a complete U.S. Army under command of 21 Army Group, something that I consider militarily necessary, and most assuredly reflects my confidence in you personally. If these things were not true this decision would, in itself, be a most difficult one.

"You know how greatly I've appreciated and depended on your frank and friendly counsel, but in your latest letter you disturb me by predictions of 'failure' unless your exact opinions in the matter of giving you command over Bradley are met in detail. I assure you that in this matter I can go no further." Eisenhower stressed that he was building up Twenty-First Army Group to carry out a major task.

"I studied the outline plan," Montgomery wrote. "It did all I wanted except in the realm of operational control, and because of Marshall's telegram that subject was closed. It put the weight in the north and gave the Ninth American Army to 21 Army Group. It gave me power of decision in the event of disagreement with Bradley on the boundary of 12 and 21 Army Groups. In fact, I had been given very nearly all that I had been asking for since August. Better late than never. I obviously could not ask for more."

On January 2, Montgomery advised Eisenhower that eliminating the Ardennes salient promised to "take some little time and that there will be heavy fighting." Once tactical victory was won, he foresaw "a considerable interval before other offensive movements begin to develop though I think it is important to try and stage Operation Veritable earliest possible. Apart from these few ideas which occur to me I have no comments on the outline plan and details can be worked out later on. You can rely on me and all under my command to go all out one hundred per cent to implement your plan."[34]

It was a good thing that Montgomery abandoned his quest for overall command. On January 7, he seriously blundered by holding an absurdly misconceived press conference regarding the Ardennes offensive. Wearing a new British Airborne Corps beret, reflecting his recent appointment as a parachute regiment colonel, Montgomery initially showered praise upon the American soldiers fighting valiantly and at great cost in the Ardennes.[35] He then claimed credit for saving the situation. Eisenhower, by casting "national considerations" aside and giving Montgomery command in the Ardennes, had turned the job over to the general most able to turn the course of the battle around.[36] "The battle has been most interesting," he said. "I think possibly one of the most interesting and tricky battles I have ever handled."[37]

Listening on the sidelines, his chief of intelligence, Brigadier Bill Williams, despaired at Montgomery's words and their delivery. "It seemed to me, well, *disastrous*. I couldn't stop it...the whole sort of business of preening made one feel extremely uncomfortable." The text of his presentation taken alone might have been viewed positively by the Americans, he thought, "but the presentation was quite appalling."[38]

Many later accounts claimed Bradley only learned of the press conference from a German propaganda broadcast that deliberately used it out of context to foment ill will. This was untrue. The conference was over no more than a few hours when Bradley was deluged by press clippings. Those of the British press lauded Montgomery while criticizing the American performance in the Ardennes and particularly Bradley's handling of the battle. Bradley quickly and sharply told Eisenhower "he could never serve under Montgomery" again.[39] Eisenhower later wrote, "I doubt that Montgomery ever came to realize how deeply resentful some American commanders were. They believed he had belittled them—and they were not slow to voice reciprocal scorn and contempt."[40] It was clear that Eisenhower would henceforth place no further American forces under Montgomery's command unless absolutely necessary.

[6]

The Small Thorn

ALTHOUGH THE GERMAN plan to force a crossing over the Maas had largely failed, it led to one incursion that quickly proved to be a thorn in First Canadian Army's side. Any major assault across the Maas was to have been implemented by Twenty-Fifth Army's LXXXVIII Korps. Generalleutnant Felix Schwalbe, the corps's recently appointed commander, thought such an idea sheer madness. He had awakened the morning after learning that the intention was serious and wondered, "Are we really going to cross the Maas, or did I merely dream it all?"[1]

Distressed to learn that it was all too true, he had taken heart in the fact that the scheme hinged on the Allied response to the Ardennes offensive. The Germans hoped for a domino reaction whereby the Americans would shift divisions from the west to the Ardennes. To maintain the Allied front's integrity, British Second Army would have to shift divisions eastward to fill in where the Americans had been. First Canadian Army should then follow suit to prevent a gap between it and the British. This would leave the Canadian Army so overextended along the Maas that Schwalbe's Korps could then pierce their defences. When 1 British Corps's grip on the Maas was instead perplexingly reinforced, Schwalbe and his superior, Heeresgruppe H's Generaloberst Kurt Student, lost all enthusiasm for the venture. Then the Russian offensive took away

Schwalbe's 711th Infanterie-Division. With that development, the idea was abandoned.[2]

The 711th had faced an unusual topographic feature on the Maas. "In a heavily waterlogged area northeast of Breda," a Canadian analysis reported, "a subsidiary channel of the Maas forms an island, about five miles long and one mile wide, along the river's south shore. Halfway along this island is a ferry crossing and harbour called Kapelsche Veer. The island is perfectly flat and without cover, except for the dykes on its perimeter and the hundreds of tiny ditches running north and south across the fields. On the eastern portion, which narrows down to less than a thousand yards, a track runs north to meet the rectangular inlet or harbour; at the north end of the track was a brick house. The current of the Maas in this area is fairly strong and the banks slope at a 45-degree angle. All approaches to the island from the south bank are under observation during daylight."[3]

The island's south shore was flanked by an extreme narrowing of the Maas that the Dutch called the Oude Maasje. This was actually the true course of the Maas, but by 1904 it had become so clogged with silt that serious local flooding was common. So the Dutch embarked on one of their most ambitious engineering projects and dug a channel to the north to create a new river course. This was the Bergsche Maas—a straight channel averaging three hundred yards wide. The ground south of the Bergsche Maas and north of the Oude Maasje became a man-made island. To enable local people to cross the Bergsche Maas, a small harbour was built on the island and a ferry service installed. The harbour was named Kapelsche Veer. "Kapelsche" referred to the nearby village of Capelle, and "Veer" meant ferry.

In winter, the island was a muddy morass of polder country. Military movement was confined to the tops of dykes, which averaged about twenty-three feet high. With no bordering trees—indeed the island was, save for one large weeping willow, virtually treeless—anybody using the dykes was completely exposed. One high dyke bordered the island's northern shore as part of the canalization of the Bergsche Maas. A second dyke of similar height cut roughly up the island's centre. Extending along the bank of Oude Maasje, a lower dyke ran from just south of the harbour for about two thousand yards westward before petering out.

A small bridge spanned the Oude Maasje, which was mostly less than one hundred yards wide along the length of the island, to join a road running across to the harbour. Overall, as the Canadian Army historian observed, the island was a "desolate spot." But it was about to become the scene of "a protracted struggle beginning at the end of December and lasting through January."

The impetus for this struggle was the arrival on the island of units of 711th Infanterie-Division on December 21. Prior to its transfer to the Eastern Front, the division was setting up outposts here to provide an anchor for the possible large-scale assault across the Maas. As the day ended, the division reported these outposts as consisting of "one company and one advanced observation post."[4] They were concentrated upon the "small, rectangular harbour...at the base of which stood a strongly-built brick house."[5]

Establishing a firm presence on the island had not been problematic, because First Canadian Army had neglected to occupy it in November 1944. As the island was so close, the consensus had been that it could be defended by gunfire from the southern shore and control of it maintained by occasional night patrols through to the harbour. There was little reason to think the Germans would bother seizing the dismal place.

But the potential offensive across the Maas abruptly increased the value of island real estate. And once the Germans took up residence there, 6th Fallschirmjäger Division's Generalleutnant Hermann Plocher decided it could serve as a decent and not too dangerous base for introducing his many young recruits to the reality of ground war. From its muddy banks they could conduct "small offensive actions" across the Oude Maasje to gain "battle inoculation during the expected lull of the winter months." Accordingly, by the end of December, Plocher had transferred responsibility for the island to his paratroopers.[6]

No sooner were the paratroopers solidly ensconced than 1 British Corps Lieutenant General John Crocker decided they must be evicted. The island itself was nameless and generally not even recognized by the local Dutch as being one. But the British, Polish, and Canadian soldiers who rotated through the front lines facing it extended the boundaries of the harbour of Kapelsche Veer to encompass the entire island. The ensuing fight would consequently be known as the Battle for Kapelsche Veer, although it was the island rather than harbour that held even the slightest strategic importance.

Major General Stanislaw Maczek's 1st Polish Armoured Division held the line in late December. Having long exhausted his ability to reinforce the division with Polish recruits found in other Allied forces, Maczek had turned to enlisting from the front. Many Poles forcibly conscripted into the Wehrmacht were all too happy to surrender at the first opportunity. Trolling prisoner-of-war cages, Maczek's recruiters rounded up any Poles they could convince to switch sides. More seemed willing than not. German field grey was quickly exchanged for the British khaki that Allied Poles wore. After the most rudimentary training, these new recruits were fed into the line.

Still, the Polish division remained woefully understrength. A report prepared after the Scheldt Estuary Campaign cited grave manpower deficiencies. The report's author, Canadian Brigadier E.O. Herbert, also thought that the new recruits were "not fighting well. They are not well trained, often bomb-shy, and very frightened of being captured. As a result more leadership is necessary; this in turn results in more [officer casualties] and the best [officers] at that." Herbert had recommended the division be withdrawn for a long rest and rebuilding, but Crocker remained so chronically short of strength on the Maas that this proved impossible.[7]

It was not only Crocker who wanted the Germans off the island, but also Maczek, who disliked having his front under observation. So he agreed with the orders. On New Year's Eve, three infantry companies backed by tanks pushed onto the island. The Poles were met by accurate fusillades of small arms from well-entrenched Germans who were able to call down even more deadly medium artillery, self-propelled gun, and mortar fire. Having taken a few paratroopers prisoner, the Poles withdrew after suffering forty-six casualties.

The following afternoon the Germans boldly ferried two self-propelled guns across the river, settling them into concealed and protected positions. When these guns proceeded to shell Polish out-posts across the Oude Maasje, Maczek reinforced his forward positions with tanks and called artillery down until the German guns ceased firing and "the situation calmed once more."[8]

Maczek attempted to eliminate the Germans again on January 7. This time he committed 9th Polish Infantry Battalion and attacked the eastern flank of the island, "where the enemy had established a small but well defended outpost."[9] By noon, the Poles had reached and won the harbour itself. But they were stopped cold there by "stubborn paratroops dug in along the dyke nearby and aided by mor-tar fire." Unable to make further gains, the Poles were obliged to withdraw from their exposed positions.[10] The battle cost the Poles dearly—133 men killed or wounded.[11]

Deciding the Poles were stymied, Crocker called upon No. 47 Royal Marine Commando to take over the job of eliminating this "as yet..small thorn [which] might develop into a prickly growth with disturbing branches." As this commando was understrength, a Nor-wegian troop from No. 10 Inter-Allied Commando was attached for the attack. Operation Horse was a night assault executed on Janu-ary 13–14. The commandos attacked from both flanks. Although the attack started well and "a few stout troops managed to reach the objective," the commando was badly exposed in the open polder ground.[12] Abandoning the ferry site, the Germans fell back into "extremely well prepared positions under the dyke...At the same time they brought extremely heavy mortar fire down on their own posi-tions from the other side [of the river], causing heavy casualties among the Royal Marines," the Argyll and Sutherland Highlanders of Canada war diarist recorded.[13] Exhausted by slogging through the thick mud, short of ammunition, and with most officers dead or wounded, the commandos were unable to make further headway.[14] After several hours of futile attempts to win the ground, they with-drew, having suffered forty-nine casualties.[15] "As it was evident that it would require a larger force to succeed, the enemy position was contained with a view to attacking it in greater strength later," con-cluded a Canadian after-action report.[16] The Argyll's war diarist moodily added that after the "complete failure" of the commando attack, "it was evidently the turn of the Canadians to tackle Kapel-sche Veer next."[17]

ON THE MORNING of January 14, Crocker gave the job to 4th Cana-dian Armoured Division. "All previous attempts to reduce the enemy [bridgehead] at Kapelsche Veer have proved abortive," his operational instruction began, and so 4th Division "will clear the enemy from Kapelsche Veer." The division's general staff war diarist dryly observed that the division was "proud, of course, to have the reputa-tion of a pinch-hitter, but the pleasure, if NOT the distinction, is a dubious one."[18]

Although Crocker wanted the job completed quickly, he empha-sized the need for thorough preparation. The attack should be made only when Major General Chris Vokes deemed the division ready. He was also to inject an element of surprise into his plan. Crocker had requested that the island be subjected to daily aerial bombing until the date of the attack and also promised that all 1 British Corps artil-lery would be available for support. This was a huge commitment of force to eliminate a piece of ground with little strategic value. Yet the German grip on the place was not easily ignored. Left to their own devices, the paratroopers might well use it as a launching point for a major spoiling attack against the troops facing them. Defeating such an attack might prove more costly than pinching out this potential launch pad. There may also have been a more dubious reason, never stated but afterwards considered by many involved as the true motive—prestige. Having thrice assaulted the island and been thrown back with significant loss, the Allies were stung by the impli-cation of German fighting superiority. So the island must be taken.[19] And it fell to the Canadians to do the taking.

Since receiving command of the division, Vokes had done little to establish a good working relationship with his divisional staff or bri-gade and battalion commanders. A big, brawny man with flaming red hair and moustache, Vokes often came across as a profane, blus-tering bully. Having led 2nd Canadian Infantry Brigade ashore in Sicily on July 10, 1943, he had been engaged in combat warfare lon-ger than most other Canadian generals. From 2nd Brigade he had

gone on to command 1st Canadian Infantry Division in Italy, and in
November 1944 had confidently expected to take over 1 Canadian
Corps. Instead, Lieutenant General Charles Foulkes had stepped off
a plane from northwest Europe with instructions to take command.
"I often wondered whether someone got the names Vokes and Foulkes mixed up," Vokes later said. "No doubt about it, I was hurt for a
few hours. On top of that, I was transferred and I didn't want to leave
the theatre...I felt I was being forced to change horses in mid-
stream...I left Italy then, to switch divisional command with [Major
General] Harry Foster...No doubt the top brass knew I'd be able to
stomach Foulkes even less well than I had [Lieutenant General
Tommy] Burns as my Corps Commander."

Foster's boots were tough to fill. He had been a popular and competent commander. Vokes also knew that he faced skepticism about
his ability to command an armoured division. His experience was
with an infantry division, and before that he had been an engineer.
Touring around the division, Vokes gave a set-piece speech aimed at
rallying the troops and convincing them he was capable. He made it
clear that much was expected of them, and he would in turn support
them. "Whatever the merits of the speech, the essential thing was
for the troops to see me and acquire a sense of identification. They
could always then say to themselves: 'There's that great rough red
hairy bastard I work for so I better Press On.'"

He was impressed by the troops, less so by his divisional staff.
Vokes thought they spent too much time lauding past combat
exploits in Normandy, Belgium, and Holland, rather than focusing
on current and future operations. After a couple of weeks, he was
"heartily sick of listening." Vokes summoned the headquarters officers and cut into them. "I will be heartily obliged if you will
henceforth refrain from telling me how many shells have been fired
out of the mouths of your tanks at Buggeroff Zoom, Sphitzen-on-
the-Floor and other places. I know a little bit about fighting and
about tanks and about what they can and cannot do."[20]

Vokes was unhappy about getting the Kapelsche Veer job. "As far
as I was concerned, the Germans could have stayed there for the rest
of the war. They were doing no harm." He believed it would inevita-

bly result in "a great waste of young lives. But I had to do it—you can't just say no when an order comes down from army headquarters." Vokes was already skating on thin ice with General Harry Crerar, and to refuse a direct order would be his undoing. From the moment he arrived in this new theatre, Vokes had been having run-ins with Crerar. Used to the casual disregard for proper uniforms, military customs, and discipline that had been one of the lasting legacies of Montgomery's years at the helm of Eighth Army, in which 1 Canadian Corps served, Vokes had little time for Crerar's fussy ways. For his part, Crerar warned Vokes he would not tolerate any "of the slack habits adopted in Italy."

Hoping to derail the operation, Vokes agreed to take it on only "if they could provide me with twenty-eight Peterborough canoes, because I had visions of sending the troops down the river in those silent craft under the cover of darkness. For a while I thought that by asking for the canoes, I might have turned the whole thing off. Well, it wasn't. The canoes were...flown in...from Canada...and I had to go ahead."[21]

The Peterborough canoe was a classic North American design that substituted canvas for the traditional birchbark and used cedar for the ribbing and planking to which it was adhered. Typically about sixteen feet long, three feet wide, and a little over a foot high, the canoe weighed about sixty-eight pounds. Because the internal ribbing torqued the planking outwards while the taut canvas compressed it inwards, the canoes were structurally very strong.

Unable to head off what was now designated Operation Elephant, Vokes ordered Brigadier Jim Jefferson on January 17 to work up the full attack plan. Vokes promised his 10th Infantry Brigade commander lavish artillery and air support aimed at blasting the Germans out of the bridgehead. But Jefferson's staff quickly gathered intelligence indicating that the approximately two companies of paratroopers dug in around the harbour were protected by "extraordinarily good field works...practically impervious to neutralization or destruction." Vokes had added an unexplained caveat to the plan. The attack must be launched no sooner than January 26 and no later than January 30. Setting January 26 as the earliest date gave Jefferson less than a week to plan the operation and train the detailed force. As for the January 30 completion deadline, this was undoubtedly intended to get the Kapelsche Veer action finished before the launch of Operation Veritable was imminent.

Although Jefferson and his staff were responsible for the detailed plan, they were hemmed in by the broad outlines that Vokes and divisional headquarters imposed. There would be a thrust from both east and west onto the island and through to the harbour of Kapelsche Veer. At the same time as these thrusts went in, the canoe-borne force would paddle downriver to land at the harbour's mouth and establish positions to prevent German reinforcement of the island. Jefferson assigned the attack to the Lincoln and Welland Regiment. Lieutenant Colonel Bill Cromb, the battalion's veteran commander, had recently left on a thirty-day leave to Canada after five years overseas. Another veteran officer, Major Jim Swayze, temporarily commanded. Jefferson told Swayze that each flanking force would be formed by one company. Sixty "specially picked men, all expert canoeists," would make up the canoe party. Swayze was extensively briefed, but for security reasons was told not to disclose full details or even the location to his officers and non-commissioned officers until the operation was imminent.[22]

Despite this proviso, Swayze's subordinate officers could hardly fail to realize the nature of the forthcoming job. The day after the briefing, Swayze and his company commanders sat down with the surviving officers of No. 47 Royal Marine Commando to glean whatever knowledge they could about that unit's attack. Two days later, the battalion began training to use man-carried lifebuoy flamethrowers. These were so named for the circular fuel tank carried on the man's back. The flame-throwers were primarily intended to burn enemy troops out of fortified positions. Refresher training in river crossings followed.[23]

Swayze disliked the operation. Operation Elephant, however, was "laid out" in such a way that all he could do was implement it as directed.[24] There was no latitude for a battalion commander to introduce changes, because of the inflexibly detailed artillery and smokescreen plans.

Jefferson and his staff were equally unhappy. Although soon poring over air photos, intelligence on the enemy, engineering reports, tidal charts, and moonrise, sunrise, and sunset schedules, they were prohibited from doing that most fundamental of reconnaissance tasks—visual inspection of the ground. As the area was still controlled by 1st Polish Armoured Division, 1 British Corps had declared that for security reasons no 10th Brigade personnel could enter the area until the day before the operation was to be launched. There would be no allowance for reconnaissance "until that time." A plan was hatched on January 18 whereby the brigade arranged for its intelligence officer to unofficially contact forward Polish units each day "to ensure that no scrap of [information regarding] Kapelsche Veer area is missed." An observation post was also established for the declared intent of "training personnel in counter mortar duties." The observation post was sited so that the intelligence personnel pretending to be learning new duties could observe enemy movement on the island and study the lay of the land. "This back door method," observed the brigade war diarist, "is unpleasant but it is the only possible way to ensure coverage and still maintain the security demanded."[25]

The finalized plan called for Major Ed Brady's 'B' Company to be ferried onto the island by amphibious Buffaloes and supported by two of the flame-thrower-equipped Bren carriers known as Wasps. After advancing due north to gain the main interior dyke, Brady would lead his men east along it to the harbour. Here they would link up with 'C' Company, under Major Jim Dandy. Having passed through a screen established on the dyke by Captain Herbert Owen Lambert's 'A' Company, Dandy's men were to clear the brick building and other fortifications with the aid of Wasps and lifebuoy flame-throwers. The canoe party, meanwhile, would have established its blocking position at the harbour's mouth. Captain Richard Fowlke Dickie, 'D' Company's second-in-command, was to raise the canoe party. Once the canoeists got under way they were to split into two groups. A seven-canoe group commanded by Lieutenant J.G. Jackson would seize the western corner of the harbour. Dickie with eight canoes under command would capture the eastern corner. They would then clear a small dyke on each side of the harbour, link up with 'C' Company, and join its attack on the harbour from the south.[26]

Because hidden movement was impossible, the troops would be concealed by a smokescreen. Three hundred guns would smother the island with fire. There would be six field regiments each deploying twenty-four guns. The 4th Army Group, Royal Artillery provided sixty-four 5.5-inch guns of four medium artillery regiments and two heavy gun batteries fielding eight 155-millimetre guns. The tanks of the South Alberta and British Columbia Regiments would also weigh in. Three platoons of the division's support regiment, the New Brunswick Rangers, would provide heavy machine-gun fire.[27] 'A' Company of 2nd Canadian Infantry Division's Toronto Scottish (MG) Regiment was drafted to fire smoke bombs with its heavy 4.2-inch mortars.[28]

Two Canadian artillery regiments—4th Division's 15th Field and 2nd Army Group's 19th Field—deployed adjacent to the village of Waalwijk immediately south of the island's easternmost point. Such a tremendous commitment of artillery required a massive logistical effort to supply the necessary tonnage of shells—particularly in light of the wretched condition of Dutch roads in this area and the miserable mid-winter weather. In addition to the smoke rounds, an even greater quantity of high-explosive shells were required—46,000 for the 25-pounders, 4,000 for the medium regiments' 5.5-inch guns, 3,500 of 75-millimetre for the tanks, 7,000 bombs for the 4.5-inch mortars, and an unrecorded small number of rounds for the heavy batteries. "When it is remembered that a 3-ton lorry can carry only 200 rounds of 25-pounder ammunition the trucking problem will be appreciated," the 15th Field Regiment's historian wrote. His regiment alone was "allotted 7,500 rounds."[29]

Inside Waalwijk, the Argylls were evaluating the security risk created by the massive buildup of military stores around the village. "Although the strictest security was maintained," wrote their war diarist, "people in town could not help but guess that something out of the ordinary was impending. Artillery ammunition was stacked up along the streets...and suddenly there were blue-patch troops in town (Toronto Scottish), in addition to the green patches the town was accustomed to see. It was generally agreed that the only way of preventing a leakage of information was to evacuate the entire population." Although most civilians had already been evacuated for their safety or because their loyalty to the Allies could not be verified, a good number of villagers and nearby farmers remained. Taking the "very drastic and complicated step" of evacuating them was ruled impossible.[30]

It was expected that the Lincs would clear the island quickly following the attack's start just after dawn on January 26. Should the operation fail to unfold smoothly, however, it might fall to the Argylls to regain the initiative and complete the job. Lieutenant Colonel Dave Stewart considered Elephant the height of stupidity. Believing 4th Division's constant demands for ever stronger patrols across the Maas was needlessly chewing up his and every other infantry regiment, Stewart had earlier written Lieutenant General Guy Simonds to express his lack of confidence in Vokes as divisional commander. The patrols, he argued, achieved little, and each one usually resulted in someone being killed or wounded.

By writing the letter, Stewart had gone a step further than anybody else had dared, but most of the division's senior officers shared his opinion. Major Bob Patterson, serving at 10th Canadian Infantry Brigade headquarters, considered Vokes "a coarse, cruel, pig-headed bastard." He didn't like how Vokes pushed Brigadier Jefferson around. Jefferson, who had previously served under Vokes in Italy as commander of the Loyal Edmonton Regiment, often got "so goddamn mad at him that he'd go out and sit in his armoured car out in the field so that Vokes couldn't get at him."[31]

Whether Stewart confronted Vokes and flatly refused to send his men into the Kapelsche Veer battle, as many Argylls later believed, is unknown. It is equally, and perhaps more, possible that Simonds disclosed the content of the letter to Vokes with or without instruction as to what should be done about an unruly subordinate. Simonds could not be expected to sympathize with Stewart's position. He strongly believed in the importance of strong, regular patrolling along the Nijmegen Salient. Simonds was also aware of First Canadian Army's effort to deceive the Germans into believing that the major offensive sure to come soon would be launched northward into Holland from 4th Division's sector. Regiments in 11

Corps's boundary were losing just as many men during nightly patrols as those in 4th Division.

Not even the increasingly vicious weather could deter Simonds from insisting his divisions maintain aggressive patrolling. As snow accumulated and temperatures dropped to below freezing, 2nd Division's 5th Infantry Brigade had resorted in mid-January to experimenting with having soldiers from the Calgary Highlanders wear moccasins. The idea was to see if moccasins provided better footing and enabled quieter movement than regular combat boots. The result was mixed. "They have been found unsuitable in soft snow and patrols prefer boots under such conditions. If, however, the snow becomes crusted or wind packed it is felt that the moccasins would be a distinct advantage for silent patrol," 5th Canadian Infantry Brigade's then acting commander, Lieutenant Colonel Julien Bibeau, reported. He suggested fifty pairs of moccasins be issued to each infantry battalion and doled out to those going patrolling when conditions favoured their use.[32]

Whether Simonds disclosed the lack-of-confidence letter to Vokes or Stewart personally confronted his divisional commander, Stewart was ordered on January 24 to report to No. 10 Canadian General Hospital for a full psychiatric assessment. In a covering note to the hospital commander, the 4th Division Assistant Director, Medical Services wrote that Stewart's condition "appears to be a straightforward case of exhaustion" and requested that he be committed to 1 Canadian Neuropsychiatric Wing. Vokes, he added, had "requested a full report on this case and so it would be appreciated if copies of the preliminary and final report...be forwarded to me at this HQ as soon as they are available." The very next day, Major Glenn S. Burton, who commanded the wing, cited Stewart's symptoms as including "inability to make decisions" and "undue concern for his men." After his examination, Burton noted that Stewart displayed some "obsessive thinking regarding the risking of his men to battle." Stewart, he wrote, showed evidence "of mental fatigue and at this time was unfit for combat duties." He recommended that Stewart be evacuated to England for further treatment and eventual employment in a non-combat post that would arouse his interest and not be overly sedentary.

Back in Waalwijk, Stewart's removal had shocked the regiment. But life continued with second-in-command Major Pete MacKenzie taking over "until a new colonel was appointed." It was clear that Stewart would not be returning. MacKenzie had no idea why Stewart had been sent off to hospital, but it was rumoured that he had too stoutly defended the regiment. Everyone was disappointed. "I guess that's putting it mildly," MacKenzie later said. "Everybody in the regiment had a very high regard for Dave Stewart, a lot of confidence in him, a lot of respect for his judgement, a feeling that if you got into trouble, he could always find a way out for you. It was a sad day when Dave Stewart left...I don't think we ever had the same confidence in anybody as Dave Stewart."[33]

WHILE 10TH CANADIAN Infantry Brigade and the Lincoln and Welland Regiment had been drafting the final attack plan, engineers of 4th Division's 9th Field Squadron had undertaken construction of a bridge across the Oude Maasje to replace those destroyed earlier by the Germans. The bridge was deemed necessary to allow tanks to come to the support of the infantry if needed. Building it was considered "a ticklish problem, as the site was only 500 yards from the enemy, and all approaches could be directly observed from the far side," reported the historian of the division's engineering units. "Fortunately the bridge itself was behind a dyke and completely hidden from the enemy." In an attempt to keep construction of the bridge secret, all building noise had to be minimal.

The bridge was to be built on top of the wrecked bridge, but to do so "a mass of twisted steel and other debris had to be removed, and the remainder of the...centre portion jacked up on...rollers and anchored into position." As the one and a quarter miles of open ground between Waalwijk and the bridge site was under German observation, it was decided to move most of the building materials up a canal on rafts at night. The engineers also deployed a rubber-tired farm cart that could carry two and a half tons of material and could be pushed and pulled along the road to the bridge site by fifteen men. This proved "a heart breaking task," the historian wrote.

Although the Germans could not see what was going on at the bridging site, they regularly blind-fired light machine guns into the area and along the length of the road. Several times, the trailer crew was caught in the open and was unable to take cover in the slit trenches bordering the road because they "were covered with ice and full of water." Surprisingly, there were no casualties, "but the wear and tear on the nerves was terrific."

At times it was clear the Germans suspected something was up, as they subjected the bridging site to indirect mortar fire. Two key non-commissioned officers, Sergeant Mervin George Durham and Lance Sergeant Henry Herbert Schell, laboured tirelessly as construction continued round the clock.[34] Durham's No. 3 Troop was responsible for each day shift. To avoid detection and drawing enemy fire, his men worked underneath the structure of the existing bridge. Several times they were subjected to severe and accurate mortar fire. Durham ordered most of the men to take cover in slit trenches, but then he and a couple of other personnel would carry on working while the bombs exploded around them. "On one occasion a mortar bomb landed in the water beside...Durham causing severe concussion and numerous cuts in his arms, legs and back. Despite this... Durham carried on with his vital work until he was relieved by the night shift," his Military Medal citation attested. At other times machine-gun fire raked the surrounding area, but Durham steadied the men and kept them to their tasks even as bullets ricocheted off steel decking and landed "around the feet of the working party."[35]

The bridge took six days to complete. Because its construction under fire had seemed a crazed undertaking and the final result was a cobbled-together structure that looked anything but sturdy, the engineers named it the Mad Whore's Dream. But the engineers had delivered a finished bridge just before Operation Elephant was to begin, and that was all that mattered.[36]

7

No Profit in It

SNOW HAD FALLEN during the night of January 26, but as dawn drew closer the clouds parted, and an almost full moon sharply illuminated the ground. In their covered positions, the assault companies of the Lincoln and Welland Regiment carried out last-minute equipment checks. Each man wore a white camouflage snowsuit—pants, a hooded jacket, and helmet cover—over the regular battledress and long woollen underwear. Combat webbing was strapped over the suit and heavy black gloves provided some warming insulation for hands that gripped the cold steel and wood of their guns. Some men wore snow overshoes. Others felt the leather moccasin-style soles provided less traction than regular combat boots.[1]

Wireless operators from the Royal Canadian Corps of Signals were scattered about alongside the three forward observation officers (FOOs) of the supporting 15th Field Regiment. One artillery officer would accompany each of the three infantry companies. As the notoriously unreliable No. 18 wireless set was even more so in sub-zero temperatures, the signallers had been equipped with sturdier, long-range No. 22 sets. Reliability carried a price. Whereas the No. 18 weighed about 32 pounds, the No. 22 was 57.5 pounds. So the signallers had mounted the sets on steel cradles that two of them could either carry or drag as a sled. The extra batteries—more than normally required because they would more quickly drain in the cold—were carried in Yukon packs shouldered by the same men.[2]

As the first rays of sunlight brightened the eastern horizon, the moon still shone overhead. At 0715 hours, everybody moved toward their start lines. Frozen snow crunched under the feet of the marching men or the tracks of the Buffaloes that carried 'B' Company. It was a noisy approach, but the thunder of the artillery, scream of shells, and blast of explosions would deafen the paratroopers hunkered in their defences around the harbour of Kapelsche Veer. Smoke smothered the island, the Oude Maasje, and Bergsche Maas.

Despite the ferocity of the bombardment, 4th Canadian Armoured Division's planners never believed it would shatter the defending force. The German defences were just too well constructed and would prove largely impervious to artillery fire. Hopes were pinned on surprise and the Lincs hiding inside and behind the smoke until they overran the German garrison.[3]

By nightfall on January 26, that garrison consisted of about 120 men serving in the 10th Company, 17th Fallschirmjäger Regiment. There was also a platoon of 15th Pioneer Company numbering about 22 men and a 28-man platoon from the regiment's 9th Company. Each platoon had been stronger originally, but frostbite and sickness had taken a toll. What remained, reported 10th Brigade's intelligence officers, was a maximum of 180 men. But factoring in more frostbite victims and other probable casualties, they estimated the garrison at approximately 150 to 160 strong.[4] Its perimeter was about two miles long and surrounded the harbour and main defensive works. Paratroopers were always heavily armed and these were no exception. Each platoon manned four MG-42 machine guns firing on fixed arcs at the main approaches to the dyke just south of the harbour that the Canadians were going to use for their approach. More machine-gun positions had been bored out of the south slope of the dyke near the river.[5]

The Germans' defensive heart on Kapelsche Veer pivoted around two brick houses. One, in which the ferryman normally lived, stood by the harbour. The second was to the east and on a rise of ground back from the river. This house was owned by the local polder association and housed its roadman. His job was to maintain the local dykes and roads. The Canadians code-named the house by the harbour Raspberry and the roadman's, Grapes. Both were solid brick structures, but Grapes was larger than the other. It had thick walls and a deep cellar.[6] Each had been strengthened to serve as a large pillbox-like bunker. A network of tunnels connected the houses to machine-gun positions on the perimeter, enabling the Germans to move freely without exposure.[7] The defenders were able to call for ample mortar and artillery support from nearby positions. There was also a strong force of paratroopers on the northern bank of the Bergsche Maas that could range in on the island and river with machine guns and light mortars. Their positions were generally sodden and conditions harsh, but their morale was relatively high and they had excellent ammunition stocks. Their motivation to fight hard had been stiffened by orders that they were to hold "at all costs."[8] There would be no boats sent to rescue them if the battle was lost. So they hunkered in their fortifications, waited for the barrage to lift, and then would race to gun positions to meet the enemy.

At 0726—just a minute late—Major Ed Brady's 'B' Company crossed its start line and rode the Buffaloes toward the island. Already the first piece of bad news had reached Major Jim Swayze's tactical headquarters in a house about a mile south of the river and behind the village of Capelle. A few minutes earlier, Captain Richard Dickie had radioed to report that ice along the river shore just east of Waalwijk was making it difficult to launch the canoes. The canoe party was not going to shove off on schedule.

On the eastern flank, 'C' Company crossed its start line at 0733, and Captain Owen Lambert radioed in at 0745 that his 'A' Company was also past its start line but had lost a Wasp that had slid into the Oude Maasje, and had difficulty getting the other one up onto the dyke.[9]

Two miles to the east, 'C' Company's four supporting Wasps also ran into trouble. Major Jim Dandy watched in frustration as the flame-thrower-mounted Bren carriers spun their tracks uselessly on the steep slope of the dyke. The weight of the tank for the flame-thrower's propellant was too much for the motor to manage when traction was poor. After the slewing Wasps ran over a couple of his men's feet, Dandy decided they needed to get rid of the heavy tank. Perhaps he could blow it off with a grenade. Dandy took the driver's position, backed the Wasp up next to the Oude Maasje, pulled the pin on a grenade, and stuck it near the brackets holding the tank. As he walked away the grenade exploded, but "just dented the metal." Dandy led his men forward without Wasp support.[10]

On the western flank, 'B' Company moved quickly without meeting any opposition. At 0746 hours, Brady's men had not only gained the dyke but advanced about six hundred yards eastward and were nearing their objective. Suddenly, the smokescreen became blindingly and suffocatingly thick. Brady radioed Swayze and asked him to get the smoke "cut off in [his] sector." The smoke was only beginning to thin at 0830 when 'B' Company finished groping its way a further two hundred yards to the objective, overlooking the harbour from a distance of about two thousand feet.[11] The men started frantically digging in, axes and shovels chipping futilely at the frozen earth. As the smoke lifted, a German machine-gun post just fifty yards distant opened fire. 'B' Company hugged the ground and threw back what fire they could, but German bullets were striking home and Lincs started dying.[12]

'A' Company, meanwhile, had paused six hundred yards short of the brick house designated Grapes at 0830 in expectation of 'C' Company's imminent arrival. Dandy and his men failed to materialize. As German fire directed at 'A' Company was rapidly intensifying, Lambert decided to lead his men straight for the brick house that was their final objective. Through the thick, cloying smoke, the house was barely visible, and in the other direction it was impossible to see any sign of 'C' Company's whereabouts.

OUT ON THE Bergsche Maas, Dickie would have welcomed any smoke he could get. The canoe party had finally got under way by breaking bodily through the shoreline ice and then dragging their boats out to where the river channel was open. Snowsuits soaked through, the canoeists paddled with the fast-moving current toward the harbour to the west. To keep free of the ice, they were forced ever farther from the southern shore. When the smokescreen suddenly dissipated, the Germans on the north bank ranged on them with machine guns. Fighting from canoes would have been hopeless in any case but was rendered moot when the men discovered the actions of their guns were frozen and useless. As "the effective fighting value of this group vanished," Dickie ordered his men to paddle shoreward. How many men died gaining safety was never recorded. Abandoning the canoes, the survivors waded through the ice and set off on foot to find 'A' and 'C' Companies. Dickie still hoped his party could complete its mission of sealing off the harbour mouth to reinforcements from the north bank of the Bergsche Maas.[13]

'A' Company had kicked over a hornet's nest moments after starting toward Grapes. Despite the smoke, they were subjected to accurate and deadly fire from multiple positions that were in turn impossible to detect. The company "was having a hell of a time... pinned right down," Sergeant Gord Brittain later recalled. Lambert sent Brittain to hurry 'C' Company into coming to his assistance. Brittain found that Major Dandy and his men had just reached the point six hundred yards back where 'A' Company had briefly paused at 0830. Dandy led his men into the blinding, choking smoke swirling outside the house at 0900. Mortar fire from the river's north bank hailed down on both attacking companies, while machine guns inside the brick building and dug into the dykes raked them. Dandy radioed for an 'A' Company situation report. A wireless operator claimed they were on the objective. Dandy didn't believe for a moment that Grapes was in their hands. Men from 'A' Company staggered past him, heading east and away from the fight. They were all choking from the smoke, a few vomiting. Dandy and his men were all coughing. He suspected that most or all of 'A' Company had either retreated or lay dead and wounded up ahead. He started moving out in front of his own company to personally see what was happening, and was wounded a few minutes later.[14]

Inside the cauldron, the two 15th Field Regiment FOOs attached to the companies were in the thick of it. Assigned to 'A' Company,

Captain Robert Spencer had lost contact with any infantry officers. He ended up twenty-five yards from the objective, "a battered ruin that was once a house." Here by sheer chance he bumped into Captain N.B. Corbett, 'C' Company's foo. Corbett had left his wireless team behind to try to get forward and assess the situation. Together the two officers "observed the scene ahead. White painted infantry carriers were trying to manoeuvre into position to flame the post on top of the dyke [an indication that at least one Wasp had managed to stick with the infantry]; infantry were trying to find cover on the hard bare ground; dead and wounded were lying everywhere; in the smoke and with all ranks dressed in snow suits, it was impossible to distinguish officers and ncos. Obviously something had to be done at once. In a hastily arranged plan Captain Corbett returned to [his] set to pass fire orders," Spencer later wrote. Corbett managed to locate a Lincoln officer—the sole surviving infantry officer, he thought—and the two men agreed on a fire plan. But when Corbett called it in, for some reason the artillery never arrived. As the mortaring and machine-gun fire grew heavier, Corbett frantically sent new orders through "to the guns, and details of the situation were passed to battalion hq."

The Lincs were being cut to pieces. Ahead of his position close to Grapes, Spencer could see no infantry at all through the smoke. He realized the infantry officer with whom Corbett had finalized the artillery support plan must have pulled them back to ensure that they were not caught in friendly fire. Looking about, Spencer saw this officer lying dead nearby and the remainder of the company straggling away from the building. Spencer gathered his wireless team and followed the retreating men. Stumbling through "the blinding choking smoke," he blundered into Corbett, and the two foo teams headed for the rear.[15]

Because of the smoke, Spencer and Corbett were unaware that a sizeable conglomeration of 'A' and 'C' Companies was still trying to gain the building. At 0945, the Germans counterattacked. Lieutenant Owen Borthwick of 'A' Company was hit. He tumbled down the side of the dyke, "literally landed beside [Lieutenant] Earl Hume and he was in terrible shape...The last thing I remember...was seeing

Owen Lambert...walking up the dyke all by himself...I'm lying flat in the ice, looking up at him and he's waving [a] pistol...swearing, cursing a blue streak and he disappeared in the smoke."[16] By 0955 hours, the Lincs' war diarist recorded, all 'A' and 'C' Companies' officers were casualties. The remnants of the two companies had been driven back by the counterattack to the position six hundred yards from the house. Here some of 'C' Company had dug slit trenches before they moved forward at 0900 hours. The counterattack was driven off, but the situation was hopeless—the Lincs on this eastern flank too shot up to possibly renew the attack or even fend off further determined counterattacks.[17]

Nothing worked. The Wasps were now all disabled. Men carrying the lifebuoy flame-throwers, "were immediately targets for the Hun snipers and none reached the objective" the 10th bridgade's war diarist acknowledged. "The smoke screen laid by us to screen off the island from the NORTH side of the river now proved to be a disadvantage to our own [troops] and was cancelled." It was clear to Brigadier Jim Jefferson that the Lincs coming at Kapelsche Veer harbour from the east had been shredded.[18]

Things were little better to the west, where 'B' Company still clung to a position two hundred yards from the harbour. Brady's men had been equipped with about ten lifebuoys, and he had lost "every goddamn man; every one of them killed. You can imagine what it was like. I think [the lifebuoys] weighed about 60 pounds. He's got army boots on with metal cleats on the heels filled with snow. He's walking on an angle...carrying this goddamn thing, trying to manoeuvre is almost impossible. And the minute they shot any flame...they were a target and every one of them got it."[19] In one recorded case, four paratroopers were "caught by a spurt of flame, rolled out the fire on their clothes and continued to fight until shot." The Lincs would refuse thereafter to use lifebuoys.[20]

Struck by a counterattack, 'B' Company grudgingly gave ground, falling back a half-mile west of its objective. When both forward platoon commanders were killed, Sergeant Lionel Charles Stewart amalgamated the two badly shredded units into one and got the men dug in. For two hours, the position was hammered by mortar fire and subjected to several counterattacks. But Stewart ensured that the men grimly held on, an effort that earned him a Military Medal.[21] Brady dashed constantly from one battered group of men to the next, offering support and directing their fire in a stellar display of command leadership, recognized by a Distinguished Service Order medal. Although Stewart and Brady's efforts stabilized the situation, 'B' Company was steadily being ground up.[22]

Back at his tactical headquarters, Major Jim Swayze did not fully appreciate how dire 'B' Company's circumstances were, despite a 1000 hours report that it was being subjected to heavy mortar fire. Fixing on a report that several German snipers had crawled into the frozen polder fields south of the dyke to fire on the company, he dispatched only a single platoon from 'D' Company at 1030 hours to reinforce Brady's men. The platoon was instructed to eliminate the snipers who had infiltrated behind 'B' Company. This was too little, too late. At 1100 hours, Brady tried to "relieve the situation" by having artillery and mortar fire saturate both the north bank of the Bergsche Maas and Kapelsche Veer harbour. The rest of 'D' Company, under Major R.T. Crawley, was sent in to establish a supporting position behind 'B' Company.

To Swayze and Brigadier Jefferson in their respective headquarters, the whole situation on the island was utterly confused. All wireless communication with 'A' and 'C' Companies had now "failed."[23] Shortly after 1100 hours, Jefferson ordered 'A' and 'C' Companies to withdraw to where they had crossed the Oude Maasje. "It was realized that attack from the right had not been successful and that complete reorganization of these two [companies] would now be necessary."[24] The anti-tank platoon was ordered to go forward as infantry and set up a blocking position to prevent any Germans from advancing off the island and to receive the withdrawing troops. Either Corbett or Spencer used his artillery wireless set to report at 1134 hours that "all personnel of 'A' and 'C' [Companies] had been evacuated from the island." Captain Richard Dickie and the survivors of the canoe party had joined the withdrawal, "their weapons [still] being frozen and useless." Major M.J. McCutcheon, second-in-command of the Lincs, raced forward to reorganize this group and sort out the butcher's bill. Once the fit men were separated from the wounded and the many men suffering frostbite, they were formed into a reserve under command of Captain John Dunlop and took up station at Waspik, a village just west of Capelle.

On the left, 'B' Company still hung on and Swayze ordered the rest of 'D' Company to reinforce them. The anti-tank platoon, meanwhile, was ordered to advance toward Grapes and soon reported having gained the position six hundred yards east of it. The platoon was too understrength to consider going farther.

At 1350 hours, the paratroopers again counterattacked 'B' Company but were thrown back. They left several dead lying on the snow in front of 'B' Company's position.[25] An hour later, the Germans tried a new gambit by landing five boatloads of paratroopers from the north side of the river next to where 'B' Company was dug in. A quick artillery barrage was called in by the FOO working with Brady. Between the artillery and fire from 'B' Company, this attack was shattered and the boats sank. The surviving Germans fell back to the harbour.[26]

CLEARLY THE ATTACK by the Lincs had failed disastrously. Actual casualties remained uncertain, but a count of 'A' and 'C' Companies' survivors turned up only sixty men out of a combined starting strength of about two hundred.[27] At 1700 hours, a "hot meal, blankets, picks and shovels" were sent up to 'B' Company. Forty minutes later, a new plan of attack was issued by Brigadier Jefferson. 'D' Company would be relieved in its positions by the combined remnants of 'A' and 'C' Companies. Major Crawley's company would then move up to 'B' Company in order to pass through it and drive on to the original objective just west of the harbour. On the left, 'A' Company of the Argyll and Sutherland Highlanders would relieve the anti-tank platoon. This would be the first step in the Argylls assuming the major role in Operation Elephant. Nobody was talking about a quick victory. That opportunity, if it had ever existed, was gone. It would be "bite and hold" now. Heavy artillery bombardments preceding short thrusts forward by infantry ideally supported by tanks. Establish a new holding position, repeat, and then repeat again until the final objective fell within the bite and was won. This was combat the Canadians knew well and had come to excel at during the Scheldt Estuary Campaign. It was grim work. Slow, tedious, and dangerous. But executed properly, it was likely to result in fewer casualties overall than those the Lincs had suffered on January 26.

"The general plan," the Argyll's war diarist recorded, "was now to work up gradually from both the east and west and literally dig out all the enemy on the bridgehead." By 2200 hours, 'A' Company had carried out the relief and dug in for the night. "The general atmosphere, cold, windy, muddy and exposed to the elements as well as to enemy fire, was as unpleasant as possible. Rations and rum were taken up to the forward troops under cover of darkness."[28]

Late in the evening, two light Stuart tanks from the South Alberta Regiment's reconnaissance squadron warily crossed the "very rickety bridge" to join the Argylls.[29] The two commanders, Sergeant Vaughan Stevenson and Corporal Matthew McSherry, quickly realized that the island was hellishly unsuited for tanks. They were confined to moving single file along the slippery road on top of the dyke. Weighing in at just over three tons, their Stuarts would quickly break through the layer of frozen ground in the surrounding polders and become stuck. The road was too narrow for them to make a U-turn, so any backward movement would have to be done by reversing—a tricky manoeuvre when the Stuart's width (eight feet) was virtually the same as the dyke's.[30]

'A' Company and the hovering Stuarts had a surprisingly uneventful night with the Germans leaving them unmolested. Lieutenant S.F. Day, who was commanding, slipped a patrol up along the dyke a little after midnight. They closed on the brick building and took a good long look around. Saw that the Germans were "dug in strongly in an interlocking system of tunnels and caves." Rooting them out promised to be "a grim business, due to the comparatively small size of the area as well as its almost complete lack of cover."[31]

Shortly after dawn on January 27, the battalion's war diarist noted with surprise that 'A' Company "had not yet suffered casualties, which did not make up for the dangerously heavy losses sustained by the Lincoln and Welland Regiment. The cold morning found the situation much unchanged with both arms of the pincer gradually closing on the enemy's bridgehead." So intricate were the fortifications with their interconnecting tunnel systems that he concluded their advantages combined to give the 100 to 150 paratroopers "the range and scope of a battalion."[32]

While the Mad Whore's Dream had enabled the Stuarts to reach 'A' Company, there was no bridge to the west for tanks to get forward to support the Lincs on the other flank. The 4th Division's engineers were consequently instructed to build a Class 40 raft during the night that could be used to float two Sherman tanks from 'A' Squadron across the Oude Maasje.[33] Late in the day, a v-1 flying bomb had crashed directly into 9th Field Squadron's lines near the river, killing one man and wounding twenty-two others. This left the squadron so depleted that No. 2 Troop from 8th Field Squadron was brought in to construct the raft.[34]

Shortly after midnight, this new team of engineers began unloading the necessary pontoons, stringers, piers, and planks for flooring. All movable parts were frozen solid, many having to be hacked or pried open with picks. Bayonets were used to scour out ice plugging holes. Some sappers had to stand in waist-deep water to connect the raft's various parts and sections together. For most of the eight gruelling hours that the engineers laboured on the raft, snow fell heavily.[35] Large drifting cakes of ice, two to five inches thick, that could easily sweep a man away posed an added danger for the sappers in the frigid water.[36]

At 0830 hours, the raft was ready. 'A' Squadron's Lieutenant Ken Little had been waiting through the night with his troop's three Shermans. As the sappers waved him forward, Little ordered his driver to creep gently down the bank to the raft. With the tide out, the raft proved too far down for the tank to reach it. When a renewed attempt was made after an untidy jumble of rubble and wood was thrown together to build an ad hoc ramp, the Sherman lurched aboard. And the raft promptly buckled in the centre and sank. After Little managed to back the tank off the damaged raft, the engineers announced it would take hours to repair and strengthen it. As the sappers set to work, a heavy German 120-millimetre mortar brought the site under fire. Whenever the fire let up, the sappers gamely emerged from slit trenches to work on the raft until the next mortar rounds fell. The process was going to be a long one, and it quickly became clear that the Lincs on the western flank would not see any armoured support on this day.[37]

Despite the lack of tanks, Major R.T. Crawley's 'D' Company pushed slowly along the dyke toward the harbour. Mortar fire from the Kapelsche Veer garrison and the northern riverbank was constant. Snipers also lurked in the polders south of the dyke. Captain A.D. Fetterly of 15th Field Regiment was with the company and continuously calling down artillery a short distance to its front. Crawley's men would stop every hundred yards and hurriedly dig in. When Fetterly finished adjusting his fire forward, another hundred-yard advance followed. In this way, by about 1300 hours, 'D' Company had reached a position about six hundred yards short of the harbour.[38] From here they made three attempts to get through to the building code-named Raspberry. Each time, they were driven back by drenching mortar and machine-gun fire.

From the Oude Maasje crossing point to just behind Crawley's rear position, the rest of the battalion's fighting units were set up in staggered positions. Their primary purpose was to intercept and wipe out any force of paratroopers attempting to cross the Bergsche Maas to attack 'D' Company from the rear. Although the war diarist reported these positions as being held by the other rifle companies, the anti-tank platoon, and the carrier platoon, the reality was less orderly. By midday on January 27, battalion adjutant Captain R.L. Rogers wrote, "there was very little left of the original organization: along the various dykes were groups of men under experienced officers with reinforcement officers assigned to help them."[39]

The covering force, however, proved its worth when two attempts were made to send boatloads of Germans across the river. Accurate and heavy artillery was immediately called down. Some boats turned back for shore, while "some of them were blown clean out of the water," one Canadian report later stated.[40]

To the east, 'A' Company of the Argylls had slowly fought through to a position within five hundred yards of the brick building known as Grapes. But it was a costly business. One Argyll was killed and nine others wounded.[41] Casualties would undoubtedly have been heavier had it not been for the supporting fire provided by the two South Alberta Regiment Stuarts and in the afternoon by two Shermans from 'A' Squadron that managed to cross the bridge and get through to the Argylls.

Darkness fell early on these cold late-January days, with the sun setting at about 1630 hours. As night closed in, the Argylls ceased further attempts to advance so that 'D' Company could relieve the exhausted 'A' Company. At 0330 hours, the rotation of infantry took place within grenade-throwing range of the German forward positions. Major Pete MacKenzie, still in command until a senior officer was appointed, had decided to switch out his forward companies regularly. He saw a twofold advantage to the approach. First, "it prevented any one company being exposed to the cold for too long a period, which would invariably result in many frostbite casualties. Secondly, it made it possible for all the new reinforcements in the companies, who had never been up against the enemy, to get accustomed to being under fire."[42]

As the changeover took place, Lieutenant Wilfred Kennedy's tank was right up with the infantry. He leaned down from the turret to speak to an Argyll officer. A shot rang out, and the sniper round struck Kennedy in the head and mortally wounded him.[43]

About the time Kennedy was shot, the engineers working on the raft declared it ready, and Lieutenant Ken Little eased his tank aboard. The Oude Maasje here was only about 450 feet wide, but as night had fallen the water had frozen over. A Buffalo was deployed to serve as icebreaker and to take the underpowered raft under tow. It took three hours for the raft to make the passage and unload Little's tank. By dawn of January 28, all three tanks had been ferried over.[44]

TANK SUPPORT IN place, hopes ran high that the battle would be won before this cold Sunday ended. On the western flank, Lieutenant Little's three tanks headed eastward along the dyke to reinforce the Lincs at about 0900 hours. With morning temperatures slightly above freezing, the frozen ground thawed slightly, and suddenly the three tanks began to wallow in sticky, thick mud. The second tank in Little's column mired and blocked the path of the third. Little ordered the other two tanks to provide what fire support they could from where they were. He then carried on with his Sherman to accompany the advancing Lincs of 'D' Company toward Raspberry.[45]

On the opposite flank, Lieutenant Ernest Hill had arrived during the night to replace the mortally wounded Kennedy. Hill had two operational Shermans and two Stuarts. Lacking obvious targets, Hill's tankers fired at any position that seemed a likely German hiding spot. Little was doing the same thing. Despite the heavy fire that the tanks threw out, the Lincs and Argylls were soon forced to ground by the paratroopers' unrelenting machine-gun and mortar fire.[46]

On the western flank the attack had fallen apart, as commanding officers were cut down one after the other. At noon, Major Crawley fell severely wounded. Moments later, his second-in-command, Captain R.S. Davis, became a casualty.[47] Having run low on ammunition, Little had stuck his head out of the turret hatch to guide his driver in backing along the dyke to the start point. A sniper round killed him. After carrying his body to where the other two tanks remained stuck in the mud of the dyke, Little's tank crew resupplied and headed back into the fight, only to get bogged down.[48] That ended the tank support for the Lincs. At 1215 hours, Captain Richard Dickie raced to reinforce the badly mauled 'D' Company with a platoon of 'A' Company. He was also to assume overall command. Dickie led a renewed attack with a small force and soon reached "the front of the ruins of the house with a handful of men." They dug in—determined to cling to their hold—but at about 1800 hours, the Germans counterattacked in strength. As Dickie fell dead, the Lincs withdrew to their start position.[49]

On the east flank, Argyll Captain Sam Chapman had managed to get 'D' Company moving again with a Wasp commanded by Lance Corporal A.R. Strom and the South Alberta tanks providing strong support. With the Wasp throwing out gouts of flame and Hill's tanks ripping loose with their main guns and machine guns, 'D' Company battered through to Grapes and reported its hold consolidated at 1530 hours. The company had suffered just four casualties. As was often the case, the threat of the flame-thrower exceeded its actual killing ability. Twelve paratroopers had emerged from fortified positions and surrendered before Strom had a chance to blast these with flame. "At this point," the Argyll historian later lamented, "prospects of a quick finish to the battle seemed excellent, but fanatically determined to hold the place, the Germans came back strongly from the second house [Raspberry] about 2200 hours and drove our people back again to the positions held before noon." Lieutenant James Henry Hall was mortally wounded. The counterattack left 'D' Company in no shape to continue the fight, so Major MacKenzie ordered 'B' Company to replace it at 0200 hours on January 29.[50]

During the course of January 28 and through the ensuing night, the Canadian artillery maintained a steady and intense rate of fire. The FOOs with the infantry called in constant targets both within the badly blasted harbour area and along the north bank of the river. Since the attack had started on January 26, Captain Robert Spencer noted, the gunners of 15th Field Regiment had been manning their 25-pounders twenty-four hours a day with nothing more than reprieves of a few minutes. Despite the intense cold, the gunners dripped sweat as they worked to meet the rates of fire demanded.[51]

"Throughout the long, cold hours of the night the troops, in many cases suffering from frostbite and exposure," a Canadian army report later stated, "stubbornly held their ground. The frozen ground made it almost impossible to dig in, and the only cover against the unceasing mortar fire were the watery shell holes which became a most welcome haven."[52] The constant din of shells exploding nearby, the piercing cold, the sodden state of uniforms and equipment, the dread of another counterattack at any moment—all combined to render sleep impossible.

At the Regimental Aid Posts, casualties were stripped of their white snowsuits, and "the pile of blood-soaked suits grew deeper" with each passing hour. "Those which were still serviceable were given to reinforcements as they went to join their companies."[53]

Dawn exposed a battlefield eerily reminiscent of the Great War. German and Canadian dead lay where they had fallen, often side by side. Everywhere one looked, a chaotic patchwork of shell craters was visible. Canadian artillery and mortar fire reached an even more feverish pitch. The 15th Field Regiment's FOOs described the harbour area as "completely chopped to pieces," but still the paratroopers clung on tenaciously. Approaches to the "two demolished houses" served as "perfect 'killing grounds' for the enemy, since there was no cover of any description." Despite this, 'B' Company of the Argylls managed to fight its way forward. Then, in the early afternoon, 'C' Company leapfrogged 'B' Company, and at 1600 hours reported closing in on Grapes. "The concentrated artillery had rid the island completely of the thin layer of snow that had covered it at the beginning of the campaign, and the white snowsuits had completely lost their value as camouflage." As a result, No. 15 Platoon was sent forward without snowsuits when the commander of No. 13 Platoon—which was out front—said he thought one more push could take the house. Lieutenant N.R. Perkins led his men into the attack, but the fierce fire killed four and wounded numerous others. Perkins and his signaller, whose wireless was riddled by bullets and useless, were the only men to gain Grapes. "They entered a small room in the cellar, while the Germans were still in an adjoining room. A spirited grenade-throwing contest ensued, but both men miraculously escaped injury and managed to reach their platoon again."[54]

During the night of January 29–30, the Germans again tried to get boats of reinforcements into the harbour. Artillery and mortar fire drove them back. At first light, the Argylls advanced 'C' Company into the maw with tanks in support. "All through the day the battle raged back and forth and the Canadian losses steadily mounted," but by evening Grapes fell to the Argylls. This time there would be no retreat. 'A' Company and the battalion's scout platoon were rushed up to bolster the badly shredded 'C' Company. These men had been in action for more than two days. "They had suffered substantial casualties and the majority of the men, cold, wet and hungry, had not slept in more than 70 hours." That night, some men from the scout platoon crept out to the west and made contact with 'D' Company of the Lincs.

With the two flanking forces having literally shaken hands on the morning of January 31, elements of the Lincs "advanced eastwards from their wet slit trenches to close the gap, and at 0900 hours the two battalions linked up and the entire area was thoroughly cleared and checked. The Battle of Kapelsche Veer," an official army report concluded, "was finally over. It ended against a backdrop curiously twisted by the natural elements, for as the troops cleared away the debris of battle and collected the dead, the intense cold seemed to disappear and the sun broke through the clouds, turning the atmosphere surprisingly warm, and then, as the rays melted the snow, dissolving the ground, already thoroughly churned by the artillery, into a vast sea of mud."[55]

The butcher's bill for such an insignificant chunk of real estate was terrible. The Lincs suffered 179 casualties, 50 fatal. Most of these men fell on the first day. The Argylls had 48 casualties, 13 dying. The South Alberta Regiment had 5 men wounded and 2 officers killed by snipers.[56] Miraculously, the 15th Regiment FOO teams had only 2 men wounded, Gunner H.B. Decou and Gunner D.A. Matthews.[57]

German losses were calculated at 145 killed, 64 wounded, and 34 taken prisoner. But 6th Fallschirmjäger Division reports captured later estimated 300 to 400 men lost as "serious casualties" and another 100 suffering frostbite. Although able to reinforce the island occasionally, it was unlikely the Germans ever had more than 160 men on the island at any given time.

Immediately, efforts were made by Allied correspondents and army public relations personnel to justify Operation Elephant as necessary to the grand scheme of things. But the arguments were weak at best. As the Canadian official historian wrote, many Canadian soldiers thought it gained only "a little patch of ground / That hath in it no profit but the name."[58] As the island on which their comrades had died was actually nameless, it had not even that value. And the harbour of Kapelsche Veer was of no strategic worth to either side.

For the Lincs, the battle constituted an epic tragedy. Captain R.L. Rogers noted that for "the remainder of the war, Kapelsche Veer was treated as the dividing point: everything was 'Before Kapelsche Veer' or 'After Kapelsche Veer.'"[59]

In the midst of the fighting, Captain Sam Chapman of the

Argyll's 'D' Company had written to his wife. He reported that the battalion was to get a new commander and that Lieutenant Colonel Dave Stewart had been sent to hospital and would not return, and hinted at the difficulties he and his men currently faced. "I wish old Joe Stalin would go just a little faster [and] meet us at Nijmegen. It certainly wouldn't hurt my feelings if we missed out on the battle into Germany."[60]

PART TWO

VERITABLE

FEBRUARY 8–21, 1945

8

A Terrific Party

FIRST CANADIAN ARMY headquarters had paid little attention to the Battle of Kapelsche Veer. In a report to Ottawa regarding the events of January 1945, General Harry Crerar never mentioned the bloody fight. Instead, after describing the long frontage he held and the consequences the Ardennes had on Allied plans, Crerar explained that Veritable had been given a green light and briefly outlined the operation. As the fighting in the Ardennes had continued into early January, Crerar's attention had primarily fixed on readying for Veritable. Plans were consequently already well advanced when, on January 16, Field Marshal Bernard Montgomery summoned Crerar to his tactical headquarters in Zonhoven. It was time, Montgomery said, for the Allies to wrest the initiative from the Germans with "a potentially decisive...operation" that had been allotted "enough forces to carry it through successfully." Montgomery had discussed the matter with General Eisenhower "that morning and been informed by telephone of [SHAEF's] acceptance." On January 18, xxx British Corps would formally return to Crerar's command, and he could begin to concentrate its divisions and other formations in staging positions. Montgomery "stressed the importance of concealing our intentions from the enemy until the last minute." Veritable was tentatively set for February 10, "on the assumption that the Ninth U.S. Army would have taken over the line south and southeast of Roermond from the Second British Army" by February 1.[1]

This requirement was critical. Veritable was but one component of Montgomery's master plan. His intention was not just to drive the Germans off the west bank of the Rhine. He wanted to trap and destroy them between two converging armies. Every German between Nijmegen and Düsseldorf was to be killed or taken prisoner. The plan would start with First Canadian Army striking from the north and shoving the Germans back between the Maas and Rhine Rivers. Then, at an unfixed date, U.S. Ninth Army would punch northeastward from the Roer River with Operation Grenade. The two armies would converge on a line running from the riverside city of Xanten southwest to Geldern. As the two armies married, a massive pincer movement would be completed. Germans west of the Rhine eliminated, British Second Army would then advance to the river, and crossings would be forced between Wesel on the right and Emmerich the left.[2]

It was a simple plan. But not set in stone. On January 16, Montgomery still did not know if Ninth Army would remain under his command or be committed to Operation Grenade. As Montgomery conferred with Crerar, General Omar Bradley was meeting Eisenhower at SHAEF's Versailles headquarters in the Trianon Palace Hotel. Bradley sought permission for his Twelfth Army Group's First and Third Armies to break through the crumbling German forces in the Ardennes and drive toward the Cologne plain. He also wanted Ninth Army returned to him, to assist this southeastward assault. If Eisenhower agreed, the Americans would play no role in Montgomery's operation.

Eisenhower had no intention of cutting Ninth Army out of Montgomery's Rhineland offensive. He noted that Lieutenant General William Simpson seemed content to remain under Montgomery's command for Grenade. There was no advantage in having Bradley regain command of Ninth Army if it was not to join his attack in the Ardennes—an attack Eisenhower would permit. This attack, however, would be secondary to Montgomery's operation. Furthermore, Bradley's primary responsibility was to guard Twenty-First Army Group's southern flank so Montgomery could concentrate his forces in support of Veritable. Bradley was chagrined. When advised of the decision by telephone, Montgomery was relieved. "Operations Veritable and Grenade will together be a terrific party," he wrote that night.[3]

Montgomery had, meanwhile, launched a small operation to better position his Americans for Grenade. Southwest of the Roer River, the Germans retained a small salient flanked by the Maas to the west and the Wurm to the east. Triangularly shaped, with an apex aligned with the fortress town of Roermond, the salient was called the Roermond Triangle. Eliminating it had been planned since November, but poor weather and the Ardennes offensive led to repeated postponements. Now, on January 15, British Second Army's XII Corps attacked. Because of the terrain, the British had hoped for "hard dry weather" to enable "armoured and other vehicles...to function adequately. As it was, it alternately froze, thawed, fogged, snowed and rained; on the other hand it never changed from being bitterly cold," the official British historian wrote. Operation Blackcock was to be a quick affair but turned into a bitter slogging fight where infantry carried the brunt of the fighting. When it ended on January 26, the British had suffered more than 1,500 casualties and lost 104 tanks, mostly flame-throwing and mine-clearing models. But the salient was eliminated, some 2,200 Germans taken prisoner, and the way cleared for Ninth Army to slip westward into the area.[4]

Another operation, considered even more vital, required capturing the Roer and Eft dams. These two dams controlled the Roer River's levels, particularly above Roermond, where Ninth Army would establish its launch point. If the dams remained in German hands, the Germans could blow them up and cause extensive flooding of the American operational ground. Consequently, Grenade could not begin until this threat was eliminated. Responsibility for capturing the dams rested with Bradley's First Army. As January wound down, Bradley kept stalling. As long as the Germans held the dams, Bradley could argue that the main operation should fall in his southern sector rather than on Montgomery's front.

Montgomery understood Bradley's game. And so did Eisenhower. But even the supreme commander dragged his feet. Only on January

21 did Eisenhower formally release Ninth Army's twelve divisions to Montgomery and commit them to Grenade. And no date was fixed for Grenade's launch. Simpson was not keen on the assignment but acquiesced to the inevitable—which Montgomery misinterpreted as cheerful willingness to serve. Simpson grumbled to his diary in mid-January that Ninth Army was consigned "to the greater glory" of Montgomery, "since he sees fit to assume all the glory and scarcely permits the mention of an Army Commander's name."[5]

Oblivious to Simpson's unhappiness, Montgomery did realize that the time for criticizing Bradley was past. He must accept what American support he received and be glad of it. But as one observer noted, "he viewed the slow progress of the attack upon the dams with grave misgiving, and was resolved to fight with his strong left arm [First Canadian Army], even if his right [U.S. Ninth Army] remained tied behind his back." It took until the end of January for Eisenhower's patience to snap. He then ordered Bradley to capture the dams with two or three First Army divisions. Bradley continued to drag his heels, only ordering the attack to begin on February 4.[6] Rather than the two Allied pincers being delivered close together with overwhelming force, Grenade was now adrift from Veritable. The Americans would surely come to Montgomery's "terrific party," but not together with or even fashionably behind First Canadian Army.

On January 21, Montgomery issued a formal directive setting February 8 for Veritable's launch. As for Grenade, its timing "could not yet be fixed."[7]

Neither Crerar nor his corps commanders—particularly xxx British Corps's Lieutenant General Brian Horrocks, who was directly responsible for carrying out Veritable—lost sleep over the Americans. It was enough for them and their staffs to ensure that First Canadian Army was able to roll on February 8. Veritable entailed massive logistical execution. In the past, Montgomery had given Crerar only the minimal number of British formations possible because of his lack of confidence in the general's ability. If Veritable were to succeed, however, First Canadian Army must be able to unleash overwhelming strength. Consequently, Montgomery not only stripped away xxx British Corps from his Second Army but pared the army's divisions to the bone and assigned Crerar the rest. While Second Army retained two corps headquarters, these commanded just four divisions and three independent brigades. Second Army's Veritable role would be minimal—to hold the centre between U.S. Ninth Army and First Canadian Army until Montgomery decided the time was ripe for it to cross the Meuse at Venlo to support American and Canadian operations.

Added to First Canadian Army were five British infantry and two armoured divisions, along with four British armoured brigades. Crerar also commanded 1st Polish Armoured Division, 4th Special Services (Commando) Brigade, the Royal Netherlands Brigade, and 116th and 117th Royal Marine Infantry Brigades. The heavy guns of five Army Groups, Royal Artillery (AGRAS) would support xxx British Corps. Specialized assault equipment—the so-called Funnies—of 79th Armoured Division were also available.[8]

With 1 British Corps remaining under First Canadian Army, Crerar now commanded three corps—unprecedented for a Canadian general. First Canadian Army comprised 449,865 soldiers. Including civilian labourers and other non-military personnel increased the number to 476,193. Vast quantities of food were required, ammunition for weapons, and POL—petrol, oil, and lubrication—for vehicles. Feeding this many people for the operation's duration was estimated to require 2.3 million rations. The ammunition need, consisting as it did of 350 different varieties ranging from 105-millimetre shells to .303-calibre rifle cartridges, was vast. If all this ammunition "were stacked side by side and five feet high, it would line a road for 30 miles," an awed Crerar noted. Just artillery shells for use in Veritable's first four days "would be the equivalent in weight to the bomb-drop of 25,000 medium bombers." Each field regiment 25-pounder was provided with 1,471 high-explosive rounds in addition to a normal daily allotment of 260 such shells. Petrol consumption was to exceed 1.5 million gallons.[9]

Virtually every necessary commodity numbered in the thousands—8,000 miles of four different communication cables, 10,000 smoke generators, 10,000 gallons of fog oil, 750,000 maps, and 500,000 aerial photos. Dozens of intelligence staff were required to study relevant photos. Intense security controlled access to maps to ensure that none detailing any aspect of the operation fell into German hands.[10]

The Royal Canadian Army Medical Corps and supporting British Army Medical Corps had to brace for an onslaught of casualties, estimated to be 1,000 per day. On the third day, Veritable casualties were to peak at between 2,300 and 5,000. A complex network of blood banks and medical store depots ran back along the entire evacuation system from the front to eight hospitals. A casualty's journey began with evacuation to his Regimental Aid Post. From here, transfers went first to casualty collection posts, then to advanced dressing stations and, as required, to field dressing stations for less severe surgery. All these facilities were provided by respective corps medical services. Beyond these, a casualty entered the First Canadian Army medical system. After being taken by ambulance to a control post, a casualty would be channelled to a particular hospital, depending on the treatment required. Three hospitals had specialized medical teams. No. 6 Canadian General Hospital had a neurosurgical team, No. 8 Canadian General Hospital had a maxillo-facial surgery team, and No. 10 Canadian General Hospital could treat serious chest wounds and provide a psychiatric team to handle severe exhaustion cases. The system was intricate, requiring thousands of personnel performing specific duties essential to caring for the wounded.[11]

The hundreds of jeep and car ambulances that would use the few roads available for evacuations constituted just a fraction of more than 35,000 vehicles jockeying for space. It took 1,600 military police to control this traffic. Drivers of the Royal Canadian Army Service Corps and Royal Army Service Corps spent such long hours behind their steering wheels "that many crashed through sheer fatigue."[12] Keeping roads open required full-time employment of nearly fifty engineer companies, three road construction companies, and twenty-nine pioneer engineer companies.[13] In addition to maintaining roads, the engineers built a hundred miles of new ones. These were crudely surfaced by laying logs side by side. The task required setting in place 18,000 logs. Although yielding a rough and bumpy ride, the log system kept vehicles from miring in the mud.[14]

Not only new roads were required. To provide additional connections into the Nijmegen Salient's forward assembling areas, the engineers threw five new military bridges across the Maas. The 1,280-foot one installed at Ravenstein was the longest Bailey bridge ever constructed.[15]

As supplies and equipment for Veritable began to move into the Nijmegen Salient, a single question dogged First Canadian Army's chief engineer, Brigadier Geoffrey Walsh: "Would the frost hold?" If it did, "the roads would carry the huge traffic load," but "if a thaw came there would be trouble. Already the floating bridges were a matter for anxiety. After the earlier floods, there had been record low-water levels in January and these had posed problems of grounding pontoons and shortened spans. Renewed flooding would reverse these trends. By 28th January the ice conditions on the Waal were very serious and the Nijmegen barge bridge was in constant danger. On the Maas conditions were not quite as bad, yet it required 50 men per bridge on a 24-hour basis to keep the pan ice passing through and to prevent ice forming on and between the pontoons."

On the night of January 30–31, just before the peak movement of men and supplies for Veritable began, Walsh's fears were realized. "In the Nijmegen area it rained; by morning the snow had largely disappeared. Within hours all roads laid over a clay base had begun to be greasy. The thaw was very rapid. By 2nd February axle-deep ruts had appeared in many places and traffic was being winched through the worst spots. In particular, roads build of *pavé* over sand, designed to withstand only light civilian traffic, went to pieces, as did tarmac-surfaced roads without real foundation. Frost boils rising nine inches above the road surface were a common sight. A culvert on the main route from Eindhoven to 's-Hertogenbosch sank four feet in a few hours and had to be replaced with Bailey bridging."[16]

The thirty-nine-year-old Walsh had never faced such difficult conditions, despite long combat service. Walsh had commanded the engineers of 1st Canadian Infantry Division through operations in Sicily and on the Italian mainland. In the Normandy and Scheldt Campaigns he had been 11 Canadian Corps's chief engineer before promotion to the army's senior engineering post. It seemed little should faze him, but on February 5 he lamented that First Canadian Army "had every disadvantage possible in weather with the highest flooding in fourteen years in November, the lowest water level ever recorded in January, a severe frost followed by very rapid thaw, bad icing conditions and now another flood."[17]

On February 1, Major Mike Tucker's 23rd Field Company took responsibility for the two bridges crossing the Waal. "The big assault is due to go in shortly," Tucker recorded. "All main arteries are closed to normal traffic during the night so that equipment to be used in the assault can be brought up during the hours of darkness without giving the enemy foreknowledge of our plans. We see many new pieces of equipment during these days, including 'buffaloes' which are armoured amphibious personnel carriers, and huge guns which are broken up into three separate components for road movement."[18]

During daylight hours, 2nd and 3rd Canadian Infantry Divisions—both deployed in the salient—maintained an illusion of normalcy. Road traffic was kept to usual volumes. Artillery and mortar fire against German positions was neither heavier nor lighter than during preceding weeks. Nightly patrol activity reflected past operations.

But from dusk to dawn, the roads "were packed with transport, moving nose to tail, and before it became light, almost like magic the units would disappear into their concentration areas." Overseeing the buildup, Lieutenant General Brian Horrocks believed that when "this concentration was complete it would have been impossible to drop even a pea into the woods around Nijmegen without hitting some part of xxx Corps."[19]

When the supply buildup had first begun, xxx British Corps ordnance corps officers had expressed grave doubts that all the shells required could be in place by February 8. It was already the end of January, and their calculations showed that this massive undertaking would require about three weeks to complete. But Brigadier Gerald Laing, 11 Canadian Corps Deputy Adjutant and Quartermaster General, insisted that the eight nights available would suffice. He seconded Captain Reginald Ralph, a Royal Canadian Ordnance Corps staff captain, to xxx Corps with carte blanche to succeed. The twenty-four-year-old had gained a lot of experience moving ammunition along muddy and often flooded roads in Belgium and Holland. Much of the ammunition was stored along the verges of roads close to the salient in December, during Veritable's first preparatory stage. These shells had remained in place while the Ardennes offensive ran its course. So Ralph's primary task was to rapidly recover these stocks and move them forward. Ralph set a strict timetable for each truck platoon—normally fielding thirty trucks—to shuttle through a specific ammunition dump. He calculated that each platoon had to be processed in just seventeen to eighteen minutes. That was a "pretty horrendous task," Ralph realized—even more so when all work occurred at night without benefit of lights. To provide some illumination, all rear axle housings were painted white and a very small light was mounted on each to serve as a distance marker for the truck behind. Labour officers pressed all surplus rear-area military personnel to load and unload trucks, but these numbers were soon deemed insufficient. The local population was levied to provide civilian labour. Each night, Ralph raced from dump site to dump site furtively monitoring the process. "Visualize the actual environment," he said later. "Night, cold, winds blowing, water lapping at the sides of the road, snow sometimes falling, more often rain...each night the roads were more broken up and worse than the previous night. As we moved the ammunition out, we replaced it with dummy bags so German air observation wouldn't realize that it was being moved."[20]

VERITABLE REQUIRED A frontal attack against well-prepared and -manned positions. Keeping the Germans ignorant "as to the force and direction" of the forthcoming attack was considered essential. If movement of xxx British Corps and the supporting formations and supplies was detected, chances of attaining surprise would be lost. "Transference of all...British formations of [xxx] Corps to their assembly areas west of the Reichswald [was] itself...a major operation of war, very difficult to conceal from the enemy's intelligence," one report noted. Several British divisions needed to travel fifty to a hundred miles to enter the Nijmegen Salient. "To move these great bodies of troops northwards to their very restricted assembly area, accessible only by two bridges across the Maas, in the short time available and with due secrecy required the most careful planning." The British divisions were discreetly slipped away from the front lines at the end of January and concentrated northeast of Eindhoven. Here they waited to be transported into the salient.[21]

With "Veritable boiling vigorously," 11 Canadian Corps Chief of Staff Brigadier Elliot Rodger wrote on January 31, his staff's "main job was dumping ammunition (very large quantities), providing covered accommodation for assaulting troops on their arrival, and controlling movement of troops across River Maas and north to concentration areas." Over the past two days, the snow, which had been six to eight inches deep, had melted. The resulting thaw had "a drastic effect on roads." Rodger spent the first two days of February driving key roads with the 11 Corps chief engineer, Brigadier D.K. Black.[22] When they encountered Brigadier Walsh at the Ravenstein bridge crossings over the Meuse, the three stared gloomily at the rapidly rising water. Walsh had ordered a floating bridge dismantled for fear it would wash away and take out a second floating bridge that had been designed for higher rates of stream flow than the one that was removed. All floating bridges were now under constant watch, with Walsh's instructions calling for each to be either strengthened or dismantled should the structure seem under imminent threat of "destruction or serious danger." Every bridge removed necessarily slowed the rate of buildup.[23]

One of the greatest challenges the planners faced was enabling British officers and non-commissioned officers to reconnoitre the grounds on which they were to soon fight. There were literally thousands of them. While wooded hills overlooked the future battleground from the Canadian lines, the Germans were accustomed to seeing little movement there. Horrocks could imagine the effect if they suddenly saw "these same hills almost covered by figures wearing a different-coloured khaki battledress (the Canadian battledress was darker than ours), studying maps, using field glasses, and so on...This unusual amount of movement could only mean one thing—an impending attack."

The only solution was "rigorous control on any movement in the area." A reconnaissance report centre was established in a Dutch military barracks at Grave, "where everyone wishing to view the bat-tlefield had to report. The staff at this centre would then control the number of people entering any particular area, by a system of passes, allowing them access to a certain view-point, for a definite period. A series of sentries were posted at intervals, to whom the passes had to be shown."[24]

Despite this system, the stream of personnel into forward areas astonished the Canadians there. The war diarist for the 4th Canadian Field Regiment declared on February 5 that their headquarters "really needed a revolving door to accommodate the horde of representatives from the advance parties of the formations coming to join us for the impending shenanigans."[25]

Traffic was that heavy in 4th Field Regiment's sector because it contained a particularly excellent observation point. "On a hill just on the outskirts of Groesbeek," the regiment's historian, Captain George Blackburn, wrote, "there stands a windmill overlooking a valley through which the border line between Holland and Germany runs. And dotted across the valley are scattered farm buildings. On the other side can be seen the Reichswald and to the left and in the distance the rolling country with factory chimneys and churches marking towns and villages. Why the Germans left that windmill intact will always be a mystery, for obviously it was the best observation post in the countryside. Certainly had they known what was going on there during the last weeks of January and the first week in February, it would not have been left standing. During that period it was filled with officers from generals down to subalterns each day planning Germany's destruction.

"The windmill had been used by regimental [forward observation] officers as an O.P. [Observation Point] to direct fire...on targets for months, but during this period they found it hard to get enough room in the top storey of the mill to observe the zone, for visiting officers from British units literally queued up to get a look at the ground they were going to attack. At first there were generals who said little, then came brigadiers and lieutenant colonels who invariably asked, 'Can you put me on the Ground?' The resident FOO would duly point out all the relevant topographical features along with suspected and known German dispositions. Lastly came majors and subalterns who discussed the details of their plans for hours studying each track, house and bush until the FOOs from the regiment knew as much about their plans as they did."[26]

In 3rd Canadian Infantry Division's sector north of Groesbeek, 8th Brigade's Brigadier Jim Roberts was notified on February 4 that Horrocks would arrive at 1400 hours to "take a personal look over the enemy lines." Roberts was excited. On January 25, he had attended an army briefing that included every officer down to brigade level. Horrocks had delivered it, and Roberts was left "deeply impressed by this fabulous character, a born leader such as I had never met before. Horrocks was brief, strictly to the point, but so overwhelmingly confident and amusing that most of the Canadian commanders felt like cheering when the general completed the outline of his plan and his intentions." He and Horrocks would now meet.

The brigade's Queen's Own Rifles was on the tip of a narrow hilltop jutting toward the German lines. A dirt track, "partly in view of the enemy but, happily, passing quickly into a wood," provided the only access. Roberts decided to take Horrocks there in his own camouflaged jeep by flooring it across the exposed ground. At 1400 hours, Horrocks arrived. "His usual bubbling self, he had the gift of stimulating everyone with whom he came in contact; I was no exception, a real Horrocks fan." Horrocks appeared interested in the details of his brigade's circumstances. "Then we moved off, just the two of us, I in my black beret and the general in his cap with scarlet band and his usual leather sleeveless jacket."

Roberts executed the dash across the open ground and gained the woods with relief. The prospect of having "a dead lieutenant general" on his hands had caused much anxiety. They soon located the Queen's Own's standing patrol on the hill. The men were in a deep hole, busily brewing tea. Horrocks immediately engaged the patrol commander in conversation and then chatted up the men. Before Roberts and Horrocks set out for the observation point, the general swapped his cap for one soldier's green beret. Plopping his general's cap on the speechless man's head, Horrocks stomped off. The two officers moved quietly, first on foot, and then crawling on stomachs to where they could see the enemy forward lines and terrain behind.

Horrocks took his time looking the ground over. Then they returned to the patrol, exchanged beret for cap, and went back to 8th Brigade headquarters.

After Horrocks departed, Roberts sat at his desk and thought of the general. "Here was a man who really led, a general who talked to everyone, down to the simplest private soldier." He called his officers by first names. By the time he and Horrocks were belly-crawling together, Roberts had become "Jim." Horrocks had leadership personality that was genuine and won the respect and affection of those he commanded. Surely this made "better soldiers of his officers and men." Somewhat guiltily, Roberts wondered why Canadian senior officers were not like him. After all, "we were supposed to be Canadians, less stiff and formal than the British." Crerar, Roberts thought, "was a good soldier, a very nice man personally...But his personality was not that of a leader of men." He always addressed officers by last names, as did Lieutenant General Guy Simonds. Roberts decided no general in the Canadian Army measured up to Horrocks. He counted it a blessing that Horrocks would be the field commander for Veritable.[27]

What Roberts had experienced was mostly Horrocks putting on a brave face. The camaraderie and personable front he presented masked the fact he was battling a recurrent and unexplained illness linked to a serious wound suffered on August 17, 1943. That day, he had been watching an amphibious landing rehearsal on a beach in Tunisia. A lone German fighter suddenly strafed the beach, and only Horrocks was hit. A slug cut into his chest, ripped down through the abdomen, to exit next to the base of his spine. Immediate surgery stabilized the wound, and five more abdominal operations followed in England, leaving him invalided for fourteen months.[28] It seemed his military career was finished. Then Montgomery called him back from the wilderness on August 3, 1944, to take over xxx Corps. Montgomery had assessed Horrocks carefully for signs of frailty and deemed "Jorrocks" battle fit.

Three weeks later, however, Horrocks was nearly incapacitated by pain, nausea, and fever. This was the persistent illness that had dogged his recovery in England. Each bout generally persisted for about a week. Horrocks had unsuccessfully tried to conceal this illness from Montgomery. Instead of evacuating Horrocks to hospital, however, Montgomery had his caravan brought to Twenty-First Army Group headquarters. For two days, Horrocks was assessed by a score of army medical specialists.[29] Although he soon bounced back, the cause of the illness remained undetermined. (Not until he underwent a seventh abdominal operation in 1947 was an elongated stone found that had developed round a piece of cloth inside his liver. The cloth scrap was a piece of uniform carried into his body by the bullet.)

In late December, the illness recurred. Montgomery noted on December 27 that Horrocks was being "nervy and twitchy with his staff" and sent him to England for a week's rest. He wanted Horrocks fit for Veritable, which would be the largest and most intricate battle the corps commander had ever fought.[30] Now with battle imminent, Horrocks was again ill, but trying to project an appearance of health and vigour. Only a few senior members of his staff knew his condition. They helped sustain the charade. But the "outward and visible sign was that I became extremely irritable and bad-tempered, yet Crerar bore with me patiently."

The two generals were in daily contact. Unlike Montgomery and many other British and even Canadian generals, Horrocks held Crerar in high regard. He considered him "much underrated, largely because he was the exact opposite to Montgomery. He hated publicity, but was full of common sense and always prepared to listen to the views of his subordinate commanders."[31]

Crerar always displayed a fine mind for grasping and considering all complexities of the modern battlefield. He carefully monitored the logistical buildup, with its meticulous emphasis on secrecy in hopes of gaining "the slightest appreciable measure of surprise." Endless hours were spent ensuring that "the technique of the fire preparation for the assault was worked out in order to ensure the closest possible integration of movement with overwhelming fire both from artillery and the air...I gave instructions to my senior officers that once the operation began, commanders of every level must be seized with the intention of keeping the initiative, maintaining the momentum of the attack and of driving on, and through, the enemy without cessation.

There should be no tendency to consider objectives on the ground as an end, rather than a means to an end. Finally I desired it to be ensured that before H-hour [the hour at which the attack would begin], all ranks taking an active part in the operation were adequately briefed and that they obtained a clear appreciation not only of what was expected of them, but of the importance of the contribution which each man could and must make."[32]

Hammering at the enemy rather than winning ground objectives was emphasized as Veritable's primary purpose. As Brigadier W.J. "Bill" Megill, 2nd Canadian Infantry Division's 5th Brigade commander, recognized, the task "for the opening phase...was to destroy the enemy on the Reichswald front, between the River Maas and River Rhine, and to break through in a southeasterly direction." His brigade "was required to destroy the enemy." Defeating the Germans was insufficient. The language emanating from First Canadian Army headquarters ceaselessly reiterated that they must be destroyed.[33]

[9]

To the Last Man

FIRST CANADIAN ARMY intelligence staff called it the Reichswald Plug. Its importance could not be understated. The plug, a
December 16 report stated, "closes the neck of the whole German
position west of the Rhine. When it is pulled, we outflank the Maas
position, the West Wall, and all the new lines in Holland and east of
the Rhine."

The Rhineland was made up of two main topographical types—
areas of flood plains and higher, relatively level ground that
contained them. Both the Rhine and the Maas had been engineered
to form single, navigable channels. Ground rising about one thousand feet on either side of the Maas restricted its flooding to a narrow
plain. But the Rhine's flood plains were wide—ranging from one to
three miles from the riverbank. Scattered about were "abandoned
channels, marsh and backwater meadows with ditches, and, near
the river, scrub in dead stretches of water. Abandoned river meanders marked by reed marsh cover this plain."[1]

Heavy winter precipitation had caused significant flooding of
these flood plains. Next to the Maas, the high ground contained the
flooding, but the Rhine was a different matter entirely. Here there
had been extensive flooding, and only the network of winter dykes
stretching from Wesel to Nijmegen contained it. If the Germans
breached these dykes, the flooding would extend until blocked by

two raised roads and an equally raised railway line. By February 2, the Rhine's water levels had receded significantly, with a resultant decrease in surface water on the flood plains. The exposed ground, however, as one intelligence analysis noted, was "now mucky and saturated with scattered pools of water in shallow depressions. Cover is generally scattered and discontinuous, the best cover being found in the compact villages surrounded by orchards."[2].

Combat in these flood plains promised to be difficult, if not impossible. Waterlogged areas were deemed impassable "without special equipment or improvement except when deeply frozen or in exceptionally dry seasons." Neither condition would exist during Veritable. The ground was "greasy and plastic when wet." Although the soil was not poorly drained clay, it possessed many identical characteristics—ideally suited to sucking tanks or vehicles into an immobilizing quagmire. The many backwaters and abandoned channels often filled with deep water. Some were like large ponds or sections of creek and must either be circumnavigated or crossed with amphibious vehicles. Movement by boat or amphibious vehicle in the inundated areas was possible, but considered quite difficult. Because of the ditches, channels, backwaters, and abandoned river meanders, the intelligence staff had decided that movement on foot "through...shallow water is precarious. The soft nature of the soil would further impede movement. Once the flooded area is drained the ground would still be impossible for a considerable time because, except during a period of continuous heavy frost, mucky conditions would prevail through the winter until artificial drainage assisted by evaporation would dispose of the surface moisture."[3]

This gloomy assessment meant that the main thrust and expectation for success lay in punching through the ground between the flood plains on either flank. On first inspection, the topography here looked more promising. In the main, the country was open and gently rolling. Despite its generally sandy and gravelly soil, much of it was arable and cultivated. Even with the woods interspersed throughout, Canadian analysts considered it "well suited to armoured warfare." First Canadian Army's final objective was the line running between Xanten on the Rhine and Geldern to the south. Here there was a good twenty miles of shoulder room between the Maas and the Rhine. Sufficient breadth existed to enable manoeuvring around enemy flanks and other initiatives.[4]

On closer inspection, this promising picture yielded many troubling details. First and foremost was the Reichswald Plug. First Canadian Army's start line for Veritable was forty miles downstream from Xanten, where the Rhine and the Maas were only six miles apart. Mook stood next to the Maas and Nijmegen beside the Rhine. Immediately across the German border lay the Reichswald—a dark, coniferous plug standing stolidly in the centre of the advance line. A state forest, it stretched about eight miles eastward to the town of Kleve. (Until the Nazis imposed spelling reforms in the 1930s, it had been Cleve. The Allies still used this spelling on maps and in all reports. For simplicity, Cleve will be used throughout the book.)

The Reichswald was a complicated feature. It consisted mainly of stands of young pine spaced about four to seven feet apart and organized in rectangular cut blocks separated by narrow access tracks. Within the forest's heart a belt of deciduous trees grew in similarly regimented blocks. About 15 per cent of all cut blocks had been harvested in recent years, had not been replanted, and had since become overgrown with low scrub. The ground in the Reichswald was undulating. Scattered at random were hummocks with occasional sudden drop-offs of ten feet or more.[5]

Extending along the northern flank and within its treeline, a feature known as the Materborn ridge ranged between 200 and 250 feet above sea level before pivoting in the northwest corner to rise to the summit of a 300-foot hill called the Branden Berg. Ridge and hill provided commanding views to the west and north and down on Cleve.[6]

Two paved roads cut north to south through the Reichswald and converged on the town of Hekkens, midway along the southern edge. No such roads ran east to west. There were only the woodsmen's tracks. Some had been roughly surfaced for use by heavy logging trucks, but most were sand-based. The forest being badly neglected, many tracks were overgrown. Vehicle movement within the forest promised to be difficult, with many parts impassable.

The ground on either flank favoured the Germans. To the south-east ran the Niers River. A tributary of the Maas, the Niers straggled out of headwaters near the fortified city of Goch to its mouth next to the village of Gennep. The Niers had overflowed its banks, spilling into a flood plain of now muddy meadows and brimming swamps. North of the Reichswald, a mile-wide expanse of cultivated land stretched from the woods to the Nijmegen–Cleve road. This road also contained the water on the Rhine's flood plain.[7] Cleve and Goch, standing as they did on either eastern flank of the Reichswald, struck some observers "as the hinges" of this area's "powerful and narrow jaws."[8] Things opened up somewhat beyond Cleve, but the ground was still uninviting for offence. It held scattered small blocks of forest, evacuated villages surely transformed into fortresses, similarly forti-fied farm compounds, and various low heights of ground. Mud everywhere. Two largish forests barred the way into Xanten. The Hochwald stood immediately south of the main road connecting Xanten and Cleve. And curving southeastward from a position almost adjacent to the Hochwald's southern edge stood the Balberger Wald.

THE GERMANS HAD allowed neither excellent defensive ground nor favourable weather to induce complacency. Even as Veritable was necessarily delayed by the Allied need to defeat the Ardennes offen-sive, the Germans in the Rhineland had continued to build their defences. There was little doubt that an attack here was inevitable. All that was at issue was timing, strength, and ultimate purpose. Hitler demanded that every inch of the Fatherland be defended. So the Germans in the Rhineland must stand their ground.

Between the German–Dutch border and Xanten were three main defensive lines—a forward line, the Siegfried Line, and the Hoch-wald Layback. The forward line ran across the western face of the Reichswald from Wyler, on the road to Cleve, south to anchor inside a small isolated stand of timber called the Kiekberg woods. The southern flank of these woods bordered a section of road running from Mook southeastward to Gennep. Although this line was con-sidered an outpost to the more formidable Siegfried Line, it was solid and well constructed. A double series of trenches provided a base.

Where these passed through the Reichswald, an anti-tank ditch had been dug to their front. All nearby farmhouses and villages had been fortified. Connecting trenches running from the forward trenches to the rear tied the system together to a depth of two thousand yards. An extensive minefield covered the front approaches. The northern and southern flanks were the most strongly constructed and manned, because they guarded the roads approaching from the Nijmegen Salient. Both roads were defended in depth by a system of roadblocks, emplaced anti-tank guns, and stretches of anti-tank ditches. The only weak point was to the north of the Nijmegen–Cleve road, where the flood plain lay. But this the Germans could flood at leisure to create a passive defensive system in its own right.[9]

Dubbed the Siegfried Line by the Allies, the second defensive line was actually part of what the Germans called the West Wall. A massive undertaking begun in 1938, the West Wall had originally faced, and was meant to match, the French Maginot Line in the Saar region. It had soon been extended to run the entire length of the German border from Switzerland to the Netherlands. The Germans touted the line as impregnable—a fact that contributed to Hitler's successfully bluffing the British and French into signing the Munich Agreement of September 29, 1938. This agreement was the first attempt to accommodate German demands rather than prompt a war. The West Wall's strength was never tested, as the Germans had invaded France and the Lowlands in May 1940.

During the early days of the war, hope for a quick victory had run high. A snappy little ditty entitled "We're Going to Hang out Our Washing on the Siegfried Line," written by British Expeditionary Force Captain Jimmy Kennedy and songwriting partner Michael Carr, was a big hit. But the Allies had grossly underestimated German aims and strength, and the invasion sent them reeling in a retreat that ended with the surrender of the Netherlands, Belgium, and France and the British evacuation through Dunkirk.

The line had since been neglected. Most of its three thousand concrete emplacements were no longer large enough to hold the bigger, more powerful weapons developed as the war progressed. The section close to the Dutch border had never been fully completed, so it lacked the intricate concrete fortification network of the part to the southeast, where the Americans were operating. Generalmajor Heinz Fiebig, whose 84th Infanterie-Division had overall responsibility for defending the area facing Nijmegen, had anxiously noted that this section of the Siegfried Line relied on "a haphazard series of earthen dugouts."[10] The main defences here ran south from Kranenburg, a village two miles east of Wyler, through the Reichswald to the road junction south of the forest at Hekkens. From here, the line then angled east and south to Goch to a point just west of Weeze. In the south, numerous "anti-tank ditches zigzagged across the whole territory from Goch south to the Maas. Northeast from Kranenburg, a similar ditch extended toward the Rhine. During the winter," a Canadian report stated, "another line had been constructed east of the Reichswald between Cleve and Goch, thus making the forest a self-contained centre of resistance. There were also continuous lines of trenches and deep, large pits containing heavy mortar and anti-tank teams along the eastern bank of the Maas."

Working from aerial photographs, intelligence staff concluded that the "only concrete constructions...in this sector were shelters and infantry pillboxes, some seventy of which had been mapped... Eight large casemates of the original Siegfried Line defences had also been observed, although they were believed to contain only machineguns."[11] Most concrete structures were concentrated around Materborn ridge. Goch presented the strongest part of the line, with anti-tank ditches, protected on three sides, encircling the city. From the village of Frasselt on the northern edge of the Reichswald, a concentrated system of fire positions extended to the Nijmegen–Cleve highway. A major anti-tank ditch extending into the flood plain and terminating at the village of Niel fronted these positions.[12]

Roughly six miles east of the Reichswald, the Hochwald Layback was recent. It ran from the west bank of the Rhine opposite Rees past the western edge of the Hochwald to Geldern. Intelligence analysis identified "some unusual features. Firstly, it consists of two and sometimes three lines of continuous trenches, between 600 and 1,000 yards apart. Secondly, there are two almost continuous belts of wire, one in front of each main trench line." Thirdly, the northern section from the Hochwald to the river was "protected by an almost continuous mine belt in front of the western line of wire and by what may be the beginning of a similar mine belt between the anti-tank ditch and the western line of trenches." Similar, less-developed features also existed in a minor defensive line running from Cleve east to Bedburg and then south to Goch.

"The main system of defence may now be regarded as complete," the analysis concluded. "The striking feature of recent work is that, instead of simply elaborating and strengthening the defensive lines, it apparently transforms their character. The principle appears no longer to be that of "defensive line," but "defensive net." The whole area is, in fact, being split up into a series of self-contained boxes enclosed by trenches with, in many cases, stretches of anti-tank ditches or river [to their front]. The intention would seem to be that each box will have [grenadiers] committed to stay there until the end, purchasing time, if nothing else. It is doubtful if there are enough troops to provide adequate [grenadiers] for all these boxes...Fitting into this system of boxes is the transformation of towns into strong points defended by elaborate trench works and anti-tank ditches."[13]

ON FEBRUARY 3, Generalfeldmarschall Gerd von Rundstedt held a senior commander conference at a mansion in a suburb of Krefeld— a city about twenty miles south of Xanten. Among those present were Heeresgruppe H's new commander, Generaloberst Johannes Blaskowitz, and his subordinate, General der Fallschirmtruppen Alfred Schlemm of the First Fallschirmjäger Army. The sixty-one-year-old Blaskowitz had succeeded Generaloberst Kurt Student—sent to the Eastern Front—on January 28. All of Von Rundstedt's senior officers and those from Heeresgruppe B were in attendance. The situation in front of OB West, Von Rundstedt declared, was critical. "An attack by the Western Powers, starting in the Heeresgruppe H area, seemed to be imminent and would extend from there to the south. The primary objective was presumed to be the Rhine and it was believed the enemy would bypass the West Wall and roll up these positions from the rear.

"The mission was to hold out to the end in order to give OKW [Oberkommando der Wehrmacht] the necessary time for carrying out the countermeasures which had been initiated to preserve Germany's last industrial area, the Ruhr and the Saar. Reinforcement from the east could not be counted on, and OB West had no strategic reserves worth mentioning. Furthermore, units of [Heeresgruppe] H were over-extended because of the lack of sufficient forces...The supply situation was equally unsatisfactory. Only one third of the required ammunition and no reserves of fuel were available. In spite of this situation, combat operations had to be carried out by using every possible means."

Efforts by 1 British Corps to deceive the Germans into thinking the forthcoming assault would be directed toward Holland had completely failed. Heeresgruppe H analysts believed the Allies understood that Holland must inevitably fall if they succeeded with a major attack into the Rhineland. Troop and supply movements detected within Twenty-First Army Group's sector had convinced Blaskowitz that a main offensive would come on either side of Venlo "with the object of reaching the Rhine at Wesel. This attack would probably be preceded by a preliminary attack by...First Canadian Army to capture Forest Reichswald, west of Cleve." The Germans also believed that Twenty-First Army Group's offensive intended to draw divisions from the American sector, which was where Von Rundstedt expected the main Allied attack. This offensive, he believed, would aim at Aachen, by attempting to create a breach in the German line between the small cities of Jülich and Düren. From here they would advance to the Rhine between Düsseldorf and Cologne.

Heeresgruppe B must contain this attack, and Von Rundstedt believed its forces—numerically far stronger than Heeresgruppe H—could do so. He was more worried about Heeresgruppe H, which must meet the British–Canadian feint offensive. First Fallschirmjäger Army would bear the full brunt here. "This army's situation" was, Von Rundstedt declared, "extremely grave." Each division held overly long fronts—ranging between seven and a half and eighteen and a half miles in length. "Although personnel were at full strength and their morale was good, and...needs of material had been satisfied to a certain extent, there was...an acute shortage of mobile anti-tank weapons." At the end of January, the army had just one battalion equipped with twenty self-propelled guns (SPGS). These were scattered across a 74.5-mile front. The army's reserves consisted of only four battalions. Supply reserves were also low, consisting of two issues of ammunition and a half issue of petrol. Although the situation was dire, Von Rundstedt could offer Blaskowitz and Schlemm little. Everything he could scrape together was being sent Schlemm's way, but movement was slow because of lack of fuel and the need to travel at night in order to evade Allied air attack. The formations that Von Rundstedt was sending consisted of four Panzer and SPG battalions, one only partially mobile anti-tank battalion, a Volkssturm artillery corps, several army artillery battalions, a rocket projector corps, a heavy assault mortar battery, and the 361st Infanterie-Division. The personnel of this division were all unarmed and had been en route to Holland for reorganization. Blaskowitz had little in the way of weapons for them. In addition to these forces, the 7th Fallschirmjäger Division was assembling at Geldern.[14]

This division would be well placed to meet the main offensive that Blaskowitz expected at Venlo. Schlemm, however, disagreed with his new boss's assessment of British–Canadian intentions. He believed First Canadian Army's attack on the Reichswald would not be a preliminary. Instead, it would be *the* attack with a drive through Cleve clear to Wesel. This way, Twenty-First Army Group would avoid having to force a crossing of the much swollen Meuse and then overcome heavier West Wall defences than existed in the Reichswald. If the Canadians succeeded, he argued, they "could then roll up the entire front from the north." Schlemm wanted all reinforcements north, but Von Rundstedt sided with Blaskowitz. Most reserves, including 7th Fallschirmjäger Division, would face Venlo.[15]

Operational command of this part of the army rested with General der Fallschirmtruppen Eugen Meindl and his 11 Fallschirmjäger Korps. Like Schlemm, Meindl was a seasoned veteran. The fifty-five-year-old Schlemm had seen bitter fighting in Russia and at Monte Cassino in Italy before being transferred to northwest Europe and command of First Fallschirmjäger Army. Only fifty, Meindl had still commanded artillery in the Great War. When Germany went to war in 1939, he was an artilleryman, but switched to the Luftwaffe's paratroop arm in late 1940. He jumped into Crete and went on to command a paratroop division in Russia and then a paratroop corps.

Meindl took over 11 Fallschirmjäger Korps in Normandy, leading its survivors through the Falaise Gap. Combat experience had sculpted both men into shrewd strategists. Although Meindl was ordered to focus on Venlo, he considered this a fool's errand. "I clung to my former assumption that a thrust would come at Groesbeek–Reichs[wald]–Cleve, as such a thrust would enable [the] enemy to gain the Rhine soonest and would lead into our open flank."[16]

Despite their disagreements, the German commanders all "looked to the near future with great anxiety. It was clear that the impending decisive battle would entail very heavy fighting without hope of outside assistance, without sufficient strategic and tactical reserves, and without sufficient support from the Luftwaffe against a superior, well-trained army. Deep penetrations and extremely critical situations, therefore, had to be expected." Yet they agreed their troops were "resolved to the last man to defend every inch of soil."[17]

With Von Rundstedt and Blaskowitz convinced that the main offensive would not be First Canadian Army's, Schlemm could not immediately strengthen his northern flank. And it was here that his army had its weakest and poorest quality troops. Responsibility for the Reichswald sector fell to General der Infanterie Erich Straube's LXXXVI Korps.[18] The caustic Straube had little confidence in either his men or the supposed West Wall defences, which he considered "a farce...It wasn't a wall, it was an idea."[19] His corps comprised two infantry divisions—84th holding the right flank in the Reichswald, and 180th Infanterie-Division deployed along the Maas on the left. Right of the 84th was 2nd Fallschirmjäger Division of Twenty-Fifth Army. This was fortuitous. In late January, Schlemm had persuaded Blaskowitz to release this division's 2nd Fallschirmjäger Regiment to him. By the February 3 meeting, the regiment's two thousand well-equipped and -trained men had slipped into the line between the Maas and the southwestern edge of the Reichswald. This placed them astride the road running from Mook to the critical junction at Gennep, from which roads ran through the forest to Cleve, Goch, and Afferden.[20]

Even with these paratroopers, Schlemm remained largely reliant on 84th Infanterie-Division to hold the line. Neither its troops nor its commander inspired confidence. The forty-five-year-old

Generalmajor Heinz Fiebig stood six feet tall and was often described as "striking and...debonair."[21] Yet despite fitting the stereotype of a dynamic Wehrmacht general, some considered him "a charming fellow to have at a party [but] the last man to lead a division in the field."[22]

The division had been formed in early 1944 by scraping together remnants of divisions recently shredded on the Russian front. Deployed to Normandy, it had been all but destroyed in the Falaise Pocket. In late September, the division was again reconstructed near Mook and had been in the defensive line since. Its strength stood at about ten thousand. The troops were a hodgepodge of soldiers, some naval personnel, and a hefty levy of seventeen-year-old raw recruits. First Canadian Army intelligence analysts believed that after several months of front-line service, "the raw troops are now fairly well trained and capable of giving a good account of themselves. Battalions should be well up to strength."[23]

The division consisted of three regiments, with 1062nd defending the Reichswald, 1051st facing the line between Groesbeek and Wyler, and 1052nd on the Rhine flood plain. Fiebig's reserve consisted of the Sicherungs Battalion Münster—a small unit of elderly men normally deployed as guards for static installations—and the 276th Magen (Stomach) Battalion. The latter battalion was composed of men with chronic digestive ailments. Fiebig had opted for this battalion over an Ohren (Ear) battalion, because he thought they might at least hear "the opening barrage of an attack." The division was weak in artillery, having only about a hundred guns of varying calibre. By February 6, it had been reinforced with thirty-six self-propelled guns of 655th Heavy Anti-Tank Battalion.[24]

Despite its weaknesses, the division was well deployed. Its frontage was divided into eight sectors, each held by a single battalion. These battalions each consisted of four companies—three being regular rifle companies and the other a heavy company whose men operated the heavy machine guns and mortars. Two rifle companies were posted forward, with the third in reserve. The heavy company was divvied up among the three companies to provide greater firepower. A further five battalions were believed to be in reserve. This gave Fiebig a total of thirteen battalions. The division's overall strength, including the added paratroopers, was estimated at about 12,500 personnel. About 6,000 of these were front-line infantry. Another 4,200 served as engineers, signallers, artillerymen, or anti-tank gunners and would mostly be engaged in active combat relevant to their specialties. A further 2,250 performed various supporting roles.

As was typical, the paratroopers were well equipped with automatic weapons. The division's three battalions were each believed to have thirty-five machine pistols, twenty-seven light machine guns, and six medium machine guns. They were also heavily armed with Panzerfaust anti-tank launchers and automatic rifles that could be used against tanks. Somewhat to the surprise of Canadian intelligence analysts, they found Fiebig's inherent infantry battalions were armed almost as well as the paratroopers. The two battalions of 1051st Grenadier Regiment, for example, boasted between them seventy-six machine pistols, fifty-eight light machine guns, twelve medium machine guns, seventy-two Panzerfausts, and possibly more than seventy-five automatic rifles. Whether infantry or paratrooper, each battalion possessed six 8.1-centimetre mortars. The combat effectiveness of this division, the analysts concluded, was not to be underestimated.[25]

JUST AS FIRST Canadian Army intelligence staff had a detailed understanding of the ground and defensive positions facing them, they possessed remarkably accurate and timely information on German forces. No sooner had 2nd Fallschirmjäger Regiment entered the line than its presence was betrayed by three deserters picked up on January 20 by a Canadian patrol. They admitted to serving in the regiment's 3rd Battalion and identified its placement in line. Within a couple of days, the 1st and 2nd Battalions were also accurately situated on Canadian maps.[26]

Carefully studying the intelligence picture, General Harry Crerar saw "strong evidence of strengthening opposition on my own front." Clearly, 84th Infanterie-Division was being bulked up, especially by paratroopers. He knew, too, that 7th Fallschirmjäger Division lurked somewhere east of the Reichswald as an immediate reinforcement, and that the 15th Panzer Grenadier Division could "be available within six hours of the assault." Furthermore, there was room within the Reichswald's "defences in depth" to absorb two such divisions.[27] Also in reserve was XLVII Panzer Korps, situated about ten miles southeast of Venlo. It consisted of two divisions—116th Panzer and 15th Panzer Grenadier. Both had taken a beating in the Ardennes and reportedly retained little more than 50 per cent of their strength. Jointly they could field no more than ninety tanks. On February 4, Twenty-First Army Group advised Crerar that Von Rundstedt might muster a reserve of eleven Panzer and Panzer Grenadier divisions. Most of these, however, would be held in the south to meet the American threat between Roermond and the Ardennes. Some were also likely to be passed off to the Russian front, where the need was considered greater.[28]

During the early phases of the buildup, Crerar had reason to believe the Germans remained uncertain of First Canadian Army's intentions. But as the concentration of troops, equipment, and supplies reached a crescendo on February 6, Crerar figured the jig was up. "I had to assume that his aircraft, flying over the Army area on tactical reconnaissance, had observed the unavoidable signs of our enterprise, especially in the district between Grave and Nijmegen, where the many hundreds of vehicles and tanks, many of them impossible to conceal as the only hard standings were roads and streets, could hardly have escaped the vigilance of the camera." Surely the Germans "had a shrewd suspicion that I was going to attack in the Reichswald sector...But in surveying the enemy's problems and possibilities, I decided that there was little he could do to improve his situation as it then stood." The Germans must initially fight with forces on hand. Crerar felt that gave him a huge edge.

It was an edge he needed. At 1700 hours on February 1, Montgomery had telephoned Crerar and said "the operation would go in [on February 8] without postponement and irrespective of the situation elsewhere." Three days later, Montgomery, Crerar, Lieutenant General Miles Dempsey, U.S. Ninth Army Lieutenant General William Simpson, and Air Marshal Arthur Coningham met. Montgomery reported that Eisenhower "had now decided that the joint offensive [operations] by the First Canadian and Ninth U.S. Armies were to be carried out as tasks of first priority. The only exception would be the operations about to be undertaken by the First U.S. Army to capture the dams controlling the River Roer." The First Army operation was a necessary precursor to enabling Ninth Army to launch Operation Grenade.

Disappointingly, Montgomery said, Ninth Army would not be as robust as initially hoped. It would only be ten divisions strong, which was just enough to meet the needs for Grenade. Montgomery had hoped to give Dempsey an American division so that British Second Army could force a crossing of the Meuse at Venlo. Such an operation would now "either not take place, or would be carried out in a somewhat tentative way." This was bad news for Crerar, because Dempsey's operation would have helped pin in place the reserves the Germans had concentrated at Venlo.

Better news was that Second Army had in effect become a robust reserve unit for both Crerar's army and Simpson's Americans. This meant Simpson need not retain any reserve of his own. He could throw all divisions into the battle and was expected to do so on February 10. Simpson vowed that even "if First U.S. Army had not captured the Roer dams by that date, his own attack would nevertheless go in, since it was not anticipated that any flooding which the enemy might cause would be of a nature to require postponement."[29]

Crerar might have looked upon this observation with a jaundiced eye. The sudden thaw at the end of January, combined with continuing heavy rains, was causing concerns at the place in the Rhine's flood plain where the advance would occur. By February 3, the Rhine was running past Nijmegen at a height of about forty feet and still rising. The Rhine had only been so swollen in six of the past thirty-four years. Earlier in the winter, the Germans had breached the main dyke at Erlekom, four miles upstream of Nijmegen. On February 6, a mighty spill of water started flowing through this breach.[30]

Until then the flood plain had been sufficiently dry that operational plans by 3rd Canadian Infantry Division had foreseen a relatively normal advance on foot, with standard army vehicles and tanks in support. By the morning of February 6, however, the situation had changed dramatically. The headquarters of the CIB's Canadian Scottish Regiment was in a large building overlooking the flood plain from a height of ground near Beek. That morning, the regiment's headquarters staff discovered they "had been invaded overnight by an overflow from the River Rhine. Excited shouts of 'The Tide's in' greeted late risers. As far as we could see, what had yesterday been dry land was now fit only for the traffic of the Royal Navy."

With Veritable imminent, 3rd Infantry Division officers anxiously watched their entire operational area become submerged. The 13th Field Regiment, whose guns were to support 8th Infantry Brigade, had started to deploy into the flood plain on February 6. Digging out gun pits was impossible because of the plain's low water table, so the gunners had squirrelled away seven thousand sandbags in nearby buildings. As the guns were placed, they and the regiment's command posts would be protected by sandbagged walls. With the field they were to have used transforming into a lake, Lieutenant William Barrett hurried to select a new position. The clock was ticking down to showtime, and the guns must be ready. "The only areas which field guns could use and still be within range for the final phase of the 8 CIB attack were now under water. The only alternative was for the regiment to deploy in the Wyler area being both within range of Millingen and on high ground not subject to flooding." There were three major problems with this plan. First, the area was still held by the Germans and would be until 2nd Canadian Infantry Division was to capture it on the first day. This would leave 8th Brigade without artillery support for critical hours. The second problem was that the area lay inside "what had been the German forward defence line during the winter and was heavily mined and booby trapped." A third problem was that the area had even earlier been occupied by the U.S. 101st Airborne Division, which additionally "had planted... many uncharted mine fields."[31]

Allied minefields had, in fact, hugely hampered preparations— particularly those enabling formations to settle in on start lines and artillery positions. Deep bands of defensive minefields had been laid during the winter along the entire Nijmegen Salient front. Many now must be cleared to allow the advance. In the week leading up to

Veritable, engineers of 2nd Infantry Division alone lifted eleven thousand mines and knew that a good number had been missed.[32]

The engineers offered 13th Field Regiment dogs to sniff out mines, but were too short on handlers to provide them. With it being essential to get guns set up quickly, the thought of a bunch of inexperienced gunners wandering around with dogs they had no idea how to handle was rejected. Regular mine detectors were also deemed useless "because the area contained so much wire and pieces of shrapnel. It was eventually decided to occupy the position in the normal manner and take the risks. It might have been argued that the risks were too great to warrant the use of artillery here but then, on the other hand, to refuse to give the infantry artillery support in their attacks would put them in a much more dangerous position." When the time came, the guns would be shunted into place and damn the mines.[33]

Within both 2nd and 3rd Infantry Divisions' operational zones, a great flurry of last-minute juggling and adaptation was soon under way. By late afternoon of February 7, the Can Scots watched warily as herds of Buffaloes, Weasels, and DUKWs arrived. The 3rd Infantry Division, which had starred in amphibious operations at Juno Beach and then later in capturing the Breskens Pocket during the Scheldt Estuary Campaign—in similarly flooded conditions—would once again live up to its reputation as the Allied force's "Water Rats."

The Can Scot officers at battalion headquarters spent much of the day arguing about whether the flooding would delay or even cancel Veritable. Lieutenant Colonel Desmond Crofton finally went to a divisional meeting. He returned to report that "any new problems were discussed and solved." Without fail, Veritable would kick off the next morning.[34]

10

Opportunity Is at Hand

"**D**o you want Cleve taking out?" General Harry Crerar had calmly asked Lieutenant General Brian Horrocks a few days before Veritable's launch. It was a city's fate that Crerar asked about. Horrocks knew "taking out" was a euphemism for "totally destroyed." Crerar had just advised Horrocks that in addition to all the resources of 2nd Tactical Air Force, Bomber Command's heavy bombers were his for the asking. All he had to do was nod.

In the darkness of night—Bomber Command's operational preference—the big four-engine Liberators and Halifaxes would appear over Cleve. Thousands of bombs would fall—a cocktail of incendiary and high explosives. Cleve's ancient buildings would be smashed apart, burned to the ground, or both. The streets, particularly the main road that ran east to west through it and was sealing Cleve's fate, would be clogged with fallen masonry and smouldering timbers. Massive fires would feed the chaos, rendering passage through the city all but impossible.

Horrocks knew a little of Cleve—knew it was "a lovely old historic Rhineland town. Anne of Cleves, Henry VIII's fourth wife, came from there. No doubt, a lot of civilians, [including] women and children, were still living there. Their fate depended on how I answered Crerar's question, and I simply hated the thought of Cleve being 'taken out.' All the same, if we were going to break out of the bottleneck into the German plain it was a race between the German reserves and the [15th (Scottish) Infantry Division] for the Nutterden feature [a heavily fortified narrow chokepoint between the Rhine's flood plain and the Reichswald through which the Nijmegen–Cleve highway ran], and the German reserves would have to come through Cleve. If I could delay them by bombing it might make all the difference to the battle, and, after all, the lives of my own troops must come first. So I said, 'Yes'—the most terrific decision I had ever had to take in my life, and I can assure you that I felt almost physically sick when, on the night before the attack, I saw the bombers flying overhead on their deadly mission."[1]

Not just Cleve would be destroyed. On the night of February 7–8, Goch faced obliteration. Also, virtually every village and small town lying in the path of First Canadian Army was to be annihilated by incendiary and anti-personnel bombs. The planners accepted that Cleve and Goch would be left with such intensive crater damage and spread of debris that movement through them by their own troops would be seriously hampered. That was the price payable for turning them into obstacles to the rapid movement of German reinforcements. The planners hoped, however, that the less destructive incendiaries and anti-personnel bombs would sufficiently reduce damage to the villages to permit easier movement by their own forces, while burning out German defensive positions.[2]

First Canadian Army had a penchant for calling in heavy bomber squadrons to support operations—so much so that in October 1944, RAF high command accused the Canadians of being "bomb happy." Every time German opposition stiffened, they declared, the Canadians called for bombers. Using heavy bombers to support army operations detracted from their true role, which was crippling German industry and transportation networks.[3]

This time, however, Bomber Command made no complaint. Crerar had been assured lavish air support and was determined to use it fully. "Given favourable weather," he wrote, "the attack was to have maximum assistance from the air. The assaulting divisions would have the support of the 2nd Tactical Air Force with a potential of 1,000 fighters or fighter-bombers, 100 medium day, and 90 night-fighters. Close-in support would be provided by 84th Group, and Bomber Command would attack targets in the enemy's battle area with up to 1,000 heavy bombers. Support was also expected from the medium bombers and the heavy bombers of Eighth U.S. Army Air Force. But given the intention to retain the greatest possible element of surprise, and as it was not to be assumed that this could be achieved if D-day were delayed by as many as twenty-four hours, the operation would be launched, if necessary, with fire support from ground weapons only...Prior to the attack an intensive programme of heavy bombing was [to be] carried out, the chief targets being the towns of Goch and Cleve, two pivotal points in the organization of the enemy's defences."[4]

Responsibility for coordinating air support was assigned to the staff of RAF's 84th Fighter Group—whose fighter-bombers and fighters normally worked with First Canadian Army. Lacking sufficient fighters to meet all the tasks for the first day of Veritable, they were allowed to draw from 83rd Fighter Group. They also determined where, when, and in what numbers light, medium, and heavy bomber allocations would be utilized.[5]

Finding the right bomb mix to inflict the desired damage while not causing extensive cratering, which hindered their troop movement, presented a major challenge. Staff from xxx Corps and 84th Fighter Group spent hours evaluating the potency and effect of one bomb type over another with various concoctions and blends considered. Wing Commander (Armament) R.B. Dashper advised that ample supplies of the 500-pound M76 Incendiary bomb were "available and that it contained benzene ignited by phosphorus. These were particularly good against houses." Liking the sound of this, Brigadier P. Jones of xxx Corps headquarters wondered if they might be used effectively "against the enemy in open emplacements" on the Netterden and Materborn features. Dashper replied that "these would be good against houses and open emplacements but not concrete emplacements." It being understood that Materborn had been heavily fortified with concrete positions, Dashper advised mixing M76's with heavy explosive bombs. This assumed, of course, that extensive crater damage was acceptable. Jones responded sharply that "cratering cannot be accepted in tactical areas of Netterden and Materborn." Twenty-First Army Group's air operations brigade staff officer Brigadier C.C. Oxborrow then cautioned that "firebombs would not produce scorched earth effect." Perhaps the best approach, Dashper offered, was to use air burst fuses on the high-explosive bombs "to get an air burst effect and the M76 bombs be mixed with these." That solution appealed to all and was adopted.[6]

Each day the air plan was honed ever sharper. By February 3, an elaborately detailed chart running to dozens of fold-out pages identified every conceivable target and its value to the Germans. The type of air asset to attack it was detailed and the desired outcome clearly noted. Railroads, roads, and bridges providing access into the Rhineland were to be cut by bombing. A large petroleum dump consisting of twenty-seven storage tanks at Emmerich was believed to hold about 16,000 tons of vegetable oil but possessed the potential to store 34,000 tons. As the city was home to a factory producing vegetable and marine oils, which intelligence reports indicated was "in full operation," Emmerich was to be heavily bombed to destroy the storage tanks and factory. Total destruction of Cleve and Goch was reconfirmed, with the last explosion in the former to occur no later than 1600 hours on D-Day and in the latter before 0800 on D+1. The Nutterden feature had been meticulously measured and assessed. It formed a rectangle approximately 1,500 by 1,800 metres in diameter. Within lay infantry "defensive positions containing many open emplacements, communication trenches, dugouts, shelters and some concrete pillboxes. Area also contains some machine-gun emplacements and radar." It was to be attacked quite late on D-Day, with the last explosions to occur before 1530 hours. U.S. Army Air Force fighter-bombers would make this attack, intended to "destroy and demoralize the enemy troops in open defended positions."

American fighter-bombers would also rain destruction upon the Germans holding the Materborn feature. This attack would also begin as late as possible on D-Day but end no later than 1600 hours. The Materborn was described as being "roughly circular in shape and covers an area approximately 750 metres [in] radius." Along with many open emplacements, communication trenches, dugouts, shelters, and concrete pillboxes, the area contained a collection of field and anti-aircraft guns. A "successful assault of the Materborn feature is the key to the operation," the plans stressed.

A particularly important target had been identified at Xanten. This was an "ammunition dump of at least 90 stacks served by road and railway." An underground storage area had been dug into a hill close by. "Bombs, shells and all types of ammunition are said to be stored there." It was guarded by only two hundred German troops. "This is the only important ammunition dump west of the Rhine and its continued existence would discount much of the advantage gained by the destruction of the Wesel bridges." These dumps were therefore to be destroyed by the heavies of Bomber Command shortly before D-Day. Wesel's rail and road bridges were also to be severed by bombing prior to Veritable's launch.[7]

The 2nd Tactical Air Force was deploying new technology that allowed its medium bombers, fighter-bombers, and fighters to accurately strike ground targets even when these were screened by cloud cover. By linking a radar unit to an anti-aircraft gun target predictor, the new Mobile Radar Control Post, operating from a boxy structure mounted on a semi-trailer, could guide aircraft to a specific target and indicate when bombs should be released for an accurate strike. Tests had shown that Mitchell and Boston medium bombers were particularly enabled to drop accurately through cloud cover when guided by operators manning this post. Its fighter-bomber Spitfires and Typhoons were also assisted by the radar direction system.[8]

Numbers of bombers and fighter-bombers expected to be in the air over the Rhineland in the lead-up to D-Day and the days following ran to the hundreds. Would the Luftwaffe threaten them? A top-secret "air appreciation" noted that the Germans had good airfields within range that would be better positioned to support the "enemy ground troops on this front than was the case on the Aachen and Ardennes fronts." They also fielded a potent tactical force consisting of 1,050 single-engine fighters, 100 single-engine ground attack planes, 100 jet aircraft, about 100 Junker 87 bombers, and 120 night fighters capable of ground attack. Most of these planes were believed to be deployed within range of Veritable's operational territory, but only about 65 per cent were serviceable and manned at any given time.

Air intelligence analysts ruled that this strength was incapable of gaining superiority over or even equality with the Allies. They also noted that German pilots were proving "insufficiently trained for effective ground attack and 'night work' was far below Allied standards." Their conclusion was that "although the [Luftwaffe] is doing its best to train and conserve pilots and aircraft for cooperation with ground forces, and is still a force to be reckoned with, it will be unable effectively to interfere with our offensive. Attacks by it may be expected by day and/or night, but these attacks, except possibly for occasional attacks by jet aircraft, will not have more than a nuisance value."[9]

THERE REMAINED ONE thing the air planners could not control. During the January 25 meeting, First Canadian Army Chief of Staff Brigadier Church Mann had asked for an accurate weather forecast, so Crerar could decide whether the "operation would go on and allow time to warn Bomber Command for operations on night of D minus 1." He was told a forty-eight-hour meteorological forecast "was not possible under present conditions, but a reasonable forecast for D-Day is possible." They would also not be able to provide "reliable information as to conditions on D plus 1." The best the meteorologists could offer was to phone predictions for the next twenty-four hours by 1700 hours on D minus 1.[10]

After careful consideration, neither Crerar nor Horrocks felt they could accept even a twenty-four-hour delay. If the weather turned sour and the air forces were grounded, the attack must proceed regardless, with the massed artillery doing the trick alone.

Major Arthur Kembar of 6th Canadian Field Regiment never doubted the artillery could singlehandedly do the job. The "artillery concentrated in our area was tremendous. Every field was occupied as a gun position, and every known calibre represented...There was no doubt about this being a big show."[11] So many guns were involved that their total number would never be accurately confirmed. Crerar understood there were more than 1,400 guns—one-third being those of British and Canadian medium-heavy and super-heavy regiments.[12] The Canadian Army's official historian calculated that there were 1,034 guns involved and agreed that a third were larger than the 25-pounders of the field regiments.[13] Britain's official army historian meticulously crunched numbers by type of gun employed and declared a total of 1,050.[14] Whatever the numbers, the artillery support was to be a "major battle-winning factor." The barrage soon to fall upon 84th Infanterie-Division would be unequalled to any against "a similar front during the entire war in the west."[15]

Carefully integrated into the fire plan were the twelve rocket projectors of 1st Canadian Rocket Battery. These projectors were equipped with thirty-two barrels and nicknamed Land Mattresses because each salvo saturated an area of approximately four hundred square yards with explosive blast. They were capable of accurate fire to a maximum range of eight thousand yards. A rocket contained approximately the same amount of explosive as the 5.5-inch shells fired by medium-artillery regiments. Brigadier F.D. Lace, 2nd Canadian Infantry Division's artillery commander, was delighted to have the battery in his support. He requested that the battery fire three salvoes against pre-identified targets that directly threatened his division's advance. An additional twelve salvoes would fire in support of the British divisions. The rockets, Lace said later, "fired on a 'ripple' system so that they would avoid colliding with each other in the air."[16]

Although rocket projectors had originally been the brainchild of British officer Lieutenant Colonel Michael Wardell, he had been unable to secure support from the War Office to render prototypes operational. But a Canadian artillery officer, Lieutenant Colonel Eric Harris, had become an enthusiastic supporter. With the War Office's agreement, Harris enlisted Wardell to work with him on developing a rocket battery for First Canadian Army. The first projector fired a successful salvo in June 1944. By September, the battery had been formed and deployed to France. It first saw combat on October 30. Operation Veritable—entailing the firing of 4,608 rockets—would mark its heaviest fire commitment to date.

Taller than most men, the rockets were unwieldy and heavy. They had to be loaded individually into the firing barrel, care being taken to avoid the rifled tube bending the rocket's fins. Each rocket was then connected to a pair of 6-volt batteries. As it took fifteen minutes to load a projector, maintaining a steady fire rate was impossible. But a full salvo from a single projector matched that of an entire artillery regiment.[17]

This was what Brigadier Lace counted on when assigning his three targets. "As the rockets have more blast than splinter effect," he said, they had the result of "stunning the enemy." To get maximum benefit from each salvo, his fire plan called for the salvoes to "take place immediately before the infantry arrived on the target area."[18]

For the past two and a half months, Lace and his staff had been carefully identifying and mapping the positions of German artillery and mortar batteries. Although the other divisions involved in Veritable were responsible for developing their individual fire plans, much of the information they used was supplied by Lace's headquarters, "which had a fairly complete picture of the situation." Drawing on information provided by sound ranging, flash spotting, and mortar location units of 2nd Canadian Survey Regiment—whose job was to prowl the front lines with their specialized equipment and pin positions of enemy artillery and mortar—Lace's staff had developed the bombardment tables that evolved into xxx British Corps's final artillery plan. "All mortar which had been active since 15 Jan[uary] were to be bombarded," Lace reported.

So that artillery could concentrate fire deep inside the German lines, a "pepper pot" was added to saturate the enemy front lines. The Normandy Campaign had revealed that not only the weight of artillery fire but also the sheer number of guns involved damaged enemy morale. Consequently, British and Canadian divisions had taken to including light anti-aircraft guns, anti-tank guns, medium machine guns, heavy mortars, and any available tanks in major barrages. Besides its demoralizing effect, such fire at close range was quite deadly. For Operation Veritable, the artillery would be supplemented by 114 Bofors light anti-aircraft guns, 80 medium mortars, 60 Sherman tanks, 24 17-pounder anti-tank guns, and 188 medium machine guns.[19]

Lieutenant Colonel E.G. Johnson, commander of the Toronto Scottish (MG) Regiment, organized 2nd Canadian Infantry Division's pepper pot. He had a squadron of British tanks, three troops of 3rd

Canadian Light Anti-Aircraft Regiment, some of the division's anti-tank guns, and his regiment's heavy mortars and medium machine guns. Johnson's intention was to "saturate with fire all enemy defences within range" of his medium machine guns, the 40-millimetre Bofors, 4.2-inch mortars, and anti-tank guns. The firing program would be maintained for five hours but not be continuous or of a set intensity. Instead, fire would be "as irregular as possible. The effect of having deliberately erratic fire come down meant that the enemy could not know when it would stop or start, and this had the desired result of reducing his morale," Johnson wrote. Pepper pots "served as a strong deterrent to free movement by the enemy, and this was very important in view of the great use which he was accustomed to make of alternative positions."

For once, the front lines the Canadians held worked in Johnson's favour. So often when planning a pepper pot, identifying targets or even sighting on enemy defences required crawling into no man's land. Here, however, "we held a reasonably easy area, from the point of view of recce, as our positions overlooked those of the enemy. Secondly, the extensive woods west and north of Groesbeek provided covered lines of approach. In both of these connections the possibilities of deployment were...unusually favourable."

There were still problems. Tanks, anti-aircraft, and anti-tank guns were all relatively short-ranged—2,000 to 5,000 yards—and fired on flat trajectories. This meant they had to be slipped into positions right on the edge of the forward defence lines in order to fire at their assigned targets. Firing from behind a protective crest was generally not possible, so they were at risk of being spotted and subjected to counter-fire. The medium machine guns were "pushed as far forward as possible" to gain maximum penetration behind enemy front lines.

A bigger problem than siting the guns was delivering the great volume of ammunition required. Only one road led to the division's position. Rain and previous traffic had rendered it impassable to trucks. Johnson rounded up a "fleet" of Bren carriers "and two full days were taken up with the transportation through the mud to the dumps. The last rounds were delivered by 2000 [hours] on the night before the attack (7–8 Feb)."[20]

As had been true for the artillery regiments, a terrific quantity of ammunition would be used. In 2nd Division's area alone, Lace calculated that they moved forward to the guns 385,400 machine-gun rounds, 13,680   40-millimetre rounds for the Bofors, and about 10,000 bombs for the 4.2-inch mortars.[21]

MORALE RAN HIGH as the countdown to Veritable began on February 7. On 3rd Canadian Medium Regiment's gun lines, Lieutenant John Reeves observed that the troops were "all eagerly awaiting the assault and it is obvious that there is only one way to keep morale high and the gunnery happy, and that is to fire their guns. The majority would give up a Brussels leave any time to stay and do some effective shooting." The regiment's intelligence officer, Reeves had a key role in directing the regiment's sixteen 5.5-inch guns. He worked alongside adjutant Captain Bill Davey. Because of the firing plan's complexity, the regiment had added a folding extension to the operation table fitted inside its mobile headquarters truck. This enabled Reeves and Davey to sit side by side. Reeves had before him a large card ruled off in ten-minute intervals with timings running down the right side. The rest of the chart was divided into five vertical columns providing coordinates for pre-arranged targets and the scale of fire assigned to each. "All tasks received to date have been recorded on this," Reeves wrote, "so...it will be possible to see at a glance, for any given ten minute period, just what our commitments are and in what area. Any task called for by Air [operators] or AGRA [Army Group, Royal Artillery] can instantly be checked against this and we will be able to tell if we have any guns available." Davey's desk area contained "target overprint maps of the battle. In addition, a lock has been placed on the door [to the truck compartment], and any casual visitor either has to stay out or phone from the Mess. This will save any unnecessary interference."

In the early evening of February 7, all regimental personnel were assembled at headquarters. After a movie, Reeves unveiled a large map and outlined Veritable. He then read messages sent by Montgomery and Crerar to every First Canadian Army unit.[22] Montgomery's displayed his penchant for awkward metaphor. The war with Germany was entering its final stage, which resembled a boxing match.

"In [Twenty-First Army Group] we stand ready for the last round. There are many of us who have fought through the previous rounds; we have won every round on points; we now come to the last and final round, and we want, and will go for, the knock-out blow.

"The rules of the last round will be that we continue fighting till the final count; there is no time limit. We know our enemy well; we must expect him to fight hard to stave off defeat, possibly in the vain hope that we might crack before he does. But we shall not crack; we shall see this thing through to the end. The last round may be long and difficult, and the fighting hard; but we now fight on German soil; we have got our opponent where we want him; and he is going to receive the knock-out blow; a somewhat unusual one delivered from more than one direction...And so we embark on the final round, in close co-operation with our American allies on our right and with complete confidence in the successful outcome of the onslaught being delivered by our Russian allies on the other side of the ring. Somewhat curious rules, you may say. But the whole match has been *most* curious; the Germans began this all-out contest and they must not complain when in the last round they are hit from several directions at the same time.

"Into the ring, then, let us go. And do not let us relax till the knock-out blow has been delivered.

"Good luck to you all and God bless you."[23]

Crerar was more direct. "Six months ago, almost to a day, history was made by formations of this Army in their southward drive which broke the 'Caen hinge' and closed the 'Falaise pocket.' The same, and other formations, shall again record great achievements in the days ahead by breaking through the 'Reichswald pivot' and turning this key sector of the Siegfried Line.

"The operations which we are about to undertake are of the greatest possible importance. Indeed, the result of them can lead to speedy and complete Allied victory. The assault will be launched with great strength and with most powerful fire support. Whatever the difficulties of ground and weather, the forward thrust through the enemy and his defences will be pressed without respite. He must be given no time or opportunity to collect his thoughts or his resources. The opportunity is at hand. Let us see to it that it is firmly seized and decisively exploited."[24]

After Reeves finished reading these messages, Lieutenant Colonel G.L.W. Macdonald gave a "pep talk which sent all the troops off to their billets very enthused." As they dispersed, "a large formation of bombers" passed overhead. Reeves had explained that on this night a large formation of bombers would bombard Cleve and Goch as Operation Veritable's opening act. The night would be short for the gunners. Reeves and Davey were to man their desk by 0330 hours and the gunners be ready soon after. The barrage would begin at 0500.[25]

MONTGOMERY HAD CONFIDENTLY declared that First Canadian Army would be amply supported by the Americans on its right. But he still had no idea when U.S. Ninth Army could launch Operation Grenade. The effect of the flooding and the spring thaw worried him greatly. On February 6, he had visited the Veritable front. "The ground is very wet and roads and tracks are breaking up and these factors are likely to make progress somewhat slow after the operation," he wrote Chief of the Imperial General Staff General Sir Alan Brooke that evening. The next day he visited General William Simpson and toured the Operation Grenade area. His evening message told Brooke that "the Roer River is very flooded. I met and talked to all the Corps and Divisional Commanders. All ten American Divisions are now assembled in 9th Army area and they are all in good shape and ready for battle. I have ordered that Grenade will be launched on 10th Feb." But Montgomery knew Grenade could only proceed when General Omar Bradley's Twelfth Army Group secured the seven dams that controlled the water levels of the Roer River, whose headwaters were nearby. Two dams were vitally important. In the early 1900s, the Urft Dam had been constructed. Blocking the Urft River downstream from Gemuend, the dam created a 42,000-acre-foot reservoir. During the mid-1930s, the Schwammenauel Dam had been added on the Roer River, a few miles north of the Urft Dam. It could impound 81,000 acre-feet of water. The Urft Dam was entirely concrete, while the Schwammenauel was constructed of earth with a concrete core. If the Germans destroyed or opened the gates of both they could flood the low-lying valley downstream at Jülich and Düren—precisely where Simpson's Ninth Army was to cross the Roer to open Grenade.

When General Courtney H. Hodges's First Army was mired in the Hürtgen Forest from September through mid-November, its line of advance had been generally toward the dams, although they had not been an objective. Belatedly, the Americans had recognized their importance and tried breaching them with bombing attacks. These had failed. The German Ardennes offensive in December scrubbed a planned ground attack. In January, capturing the dams was assigned to the newly appointed commander of First Army's V Corps, General Clarence Ralph Huebner. On the evening of February 2, he summoned Major General Edwin G. Parker Jr. of 78th U.S. Infantry Division. Huebner told Parker his mission to capture Schwammenauel Dam "was the most vital at that time on the entire Western front; until the dam was in hand, the Ninth Army dared not cross the Roer."

The 78th's attack was set for the early morning hours of February 5. In preparation, U.S. 9th Infantry Division easily captured the Urft Dam intact after, as the American Army official historian put it, "little more than a cross-country march." Parker's division enjoyed no such luck. Although opposition was relatively light, roads proved to be blocked by mines and obstructions. This forced the division to advance cross-country through increasingly rugged terrain. Parker had a hard time controlling his battalions. By February 6, the advance had bogged down so badly that Hodges burst into the division headquarters that morning and demanded that Parker get "cracking" or be sacked. With German resistance rapidly stiffening, the threat was meaningless. As night fell on February 7, Parker's division was still far short of the dam. Nobody knew when the dam would finally be taken or what its condition would be. The U.S. Ninth Army could only sit and wait as Veritable got under way on its left flank.[26]

CLEVE HAD NOT been previously untouched by Allied bombing. On the nights of September 23 and 26, 1944, the city of about 21,000 had been bombed. St. Antonius Hospital, the city hall, and the mint suffered extensive damage. Following these attacks, about one-third of the population fled to central Germany. Then—on October 7—351 bombers reduced three-quarters of the urban area, measuring 480 acres, to ruin. More than a million cubic yards of rubble choked city streets. About five hundred people died, roughly one in thirty of its then population.[27] The night of February 7–8 saw Cleve's destruction completed—rendering it the most bomb-damaged German city for its size. Its famous castle and cathedral were left in ruins.

At 2200 hours on February 7, another 286 heavy bombers dropped 1,397 tons of high explosives. The few buildings still standing in its centre and southern sectors were shattered.[28] Because of extensive prior damage, most of the remaining civilians had been evacuated three miles to a tent encampment in a muddy field outside the village of Bedburg. Aboard an RAF Lancaster of 153rd Squadron, BBC reporter Richard Dimbleby recorded his impressions of the destruction. The city's historic spires were toppled, devastation everywhere to be seen—a "staggering sight." Dimbleby, who had accompanied British bombers on many raids, declared that "Cleve is blazing...lit like London on its brightest day." The bombing had lasted just twenty minutes.[29]

Horrocks saw the bombers pass overhead. Neither he nor Crerar fully understood how badly the town had been damaged earlier. Fixated on creating a chokepoint to German traffic, each believed the horrendous damage resulted from the single raid they had ordered. After the war, Horrocks suffered years of nightmares that "always concerned Cleve. Unfortunately, [the destruction] was even worse than I had imagined."[30]

Goch was also struck that night by 151 bombers dropping a fairly modest 475 tons of bombs on roads and defensive positions. About midnight, south of Cleve and Goch, 95 Halifax and Stirling medium bombers struck known German billets and defensive positions at Calcar, Üdem, and Weeze.[31]

Standing outside 4th Field Regiment's headquarters at Rusthuis, Captain George Blackburn joined the regiment's new padre, Captain Marsh Laverty, to watch the show. The night was intensely dark, a light drizzle falling. At first the southeastern sky was lit by the flares of pathfinder planes marking Cleve. A small amount of anti-aircraft fire sparked skyward. Then the bombers growled loudly as they passed invisibly overhead. Moments later came the "ground-shudder-ing string of crumps." Blackburn figured Cleve was about ten miles distant, "but the violence of the flashing explosions at times lit up the whole cloudy dome of the sky; and soon the reddish glow of fires, mounting higher and higher like an early sunrise along the eastern horizon, made it appear much closer." It was the heaviest bombing he had seen since Normandy. Blackburn remembered "the awful tumble of rubble in Caen and other Norman towns," and thought, "Cleve and the Rhineland targets will look like that."[32]

Not long after the bombers departed, First Canadian Army stirred. Thousands of men in five divisions under xxx British Corps command formed in the darkness to move toward forming-up posi-tions for the attack. The two Canadian divisions were on the left flank, with 3rd Division on the far left and 2nd Division adjacent. Next to the Canadians, 15th (Scottish) Infantry Division was in the centre. To its right was 53rd (Welsh) Division, and 51st (Highland) Division was on the far right flank. Each division was supported by tanks of armoured brigades and units of 79th Armoured Division. The British 34th Armoured Brigade supported 51st and 53rd Divi-sions, 6th Guards Armoured Brigade the 15th Division, and a regiment of 8th Armoured Brigade backed up the Canadians.[33]

Because of the constricted frontage and extensive flooding before it, 3rd Division would not enter the fray until 1800 hours. The other four divisions would cross their start lines much earlier, at 1030. Brigadier Bill Megill's 5th Brigade would lead 2nd Division's attack with two battalions forward—the Calgary Highlanders and Le Régi-ment de Maisonneuve.[34] The Maisies started assembling at 0300 hours and were pleased to see that the sky had mostly cleared, offer-ing the promise of a fine day.[35] Earlier, the troops had spent hours surveying their advance route and studying a detailed sand-table model of the ground. Everybody knew his job.[36] Men quietly checked weapons and battle kits. Many chain-smoked. Jokes were exchanged. Some scribbled letters. Eyes strayed regularly to the eastern horizon.

Shortly before 0500, Lieutenant General Brian Horrocks climbed into his command post. This was a crude platform halfway up a large tree. It was on a ridge a short distance outside of Groesbeek. "From here I could see most of the valley in front, and I was connected by line with a group of small scout cars below me at the bottom of the tree, each of which was tuned in on the same wireless link with a similar vehicle at the advance HQ of each...division taking part. From my viewpoint, I could follow the progress of the attacks by the lifts in the barrage." Like those of the soldiers he commanded, Horrocks's eyes turned eastward and he waited for hell to be unleashed.[37]

11

Never to Be Forgotten

IN THE PRE-DAWN darkness of February 8, Captain George Blackburn walked toward 4th Canadian Field Regiment's 2nd Battery Command Post. It was cold, the persistent drizzle of the night just ending. On their gun lines, Blackburn thought the crews would be wet and miserable. For several hours they had been taking shells out of cases, "removing safety caps, and stacking them in piles handy to the guns." Blackburn stumbled through mud and deep water-filled ruts left by the heavy transports. As he passed the guns of two other 4th Field batteries, Blackburn saw that British field and medium regiments had "slotted into spaces behind and beside them during the night." Voices softly issued orders. There were "brief, glowing flickers of subdued light from hooded [flashlights] hovering over dial-sights of guns getting a final check of their 'parallelism'—making sure all [were] perfectly on line.

"Silhouettes of gun muzzles [poked] up against the night sky where previously there were only scrubby pines. Unseen hordes of gunners" were "now standing to their guns as they [carried] out last-minute tasks." Some nine thousand gunners stood to their guns, awaiting H-Hour—just five minutes away.

Blackburn pushed aside a sodden tarpaulin covering the log and earth dugout's entrance. He was nearly blinded by electric lights illuminating the artillery boards that men hunched over. Captain Les

Hutcheon commanded. At 0459, he calmly started counting down over two phones linked to the gun lines. Blackburn stepped outside.

"For a few seconds there is deep silence, broken only by the slight rustle of wind...covering up the sounds of nearby Tannoy speakers... now...carrying voices of countless GPOS [gun position officers] counting down the seconds to their gun sergeants.

"One faint, distant voice yells, 'Fire!' And for a split second there's a rising chorus of urgent voices on all sides yelling 'Fire!' before the night is overwhelmed by furious, flashing, roaring waves of sound and concussion, rending and tearing the darkness with monstrous theatrical effects."[1]

"It was a fantastic scene, never to be forgotten," a British 4th/7th Royal Dragoon Guards officer wrote. "One moment silence and the next moment a terrific ear splitting din, with every pitch of noise imaginable, little bangs, big bangs, sharp cracks, the rattle of machine-guns and the ripple of Bofors, intermingled with the periodic swoosh of a rocket battery. The night was lit by flashes of every colour and the tracer of the Bofors guns weaving fairy patterns in the sky as it streamed off toward the target."[2]

Gunner J.P. Grady, a Métis with 4th Medium Regiment, later wrote that when the guns of his 50th Battery joined in, "previously registered German strongpoints are smothered in a tornado of fire. Gunfire rolls incessantly...The outer Nazi defences have crumbled in a terrible inferno of fire and destruction." For the next thirteen and a half hours, Grady's battery fired steadily.[3]

The bombardment delighted the Calgary Highlanders. Passing among the troops, doling out a ration of tea and sandwiches, Regimental Sergeant Major Vince Bowen thought he had "never seen the battalion in better spirits." Lieutenant Howard Powell, the battalion's new intelligence officer, recorded that the bombardment "was good to see and hear, especially to any of the old timers, as so many times we have gone in and would like more support than we got." Shortly after the bombardment began, Lieutenant Colonel Ross Ellis walked through the company lines. He found "the men in the best of spirits and very happy about the heavy barrage...falling."[4] Ellis calculatedly projected an aura of calm: balmoral rather than a helmet, uniform precisely pressed and pants tucked into polished black boots, swagger stick tucked under an arm. 'B' Company commander Major Francis H. "Knobby" Clarke and 'C' Company's Major John Campbell chatted in the former company's area. Campbell had only returned a few days earlier. He had been badly wounded in the thigh by a sniper bullet on July 24, 1944, at Verrières Ridge. This would be his first fight since. A piper was playing, barely audible over the thunder of the guns. In the distance, the steeple of Wyler's church could be seen. "I'll see you and we'll have our rum together in the church," Clarke told Campbell.

Powell was awestruck when 1st Canadian Rocket Battery threw a full twelve-projector salvo down upon a farm and grove of trees near the Calgary objective of Wyler. "I never saw anything like that in my life. The ground just rocked...That was the first time I saw those multiple rockets fired...that place just disintegrated, all in one smack."[5]

Canadian war artist Alex Colville and 2nd Division's historical officer, Captain R.F. Gray, stood near a medium artillery regiment about a mile north of Groesbeek. Gray thought the "sight of the air-bursts and tracer in the sky, against the yellow light of the rising sun was very impressive. There was continuous roll of heavy gunfire punctuated by staccato bursts of MG fire from all sides...At 0740 hours, almost a complete silence descended on the entire front for a period of a full ten minutes...to enable the Flash Spotters and Sound Rangers to locate active enemy [batteries] not previously known."[6]

The 2nd Canadian Survey Regiment's historian declared this exercise "highly unsuccessful." Most German gunners opted not to expose their positions by returning fire or had already been knocked out by the bombardment. Twenty-three positions, primarily mortars, did retaliate and were quickly silenced by a deluge of fire.[7]

When the ten-minute period of silence ended, Gray saw that "a few birds were still flying across the sky in a bewildered manner," as the artillery resumed firing. "Beyond the occasional airburst, and the odd round over a wide area, there was little reply from the enemy and, at this stage, the spectator was left with the impression that hostile positions were being simply smothered.

"The gaunt trunks and torn branches of trees, ruined farm buildings, and the smoke and cordite fumes that swept across the area all contributed to the strangely fascinating panorama of war.

"As H-Hour approached, if anything, the noise increased and a new note was added by the sound of armour moving forward and planes passing overhead. The combined effect produced a vivid picture of a war of machines—a war of calculated and terrible efficiency.

"A wounded soldier, with face covered by a field dressing, was directed to a nearby RAP [Regimental Aid Post] as pockets of smoke began to fill the contours in the ground." Gray and Colville "were compelled to shout in order to be heard above the noise. Carriers with Red Cross flags prominently displayed clattered by. A troop of Cromwell tanks camouflaged with straw, which had been hidden beside the walls of a demolished barn, suddenly rolled forward. Churchill and Sherman tanks began to move east along the draw... through the scattered debris of gliders that remained from the airborne attack of the previous September.

"At 0950 the barrage, which represented the climax of the preliminary bombardment, was observed to be beginning...Besides the orthodox types of tanks, there were 'Flails,' 'Crocodiles,' 'AVRES,' all with their fluorescent panels (for identification from the air) glowing like red hot plates against the dull background. A tank officer enquired anxiously about minefields but could not be satisfied. The armour lurched forward with all vehicles stripped for action—one tank still had a frying pan dangling from the back of the turret. An Air OP [Air Observation Plane] flew slowly overhead, and smoke shells continued to drop a short distance in front, as the deafening noise increased. Some enemy rounds dropped about 300 yards distant and personnel took cover, but the armoured advance went on without hesitation. There was an air of urgency and tense expectation evident everywhere as H-Hour approached."[8]

While the bombardment prompted Gray to expend hundreds of words trying to describe it, Colville sketched. After pausing for breakfast, he returned to his vantage point. "The rest of the day, I spent painting *Before Zero Hour*, a nocturne," he wrote in his monthly report.[9]

AT 1030 HOURS, 50,000 troops stood on start lines, supported by 500 tanks and about 500 "Funnies" of 79th Armoured Division. To the northeast, 10,000 men of 3rd Canadian Division waited to begin their late afternoon advance. In reserve, XXX British Corps held another 15,000 front-line troops and more than 500 more tanks.[10]

Smoke shells, mixed with the high explosives, cast "a protective white screen [that] blanketed the north-western edge of the Reichswald and effectively concealed the assault battalions of four divisions as they emerged from the woods behind Groesbeek and advanced down the forward slopes to their start-lines. If the enemy took this smoke as prelude to an attack, after his earlier experience he was reluctant to retaliate," the Canadian Army's historian wrote.[11]

The long line of soldiers stretched across a broad six-mile front from the Nijmegen–Cleve highway south almost to Mook. For the last few days, this line had been held by just two 2nd Canadian Infantry Division brigades. Now thousands of British soldiers "simply passed through" these men and strode through swirling smoke toward the Germans. Only 2nd Division's 5th Canadian Infantry Brigade joined the advance. Its task was "to clear a small triangle of territory south of the Nijmegen–Cleve road in the vicinity of Wyler, considered to be a corner stone in the enemy's first line, and to open two roads for the use of 15th Scottish which would take over the sector, the Canadian division then going into reserve."[12] Success was considered essential to enabling 15th Division to "breach the Siegfried Line and secure the high ground west of Cleve," Brigadier Bill Megill had stressed in an earlier battalion commander briefing.[13]

Running along a low escarpment overlooking the Rhine flood plain, the road provided a vital route for British armour to support 15th Division's push to Cleve. Failure to take Wyler and clear the enemy positions along the road to its east would turn the advance on Cleve into a bloody cross-country slog by infantry only, as the rough, muddy terrain was largely impassable to tanks.[14]

Following guides from their pioneer platoon, Le Régiment de Maisonneuve had moved toward forming-up positions at 0600 hours. The men cursed the "terrible muddy, bumpy, and awful ground conditions." They knew with grim certainty that as the ground beyond the start line had additionally been churned up by artillery, the going would only get worse. The Maisies reached the forming-up position at 0730. There they waited until 1030 and H-Hour. Then the artillery carried out its first lift, and the French Canadians surged forward. "It is from that moment that we began to do a real job," their war diarist wrote. As they went forward, Lieutenant Louis Fontaine was wounded.[15] With blood oozing through a hastily applied bandage, he ignored the pain. Fontaine declared he would not be evacuated until his platoon took its objective.[16]

Direct support was provided by a squadron of tanks from 13th/18th Royal Hussars, a squadron of Flails (79th Armoured Division tanks with a rotating drum to which long chains were attached for detonating mines), a British engineer squadron mounted in AVRES (Armoured Vehicle, Royal Engineers), and the 7th Field Company, Royal Canadian Engineers.

Thinking the Germans would expect any attack on Wyler to come straight along the Nijmegen–Cleve road, Megill had instead ordered the Calgary Highlanders on the left to bypass Wyler to the south, cut the road behind it, and then attack from the rear.[17] This "fanwise sweep with the left wheel movement" would be executed by the battalion's 'C' and 'D' Companies. Left of these companies, 'A' Company would get astride the road to Cleve and push on toward Kranenburg to link up with elements of 15th Division.[18] If successful, the Calgaries would not only surprise the Germans in Wyler but cut their line of retreat. Right of the Calgaries, the Maisies would punch through the hamlet of Den Heuvel and gain the road west of Hochstrasse. The Germans had transformed both Wyler and Den Heuvel into major strongpoints surrounded by minefields. Megill knew that Wyler would "be the hardest nut to crack."[19]

At precisely 1030 hours, two Maisonneuve companies headed for Den Heuvel. The French Canadians "crowded the barrage" so closely they burst into the village almost the moment the artillery lifted to its next three-hundred-yard line.[20] Den Heuvel was a rat's nest of dugouts and fortified buildings. A sharp, close-quarter firefight ensued. Major François de Salle Robert's 'D' Company had no sooner entered the village than intense rifle fire struck it from behind. Private Joseph Lefebvre, a wireless signaller, spotted the source of the fire. Thrusting his No. 18 wireless set into the hands of another signaller, Lefebvre grabbed a Sten gun and four grenades off an infantryman and worked his way back toward a dugout that 'D' Company had failed to check when passing by. Firing the Sten from the hip, Lefebvre ran to the dugout and chucked a grenade inside. He then shouted for the Germans to come out. Not getting a response, he threw two more of the grenades in and "dashed inside firing his Sten gun." A few minutes later, Lefebvre emerged with four prisoners. The private never revealed how many German dead remained behind. His action earned a Military Medal.[21]

Many Germans in Den Heuvel seemed dazed by the bombardment. A German officer with arms raised stumbled up to one Maisie. "It was terrible," he stammered.[22] One of the regiment's officers counted forty-six German dead strewn about in a small area. Many more lay inside the bunkers and trenches.[23] A captured letter apparently hastily scribbled within minutes of the bombardment's end read, "When Tommy began his attack he started such a terrific artillery barrage that we took leave of our senses. I shall not forget my experience in the Reichswald for a long time."[24] The Toronto Scottish (MG) Regiment's Lieutenant Colonel E.G. Johnson, who had organized 2nd Division's pepper pot, recorded that many prisoners were "completely addled." Their guards reported that most had come "out of their trenches with...hands up and offering no resistance to our troops."[25]

From where he served a gun in 4th Medium Regiment's 50th Battery, Gunner J.P. Brady had earlier watched a British battalion advance toward the Reichswald. Soon, he saw, "corpses are being brought back lashed to the tops of ambulance jeeps...Later, long lines of prisoners come in. Some reel drunkenly, others stare vacantly; some shamble along in tears, while others laugh hysterically. The prisoners who are articulate say they were overwhelmed by an annihilating fire and could not make a defensive stand in their front line."[26]

At 1123, the Maisies reported Den Heuvel secure and that they were advancing on the nearby German border. Major G.F. Charlebois, commanding 'A' Company, radioed back to regimental headquarters at 1150 hours that "No. 7 Platoon led by Lieutenant Bud

Delorme [was] the first fighting group to put steps on German soil... after having cleared their objective in 15 minutes."[27]

Although the advance continued quickly and steadily, there were still Germans able and determined to fight. Private Albert Lacoste, batman for one of 'A' Company's lieutenants, was killed. He was two months shy of his twentieth birthday.[28]

The company in which Private Hector Lefebvre served as a sniper came under heavy machine-gun fire just as some rare German artillery shells fell nearby. "Despite flying shrapnel and a continuous hail of bullets," Lefebvre "worked his way to a vantage point. Still under fire, he coolly pinpointed the enemy machine-gun post and successfully silenced it, killing one and wounding two of the crew," his Military Medal citation declared.[29]

Lieutenant Louis Fontaine, increasingly weakened by his wound, was closing on the regiment's final objective just west of Hochstrasse when a machine gun opened fire and drove his men to ground. Realizing the gun was sited so it could inflict heavy casualties and stall the advance indefinitely, Fontaine and one man crawled through "continuous enemy fire" to a position close to the gun. Then the two soldiers, "with determination and great gallantry rushed it and killed the three occupants." Fontaine, who only agreed to be evacuated at 1320 hours, was awarded a Military Cross.[30] The Maisonneuve attack had been so well executed that their casualties were surprisingly light: two men dead and twenty wounded.[31]

THE CALGARY HIGHLANDERS were less fortunate. Twelve minutes late crossing the start line, 'A' Company to the right and 'D' Company on the left led the advance. 'C' Company tucked in close behind Major Del Kearns's 'A' Company, while 'B' Company remained in reserve. Despite the late start putting them well behind the creeping barrage, the battalion's officers were not concerned. They had been told to expect "no enemy resistance...between the [start line] and Vossendaal."[32] Kearns directed his men along a muddy road toward the hamlet. Closing on Vossendaal at about 1100 hours, 'A' Company suddenly confronted a minefield just as it came under heavy mortar fire. At first glance the minefield looked haphazard—a large number of Schützenmines scattered on the surface rather than buried. As the lead platoon started dodging around the visible mines, however, some men triggered buried ones. The mortar rounds also exacted a toll. Within a few minutes, all members of the platoon's leading section, except its commander, Lance Corporal Robert Allan McMahon, were either dead or wounded.

From two buildings on the edge of the hamlet, machine guns commenced firing. Realizing that his badly exposed platoon—now completely mired in the minefield—faced destruction, McMahon picked his way past the remaining mines. Once clear of the field, he ran to the buildings. Working his way from one to the other, McMahon killed a number of the Germans inside, wounded several more, and took one officer and twenty-two men prisoners. When the officer realized that McMahon was alone, he "attempted to stir up an insurrection." As his Distinguished Conduct Medal citation put it, McMahon "stopped [this] with his fists."[33]

When McMahon escorted the prisoners back, he made them pick up and carry out his wounded. Two Germans tripped mines and were "blown up." Once McMahon finished this task, he rushed back to 'A' Company.

The company was in a bad way. It had suffered twenty-eight casualties in mere minutes.[34] Most, including McMahon's section, were in Sergeant Carol Edwin Anderson's platoon. While McMahon had engaged the Germans, Anderson had dashed recklessly about the minefield giving first aid to wounded men. Once he had treated the wounded, Anderson ran back to warn Kearns to keep the rest of the company out of the minefield. He then returned to his platoon and led the survivors through the mines to Vossendaal. While Anderson's men cleared the hamlet, Kearns led the rest of 'A' Company around its right flank and headed toward the main road that was its objective. Meanwhile, the moment Anderson's platoon emerged from the hamlet, it drew fire from another machine-gun position. While a Bren gunner provided covering fire, Anderson rushed it, killing the four-man crew with bursts from his Sten gun and several grenades. No sooner did the platoon renew its advance than a new machine gun opened up from ahead. Anderson crawled forward alone and killed the Germans manning the gun. He then led his "depleted platoon to its final objective." Anderson's actions were recognized with a Military Medal.[35]

By noon, 'A' Company had reached the road. In doing so, Kearns and his men cut the only route of escape for the Germans defending Wyler. At 1330 hours, a company of Maisonneuves relieved it. Kearns then led his men toward Wyler from the rear.[36]

'D' Company's lead platoon, meanwhile, had just passed Vossendaal on the left when intense mortar fire struck. The platoon commander was killed and his men driven to ground. Realizing such hesitation could be fatal, Sergeant Emile Jean "Blackie" Laloge shouted at his following platoon to keep moving. Laloge's men passed the frozen platoon, advanced through a minefield, and gained the Nijmegen–Cleve highway. Laloge was a tough, experienced platoon leader, who already held a Distinguished Conduct Medal for bravery. When several of his men were cut down by machine-gun fire, Laloge realized the German position was impossible to outflank. So he charged straight at it and gunned down the four-man crew with bursts of Sten-gun fire.

As the platoon led 'D' Company up the road toward Wyler, it was again engaged by a machine gun. This time Laloge threw a section out on the flank to infiltrate behind it while he kept the gunner's attention fixed on himself by repeatedly moving into the open to draw fire. The section soon overran the gun and took its crew prisoner. To the amazement of his men, Laloge had not been injured despite his clothes being riddled by bullets. Laloge added a Military Medal to his decorations.[37]

Major John Campbell's 'C' Company—which had been following 'A' Company—had turned off early to follow a narrow secondary road into Wyler from the southeast. Just outside the village, the road forked, and the plan called for one platoon to go right toward the church while another moved left to clear its western outskirts.[38]

'C' Company advanced with its three platoons in line. As they closed on Wyler, several mines went off underfoot. When the platoon commanders directed their men away from the minefield, they drew fire from gun pits on either side manned by Germans well armed with MG-42 machine guns. A deluge of mortar fire brought the dread realization that the company had been herded into a prepared killing ground. Unable to move quickly because of the mines, the company could not escape the German crossfire. Men started falling wounded and dying. Lieutenant Sidney Kemp of No. 15 Platoon, his platoon sergeant, and both section leaders fell dead. Major John Campbell and his company headquarters gained the cover of a trench nearby. The cover it offered, however, was illusory—the entire length was exposed to fire from overlooking buildings on the edge of Wyler. Campbell was killed by a sniper's bullet and his headquarters section shredded. Men "desperately sought shelter in shell holes or anywhere they could find it," Private John Shaw remembered. No. 14 Platoon's Lieutenant Ed Ford took command.[39] He no sooner retrieved the wireless set from the trench where Campbell had died than a message came asking if he required artillery support. Ford feared artillery or heavy mortar fire would end up hitting his people. "No," he said, it's "an infantry job," but reinforcements would be welcome. Back at battalion headquarters, Lieutenant Colonel Ross Ellis ordered Major "Knobby" Clarke to send one 'B' Company platoon to 'C' Company's position.[40] Clarke sent the platoon commanded by Lieutenant Dan Shiell.

Ford realized that unless the Germans in the overlooking buildings were taken out, the company would be cut to pieces. He shouted to Sergeant Michael Melnychanko, commanding No. 13 Platoon, to assume company command and its wireless set. With part of No. 14 Platoon throwing out covering fire, Ford led a few men running to the buildings. They cleared them with grenades, Sten guns, and rifles. Once the Germans in the buildings had been driven off or killed, Ford worked his way under fire to where 'D' Company was pinned down in front of a sunken road. Ford found Major Alex Keller "ashen faced and tight lipped." Keller's wireless was damaged. He asked Ford to relay to battalion headquarters a request for covering smoke behind which his men could charge across the road and break into Wyler. Ford started back toward 'C' Company.[41]

Platoon in tow, Shiell had arrived and found only a small nucleus of the company headquarters. "What's going on?" he asked. The sergeant [presumably Melnychanko] told him Campbell was dead and he had no idea where most of the men were. "I'm here by myself. I don't know if we have anybody left or what's going on."

At battalion headquarters, a deeply concerned Ellis decided he must go forward and personally determine what was happening. He had no wireless contact with either 'D' or 'A' Company. What he knew of 'C' Company's situation suggested it was in grave trouble. The wireless signals from Melnychanko indicated that 'C' Company "had become disorganized and was not sure of its own location." Ellis arranged a fire plan utilizing 5th Field Regiment's 25-pounders and the Toronto Scottish Regiment's 4.2-inch mortars to be on call. He then told Clarke to bring up the rest of 'B' Company to reinforce 'C' Company.[42] Setting off alone, Ellis navigated the minefield while under small-arms fire and reached 'A' Company. He then moved to where 'C' Company was pinned down.

Ford had not yet returned, but Ellis found Melnychanko and decided 'C' Company was pretty much shot. Yet if he could establish a viable start line for 'B' Company, the Calgaries might regain the initiative. He told Melnychanko to send ten men from No. 13 Platoon to bolster the mangled No. 15 Platoon.[43] The sergeant was to take his remaining six men and wrest a start line from German control.

Melnychanko and his men crawled into a complex network of trenches, killing or taking prisoner any Germans encountered and silencing three machine guns. Closing on a house lousy with snipers, the sergeant ordered his PIAT man to punch a bomb into the building. The cumbersome Projector, Infantry, Anti-Tank launcher fired a two-and-a-half-pound bomb intended to disable a tank, but it was routinely used to open holes in buildings. Once the round exploded, Melnychanko and three men dashed to a communication trench that allowed them to outflank the house. Leading from the front, he burst through a door, killed two snipers, and took the surrender of the remaining eighteen. "The job finished, he reorganized his platoon on its objective, enabling another company to pass through," his Military Medal citation subsequently stated. The platoon had taken seventy-five prisoners and killed a good number more.[44]

While Melnychanko had been at work, Clarke had arrived with 'B' Company. Ellis told him to be ready to pass through 'C' Company when the creeping barrage he was calling arrived. He then headed for 'D' Company's lines. Ellis advised Keller that the artillery and mortar fire was on the way. 'D' Company was to push through to Wyler and support Clarke's men. Returning to 'C' Company's lines, he grabbed the wireless there and implemented the fire plan.

At 1725 hours, artillery and the 4.2-inch mortars battered Wyler. The "co-ordinated movement of 'D' and 'B' Companies was suffi-cient to clear Wyler of all organized resistance by 1745 hours," Brigadier Megill wrote. 'B' Company relentlessly hunted down the few remaining snipers. At 1830 hours, Clarke reported all resistance eliminated. By this time the weather had deteriorated and a cold rain was falling.

Megill credited the success of the Calgary attack "to the fact that the obvious line of approach had been avoided and also that, by strik-ing at the enemy from the south-east, it had been possible to seal off the force in Wyler to prevent its escape." But the number of Germans trapped inside Wyler had been larger than expected. The complex network and extent of defensive positions—all interlinked by com-munication trenches—had proven stronger than anticipated. Trenches were discovered running from Wyler to Den Heuvel, pass-ing through Vossendaal en route. Two Calgary Highlanders officers and eleven other ranks were killed. Another officer and sixty other ranks were wounded. Megill reported that 40 per cent of the Calgary casualties had occurred inside the minefields during the initial assault.

The brigadier criticized Ford's leadership, characterizing him as "a much less aggressive officer" than Campbell. He also believed a map-reading error had led Ford to incorrectly report 'C' Company's position. This led to a delay in artillery support, which was obviously required to break the Germans. In future operations, Megill won-dered if it would not be better to build in a pause for reorganization just outside the objective. Then, behind a new artillery barrage, the battalion could again advance. Ford, he said, had initially insisted he "was quite confident that he could finish the battle without support and, in fact, preferred to dispense with support. When he had failed, and another company was put in—following a quickly laid fire plan—all organized resistance ended very quickly."[45]

Neither Ellis, awarded a Distinguished Service Order for his work at Wyler, nor the battalion's second-in-command, Major Dalt Heyland, agreed with Megill's criticism.[46] The thirty-one-year-old Ford had served as a platoon commander in Normandy until being briefly evacuated with battle exhaustion in August. When he returned in September, Ford became the battalion's intelligence officer—a common posting for junior officers recovering from battle exhaustion. On November 2, Ford had taken command of No. 14 Platoon.[47] Heyland and Ellis did not consider his medical background a factor in Ford's performance. They felt he had done as well as could be expected in extremely difficult circumstances.[48] And the Calgaries had won, taking more than two hundred prisoners. The 5th Brigade's attack on the Wyler triangle netted a total of 322 Germans captured.[49]

Even as the fight for Wyler raged, sappers of 7th Field Company, Royal Canadian Engineers had worked to open the Nijmegen–Cleve highway running southeast from the village. They were often under fire from snipers in Wyler and dugouts near the road that had not been mopped up yet by the Maisies, who controlled the road. The Veritable plan had called for the highway to open through to Kranenburg by 1600 hours. Hampered by German fire and even more so by "thickly sown minefields," the sappers did not complete the task until 2100 hours. When that was done, 2nd Division's role in the opening phase of Veritable ended. The Calgaries and Maisies held in place. There was insufficient elbow room for 2nd Division to join the continuing effort.[50]

[12]

Into Hitler's Germany

O N THE MORNING of February 8, most divisions of xxx British
Corps had initially met light resistance. The attack's sheer
magnitude combined with the opening bombardment's severity had
overwhelmed and stunned the defenders. As General Harry Crerar
reported, "resistance offered by a dazed and shaken enemy proved to
be a lesser handicap than the appalling conditions of the ground."[1]
There was, however, no rout. Just as 2nd Canadian Infantry Division
had faced a tough fight, the three British divisions had also encountered Germans ready for battle.

To the Canadian right, 15th (Scottish) Infantry Division had
sought to storm the Siegfried Line north of the Reichswald and seize
the key ground around Cleve. Its attack with two brigades across a
very narrow front went well at first. Enemy opposition was ineffec-
tual and casualties were light. "The main obstacles to the advance
were mines of all types and the ground." Flails helped clear mines in
the southern sector, but to the north they mired in the mud and were
unable to operate.[2] Delay piled upon delay until the division was
badly behind schedule. The 46th Brigade on the right became entangled in clearing the long straggling village of Frasselt—a task that
continued until nightfall. On the left, Kranenburg fell to 227th Brigade at 1700 hours—much later than intended. The 44th Brigade
was to have passed through the leading brigades to sever the Sieg-

fried Line. When the almost three hundred heavy armoured vehicles supporting it were "brought to a standstill along the rough track which had been carrying traffic of the two leading brigades for most of the day," the attack stalled. Bulldozers were required to carve out a detour for the vehicles, and the brigade's attack was pushed back to 0400 hours on February 9.[3]

Tasked with seizing the northern half of the Reichswald and particularly the Branden Berg and Stoppel Berg features, 53rd (Welsh) Division advanced on such a narrow front that only its 71st Brigade led. Once this brigade took the Branden Berg, the 160th Brigade was to pass through, force the Siegfried Line, and seize the Stoppel Berg. Mines and soggy terrain again proved the "chief obstacles." The broader-tracked Churchill tanks could find traction, but other vehicles got bogged down in the quagmire. When the infantry reached a major anti-tank ditch, it proved less formidable than feared. As the men scampered across, some Churchills were able to follow. The Branden Berg was in British hands by 1400 hours. As night set in, 160th Brigade passed through. Although searchlights bouncing off overhead clouds created "artificial moonlight," the drenching rain was so heavy that there was still only scant illumination. All but one tank squadron had mired in mud, so the infantry advanced largely alone. A little after midnight, faced with only light resistance, the brigade reached the Siegfried Line's defences.[4]

It was on the far right of the offensive that the British met their toughest resistance. The 51st (Highland) Division's job here was to capture the southwest corner of the Reichswald and open the Mook–Goch road. Out front, the 154th Highland Brigade locked horns with 180th Infanterie-Division's 1222nd Grenadier Regiment. This regiment had been thrown into the line the previous evening. The grenadiers offered defiant stands from inside every one of the small villages dotting this area. It was 0400 the following morning before the Highlanders secured primary objectives. Facing them remained a "strong body of Germans."[5]

The Germans suffered heavily. In the 84th Infanterie-Division, upon which the majority of the offensive had fallen, six battalions were virtually destroyed. More than 1,200 prisoners were taken on

February 8 and a large, uncounted number of Germans killed. Such losses were unsustainable.[6]

ALWAYS SOMEWHAT BEHIND schedule, Operation Veritable was still achieving its initial goals. At 1800 hours on the first day, 3rd Canadian Infantry Division had joined the effort. Its front lay between the Nijmegen–Cleve road and the Rhine River. This front was considerably wider than any other and was also almost entirely underwater. The only silver lining was that the many German anti-tank ditches, wire barriers, and mines "were largely lost." But it meant the Canadians could seldom march to the attack or be accompanied by tanks. Instead, 3rd Division relied on amphibious vehicles—114 Buffaloes and 50 Weasels of the British 79th Armoured Division.[7]

Major General Dan Spry planned a two-brigade-wide attack, each advancing two battalions. Spry had celebrated his thirty-second birthday on February 4 and remained the youngest general in the Allied forces. Spry was an avid follower of the Boy Scout movement. Many friends and the troops he led believed his behaviour was modelled on Boy Scout values. Always a gentleman, he was temperate in both speech and manner. Since taking divisional command on August 18, 1944, he had proven popular with the men and developed a reputation as a general who did his best to keep them alive.[8]

The 3rd's task was to clear the flood plain between the Nijmegen–Cleve road and the Rhine through to a railway line running northeast of Cleve to Griethausen. To the right, 7th Infantry Brigade would advance with 8th Brigade on its left.[9] The Regina Rifle and Canadian Scottish Regiments would lead for 7th Brigade. Their first objective was the mile-long Quer Damm that blocked the line of advance. The Germans had strong defensive positions dug into the dam's banks. At the dam's northeastern corner, a particularly strong fortification was code-named Little Tobruk. The Can Scots were to capture this fortification with one company. All the German digging into the dam had seriously weakened it. With floodwaters spilling out from the Rhine, a section of the dam had collapsed on the morning of February 8. Water poured through the break and rushed toward the villages of Zyfflich and Leuth.[10] Zyfflich was the Regina

Rifles' objective beyond the dam. Although the Can Scots were to win Little Tobruk, their main objective was to seize the village of Germenseel and then hook northeastward into Niel. This village would provide a firm base for 7th Brigade to clear the flood plain through to a line running between Duffelward and Donsbrüggen, which were both just west of Cleve.[11]

Left of 7th Brigade, the morning's collapse of the Quer Damm had caused consternation amid the ranks of 8th Brigade's North Shore (New Brunswick) Regiment. The two companies that were to lead had assembled in their assigned area at 0550 hours and settled in to wait for the launch time. Anxiously watching the rising flood-waters, Lieutenant Colonel John Rowley warned the men of 'A' and 'B' Companies at 1045 hours to prepare to fall back to higher ground. Thirty minutes later, he ordered them to flee. Although the Buffa-loes could easily float to the new location, the North Shores had brought up a number of their Bren carriers. Men had to frantically drive these to higher ground through swirling floodwaters and mud that threatened to mire their tracks. All got through safely.[12]

Brigadier Jim Roberts had watched the chaotic retreat. Before the waters unexpectedly began to rise, he had been thinking that in "actual combat it is wise to keep your plan simple. Too detailed a plan usually comes unstuck. And yet, in my plan for 8th Brigade, it was very difficult to be simple, given the flooded conditions of the terrain. The flood waters were rising every hour."

At 1800 hours it would be pitch dark, one reason for the attack to happen then. His battalions would benefit from the concealment of darkness. But operating at night also brought the risk of officers becoming lost or other calamities arising. His plan called for Buffa-loes to carry two North Shore companies across the flooded polders to a dyke running north from the Quer Damm to the Rhine that lay not more than three hundred yards from the new launch point. Le Régiment de la Chaudière would, meanwhile, employ "canoe-like skiffs" and paddle to a flooded orchard about 150 yards shy of the dyke and right of the North Shores. They would wait there until the North Shores signalled with a flashing light that they were in place. Once the Chauds gained the dyke, the two battalions would clear it from the juncture with the Quer Damm almost to the Rhine. Then the North Shores would head northeast toward Zandpol while the Chauds made for Leuth.

Roberts considered the plan sound, despite many complicating factors presented by operating in darkness and over badly flooded ground. He was excited to be part of Operation Veritable and believed his men felt the same. They would clear the "flooded area north of Cleve and up to Emmerich. These names were heady stuff to us. We were thinking of and moving towards German cities and the Rhine was on our immediate left flank. One could almost smell the great opportunity for the final break through into Hitler's Germany."

With a pepper pot "falling with unbelievable power and noise on the German position," 8th Brigade crossed its start line. Roberts stood next to the deserted brick kiln serving as his headquarters. Twelve Buffaloes loaded with North Shore soldiers rumbled toward a dyke that shielded them from enemy detection. The Buffaloes were accelerating hard, seeking maximum protective cover from the pepper pot. Roberts watched in dismay as "the tracks of the Buffaloes dug into the wet earth...and proceeded to dig themselves, deeper and deeper," into the embankment. The British major in charge "was doing everything possible to disengage his machines from the soft mud, but nothing happened." Roberts grabbed the wireless handset that linked him to divisional headquarters and pleaded for a ten-minute extension of the pepper pot. When the guns kept firing, Roberts dashed to the British major and shouted for him to reverse the Buffaloes off the embankment and try climbing it on a diagonal slope. "I was deeply relieved when the gouging tracks cut into the earth on the diagonal and, one by one, the machines crested our [dyke] and plunged into the flooding waters on the other side."[13]

The Chauds had, meanwhile, pushed off in their skiffs with 'A' and 'D' Companies out front and the other two companies following. Captain Leo Larose, 'A' Company's second-in-command, was in a skiff with seven of his men. Suddenly, either a friendly or German shell exploded in a nearby air burst. Shrapnel slashed holes in the skiff but hurt none of the men aboard. Spotting a half-submerged farmhouse to one side, Larose ordered everyone to paddle hard toward it. They pulled up level with the building's second storey just in time to scramble through a window as the skiff sank. The rest of the battalion carried on to the small wood and awaited the signal from the North Shores to continue on foot.[14]

Everything went as planned until Major F.F. "Toot" Moar of the North Shore's 'A' Company radioed battalion headquarters at 1835 hours that his Buffalo had broken down halfway to the dyke.[15] Moar had the critical signal light. Consequently, the Chauds remained in the woods awaiting a landing signal the North Shores were unable to send and missed the assault on the dyke.[16] The rest of the North Shore Buffaloes sailed on to the dyke. Most of 'A' Company disembarked and, following a short skirmish, reported it taken at 1850 hours. They had rounded up sixty prisoners.

Roberts was pleased to learn the dyke had fallen without much fuss despite the missing Chauds. The defenders proved to be a unit of Volkssturm, "most of them World War 1 veterans, with Mauser rifles of their generation, grey grizzled beards, and a look of dazed shock on their faces—no wonder, considering the terrific bombardment they had received for a full 20 minutes! They came out of their dug-outs, not with their arms raised in surrender, but holding their ears with their hands, rolling their heads from side to side, and drooling at the mouth," an 'A' Company report claimed.[17] 'A' Company sent back sixty-nine prisoners.

'B' Company arrived fifteen minutes after the fight concluded, landing to one side of 'A' Company. A series of navigational mishaps had separated the Buffalo carrying Captain Charles Richardson from those carrying most of his men. As a result, Richardson's Buffalo landed several minutes early. Richardson's runner, Private Russell Geoarld Munroe, raced to the top of the dyke just in time to fire down upon a cluster of Germans closing in on the small headquarters. Crawling through heavy machine-gun fire, Munroe gained the lines of 'A' Company and advised the men there of 'B' Company's position. By the time he returned to Richardson, the rest of the company had landed. The machine gun was still firing, and the leading platoon with Richardson's headquarters section following moved toward it, only to enter a minefield. Four men, including Lieutenant

Louis Joseph Walsh, triggered mines and were killed. Several other men fell wounded. Munroe dashed repeatedly into the minefield to carry each to safety. He then grabbed a PIAT and tackled the machine gun. Despite being completely exposed, Munroe set up on top of the dyke and "blasted the machine-gun position into submission." Munroe's gallantry garnered a Military Medal.[18]

It was 2015 hours when the last resistance on the dyke was quelled. 'B' Company had nine prisoners to add to 'A' Company's total. Suspecting Zandpol might be more heavily defended than the dyke, Richardson asked that it be heavily shelled. Major T. O'Shea of 13th Field Regiment, the artillery representative at battalion headquarters, happily obliged. 'B' Company's Buffaloes sailed toward the village under cover of the shelling and reported their arrival at 2055 hours. They found no enemy there.[19]

The Chauds were to have been advancing on Leuth by this time, and once Zandpol was in hand, the North Shores' 'C' and 'D' Companies would pass through and strike northward for Kekerdom. With the Chauds still waiting for the signal from 'A' Company, this plan was delayed until Roberts was able to send orders for the French Canadians to get going.[20] 'B' and 'C' Companies duly set off on foot, wading through three-foot-deep water and sinking to the tops of their boots in the mud beneath.[21] Gaining the dyke, the two companies secured their assigned sections as originally planned—although the North Shores had already cleared this area. 'A' and 'D' Companies then passed through and advanced to Leuth. Meeting only light opposition, they quickly cleared the village and took twenty prisoners. By dawn of February 9, their operation was successfully completed. Leuth, however, was rapidly being submerged under rising water. The men were forced to take refuge in the upper storeys and on the rooftops of several buildings.[22]

With Leuth and Zandpol in hand, the North Shores advanced on Kekerdom with 'C' and 'D' Companies aboard Buffaloes. After a short shelling, the North Nova Scotia Highlanders moved in. They met no opposition and took seven Germans prisoner. Three factories on Kekerdom's outskirts were to have been cleared in the next phase. As these were badly flooded, such effort was deemed unnecessary.

By mid-morning, the North Shores considered their part in Veritable over. They had one officer and nine other ranks killed, another officer and twelve men wounded, and four soldiers with battle exhaustion, who were evacuated. The battalion's total prisoner count was ninety-five.[23]

About noon, Roberts sent the Queen's Own Rifles to pass through Leuth and proceed to Millingen. Three companies advanced toward the village, which stood next to the Rhine. Normally, a large dyke held back the river, but a gap had been blown in it by the Germans. The village and surrounding area were badly flooded, and the water was rising at a rate of about five inches every three hours. The Queen's Own met no opposition in Millingen, rounding up eleven German soldiers and a couple of civilians.[24]

Rising water proved to be 8th Brigade's biggest problem on February 9. By mid-afternoon, plans were afoot to evacuate the Chauds from Leuth, as the situation there was untenable. Things were little better at Kekerdom and Zandpol. The North Shores in these villages were shrinking their lines inward. By nightfall, the troops in Kekerdom had abandoned the village and found refuge on top of the dyke next to the Rhine.[25]

Back at headquarters, Roberts thought his battalions had got through Veritable's opening with little real difficulty and surprisingly few casualties.[26] Circumstances might have been entirely different had the brigade not enjoyed the protection of a massive smokescreen that blinded the Germans on the opposite side of the Rhine, particularly those in the Hoch Elten—a 270-foot-high wooded ridge west of Emmerich that overlooked 3rd Division's operational area. Hoch Elten bristled with artillery, mortar, heavy machine-gun, and sniper positions. The plan was to so obscure the Germans' view from here to the flood plain that no amount of flares or star shells would illuminate the advancing Canadians.

The smokescreen was the creation of 11 Canadian Corps's chemical weapons technical officer, Captain J.C. Bond. Initially, "a smoke haze" to cover the entire flood plain from Nijmegen over to Cleve had been desired. Rather than conceal the troops at the head of the advance, the intention was to screen the rear areas to allow the supporting forces unimpeded movement. Bond quickly realized "that it was impossible to produce smoke haze over this large flat area but that a linear screen, which would prevent enemy observation... would be equally effective." He "crystalized" the plan by studying air photographs and maps, dividing the "smoke emission lines" into eight sectors. Bond had three 11 Canadian Corps companies of pioneers trained and equipped for the task, using ninety-six Esso smoke generators and fifteen smaller Besler generators. "As a measure of the stores necessary," Bond wrote, "an Esso generator requires from four to five tons of oil per day, while a Besler requires half that amount. The type of oil used is known as 'fog oil,' having a low flash point, low vapour pressure and no carbonization during combustion." This last point meant the oil did not burn inside the generator. Rather, it spewed forth as a white vapour.[27]

AT THEIR FORMING-UP position south of 8th Brigade's lines, the Can Scots had spent the daylight hours of February 8 watching the cab rank "of Allied fighters and fighter-bombers circling overhead and swooping down to blast the enemy upon call from the infantry. The artillery and mortars, firing on request, kept up an almost continuous racket as they hurled shells and bombs into German posts still resisting after the major bombardment." As word came in the late afternoon that 2nd Division was doing well on their right flank, the quartermaster issued emergency rations. It was judged impossible to provide food as normal because of the operation's amphibious nature. The issue included a twenty-four-hour ration containing various tinned and dried foods that two men split, a "Tommy Cooker" to heat some of it with, and Hexamine tablets as the heating fuel. Tins of self-heating cocoa and soup were passed around. At 1530 hours, the men were told to get ready. They "began to buckle on their equipment, gave a last check to make sure they had enough grenades, Bren gun magazines, mortar bombs *et cetera* and then started off along the muddy road to their assembly point with the Buffaloes," the Can Scot historian recorded.

The attack on Little Tobruk was to be carried out by Major Earl English's 'B' Company. Only Lieutenant L. Hobden's No. 11 Platoon was to go forward aboard Buffaloes. The rest of the company would approach on foot along the Quer Damm.[28] As English led his men forward, the Regina Rifles would strike out for Zyfflich with tanks of the 13th/18th Royal Hussars in support. Artificial moonlight would provide some illumination, but it was hoped not enough to enable the German defenders to zero in on the advancing troops.[29] The use of searchlights playing their beams upward to bounce off clouds had been used so often since Normandy that it no longer impressed the Canadians. They viewed it as simply "usual for night attacks."[30]

On this night, however, the technique proved "not altogether satisfactory, due to the high cloud level and scarcity of searchlights," reported 7th Brigade's diarist.[31] The Reginas kicked off at 1800 with 'D' and 'B' Companies leading.[32] A Flail tank was out front to clear mines. Despite the mud and flooding, the Flail never bogged down and neither did the supporting tanks. Very rapidly the leading companies cleared the majority of their section of the Quer Damm, opening the route the Can Scots were to use to attack Little Tobruk. Forty-five minutes after pushing off from the Regina start line, 'D' Company entered the outskirts of Zyfflich. 'B' Company passed through. Although resistance was light, the process of clearing houses and small factories was time-consuming. It took until 2000 hours for the company to reach its objective of the town's church.[33] When Captain Gordon Baird's 'C' Company jumped past 'B' Company to clear the eastern part of the town, things got sticky.

Flooding was so bad here that Baird realized, when only thirty yards from what appeared to be a strong German position, that his intended route of approach was impassable. Calmly, he set about checking other streets for one the tanks could navigate. Baird then guided the tanks singly into various positions from which they could fire on targets he pointed out. He purposefully stood in the open, despite knowing that in a confused night action, 'C' Company must have bypassed a good number of Germans—especially snipers. Baird's coolness under fire would garner a Distinguished Service Order.

One of the biggest obstacles facing 'C' Company was a large cheese factory. Baird sent No. 14 Platoon to clear it. Lance Sergeant

Gerald Royce Langton commanded the leading section. As his men closed in, Germans inside the factory opened up with heavy small-arms fire. Langton and several men were wounded. Ignoring his wound, Langton entered the factory alone "and engaged the enemy in close quarter fighting during which he killed and wounded several others. Such was the fury of his attack that he succeeded in driving the enemy into the cellar. Bringing the rest of the section forward, they successfully took the remainder, fifteen in all, prisoners of war," his Military Medal citation reported. Although Baird ordered him to the rear, Langton stayed to clear several adjacent houses, from which his section took another eighteen prisoners. Only when the position was consolidated did Langton consent to evacuation.[34]

At 2245 hours, Lieutenant Colonel Al Gregory moved his battalion tactical headquarters into Zyfflich. He immediately ordered Major Art Gollnick to load 'A' Company in a collection of Buffaloes and older Alligators. The company sailed due east about two miles to assail the village of Mehr. Intelligence reports had deemed it a key component of the Siegfried Line. But the flooding had completely submerged any mines or obstacles, such as wire. The Germans had also decamped.[35]

AS SOON AS the Reginas had secured the southern sector of the Quer Damm, 'B' Company of the Can Scots—less No. 11 Platoon, which was moving separately in Buffaloes—started toward Little Tobruk. Lieutenant W.G. MacIntosh's No. 10 Platoon was on point. Only a very narrow part of the dam's top had escaped flooding, so the three company sections were forced to follow each other rather than deploy into line abreast. The men quickly overran several dugouts and sent back twenty-three prisoners. Then they came face to face with a powerful strongpoint that consisted of a large blockhouse, a concrete pillbox, and field defences. The only way forward was through this position. As MacIntosh ordered the platoon to advance, deadly fire from several machine guns lashed out from the strongpoint. Several men fell wounded. Lance Corporal Edwin Fiddick and Corporal Arthur Sidney Low were both killed. Private Mayeso Mayes tried to rescue Low from the killing zone, and was also mortally wounded.

The company's PIAT team pounded the bunker but merely scratched its concrete. MacIntosh realized that taking the position head-on was hopeless. After a frustrating delay establishing wireless contact with No. 11 Platoon, he managed to get its Buffaloes brought to the edge of the dam next to his company headquarters. MacIntosh intended to transform the Buffalo into a floating bunker-buster. He loaded Sergeant L.A. Cummings and five men from No. 12 Platoon aboard. They were armed with Bren guns and a PIAT, while the Buffalo brought to bear its 20-millimetre and 50-millimetre machine guns. While the Buffalo was being readied, a section from No. 10 Platoon cleared a house to the right of the pillbox. The section captured five Germans and eliminated one machine gun. They were now positioned to bring flanking fire against the pillbox. The Buffalo made a wide circle out into the darkness and then bore down upon the fortification from the left and rear. As the men on the Buffalo let loose with heavy volleys of fire, No. 10 Platoon put in an assault that captured the pillbox. In the process, one of the battalion's old-timers, Private George Robertson, was killed.

It was well past midnight. 'B' Company was badly behind schedule. No. 12 Platoon moved through the strongpoint with Sergeant David Janicki's section leading. A popular twenty-four-year-old from Vernon, British Columbia, he was one of the few remaining D-Day veterans. Janicki and his men could only push up the length of the dam toward Little Tobruk. They soon broke into the major fortification and captured three officers and sixty-one soldiers while killing a good number more. Janicki was rounding up prisoners when a sniper shot him dead.

One of the surrendered officers, a captain, struck Major English as being very antsy. Suspicious, English ordered his men out of the fortification and down one of the dam's embankments. Minutes later, Little Tobruk was smothered by German artillery shells. The German captain had sent a signal that the fort would soon be swarming with Allied troops. English figured his company could have been easily wiped out.[36] Instead, they were in good shape and had a firm hold on Little Tobruk. They had, however, taken far longer to win the position than expected.

The original plan called for the battalion's 'A' and 'D' Companies to wait for 'B' Company to complete its mission before embarking on theirs. With Zyfflich taken by the Reginas and no sign that Little Tobruk was going to fall quickly, 7th Brigade's Brigadier J.G. "Jock" Spragge had ordered the Can Scots to make for their objective of Niel at about 2300 hours. The Can Scot war diarist thought the "heavily-laden" men in the two companies seemed "glad to get going." Off they went "sailing into the dark unknown." Their sailing time was estimated at thirty minutes, and all that time artillery pounded Niel.

As soon as the Buffaloes were under way, all wireless communication with the flotilla ceased.[37] It took four Buffaloes to carry a company—twenty men in each. The pilot in the flotilla's lead Buffalo was finding navigation "difficult in the murky darkness."[38] As a number of buildings were burning inside Zyfflich to the left and lighting "up the surrounding water-covered fields like a lighthouse," he directed the Buffaloes to make a wide detour rightward to remain hidden in the darkness. The Buffaloes were ungainly craft. Occasionally, a track would strike ground, a fence, shrub, or other obstacle being passed over and the Buffalo would spin completely around. Hunkered inside, only their lower bodies protected by the thin armoured sides, the infantrymen felt terribly vulnerable.

While the detour concealed the Buffaloes, it also took them well off the intended course. The flotilla set down on muddy ground too far to the right on a road running into the tiny village of Germenseel, about a mile and half south of Niel. 'A' Company's Captain Joseph James Andrews and 'D' Company's Major Dave Pugh huddled, trying to decide if the cluster of fifteen to twenty houses visible in the distance was their objective. Skeptical, Andrews jumped on a Buffalo and set off to probe the village from the north, while Pugh sent a patrol along the raised road to enter it directly. Neither party encountered any enemy. Andrews found an anti-tank ditch cutting across the road running north out of the village. His map showed such a ditch at Germenseel rather than Niel. He returned to find that Pugh had also determined they were at the wrong village. It was 0430 hours when the two companies sailed for Niel. They were unable to raise battalion headquarters to report their situation.[39]

WITH THREE COMPANIES out in the blue, and lacking wireless links to any of them, Lieutenant Colonel Desmond Crofton had been growing increasingly anxious and impatient. At about 0015, the war diarist recorded, he ordered "the remainder of the battalion to 'get cracking.'" Loading his headquarters section aboard two Buffaloes, Crofton set off for Niel. The Buffalo carrying Crofton led. A pre-dawn light was just appearing on the eastern horizon as the two amphibious vehicles approached the village. Crofton saw two large buildings ahead that were isolated from Niel by the floodwaters. A raised strip of ground connected the two buildings. As the lead Buffalo passed between these buildings, "fire belched" from the dry ground ahead. An explosive charge from a Panzerfaust struck the lead Buffalo, setting it on fire. The explosion killed the British officer helming the Buffalo and Can Scot Privates Bernard Merlyn Krislock and Max Bradie Brown.[40] Crofton suffered a bad compound fracture of his right arm.[41] His intelligence officer, Lieutenant T.A. Bruge, was blinded. Major Herbert Cecil James Morison, a 6th Field Artillery officer, was terribly wounded.

When the following Buffalo attempted to assist the men who had tumbled out of the burning vehicle, it was driven back by intense fire. No fire was directed at the survivors in Crofton's group. Several took cover in one of the large buildings while Crofton, Bruge, and Morison struggled through deep water toward a nearby barn. Just short of the barn, Morison succumbed to his injuries. Crofton and Bruge crawled into the building and took cover. The two badly wounded officers would not be found and evacuated for twelve hours.

Despite having been wounded and somewhat dazed by the explosion, Corporals R.G. Allan and O. Quesseth mustered "sufficient strength to swim, wade, and crawl past the buildings to a road covered in [three] feet of water." Although often wading through chest-high water, the men followed the road back to the Can Scot command post near Beek and reported to Major Bill Matthews before being sent to the Regimental Aid Post for treatment.

The surviving Buffalo in Crofton's party, meanwhile, had fallen back to Zyfflich. Lieutenant C.P. Shoop, the senior officer aboard, used the Regina Regiment's wireless to report the tragedy that had befallen Crofton's Buffalo. Major Larry Henderson immediately assumed battalion command, and Matthews became his second-in-command. Although sporadically in touch with 'B' Company at Little Tobruk, the two officers had no idea what was happening with 'A' and 'D' Companies. They dispatched a Weasel to pass through Zyfflich and attempt to evacuate the survivors of Crofton's Buffalo.[42]

The two missing companies, meanwhile, had approached Niel shortly after dawn on February 9 and put in their attack. A cold, hard rain fell from dense cloud cover. 'A' Company struck from the southwest and 'D' Company the northwest. Captain Andrews and Major Pugh had split the village in half and set the church as a meeting point. More than a hundred Germans defended Niel, but most quickly surrendered. The others were hunted down and killed in brief exchanges of grenades and rifle and machine-gun fire. By about 0700 hours, the village was mostly secure. They had taken about 110 prisoners at little loss to themselves. 'A' Company raised its battle flag on top of a building in honour of its first successful action on German soil.

Andrews and Pugh huddled beside the church to coordinate company dispositions. As the two men parted, the courtyard by the church was severely shelled by a German artillery battery firing from near Cleve. Despite several shells exploding just feet from Andrews, the 'A' Company commander and all the men with him were unscathed. Major Pugh's party was not so lucky. Pugh and his runner fell badly wounded, while 'D' Company's acting second-in-command, Lieutenant Donald Neville Fergusson, and Private Eric Selcov Hansen were killed.

After this short bombardment, Niel was not shelled again. It took all available Buffaloes to evacuate the Can Scot wounded and German prisoners. Shortly after the Buffaloes departed, the remaining men realized that the previously dry land upon which most of Niel had stood was being increasingly submerged by the floodwaters. With every passing hour they were forced to circle their defensive positions ever tighter, and eventually some men retreated to the second storeys of buildings when the main floors and basements were inundated.[43] At about 1800 hours, Captain Harvey Bailey, who as the company's normal second-in-command had been Left Out of Battle, arrived in a single Buffalo to take over the company. He found the men uniformly miserable and that "thoughts of food ruled their minds." Attempts by Henderson to arrange for Buffaloes to ship food, cookers, and other kitchen equipment to the stranded companies were rebuffed, as the first priority set by brigade for use of these vehicles was to support ongoing combat operations—particularly those of the Royal Winnipeg Rifle Regiment.[44] This regiment had advanced its battalion tactical headquarters and two companies by Buffalo to a cluster of farm buildings on the northern outskirts of Niel at 0945. By 1245, Lieutenant Colonel Lockhart "Lochie" Fulton had his command post well established outside Niel and had sent 'A' and 'B' Companies on their way toward the battalion's objective of Keeken—a village east of Millingen and also on the edge of the Rhine. Keeken was taken without incident at 2000 hours. 'B' Company moved west along the dry ground of the main river dyke and established contact with the Queen's Own Rifles, who were patrolling eastward from Millingen. 'C' Company was then brought up in Buffaloes and set about pushing along the river to turn the northern flank of the Siegfried Line by capturing a customs house that served as an anchor point. They met "stiff opposition," but by midnight Captain Frank Battershill radioed back that the customs house was secure and 'C' Company had suffered only light casualties while taking some seventy prisoners. The battalion settled down for the rest of the night in buildings surrounded by rising water and endured sporadic heavy mortaring and shelling.[45]

The Can Scots inside Niel and the Winnipegs to their north had no contact with each other because the floodwaters presented an effective barrier to movement on foot. In fact, their respective war diarists never mentioned the presence of the other battalion at all. For the Can Scots, that night was a time to count their casualties. These consisted of one officer and seven other ranks killed, three officers and fourteen men wounded, and one man listed as missing.[46]

While 'B' Company had departed Little Tobruk on the evening of February 9 and returned to battalion headquarters at Beek, the troops in Niel remained "marooned in the backwash of battle."

Throughout February 10, Bailey was in sporadic wireless contact with the Can Scot headquarters and given various times for a planned evacuation from a village rendered "tactically useless" by flooding. Each promised time passed without any Buffaloes showing up. By the following day, Bailey was desperate to get the two companies rescued. When 1000 hours, the promised time for a lift, came and went, he took to "frantically trying to hail all passing Buffaloes, who mistook the signals for friendly greetings and waved cheerily as they passed by! Finally three Buffaloes appeared and someone asked if the men were marooned. He received the answer: 'What the hell do you think?'" The Buffaloes rescued part of 'D' Company, but the rest of the force remained stranded in Niel until ten Buffaloes evacuated them in the early morning hours of February 12. They arrived at Beek to find the rest of the battalion preparing to march into Germany, and that the war that had temporarily passed them by was well advanced.[47]

[13]

The Water Rats

N ITS FIRST two days, Operation Veritable shattered the Germans'
first line of defence and reached the Siegfried Line fortifications.
Both days had seen the British and Canadian divisions more impeded
by weather than the enemy. As well, on February 9, low-hanging
cloud and heavy rain curtailed the air support that had been so bene-
ficial during the first day, when 2nd Tactical Air Force flew more than
a thousand sorties. General Harry Crerar observed that while "opposition continued to be light, the going through the water-logged fields
and the narrow rides of the [Reichswald] was heavy, progress was
limited, and it became increasingly apparent that the main problems
of the operation would be those of deployment and supply."[1]

To the right of the Canadian division, all three British divisions
had gained ground on February 9. At first, 15th Scottish had been
left idling in front of a major anti-tank ditch blocking entry into Frasselt. Its brigades awaited a special armoured breaching force
consisting of Flails and AVRES equipped for bridging operations.
Frasselt was on the Reichswald's northern flank. Five tracks
approached the anti-tank ditch, and the breaching force advanced
along all of them. "At once Flails began to bog down, and soon three
of the lanes were useless," the division's historian recorded. AVRES
on the other two gained the ditch and created crossings. As dawn
broke, this enabled the King's Own Scottish Borderers to cross the

ditch.[2] The infantrymen had been brought forward in an eight-hour journey from Nijmegen aboard Kangaroos of 1st Canadian Armoured Personnel Carrier Regiment. The British battalion's commander personally remarked on the "remarkable display of skill and endurance by the drivers" of the carriers. By 0800, the Borderers had seized Schottheide and Koningsheide, about five hundred yards east of the anti-tank ditch.[3]

To their left, 2nd Battalion of the Gordon Highlanders had captured an intact bridge crossing over the anti-tank ditch, allowing the battalion to advance along the main road from Kranenburg to the outskirts of Nutterden. Large trees lining the Nijmegen–Cleve road had been wrapped with necklaces of explosives so they could be brought down to bar traffic. None of the charges had been triggered, a sure sign that the heavy bombardments "had completely disorganized the defence." Hampered only by deep mud and a few mines, the Gordons finished clearing Nutterden by 1000 hours. They routed about two hundred "bomb-happy" Germans from a large concrete bunker, taking all of them prisoner. Had the enemy made a stand, a costly battle would have been assured.

The division's plan had called for its three brigades to leapfrog each other as one objective fell after another. That scheme unravelled when the following brigades became mired on roads chewed to pieces by the one leading. Jumping back on their Kangaroos, the Borderers retained the lead. They headed for a hill called the Wolfs-Berg, a little south of Nutterden. At 1115 hours, the Borderers reported the hill taken. They had captured 240 Germans and an artillery battery. Two hills—collectively called the Materborn feature—now faced 15th Scottish and barred the southwest approach to Cleve. An expected hard fight never materialized, and the Borderers pushed past the feature toward another hill at Bresserberg. This obstacle held the key to Cleve. Unaware that they were engaged in a race, the Borderers took Bresserberg at 1500 hours, just as elements of 7th Fallschirmjäger Division approached it from the east. With dusk falling, the Borderers and paratroopers fought a short, sharp action before the Germans withdrew toward Cleve. The Borderers "had won a decisive success."[4] But when the division's 15th Reconnaissance Regiment attempted to break into Cleve, it was driven off.

South of 15th Scottish, 53rd (Welsh) Division had bulled into the Reichswald, occupying the high ground southwest of Materborn. Further advances were frustrated, however, when the muddy track being used to bring supplies forward "gave way completely and had to be closed for repair." The division shifted its traffic to the already overburdened Nijmegen–Cleve road that 15th Scottish relied on. With sections of this road also flooded, movement of men and supplies for two divisions slowed to a crawl.

Right of the Welsh, 51st (Highland) Division had met the stiffest resistance. Still, an advance along the southern fringe of the forest to a point about one mile north of Hekkens cut the Mook–Gennep road.

By day's end on February 9, XXX British Corps estimated it had taken 2,500 prisoners during Operation Veritable's first two days in exchange for about 500 Canadian and British casualties.[5]

THE THUNDER OF the massive February 8 artillery bombardment had abruptly awakened First Fallschirmjäger Army's General der Fallschirmtruppen Alfred Schlemm at his headquarters in Dinxperlo on the Dutch–German border north of Rees. Although they were eighteen miles from First Canadian Army's gun lines, Schlemm appreciated the immensity of fire his troops holding the Reichswald endured. Within minutes, Schlemm was racing toward the gunfire in his Kübelwagen scout car. Schlemm quickly confirmed that this was the expected big offensive out of Nijmegen. When a liaison officer suggested the bombardment was a massive deception to divert troops away from the Venlo area where the main offensive would actually fall, Schlemm discounted the notion. He knew *this* was the offensive.

Upon returning to his headquarters in the early afternoon, Schlemm telephoned Generaloberst Johannes Blaskowitz at Heeresgruppe H and reported that First Canadian Army had struck 84th Infanterie-Division with an all-out attack. On his own initiative, Schlemm had alerted the only nearby reserve—7th Fallschirmjäger Division. In the late evening of February 8, these paratroopers were trucked to a rallying point near Gennep. From here, they were to counterattack the advancing Canadian Army's southern flank.[6]

Despite reports confirming that 84th Infanterie-Division had been struck "by the heaviest barrage hitherto experienced [on the western front] and by heavy attacks of strong formations of four-engine bombers on the area immediately behind [its main line of resistance]," Blaskowitz rejected Schlemm's conclusion. He believed it still necessary to "consider the possibility of a British attack via Venlo until...it was clearly established that the bulk of British forces were in the Cleve area." He also wanted to secure the army group's left flank against an American breakthrough at its juncture with Heeresgruppe B. For these reasons, Blaskowitz rejected sending further reinforcements to Schlemm.[7] He even ordered 7th Fall-schirmjäger Division's return to Venlo.

If it had been up to Schlemm, not only would the paratroopers be racing toward the Reichswald, but XLVII Panzer Korps and its 15th Panzer Grenadier and 116th Panzer Divisions, currently stationed east of Venlo, would join them. Schlemm was certain there was no threat of a stronger attack by British Second Army falling there. The British and Canadians were not strong enough to simultaneously mount two offensives. All their cards were on the table in front of the Reichswald. The longer Heeresgruppe H delayed in reinforcing that area, the more likely the game there would be lost.

Blaskowitz had given Schlemm a direct order. Should he ignore it? Could he? In the end, Schlemm temporized. He ordered 7th Division halted halfway between Venlo and Gennep. This put the division in Kevelaer, about fourteen miles east of the fighting. By late evening or early the following morning, he hoped Blaskowitz or his superior, Generalfeldmarschall Gerd von Rundstedt, would agree to release the desperately needed reinforcements.[8]

The chief problem facing the German command was their inability to situate XXX British Corps. Their intelligence staffs could only declare its "whereabouts unknown." Blaskowitz and Von Rundstedt thought it lurked behind the front near Venlo. This led to their insistence that 84th Infanterie-Division was being attacked by only two Canadian infantry divisions and 2nd Canadian Armoured Brigade. Schlemm was sure it was XXX Corps attacking with at least four divisions—two British and two Canadian. Only reluctantly, on the evening of February 8, did Blaskowitz reverse the order pertaining to

7th Division. Schlemm hurriedly got the paratroopers back on the move. Hampered by insufficient transportation and roads badly damaged by aerial bombardment, they arrived piecemeal by battalion and began to organize a solid defensive line to the left of the mauled 84th Infanterie-Division between Asperden—immediately west of Goch—and the Maas River. Some elements of this division, however, were sent to help stabilize the line to their north. It was one such unit that had attempted to occupy Bresserberg Hill, outside Cleve, which the Borderers had reached on the evening of February 9.

Although the presence of both the British 51st and 53rd Divisions had been confirmed earlier that day, German intelligence staff doggedly insisted the big push would come at Venlo.[9] By this time, Schlemm had been stripped of whatever command freedom he had possessed. Late that evening, "Berlin had taken an interest in the matter," he later told Allied interrogators. Schlemm, they wrote, "merely became a receptacle for the passing of orders. The Reichswald battle from that time on was to become for Schlemm a nightmare of excuses, entreaties and explanations. His first indication that he did not have a free hand came with the order that under no circumstances was any land between the Maas and the Rhine to be given up without the permission of Rundstedt, who would first ask Hitler. This prohibition on his freedom of movement considerably restricted Schlemm's plans. He realized that if the Allies captured the west bank of the Rhine, his complete army would be trapped. His own plan was to build a series of lines facing north, between the Maas and the Rhine, and retire slowly from position to position, exacting as heavy a price as possible for every loss of ground. These tactics were not permitted, however, and [LXXXVI Korps] was ordered to stand where it was and not yield an inch." Whenever a withdrawal proved necessary, Schlemm had to send "a detailed explanation" to gain approval.[10]

Schlemm did receive one good piece of news on February 9. During the day, U.S. First Army's v Corps had been advancing slowly against stiff resistance toward the Schwammenauel Dam on the Roer River. As night fell, 78th Division's 311th Regiment approached the dam in two groups. One was to seize the top of the dam and cross it, while the other took the power house on the lower level. Both groups consisted of elements of the regiment's 1st Battalion, and the one making for the dam's top was supported by a team of 303rd Engineer Battalion. The troops headed for the lower level approached slowly and warily. In the words of the U.S. Army's official historian, they seemed "particularly apprehensive lest the Germans at any moment blow the dam, sending tons of concrete, earth, and water cascading down upon them."

Events progressed more quickly above them, as the engineers—specially briefed on the dam's construction and operation—sought to reach the spillway and then descend into an inspection tunnel that reportedly ran the length of the structure. Crouching low to avoid continuing rifle fire, the engineers raced forward until stopped by a section of blown spillway. "There was only one other way, to slide down the 200-foot face of the dam and gain the tunnel through its bottom exit. Although the task was slow and treacherous, the engineers accomplished it. Entering the tunnel, they expected at any moment to be blown to kingdom come. The explosion never came. Subsequent investigation revealed that the Germans already had done all the damage intended. They had destroyed the machinery in the power room and had blown the discharge valves. They had also destroyed the discharge valves on a penstock that carried water from the upper reservoir on the Urft to a point of discharge below the Schwammenauel Dam, which explained why they had allowed the Urft Dam itself to fall into American hands intact. Together the two demolitions would release no major cascade of water but a steady flow calculated to create a long-lasting flood in the valley of the Roer."[11]

The effect was immediate—the water rose between three and four feet and spilled over the Roer's bank, in front of the entire U.S. Ninth Army front. There was also a lesser rise of the Maas in First Canadian Army's sector. In consequence, the scheduled launch of Operation Grenade on February 10 was cancelled. The Americans would have to wait for the flooding to abate. Reluctantly, Field Marshal Montgomery issued orders postponing Grenade to the 14th or 15th at the earliest. He feared the delay might be far longer. And as long as Grenade was delayed, the Germans were free to concentrate entirely on First Canadian Army. By midday on February 10, Von Rundstedt grasped this. Although still reluctant to believe that the Reichswald offensive was a singular one, he directed XLVII Panzer Korps to take control of the battle and bring its two divisions into play. Earlier, the 6th Fallshirmjäger Division had also been ordered to send its 16th Regiment from a holding area west of Arnhem.[12]

EVEN AS THE flooding Roer forced Operation Grenade's delay, the Rhine water spilling across the western flood plain was increasingly plaguing First Canadian Army. By the morning of February 10, long stretches of the Nijmegen–Cleve road between Wyler and Kranenburg were so flooded that 2nd Canadian Infantry Division engineers closed it to further traffic. At the same time, most alternative routes—largely dirt tracks—became so badly broken up that the sappers could barely keep them operational. Nose-to-nose traffic crept along each track, with weary provosts hard put to keep various formations jockeying for place in line from becoming entangled.

To ensure that priority traffic—particularly ambulances carrying the wounded—was not caught in the jams, the engineers of 2nd Field Company established four ferry services with launching sites near Wyler. The ferries shuttled from here to where the main road emerged from the floodwaters three hundred yards east of Kranenburg. "These ferries," reported 2nd Division's chief engineer, Lieutenant Colonel L.G.C. Lilley, "traversed areas that were flooded to a depth of from 8 to 10 feet. The only serious problem that arose in connection with their use was the necessity of a careful survey of the route which they took in order to clear hedges, fence posts, and other obstructions."[13]

Despite these efforts, by February 10 all divisions under XXX British Corps command were greatly hampered by rising water and mud. Heavy, continuous rain worsened conditions. General Harry Crerar lamented that although the advance continued, it did so "more slowly as the difficulties of the ground, together with stiffening enemy resistance, began to have their effect."[14] The day's plan had envisioned 3rd Canadian Infantry Division advancing to the Spoy Canal, running in a straight line north from Cleve to the Rhine. At the same time, 43rd (Wessex) Division was to pass through the 15th (Scottish) Infantry Division and capture Goch, Üdem, and Weeze—towns all well to the southeast of the Reichswald. The 15th Scottish would, meanwhile, sweep through Cleve and rush mobile columns eastward to Emmerich and Calcar. South of these divisions, 51st (Highland) Division was to mop up German forces east of the Maas and open the way for the 43rd Wessex advance on Goch.[15]

The plan was remarkably ambitious, given the conditions and slowness of advances attained in Veritable's first two days. But Lieutenant General Brian Horrocks was encouraged by news that during the night of February 9–10, the Scottish Division had captured the Nutterden feature and reached Cleve's outskirts. Accordingly, he wrote, "I unleashed my first reserve, the 43rd (Wessex) Division, which was to...burst out into the plain beyond [Cleve] and advance toward Goch."[16]

In fact, most of 15th Scottish faced strong resistance outside Cleve and won very little ground throughout a day of bitter fighting that stretched into the night. February 10 was, wrote the division's historian, "a day of frustration. The weather was shocking; the going deeper than ever...traffic congestion had made troop movement impossible. Golden opportunities...slipped by in consequence—and all the time the enemy front was hardening."[17] Not until just after midnight on the night of February 10–11 did 15th Scottish gain the outskirts and start fighting their way into Cleve.[18]

The 129th Infantry Brigade had led 43rd Wessex's advance out of the Nijmegen Salient toward Cleve. Very shortly, Horrocks realized the division was caught in "one of the worst traffic jams in the war." Advancing this division, he concluded, was "one of the worst mistakes I made in the war...My only excuse is that all too often during the war I had witnessed a pause in the battle when one division was ordered to pass through another, which allowed the enemy time to recover."[19]

Despite tangled traffic and the necessary shift from one route to another as vehicles mired and German roadblocks prevented forward progress, the division's 129th Brigade reached Cleve by dawn. As its battalions pushed into the ruins, they met heavy resistance from the newly arrived 6th Fallschirmjäger Division's 16th Regiment and elements of 84th Infanterie-Division supported by several self-propelled guns and tanks. Fighting raged through the day as the British troops fended off repeated counterattacks. At nightfall, 129th Brigade was pinned down in the ruins.[20] South of Cleve, 214th Infantry Brigade and the division's reconnaissance regiment had struggled through the Reichswald to gain the village of Materborn, only to find it held in strength by Germans. Bitter, often hand-to-hand, fighting ensued. "Owing to the appalling condition of the trackways and the frightful congestion of the traffic of two divisions, the third of the Wessex brigades (130 Infantry Brigade) was ordered to remain in Nijmegen," a Canadian report noted. "Seldom has a major battle been waged under such difficulties."

Things had gone little better for the other British divisions. The 51st (Highland) Division also met heavy resistance and by day's end had only taken Ottersum and Zelderheide in a one-mile advance. Patrols sent north managed to link up with elements of 53rd Welsh.[21] This division's operations had been largely confined to mopping up resistance within its dense sector of the Reichswald and readying to forcibly cross the road running southwest from Cleve to Hekkens in a drive directed on Goch.[22]

ON THE FLOOD plain, 3rd Canadian Infantry Division's advance on February 10 was led by 9th Brigade. Brigadier John "Rocky" Rockingham and his tactical headquarters unit had led, sailing from Beek at 0730 hours aboard two Buffaloes and one Weasel. Following along in an assortment of amphibious vehicles were the tactical headquarters parties of the Stormont, Dundas and Glengarry Highlanders and the Highland Light Infantry Battalions, which together would be on point. The straggling amphibious convoy headed for Mehr, launch point for the brigade's advance toward the Spoy Canal. A few feet higher than the ground surrounding it, the village resembled a low-lying island.[23]

Passage to Mehr was not without mishap. The Weasel carrying Glens signals officer Lieutenant W.D. Eley sank, leaving everybody aboard "marooned" for several hours. Then the Weasel bearing

Lieutenant F.K. Pelton—currently serving as the battalion's liaison officer to brigade headquarters—also sank. Pelton was left "perched precariously on top," awaiting rescue.[24] The Buffalo carrying Pioneer Platoon Captain J.P. Donihee and a section of men equipped with the Glens' mortars mired while crossing a dyke. They would remain stuck there until being dragged free at midnight by engineers in an assault boat. After going no more than a thousand yards, the Buffalo then ran over a submerged fence post that ripped a four-inch hole in its bottom. Water fountained in until someone plugged the hole with a ground sheet. The vehicle finally lurched into Mehr at 0700 hours on February 11—by which time the Glens had long gone into the attack.[25]

As the brigade's various tactical headquarters were set up in buildings at Mehr, the large grouping of officers had realized "there were no friendly troops" ahead. Just as this information sank in, several armour-piercing shells tore away a chunk of roof on the house Glens Lieutenant Colonel Roger Rowley had selected for his headquarters. Rowley climbed out onto the roof in order to identify the German gun's firing position, while Captain W.J. Franklin took station on the stairs. As Rowley shouted coordinates, Franklin passed these to an artillery officer manning a wireless on the ground floor. Because of the extensive flooding to the west, 9th Brigade was well beyond range of any field artillery regiments. So a medium battery zeroed in, and a few minutes later the German gun was knocked out of action. As the 9th Brigade war diarist recorded, Rowley's approach here was not "according to the pamphlet."[26]

It was, however, typical of the man. The thirty-year-old had taken over the Glens in Normandy and established a reputation for almost reckless audaciousness. His leadership during Boulogne's capture garnered a Distinguished Service Order, to which was added a bar for taking Breskens during the Scheldt Estuary Campaign. Roger's brother John—two years older—had commanded the North Shore (New Brunswick) Regiment since December 1944. This led to their being nicknamed "the brother act." John was only slightly less dashing and a little more serious than Roger. The North Shores called him the Good Shepherd because he carried a long Scottish walking staff.

Both Rowleys were considered exemplary battalion commanders.

The 9th Brigade plan had the Glens advancing from Mehr aboard Buffaloes at 1630 hours, with 'A' and 'C' Companies leading. At the same time, the Highland Light Infantry would push out from the village of Keeken. The Glens headed for Rindern, about three miles east of Mehr, while the HLI were to seize Duffelward. This village was adjacent to a short section of the original Rhine riverbed circumvented when German engineers straightened the river's course in the early 1900s. The riverbed remnants left behind were collectively designated the Alter Rhein. Normally, this section held some water most of the year, but the flooding on either side had transformed it into a deep channel within a low-lying lake. Duffelward remained above water level, as did a dyke bordering the Alter Rhein between the village and the HLI start line. Although Duffelward was only about a mile distant, Lieutenant Colonel Phil Strickland recognized that approaching it would be difficult. Lacking sufficient Buffaloes, the leading 'B' Company must "attack along the main river dyke." Thereafter, 'A' Company would pass through and finish clearing it. Complicating the job was the fact that no artillery could support the attack because the field guns were out of range. Company commanders were instead told that they would have to "rely on their own weapons to get...into Duffelward."[27]

One blessing for Canadians on the flood plain was the continued smokescreen along the Rhine from Nijmegen to 3rd Division's front lines. As the advance continued, more smoke-generating devices were deployed to maintain the screen's integrity. All equipment and fuel had to be moved by Buffaloes to points along the main dyke bordering the Rhine. These were then loaded onto Bren carriers of the division's 17th Duke of York's Royal Canadian Hussars Reconnaissance Regiment. The carrier crews carefully picked their way along the mine-infested dyke to resupply existing smoke generators and enable crews to deploy the new ones as the advance continued. It was slow, dangerous work requiring repeated daily runs by Buffaloes and carriers to feed the necessary daily fuel supply of about 120 tons.[28] Although the Germans across the Rhine were blinded by the smoke, they tried to disrupt the smoke-generating operation. Machine guns routinely fired bursts on fixed lines, and snipers were also active, but because those firing were unable to pick specific targets, this fire was more nuisance than hindrance to the smoke crews.[29]

Sheltered by this screen, the HLI's 'B' Company at first made good progress approaching Duffelward. Then, just short of the village, it came under heavy machine-gun fire from positions that, as the HLI diarist recorded, "had our line of advance well covered." Eighteen men were killed or wounded and the company driven to ground with no prospect of continuing.[30]

Strickland sent 'A' Company in on 'B' Company's right at 1700 hours. The company had to cross nine hundred yards "of ground already saturated and knee deep in mud, in order to approach the town." Fortunately, the men were cloaked by darkness and managed "to plow through the mud and gain a foothold on the outskirts of the town without serious opposition." Quickly reorganizing, 'A' Company started the slow work of clearing Duffelward.[31] The job proved tough, for the village was a maze of pillboxes and fortified houses. Even several artillery concentrations fired by medium guns with sufficient range failed to break the German hold.[32]

The Glens, meanwhile, had advanced 'A' and 'C' Companies in Buffaloes toward Donsbrüggen, a village on the edge of the Reichswald about midway between their start line and Rindern. Although opposition was initially light, Private Edmund Robert Malone was killed. Approaching the village, 'C' Company was fired on by a machine gun. The men piled out of the Buffaloes to engage it. Sergeant G.E. Wilson's platoon quickly overwhelmed the gun crew. When another machine gun started firing from a low densely wooded hill within the Reichswald, Wilson ordered his men to take cover. He then charged the gun and killed its crew with bursts of Sten-gun fire. With the right flank secured by Wilson, the company pushed into Donsbrüggen and easily cleared it.

On foot, the two companies advanced along a road leading to Rindern.[33] About two hundred yards past Donsbrüggen, Germans in four houses lining the road opened fire. Shouting for his section to cover him, Corporal Ernest William Baker dashed into the nearest house and killed the Germans there. He then single-handedly cleared the other three buildings. "This aggressive action resulted in the death of five Germans and the capture of sixteen," his Military Medal citation noted.[34]

Pushing on to Rindern, the Glens overran a 75-millimetre gun on its outskirts. Entering the town shortly after midnight, they became entangled in a fight for control of a system of trenches anchored on fortified houses. Despite this opposition, Rowley ordered 'A' Company to continue straight along the main road through the town to gain the Spoy Canal. Leading the way, No. 7 Platoon was soon cut off by Germans firing from bypassed buildings. Rowley realized he needed both companies to clear Rindern. The rest of 'A' Company turned to this task, and Private Ernest Joseph Bourgon was killed when he attacked one building with a lifebuoy flame-thrower. The company commander, Major J.W. Braden, suddenly came face to face with a German. Braden squeezed his 9-millimetre Browning pistol's trigger, only to have the weapon jam. Throwing the gun with all his strength, Braden scored a dead-on facial hit that stunned the German. Braden took the man prisoner. Soon thereafter the village was taken and an attempted counterattack by German paratroopers beaten off.[35]

Opposition to 9th Brigade's advance had so far been offered by 1052nd Grenadier Regiment of 84th Infanterie-Division, but now elements of 6th Fallschirmjäger Division were appearing. As Cleve fell to the British on the Canadian right in the early morning hours of February 11, resistance began to slacken. There was, the Canadian Army's historian noted, "no great incentive for a sacrificial defence of the scattered 'island' villages in the flooded river flats." The 84th Infanterie-Division had been butchered. On February 11, only about a thousand combat troops remained in the field. As the day progressed, they generally gave ground before being attacked.[36]

At first, this faltering resolve was little evident on 9th Brigade's front. In Duffelward, the HLI's 'A' Company at 0430 hours came up against a large strongpoint in the central square.[37] Reinforcing the company was initially impossible, because early that morning German engineers had blown the sluice-gates of the Spoy Canal, breaching the western dyke of the Kalflach Canal to the east of Cleve near Huisberden. Water on the already inundated flood plain rose alarmingly. Prior to this, Canadian engineers had been trying to drain the flood plain. As the Waal River was lower than the flood plain, they had breached its main dyke at Nijmegen to allow the flood plain waters to flow through. Now that water was rising faster than their breach could drain it.[38] Major General Dan Spry had personally witnessed the explosion that created the 165-foot breach in Kalflach Canal's dyke. Seeing a thick chunk of earth fly skyward and then fall back to earth, Spry telephoned his chief engineer and architect of the Canadian draining effort, Lieutenant Colonel Alec McTavish. "Did you see what I saw?" Spry asked. "Well, try sticking your finger in that!"[39]

By early morning, the muddy field that HLI's 'A' Company had crossed to gain Duffelward was submerged under three feet of water. Rounding up several Buffaloes, Lieutenant Colonel Strickland mounted his 'D' Company and sent it out from Keeken. When the Buffaloes arrived about mid-morning, they sailed down Duffelward's streets to reinforce 'A' Company. German resistance was quickly broken and the town secured.[40]

The leading companies of the Glens had also been reinforced during the morning of February 11. 'B' and 'D' Companies, along with Captain J.P. Donihee's mortar section, had departed Mehr aboard Buffaloes at 0700 hours. Unloading outside of Rindern, these troops advanced through a thousand yards of waist-deep, ice-cold water. As 'B' Company secured Rindern from Germans lurking in the nearby Reichswald, 'D' Company caught up to 'A' and 'C' Companies. These three companies pressed on toward the Spoy Canal against initially stiff opposition concentrated in scattered but heavily fortified farm buildings. By 1100 hours, they signalled that Spoy Canal was just three hundred yards distant. Still, it took until 1345 to win through to it. Two Glens were mortally wounded in this advance—Sergeant Sherman Roger Hill and Private Robert Eugene Arbuckle.[41]

On the HLI front, 'D' Company had advanced from Duffelward aboard Buffaloes in the early afternoon and by nightfall secured Wardhausen, on the western edge of the canal, without suffering casualties.

Anxious to maintain the momentum, Brigadier Rockingham ordered the HLI to keep going and the North Nova Scotia Highlanders to pass through the Glens. The HLI's 'C' Company set off in the pre-dawn hours of February 12 and by sunrise controlled Griethausen. This village stood adjacent to a railway bridge across the easternmost extremity of the Alter Rhein. The troops found a number of German civilians, but they remained passively in their houses.[42] As the ground between the Alter Rhein and the Rhine itself was completely submerged, there was no need or thought given to trying to secure it. Only a small finger of raised ground running from Griethausen to a point just southwest of Emerich remained to be cleared.

Water and operating in pitch-black darkness slowed the North Novas' advance. Lieutenant Colonel Don Forbes had intended for his tactical command team to advance in concert with 'B' Company. Preceding this group, 'A' Company gamely set off with Major A.W. Jefferson and second-in-command Captain Dave Dickson riding in the same Buffalo. With all landmarks submerged, the two officers tried using a naval compass to set their course. But the magnetic needle appeared confused by the metallic confines of the Buffalo and spun wildly. The Buffalo circled lost in the night, with the rest of the flotilla trailing behind.

Meanwhile, the Buffalo carrying Forbes and his men had become separated from those of 'B' Company and then mired in a hole under several feet of water. Forbes and his party waded to Rindern. Somehow the artillery officer accompanying Forbes had got his Bren carrier driven through to the village. Everybody loaded up, setting off along a submerged road running toward the canal. A short distance out, the carrier slid into a ditch. Vehicle drowned, Forbes led his once more thoroughly soaked and freezing party back to Rindern.[43]

'B' Company, meanwhile, had crossed the Spoy Canal and gained the railway running from Griethausen to Cleve without meeting any resistance. It was soon joined by 'C' Company. 'A' Company eventually turned up at the North Novas' headquarters in Rindern at about 1000 hours on February 12. Forbes immediately dispatched it and 'D' Company to cross the railway and proceed into the battalion's final objective of Kellen. By early afternoon, the village was secured without incident.[44] This concluded 3rd Division's major flood-plain operation. Major General Spry ordered 9th Brigade to limit further actions to small patrols into the dry ground due east. Although this area and two villages within it would eventually have to be cleared, there was no urgency, the ground being isolated from the rest of the German front by a wide stretch of deeply flooded terrain.

As 9th Brigade settled in, 7th and 8th Brigades withdrew entirely from the flood plain. Spry had spotted some men from these brigades "sitting on rooftops of farmhouses and barns or standing in water holding their weapons above their heads."[45] In places, the water was five feet deep. Even the Water Rats were unable to conduct combat operations in such terrible conditions. Fortunately, their time here was mostly done. Cleve had fallen. The Germans had been mostly driven out of the Reichswald. Veritable moved into a new phase.

14

Heavy Going

A T 2330 HOURS on February 12, Field Marshal Bernard Montgomery sent his nightly signal to General Sir Alan Brooke in London. Since Veritable's launch, some five thousand prisoners had been taken and many other Germans killed or severely wounded. The Reichswald and Cleve had fallen. British and Canadian casualties totalled about 1,100. At first blush, all the news seemed good. But Montgomery had spent the day visiting the American front on the Roer River. There, things were anything but good. "The conditions in the river valley are appalling and Grenade is quite impossible for the present and it may very well be a week or more before we can launch it. Meanwhile Veritable must carry on alone and it is therefore bound to go slowly unless it can be strengthened and this I propose to do...I shall in fact put all the strength I can into Veritable and will go on driving hard to the southeast until Grenade can be launched." Montgomery closed by pointing out that Veritable was drawing most of the German reserves toward it, and once Grenade began, these thousands of troops could be eliminated in a classic anvil-hammer operation.[1]

In truth, Montgomery had few resources with which to strengthen Veritable. General Harry Crerar and his planners had built into Veritable responses to two potential scenarios. The optimistic scenario envisioned the battle loosening once XXX British

Corps broke out of the Reichswald and the British Guards Armoured Division could be released for a spirited drive from Cleve through to Calcar and Üdem. If things got "sticky" and no opening was presented for the Guards, Crerar's second scenario foresaw bringing in more divisions by having 11 Canadian Corps take over the left flank from xxx Corps.[2] As they were already deployed in the area, the 43rd (Wessex) and 15th (Scottish) Infantry Divisions would come under Lieutenant General Guy Simonds's command. He would also bring 2nd Canadian and 3rd Canadian Infantry Divisions to bear and keep 4th Canadian Armoured Division on standby to exploit any breakout opportunity. Simonds's advance would follow a southeast axis running from Cleve to Üdem. Lieutenant General Brian Horrocks would meantime thrust xxx Corps along a line running through Goch toward Weeze and beyond to Kevelaer. Initially, the 53rd (Welsh) and 51st (Highland) Divisions would carry out this thrust. As more Canadian divisions came into the line and shoulder room grew, 43rd Wessex and then 15th Scottish would revert to his control.[3] Meanwhile, Horrocks received welcome reinforcement in the form of 52nd (Lowland) Infantry Division, which Montgomery pulled from 11 British Corps. This division took over the right flank from the 51st (Highland) Infantry Division, enabling it to concentrate on attacking Goch from the northwest. Although Cleve was in hand, Goch and Üdem remained beyond reach. And German resistance was mounting alarmingly as more divisions faced off against First Canadian Army.[4]

Crerar noted on February 12 that the number of Germans "along the whole front" was increasing.[5] Although on the previous day the 15th Scottish had relieved the besieged 43rd Wessex's 129th Brigade in Cleve, the city had only fallen that morning, after a last counterattack by paratroopers had been driven off and 180 prisoners taken. The city now passed to 3rd Canadian Infantry Division's control, so the two British divisions could push toward Bedburg and cut the Cleve–Goch road. The German response to these threats on Calcar and Goch was fierce and reflected their determination to retain control of these pivotally important towns. Soon the British were checked by a hastily improvised line of entrenchments running from Moyland Wood across open terrain to Cleve Forest, where it intersected with an existing line anchored on the Cleve–Goch road.

These developments troubled Crerar, but not as much as the fact that 53rd (Welsh) Division had run straight into the teeth of four counterattacks while completing the clearing of the southeastern corner of the Reichswald. The counterattacks had been mounted by xLVII Korps's 116th Panzer and 15th Panzer Grenadier Divisions and were intended to recover Cleve and the ground immediately west of it.[6]

However, the German divisions were greatly delayed by "strong harassing fire on crossroads and important terrain points by enemy artillery," and their attack ran straight into the advancing 53rd Welsh. As one senior German corps staff officer later wrote, the Welsh met the Germans "energetically and soon were able to commence their own attack." By late afternoon, the 53rd had broken the seam linking the two German divisions. The situation for 15th Panzer Grenadier Division "became critical. Hurriedly raked up emergency units had to be committed in the north in order to establish a block."

Things deteriorated rapidly for the Germans. The "actions in the woods broke the fighting power of the 15th [Division] for the coming weeks." A wedge had been driven between the remnants of 84th Infanterie-Division and the two LXXXVI Korps divisions with the late-day capture of Bedburg by 43rd Wessex. In consequence, the Germans had "suffered a severe loss of fighting power [and] in addition ran into a very difficult tactical situation."

The Germans believed they now faced a southeastern drive along the Cleve–Calcar road toward Goch and Üdem in conjunction with a thrust out of the Reichswald. This two-pronged attack would attempt to "annihilate the main body of the corps." All available reinforcements were rushed to strengthen 116th Panzer Division to meet the attack from Bedburg, while 84th and 15th Divisions were to be reorganized. "By the night of 13 February," the officer wrote, "there was no more talk of major counterattacks, but a defensive stalemate had been temporarily achieved."[7]

This was the most that General der Fallschirmtruppen Alfred Schlemm had hoped to achieve. Schlemm just had too little to work with to offer more than a spirited defence. Generalmajor Heinz Fiebig's 84th Infanterie-Division existed as only ragged elements. The 7th Fallshirmjäger Division was in place, and 6th Fallschirmjäger Division was coming into play. Under XLVII Korps's command, these divisions and its inherent 116th Panzer and 15th Panzer Grenadier Divisions would hold the line from the Rhine to Goch, while LXXXVI Infanterie Korps with both its 180th and 190th Infanterie-Divisions assumed responsibility for the ground south of this city through to the Maas.

Schlemm would soon reinforce his badly extended forces by drawing 8th Fallschirmjäger Division away from the Roermond area. But the transfer would take several days to execute. Withdrawal of the paratroopers from Roermond would also badly weaken this front facing the Americans. Given the critical situation developing around Goch, the risk must be taken. It was a case of making do with all too little. Yet Schlemm knew better than to tell his superiors this.

Although he had a reasonable amount of artillery and mortars—by mid-February it amounted to about 1,000 guns and 300 mortars—he could not hope to match the British–Canadian daily rates of fire. His intelligence staff reported the Allied artillery fired an average of 80,000 to 100,000 rounds daily. Ammunition shortages imposed expenditure rates on his artillerymen of only 8,000 to 10,000 rounds. Although the mud, the density of the Reichswald, and the inundation of the flood plain had rendered tanks largely useless so far, Schlemm knew he would face an armoured juggernaut as soon as conditions allowed. First Canadian Army was believed capable of fielding about 500 tanks, whereas the Germans were lucky to have 40 to 50 operational tanks on any given day. So it came down to the determination of his infantry and the skill of their officers in mastering a "critical situation." Schlemm believed his army still possessed good "discipline and order."

The terrible weather was a godsend for Schlemm. The low cloud and almost constant rain rendered Allied air superiority largely irrelevant. On many days the dreaded 2nd Tactical Air Force fighter-bombers were not seen. But this weather was unlikely to hold. Any day, the skies might clear and the *Jabos*, as the Germans called the fighters, would swarm in and wreak havoc upon Schlemm's troops and supply lines. For now, though, they were absent, and his vital bridges at Wesel had been neither destroyed by bombing nor seriously damaged. This left his supply lines intact. All things considered, he anticipated preventing any decisive breakthrough and either imposing a stalemate or conducting a slow, fighting withdrawal.[8]

While a stalemate would suit the Germans, it was the last thing Twenty-First Army Group could afford. Both British and Canadian armies suffered reinforcement shortages. The previous December, Prime Minister Winston Churchill had sought to alleviate the British problem by ordering 250,000 men transferred from other arms of the country's military service. Canada's overseas army often dredged the barrel to keep its divisions—particularly the infantry brigades—up to strength. With air superiority assured, some anti-aircraft battalions were decommissioned and their troops sent to the infantry. Other battalions were reformed whole into fresh infantry units. Rear areas were scoured for surplus men who could be sent to the front. Cook, baker, typist, mechanic, whatever—anybody was a candidate for a ticket to an infantry battalion. For many such men, years had passed since basic training, and whatever knowledge of weapons or tactics they might have received was long forgotten. Their sudden presence at the side of veteran infantrymen was often unwelcome for fear that inexperience jeopardized everybody.

The new soldiers coming to the British divisions were especially poorly and hastily trained. And there were few vitally needed junior officers or senior non-commissioned officers. By February 14, Veritable had cost 2,400 Canadian and British casualties. These included 176 officers who could not be fully replaced. With German resistance stiffening, the prospect of overwhelming casualties was extremely worrisome.[9]

On February 14, Crerar lunched with Simonds and told him to take over the left sector from xxx Corps by noon the following day. Simonds interjected with a suggested alternative plan he had worked up in concert with Major General G.H.A. MacMillan, who commanded 49th (West Riding) Infantry Division. This division was deployed in the Nijmegen Island and had no role in Veritable. In December, the two generals had concocted a scheme to force a crossing of the Nederrijn at Arnhem and take the entirety of 11 Canadian Corps up the Rhine's east bank. This would effectively render continued German defence of the Rhineland untenable. It would also enable 11 Canadian Corps to avoid getting fully entangled in Veritable, which Simonds believed destined to devolve into a costly set-piece slugging match of Great War proportions.

Simonds had floated this idea in December, but neither Montgomery nor Crerar had shown interest. However, the last two days of Veritable had revealed that the operation was becoming a slow, day-to-day grind where ground was won foot by foot and at great cost. Simonds thought the moment ripe to again propose Operation Wallstreet.[10]

Although an attractive scheme and not without merit, Crerar told Simonds, "it was of secondary importance to the immediate responsibility of completing what we have set out to do in Operation Veritable." Maximum strength needed to be brought against the Germans, which meant maintaining as wide a front as possible. And that required 11 Canadian Corps's fresh divisions.[11]

ON THE MORNING of February 14, the skies partly cleared, allowing squadrons of 2nd Tactical Air Force to swarm aloft. Nine thousand sorties—the most since the Normandy Campaign—were flown. The Spitfires of No. 126 (RCAF) Wing put in their busiest day of the war with 237 sorties. Typhoon fighter-bombers from No. 440 (RCAF) Wing sortied 55 times. The overall support provided by Canadian squadrons was calculated at 1,500 sorties and deemed in one report to be "historically significant," because it was the first time there had been such "close coordination...on such a scale between Canada's air and ground forces."[12]

The Luftwaffe put in a very modest appearance, with about ten new jet-propelled ME-262 fighters. Although the jets could carry 1,000 pounds of bombs, they were designed as fighters. With a top speed of 540 miles per hour and a cruising speed of 460, they were wildly inaccurate as fighter-bombers. The jets scattered bomb loads apparently at random while dodging a storm of anti-aircraft fire. In "seeing them off," 3rd Canadian Light Anti-Aircraft Regiment loosed about 3,500 rounds.[13]

From where they mustered in Kellen to attack the unflooded triangle between the Alter Rhein and the Rhine, the North Nova Scotia Highlanders watched one jet drop its bombs into the ruins of Cleve before whooshing away at great speed. There seemed little point to the effort.[14]

The North Novas were little concerned about the day ahead. It seemed easy enough. Go forward in Buffaloes, unload when they reached the mud of the triangle, and then squelch up a muddy road past first Warbeyen and then Hurendeich. The latter village stood next to the Rhine and looked across to the battered city of Emmerich. Little German opposition was expected because the triangle was defensively untenable. Lieutenant Colonel Don Forbes sent three companies forward in Buffaloes at 1200 hours, intending to quickly overwhelm any resistance. Through 9th Brigade's Brigadier Rocky Rockingham, Forbes had teed up "terrific fire support from field and medium artillery." The Buffaloes would also have their machine guns blazing. 'C' Company was to set down to the left of the road, 'A' Company to the right, and 'B' Company was to go straight up it to Warbeyen. Problems with the last company's Buffaloes caused it to touch down ten minutes behind the other two. Major J. Weston Campbell hustled his men up the road, and soon the three companies advanced in line abreast.[15]

The only opposition en route was sporadic machine-gun fire from positions across the river in Emmerich. After securing the village, the North Novas pressed on toward Hurendeich. As that village lay to the right of the road, 'C' Company had carried on past it. Trees lined either side of the road, and its raised bed was the only ground not deep in mud. So Captain Jack Veness led the company along it with platoons in line. Closing on Hurendeich, Veness slipped one platoon, under Sergeant George Stewart, across the mud to gain the top of a dyke bordering the Kalflach Canal. Road and dyke almost converged at the little village. Approaching the village, the company suddenly came under fire from the first cluster of buildings.[16]

Lieutenant Bill Myers and Veness drew pistols and charged with the lead platoon in their wake. The North Novas went forward in bounds, using trees for cover. Bullets slashed splinters from trees and kicked up splashes in the muddy water alongside the road, but for the most part proved wildly inaccurate. As the men led by Veness broke into the village, about twenty Germans dashed out. They ran across the dyke in front of the 'C' Company platoon there. Caught by surprise, Sergeant Stewart and his men only opened fire as the Germans plunged into the canal's icy water and tried to swim to the other side. "I figure we got a few of them," Stewart told the battalion's intelligence officer. The North Novas reported one German dead, plus an unknown number killed crossing the canal, seven wounded, and eighteen taken prisoner. Their own casualties in what was to have been an easy day totalled four killed and eight wounded. Major Campbell was among the dead.[17]

Also killed was twenty-six-year-old Sergeant Eric Greene. When war was declared in 1939, Greene had left the little outpost of Burgeo, Newfoundland, and travelled to Canada to join the army. When the fight for Hurendeich ended, Greene's platoon took over a farmhouse on the outskirts facing Emmerich. Greene climbed the stairs to the upper storey and settled in a chair with a view out a window to the Rhine. A few minutes later, wireless operator Corporal Keith Johnston appeared at the top of the stairs lugging his heavy set. Seeing that Johnston was obviously exhausted, Greene stood to let him sit down. Suddenly, a sniper bullet through the window struck Greene in the head. Several men rushed to break his fall, but Greene was already dead. Johnston considered Greene his best friend. He was devastated that Greene should die performing such "an unassuming act of kindness and friendship."[18]

ON THE OTHER side of the flooded ground and due south of the North Novas, 15th (Scottish) Infantry Division's 46th (Highland) Brigade had reached the improvised defensive line running from Moyland Wood to the Cleve Forest. The brigade had advanced from Hasselt, with its objective being the village of Moyland. Hasselt and Moyland were directly connected by the highway running from

top · A gun crew of 5th Field Regiment's 'B' Troop fires a 25-pounder in the Nijmegen Salient during the winter of 1944–45. Michael M. Dean photo. LAC PA–168908.

bottom · A canoe party of the Lincoln and Welland Regiment rehearses on January 26, 1945, for the Kapelsche Veer assault. Jack H. Smith photo. LAC PA–114067.

top · Lincoln and Welland Regiment soldiers fight the bitter cold in winter camouflage suits after the Kapelsche Veer battle. Harold G. Aikman photo. LAC PA–175530.

bottom · Lieutenant General Guy Simonds, Field Marshal Bernard Montgomery and General Harry Crerar take a break from an Operation Veritable planning session at Montgomery's advanced command post. Photographer unknown. Photo in the author's possession.

top right · This aerial photo of Cleve was taken a few days after the town was heavily bombed on the night of February 7–8. Note the extensive flooding immediately north of the ruined city. Barney J. Gloster photo. LAC PA–145756.

bottom right · An armoured bulldozer and two scissors bridge units gather on the Operation Veritable start line near Nijmegen on February 8, 1945. Michael M. Dean photo. LAC PA–137988.

top left · First Canadian Army engineers on February 8, 1945, unload stone to cover the corduroy base they made with logs to create a usable approach to the Veritable start line. Ken Bell photo. LAC PA–145765.

bottom left · Canadian Scottish Regiment's 3-inch mortar platoon participates in the Veritable pepper pot barrage during the opening hours of Operation Veritable. Note the large stacks of ammunition beside each gun tube. Ken Bell photo. LAC PA–161317.

top · North Shore (New Brunswick) Regiment troops board a Buffalo to begin their advance into the Rhine flood plain on February 8. Colin Campbell McDougall photo. LAC PA–145769.

bottom · Le Régiment de la Chaudière soldiers—partially screened from observation by smoke—advance along a dyke toward Cleve on February 10, 1945. The Canadians of 3rd Division were confined to moving along these exposed dykes by the adjacent floodwaters. Colin Campbell McDougall photo. LAC PA–159561.

top · As 3rd Canadian Infantry Division's forward troops advanced into the Rhine flood plain, moving supplies forward and evacuating wounded became acute problems. On February 13, this supply column carefully inched along a flooded road as men watched for hazards hidden beneath the water. Colin Campbell McDougall photo. LAC PA–143946.

bottom · An amphibious vehicle resupply convoy follows a tree-lined road so submerged it can't be used by regular vehicles. Barney J. Gloster photo. LAC PA–132422.

top · Hundreds of smoke generators blanket the Rhine to screen the Canadian advance from German forces on the opposite bank. This photo was taken from across the inundated flood plain constituting 3rd Division's operational area. Barney J. Gloster photo. LAC PA–145754.

bottom · A Royal Winnipeg Rifles platoon musters in Cleve before advancing toward the Moyland Wood and Calcar–Goch road attack. Colin Campbell McDougall photo. LAC PA–145772.

top · A South Alberta Regiment tank advances along a muddy track near Calcar on February 26. One wrong move and the tank will bog down in the raised mud bordering the track. Jack H. Smith photo. LAC PA–113675.

bottom · Algonquin Regiment infantry ride on South Alberta Regiment tanks struggling through deep mud during the opening of Operation Blockbuster, February 26. Harold G. Aikman photo. LAC PA–113672.

above · This aerial view shows Siegfried Line trenches in the Goch–Calcar road. The surrounding extensive cratering was caused by Allied artillery and aerial bombardment. Barney J. Gloster photo. LAC PA–145756.

left · Sergeant Aubrey Cosens, Queen's Own Rifles, was killed on February 26 at the hamlet of Mooshof after a gallant action for which he received a posthumous Victoria Cross. Photo courtesy of the Queen's Own Rifles Regimental Museum.

left · Canadian troops amid the ruins of Üdem. The armoured bulldozer has been clearing rubble off the muddy road. Donald I. Grant photo. LAC PA–170262

top · On March 1, Major Fred Tilston of the Essex Scottish Regiment earned a Victoria Cross for action during a bitter fight on the edge of the Hochwald. Tilston was gravely wounded, and the battle marked his first and last day as a combat company commander. Michael M. Dean photo. LAC PA–132827.

bottom · German prisoners march to the rear on February 26. The third-from-left man in the nearest row is wearing civilian clothing and wooden clogs. Jack H. Smith photo. LAC PA–145761.

above · This German anti-tank gun was captured during the action fought by the Essex Scottish. The gun enjoyed an excellent field of fire toward the plain across which the Essex attacked. Ken Bell photo. LAC PA–113683.

right · Snaking across the front of the Hochwald just inside the tree line, where the Essex Scottish attacked on March 1, this trench was heavily defended. Ken Bell photo. LAC PA–137036.

top left · Soldiers inspect captured German weapons in a field close to the Hochwald and Hochwald Gap on March 3. In the foreground is a pile of Panzerschrek launchers. Ken Bell photo. LAC PA–166595.

bottom left · Medical personnel unload wounded from an ambulance jeep on March 6 in Sonsbeck. Jack H. Smith photo. LAC PA–113872.

top · A 4th Canadian Armoured Division column pauses in the mud of a small forest near Sonsbeck. Throughout the Rhineland Campaign, the mud was as much an enemy as the Germans. Jack H. Smith photo. LAC PA–138353.

bottom · German artillery fire falls on 4th Canadian Armoured Division troops advancing toward Xanten and Veen on March 7. Donald I. Grant photo. LAC PA–113681.

top · Padre G.J. Murphy of 4th Canadian Infantry Brigade leads a small burial service near Xanten on March 10. Ken Bell photo. LAC PA–167693.

bottom · Playing his trademark left-handed pipes, Essex Piper Archie Beaton pays tribute to fallen comrades at Xanten on March 9. Ken Bell photo. LAC PA–137464.

Cleve to Calcar, but the ground on either flank was badly flooded. So Brigadier R.M. Villiers shifted the axis of advance one thousand yards to the right, sending one battalion along a road a mile south of the highway and another along a ridge between the two.[19]

The 46th Brigade moved into Moyland Wood, which drew its name from the small village. One Canadian Army report described it as "a long, largely coniferous wood, with many clearings, and roads or tracks, running across and through it. The trees are for the most part small, hence there were no obstacles to armoured vehicles. There is a ridge running length-wise along the northern half of the wood, dropping off sharply to the north edge."[20]

This description was deceptive. Moyland Wood was far more complex. Standing on a low escarpment, it overlooked the surrounding countryside—particularly the open farmland to the south. Mostly a mix of fir and pine organized in fairly orderly fashion, the wood also contained smatterings of deciduous trees growing amid these stands and in small pockets of their own. Nowhere did it resemble the normal meticulously organized German state forests. Undergrowth was thick in places and the ground irregular. The forest was about three miles long. Its width varied and was broken by intervening patches of open ground. Some forested sections were a third of a mile wide, others up to a mile. The German paratroopers had transformed this tangled natural obstacle into a deadly trap. Booby traps and mines were plentiful. Tangles of barbed wire snaked between the trees. Machine-gun positions were cleverly camouflaged and spaced to ensure interlocking lines of fire. Artillery and mortar fire could be called on any part of the forest with extreme accuracy. Moyland Wood, as the 15th (Scottish) Division's historian later wrote, was considered by the Germans to be "the key to the defence of the Rhineland."

The 46th Brigade met heavy fire even as it slogged through the seemingly perpetual mud toward the wood. Fighting their way in, the leading battalions became mired in close, bitter battle. Their advance ground to a halt. Attacks met counterattacks. Ground was taken and lost. Some companies were cut off entirely from their battalions and remained so for days. "The ferocious resistance of the German paratroopers" stunned the Scots, as an "unprecedented weight of artillery and mortar-fire" fell upon them. "Moreover, since so much of the fighting took place in woods, the airburst effect of the enemy's fire was unusually deadly. In the woods, too, wireless was wholly unreliable, while cable was being perpetually cut, so runners became the only sure means of keeping in touch. But above all there were the mud and the floods, though the weather itself was fine at last."[21]

On February 15, Lieutenant General Simonds and 11 Canadian Corps officially entered the battle. Major General Dan Spry's 3rd Canadian Infantry Division reverted from xxx Corps to Simonds's command. As 46th Brigade was entangled in Moyland Wood, to be included in 3rd Division's operational area, it came temporarily under Spry's control, while the rest of 15th (Scottish) Infantry Division moved into xxx Corps reserve to rest and refit.[22] 11 Canadian Corps consisted of 2nd Infantry Division, 3rd Infantry Division, and 2nd Canadian Armoured Brigade. The 4th Canadian Armoured Division remained deployed on the Maas under 1 British Corps command. Major General Bruce Matthews's 2nd Division was concentrated in Nijmegen, but was under orders to prepare to advance through 3rd Division to take Calcar. Spry's 3rd Division was currently scattered, with 7th Brigade deployed amid the ruins of Cleve, 8th Brigade's battalions distributed among villages in the flood plain or along its edge, and 9th Brigade holding Kellan, as well as Griethausen east of the Spoy Canal, and the triangle facing Emmerich. It was going to take time to gather these brigades together, but there was currently room in 11 Canadian Corps's sector for only one brigade to support 46th Brigade. That brigade would be Brigadier Jock Spragge's 7th Brigade.[23]

Thirty-seven-year-old Jock Spragge was a veteran at the apex of a distinguished career. He had entered the Cadet Corps in 1921 while attending Trinity College School in Port Hope. Graduating in 1924, Spragge enlisted as a rifleman in the Queen's Own Rifles the following year. He was soon promoted to corporal and steadily progressed up the ranks until making captain on October 26, 1932. Spragge went overseas with the regiment and on April 16, 1942, was promoted to lieutenant colonel and the regiment's command. On

August 26, 1944, at the end of the Normandy Campaign and after garnering a Distinguished Service Order, Spragge took command of 7th Brigade.[24]

Since landing in Normandy on June 6, Spragge had seen almost constant service in demanding command roles. Recently, there had been some discussion by Crerar and other senior First Canadian Army officers that it was time to send Spragge to a non-combat posting for some badly needed rest so he could recover from the stress of commanding a fighting brigade.[25] The pace of operations and lack of obvious replacement led to this decision being repeatedly postponed.

Spragge had established his headquarters inside a rare undamaged house in Cleve on February 13. Here he met Simonds and Montgomery on the morning of the 15th. It was a cool, cloudy day. Spragge took his two superiors on a city tour.[26] Cleve, as the Canadian Scottish Regiment's official historian described it, "was a mess. It had been thoroughly clobbered by the air force and the wreckage and ruins reminded the [men] of Caen. The town was crowded with a mass of British and Canadian troops and vehicles, but there were numerous houses with deep, strong cellars which provided good accommodation for the men during the four days they remained there waiting for return to battle."[27] Spragge, Simonds, and Montgomery soberly looked over the damage, inspected several underground billets being used by the brigade's battalions, examined a couple of remaining bridges, and observed the extent of flooding in and around the city.

Before visiting the battlefront, Simonds had issued a flurry of orders intended to get Veritable marching along smartly. Fifteenth Division's 46th (Highland) Brigade was to clear Moyland Wood and the ground before Louisendorf. Mounted in Kangaroo armoured personnel carriers and supported by a tank regiment drawn from 6th Guards Armoured Brigade, Spragge's battalions would then leapfrog through and seize this village. Thereafter, 2nd Division in company with 2nd Canadian Armoured Brigade would press on to Calcar.[28]

Having seen things close up and taken the measure of how the battle in Moyland Wood was going, Simonds realized that these plans were overly ambitious. Recasting, he assigned the brigade's Royal Winnipeg Rifle Regiment with two squadrons of tanks to advance along the right side of the woods. At the same time, the Regina Rifles with one tank squadron would come up to the left of 46th Brigade and help clear the wood. This attack would take place the following day.

The 7th Brigade attack was to follow on the heels of 43rd (Wessex) Division's 130th Brigade winning a height of ground overlooking Louisendorf and the Calcar–Goch road. Also prior to 7th Brigade going in, 46th Brigade would gain control of the part of Moyland Wood bordering the highway running from Cleve to Calcar. The two British brigades launched these attacks the night of February 15–16.

At 0600 hours on February 16, Spragge moved his tactical head-quarters to Bedburg, establishing it in a building inside the Rhineland Province Insane Asylum. The brigade's concentration area for the attack was immediately east of the village. A road running from Cleve to Bedburg was closed to all but 7th Brigade's traffic from 0800 to 1000 hours to enable its battalions to get into position. News flowing in from the two brigades fighting out ahead was mixed. On the right, 130th Brigade had taken the heights as planned during the night. But 46th Brigade remained locked "in confused fighting in the woods." As the morning wore on, reports from this brigade became increasingly vague and contradictory. Spragge decided he could post-pone no longer. The Little Black Devils—as the Winnipeg regiment was known—and the Reginas would kick off at 1330 hours, regard-less of what was happening in Moyland Wood.[29]

Because of the high ground between, Lieutenant Colonel Lock-hart "Lochie" Fulton and the other Winnipeg officers could only see the upper storeys of buildings and the church steeple of Louisendorf. What German defences lay behind the high ground was unknown, so planning a route of attack was pretty much impossible. Although many regiments had previously ridden Kangaroos into battle, this was a first for the Little Black Devils. The Kangaroos were the inspired brainchild of Lieutenant General Simonds. During the Nor-mandy Campaign, he had realized the need for infantry to be provided with some protective transportation that would enable their keeping pace with tanks. By removing the 105-millimetre gun from American M-7 self-propelled guns, sufficient room was created inside to carry a clutch of soldiers. The Canadians had since fielded an entire specialized regiment, the 1st Armoured Personnel Carrier Regiment, equipped with Kangaroos. In addition to converted M-7's, the regiment also used Ram tanks with removed turrets as armoured personnel carriers. This regiment's squadrons went wherever they were called by Twenty-First Army Group and had won the hearts and minds of many a British and Canadian infantryman. On February 16, its 'A' Squadron, under command of Major F.S. Corbeau, loaded Fulton's men aboard.

Leading the attack were Churchill tanks of No. 3 Squadron, 3rd Scots Guards of 6th Guards Armoured Brigade, and several Flails. The Kangaroos followed with 'A' and 'C' Companies forward and 'B' and 'D' Companies behind. German artillery and Nebelwerfer rocket fire fell around the advancing column, but the Kangaroos' armoured hides protected the soldiers inside.[30] "We rode right to our objectives," Fulton said later, "capturing many German paratroopers...We had practically no casualties of our own."[31] Most of a battalion of paratroopers had been holding Louisendorf. They offered some resistance, and Lieutenants D.F. Harvey and T.M. Dickson of 'B' Company were wounded in the fire. But the majority appeared so shocked by the speedy deployment from the Kangaroos and the fire of the supporting tanks that they just gave up.[32]

'A' Company happened to attack in a sector in which the Germans did put up a fight. The company had run into trouble en route to Louisendorf when two Kangaroos were disabled by shellfire. Only the Kangaroo carrying Lieutenant Harry Badger's No. 9 Platoon reached the company objective. As Badger and his men jumped out fifty yards from the first buildings, they came under machine-gun fire. The platoon charged the buildings and quickly killed the German gun crew. A concrete blockhouse to the right of their position suddenly erupted with gunfire. Realizing his men would be cut to pieces trying to cross the open ground in front of the blockhouse, Badger dashed across the bullet-swept field to reach a troop of Churchill tanks. When he pointed out the blockhouse, the troop commander agreed to send a tank to help. With the tank between him and the Germans firing from the blockhouse, Badger returned to his men. As the tank pummelled the blockhouse with shells, Badger and his men charged in and took the surrender of fifty Germans. Only two of his men had been wounded. Badger was awarded the Military Cross.[33]

Altogether, about 240 paratroopers were rounded up in Louisendorf. The Little Black Devils then set up inside the battered village and awaited news of how the battle had progressed in Moyland Wood.

AS THE CLOCK had ticked down to 1330, the attack deadline of 7th Canadian Infantry Brigade's Brigadier Jock Spragge, a report from either the 15th (Scottish) Infantry Division or 46th Brigade headquarters had reported that "everything [was] going well, against light opposition" in Moyland Wood. The wood, in fact, was said to be completely clear all the way east to a road that cut across the wood from the village of Moyland to intersect the secondary road running from Bedburg to Calcar. About 550 yards west of this road was a narrow track selected to serve as the Regina start line, and it fell well inside the purportedly cleared area.

Like many 3rd Canadian Infantry Division regiments, the Reginas were not at the top of their combat effectiveness. Many veterans fighting since D-Day on June 6, such as Major Gordon Brown who led 'D' Company, "were near exhaustion." Casualties in the eight months since "had been horrendous. Regiments lacked trained and experienced officers and non-commissioned officers, and many soldiers had no battle experience." Brown felt the "gung-ho spirit of 1944 had been replaced with caution and apathy." Some of this malaise resulted from the static period of warfare on the Maas that had stretched from November to the kickoff of Veritable. But it was also a symptom of knowing the end of the war was near, and nobody wanted to be last to die. That kind of thinking made men averse to unnecessary risks and encouraged officers to think as much about avoiding casualties as winning battles. Yet, as "understrength, cautious and lethargic" as they were, Brown also knew that "7th Canadian Infantry Brigade...had a reputation of being highly successful in the heavy going." On February 16, he expected the Reginas would live up to that reputation.[34]

Brown had no idea how badly the cards were stacked against his regiment. As the companies marched to their start line, German machine guns opened up from a small wood behind and to the north of them. This was an area supposedly cleared by 46th Brigade. Lieutenant Colonel Al Gregory had Captain Doug Howat wheel 'B' Company about to drive the Germans off.[35] Howat's men were still so engaged when the brigade's attack was ordered to proceed at 1330 hours. Consequently, the pre-arranged heavy bombardment by field and medium artillery regiments on "all enemy localities and objectives" ended well before the Reginas crossed their start line, and they lost any value it might have yielded.[36]

The battalion plan called for Major Art Gollnick's 'A' Company to push northward across the secondary Cleve–Calcar road and clear the woods ahead through to the northern edge of the escarpment that looked out upon Moyland village. Gollnick's men would then move eastward to "clear the north side of the wood."[37] Recently promoted from captain, Major Gordon Baird would lead 'C' Company's simultaneous advance along the road bordering the wood's southern flank to the "high ground overlooking Heselerfeld and Rosskamp— farmsteads about half a mile south of the Calcar end of Moyland Wood."[38] This ground was the furthermost Regina objective for February 16, and behind it all of Moyland Wood was expected to have been cleared.[39]

Meeting little resistance, Gollnick's men reached the section of forest on the northern flank from which they were to swing eastward to clear the high ground through to the southern extent of Moyland Wood. Suddenly, the forest around Gollnick's men erupted with machine-gun and mortar fire. With men falling dead and wounded, Gollnick ordered the company to dig in. All but surrounded, 'A' Company could go no farther.[40]

'C' Company, meanwhile, made surprisingly good progress along the road with several tanks in support. No. 14 Platoon was on the left-hand flank, advancing with men partly in the thin bush alongside the road and the rest on the road itself.[41] Covering about two thousand yards, the company came to a small stream flowing from the forest a short distance from the southeast corner of Moyland Wood.[42] Although Baird thought the advance's pace meant 'C' Company had caught the Germans off balance, he felt uneasy. To determine whether anything lurked in the woods, Baird sent Lieutenant Frank Shaughnessy's No. 15 Platoon on a reconnaissance. The dense forest seemed to utterly swallow Shaughnessy and his men. After a few minutes, Baird realized he had lost all contact with them.[43] Before he could send anybody to find them, the Germans sprang a cleverly executed trap. While 'C' Company had been advancing, the Germans in the woods had allowed it to pass by—"simply moving from the low to the high grounds, and closing in behind them as they passed." Now, they attacked from the woods to their side and rear.[44]

In the forest, Shaughnessy's men had come upon some abandoned trenches in a small clearing. Like the rest of the Regina platoons, this one was badly understrength—just twenty men instead of the normal thirty-seven. The platoon had just dropped into the trench system to search it when a large number of Germans waving white flags emerged from the woods around them. Believing the Germans were surrendering, the platoon allowed them to close right in. When the Germans standing directly above the men in the trenches pulled guns from under their coats and pointed them down at the hapless Reginas, they could only raise their own hands in surrender. Later that night, one platoon member managed to escape and report the fate of the rest, but his report was sufficiently vague that the German deception was not recorded.[45]

The rest of 'C' Company was caught in a terrific firefight after taking cover amid a cluster of farm buildings. Sergeant Edward Stanley Tenklei had taken over No. 13 Platoon after its platoon commander was wounded in the advance. He led the platoon in three separate charges to eliminate German machine-gun positions. His superb leadership during this chaotic battle would garner a Military Medal.[46] Despite such efforts, 'C' Company was unable to make further headway. At about 2000 hours, Baird pulled what was left of the company back to the start line and they dug in for the night.[47]

At the same time as the Germans sprang their trap on 'C' Company, they had also struck 'B' Company. Captain Howat had just led it into the forest to the left of 'A' Company's assigned line of advance and was fairly close to the secondary road. The company was struck by machine-gun fire from "the left-rear, left-front, and immediate front."

Scattered through the woods around 'B' Company's perimeter lay corpses of men from 46th Brigade. In the middle of the fighting, an officer and five men from one of the brigade's battalions slipped in. The officer reported that they had been hiding among the dead for the past twenty-four hours. Howat incorporated them into his defensive circle.[48]

Brigadier Spragge decided to spend the night putting together a new attack plan for the next morning.[49] The Canadian Scottish Regiment had moved up to positions to the rear of the Winnipeg Rifles. "We were in the midst of a stretch of open ground," wrote the Can Scot war diarist, "and seemed under the eye of the enemy on the higher ground to the north, south, and east."[50] In Louisendorf, the Winnipeg Rifles were sitting tight. The Reginas were badly disorganized after their failed attack. German artillery and mortar fire pounded all the battalions.[51]

One thing was clear. The Germans realized that Louisendorf provided a potential jumping-off point for a further advance eastward through the Rhineland. Lacking troops to immediately counterattack and regain control of the village, they were keen to disrupt any such advance by drenching the area with artillery, mortar, and rocket fire.[52] And they were determined to retain their grip on Moyland Wood. So long as the wood remained in their hands, the advantage the Canadians had gained by winning Louisendorf could not be exploited.

Intelligence gathered during the day identified the Germans inside Moyland Wood as troops from the 346th Fusiliers Battalion of 346th Infanterie-Division, and II Battalion, 60th Panzer Grenadiers Regiment of 116th Panzer Division.[53] Yet both the Reginas and the soldiers of 46th Brigade's battalions insisted they had locked horns with paratroopers from 6th Fallschirmjäger Division.

15

Into Hell

TO THE RIGHT of II Canadian Corps, XXX British Corps had launched a concerted drive toward Goch on February 16. The small city was an anchor point in the German defences, surrounded by strongpoints, entrenchments, and anti-tank ditches. An escarpment a mile north overlooked the Niers River and the city. This escarpment was 43rd (Wessex) Division's objective, and its brigades approached by hooking around the east side of Cleve Forest. In heavy fighting lasting well into the next day, the Wessex pushed 15th Panzer Grenadier Division back almost five miles to gain the escarpment and also sever the Calcar–Goch road. This opened the way for 15th (Scottish) Infantry Division to advance on Goch. The 51st (Highland) Division, meanwhile, had advanced from Kessel toward Asperden. On its right, 52nd (Lowland) Division joined Veritable on February 16, determinedly driving toward Afferden alongside the Maas. Operating between 51st and 52nd Divisions, 32nd Guards Armoured Brigade seized the village of Hommersum and then headed for Hassum, about 2,500 yards beyond. Everywhere the fighting was heavy, the Germans desperate to maintain the Goch–Calcar defensive line.[1]

General Harry Crerar's battle plan for February 17 called upon 3rd Canadian Infantry Division's 7th Brigade and 15th (Scottish) Infantry Division's 46th (Highland) Brigade to finish clearing Moyland Wood. The 2nd Canadian Infantry Division's 4th Brigade would pass through the Royal Winnipeg Rifles at Louisendorf and cross the Calcar–Goch road near Verkält—about midway between these cities. The rest of 2nd and 3rd Divisions' brigades would enter the battlefield between February 17 and 20. Right of the Canadians, 43rd (Wessex) and 53rd (Welsh) Divisions would complete the Cleve Forest encirclement. The 43rd would then send its 130th Brigade in from the north to clear these woods. To the south, 51st (Highland) Division was to secure Hassum and advance on Goch, while 52nd (Lowland) Division would continue toward Afferden. Except for its 46th Brigade, 15th Scottish was withdrawn. So, too, was 6th Guards Armoured Brigade.[2]

The attempt to take Moyland Wood was badly coordinated. While it was evident that 46 Brigade's three battalions—the 9th Cameronians, 2nd Glasgow Highlanders, and 7th Seaforth Highlanders—had been stopped short of the road running through the wood between Moyland village and the Bedburg–Calcar road, their precise location was unknown to the Canadians. A 11 Canadian Corp report placed the 46th Brigade's battalions between the hamlets of Rosendahl and Tillemannskath in the wood's northwestern sector. If true, they were then behind where the Regina Rifles had attacked on February 16.[3] The battalions were also reportedly so beaten up they were incapable of further advances.[4]

Although three Regina companies had failed to make progress in their first attack, the plan for February 17 required Major Gordon Brown's 'D' Company, with the badly shot-up 'B' and 'A' Companies in support, to attack alone.[5] Two 'C' Company Reginas had escaped captivity the previous night and warned brigade intelligence officers there were about 210 Germans in the wood. Normal Canadian infantry company strength was 127 men. 'D' Company counted fewer than 100. Brown led his men forward at 1000 hours through low-hanging fog.[6] His men were to pass through the position where 'B' Company remained dug in, cross a small clearing and the road from Moyland village to the Bedburg–Calcar route, and then seize a section of wood with clearings to its north and south.[7]

'D' Company advanced single file with Lieutenant Warren "Buzz" Keating's platoon leading. Brown and his runner, Rifleman Francis

"Frenchy" Paulin, were up with Keating. The company had no sooner started walking than it came under heavy artillery and mortar fire. Most of the high-explosive rounds detonated in treetops, spraying down deadly shrapnel. A number of men were killed or wounded. When the company reached Captain Doug Howat's 'B' Company, it was met by machine-gun, rifle-grenade, and rifle fire seemingly from every direction. 'D' Company went to earth, the men lying among dead Scottish and 'B' Company Reginas. Brown crawled over to Howat, crowding into his slit trench. Pointing to the clearing, Howat warned it was a prepared killing ground. He had located only a few German positions. The enemy held all the cards. They were dug in and well camouflaged. The moment the Reginas entered the field, they would be cut to pieces. The weight of fire led Brown to estimate that he faced about four hundred enemy. Hell, he thought, a "determined force of 200 defenders, in heavy woods, can hold off hundreds of attackers who simply cannot see their enemy."

While he was conferring with Howat, Keating's platoon dug in alongside 'B' Company. Brown shouted back to his other two platoons for the men to also take cover. With so many dead good guys lying around, Brown could feel his Reginas falling away. Many corpses were badly mangled, missing limbs or with gaping wounds exposing internal organs. Brown "was appalled by the situation."

When he tried to raise Lieutenant Colonel Al Gregory, the wireless failed. Scribbling a message, Brown sent runner Paulin on a one-mile dash back to battalion headquarters.

Brown saw no way to win. The woods were too dense for tanks. Three Churchills assigned to fire their machine guns and main 75-millimetre guns from hull-down positions on the edge of the woods were still firing blindly. Brown figured their fire hurt only trees. Artillery might have helped, but the Reginas had no forward observation officers. So artillery was going to be inaccurate, as likely to strike Reginas as Germans.

The clearing formed a rough triangle. "They had placed machine-guns along their two sides of the triangle, while we were pinned down among the dead on our side. We were being invited out into the open where we could go nowhere but into hell." Brown thought things over, and by the time Gregory summoned him to headquarters in the late afternoon had a plan that could be executed the next morning.[8]

AN HOUR BEFORE 'D' Company's abortive attack, German artillery had started pounding Louisendorf—a bombardment that continued through the day. "This is the heaviest shelling the battalion has ever been subjected to," the Royal Winnipeg Rifles war diarist recorded.[9] Through this fiery storm the Little Black Devils pushed 'C' and 'D' Companies, with the Carrier Platoon supporting, only a few hundred yards east of the village to cover the approaches.[10]

Left of Louisendorf, 7th Brigade's Brigadier Jock Spragge had ordered the Canadian Scottish Regiment to advance across open country and seize the high ground overlooking Heselerfeld and Rosskamp. These farmsteads were a half-mile south of Moyland Wood's southeastern corner.[11] 'B' Company was already dug in behind the road that had served as the Royal Winnipeg Rifles' start line on February 16. Lieutenant Colonel Larry Henderson sent 'A' Company under Captain P.F. McDonnell and Captain Harvey Bailey's 'D' Company through 'B' Company's position. To gain the farms, they must advance about 1,500 yards. About every 700 yards in this country south of Moyland Wood, a road branched off at right angles from the Bedburg–Calcar road. There were about a half dozen of these. One provided the Canadian Scottish start line, and another lay midway to their objective. A small cluster of buildings alongside this road would need to be secured. The attack was to be supported by a 3rd (Armoured) Battalion, Scots Guards tank squadron. During Henderson's morning Orders Group, the tank officer had said, "Of course... we shall want to go ahead of you when you get to those houses."

"I've been looking for someone like you all during the War!" Bailey quipped. "I've never found anyone who wanted to get ahead of me in the attack."

The tanks actually led the way from the beginning, finding the spongy ground still sufficiently firm to provide fair going. Smoke shells completely obscured the buildings in order to blind any defenders. More artillery was falling on the two farmsteads. As one tank troop swept out left and then wheeled to fire on the buildings,

Bailey's 'D' Company rushed in and cleared them without difficulty. Consolidating a hundred yards beyond the buildings, Bailey fired a red flare to call the tanks to him. The moment the flare shot up, the Germans began shelling the buildings. The fire struck just as 'A' Company was passing by. Several men were hit. 'A' Company formed up on 'D' Company's right and, tanks again leading, the attack continued up a gentle slope.

There was no opposition in the open ground itself, but intense machine-gun fire poured from Moyland Wood to the left. Some machine guns also fired to the right. The rate of artillery and mortar fire falling increased the closer the companies got to the objective. When the two companies gained the high ground's summit and started frantically digging in, one tank troop commander came alongside Bailey's slit trench and shouted that the tanks intended to withdraw, as they seemed to be drawing the mortar and shellfire. Bailey agreed, but asked that they go back only eight hundred yards and provide supporting fire. "That's quite all right, old boy," the troop commander shouted. "We shan't leave you with your suspenders unbuttoned."[12]

As night fell at 1600 hours, the tanks withdrew completely. "That night there was no sleep," Bailey said later. "The enemy shell fire... continued, ably assisted by sniping on the part of fanatic German troops. Movement was restricted and both companies were content with holding what they had." Several supporting artillery shells fell on the Can Scots. "This only added to the nervous strain already caused by enemy shelling."[13] It had been a costly attack. One officer wounded, twenty-six other ranks wounded, and six killed.[14]

IT WAS DARK when Major Gordon Brown returned to the Regina's headquarters. Lieutenant Colonel Al Gregory offered "a friendly smile" and shepherded him into a separate room so they were alone. There was great impatience from up the command chain, Gregory said. Corps was demanding Moyland Wood be cleared without delay. Division HQ was snapping at Brigadier Spragge, who in turn insisted that Gregory order 'D' Company to attack immediately. Brown warned this would mean "frittering away one company after another while achieving little or nothing."

Brown set out his alternative. Station tanks on either side of the wood. Two Regina companies follow the tanks on one side and two Winnipeg Rifle companies the tanks on the other flank. Bypass the triangle entirely under cover of darkness and enter the woods behind. The result should panic the Germans and possibly split their force in two. In the dark, the tanks would be less vulnerable. No sign of German armour or anti-tank guns had been detected in the woods, so the British tanks should be relatively invulnerable. This joint tank-infantry assault was more likely to succeed than any infantry attack against Germans as well dug in as these were.

Finished, Brown advised Gregory that he refused to lead 'D' Company into the triangular killing ground. Take the plan up the chain. Get it or something similar approved and Brown would commit his men. Gregory warned that Brown was playing with fire, refusing a direct order. He could be court-martialled.

Better that than lead men to slaughter, Brown replied. Gregory "shook his head and smiled grimly." Then he said, "Okay, Gord, you've convinced me that we must have a new plan, along with an artillery barrage and an aerial bombardment. I don't know how the brigadier will take to the idea, but I'll let you know. Wish me luck."

A few minutes past midnight, Gregory called an Orders Group. Gregory took Brown aside. Both of them, he said, "were in serious trouble for taking such strong stands against the brigade plan." Despite much argument, Gregory had won only a compromise. Three Regina companies would attack at first light, supported by the battalion's flame-throwing Wasp carriers and its carriers mounted with machine guns. During the pre-dawn hours, these companies would slip back undetected from their current positions. They would then use the predictable morning fog to cover a move across open fields to the point alongside Moyland Wood that 'C' Company had reached on February 16. 'B' Company would lead off from here by attacking into the wood block that brushed up against the Bedburg–Calcar road. Once 'B' Company was four to five hundred yards into the trees, 'D' Company would leapfrog it and take a wooded ridge about a hundred yards beyond. At the same time, 'A' Company would enter the woods left of 'B' Company and strike the Germans guarding the triangle from behind.

262 / FORGOTTEN VICTORY

The plan was non-negotiable. And once carried out, Gregory and Brown must report to brigade headquarters. Brown disliked the scheme. It struck the Germans from only one flank. They would be able to shift men to block 'B' Company's advance and then shred the other two companies as they came forward. Still, better than sending 'D' Company head-on to its doom inside the triangle. Brown told Gregory he hoped to be alive and unwounded in order to accompany Gregory to the brigade meeting.

Withdrawing from in front of the triangle went off smoothly, and Brown was reasonably sure the Germans had not detected their leaving. February 18 dawned with the expected thick fog that cloaked the Reginas as they walked silently to the right of the road where some farm buildings provided a start line.[15] This was just opposite the northwestern corner of where the wood brushed up against the Bedburg–Calcar road.

THE PRECEDING NIGHT, whatever German forces were deployed in Moyland Wood had been reinforced by 1st Battalion, 18th Fallschirmjäger Regiment of 6th Fallschirmjäger Division.[16] On February 16, this paratroop division had started relieving the devastated 84th Infanterie-Division between the Cleve–Calcar highway and the Rhine. At first, the division's 16th Regiment, elements of the 346th Infanterie-Division, and some companies of 7th Fallschirmjäger Division were available. But the following day, the full strength of this last division's 19th and 21st Regiments arrived. By the night of February 17–18, 6th Division's 17th and 18th Regiments had also entered the line.[17]

Most paratroopers in these divisions had never parachuted into battle. They were paratroops only in name, performing a purely ground infantry role. But the identity mattered. They were "the cream of German manhood," recruited into the Luftwaffe to serve as paratroopers—indoctrinated into the cult of the German fighting man, convinced of the rightness of their cause and of their superior fighting skill as opposed to that of any enemy.[18]

Major Gordon Brown believed they "were probably the best troops we had faced, and they were now fighting in defence of their homeland. They were not wild-eyed Nazis like the ss back in France, but brighter and just as dedicated."[19]

To the left of these paratroop divisions, 116th Panzer Division was slowly being forced to give ground. Passing some of its frontage to 6th Fallschirmjäger Division's Generalleutnant Hermann Plocher's troops, however, enabled this division to consolidate and remain a potent, deadly force. Yet as the Germans backed away toward the Calcar–Goch highway, they retained Moyland Wood as a salient of resistance—a salient that kept the Cleve–Calcar highway closed and prevented 11 Canadian Corps from committing more divisions to the battle. This was why Lieutenant General Guy Simonds was clamouring for the Regina Rifles to get it cleared.

Delays in teeing up the attack pushed it back to 1230 hours, by which time the fog had long since lifted.[20] As 'B' Company crossed the start line, it came under intense shell, mortar, and small-arms fire. On the right, No. 10 Platoon's commander, Sergeant William James Shaw, realized that the worst fire was coming from the woods directly ahead. Fearing his men would go to ground, Shaw rushed to the head of the lead section and directed the men into the woods. A fierce close-range gunfight, often degenerating into hand-to-hand fighting, ensued. Shaw "was seriously and painfully wounded" but continued to lead the platoon to its objective about four hundred yards inside the wood. Only then did he agree to evacuation. His bravery was recognized by a Military Medal.[21]

The leading platoon to the left of Shaw's platoon suffered many casualties during the advance and began to falter. Seeing this, Captain Doug Howat ran across the bullet-swept ground and through shell bursts to rally the survivors. Once the platoon was tied in with Shaw's men, Howat went back and brought the reserve platoon forward. Badly cut up in the advance, 'B' Company continued to take casualties as it was battered by continuous shellfire. Having dug in, Howat and his men waited for the other two companies to pass it by and take the pressure off.[22]

'D' Company's two leading platoons, led by Lieutenant "Buzz" Keating and Sergeant Hunt Taylor, soon charged through 'B' Company's lines and made for the forested ridge a thousand yards distant.

The company had been heavily shelled and fired upon by a sniper even before they reached the woods. Rifleman Chris Vogt was number two man on a Bren gun team in No. 16 Platoon. The platoon was soon closing on its objective when a barbed-wire fence on top of the ridge that faced a small clearing blocked the way. A German machine gun opened up, and Vogt dropped to the ground in front of the wire, bullets pinging off the strands above his head. Suddenly, the Germans manning the gun bolted, abandoning the weapon. No. 16 Platoon hurtled the wire and dashed into the now empty trenches. Keating shouted at Vogt to turn the German machine gun around and fire its ammunition off in the direction of the enemy.[23]

Brown had accompanied the reserve No. 17 Platoon, made up mostly of inexperienced men. Almost immediately after 'D' Company passed through 'B' Company, the officer lost sight of his forward platoons in the dense, dark woods. His group veered off course to the left and almost stumbled into the triangular killing ground. Having spun their machine guns about, paratroopers guarding the field lashed out with a hail of bullets and began chucking grenades at the startled Reginas. Several men fell dead or wounded, while the rest dived for cover behind the nearest tree. Brown ordered the platoon to fall back to 'B' Company and reorganize. "There was a lot of firing going on and chaos reigned supreme." The Wasps had tried to advance with the rifle companies, but the dense woods blocked their way. One Wasp commanded by Sergeant Milton Adolph managed to navigate just past 'B' Company's position before throwing a track. Seeing a paratrooper crouched behind a large tree, Adolph jumped down, punched the man, and wrestled his rifle away. The German stumbled off, almost ran into Brown, and became the company's first prisoner in the battle.

Brown had no idea where his other two platoons were. He and Howat tried several times to go forward and find them. "We were met by grenades and bullets, escaping death only by crawling on our stomachs. It was pointless." A shell smashed into a tree close to them. Brown felt blood trickle down his forehead and wiped it away. A shrapnel fragment "had gone through my steel helmet and stopped on my forehead. I was able to pick it off, but I was exhausted and badly shaken." Brown decided there was nothing more he could do here. It was time to go back and report to Lieutenant Colonel Gregory. To hold their tenuous gains, the companies needed reinforcement and an infusion of those officers kept back as Left Out of Battle.[24]

Back at headquarters, Brown discovered there was no further talk about him and Gregory being called on the carpet for disobeying orders. The situation in the wood spoke for itself. At this point, the Reginas were going to be lucky to hold out.

As No. 17 Platoon had fallen back to 'B' Company's lines, two of its men were inadvertently left behind—Rifleman Dwight Small, a Bren gunner, and his second. They had been pinned behind a small bush by fire from three machine guns. Realizing there were suddenly no Reginas on either side of him, Small asked the other man where everybody had gone. The man had no idea. Taking all the Bren magazines, Small said that once he started firing, the man was to run about 150 yards to some dense brush, which would provide cover. Small opened up and the man ran for it. When the man was safe, Small snatched up the Bren and followed him. Bullets swarmed about, but none struck home.

The two crept through the forest until they bumped into a Regina sergeant. When they said they were from 'D' Company, the sergeant said, "You're with 'A' Company now." They dug in alongside 'A' Company, which was to the left of 'D' Company. Sometime during the night, No. 17 Platoon's officer came and retrieved his two lost soldiers.[25]

As darkness closed in at 1600 hours, the Reginas in Moyland Wood were in rough shape. 'B' Company numbered only about thirty-two effectives.[26] Out on the ridge, 'D' Company counted twenty men in the two platoons. Keating was their only officer. They were cut off and under constant counterattack. The Germans were, in fact, relentlessly counterattacking all three company positions and trying to infiltrate between 'D' and 'B' Companies. To counter this, 'C' Company sent a depleted platoon to fill the gap. "Resistance from the enemy never slackened," stated one report. "Counterattacks, mortar, artillery fire, and snipers prevented any further forward movement. All the Reginas could do was cling to the ground won."[27]

Yet, as Regina Major Eric Luxton wrote, "Brigade headquarters were screaming that the wood 'should have been cleared by now and what were we doing about it.' The huge casualty list was a mute answer."[28] As their third day in Moyland Wood closed, the Reginas reported more than a hundred casualties.[29]

AT 1330 HOURS on February 18—an hour after the Reginas had launched their disastrous attack—the Canadian Scottish's 'B' Company had kicked over another hornet's nest. Commanded by Major Earl English, the company had advanced toward the high ground won the previous night by 'A' and 'D' Companies. This ground overlooked the Rosskamp and Heselerfeld farmsteads east of Moyland Wood. Both companies had been hunkered down in slit trenches to escape unrelenting mortar and shellfire ever since reaching their objective. As the regiment's historian put it, they were "out on a limb to an extent where on their left they could overlook the wooded hills which [was] the final objective for the Reginas. The intervening ground, open and undulating, also came under the observation of the enemy so that 'B' Company...was up against a tough proposition when it was ordered to push forward to seize the crossroads at [Rosskamp,] a few hundred yards beyond Heselerfeld."[30]

As 'B' Company sought to reach the forward companies, the men walked through heavy artillery and mortar shelling. Company Sergeant Major James Little Nimmo sent three men back because they "couldn't take any more of the punishing shelling...The going was tough. The soft ploughed fields deep in mud." Reaching the summit, the company formed up to begin its attack. A supporting barrage began to fall on Rosskamp and Heselerfeld. Nimmo thought this was just fine, but the company "couldn't seem to get going to take full advantage of it. The enemy MG and mortar fire was hellish. In no time at all we had lost half our lead platoon and the attack threatened to bog down." English sent Nimmo to see what was holding things up. Reaching the lead platoon entailed crossing about two hundred yards, and rounds from a sniper snapped past his head the whole way. "Damn lucky not to be hit!" he thought.

Using the platoon's wireless, Nimmo summoned English, as "the situation was really grim. Then all hell broke loose again. The ground was literally covered by a mass of singing lead. As we were in fields and soft ground we dug in bloody fast. Casualties were mounting and that didn't help matters...In the circumstances, we couldn't move one inch."[31]

'B' Company was only about a hundred yards ahead of the other two companies. Staying put was suicide. English decided the company must push on. To the left, the Germans had turned a building into a blockhouse. To the right, about three or four hundred yards distant and between positions held by the Can Scots and Winnipeg Rifles, a cluster of buildings sheltered several machine guns. Dashing back and forth from his company to those behind, English arranged for supporting cover fire.[32] Once this was ready, he sent Nos. 10 and 12 Platoons forward at about 1700 hours to seize the blockhouse. No. 11 Platoon threw out covering fire. "It was a hell of a fine effort," Nimmo remembered. Although No. 12 Platoon was quickly pinned down, No. 10 Platoon got through. They sent back twelve prisoners and word that "they intended to stay for the duration."[33]

Once the attack was well along, an 'A' Company platoon under Lieutenant J.H. Gray had rushed the cluster of buildings to the right. Gray's men set up a defensive position inside the houses. Exhausted, perhaps deriving a false sense of security from the protection of stout walls, most of the men soon fell asleep. Just before midnight, the Germans silently counterattacked. Only three Can Scots escaped. The rest, including Gray, were taken prisoner. It was a hard blow for 'A' Company, slashing its strength to about thirty men.

Things were no better for the other two companies. 'D' Company counted only about 30 men. 'B' Company had suffered 40 casualties. At most, 150 Can Scots were out in the blue.[34] Their situation was tenuous. Nimmo had managed to tie 'B' Company's platoons together in some semblance of a defence based on the blockhouse. He had men crawling through the darkness to scavenge ammunition and grenades off the dead and web belts discarded during evacuation of the wounded. A plan to bring up a food truck had gone awry when it strayed right past the companies. Realizing something was amiss, 'B' Company's Quarter Master Sergeant R. Fitzgerald had the driver stop as the truck approached an apparent sentry. Fitzgerald's request for directions was met by gunfire. He and the cook, Private W.A. Thorsen, were wounded. Fitzgerald crawled back alone to the Can Scot lines. Unscathed, driver Private S. Berry could have, as the Can Scot war diarist later wrote, "come back by himself and...been congratulated for having escaped...almost certain death; but he preferred to stay and accept the greater risks involved in aiding his comrade." Berry managed to carry Thorsen safely back.[35]

English was the senior surviving officer out front, so he went back to battalion headquarters for instructions. All three 'B' Company lieutenants had been wounded, leaving Nimmo in charge. This was of no concern. Nimmo was a seasoned and competent non-commissioned officer.

At battalion tactical headquarters, Lieutenant Colonel Larry Henderson told English and 'C' Company's Major R.H. Tye that his orders from Brigadier Jock Spragge were to renew the advance. Captain Harvey Bailey's 'D' Company would pass through 'B' Company's battered ranks and descend a steep slope to seize Rosskamp. At the same time, 'A' Company would advance on the right and capture a German strongpoint that was harassing 'B' Company. These limited objectives made some sense. 'C' Company, however, was to turn about and punch northeast along a narrow road running from Louisendorf to intersect the Bedburg–Calcar road. This would bring the company up to the easternmost extent of Moyland Wood and a farmstead called Rosenboom. The disjointed attack, with two companies going off a good half-mile from 'C' Company's objective, was to start at 0730 hours on February 19. A fifteen-minute barrage on all objectives was to provide some support. The heavy mists of morning were also expected to give a little cover. Henderson made it clear to English and Tye that he had vigorously protested the 'C' Company orders, but Spragge had been adamant.[36]

SPRAGGE'S ORDER WAS the desperate response of a man without options. Attendees of the meeting Spragge had called that evening in his Bedburg insane asylum headquarters included the division's Major General Dan Spry and Lieutenant General Guy Simonds. General Harry Crerar was planning for First Canadian Army to regroup in order to reinvigorate the campaign with a new operation, code-named Blockbuster. But this could not proceed until II Canadian Corps uncorked the bottleneck created by Moyland Wood.

"Simonds was pushing me and I was pushing the brigadiers and battalion commanders," Spry said later. "He was very determined. Just by the glint in his eye and the set of his jaw you knew what he wanted. When he was angry, he became icy."[37] At Verrières Ridge in Normandy, in the flooded polders of the Scheldt Estuary, and now here amid the mud and dense woods of Moyland Wood, Simonds's impatience manifested itself. Rather than admit a need to reorganize for a major divisional-scale offensive against Moyland Wood and the ground east of it, Simonds insisted that exhausted and depleted battalions immediately win the day. And he was ready to take scalps to make it happen. During the meeting, it became clear that Spragge's head was on the chopping block and Spry's likely to soon join it. Simonds condemned both for being overly cautious, too worried about avoiding casualties, and lacking verve. The failure was theirs and nothing to do with unsound tactics coming down from their superiors.

So there would be attacks on February 19, even if they were almost sure to fail. There must be action. The Reginas would hold, face down the unrelenting counterattacks. And the Can Scots must attack.

Making the decision especially exasperating to Spry and Spragge was the fact that Simonds had earlier cut orders that promised to relieve some pressure on the embattled battalions of 7th Brigade. Why not just wait for these to develop? Simonds had ordered that at noon on February 19, 2nd Canadian Infantry Division would enter the operation. First, its 5th Brigade would relieve the worn-out 15th (Scottish) Infantry Division's 46th Brigade from their holding positions in the western part of Moyland Wood.[38] The Scottish brigade's troops emerged from the forest "dead tired, unshaven, unwashed, hungry and thirsty...All were to agree that it had been the worst experience they had endured since the campaign began."[39]

While relieving the Scots tidied things up by returning them to where their division was currently resting up for participation in a forthcoming assault on Goch, it did nothing to improve the situation of II Canadian Corps. Simonds hoped 2nd Division's 4th

Infantry Brigade would achieve that. The 4th Brigade was to attack from the ground held by the Winnipeg Rifles at Louisendorf to reach the Goch–Calcar highway and its intersection with a road running from Bedburg to Üdem.[40] This thousand-yard advance would relieve the Little Black Devils so that they could launch a renewed 7th Brigade effort against Moyland Wood. The attack would be carefully developed, properly supported, and initiated on the morning of February 21.[41]

[16]

Pitched Battle

INSIDE MOYLAND WOOD, the ragged three Regina Rifle Regiment companies met the fog-shrouded dawn of February 19 somewhat surprised to be still alive. Throughout the night they had repelled numerous counterattacks. Their situation had been slightly improved when Captain Dick Roberts—having taken over 'D' Company from Major Gordon Brown—led No. 17 Platoon through to join the rest of the company.[1]

Lieutenant Buzz Keating and Sergeant Hunt Taylor had held the two isolated platoons together until this relief. Hunkered in a slit trench, Keating would raise his head just high enough to see. When the paratroopers emerged through the fog or out of the cover of the trees, long grey greatcoats flapping and coal-bucket helmets unmistakable, Keating waited a few seconds to let them come well into range. "Up!" he then yelled. Rifleman Chris Vogt and the others would rise with guns blazing, grenades flying. Each time, the Germans melted back into the fog or treeline, leaving some dead and wounded behind. One paratrooper, braver and clearly more determined than most, overran a Regina position and tried to take prisoners. Using Keating's shoulder to brace his rifle, Taylor shot the German dead. Lowering the rifle, Taylor politely thanked the lieutenant for standing still.[2]

All three companies had new commanders drawn from Left Out of Battle cadre normally retained for rebuilding the battalion should it suffer disaster. Major Len McGurran had replaced Captain Doug Howat at 'B' Company and Captain Bill Jansen took over 'A' Company from Major Art Gollnick. As Major Gordon Baird's 'C' Company had spent most of the previous day in reserve, he was deemed fresh enough to take the tiller. With so many platoon officer and sergeant casualties, there were insufficient replacements to relieve those who survived.[3]

A good number of men in the Reginas were being brought out of the line. "Although not actually casualties," the war diarist recorded, they were "suffering from exhaustion due to the continual shelling and the nature of the woods."[4]

CANADIAN SCOTTISH REGIMENT Captain Harvey Bailey of 'D' Company and 'A' Company's Captain P.F. McDonnell launched the battalion attack on time at 0730 hours on February 19. The two companies headed down the slope toward Rosskamp and Heselerfeld, while 'C' Company moved along the road from Louisendorf toward Rosenboom and Moyland Wood.[5]

'C' Company had spent the night supposedly behind the other Can Scot companies. But its position had suffered endless shelling that by dawn had resulted in seven casualties and several more men evacuated for battle exhaustion. Major R.H. Tye led just sixty-seven men out into the mist. Company Sergeant Major Campbell "Chum" Morgan kept close beside Tye. Morgan was worried. The heavy shelling and fighting had "many of the men in quite difficult nervous condition," he wrote. "This condition is no novelty on the battlefield where every soldier going into battle is afraid; he is not human if he has no mental disturbances before action begins."[6] This time, however, an aura of doom seemed to hang over them.

It was eight hundred yards to the objective. Nos. 13 and 15 Platoons led, each spread out on opposite sides of the road. The ground was gently rolling and too muddy for tanks. A smokescreen fired by mortars and a concentration of artillery on and around Rosenboom was to help them. Tye had been assured there were few Germans. It was the shelling, not German infantry, that had inflicted so much damage on the Can Scots.

Three hundred yards out, this assertion was proved wrong when a line of machine guns concealed in camouflaged slit trenches on the edge of the woods unleashed a terrific fire. Both leading platoons hit the dirt, and a call for more smoke was issued. The mortars responded instantly and accurately. The Can Scots got up, moved on and crossed the Bedburg–Cleve road. They started up the gentle slope leading to the woods and the farmstead "in a magnificent show of steadiness," as their regimental historian observed. The enemy fire never slackened. In fact, it increased as more guns from the front and the right flank joined in.

About two hundred yards behind the leading platoons, Major Tye, his command section, and No. 14 Platoon were just crossing the Bedburg–Cleve road when the guns on the right flank found them.[7] A burst of machine-gun fire punched into Tye's thigh. "He was unable to do more than crawl to a shell crater from where he directed as much of the remaining action as possible," Morgan wrote. "I was also hit but only slightly injured, so took over the company and crept forward to observe the two platoons, which had by now disappeared over the crest of the ridge. The machine-gun fire seemed to increase in intensity, forcing me to change my mind about reaching the platoons."[8]

'C' Company was divided into two by "withering fire coming at right angles between the leading and follow-up" parties. Tye tried to call for more smoke, but the wireless was broken.[9] "During all these desperate minutes," Morgan reported, stretcher-bearer Private Dan Elder "moved around among the wounded men as they writhed in their pain. He was bravely oblivious of the MG slugs and shrapnel which buzzed about him. As he went from one casualty to the other he carried a Red Cross flag on a stick which he placed in the ground as evidence to the enemy that he was doing non-combatant work; it was to no avail as they continued to snipe at him."

Morgan was helping to treat the wounded men Elder brought to the shell hole when he saw some fifty Germans emerge from the direction of the forward platoons. Tye and Morgan assumed those platoons had been surrounded, taken prisoner, or killed. Realizing that 'C' Company was all but eliminated, Tye told Morgan to try taking Lieutenant Colonel Larry Henderson the news. Morgan shouted for any men able to retreat to do so. Several joined Morgan in a mad dash across the road. "All the way we were chased by MG bullets which tried to prevent our escape. However, luckily no more casualties were caused." When Morgan reported 'C' Company's fate to Henderson, the battalion commander pushed the support company forward to plug the gap created by the disaster.[10] "Only six men escaped from the holocaust into which they had stepped," the Can Scot war diarist reported.[11]

To the east, 'D' Company had advanced a short distance past 'B' Company's position to a burned-out barn at the crest of the hill leading down to Rosskamp. Here, it was drenched by machine-gun fire. The fire came from close by. Captain Harvey Bailey realized that during the night the Germans had infiltrated ground previously considered won. In fact, the paratroopers had been readying an attack on 'B' Company when Bailey's men approached out of the mist. One Bren gunner had his weapon smashed when a Panzerfaust rocket struck it smack-on without exploding. The gunner suffered not the slightest injury.[12]

Bailey saw Lieutenant K. Spencer fall wounded while leading the forward platoon "into the pitched battle. Obviously the element of surprise was lost so an operation based on stealth was impossible. The barrage was not due to come down for 15 minutes and already the fighting had begun." Bailey ordered a withdrawal back on 'B' Company's position.[13] 'A' Company had, meanwhile, reached its objective of the small building to the right where the Germans had established a strongpoint. But McDonnell had no strength to do anything more. All told, the three companies overlooking Heselerfeld numbered 130 men of all ranks. In the failed attack, one officer had been wounded, and twenty other ranks were dead, with seventeen wounded. Another three officers and forty-one other ranks from 'C' Company were missing and presumed captured.[14]

As an offensive unit the Canadian Scottish were finished. German fire continued to slash them. Any movement invited immediate shots from snipers, and machine-gun bursts. Men continued to die or be wounded. "There was no reserve force left... and with all companies so thin on the ground and attempting to defend such an exposed area the situation was precarious. There was little the unit could do by itself except dig in and hope that other attacks planned by the 2nd Division on the right would relieve some of the pressure on the [their] front."[15]

THE DESIRED RELIEF by 2nd Division materialized at noon. It was an all-out effort—nothing remotely resembling the piecemeal attacks required of 7th Canadian Infantry Brigade. Fourteen field regiments from five divisions, seven medium regiments, two heavy batteries of artillery—about 470 guns—and 1st Canadian Rocket Battery unleashed a withering barrage. The Toronto Scottish (MG) Regiment's medium Vickers machine guns and 4.2-inch mortars also lent indirect fire support toward enemy positions around the hamlets of Brunshof and Göttern.

Most of the guns—those of ten field and six medium regiments—provided a rolling barrage.[16] This was timed to advance in lifts of a hundred yards every minute and a half to match the standard pace of armoured vehicles.[17] Because the ground was so open, the leading two companies of 4th Canadian Infantry Brigade's attacking battalions rode inside Kangaroos. For the Essex Scottish Regiment on the right, 'A' and 'D' Companies were out front. On the left, the Royal Hamilton Light Infantry's 'A' and 'B' Companies led. Both battalions' other companies advanced behind on foot to mop up pockets of resistance the men in the Kangaroos had bypassed during the race to the objective—high ground east of the Calcar–Goch road. The Essex Scottish headed toward Brunshof and Göttern, while the Rileys centred on Schwanenhof and a scattering of farmhouses just northeast of Ebben.[18] Support company Bren carriers and flame-throwing Wasps protected the flanks of the marching infantry.[19] Advancing with the mounted infantry of each battalion was a squadron of tanks—each fielding sixteen Shermans—of the Fort Garry Horse Regiment. It was a heady day for the Garrys. They would be the first Canadian tankers to enter battle inside Germany.[20]

It had rained heavily the preceding night and at noon was still bitterly cold, with heavy cloud threatening more precipitation. As the Royal Hamilton war diarist noted, such weather "was not very promising for an attack...Road conditions were bad making vehicle movement slow."[21]

Looking southeastward from Louisendorf, Lieutenant Colonel Denis Whitaker could see a "narrow country road, hard-surfaced, dead straight, with barely space for two tractors to pass, connecting the market towns of Goch and Calcar." It was utterly ordinary. "I could plainly see across the stubbled brown field sloping gently upwards to the road 2,000 yards away. Dotted here and there were farmhouses and sheds. To reach our objective my men had to cross that open stretch. But 'upwards.' I recall a disquieting thought: we were on the forward slope. What lay over the top?"

Whitaker's greater concern was his exposed left flank. With fighting still under way in Moyland Wood, he had no idea how many Germans lay in wait in the open ground to that side. That was why the support company Brens and Wasps advanced alongside the marching infantry. He had also sent a section of the battalion's anti-tank platoon to each forward company and the third to 'C' Company; which would be on the left to the rear.

As the barrage began, Whitaker scrambled onto Major Harvey Theobold's Sherman and climbed inside. Theobold's 'B' Squadron was supporting the Rileys, while Major Bruce MacDonald's 'A' Squadron backed the Essex Scottish. Like most infantrymen, Whitaker hated riding in tanks. Felt helpless inside one. But he wanted to get to the Calcar–Goch road just behind the forward companies and set up a tactical headquarters inside a milk plant alongside it. From there, he could better monitor and support the advance toward Schwanenhof. Burdened by his battle gear and map case, Whitaker squeezed into the narrow co-driver's seat and took in the limited view offered by a thin vision slit. Whitaker imagined that if the tank was hit and started to burn, all his gear would make escape impossible.[22]

The success of the attack, one army report concluded, ultimately "depended on whether the armoured vehicles could negotiate the boggy ground on the way to the objective." Both the Kangaroo squadron's commander and Fort Garry Lieutenant Colonel Eric Mackay Wilson were confident "they would have no trouble." As the Shermans and Kangaroos crossed the start line, however, they wallowed through ever-deepening mud. Several became stuck, but the others pressed on.[23]

On the Essex Scottish front, Sergeant Don Elvy headed up the crew of one of the battalion's 6-pounder anti-tank guns. Normally, a carrier would have towed the gun, but on this day it was hitched behind a Kangaroo with the crew inside. Well short of the objective, the Kangaroo mired. Elvy and his men unhooked the gun, flagged down a passing carrier loaded with ammunition, and hitched it up. Even towing the 2,640-pound gun, the lighter carrier rode easily over the ground toward the objective. Elvy was concerned to see that a lot of 25-pounder artillery shells were burying into the mud before detonating, greatly reducing their effect.[24]

Halfway to the Goch–Calcar road, the Canadians started taking fire from "a strong anti-tank screen...which included many 88-millimetre guns in well-sited positions and ably protected by infantry of [12th Fallschirmjäger Reconnaissance Regiment]." The guns and mines started taking a toll on the Rileys' Shermans and Kangaroos.[25] As Lieutenant Gordie Holder guided the support company carriers and Wasps to the left of the advancing troops in an attempt to engage the German guns, he was killed in the "first slashing burst of fire from the German 88's."

Major Joe Pigott, commanding 'C' Company, saw many of his marching men fall. Suddenly, "we were taking one hell of a licking. The 88's made it so hot for the Kangaroos that some of the companies were dropped short of their objective. We finally got there, but we had about fifty percent casualties."[26]

When Theobold's tank arrived at the milk plant by the Goch–Calcar road, Whitaker saw the leading troop of the Fort Garry Horse's 'A' Squadron moving into open ground ahead. Suddenly, two of the troop's tanks exploded in flame, and 88-millimetre shells disabled the other two. Glancing left, Theobold thought all the Riley carriers burned. "Then I saw the German 88s. Our radio net was jammed—it seemed as if 75 people were trying for the same airtime! I was screaming, trying to get on the air to the fellows and warn them." Whitaker heard Theobold shout at his driver to reverse. Two shells narrowly missed the tank before it reached the protection of the milk plant.[27]

As Theobold was stopping his tank alongside an abandoned 88-millimetre gun, Whitaker shouted, "Let me out of this tin can." The relieved infantryman dashed into the creamery and was soon joined by his tactical headquarters team. Theobold, meanwhile, was still finding it almost impossible to communicate with his other tanks. The Garrys had gone into the attack with wireless sets all operating on one frequency—known as the "regimental system." This system was normally used when a regiment's squadrons were each supporting a brigade and so separated that messages passing within each squadron would not be intercepted by the tanks of a different squadron. But here, with 'A' and 'B' squadrons operating almost side by side, the single frequency kept jamming. Every time Theobold tried to communicate, the net was clogged with excited voices of men from 'A' Squadron. It appeared things were going badly on the right flank of 4th Brigade's attack, but Theobold could not determine whether the situation there was worse than his own.[28]

Out front in the Rileys' sector, Major Duncan "Dunc" Kennedy's 'B' Company was on the left. The Kangaroos had carried it about two hundred yards past the road before the fire so thickened that the infantry were ordered to bail out. Kennedy told Lieutenant John Williamson, commanding No. 10 Platoon, to provide fire support while he led the rest of the company to the farmstead of Schwanenhof. In particular, Williamson was to provide covering smoke with the platoon's 2-inch mortar. When the platoon turned up only thirteen smoke bombs, Williamson had those fired off. Seeing the company disappearing amid some farm buildings just short of Schwanenhof, Williamson led his men running to catch up. A machine-gun bullet struck Williamson in the leg and he collapsed in a shell crater. A stretcher-bearer put some sulfa powder on the wound and bandaged it. His men having gained the cover of the farm buildings, Williamson hobbled through the fire to join them. The company dug in, already having to fend off Germans trying to infiltrate the position by coming up a ditch 150 yards to the front of the buildings. A steady exchange of rifle fire followed. Williamson limped over to Kennedy to report, finding him standing next to a piece of farm machinery. As Williamson came up beside the major, a bullet rico-cheted off the machinery and pierced Kennedy's stomach just below his belt. He was quickly carried to the shelter of a basement, which the major declared would serve as his company headquarters. Ken-nedy made it clear he was not being evacuated. He would fight from this hole in the ground.

Behind the lead companies, 'C' Company was shredded by intense machine-gun and anti-tank-gun fire striking its exposed left flank. The machine guns were in a hedgerow and the house and barn of a small farm. Between the company and this position was only open ground. Most of the men were poorly trained reinforce-ments. Major Pigott tried to keep them moving, pushing on to the objective despite the rain of fire. Falter, he had warned, and you die. They were to do what he did. Now he was running forward and the men around him were hitting the dirt.

At this critical moment, three Wasps emerged out of the smoke with Sergeant Pete Boles in command. Pigott pointed to the hedge-row, the barn, and the house. "There are Germans in that house!" he shouted. "Go and burn the bastards out!" The carriers ground toward the little farm and let loose their deadly flame. "The fuel was a black jelly that stayed in a mass like a tube of toothpaste," Boles recounted. "You'd fire it on the ground—that damned stuff, it would crawl along the ditch and over the top...It would stick and burn and keep on burning. If you ever got it on your clothes you were a goner. It was devastating." Boles burned the barn and house to the ground. The fire spread to the hedgerow as 'C' Company came through it. 'C' Company moved on to another farm and captured it. As the Wasps were out of flame, Pigott ordered Boles to go and rearm.[29]

Pigott started getting 'C' Company dug in around the second farmyard. Unlike most of his men, Pigott had years of combat expe-rience. He had fought with a British battalion in North Africa under a plan providing Canadian officers with fighting experience. He had landed with the Rileys in Normandy, fought through that campaign, and survived the bloodbaths of the Scheldt Estuary Campaign. Pigott had one eccentricity. He stubbornly wore an experimental type of body armour issued in Normandy. Over three thousand British-made light armour protection units had been supplied to 2nd Canadian Infantry Division for testing. Consisting of three sections of canvas-covered, one-millimetre-thick manganese steel plate linked by webbing that offered general protection from the shoulders to just above the groin, each weighed two and a half pounds. The plate material matched that of the standard-issue British helmet. Designed to be worn under the uniform, the body armour was well padded.[30] But it still chafed and promoted heavy perspiration. This had led most soldiers to jettison it long before. Nobody knew anybody but Pigott who still wore the armour, which he claimed had saved his life on many occasions.

As the company dug in, Company Sergeant Major Stewart Moffatt was knocked to the ground by a sniper bullet that tore through his jaw. Having been wounded on August 1, 1944, this was his second serious injury. Pigott, who had been standing at his side, picked Moffatt up and headed for the farmhouse. He planned to leave him in the house for the stretcher-bearers to pick up. "When I opened the door, there was a German standing there with a stick-grenade in each hand. We stared at each other. He was pretty scared, I guess, and I think that if I had yelled at him he would have surrendered. Anyway, he flipped the grenade. It hit me on the chest and exploded."[31]

The grenade blew a huge dent in Pigott's body armour that left his chest black and blue for six weeks. But the armour saved him from being torn apart. A metal shard of the grenade, however, pierced Pigott's windpipe and the explosion threw him into the farmyard. Moffatt had also survived the grenade. For both men the war was over.[32]

'C' Company was in terrible shape. Pigott was gravely wounded. Lieutenant George Ratchford Thomson was dead. Lieutenant J.R. Sams had been wounded, suffering severe powder burns to his eyes. Moffatt, the senior sergeant, was down. Lieutenant R.W. Wright of the pioneer platoon had accompanied the company, so he assumed command until its second-in-command, Captain Ben Bolt, could come up from the rear.[33]

Despite its inexperience and the loss of so many leaders, once 'C' Company dug in, the men steadied. They drove off repeated German counterattacks, holding their "positions with determination," as the Rileys' war diarist acknowledged.[34]

ON THE RIGHT flank, the momentum of the Essex Scottish attack had carried it to about two hundred yards short of its objectives of Göttern and Brunshof. Here, deepening mud and intensifying fire forced the Kangaroos to unload the infantry. Two Shermans supporting Major Ken MacIntyre's 'A' Company had been knocked out and a third disabled. The rest of the 'B' Squadron tanks stood off from the farmsteads and slammed them with fire while, "under a heavy hail of shrapnel and small-arms fire," the infantry stormed in.[35] By 1345 hours, elements of the lead companies were established inside the farmsteads after a very stiff and confused fight in which 'A' Company suffered heavy losses. The losses included the men of one section taken prisoner when a German tank overran their position. Both 'B' Company's Major Francis Chauvin and 'C' Company's Major Stanley McDonald were wounded short of the farmsteads. McDonald's company was on the Essex right flank and had come under terrific fire from German positions south of it. This was unexpected, because the Essex Scottish had understood that 214th Brigade of 43rd (Wessex) Division was to be advancing alongside and protecting their flank there. But the British troops were nowhere to be seen.[36]

The 4th Brigade's Major Charles Barrett, posted to 2nd Division headquarters, claimed that 214th's Brigadier H. Essame had decided the Canadians could handle the situation and directed his efforts toward supporting 43rd Wessex's advance on Goch.[37] Essame's brigade had been part of a three-division assault that had started on the night of February 17–18. The brigade had forced nine crossings over the major anti-tank ditch protecting Goch's northern flank. By February 19, British troops were fighting the Germans amid Goch's bomb-damaged ruins. During the day, the German garrison commander surrendered his troops. But confused fighting raged outside Goch, particularly to the south, for forty-eight more hours. On February 20, 214th Brigade would shift direction and seize the village of Halvenboom to the south of the Canadian flank. Although the Canadian Army's official historian credited this move with "helping to shield the right flank of the hard-pressed 4th Canadian Brigade," the British troops were a mile south of the Essex—more than sufficient room for the Germans to operate with virtual impunity between.[38]

Whatever the reason for the British absence on February 19, by 1500 hours the Essex had 'A' Company inside Göttern, 'D' Company at Brunshof, and 'B' Company immediately right of Brunshof amid the buildings of another smaller farm. Even as the situation appeared to be stabilizing, the Germans counterattacked with infantry and tanks. Because the Essex right flank was exposed, the counterattack struck from both the front and south.[39]

The tanks of 'A' Squadron had expended their smoke rounds covering the Essex advance, and in Major Bruce MacDonald's Sherman the other ammunition types were being burned through at a furious rate. Seeing German infantry running toward the farm buildings the Essex were in, the tanks in MacDonald's headquarters troop lashed them with coaxial machine-gun fire. German artillery and mortar rounds were exploding around the Shermans and among the farm buildings. Soon the loader in MacDonald's tank shouted that they had only four rounds of armour-piercing shell left and 150 rounds for the coaxial machine gun. A second later, a high-explosive shell scored a direct hit on MacDonald's Sherman and smashed one radio aerial. This severed his communication with the infantry. The counterattack was strengthening by the minute. MacDonald realized the Germans were using a depression to his left to close in on the farm buildings. He ordered the Sherman of No. 3 Troop mounting the 17-pounder gun—more powerful than a standard 75-millimetre gun and intended as a German tank killer—to engage the Germans in the depression. The tank had just passed MacDonald's tank when its track was shot off. Despite being immobilized, the tank crew made "many 'good Germans'" out of the counter-attacking force," MacDonald said later.

The situation for 'A' Squadron and the Essex was rapidly deteriorating. MacDonald's wireless woes had so increased that he was only able to communicate with his No. 1 Troop. The troop commander reported that the two following Essex companies were pinned down and taking heavy casualties. MacDonald's 17-pounder tank took another direct hit and the crew bailed out. Then a shell smashed into his Sherman. Ammunition all but exhausted, MacDonald "with more alacrity than dignity" ordered everyone out of the disabled tank.

"Immediately we hit the ground, we were sniped at." MacDonald contacted the artillery forward observation officer supporting the Essex. All 'B' Company officers were either dead or wounded, the man said. He had been commanding the company until also being wounded. MacDonald ordered the artilleryman to the rear. The Essex battalion's signals officer, Lieutenant Kenneth Jennerette, joined MacDonald in a slit trench. MacDonald saw his tank crew heading to the rear. He and Jennerette stayed, hoping to link up with the infantry. Jennerette started digging with a shovel toward a nearby slit trench in the hope of reaching the soldiers there. Germans inside a nearby building were firing from its attic. A bullet pierced Jennerette's wrist. "He tried to jump from one slit into another so that he could get bandaged, and with the second shot, the sniper hit him in the abdomen. He was...in considerable pain and I passed him my morphine Syrette...There was then little we could do but watch and wait...The sound of our artillery passing overhead was some solace, and we kept our ears cocked, hoping momentarily to hear the rumble of relieving tanks, plus 'C' and 'D' Companies. They didn't come, but the Boche did, throwing hand grenades into our slits from 50 feet away and after most [of the nearby Essex] were wounded, one stood up with his hands in the air and the rest of us followed suit."

Before surrendering, MacDonald tore off his rank badges and got rid of any documents indicating he was an officer. The prisoners were marched into the German lines on what would be a ten-mile trek. Pretending to suffer shell shock, MacDonald staggered listlessly along and fell slowly farther and farther back from the main column. There were only about three guards in charge, and they paid his lagging little heed. Seeing a slit trench beside the road, MacDonald slipped in and lay down. The column was two hundred yards distant before the Germans realized he had disappeared.

Although the guards came back, they were unable to find him in the darkness and soon gave up. MacDonald returned to the Canadian lines the following day, bringing with him much intelligence on locations of German artillery and other positions. His actions in supporting the Essex attack and escaping captivity garnered a Distinguished Service Order.[40]

DESPITE MOUNTING CASUALTIES and losing some men as prisoners, 'A' and 'D' Companies of the Essex Scottish retained a tenuous grip on the two farmsteads of Göttern and Brunshof. To their left, the Rileys also clung to the ground won. Even when the Germans committed fresh formations, the two battalions fought on. At about 2000 hours, a battle group of Panzer Lehr Division attacked the Rileys, while fresh troops of 116th Panzer Division struck the Essex. The Panzer Lehr had deployed on the Rhineland front during the evening of February 18, establishing its base at Marienbaum—a village midway between Calcar and Xanten. Once one of the army's most elite armoured divisions, Panzer Lehr had been badly mauled during the Ardennes offensive and only recently rebuilt with an infusion of young and ill-trained recruits. The division was, however, "still capable of fierce fighting." While fielding only twenty-two tanks on the night of February 19, it had plenty of infantry.[41] Panzer Lehr had mustered three regular infantry battalions, a reconnaissance battalion, and an engineer company. It had also added a battalion of artillery to the mix. Some of these guns were self-propelled, enabling them to play a limited but potentially deadly role as mobile armour.[42]

According to standard Allied practice and because most tanks had exhausted their ammunition, by 2000 hours the Fort Garry Horse had returned to their regimental harbour to replenish and carry out necessary maintenance. This left the Rileys and Essex to fight alone. As the night "wore on more counterattacks began to come in against the Canadians," one report later stated, "and all supported by heavy artillery and mortar fire, which caused many casualties. At least seven of these attacks were thrown in against [the Essex], each with renewed vigour." At about 2300 hours, Lieutenant Colonel John Pangman "reported that the situation about him was becoming critical; his forward area had been overrun, and enemy tanks were firing on his headquarters." The Rileys reported "fighting fiercely to beat off two counterattacks against [their] left flank, which had penetrated the forward defences and were slowly overrunning 'C' Company."[43]

Pangman and his battalion tactical headquarters had followed the Essex infantry companies aboard a Kangaroo. When the Kangaroo was disabled just to the rear of the forward companies, Pangman and his party had set up in a farmhouse. By 0300 hours on February 20, the building was surrounded by German tanks and infantry. Pangman and his men were in the building's cellar, which had a strongly built ceiling. Lieutenant Horace Tucker, the Essex intelligence officer, stayed above ground with a small number of men to engage the Germans. Tucker cut down several enemy troops with bursts from a Bren gun until he fell seriously wounded. The defenders were forced back into the basement, two men from the Carrier Platoon setting up a Bren gun at a bend in the stairway. After they killed six Germans descending the stairs, the enemy pulled back. A short time later, a Panzerfaust round struck the farmhouse and set it on fire. Then a tank smashed through an outside wall and ground back and forth on the main floor in an attempt to collapse the cellar ceiling. Corporal Armand Kain, one of the two men manning the Bren, grabbed a PIAT and ran up to the main floor. He fired two rounds in an unsuccessful effort to knock out the tank before being driven back into the cellar by heavy fire. Desperate, Pangman burned his papers and maps. He then ordered the two men manning the Bren gun to begin the process of surrendering. Kain, who was one tough soldier, said he didn't believe in surrender and refused. The dire situation was saved by Major Joe Brown of 4th Canadian Field Regiment, who was Pangman's forward observation officer. He managed to raise his regimental headquarters and asked Lieutenant Colonel MacGregor Young to fire artillery directly on the farm building.[44] When Young asked if Brown was certain, the FOO replied, "It's our last resort...position overrun by tanks and infantry."[45] All of 4th Field's twenty-four guns drenched it with shells that caught many Germans in the open. The immediate pressure on the battalion headquarters eased.

In Göttern, Major Ken MacIntyre's 'A' Company had been reduced to thirty-five men capable of fighting and a number of immobilized wounded. A surviving remnant of 'D' Company was also still in the fight amid the battered buildings of Brunshof. 'B' and 'C' Companies were not much better off. The platoons of both were scattered in slit trenches such a distance apart that they were unable to support each other. These companies, however, were not surrounded and had established communication links back to 4th Brigade headquarters. They reported holding at the Calcar–Goch road but having no contact with their battalion commander. "The early hours of the morning were grim ones," the Essex war diarist wrote. "Isolated company groups fought on, short of ammunition, burdened with casualties which could not be easily evacuated and lacking support of the anti-tank weapons with which to deal with the [Mark IV] tanks the enemy had marshalled for his counterattack."[46]

To the left of the embattled Essex, Lieutenant Colonel Denis Whitaker was swamped by reports of relentless counterattacks. At Schwanenhof, Major Dunc Kennedy's 'B' Company had been attacked head-on by tanks, and German infantry were swarming in from the flanks. Crawling out with a PIAT, Lieutenant D.W. Ashbury managed to knock one tank out. But the infantry were soon infiltrating through the company lines and threatening to overwhelm it. From his platoon's position, Lieutenant John Williamson thought the farmhouse in which the badly wounded Kennedy had established his company headquarters had fallen. He managed to reach Whitaker by wireless and reported that the "situation was desperate."[47]

It was 0135 hours. Whitaker reported to brigade headquarters that he had a company overrun and was counterattacking to save it.[48] Whitaker's only possible reinforcement consisted of the battalion's scout platoon—about twenty-five men under Lieutenant Johnny Lawless. The scouts crept silently through intervening German troops and surrounded the Schwanenhof house where Kennedy was holed up. When Lawless gave the signal, the scouts "started yelling and making a terrific noise, throwing many grenades through the windows before rushing in. The operation was a complete success. Twenty-five Germans were killed or wounded and another 50 taken prisoner; our only casualty was Lawless, who was slightly wounded by shrapnel from one of his own grenades. 'B' Company position was finally stabilized," Whitaker reported.[49]

[17]

Sheer Guts and Determination

A COUPLE OF HOURS before midnight on February 19, Brigadier
Fred Cabeldu had advised 2nd Canadian Infantry Division's
Major General Bruce Matthews that 4th Brigade was in dire straits.
Matthews immediately placed 6th Brigade's Queen's Own Cameron
Highlanders temporarily under Cabeldu and ordered them to "stand
by for counterattack role or to relieve elements of 4th Brigade."[1]
Cabeldu decided to have the Camerons take over the brigade's firm
base position from the Royal Regiment. He could then send the Roy-
als to save the Essex Scottish Regiment.

Teeing up the rescue effort took time, leaving the Royal Hamilton
Light Infantry and Essex Scottish fighting on alone through to dawn.
The situation continued to worsen alarmingly. At 0315 hours, 'D'
Company sent a message to brigade that it was withdrawing from
Brunshof with just thirteen men combat effective.[2] Company Sergeant Major Les Dixon and Lance Sergeant Bill Moriarty had played a
major role in preventing this small group from being overrun. The
men had taken refuge in a cellar. When German infantry, covered by
machine-gun fire from supporting Panzers, rushed the building,
Dixon and Moriarty met them with Bren gun bursts and PIAT
rounds. After a grenade blast threw both men down the stairs, they
rushed back to the entrance. Several tanks then tried to close in, but
Dixon drove them off with the PIAT. The tanks then stood off and

proceeded to "reduce the house to a mass of rubble...but despite a veritable hail of shrapnel and splinters the intrepid pair remained at their post." When the Bren gun jammed, Dixon shoved it down the stairs for somebody to clear, and the two men fought on using German grenades and rifles taken from men they had killed.[3] Finally, the Germans—demoralized by the heroic stand—pulled back. This enabled 'D' Company to extract itself. Dixon—a decorated veteran of the Dieppe raid—was awarded a second bar to the Military Medal he had won in 1942.[4] This made him the only Canadian soldier in the war to win the decoration three times. Moriarty also received a Military Medal.[5]

Cabeldu had been busy at the Royal Regiment's headquarters. He told Lieutenant Colonel Richard Lendrum that if the Royals "could get in quickly they might recover a good many Essex Scot[tish] who would be pinned down in slit trenches." The attack was set for 0900. After Cabledu left, Lendrum sat down with 4th Canadian Field Regiment's commander, Lieutenant Colonel MacGregor Young, to organize a supporting artillery program. Young was exhausted. During the past day and night he had directed delivery of artillery involving at varying times the guns of up to twenty regiments "with scarcely a halt."[6]

A half hour late, 'A' and 'C' Companies crossed their start line with the Fort Garry Horse Regiment's 'C' Squadron. "The advancing Royals found that shell and mortar fire constituted the principal hazard in this attack," wrote the battalion's official historian.[7] Despite inevitable mud, none of the tanks bogged down and they provided such close support that casualties were initially light. No tanks were knocked out, but 'C' Company had several men wounded by a Panzer firing from hull-down position. 'A' Company soon reached the Calcar–Goch road, and the tanks knocked out a 75-millimetre anti-tank gun and a half-track mounting a smaller anti-tank gun.[8]

By 1030 hours, 'C' Company's Major Jack Stother was in wireless contact with Essex Scottish commander Lieutenant Colonel John Pangman. The Essex battalion headquarters party, he informed Lendrum, was trapped in the cellar of a demolished house. Stother then advised Pangman that "relief was on the way...and to keep his head down." Soon 'C' Company arrived. Eighteen men were holed up in the cellar. Several, including Essex intelligence officer Lieutenant Horace Tucker, were badly wounded.

Before Stother could arrange for carriers to evacuate Pangman and his people, the Germans counterattacked. When Stother said he must withdraw to reorganize his men, Pangman and the other fit Essex refused to leave the wounded. The eighteen men hunkered back in the cellar. When a German officer holding a grenade appeared at the top of the stairs, an Essex corporal shot him dead. Although the Canadians kept a wary watch, they were paid no further attention.

At about 1400 hours, Stother's 'C' Company returned with carriers in tow. The wounded were loaded and carried away. After looking the position over carefully in the light of day, Stother declared it "a poor one tactically as enemy tanks could come up very close to it unobserved and fire on it from hull-down positions." Leaving one platoon in place to cover the withdrawal, he pulled 'C' Company and those of Pangman's party fit to walk back to a more secure position. The remaining platoon then withdrew from the ruined farm.

Cabeldu and Lendrum were in agreement that the Germans between the Calcar–Goch road and the Essex objectives of Göttern and Brunshof were too strong for one battalion to defeat. The Germans continued to plaster the ground with shell and mortar fire. Throughout the morning and afternoon, both the Rileys and the Royals were forced to repel counterattacks. But their grip on the Calcar–Goch road remained unyielding. It was soon evident that the Germans could keep punching away, but the Canadians were not going to give ground. They were, as 4th Brigade's war diarist declared, "proud holders of the ground won, ground strewn with the enemy's dead and equipment."

The last gasp by Panzer Lehr struck the Rileys at 1800 hours, when troops and tanks charged from the northeast. Cabeldu responded by sending 'C' Squadron of the Fort Garry Horse into the darkness to bolster the Riley defence. A company of Queen's Own Camerons was also rushed in. Two hours later, the German attack collapsed. At 2000 hours, Lieutenant Johnny Lawless and seventeen men of the scout platoon sallied out of 'B' Company's position inside

Schwanenhof to raid a position the Germans had used for forming up attacks. They caught the Germans off guard, killed about twenty-five, and captured about fifty. One prisoner said the remains of his company, No. 5 of the 902nd Panzer Grenadier Regiment of Panzer Lehr, had been destroyed by the scouts.[9]

The Germans conceded the loss of the highway. On the night of February 21–22, Panzer Lehr—having lost many men captured and an untold number killed and wounded—withdrew to the west of Üdem. Most of the eleven German tanks and six 88-millimetre guns confirmed as knocked out by 4th Brigade's stubborn stand were from this division. Panzer Lehr soon departed the Rhineland to join Heeresgruppe B.[10]

Essex Scottish continued to emerge. Men who had hidden out until finding an opportunity to escape, sections that fought their way through the Germans, and, the next day, the remnants of an entire company all came in. The battalion's adjutant, Captain Fred Tilston, organized them. At 1035, the battalion counted its strength at only 6 officers and 140 other ranks out of 25 officers and 540 men who had gone into the attack. By day's end, the numbers increased to 17 officers and 395 other ranks.[11] Then, at 0300 hours on February 21, Major Ken MacIntyre and Lieutenants M.C. Millan and P.F. McDonnell "returned from what was thought to be the land of the missing." MacIntyre had received no instructions to withdraw, so 'A' Company had stubbornly held Göttern until it was clear the Germans had either fled or died. The company's 35 fit men brought their wounded out in a slow, methodically executed withdrawal. "All their deeds of valour can never be recorded but each man came out, after nearly two days of close unsupported combat with the enemy, a veteran," the Essex war diarist wrote.[12] MacIntyre's courageous leadership was recognized with a Distinguished Service Order, an award also given to Pangman. In all, eight Essex Scottish—including Dixon and Moriarty—earned medals.

The Essex final casualty total was set at 55 killed, 99 wounded, and 54 lost as prisoners. The Rileys reported 125 casualties. Six of its number garnered awards for their valour, including Lieutenant Colonel Denis Whitaker, who added a bar to the DSO received for heroism during the Dieppe raid. All too often the contribution of anti-tank units was overlooked, but for this day Lieutenant David Heaps of the 18th Canadian Anti-Tank Battery's 'C' Troop received due recognition. He and his crews, manning 17-pounder anti-tank guns—working in support of the Rileys—were credited with seven German tank kills, and Heaps was awarded a Military Cross. The Royals suffered sixty-four casualties steadying the line. Including some Queen's Own Camerons casualties, 4th Brigade's final casualty tally for February 19–20 was precisely four hundred.[13] "All units have done an exceptionally fine job of fighting," the brigade's diarist recorded. The Rileys were particularly singled out for their "outstanding example of a well planned and executed operation and of the ability of our troops under good leadership and by sheer guts and determination to take and hold difficult ground against the enemy's best."[14]

WHILE 4TH INFANTRY Brigade had fought to retain its foothold on the Calcar–Goch road, 3rd Division's 7th Brigade had remained at Moyland Wood. Inside the forest, the Regina Rifles were continuously pounded by artillery, mortar, and Nebelwerfer fire. They repelled regular counterattacks. Like most other Reginas, Rifleman Dwight Small of 'D' Company's No. 17 Platoon had been fighting relentlessly for two and a half days and three nights by February 21. Hunched behind his Bren gun, Small thought "it was a miracle we held off the Germans! We were firing on the Germans almost constantly and throwing more grenades than I ever had in my life." Small had little idea what happened beyond the slit trench he shared with his Bren crew second. Once a day, the platoon commander and his runner passed over a supply of ammunition and a can of bully beef. Lying in his slit trench on February 21 with the routine morning mist cloaking the woods, Small checked the action of the Bren gun and expected to start firing any moment. He saw no end to the ordeal.[15]

Both the Reginas and the equally embattled Canadian Scottish Regiment on the high ground to the right were too beaten up to do more than cling to the ground won. The Can Scots had fended off a strong counterattack on the early morning of February 20 and then met another directed at 'B' Company alone. The enemy involved in the last counterattack were forced to ground seventy yards short of the company's position. The Germans took cover in a depression "from which even the heaviest artillery concentration could not budge him." Wasp flame-throwers found the ground too muddy to attack. The paratroopers were finally left where they were.[16]

Plans had been afoot since late afternoon of February 19 to relieve the situation by having 7th Brigade's third battalion, the Royal Winnipeg Rifles, attack the wood. Brigadier Jock Spragge had been much involved in planning the attack, but he was not to see it implemented. At 1400 hours on February 20, Spragge gave a final Orders Group to coordinate the role of artillery, tanks, and infantry in the operation. Spragge then left to assume command of an infantry-training brigade in England.[17] Lieutenant General Guy Simonds had swung the axe, relieving Spragge in the normal Canadian Army manner by either promotion or a cross-posting. Either way, the result was transfer to non-combat command. Only in the most egregious circumstances was a high-ranking commander demoted or dismissed.[18] Although the Moyland Wood debacle arose from a failure by corps headquarters staff to first recognize that the Germans held it in strength and then to provide adequate reinforcement when the situation was better understood, Spragge—a popular and highly experienced combat officer—served as a convenient scapegoat. Lieutenant Colonel Al Gregory assumed temporary brigade command until a replacement from England arrived.

The area of Moyland Wood held by the Germans had been carefully divided into sectors running west to east and identified alphabetically from A to E. Each sector was three hundred yards wide. A fire plan called for the wood to be saturated beginning thirty minutes before the attack. Artillery, 4.2-inch mortars, anti-tank guns of all 7th Brigade battalions, along with the medium machine guns of the Cameron Highlanders of Ottawa, were to participate. The Camerons would be firing their Vickers machine guns over open sights. Most of the bombardment preceding H-Hour was to be directed on the sector of forest facing the start line—Sector A. When the attacking force crossed the start line, the lighter-calibre guns—the anti-tank guns, mortars, and machine guns—would lift their fire to B Sector for forty-five minutes, then to C Sector for thirty minutes, D Sector for forty-five minutes, and finally E Sector for thirty minutes. The field and other artillery supporting the attack would shift fire to concentrate on "known, and likely, enemy positions, north and east of the wood."

'B' Company on the left and 'D' Company the right would lead. Because the woods were so dense, only four tanks from 'B' Squadron of 2nd Canadian Armoured Brigade's Sherbrooke Fusiliers Regiment were in support. Two Shermans would operate alongside each leading company. Twelve Wasp carriers, which were more nimble, were also provided—six being those inherent to the Winnipeg battalion and the other six drawn from the Can Scots. The plan was for Wasps to support the leading companies. Operating in relays, one group of Wasps would work with the infantry, while the other was reloading its deadly mixture of flammable fuel. In this way, the leading infantry should enjoy continuous support. H-Hour was set for 1000 hours.[19] When the idea was first broached, Lieutenant G. Ran Wybourne, commanding the carrier platoon, had objected strenuously to the unorthodox plan. Carriers were not normally deployed in heavily wooded areas, he argued. Royal Winnipeg Rifle Regiment commander Lieutenant Colonel Lochie Fulton had smiled, and "reassured the young officer that everything would be all right."[20]

By 0800 hours, the Little Black Devils were forming behind the Regina Rifles inside the wood. The men hurriedly dug in, correctly anticipating their arrival had been noted and would draw defensive artillery fire. Three machine guns to their left began firing from woods on the other side of a clearing. These guns had been harassing the Reginas for days. Fulton decided they needed to be silenced before the attack went in, so Major Hugh Denison's 'D' Company was sent to do so. Denison's men quickly carried out this task and fell back to their start line just five minutes before the attack began. With the company somewhat muddled, the attack was shifted back. Instead of 1000, the two companies went forward at 1012 hours.

To avoid getting into the woods and becoming easy prey for paratroopers packing Panzerfausts, the Sherbrooke tanks established firing positions on higher ground, where the road running through the forest to Moyland village intersected a narrow track next to the open ground on which 'D' Company had cleared off the German machine-gun crews. The tanks threw out a terrific rate of fire with their 75-millimetre main guns and 30-calibre coaxial machine guns.[21]

As soon as the Little Black Devils started advancing, the Germans opened with their artillery and mortars, dropping shells behind the Canadian barrage in sure knowledge that infantry were moving there. As the Reginas had experienced before them, the shells exploded in treetops, creating a shrapnel rain of steel and wood fragments. 'B' Company's recently promoted Major Harry Badger and all its platoon commanders fell wounded.[22] Lieutenant Bob Gammon in 'D' Company was killed. Many men in both companies were left dead, dying, or wounded. The advance never faltered, and the two companies cleared the Germans before them until reaching the far edge of Sector A. This was their objective. Seeing paratroopers running toward a farm building in the direction of Moyland village, 'B' Company loosed a volley of Bren gun fire that dropped several of them.

February 21 had proved to be a rare clear, sunny day. The overcast skies and rain of the previous five days had grounded the fighter-bombers of 2nd Tactical Air Force. But today they were out in strength, with No. 84 Group directly supporting the Moyland Wood attack. Having spotted the Germans fleeing into the building, several Typhoons swept down and savaged it with rockets. Forty minutes after crossing the start line, the two companies reported their objectives clear and secure.[23]

'A' and 'C' Companies moved past the leading companies and entered Sector B. Six Wasps slithered through the mud, spouting flame at conceivable hiding places for Germans. The sector was cleared without meeting any opposition, the flame-throwers credited with having "terrified the enemy." Leapfrogging in freshly loaded Wasps to replace those with exhausted fuel worked like a charm. "It proved of double value," one report stated later, "to bolster the morale of our troops while undermining that of the enemy. The fire plan was still carrying on, and the attack was running to schedule." Things got rockier when the two companies entered Sector C and came under renewed and deadly artillery and mortar fire. The shrapnel rain cut men down, while the well dug-in Germans were impervious to the Canadian artillery.[24] German snipers shooting from well-concealed holes exacted a terrible toll on officers easily identified by their efforts to direct the men through the thick woods. All of 'A' Company's officers were struck down. A sniper wounded Captain J.R. Morgan and one other officer, and Lieutenants Frederick Ernest Walsh and Kenneth Patterson Pritchard were killed. Sergeant Alf Richardson took over the company. 'C' Company's Lieutenant E.E. Gridley fell with a wound, his third suffered in combat. Lieutenant A. Bruce MacDonald, recommended for a Military Cross for heroism on February 9 during the battalion's attack on Keeken in the Rhine flood plain, was also wounded.[25]

"The advance was painful and step-by-step, with close-quarter fighting controlled by the remaining NCOs [non-commissioned officers]," a Winnipeg report recorded. "The enemy positions were revealed only when they opened fire at close range. The German paratroopers were well dug in and camouflaged, and the advancing troops had to crawl forward determinedly to reach cover and fire back."[26]

'A' and 'C' Companies grimly cleared D Sector. Men were being cut down all the way through this block of woods. When they reached the other side, 'C' Company had two officers and forty men left. 'A' Company counted no officers and just twenty-five men.[27]

Ahead of 'C' Company was a well-prepared position on a height of ground held by two hundred paratroopers. Major Charlie Platts led his men forward with the Wasps rolling along beside. The Germans were "dug in and supported by mortar fire and air-burst artillery, its position ringed with mines and trip wire. But with flame, heavy machine-gun fire and assaulting infantry, the position was stormed and overrun. Some were killed, a number escaped, and only five were taken out alive."

'A' Company had gained and seized a position on the high ground, and Sergeant Fred Bragnalo's point platoon looked down upon a stretch of open ground and a small wood about two hundred yards to the east. From these woods the paratroopers came in groups of thirty to forty in three successive counterattacks, "but were caught in the open by artillery fire directed by a forward observation officer in the 'A' Company position. A heavy toll was inflicted," the Winnipeg report stated.[28]

'B' and 'D' Companies firmed up on the two leading companies. 'B' Company counted about fifty men, so Fulton assigned it to consolidate the battalion hold on the high ground. Carrier Platoon's Lieutenant Wybourne reinforced 'A' Company with those of his men not crewing the Wasps and assumed its command. Sector E remained to be cleared. Only 'D' Company was strong enough to make the attempt. At 1400 hours, Major Hugh Denison led the company out of 'C' Company's lines. Sector E proved to be defended by two machine guns on the eastern edge and by "riflemen in pits" all through the woods. Three Sherbrooke tanks provided closer support in this attack because the woods were less dense here, and a boundary track running east to west allowed good access for the tanks to operate single file.[29] The fourth tank supporting the infantry had earlier run over a powerful mine and brewed up. The co-driver, Trooper Robert James Elliott, was killed and three other crewmen wounded.[30] The wood here proved to be heavily mined with both anti-tank and anti-personnel charges. But they were not planted in any real pattern, being hastily "and promiscuously laid." Still, they caused many casualties.

Despite the opposition, Denison's men cleared Sector E. The eastern edge of this sector was the terminal point of Moyland Wood. Here it came to a narrow point. From the cover of the trees, 'D' Company looked out at a row of houses. They bristled with paratroopers. There were so many anti-tank mines identifiable in front of all the exits from the wood that the tankers warned Denison they could not help with clearing the buildings. The Sherbrookes withdrew to the right, where some buildings provided sheltered positions for them to offer limited flanking fire. No sooner had the tanks moved away than about twenty-five "enemy launched a wild counterattack. Throwing grenades and firing Schmeissers from the hip, they charged our positions, yelling in English: 'Get your hands up!'" At this desperate moment, the Bren gun in the position of the most forward platoon section jammed, and the men there were overrun and killed. The rest of the platoon shot down many of the Germans before they with-drew.[31] During the height of the fight, Lieutenant George Aldous, commanding this forward platoon, was temporarily blinded by gre-nade fragments. After a stretcher-bearer cleaned his eyes, Aldous regained his vision and continued to lead the platoon. His effort earned a Military Cross.

Although this opposition to 'D' Company's hold on the woods was limited for some time to small-arms and 5-centimetre mortar fire, casualties continued to mount. 'D' Company's stretcher-bearers, despite visible Red Cross armbands, were a magnet for sniper fire. Rifleman Mervin Milson had a bullet punch through his helmet, causing a bad scalp wound. But he continued to help the casualties. His selflessness garnered a Military Medal.[32]

Just before nightfall, the Germans counterattacked again, only to be driven back with the loss of six men. With signs that the para-troopers had shot their bolt, the tanks came up alongside the wood to provide closer support. As night fell, the battalion's scout platoon crept toward the buildings. Running straight into another counter-attacking force, the scouts shot down six more Germans and broke up the attack.[33] 'D' Company had been reduced to three officers and fifty men.[34]

"Thus," concluded the army's official historian, "the obstacle of Moyland Wood had been overcome at last."[35] But the cost had been terrible. The Little Black Devils entered the battle on this day heavily understrength with just 207 men in the four rifle companies. In the woods, 105 men had become casualties, 26 killed—a 40-per-cent casualty rate.[36] The last two casualties struck many as particularly tragic. After dark, 'D' Company's second-in-command, Captain Bill Ormiston, and driver Corporal George Quovadis were bringing food forward in a carrier. Getting a good meal up to the men was a typical action for Ormiston. The carrier hit a mine and both men were killed in the explosion.[37]

In the four days leading up to February 21, the battalion had suf-fered another 78 casualties. It was the same story for the other regiments of 7th Canadian Brigade. The Canadian Scottish had 168 casualties and the Reginas lost 134.[38]

One thing that struck the Canadians in the battle's aftermath was how few prisoners were taken. Usually, prisoner cages filled as a battle progressed, many Germans opting to give up rather than face death. But the paratroopers had fought to the bitter end. In its attack on the position reportedly held by two hundred paratroopers, 'C' Company had taken just five prisoners. And the position had been strewn with dead.[39] When Regina's Major Gordon Brown and Lieutenant Buzz Keating returned to the wood after the battle ended, they found many enemy corpses spread out through the conifers. For the Reginas, their time in Moyland Wood saw the second-worst casualty rate of the war, just behind their losses at the Leopold Canal in the Scheldt Estuary Campaign.[40]

One-third of 7th Brigade was lost. The Royal Regiment relieved the Can Scots from their positions next to Moyland Wood. Of the three rifle companies out front, only 120 to 130 men remained. The men walked back to the battalion's tactical headquarters and took off their small battle packs. They loaded these and the heavy weapons into trucks. A piper led each company in a march back to the Can Scot headquarters near Bedburg. "The shrill, triumphant sound of the pipes gave something to the men that nothing else could," wrote the regiment's historian. "Almost automatically the bone-weary soldiers began to march in step...with pride in every step. Swinging into their rest area the companies were greeted by the pipes and drums of the whole battalion. It was an electrifying moment, one charged with great emotion as the throbbing drums and ancient Highland pipe music cut through the darkness to bring the battle-weary troops a message of praise and admiration for a job well done. No battle had been tougher, and none had exacted such a heavy toll in dead and wounded...The pipers blew as if their lungs would burst, and in the darkness pride and sorrow were expressed in handclasps and released, by some, in tears."[41]

Among those watching with a catch in his throat was Major Bill Matthews, battalion second-in-command. Matthews was a young officer, and as chance would have it he watched the parade of so few returning next to a grizzled and tough pipe major of the 15th (Scottish) Infantry Division, still extracting men from the Moyland Wood killing ground. The pipe major was silhouetted against a moon that nobody had seen for days. Tears rolled down the older man's cheeks as the thin ranks of Can Scots passed. "Makes you fucking think, don't it kid?" the pipe major observed ruefully. Matthews had no answer.[42]

Early on the evening of February 21, 5th Canadian Infantry Brigade's Le Régiment de Maisonneuve probed along the highway running from Cleve to Calcar. When they moved into the shattered streets and buildings of Moyland village, they found it abandoned. The 6th Fallschirmjäger Division had quit the place, falling back to a line extending northeastward from Calcar to the Rhine at Hönnepel. The way to Calcar was open.[43] And Operation Veritable was done.

PART THREE

BLOCKBUSTER

FEBRUARY 22–MARCH 10, 1945

18

All This Is Good

OPERATION VERITABLE HAD progressed more slowly than hoped, because of weather conditions that "could scarcely have been worse." And "the enemy, fighting on the soil of Germany and in the valley of the Fatherland's great river, had resisted with fierce determination." Flooding the Roer River to delay U.S. Ninth Army launching Operation Grenade had freed the Germans to concentrate all their resources against the Anglo-Canadian advance.[1]

Despite all, xxx British Corps and 11 Canadian Corps had clawed their way fifteen to twenty miles into Germany. A bottleneck front just six miles wide now stretched twenty miles, with the army's shoulders brushing both the Maas and Rhine Rivers.[2]

Veritable had exacted a bloody toll. Between February 8 and 26—launch date for Operation Blockbuster—First Canadian Army reported 490 officers and 8,023 other ranks killed, wounded, or missing. Of these, 111 officers and 1,683 other ranks were Canadian, 379 officers and 6,325 other ranks were British (about 900 lost between February 22 and 25), and 15 other ranks were from other attached Allied formations. German losses were far greater. Up to midnight of February 25–26, a total of 11,778 Germans were taken prisoner. German dead were "estimated as at least equal to the number of prisoners taken." The primary intention of Veritable—killing or capturing German troops—had been achieved.

More killing lay ahead. First Canadian Army faced a still unbroken front anchored on the Germans' last major defensive line, which the Allies called the Hochwald Layback. Blockbuster was to shatter this and drive to Xanten.

Before Blockbuster could begin, First Canadian Army needed to regroup. This provided the soldiers with a welcome breather. "To the commanders...these few days...represented precious hours in which final and detailed preparations must be made for the continuation of the advance."[3]

On February 19, General Harry Crerar had sent warning orders to all corps and divisional commanders.[4] "It was now my intention to transfer the weight of Army's effort to its left...with [11] Canadian Corps to mount a deliberate assault across the plateau between Calcar and Üdem against the strong enemy defences of the Hochwald." The 11th British Armoured Division was transferred from British Second Army and 4th Canadian Armoured Division from 1 British Corps to 11 Canadian Corps. Lieutenant General Guy Simonds also received 43rd (Wessex) Division from xxx Corps to protect the left flank of the attacking Canadian divisions via a limited advance in the Rhine's flood plain. "If the situation developed propitiously... Simonds was to carry his armoured thrust to Xanten and secure the town and the high ground to the south." Lieutenant General Brian Horrocks's xxx Corps, "keeping well up on his left, was to give protection to the [11] Canadian Corps' right flank. He was also to exploit to the southeast and south should opportunity offer."[5]

On February 22, Simonds fleshed out the plan before his divisional commanders. The Germans, he said, had committed "every reserve" they could "lay hands upon." With U.S. Ninth Army planning to cross the Roer on the morrow, the Germans would have to divert some of this strength to meet that offensive. 11 Canadian Corps would then strike on the 26th "with the object of capturing the high ground south of Calcar and Üdem and then to exploit through the enemy positions toward Xanten and Wesel." Simonds was delighted to have "two fresh armoured divisions available," pointing out "that seldom, if ever, will such an opportunity present itself." Rather than "dribble in his fresh reserves...now was the time to strike hard at the enemy in an all-out effort."

Blockbuster would open with a massed artillery bombardment and—weather permitting—"all available air support." Because Calcar was a key hub, Simonds expected the Germans to fiercely defend it. The high ground running from Calcar to Üdem also held the main German infantry defences. Behind these, an anti-tank ditch formed a critical part of the Hochwald Layback.[6]

Like Veritable, Blockbuster would be hampered by a road shortage. There were three possible routes. The Cleve–Calcar–Xanten highway was the best, so the Germans could be expected to strongly block it. Aerial photographs revealed that the highway was actually in poor shape. Bombing had badly cratered long sections, and flooding to the left made movement of troops on that flank almost impossible. The road from Üdem east to Kervenheim and then northeast to Sonsbeck overlapped the q between II Canadian Corps and XXX British Corps. Both would vie for access, creating the same problem that had arisen on roads through Cleve during Veritable. Running on an angle directly through the Canadian operational area was the Goch–Xanten railway. Its tracks followed a raised embankment reported free of mines or sections destroyed by demolition. Simonds decided that his engineers would follow behind the leading troops—ripping up tracks and transforming rail bed into road as they went.[7]

The corps engineers planned to use explosives to separate metal tracks from wooden supporting ties. Long lengths of cordex (an instantaneous fuse) were stretched out next to each rail. Four-ounce cartridges of plastic explosive were then slit, slipped over the fuse, "and rammed between the rail and tie-bolt of each tie. When the circuit was detonated, the 90-pound rail was usually found quite free of the steel ties. The rails were then pushed off the grade and the ties collected for later use." The bed was then graded for road use.

More problematic was creating and maintaining roads running up to the Blockbuster forming-up positions. "These roads exist in theory only and maintenance consists of dumping endless quantities of rubble into a bottomless mass of mud," complained 7th Field Company's diarist. Cleve's hundreds of destroyed buildings yielded a ready source of rubble. Most buildings had been of stout masonry that could be scooped into dump trucks and hauled to where repairs or road-bed construction was under way. Although the engineers quickly deduced that "the best and most easily obtained fill was on the sites of bombed churches," 11 Canadian Corps issued an order forbidding the use of "ecclesiastical rubble" for road fill.[8]

There were never enough trucks to haul all the rubble from Cleve, so when possible, sappers demolished any nearby farmhouses for material. This, as a 3rd Canadian Infantry Division engineering report noted, was done "not, it is to be feared, without some suspicion of hard feelings from the tenantry." Inspiring hard feelings among German civilians little bothered the engineers. When some British Guards Armoured Division troops tried to prevent a farm building's destruction, a "skirmish" ensued that "involved some high flights of rhetoric on both sides. However, the bulldozer moved in, the Guards moved out, and all was happily resolved."

Often working "under desultory mortar and artillery fire," the engineers chalked up eighteen- to twenty-hour days readying the roads for showtime on the night of February 25–26.[9]

simonds intended to deceive the Germans into believing the attack's main objective was gaining control of the Cleve–Xanten highway by launching a powerful thrust toward the high ground immediately south of Calcar. If the Germans took the bait and shifted men to block him, the southern end of these heights at Üdem would become less heavily defended. The attack at Calcar was given to 2nd Canadian Infantry Division, with two regiments of 2nd Canadian Armoured Brigade in support. This kick-off would start at 0430 hours on February 26. Two of Major General Bruce Matthews's infantry brigades along with the tanks would cross the Calcar–Goch road and hook behind Calcar. At the same time, 3rd Canadian Infantry Division's 8th Brigade would seize the heights just north of the village of Keppeln, which formed "an intermediate strongpoint between Calcar and Üdem where the enemy's flanks were anchored." Once the ridge was secure, 3rd Division would take Keppeln. At the same time, 2,500 yards northeast of the village, a 4th Canadian Armoured Division battle group would advance through 2nd Division's front. Driving southward between the two infantry divisions, the battle group would widen the grip on the ridge by taking Todtenhügel. Sometime in the mid-afternoon, the next phase of Blockbuster would involve 11 Canadian Corps thrusting southward with 3rd Division's

9th Brigade toward Üdem, while the 4th Division armoured battle group approached from the northeast. To complete Üdem's envelopment, 11th British Armoured Division would pass to its south and clear the southernmost part of the ridge where it trickled down to level ground northeast of Kervenheim.

With the ridge overcome, the two armoured divisions would break out into the plain beyond. The Canadians would advance astride the railway to reach the so-called Hochwald Gap. This narrow stretch of open ground divided the Hochwald from two smaller forests to the south—the Tüschen Wald and Barberger Wald. The railway itself cut through the Tüschen Wald before crossing the open country east of the Hochwald to reach Xanten. While the Canadians won the gap and cleared the adjacent woods, the British armour would seize Sonsbeck and establish a brigade on the high ground north of the village. Further exploitation would depend on developments, but Simonds hoped to drive the armour directly toward Xanten and Wesel. The Canadian infantry divisions during this period would protect the flanks of their armoured brethren.[10]

OPERATION VERITABLE HAD well pleased Field Marshal Bernard Montgomery, despite its winning less ground than desired. But the plum in the pudding was First Canadian Army's drawing eleven divisions before it. "All this is good and is sowing the seeds for a successful Grenade," he signalled General Sir Alan Brooke.

On February 21, Montgomery had visited U.S. Ninth Army's Lieutenant General William Simpson. The two generals agreed to launch Operation Grenade before dawn on February 23.[11] Simpson's engineers had been monitoring the rate at which the reservoirs opened by the Germans upstream were draining. They estimated the reservoirs would be fully drained by February 24. The day before, however, the Roer River would have receded eight to fourteen inches below its highest flood peak and be running at less than six miles per hour. These conditions were sufficient for Simpson's attack to possibly gain "some measure of surprise."[12]

When the attack went in on a two-corps-wide front at 0330 hours the morning of February 23, this proved to be the case. Having denuded this part of the front to oppose Veritable, the Germans offered slight resistance. By day's end, the Americans had twenty-eight infantry battalions across the river and seven bridges were carrying traffic. Opposing them were only four infantry and Volks-grenadier divisions, and 1,100 of their men surrendered on the first day. Pushing hard beyond the river, by February 26, all of Ninth Army's three corps were fully engaged. They had taken 6,000 prisoners at a cost of 3,368 casualties and were sweeping toward the Rhine.[13]

Until February 24, the German high command had clung to hope that the American operation "was not designed to converge with the Canadian thrust southeast from Nijmegen." That day, however, they "were at last impelled to face reality. Operation Grenade at that point clearly was the hammer aimed at crushing the southern wing of [Heeresgruppe] H against the anvil" of First Canadian Army. Heeresgruppe B's Generalfeldmarschall Walter Model could barely reinforce this front. All he had on offer was Panzer Lehr Division, which "was severely bruised from its fight against Operation Veritable and in any event could make no appearance in strength for several days."

On February 25, Generalfeldmarschall Gerd von Rundstedt appealed to Hitler for permission to conduct minor withdrawals to improve the German situation. Hitler refused. Heeresgruppe H's endangered southern wing was to hold where it was. "Withdrawal behind the Rhine was unthinkable."[14]

First Fallschirmjäger Army's General der Fallschirmtruppen Alfred Schlemm had four corps to prevent two Allied armies from converging upon Wesel from different directions. On his right, General Panzerdertruppen Heinrich Freiherr von Lüttwitz's XLVII Korps faced the Canadians at Calcar. To his left, II Fallschirmjäger Korps, under the extremely capable General der Fallschirmtruppen Eugen Meindl, was responsible for the Üdem–Weeze area. From Weeze south to Venlo, the line was held by General der Infanterie Erich Straube's very weak LXXXVI Korps. The LXIII Korps was responsible for the line running south from Venlo to Roermond.

Von Lüttwitz defended Calcar with 6th Fallschirmjäger Division. Both its 17th and 18th Fallschirmjäger Regiments were near full strength and fighting fit. Centred on Keppeln, the 116th Panzer Division held the ground to the left. This division had received an infusion of troops, tanks, and artillery. Üdem was held by 2nd Fallschirmjäger Division's 7th Regiment.

South of Üdem, Meindl commanded a mixed lot of divisions. His 7th Fallschirmjäger Division was good and strong, while the men of 8th Fallschirmjäger Division were mostly green. There were also remnants of 15th Panzer Grenadier Division and a fewer number from 84th Infanterie-Division. With so few men, Meindl deployed them by stringing weak outposts along his front while retaining the bulk in reserve within woods southeast of the town. These would rush to counterattack any Allied attack.[15]

Although Simonds intended to deploy the might of two armoured divisions during Blockbuster, the terrain little favoured tank movement. Directly east of Moyland Wood, the Rhine's flood plain extended past Calcar to Xanten. Some of this ground was inundated, and all of it was deep in mud. Immediately south of Calcar stood the low ridge that had been 4th Canadian Infantry Brigade's objective during the February 20–21 fighting. This ridge, one army report noted, "continues in the shape of a drawn bow to the eastern outskirts of Üdem, then crosses the railway to the...north of Kervenheim. Between Kervenheim and Weeze lie well watered farmlands bound in by the...Niers River. Forestation is plentiful and especially thick south of Weeze...East of the Calcar-Üdem escarpment there exists an arable valley which...winds thinly to the south through Üdemerbruch and on again toward the areas north of Winnekendonk and Kapellen. Beyond to the east lies the vast greenness of the Hochwald Forest covering the quickly rising ridge which takes shape south of Marienbaum and stretches southwest to the line of the railway, where a small gap separates it from the lesser Balberger Wald. From here the high ground continues and turns slightly east to end northeast of Sonsbeck. From the line of the large forests toward Veen and Winnenthal on to the banks of the Rhine, innumerable farms dot the landscape." This plain was broken by small, mostly state-managed pockets of forest. As the plain extended eastward, "the vegetation gradually thins out and the ground becomes open and liable to flooding. It was against this choice background that the Hochwald 'layback' defence line had been placed."[16]

The Germans had actually named this line the Schlieffen Position, after Generalfeldmarschall Alfred von Schlieffen—mastermind of the grand strategy implemented to invade France and Belgium at the outbreak of the Great War. The Schlieffen Position boasted three anti-tank ditches about five hundred yards apart. These trenches were the strongest feature. The most easterly extended from Kehrum along the westerly edge of the Hochwald and Balberger Wald to more woods one and a half miles west of Sonsbeck. This trench was dug into the high ground's forward slope and was strongest at its northern extent. Here it overlooked a series of forward outposts about a mile to the west. In the area of the vital railway Simonds intended for his major road, woodlots east of Üdem offered good concealment, and the heights southeast of the town provided excellent observation points. South of Üdem, the ground was mostly open and worked against the defence. Many of the defensive trenches and dugouts throughout the Hochwald Layback were in poor shape, some being partly collapsed. Wire entanglements varied in density and effectiveness.

In a desperate effort to strengthen this weak line, Schlemm had brought in about fifty additional 88-millimetre guns—drawing them from defences between Geldern and Roermond that faced the Americans. Schlemm had done this without either attaining authorization from or informing higher command. While the guns added formidable strength, their crews were inexperienced and undisciplined.[17]

IN THE FOUR days leading up to Blockbuster, XXX British Corps had made a concerted effort to advance from Goch to Weeze. Despite a two-pronged effort involving both the 15th (Scottish) and 53rd (Welsh) Infantry Divisions, the attack went badly. Opposition was extremely heavy. Inevitable mines, mud, and an anti-tank ditch added to British woes. Every advance was met by fierce counterattacks. On the 25th, Horrocks ordered his divisions to stand down two thousand yards short of Weeze. Blockbuster was imminent, and his corps artillery must divert to support the Canadian attack. The four days' fighting had cost nine hundred British casualties.[18]

Six hundred guns supported Blockbuster. Twelve field, six medium, and three heavy regiments backed 2nd Canadian Infantry Division, and seven field and two medium regiments weighed in for 3rd Canadian Infantry Division. The plan was to maintain this level of artillery commitment for the operation's duration.

Despite continuing poor weather that greatly hindered air operations, twenty-four specific targets had been selected for bombing immediately prior to Blockbuster's launch. Fighter-bombers would strike eighteen targets, all likely strongpoints extending from the Calcar–Üdem ridge to the western fringe of the Hochwald and Balberger Wald. Medium bombers would attack targets north of Kervenheim and inside the Hochwald and Balberger Wald with anti-personnel bombs.[19] Given repeated groundings of the air force during February, one army analyst wrote that "it became the object of honest prayer on all levels that the weather would clear for the II Canadian Corps operation."[20]

The XXX Corps failure to take Weeze worried Crerar. Weeze's capture had been intended to open the road running south from this town to a crossing of the Maas at the village of Well. Once this road was available, British engineers had intended to build a bridge over the river. Supplies could then flow through Wanssum on the south bank. Crerar warned his two corps commanders that lack of this bridge and the alternative supply route the road provided could limit the operation to a "partial" Blockbuster. If by the second day the attack lost steam, Blockbuster might only entail securing the high ground east of the Calcar–Üdem road. During those first two days, XXX Corps had the "principal responsibility" of securing II Corps's right shoulder. If Blockbuster lagged, however, "the weight of the Canadian Army effort [would] then be transferred to XXX Corps—which...will then proceed to secure the Well-Weeze road, and eliminate the enemy remaining to the north of it."[21]

Simonds had no intention of allowing Blockbuster to peter out into something "partial." He deduced from Crerar's warning that it was up to his corps "to carry the ball through to Xanten." Simonds judged it "unlikely...that the [3rd British Division immediately to his right] would strain every nerve when the [xxx Corps's] role was only to provide a defensive flank."[22] Conceivably, a gap might emerge between the two corps as Simonds advanced, but he had no intention of slowing the pace. Blockbuster would start on time and he would drive hard toward Xanten.

Nobody was under any illusions. Blockbuster would be tough. In briefings at all levels, that point was made clear. Major Dick Medland, commander of the Queen's Own Rifle Regiment's 'D' Company, warned that elite paratroopers waited opposite the battalion's start line. Medland had studied the ground that must be crossed. It was gently sloping and open, dotted with farmhouses surely fortified. The battalion's objectives were three small hamlets whose buildings offered more forts. Medland told his men they "had done this sort of thing before. Always it had been costly. I didn't try to kid anyone." His biggest concern was that the platoon commanders were all new and had little combat experience. It was the same with most of the men. But there was a core of battle-hardened soldiers, and the non-commissioned officers were all seasoned. Medland encouraged the officers and men "to lean a little on the older veterans." Someone asked how many casualties he anticipated. "This could be the toughest scrap we've ever been in," Medland replied. "A lot of us won't make it. Those who do, well, they'll remember it for a long time."[23]

Near where Medland briefed his troops, the Catholics in the North Shore (New Brunswick) Regiment had gathered in a barn. Padre R. Miles Hickey said mass and gave the men general absolution and then Holy Communion. Hickey tried to do this before every battle, considering it an essential act. Then should he have to inform a man's family of his death, Hickey could truthfully write that the soldier had "died prepared, for...with all the others, he [had] knelt and received Holy Communion before going into action."[24]

On the night of February 25–26, all 11 Canadian Corps formed up as planned. Anti-aircraft guns firing tracer rounds along fixed lines would provide directional aid, and aritificial moonlight would light the way. In a departure from rote, all three of 2nd Division's 6th Brigade battalions would advance in line instead of one being held back as a reserve. The two battalions on either flank would be in Kangaroos, while the one in the middle rode on the outer hulls of supporting tanks.[25] Two battalions of 2nd Division's 5th Brigade and—again departing from the norm—3rd Division 8th Brigade's three battalions would advance on foot.

In the darkness, the Canadians moved to forming-up positions in muddy fields facing the ridge. Having detected movement, the Germans subjected the fields to fairly constant shelling. Then, in the early hours of February 26, a strong force of paratroopers from 26th Fallschirmjäger Regiment, supported by about six tanks, struck 2nd Division's far right flank, which was guarded by the Royal Hamilton Light Infantry of 4th Infantry Brigade. The attack fell on Major Louis Froggett's 'D' Company. A fierce firefight broke out. Froggett's men suffered heavy casualties, but they "stood firm and each attack was repelled." In the midst of the fight, Froggett personally killed three paratroopers who had infiltrated his company headquarters.[26] The appearance of a troop of Fort Garry Horse tanks saved the situation, the Shermans knocking out one Panther. After that, the paratroopers melted into the night.[27] Froggett declared this the "grisliest day of the war." He received a Distinguished Service Order for his leadership.

As the Germans withdrew, the battleground fell strangely silent. Fifteen minutes later, at precisely 0345 hours, Allied artillery shattered the night.[28] Operation Blockbuster began.

19

Toughest Scrap

T 0430 HOURS, 2nd Canadian Infantry Division's five battalions advanced across muddy fields through heavy rain. "An
eerie light was added to the whole scene by the searchlights, Jerry
flares and burning farm buildings," South Saskatchewan Regiment's Major George Buchanan wrote.[1] Private Charles "Chic"
Goodman was one of two signallers in Major Fraser Lee's 'B' Company headquarters section. Lee and his men were crowded into a
Kangaroo. The Sasks were on 6th Brigade's left flank. Their objective was a pimple-shaped feature dominating the highway running
from Calcar to Xanten. In the centre, Les Fusiliers Mont-Royal had
less distance to travel—just beyond the intersection where the road
to Üdem branched off the Calcar–Goch road. The French Canadians
clung to the outside hulls of the Fort Garry Horse Regiment's 'A' and
'B' Squadron tanks. To the right, the Queen's Own Cameron Highlanders were in Kangaroos. Their objective was more high ground
east of the pimple.[2]

Private Goodman was excited. With the other signaller manning
the wireless, the eighteen-year-old was free to look around. Everywhere, Kangaroos were moving. The racket was incredible. Engines
roared, tracks clattered, shells shrieked overhead, explosions thun-
dered, machine guns chattered. Goodman had never ridden into an
attack. And he was "delighted because there was a Browning

machine gun mounted on a spigot" in the Kangaroo. Goodman had appropriated the Browning and a good supply of belts of .303-calibre ammunition for it.[3]

The Sasks reached the Calcar–Goch road quickly. About a hundred yards beyond the road, they started up the gradual slope in deepening mud.[4] 'B' Squadron of the Sherbrooke Fusiliers Regiment was supporting the Sasks, and 'A' Squadron worked with the Camerons.[5] One tank mired in the mud, as did four Kangaroos. The men from these boarded others passing by. Intense small-arms and mortar fire started coming in. The Germans were firing off dozens of flares. Farm buildings burned on every side. Smoke became so dense that Saskatchewan Lieutenant Colonel Vern Stott signalled back for the anti-aircraft guns to double the rate of tracer fire to provide better directional guidance.[6]

Through the smoke, Goodman saw the tree-lined road running from just south of Calcar to Üdem. A lot of Germans were marching southward, obviously evacuating Calcar. Goodman unleashed the Browning. "I kept shooting at them. No idea whether I hit any of them or not. But think I must have frightened some."[7]

As the Sasks closed on the pimple, they came under fire from four 88-millimetre guns on the summit. Captain George Stiles and 'D' Company piled out of the Kangaroos and charged the rightmost gun. Capturing it, they removed a demolition charge the German crew had attached to the gun before it exploded. Captain H.A. Robertson and the battalion's support company platoons, riding on Bren carriers, overran the position containing the other three 88s and also captured them intact.

'D' Company had carried on, sweeping through a group of burning buildings. Stiles saw that a number of Germans had taken refuge in their cellars. Suddenly, "one kid in civvies, about fifteen years old, threw a grenade at our gang and wounded four," Stiles recounted. "This [was] the first instance we...encountered of a civilian offering resistance. We let him have it."[8] It was 0650 hours. The Sasks were on their objective, looking over the Calcar–Xanten road and parallel railway.[9]

'B' Company's section set up inside a farmhouse. Three or four

German soldiers lay dead on the main floor. Company Sergeant Major Frank Cunningham disliked using the house. "It's going to be a big target," he cautioned Goodman. "Let's look at the barn." The two men went over to the stoutly built structure, which had a lower profile than the big house. Cunningham pointed to a trap door leading to a cellar. "We can go down there when the shelling starts up," he said. After opening the trap door, Goodman paused and peered into the dark interior below. He and Cunningham exchanged glances, considering. "Better throw a grenade down," Cunningham advised. "Yeah, but this is a farm. We don't want to kill women and children," Goodman answered. Goodman shouted loudly, "*Raus. Raus.*" Up the stairs came "four of the biggest paratroopers I had ever seen. They were huge guys and the Sergeant Major and I were both little guys. We started escorting them back to where one of the platoons was holding prisoners. And one of the guys kept lagging behind. I thought, 'The son of a bitch is up to something.' So I fired a burst of Sten gun into the ground in front of him and he got the message."[10]

At 0705, 'B' Company had just finished deploying defensively when about forty Germans counterattacked. Major Lee had his men hold fire until the paratroopers nearly reached their lines. A deadly volley of fire killed about thirty and sent the rest running. The Sasks captured sixty-nine Germans, killed at least forty, and wounded another fifty. In the early afternoon, they observed about three hundred Germans marching in ranks of three eastward from Calcar toward Xanten. Artillery was called in. The German column scattered, a good number of dead and wounded left sprawled on the road.[11]

RIGHT OF THE Sasks, the tankers carrying Les Fusiliers Mont-Royal had found it virtually impossible to maintain course amid the thick, roiling smoke. Fort Garry Horse Lieutenant Lloyd Queen's 'B' Squadron troop was on point. This put Queen, as his Military Cross citation stated, in "one of those rare occasions when the success of a major operation hinged upon the judgement of a junior commander." Queen could only guide the force by regularly jumping out of the tank and walking ahead to take compass bearings.[12] Queen's work was soon done. Despite losing ten tanks to mud and another to a mine, the Fusiliers were tight on their objective at 0510 hours.[13] Casualties were surprisingly few. But Major Gaétan Giroux was severely wounded when his 'A' Company met sharp resistance from a clutch of paratroopers.[14]

While Blockbuster opened well for the Fusiliers and Sasks, the opposite proved true for the Queen's Own Cameron Highlanders. Advancing on the brigade's right with 'A' Squadron of the Sherbrookes, the Kangaroos and tanks wallowed through ever-deepening mud until running into a thick minefield alongside the Calcar–Üdem road. Finding safe passage through the mines would leave the Camerons far behind the battalions advancing on either flank, so Brigadier R.H. "Holly" Keefler ordered Lieutenant Colonel Ernest Payson Thompson to swing north and advance through the position just taken by the Fusiliers. At twenty-four, "Tommy" Thompson was the Canadian Army's youngest battalion commander. He had recently married a Scottish lass from Kirkaldy, Fife. Three days before Blockbuster, Montgomery personally pinned a Distinguished Service Order medal on Thompson's chest for bravery in the Scheldt Estuary Campaign.[15]

Changing the axis of the advance worried Keefler, even as he accepted there was no alternative. "The carefully studied landmarks no longer served to guide them and...the visibility was becoming extremely bad, due to many burning buildings. At this point, the determination and resourcefulness of all concerned were to be taxed to the limit, as the immediate barrage support had disappeared." Thompson ably swung his battalion about eight hundred yards northward. At 0700 hours, the Camerons passed through the Fusiliers and were "making good progress with the leading company fighting their way toward the objective." Then an 88-millimetre shell slammed into Thompson's Kangaroo.[16] In the ensuing confusion, those who survived emerged with conflicting reports of what happened. Some thought Thompson was shot dead by a sniper's bullet outside the Kangaroo.[17] Others reported he was killed by the 88 shell. His intelligence officer, Captain K.A. Smith, was wounded by shrapnel.[18] Casualties in the headquarters section were so heavy the battalion was left momentarily rudderless.

Major David Rodgers of 'A' Company had been close to the battalion headquarters when disaster struck it. He took over and soon got the headquarters marginally functional. Then he led his company onward. It was 0830, and half the Camerons were meeting heavy resistance. Fire from a nearby building swept the battalion headquarters group. Realizing the surviving men there were going to be wiped out, Rodgers ran back from his company and charged the building alone. After killing the machine-gun crew, he went on to clear two more buildings of snipers, delaying his company's advance. His actions garnered a Distinguished Service Order.[19]

Only thirty-four men of 'B' Company reached their objective. The Kangaroos carrying the rest had bogged down or become lost. With two Sherman tanks firing machine guns in support, the small group attacked the buildings before them. They took the position and 116 prisoners. Seven Camerons were wounded. Two might have died had Lance Corporal J. Plantje not rescued them.

Such are the vagaries of battle that while 'A' and 'B' Companies had to fight hard, 'C' and 'D' Companies rolled into their objectives unopposed. The Camerons started digging in and preparing to fend off expected counterattacks. At 1800 hours, Major R.H. Lane—the second-in-command—arrived and took over from Rodgers.[20]

The 6th Brigade's attack had gone off exceedingly well. "It was an example of what detailed planning, a high standard of training and excellent morale can accomplish," the army's official historian declared. "At a cost of only 140 casualties (including three of the supporting armour) the brigade had taken between 400 and 500 prisoners and accounted for many enemy killed."[21] Brigadier Keefler reported that although the Germans launched seven counterattacks, none were successful. By noon, all brigade assignments had been achieved.[22]

LEFT OF 6TH Brigade, things had gone less well for 5th Brigade. Le Régiment de Maisonneuve and the Black Watch Regiment were partly intended to support 6th Brigade but more importantly to open a route through which 4th Canadian Armoured Division's battle group could advance toward Üdem. Tank support was limited to 1st

Hussars Regiment's 'A' Squadron. Its tanks, however, were entirely assigned to the Black Watch's 'B' Company, which would enter the operation only after the regiment's other three companies had won their objectives. No tanks were given to the Maisies because, as they were relieving the Royal Hamilton Light Infantry of positions taken earlier, they were not expected to meet stiff opposition.[23]

The relief was concluded with clockwork precision by 0400 hours. From here, 'D' Company advanced into contested territory to occupy a U-shaped wood on the ridge just beyond the Calcar–Goch road.[24] A 2,500-yard-wide, gradually rising open field separated the company from the wood. Major G.F. Charlebois led his men forward in an extended line behind lifts of an artillery barrage. A hundred yards short of the woods, they were "met by a heavy line of enemy dugouts filled with fanatic paratroops." With dawn breaking, the two forward platoons were caught "in the open and went to ground in shell holes and whatever slit trenches were available. To move for them was utterly impossible," reported the battalion's war diarist. Cutting around the left flank, the third platoon bypassed the dugouts only to be halted by a shower of grenades twenty-five yards short of the wood. The platoon took refuge in a nearby house.[25]

Lieutenant Colonel Julien Bibeau reported 'D' Company's situation to Brigadier Bill Megill, who judged it critical but not dire, despite the fact that the company was being "shot up from all sides" and entangled in "a very slow infantry fight in close contact with the enemy." Still, Charlebois's men were "containing the locality and the trouble experienced...was not dislocating the advance in other directions. Consequently, all available tanks were kept disengaged in order to support [the Black Watch,] who had the vital job." When that job concluded, Megill would send tanks to help rescue 'D' Company.

The Black Watch, meanwhile, had hit trouble at the outset. Ever since Verrières Ridge, in Normandy, where most of its men had been slaughtered in a badly conceived and executed attack, the Black Watch had been a hard-luck battalion. Difficulties had erupted even off the battlefield in a clash between the brigadier and its battalion commander. Megill had wanted fresh blood from another battalion, someone with a good, tough reputation for sorting out deadwood and keeping the best. Then Lieutenant Colonel Bruce R. Ritchie had been appointed. Despite—or perhaps because of—Ritchie's deep Black Watch roots, the two men disliked each other. Megill criticized Ritchie's leadership. He blamed the regiment's officers for the disasters that habitually befell them, while many a Black Watch considered Megill the problem. In four days of fighting in October 1944, the regiment had suffered almost 250 casualties. When the smoke cleared, most of its experienced officers were dead, wounded, or lost as prisoners. Morale at all levels was poor. The men had lost confidence in their commanders, and there was little to inspire new officers and men inducted into the battalion.

The development of the attack on February 26 was typical of Black Watch operations. At midnight Ritchie, accompanied by an artillery forward observation officer, selected his tactical headquarters: 'C' Company's forming-up point. On his return to battalion headquarters, he was unable to find either his intelligence officer or signals officer there and sent a message that they were to go ahead and ensure that the tactical headquarters was functioning upon his arrival. Organization of the headquarters was still under way when Ritchie arrived, and he was left scrambling to get the attack teed up. It was 0415 hours before the tactical headquarters opened for business. The attack was just fifteen minutes away.[26] Although artillery support would be criticized after the fact, it is equally possible the FOO was unable to situate himself in time to summon accurate fire.

THE BLACK WATCH had four objectives—road junctions with adjacent building clusters.[27] The closest was code-named Gull, the one beyond Eagle, then Ottawa, and finally Raven.[28] This last objective was "a built-up road junction one mile south of Calcar."[29] Megill's intelligence showed Gull as "free of enemy prior to the attack." So "it had not been considered necessary to bring down additional fire on that locality." Instead, Gull and Eagle were "swept by a fast barrage" that was actually supporting the adjacent 6th Brigade attack. "In reality," Megill reported later, "the enemy had moved troops into the area and, as soon as the companies proceeding to 'Eagle' and 'Gull' began their advance, they ran into fire from 'Gull.'"[30] 'D' Company's Major

E.W. Hudson was severely wounded.[31] Hudson's loss struck the Black Watch "a heavy blow," wrote their war diarist, "for he was an excellent leader of his men, a most enthusiastic soldier, and what we need now is enthusiasm...through this campaign, the success of which depends so much on our punch and verve."[32] Ritchie told Megill it "was quite obvious that 'A' and 'D' companies...had to be reorganized with a fire plan to get onto 'Gull,' and it was also apparent that the position had to be secured quickly or the result would be a slowing down of the whole Corps battle." The Black Watch's only break so far was that 'C' Company, moving behind a "slow barrage," had secured Ottawa and were digging in.[33] 'D' Company, meanwhile, which had been leading the attack on Gull, fell back to 'A' Company's position.[34]

At 0745 hours, Major Bill Robinson of the 1st Hussars 'A' Squadron "received orders to push on immediately through to our objective regardless of previous circumstances." Because the Black Watch's pre-dawn attack had failed, the route required by 4th Canadian Armoured Division's battle group remained closed. So the earlier plan, whereby 'A' Squadron would advance to Raven in support of 'B' Company, "had to be scrapped." Robinson's squadron was to mount "a direct assault with the tanks leading across the open fields around 'A' Company's position and then straight on to the objective."

A hurriedly attached artillery FOO promised a barrage by half a field regiment, and half a medium regiment would hammer Gull and Raven for fifteen minutes after the force crossed its start line. Robinson and the FOO estimated that when the artillery program ended, the tanks would be two hundred yards from Raven. The attack was set for 0800. As 'A' Squadron moved toward the start line, Robinson had the tanks heavily shell Gull.

Four Shermans bogged down before reaching the start line. Robinson regrouped, breaking the squadron into two troops of four tanks and a four-tank headquarters troop. The leading troop was to make straight for Raven rather than tackling the Germans at Gull, which the second troop would charge. A platoon of Black Watch's 'B' Company would follow each tank troop.

Tanks and infantry found it heavy going up the muddy slope. Then three Shermans in the leading troop lost tracks to mines. Robinson ordered the headquarters troop to take its place. What was left of 'A' Squadron was still four hundred yards short of Raven when the barrage ceased. Robinson requested a five-minute extension. During the lag that ensued between request and resumption of the barrage, the tanks fired main guns and machine guns to support the infantry clearing buildings at Gull and heavily engaged paratroopers in adjacent dugouts. When the artillery barrage lifted a second time, the Black Watch and 1st Hussars rolled into Raven. The surviving tanks circled in order to fire in all directions while the infantry set up on the forward slope. It was 0830 hours. More than two hundred paratroopers from 6th Fallschirmjäger Division surrendered. The small force had also knocked out two 88-millimetre and two 75-millimetre anti-tank guns. No sooner had the position fallen than the Germans pounded it with "very heavy shelling and mortaring which proved the enemy had far more artillery than had been anticipated," Robinson reported.[35]

Robinson's subsequent Distinguished Service Order citation commended the "skilful manoeuvring of his tanks to give intimate support to the troops assaulting the final position." It also noted that because the Black Watch were unable to bring their anti-tank guns up to Raven, Robinson decided to keep 'A' Squadron with the infantry, remaining in place for more than eight hours despite the terrific weight of artillery and lack of cover for his tanks.[36]

Once the situation facing the Black Watch was resolved, Brigadier Megill had intended to send 'A' Squadron to assist Les Régiment de Maisonneuve's rescue of its embattled 'D' Company. The company had been pinned for several hours in front of the U-shaped wood overlooking the Goch–Calcar road. With Major Robinson still supporting 'B' Company at Raven, Megill was short of tanks. He could send only a single 1st Hussars troop formed by the tanks that had bogged down earlier.[37]

Lieutenant Colonel Bibeau had been waiting impatiently for his armour. When they arrived at 1400 hours, he personally led 'B' Company and the battalion's Wasp flame-throwers into the attack. The Maisies advanced through fire from three sides, Bibeau inspiring his men by showing "complete disregard" for personal safety. He dashed through flying bullets, shrapnel, and nearby explosions to direct the Wasps and tanks into firing positions on enemy dugouts.[38] "In some instances," Megill reported, "the enemy preferred to stay in their slit trenches and fight it out to the end without surrendering."[39] When Bibeau's force reached 'D' Company, he rallied the men there to come out of their holes and join an assault that cleared the Germans from the woods ahead. Bibeau's bravery was recognized with a Distinguished Service Order.[40]

The Maisies suffered heavily. Twelve men were killed, two more suffered mortal wounds, and seventy-nine others were injured.[41] Ten 'D' Company men died and eighteen were wounded. Two 'B' Company platoon officers, Lieutenant J.A.M. Prudhomme and Lieutenant L. Guay, suffered wounds. Lieutenant G. de Merlis was wounded right beside Bibeau.[42] A few days earlier, Bibeau had pulled strings to have de Merlis sent to England to attend an intelligence officers' course. Although the officer had gone through six months of combat "scratchless," Bibeau worried his luck was expended. He was hit by a grenade fragment and then a bullet to the leg. Fearing medical evacuation would deny him the opportunity to go to England, de Merlis convinced the battalion's medical officer to bandage him up and pretend the wounds had never happened. He gave the doctor a bottle of champagne in exchange.

Losses for the Black Watch were less severe than befell the Maisies—thirteen killed and thirty-three wounded. For both battalions, however, February 26 proved the most costly day of 1945.[43]

TO THE RIGHT of 2nd Canadian Infantry Division, 3rd Canadian Infantry Division's 8th Brigade had also attacked the Calcar–Üdem escarpment. Brigadier Jim Roberts had wanted to employ Kangaroos but was rebuffed. There were not enough armoured personnel carriers to go around. "Our army should have made up at least one more 'Kangaroo' regiment," he said later. "We, in the infantry, needed it badly and many Canadian infantry lives could have been saved by greater availability of this Canadian invention."[44] Even tank support was limited to only two 1st Hussars squadrons.

The brigade's plan deviated from normal Canadian procedures, whereby at least two battalions advanced shoulder to shoulder with tank and artillery support. Instead, each of the brigade's three battalions would go forward separately at different times. The Queen's Own Rifles would lead at 0430 hours and advance on the brigade's right flank to capture the small hamlets of Mooshof, Wemmershof, and Steeg. The battalion's line of advance was slightly to the northeast and timed to accord with 2nd Division's 6th Brigade on its left.[45] The argument for committing the Queen's Own before the rest of the brigade was that its job was distinct from that of the other battalions. They were to take Keppeln, whereas the Queen's Own was protecting 6th Brigade's flank. Then, having gained the three hamlets, they would provide covering fire that would guard their sister battalions' left flank.[46]

Only at 0830 hours would Le Régiment de la Chaudière advance on the brigade's left. Fifteen minutes later, the North Shore (New Brunswick) Regiment would move out in the centre.[47] The Chauds were to seize the hamlets of Halvenboom, Hollen, and Bomshof, all directly east of Üdem. In the alley created by the two flanking battalions, the North Shores' objective was Keppeln—known to be heavily fortified and astride the road branching off the Calcar–Goch road leading to Üdem.[48] Each battalion's line of advance was such that most of the time, the North Shores would be as much as 1,500 yards south of the Queen's Own Rifles.

The latter battalion's Lieutenant Colonel S.M. "Steve" Lett disliked the scheme intensely. He felt the Germans "had all that could be desired for a defensive position"—flanks well anchored with Calcar to the north and Üdem to the south and the strongpoint of Keppeln between. "The country is open and flat. Behind this excellent tank country lies the horse-shoe shaped Calcar-Üdem escarpment, while still farther to the east lies the Hochwald, an ideal gun area." Lett's headquarters was in the hamlet of Wilmshof, just back from the battalion's start line between two other hamlets— Hofmaunshof and Ebben. His hope to effectively reconnoitre the ground ahead was scuttled by the "flat open country [being] completely under enemy observation." It proved impossible to see the objective hamlets or any of the German strongpoints surely lurking just over the crest of the escarpment.[49]

At 0330 hours, the battalion roused after what had been for most a fitful night's sleep. Men gathered equipment while drinking hot coffee laced with rum and munching on cold sandwiches. At 0400, the barrage started—hundreds of guns firing in support of both 2nd and 3rd Divisions. The men trudged through the chilly darkness toward the start line. They followed lines of white tape that brought each company to their precise starting point. Artificial moonlight reflected off thick cloud, creating a false dawn.[50] There was no ground mist. The soldiers could see across the mile or more of open ground ahead. Its gradual slope was dotted with several farms. Everybody knew there were paratroopers waiting in their buildings.

Lett formed the battalion in standard formation, two companies up and two back. Major Allen Nickson's 'C' Company led on the right, and 'D' Company under Major Ben Dunkleman was to the left. Major Dick Medland's 'A' Company followed Nickson's, and Captain D.B. Hamilton's 'B' Company trailed Dunkleman's.

The first thing to go awry was that, just as it had for 6th Brigade's Queen's Own Cameron Highlanders, the ground presented a boggy obstacle for tanks. Major John "Jake" Powell's 'C' Squadron, 1st Hussars found it impossible to match the infantry pace. They were still wallowing toward the start line when Lett ordered the advance at 0440 hours.[51]

"Right away they drew small arms fire," Major Medland said. "The fight was on." German artillery and mortars hammered rounds down behind the creeping barrage 'C' and 'D' Companies followed. Several shells struck Medland's 'A' Company as it approached the start line. Seven men fell dead or wounded. Medland could no longer see 'C' Company through the smoke, and no wireless reports were coming in from Nickson.[52] The near constant sheet-ripping sound of MG-42 machine guns and exploding grenade blasts told him there was heavy fighting out there.

'C' Company had been struck by murderous defensive fire from paratroopers holding nearby farm buildings and adjacent dugouts. No. 15 Platoon was pinned down until one section slipped out to the right and drove in with bayonets fixed to take the buildings from the rear. "Hand-to-hand fighting resulted. The rifleman's sword, so seldom used in battle, here came into action. The enemy fought bitterly, tenaciously. The other two platoon sections came up, and eventually after suffering many casualties, were victorious." With the remnants of No. 15 Platoon providing covering fire, No. 14 Platoon gained the second group of buildings beyond. This platoon was greatly assisted by the timely arrival of a troop of 'C' Squadron. As 'C' Company began consolidating on its objectives, German artillery and mortar fire struck, the first salvo killing the platoon's lieutenant and sergeant. But the men held steady.

On the left flank, 'D' Company's two lead platoons, Nos. 16 and 17, had quickly managed to seize their assigned clutches of buildings in the village of Mooshof. But no sooner were the paratroopers evicted than the predictable retaliatory artillery and mortar shower began. As No. 18 Platoon passed through Lieutenant Don McKay's No. 16 Platoon, it strayed to the right behind a couple of tanks. This exposed McKay's platoon to an attempted infiltration by paratroopers. A fierce gunfire exchange followed before the Germans broke off. Several artillery salvoes fell, badly wounding McKay and wiping out one entire section. What remained of the platoon fell back on No. 17 Platoon's position.[53]

Rifleman Norm Selby was pulling back slowly when Lance Corporal Edward William Fraser shouted, "Speed it up, you guys." Dashing around the corner of a building, Fraser was passing a window when a German inside fired a Schmeisser burst. Fraser fell dead. Selby chucked a grenade through the window. A glance inside revealed the German lying dead, both hands still gripping the machine-pistol.

Sergeant Aubrey Cosens took over the platoon. He was twenty-three and hailed from the northern Ontario village of Porquis Junction (now part of Iroquois Falls). Selby recalled that Cosens "wore a tank suit, lots of pockets, carried a pistol. I never saw him with a rifle or a Sten."[54] Despite No. 16 Platoon's losses, Cosens led it in two attacks on the last three farm buildings. Each time they were beaten back. The platoon was in terrible shape. About thirty men had crossed the start line. Now just Cosens and four riflemen remained fighting fit.

Cosens was undeterred. Those buildings were going to be retaken. Ordering his four soldiers to provide covering fire, Cosens armed himself with a Sten gun and grenades. Then he dashed across twenty-five yards of bullet-swept ground to reach the tank commanded by Sergeant Charles Anderson.[55] Cosens grabbed the outside phone attached to the tank's hull and directed Anderson to attack the buildings with main-gun and machine-gun fire. After some heavy fire had been thrown out, Cosens told Anderson to ram the first building in order to collapse a wall. Trooper Bill Adams, the driver, was wary. "I was pretty careful about ramming those stone walls. Usually there's some kind of basement. We wouldn't be much use to anyone with a thirty ton Sherman tank lying around in a farm cellar."[56] As the tank slammed into the building, Cosens dashed through the opening created. The sergeant fought his way through "the three buildings in turn, alone, and killed or captured all the occupants."

During his solo rampage, Cosens killed at least twenty Germans and captured about the same number. As the survivors of No. 16 Platoon re-established themselves amid the buildings, Cosens moved across a small clearing to report to Major Dunkleman. A shot rang out. Cosens fell, the sniper's bullet striking him in the head and killing him instantly. Sergeant Aubrey Cosens was posthumously awarded the Commonwealth's highest medal for valour, the Victoria Cross.[57]

'D' Company had been badly mauled. Dunkleman counted only 36 out of 115 men still standing.[58] It required assistance from the following 'B' Company to fully secure Mooshof.[59]

On the right flank, 'C' Company had been equally shredded. Although unable to contact Major Nickson, Major Medland could see a close-quarters fight going on in the hamlet ahead. Deciding that 'C' Company likely had the situation in hand, he told his 'A' Company's Nos. 7 and 9 Platoons to sweep out to the left and bypass 'C' Company's position. "The Germans contested every foot. They put up one hell of a fight. They threw everything at us. We did the same to them. For a solid two hours it was sheer madness," Medland said.[60]

No. 7 Platoon's objective was a fortified farmhouse concealing an 88-millimetre gun and several protecting machine guns. Lieutenant Donald David Chadbolt—just twenty-one—led the platoon. By 0600 hours, it had taken the building and silenced the German guns in a fierce battle that claimed Chadbolt's life. Platoon Sergeant

Joe Meagher suffered a bad spleen wound. Lance Sergeant Harold Clyne took over and led two men in a fight for a second building sheltering another 88-millimetre gun. They won the place at 0730, but Clyne was dead.

All 'A' Company platoons suffered terrible losses. Lieutenant Edward Leslie Nicholas Grant was killed in No. 8 Platoon's fight for a first building. Sergeant Bill Lennox kept the platoon going and they won their objective. But at least half the men were killed or wounded.[61]

Beyond the buildings taken by Nos. 7 and 8 Platoons stood another cluster. Twenty-two-year-old Lieutenant John James Chambers led a charge. Chambers had joined the regiment just two weeks earlier. He died in that morning's fight.[62] Despite suffering an arm wound, Corporal Bob Dunstan led the survivors in clearing the buildings. Corporal Bert Shepherd, a rough and argumentative veteran of D-Day, oversaw the platoon's consolidation in the place.

Medland established his company headquarters in the farmhouse taken by Chadbolt's platoon. A quick count revealed that he was the only surviving officer in 'A' Company and commanded just forty-two men. That included two non-commissioned officers, Company Sergeant Major Charlie Martin and Corporal Shepherd. The building was crowded with wounded men.[63] 'A' Company had lost three officers, with twenty other ranks killed and another thirty-nine wounded. Among the dead was Rifleman Ole Herman Thorell, Medland's wireless operator. Thorell, Medland, and Medland's runner/batman had been running forward by bounds through heavy fire when Medland saw a German helmet to his left. He shouted, "Down!" Medland and the runner dropped to safety, but Thorell was hit by a Schmeisser burst. Medland crawled over to him. Thorell was dead, the wireless set riddled by bullets. Medland and his runner mercilessly hunted and killed the German. "When you've lost in action somebody like Thorell you become a different person," Medland said.

With the wireless lost, Medland managed to get a message relayed through the artillery net being used by forward observation officers. He told Lieutenant Colonel Lett that he needed the company's jeep and carrier to evacuate the wounded. He also wanted extra Bren guns, ammunition, and rum. Medland got all that and also a new wireless with signaller attached. When Medland raised Lett, the battalion commander told him 'A' Company must finish the battle by taking Steeg. Medland protested that Steeg was a 'C' Company objective. Didn't matter, Lett replied, 'C' Company was done. Medland, Martin, and Shepherd got busy on a plan. The major had expected an argument from Shepherd, normally always up for griping and playing barracks lawyer. Medland could see that Shepherd "thought I'd gone over the edge." But the corporal kept his silence.[64]

Medland asked Lett for tanks, only to learn that 'C' Squadron had been sent to help the North Shores, who had attacked Keppeln and been caught in a firestorm.[65] Lett sent Sergeant Wilf Mercer with the battalion's Wasp flame-thrower carriers and promised to try calling in some Typhoons. He also promised heavy artillery support.

Mercer told Martin that the Wasps would go forward with the leading section. They had to get in close to be effective.[66] Shepherd led that section of a dozen men. Martin had the rest of the company divided into a following section and a small fire group that would remain with Medland.

"I can't describe my feelings as they moved out," Medland recounted. "We were all filthy and covered in mud. Bert and his men were being asked to behave as if they were five times as many. They went into the job with courage and heart. Shepherd had been with us from the start, one of the best marksmen in our 3rd Division, irreverent but always reliable, and this was a case where his regard for duty was over-riding his common sense.

"So I was feeling very badly, staying with my cover-fire group, my signaller and the artillery FOO, ready to coordinate support for this brave but rather feeble group." Martin headed out to follow Shepherd's group. "He didn't say anything, just gave me a hand wave."[67]

The remnant had about five hundred yards to cover—open, bare ground. In a matter of seconds, 88-millimetre guns knocked out all the Wasps save the one with Mercer aboard. It struck a mine that tore off a track. Mercer was pinned in the wreckage by a mangled leg. Two riflemen and Martin ran to his aid. Martin drew a morphine syringe while the two riflemen tried to free Mercer. When they were unable to do so, Martin jabbed the syringe through Mercer's uniform and injected the morphine. Mercer was shouting at them to get away, to leave him. Any moment the flame-thrower's fuel would cook off. They would all be burned alive. Somehow they freed Mercer. The four men were twenty yards from the Wasp when it exploded. Their clothes were scorched, but they were otherwise unharmed.

As the riflemen and a stretcher-bearer carried Mercer from the field, Martin turned back to the attack. And there before him was the most beautiful sight. The two sections were closing on Steeg, and all over, white pieces of fabric were waving. A huge throng of Germans, far outnumbering the ragtag group of Queen's Own Rifles, stumbled out of buildings with raised arms. "To a battered and shattered under-strength rifle company the sight of those flags was like rain in the desert."[68]

It was about 1500 hours, and the battle was done. In the various company areas, survivors dug in and prepared to weather the inevitable retaliatory shelling and likely counterattacks. Four officers and twenty-eight other ranks were dead. Another five died of their wounds. Three officers and sixty-one other ranks were wounded. The Queen's Own counted three hundred Germans taken prisoner and an unknown number killed. Those who survived generally agreed that February 26 was "their toughest scrap" of the war.[69]

Dash and Simplicity

NORTH SHORE (NEW Brunswick) Regiment Padre Miles Hickey thought the two thousand yards his battalion must cross to reach the fortified village of Keppeln resembled a "baseball diamond." The Canadians stood in the batting box, looking toward a widening triangle with Keppeln somewhere near the back bleachers and concealed by a ridge crest. Hickey suspected a trap. He thought of places soldiers of other battalions had dubbed Hell's Corner. Such places potentially lay "around every bend in Europe. Every unit in action went through one." So far, the North Shores had escaped finding one. But now Hickey feared Keppeln would be their Hell's Corner.[1]

Brigadier Jim Roberts knew the danger his two battalions faced. Situated on the Calcar–Üdem road, Keppeln "would be strongly held by the enemy as the centre of communications in this defensive position." Roberts had hoped to gain a slight edge for the North Shores by having the Queen's Own Rifles Regiment attack several hours earlier. They were to have secured the left flank eastward to Steeg before the North Shores advanced. With the Queen's Own providing covering fire, resistance should have been lessened. By having Le Régiment de la Chaudière advance fifteen minutes ahead of the North Shores, he also hoped to partially secure their right flank. If Kangaroos or even tanks were available for the North Shores to ride some of the way, the situation might have seemed less hopeless. But 2nd Canadian Armoured Brigade was overextended. 'B' Squadron of the 1st Hussars Regiment supported the Chauds. Nobody backed the North Shores.[2]

A troop of self-propelled guns and a troop of towed anti-tank guns from 3rd Canadian Anti-Tank Regiment, as well as the medium machine-gun company and 4.2-inch mortars of the Cameron Highlanders of Ottawa (MG Battalion), had been promised for the Chauds.[3] North Shores' Lieutenant Colonel John Rowley could not understand why he got nothing. When asked, Roberts could only advise that there were no tanks available. Nor "were the anti-tank guns or mortars of the battalion support company to be brought forward, to avoid congestion on the roads. There was however a plan for heavy artillery support. The action therefore resolved itself into a straight infantry attack over a wide, open front."

Rowley was a bold commander. But his nickname, Good Shepherd, alluded not purely to his carrying a long Scottish walking stick. It reflected on his concern for the battalion's welfare. Given the handicaps he faced, Rowley planned to cut straight to the heart. No dicking around with intermediary objectives and carefully passing one company through the other. Instead, Major Bill Parker's 'B' Company and Major Jim Currie's 'C' Company would charge straight to Keppeln and carve a path through it.[4] The support company's Bren carriers and Wasps were to trail about two hundred yards behind 'B' Company, ready to assist. 'A' and 'D' Companies would remain on the start line until Rowley deemed it opportune to advance them. He hoped these companies and his tactical headquarters would walk up that long slope unmolested and enter a subdued Keppeln.[5]

A subdued Parker and his friend Lieutenant Harry Nutter chatted while looking toward the ridge crest. "What do you think of this one?" Nutter asked. The twenty-nine-year-old major, nicknamed Billy, replied, "Harry, this is my last go. This is going to be one of the worst." Nutter tried "to kid him, but he just smiled at me."[6]

Off to the right, the Chauds made their own preparations. Lieutenant Colonel Guy Taschereau did not think the Chauds bountifully supported. Same open ground and certainty that the little hamlets of Halvenboom, Hollen, and Bomshof would be fiercely defended by capable 6th Fallschirmjäger Division paratroopers. Hollen was larger than the other two, so despite being in the middle, it was the primary objective.[7] The Chauds were woefully understrength and short of officers. 'B' Company's commander, for example, was a lieutenant jacked up to acting captain. William Atkinson was a very able young man, but not a seasoned leader.[8] 'B' Company would be on the right, with 'A' Company opposite. Another captain, Robert Rochon, led that company. Each company had two preliminary objectives. Once these were taken, 'C' Company under Major Armand Ross would pass through 'A' Company, while Major Jacques Castonguay's 'D' Company advanced through 'B' Company to the primary objective.[9]

FOR REASONS NEVER explained, the Chauds started late—at 0845 instead of 0830. At precisely the same time, the North Shores set off. Both battalions advanced on either side of a road running directly to Üdem. The road cut through Bomshof, which lay just a few hundred yards south of Keppeln.

All went smoothly at first and hopes lifted. Artillery was on target and on time. 'B' Squadron rolled along with the Chauds, firing at any potential target. The two leading Chaud companies got through Halvenboom with only a slight skirmish.[10]

Forty-five minutes out, the Chauds were closing on Hollen and the North Shores were just crossing the ridge crest. The North Shores could see Keppeln now, particularly a barn on its edge. About 150 yards left. The supporting barrage struck the village sharply and then ceased according to plan, to avoid falling on the North Shores. Immediately, things went to hell. Two self-propelled guns inside the barn spouted fire. Machine-gun crews lashed out from a well-concealed trench system that cut across Keppeln's front. Mortar and artillery fire fell.[11] Heavy machine-gun fire from Hollen and Steeg slashed their flanks. Both hamlets were to have been taken much earlier. But the Queen's Own still fought at Mooshof, and the Chauds had gone to ground in the face of heavy opposition anchored on Hollen.[12]

'C' Company's Lieutenant Don MacPherson led his platoon in a charge on the trenches. MacPherson was killed. The platoon's survivors did the only thing possible and hit the dirt. So did everybody else. Most took refuge in shell craters. The Wasps tried to get forward. Only Sergeant Horace Boulay's Wasp escaped being lost to mines or anti-tank fire.[13] Boulay steered it up to the barn. Flames sprayed out to destroy one self-propelled gun, a Panther tank, and an armoured scout car while also driving the paratroopers away. This enabled a 'C' Company platoon to seize the barn, but there was no question of the North Shores carrying on into Keppeln.[14] While the action earned Boulay a deserved Military Medal, it failed to break the German defence. Fuel for the flame-thrower exhausted, Boulay withdrew, refuelled, and reported to battalion headquarters for orders.[15]

Facing Hollen, the Chauds were being ripped apart by fire out of Keppeln. The paratroopers in Hollen and Keppeln were skillfully supporting each other, creating a broad-front defence. Only on the right flank did the Chauds enjoy slight success. Captain Rochon's 'B' Company captured both its objectives—a small farm and then a crossroads—taking about forty-five prisoners. Taschereau decided to exploit this gain to relieve some of the pressure from his heavily engaged 'A' Company, which directly faced Hollen. He ordered Major Ross to pass 'D' Company through the 'B' Company position and seize a group of buildings to the right of Hollen. Ross and his men advanced across ground swept by fire and were closing in when a white flag appeared. Believing the Germans were surrendering, the men relaxed just as three Panther tanks cut into the company with their machine guns. Many men fell dead or wounded, and the survivors ran back to 'B' Company's lines.[16]

In front of Hollen, 'B' Squadron's Shermans locked in an uneven duel with well-hidden tanks and anti-tank guns. As soon as one enemy gun was knocked out, another seemed to sprout up. So much machine-gun fire whipped around the tanks that crew commanders were forced to hunker down inside the turrets, and communication with the Chauds became impossible. Lieutenant A.M. Spencer tried to work his No. 3 Troop around to the right of a hidden 88-millimetre gun that had knocked out a No. 4 Troop tank. Spencer was still trying to locate the gun when it fired a shell that set his tank burning. The tankers realized the situation was stalemated and pulled back.[17]

At his headquarters, Lieutenant Colonel Rowley realized that any impetus the attack had enjoyed was lost. "It was apparent that some new element must be introduced to regain the initiative." Brigadier

Jim Roberts suggested Rowley send his remaining two companies through the Chauds and attack Keppeln from either the south or the rear. Rowley wanted to stick to the original plan, but "with the aid of armour."[18] Roberts agreed. But the only tanks available were the 1st Hussars 'C' Squadron, still with the Queen's Own Rifles.[19]

At 1100 hours, 'C' Squadron was ordered to withdraw. Thirteen of nineteen Shermans were battle-worthy. While these tanks rearmed, Major Jake Powell hurried to Rowley's headquarters.[20] Having worked their way back from Keppeln, Major Bill Parker and Major Jim Currie were also present. Both company commanders reported counting about ten tanks prowling inside the village, mostly Panthers.[21] These tanks appeared to have concentrated around the church square.[22] Rowley believed that his plan, "while unorthodox, had the advantage of dash and simplicity."

One 'A' Company platoon, riding on Powell's tanks, would barrel directly into Kepplen—passing right by the two pinned-down lead companies. The moment the tanks were out front with the platoon still aboard, Parker and Currie would move their men forward behind the tanks. The rest of 'A' Company and all of 'D' Company would be advancing on foot "with all possible speed" to join the battle. The attack was set for 1415 hours. It was now 1320. Meantime, the guns of both a field and medium artillery regiment would batter Keppeln to try neutralizing the tanks. Rowley had asked for fighter-bombers as well, but weather conditions had grounded them.[23]

The scheme shocked Powell, who returned to his tank. He raised 1st Hussars Lieutenant Colonel Franklyn "Frankie" White by wireless, and warned the attack "would be nothing short of suicide." But it might create a sufficient diversion to enable the North Shores to gain Keppeln.[24]

Parker and Currie headed up the slope to join their companies. As Parker had predicted to Lieutenant Harry Nutter, Keppeln proved to be his last show. A German shell killed him out on that open ground.[25]

IT WAS NUTTER'S platoon that was ordered to ride the tanks. Nutter gathered his forty-two men and told them "this would be bad, the worst yet, but we would do it. I remember their faces, their trust was terrifying. I told them that some of us would make it, and we would all do our best. They were wonderful men and after that day my faith in human nature would never fail."

The platoon climbed onto the growling Shermans. Other men passed up all the company's PIAT guns and ammunition. Nutter was sure he was going to die. With two other men, he rode the third tank in line.[26] As the tanks surged out at 1415 hours, they came under German artillery fire. But so much dust and smoke boiled around Keppeln that the German observers were firing blind, and the shells fell harmlessly behind the thirteen racing tanks.[27]

"We went tearing across the start line and it was a naked feeling to be on top of a tank." The tanks were going flat out at twenty-five miles per hour. Closer to Keppeln, the accuracy of German artillery and mortar fire improved. Nutter saw Private Waldo Leroy Richardson tumble dead off a tank. As the tanks reached 'B' and 'C' Companies, they swung away from the road to avoid running over dead and wounded North Shores lying on it. "Then we hit the enemy trenches and our tank stalled in the mud right there. My men had been shooting like mad as we slowed speed and we took a heavy toll of the trench garrison...Our tank was free in a moment and we roared on. Two German tanks were dug in behind a house just beyond the trenches and our tanks blasted away at them as they could not swing their guns enough to fire back...Some of our tanks blew up there on mines. The rest, including the one I was on, went on as fast as possible, swinging out around the town. A German tank dug in behind the church began picking off the first tanks and I could see my men jumping off as tanks were hit and I beat my tank commander over the head with a Sten gun to get him stopped. We jumped off."[28]

Only five Shermans reached Keppeln. Behind them others burned or had lost tracks to mines. A couple were stuck in mud. Powell's had pitched into a shell hole just outside the village. Lieutenant David Eggo's tank was the only one in his troop to reach Keppeln. His infantry had dismounted. He could raise no fellow tankers on the wireless. When Eggo ordered the driver to go deeper into the village, the tank was immediately struck "by a hail of fire from enemy infantry, panzerfaust, and armoured fighting vehicles. So determined, however, was his advance that the enemy were forced to withdraw, leaving behind many dead and wounded," stated his Military Cross citation.[29]

Nutter's platoon and the tankers were scattered. The remnants of the infantry fought in small groups or sometimes alone. Sometimes a tank weighed in alongside. Nutter had five men with him, one with the last name Jagoe. As Nutter and his men took shelter in a shell crater, the man's cousin—Private Donald Charles Jagoe—"was blown right over our heads by a shell burst and killed." Buildings burned and Nutter thought of withdrawing under the cover of the smoke.

"Corporal Jack Tree shook his Sten gun at me in a rage and showed me a shrapnel hole through the mechanism. So I gave him mine and resorted to my pistol. There were four Germans in the first trench we reached and they never fired a shot but were lying in the bottom of their hiding place. Out they came with hands up and raced back as we pointed the way for them to go. We ran into the town then, shooting at any Germans we saw, had luck all the way, and kept booting prisoners back toward our advancing troops. We obtained good positions by our attack and were firing up the main street... when our troops finally arrived."

As the men of 'B' and 'C' Companies poured into Keppeln, six German tanks fled toward Üdem. At 1600 hours, Keppeln was reported secure. The slow task of silencing a handful of stay-behind snipers was all that remained to be done.[30]

Nutter's platoon numbered only nine men. The sergeant's back was peppered with shrapnel. One private had lost an arm, another had an arm paralyzed.

Walking alone to Keppeln, Lieutenant Colonel Rowley passed Lieutenant Owen Kierans crouching by a wall. Kierans could not believe Rowley was walking in the open. "He was in super-fine battle dress with brass gleaming, binoculars on his chest and map-board by his side. 'Where is your platoon?' he asked. I crouched closer to the wall as a mortar landed very near and answered him. 'Well, Kierans,' he remarked, 'I'm glad to see that things are well in hand.' He began to talk about the possibility of a counterattack, as if he were standing in a railway station, while I felt the most dangerous place in the world right then was the centre of main street in Keppeln. As much as I admired his courage, I didn't want to be near him while snipers were still active in the place."[31]

ONCE KEPPELN FELL, Le Régiment de la Chaudière could advance on Hollen. "This move was made so quickly that a German half-track full of ammunition was captured intact. One 88-millimetre and two 50-millimetre guns were captured here, together with 84 prisoners of war; 15 enemy dead were found," the battalion's second-in-command, Major F.J. L'Espérance, reported. Bomshof fell at 1630 hours, and another anti-tank gun and a German lorry loaded with loot were captured. A barn thought to conceal another anti-tank gun was set afire. It proved instead to be a quartermaster's store, and the large ammunition dump contained therein exploded spectacularly. By 1900 hours, the Chauds had secured all objectives.

"The fighting by the battalion this day," L'Espérance wrote, "was as hard as any it has met to date. It accomplished much. A total of 225 prisoners were taken...The casualties for the day were 15 other ranks killed and 3 officers and 52 other ranks wounded."[32] The Chauds would soon grieve another death. On February 28, the regiment's padre, Major Joseph Remi Archibald Dalcourt, was collecting dead from the battlefield when his jeep struck a mine and he was killed.[33]

North Shore casualties were heavier. Two officers killed, four officers wounded, one officer evacuated with battle exhaustion, twenty-six other ranks killed, fifty-six wounded, and three missing.[34] Rowley received a Distinguished Service Order and left the following day for well-deserved leave. The battalion's second-in-command, Major Neil Gordon, temporarily took command. Nutter was put in for a Military Cross, but the recommendation was refused. On the day following the battle, the North Shore's Padre Miles Hickey watched "with a weary heart as German prisoners...dug twenty-six graves in the military cemetery at Bedburg." The North Shores had found their Hell's Corner.[35]

For the 1st Hussars, February 26 inflicted the largest number of casualties suffered in a single day. Sixteen men were killed and eleven wounded. February 26 also brought the regiment its highest number of gallantry awards for one day—six in total. Major Jake Powell was recommended for a Victoria Cross. Although every commander along the chain of command up to First Canadian Army's General Harry Crerar approved it, Field Marshal Montgomery personally knocked it back to a DSO with a pen stroke.[36] Nine tanks had brewed and burned. Four tanks were damaged by mines. Another four were knocked out by Panzerfausts or anti-tank guns but proved repairable. Five tanks had bogged down and necessitated being towed free by recovery teams. The tankers were well pleased with the day's results, despite the losses in men and equipment. A 1st Hussars report noted that more than seven hundred prisoners had been taken. They had knocked out two Mark IVs, one Panther, and one self-propelled gun, as well as capturing at least three anti-tank guns.[37]

More importantly, the battle fought by 8th Canadian Infantry Brigade opened the way for 9th Canadian Infantry Brigade to pass through and attack Üdem. Bomshof was to serve as the start line of the attack, which would begin that night.

The attack was to be coordinated with one coming from the northeast by the 4th Canadian Armoured Division battle group. About mid-morning, the Canadian tank division had launched its part in Operation Blockbuster by advancing from ground that 2nd Canadian Infantry Division had won south of Calcar. Üdem was surrounded by anti-tank ditches and known to be heavily fortified. As the town was the last true bastion in front of the Hochwald Layback, a stiff fight was expected. The coordinated attack was also the third phase in the Blockbuster plan for February 26.[38]

THE 4TH CANADIAN Armoured Division's attack was aimed at seizing high ground overlooking Üdem from the northeast. Lieutenant General Guy Simonds had anticipated that 3rd Canadian Infantry Division might be unable to breach the town's defences as long as the Germans retained a firm grip on these heights. So once 2nd Division had forced the Germans back about 1,500 yards from the Calcar–Üdem ridge, the armoured battle group was to pass through its lines. This force would then advance about four miles in a bow-shaped curve to pass east of Keppeln and seize the heights.

This was Major General Chris Vokes's first major armoured operation. He was determined to see the division excel in the task. His written orders ended with a "tactics and thrust" lecture. "This will be an all-out effort...strip[ped] to the absolute minimum of wheeled vehicles within units. The troops must be impressed with the vital necessity to get on to destroy the enemy. Subordinate commands must act on their own initiative. Don't sit on the objective, if you can press on. Be prepared to go hungry but make every effort to see adequate food is available. Tanks should try to carry extra to feed infantry. Every vehicle should contain rations and spare petrol. Tanks must be topped up in forming-up positions. Don't waste ammunition. The Bosche is in a bad way compared to ourselves and is fighting in sheer desperation. He gives up easily when cut off. This is our opportunity—we must make the best of it."[39]

Primarily a tank show, the division's 4th Canadian Armoured Brigade was under the overall command of Brigadier Robert Moncel. Its three tank regiments formed the core of Tiger Force, with infantry drawn from the Lake Superior Regiment (Motor) and two battalions of 10th Canadian Infantry Brigade. Tiger Force packed a lot of mobile punch. But Moncel's complex plan divvied it into five sub-groups—each having separate objectives. Two sub-groups were formed around armoured regiments (less one squadron sent to one of the other sub-groups) accompanied by infantry companies. Lacking Kangaroos, the infantry rode in a mix of Crusader and Ram armoured gun tractors provided by 5th and 6th Canadian Anti-Tank Regiments. These tractors normally towed the regiments' 17-pounder anti-tank guns.[40]

Leading on the left would be Gerry Force, anchored on the British Columbia Regiment and under command of its Lieutenant Colonel Gerry Chubb. Two Lincoln and Welland Regiment companies and one Flail tank troop were attached. To the right, Lieutenant Colonel Hershell "Snuffy" Smith's Canadian Grenadier Guards, two companies of Argyll and Sutherland Highlanders, and a Flail troop formed Snuff Force. Behind each of these followed two more. Jock Force consisted of Argylls (less the two companies, so quite weak), a Grenadier squadron, a self-propelled anti-tank gun troop, and a troop of flame-throwing Crocodile tanks. Its commander was Argyll Lieutenant Colonel Fred Wigle. Cole Force had the same composition, with the Lincs providing the infantry and the Dukes (the British Columbia Regiment) a tank squadron. Lincs' commander Lieutenant Colonel Rowen "Ron" Coleman was in charge. These two forces were to mop up enemy resistance pockets bypassed by the armoured forces. Bringing up the rear was Smith Force, made up of the Governor General's Foot Guards, the Lake Superior (Motor) Battalion, a Crocodile troop, and another self-propelled anti-tank gun troop.

Moncel emphasized that Snuff and Gerry must "push on for the objective, stopping for nothing. Enemy pockets would be mopped up by Jock Force on the right and Cole Force on the left." The first objective was a line roughly parallel with Keppeln and centred on a shell-torn orchard next to Todtenhügel. Once Snuff and Gerry reached this, Smith Force would pass through to carry the advance to the heights overlooking Üdem.[41] Following well behind Tiger Force would be the rest of 10th Canadian Infantry Brigade, formed into Lion Force and under command of Brigadier Jim Jefferson. Tiger Force was formed primarily around the Algonquin Regiment, with its tank strength provided by the division's reconnaissance unit, the South Alberta Regiment. If all went well, it would seize a hill dominating the western end of the Hochwald Gap.[42]

Commenting on the plan later, Coleman said, "I remember my irritation at the time and the irritation of all my fellow commanders. Here we are being divided up into little segments...Yes, it was complicated, unnecessarily complicated from the standpoint of a commander...I found myself halfway up the wall...I thought, 'Good God, how mixed up can you get?' I was really wild with impatience and anger as anybody who was with me will attest."[43] There was little Coleman could do but salute and play the good soldier. Moncel was not a man easily dissuaded.

Not a soul involved on February 26 would ever forget the mud. It took hours for the battle group to cover seven miles to reach its start line. Tanks and tractors created a sea of churning mud. Waiting on the start line two thousand yards from Calcar on the west side of the road running to Goch, tanks sank "belly deep in the wet clay."[44] At 1015 hours, the advance began.[45]

"The slippery going in the soupy mud—bad enough for the leading tanks but nearly impossible for those behind—slowed the pace of all," the Grenadier Guards historian later recorded.[46] It took two hours to cover just five hundred yards.[47]

Guardsman Stuart Louis Johns was in a Grenadier Guards Sherman in No. 2 Troop of No. 2 Squadron. Today, however, his tank was seconded to the squadron's headquarters troop. To ensure that all the brigade's officers got some battlefield experience, Moncel had assigned several rear area officers to command tanks in Tiger Force. Captain Doug McGowan, a Royal Electrical and Mechanical Engineers officer, was Johns's crew commander. The squadron's commander, Major Curtis Greenleaf, had assigned McGowan to Johns's tank because the crew was experienced and competent. Greenleaf told the crew to keep McGowan out of trouble and the officer to follow their instructions.

Not far from the start line, the tank's right track ran "into a mine. It was so deep in the mud," Johns remembered, "that the bottom of the track was lower than the mine. So we didn't run over it, we ran into it. The mine was between the drive sprocket and the first bogie wheel. When it exploded, the tank just stopped completely. The track was separated. A couple of the links had been blown off. The bottom was fine because the weight of the tank just held it. But the top part had been thrown around and it had rolled back on the rollers and was partly lying out in the field right behind the tank."

To avoid getting mired in ruts created by the leading tanks, each crew had tried to avoid following behind another. In every direction, Johns saw tanks bogged down or immobilized by mines. Others came up and rolled on by. McGowan normally commanded mechanics. "I think we can fix this," he told the crew. Johns and the others doubted it. They also pointed out that McGowan was today's squadron second-in-command. His place was with Greenleaf, not playing mechanic in a muddy field. They flagged a passing tank and put him aboard.

Guardsman Bill Mackie, the driver in Johns's tank, was a competent mechanic. He said it might be possible to fix the track if they hooked a cable to it and then got another tank to pull it back onto the rollers. They could then replace any broken links and be good to go. Looking more closely, Mackie realized the explosion had flattened the most forward bogie wheel. Normally, the track would jam as it passed over the damaged wheel. But the mud might work in their favour, acting like a constant grease to keep the track slipping past the front bogie. "We might be able to move," Mackie said.

A Fort Garry Horse troop was coming back from an attack, so Johns waved one down. The sergeant commanding tossed down a headphone and microphone set. Johns explained their idea. "I think you guys are crazy. I think if I was you, I'd sit on my ass and wait until you get picked up." Johns said they were determined. The moment Johns started back toward his tank, a shot rang out and he was barely missed by a sniper bullet from somewhere to their left. No way could the crew work in front of the tank without getting shot. The Garry sergeant had the solution. "If you guys are going to do this, we'll do it right," he shouted. Once his tank pulled the track into place, he would roll out to the front of their tank and provide a shield. The job took just twenty minutes. After replacing three links, "we shovelled a bunch of wet, wet mud onto the inside of the track. Then Bill Mackie scrambled into the tank and started it and moved forward. That first bogie wheel, that had a flat circumference on it, it just turned until it sat on the inside of the track and it never moved after that. But the mud was so sloppy that it kept that thing from seizing up on us. Only problem was we couldn't reverse. Soon as we did, instead of that loop being between the drive sprocket and the flat bogie, it would become tight and bind." Setting off, the tank crew soon rejoined No. 2 Squadron's headquarters section. McGowan resumed command.[48]

Tiger force met steadily increasing opposition from the paratroopers, who took a toll on the Shermans with Panzerfausts. Also more active than usual were Panzerschreck anti-tank rocket-launcher crews. Firing an 88-millimetre rocket, the Panzerschreck had an effective range of about 450 feet. Unlike the Panzerfaust, the launching tube was reusable. At 24.25 pounds, the launcher was heavy, and its 64.75-inch length made it unwieldy. The 88-millimetre rocket presented a deadly threat though.

On the left flank, Gerry Force ran into particular trouble. The tanks of both the commander and second-in-command of the British Columbia Regiment's 'C' Squadron were knocked out early on. Major Jim Tedlie of 'B' Squadron brought the other squadron under his command and continued the advance.[49]

"We were losing Shermans; they were running over mines, blowing tracks, getting stuck," Lincoln and Welland Regiment Corporal Ken Hipel said. His 'C' Company commander, Major C.K. Crummer, found that every house encountered was fortified and held by half a dozen paratroopers. But despite the heavy losses, even when a single tank remained in support, it "could just take a house out like that in no time...Put several amour piercing right through the basement window and an HE [high-explosive shell] following it and it's all over... It was mostly firepower that did it."[50]

Following behind the lead groups, Lieutenant Colonel Fred Wigle commanding Jock Force was dismayed by how many small skirmishes his Argyll and Sutherland Highlander infantry were fighting for individual buildings or farm clusters. The tanks up front were pounding these, but there always seemed to be paratroopers who survived. Each action generated twenty to thirty prisoners, which showed that Crummer little appreciated how strongly the positions were held. And each skirmish pushed back "the contemplated time for the completion of this task," Wigle complained.[51]

It was already mid-afternoon. Tiger Force was well behind schedule. To Wigle's front, Snuff Force was climbing a gradual slope toward Todtenhügel. The Argylls in the Ram tractors were lagging badly as the heavy vehicles churned through mud. Guardsman Stuart Johns peered through a periscope. He saw a Sherman to the left shudder, and knew it was hit. Seconds later the crew bailed out. Swivelling the periscope right revealed a couple more knocked-out Shermans. Johns wanted to hit back, but there were no targets. The Germans were up the slope in hull-down positions. Lieutenant Colonel Hershell Smith came on the air with orders for the tanks to fire smoke rounds. He also called in artillery smoke. The Grenadiers were to fall back, regroup, and put in a charge. Reversing down the slope as the other tanks did was not possible for Johns's tank, as the flattened front bogie would jam the track. So Captain McGowan ordered the driver to make a long slow turn to the right. In his loader/operator seat, Johns kept looking through the periscope. In the distance, about five hundred yards off, was a farm. Johns thought he saw a German tank backed into the guts of a smaller building behind the farmhouse. As the Sherman rolled into a cloud of smoke, McGowan reported seeing a muzzle flash from the building.

Reaching the regrouping tanks, they carried out another slow turn and joined the charge. McGowan carefully minded the left flank, certain there was a tank out there. Johns was equally vigilant. At the same time, he argued with gunner Guardsman Oliver McLeod. McLeod wanted to switch an armour-piercing round into the 75-millimetre gun breech, while Johns favoured retaining the normal high-explosive. McGowan said to leave the HE in place. If they fired an AP round and missed, they would have nothing to show for it. At least the HE might knock some of the building down on the Germans.

As the Sherman emerged from the smokescreen, they saw the German tank. It was jockeying forward, trying to get to where the turret could swivel to engage them. McLeod fired. The shell "knocked out part of a wall and a bunch of debris fell on the tank." Johns had his legs wrapped around three AP shells and one HE, so they were right at hand. He snatched up an AP shell, slammed it into the breech. The breech slammed back, pushing Johns's hand out of the way hard. Only a few seconds passed before all three AP shells were gone and then the HE round. "The final high-explosive caught the German crew dismounting out of their tank. That is the only tank that we can lay claim to. We never came one-on-one against a German tank after that. It was a Mark IV."[52]

All around, Johns saw Shermans burning or knocked out. Their victory had obviously not won the day. Out front, Lieutenant Colonel Smith could see Snuff Force's objective about a thousand yards away. It was just a row of orchard trees. Suddenly, three tanks were knocked out in a row, "very quickly, just bang, bang, bang." One of them was Smith's. "I was in the lead tank. It brewed up. All I can remember is that when it got hit, I looked up and the thing was on fire. Looking up at the turret, I could see daylight but it was like looking into a cone of fire. I'm on the floor. I went to stand up and fell down...because I don't know what the hell is wrong with me. But I knew I didn't have long to get out of there. So literally pulled myself up and slowly and surely pulled myself out and then fell on the back of the tank. And then I saw my foot was dangling, but the bones were all gone. Shell had gone through the tank. I jumped down on the ground and rolled over. I took the boot laces out of my other boot and tied it as tight as I could around my other leg as a tourniquet and think that saved my life... bleeding·something vicious, arteries in body not going to take long running out of blood. Everything quietened down and they lifted me on to a light tank and I hung on the side...and they loaded other casualties on and took us back." Everybody in his tank had escaped, but one was badly burned. Smith lost the lower part of his leg.[53]

Command of Snuff Force passed to Major Greenleaf, who told Captain McGowan he had charge of No. 2 Squadron. Night was falling. The Argylls had caught up to the tanks. They were on the objective, Todtenhügel over to the left. There was still scattered fighting, infantry and tanks taking on various pockets of resistance. McGowan started dismounting from the tank to talk to a nearby Argyll lieutenant about tackling one pocket. Suddenly, a hidden German fired a Schmeisser burst. Three rounds went through the left side of McGowan's neck and a couple pierced his cheek. In the time it took Johns and the others to dress his wounds, McGowan lost a lot of blood, but he would survive. Johns got on the wireless and reported that No. 2 Squadron had no officers left. The order was for his tank to continue leading until the fight concluded. So the four men got back in the Sherman and led the squadron through the last small fight. A lieutenant took over as the Grenadiers came together at about 2000 hours. Snuff Force's battle was over.[54]

Across the way, Gerry Force was on its objective and Jock and Cole Forces were mopping up behind. They would soon report taking 350 paratroopers prisoner.[55] On the left flank, Gerry Force had come under heavy shell and mortar fire. Major Jim Tedlie repeatedly dismounted from his tank to guide what was left of the British

Columbia Regiment tanks into positions that would enable them to support the infantry of the Lincoln and Welland Regiment. In the middle of this process, the Germans launched a counterattack. Tedlie called in artillery and then twice deployed a small reaction force of tanks and infantry to drive the Germans back. The reaction force overran a number of Germans armed with Panzerschrecks and destroyed a self-propelled gun. Finally, the counterattacks ceased. Tedlie's actions earned a Distinguished Service Order.[56]

Push On Through

E VEN AS THE rest of Tiger Force was still mopping up its objectives, Smith Force crossed its start line at about 1530 hours. At first it faced only the ubiquitous mud that bogged down several of the Governor General's Foot Guard tanks and half-tracks carrying the Lake Superior (Motor) Battalion. Unlike most Canadian infantry battalions, the Superiors had inherent mobility provided by half-track armoured-personnel carriers that each carried ten men. At 1600 hours, the force came under intense fire from Panzerschrecks and 88-millimetre guns. Ten Superior half-tracks were destroyed.[1] Seven of eight tanks in the Foot Guards' leading troop of No. 2 Squadron were hit and five crewmen killed outright or mortally wounded.[2] "All around were crashing shells, burning buildings, and gaping holes filled with water," the Superiors' official historian recorded. "The armoured vehicles floundered in the mud, and with increasing casualties both of men and armour and constant interference with radio communications, control became practically impossible...As the attack withered and died, the men sought refuge among the stark and splintered trees of a nearby orchard where they dismounted and prepared to organize their defences on the ground."

At 1750, under cover of darkness, the attack was renewed. 'C' Company and No. 3 Squadron led. "Again the vehicles of the Lake Superiors became bogged down and had to be abandoned...the men clambered aboard the jolting, lumbering Sherman tanks of the Foot Guards; again they were fired upon by the enemy's anti-tank defences; again they dismounted to organize ground attacks upon their determined opponents. Every man was weary, for few of them had had any sleep the previous night, yet every man was aware of what he had to do. It was the kind of fighting in which the Canadians showed to the best advantage, the kind that demanded adaptability and initiative, not only on the part of the officers but on the part of every non-commissioned officer and man. In spite of every difficulty the Lake Sups and the Foot Guards groped their way forward...Then, at last they were on the hill. In the darkness, the fighting was, of necessity, marked by confusion; there was, however, some comfort in the fact that the enemy must have been just as confused as the Canadians, probably even more so."

The Germans counterattacked repeatedly during the night of February 26–27, each time being flung back. As dawn broke the next morning, Superiors and Foot Guards "could lift their heads in the sharp, chilling wind, to view the field of battle. It was a scene of desolation. Enemy dead lay thick about the ground; enemy anti-tank guns stood at crazy angles; and two enemy tanks were still burning nearby. But the price the Germans had demanded had been high. Not only were there many Canadian vehicles sunk deep in the mud, there were no less than thirty-three Shermans smashed, or burned, as mute evidence of the strength of the enemy resistance."[3] The Foot Guards had ten dead.[4] Lake Superior casualties went unrecorded. By daybreak on February 27, the entire stretch of heights from Calcar's outskirts to the east of Üdem was in Canadian hands. And Üdem itself had been taken in a sharp action involving the Stormont, Dundas and Glengarry Highlanders and Highland Light Infantry of 3rd Division's 9th Brigade.

The Glens had attacked at 2100 hours with 'B' Company on the left and 'D' Company the right. There was the usual artificial moonlight and heavy fog. Left of the Glens, the Highlanders advanced 'D' and 'C' Companies. Progress was good. By 2240 hours, the Glens' 'B' Company was on the outskirts. Soon both battalions were fighting in the town streets. It was slow, dangerous work.[5]

Private Glen Tomlin was in the Highland Light Infantry. The men in his section had taken momentary shelter in a deep anti-tank ditch that circled Üdem. Nearby, Private Kenneth Arthur Lumley stood with his back to where the ditch turned a corner. Tomlin saw a German step around it and fire a Schmeisser into Lumley's back. Lumley cried out, "I can't move. I'm paralysed." The man's "helmet was full of blood and everything else." Seconds later Lumley died. Tomlin and another man "started shooting back toward the corner...We even threw a hand grenade around that corner to keep anything back." Then an officer appeared dragging a German prisoner. "I think that was the closest I ever came to committing murder in my life. I had a bead on the bugger and I was going to shoot him...and the sergeant just walked in front of us." At the time, Tomlin was angry at the sergeant's interference, but later he was "glad it didn't happen."

The section went on, clearing houses. When they got to one large house, Tomlin took his web kit off and leaned the rifle against a wall. He was just beginning to relax when "the Germans came in the back of the house. They threw a counterattack at us, and they threw a grenade because I heard the click, you know, when the firing pin hit the detonator. And it lit down between my rifle...and the wall. And I made a grab for the rifle and she blew it out of my hand. And the guy on either side of me...got hit with shrapnel from the grenade. And my rifle deflected it. I never got a mark on me...And one of the guys threw a grenade in the back room...and we got a couple Germans back there."

Next to Tomlin, a Bren gunner was riddled with bullets and fell dead. The section's survivors, about five men, took refuge in a room. Tomlin's rifle was gone and another man had one jammed. Tomlin managed to clear it. They expected a fight to the death, but soon realized the Germans had slipped away.[6]

Tomlin's experience was typical of that night's fighting amid the ruins. Glens Private Harold Snyder had been tasked with covering one side of the perimeter after 'A' Company cleared its objectives. Lacking any logical position, he built a parapet on the sidewalk and got behind it. When the Germans counterattacked, Snyder fought them alone. He maintained a steady rate of accurate fire that broke the attack and left three Germans killed and another six wounded.

The Germans retaliated by firing a Panzerschreck at him. Despite being wounded by the blast, Snyder met a charge of about thirty men. He shot two dead and wounded three more. That broke the German counterattack. Snyder garnered a Military Medal for his stoic stand.[7]

At about 0400 hours, resistance from the hard-fighting 7th Fallschirmjäger Division dwindled away to occasional sniping. The North Nova Scotia Highlanders passed through to clear the southern sector of Üdem. Sporadic fighting would continue through the mid-afternoon of February 27, but by 0930 hours, the Goch–Xanten railway on its southern outskirts was reported secure. With the long stretch of heights running from Calcar to Üdem successfully taken on the first day of Blockbuster and the towns now also, the way was open for the thrust to the Hochwald.[8]

February 26 was one of the biggest and hardest days of battle Canadians fought in World War II. With all II Canadian Corps engaged, it yielded more decorations for bravery than any other single day. Forty in all—eight to soldiers of 2nd Canadian Infantry Division, ten to 3rd Canadian Infantry Division, ten to 4th Canadian Armoured Division, and twelve to the three tank regiments of 2nd Canadian Armoured Brigade.[9]

YET THE DAY was not fully done when 4th Division's Lion Force, under Brigadier Jim Jefferson, advanced toward the Hochwald. This force was organized around a core provided by the South Alberta Regiment and Algonquin Regiment. Attached was the division's support battalion, the North Shore (New Brunswick) Regiment, and one squadron each of Flails, AVRES, and Crocodile flame-throwing tanks. Lion was to be reinforced early on February 27 by release of the other two 10th Canadian Infantry Brigade battalions from Tiger Force. Algonquin Major George Cassidy noted that Lion's initial composition, "while relatively small in numbers, packed quite a wallop in fire power and mobility, and would doubtless come as an unpleasant surprise to an exhausted enemy battered by so much previous power. Its success, however, would depend largely on its ability to get forward while the battle was still raging, find its jumping-off point, and strike."[10]

This accorded with Lieutenant General Guy Simonds's intention that Blockbuster be a continuous operation—denying the Germans any respite to regroup.[11] The limiting factor, of course, lay with Lion's "ability to get forward." On the night of February 26–27, this proved extremely difficult. Lion Force had spent the day pushing through the mud behind Tiger Force. Although Jefferson commanded, he remained at 10th Brigade headquarters to coordinate communications and provide overall operational direction. Algonquin commander Lieutenant Colonel Robert "Bob" Bradburn controlled the sharp end. With South Alberta Regiment's commander, Lieutenant Colonel Gordon "Swatty" Wotherspoon, temporarily running the division's battle school, Major Bob Coffin commanded the tankers. Nightfall found Lion about three thousand yards north of Keppeln. Information from the front was sketchy and confused.

Calling a halt, Bradburn sent his four company commanders to try to determine what lay ahead. They "floundered in mud across fields, around burnt-out tanks and carriers, map-reading only by intervals with a flashlight or a hurriedly-lit match...It was impossible to get even a notion of who was where, or which routes would serve to move a heavy force."[12] Effort fruitless, the dejected officers returned to say that no matter which route they took, the Algonquin vehicles were going to get "bogged down."[13]

The original Lion plan called for an advance from the heights to the valley floor and then through to a rounded hill sitting like a small plug close to the centre of the Hochwald Gap's western entrance. This was Point 73—code-named Albatross. Two Algonquin companies were to gain the northern edge of the gap and then the other two would leapfrog through to Point 73. Each infantry company would be supported by a troop of 'B' Squadron tanks. 'C' Squadron would remain on the heights to provide fire support. An unusual aspect of the plan called for 'A' Squadron with the Algonquin carrier platoon to carry out a right hook by skirting Üdem to cross the railway southeast of the town and advance along a narrow road leading to Üdemerbruch. This hamlet stood just outside the gap, and the plan called for the hooking force to seize the southern edge of its entrance. The right hook meant an advance through enemy-held territory, but the 11th British Armoured Division was to be advancing south of Üdem and positioned to provide partial flank protection.[14]

This division, however, had encountered extremely heavy opposition and also delayed its advance by waiting for 9th Canadian Infantry Brigade to get well along in clearing Üdem. Consequently, its advance began at 1800 hours on February 26. After a night of fierce fighting that yielded 350 prisoners, the leading battalions had only reached the railway southwest of Üdem by 0500 hours. Here the division paused to regroup with no intention of conducting further operations until the morning of February 28.[15]

From the outset, the South Alberta and Algonquin commanders had opposed the right hook. "This attack will be made in spite of our protestation—it is a brigade order," the South Alberta war diarist wrote. Originally, the attack was to be timed so that Lion crossed the valley floor in darkness, because the ground was so open that "a day show would be bound to fail."[16]

By the time the Algonquin company commanders returned from their futile reconnaissance, however, any possibility of a night attack was fast disappearing. Realizing this, Bradburn and Coffin asked to delay the attack twelve hours.[17] With dawn approaching, Brigadier Jefferson responded after having taken the matter to Major General Chris Vokes. "You will, regardless of [a] possible confusing situation quite probably existing when you are ready, push on through. It is imperative that your force cross the valley by first light. You are ordered to secure your objective by that time. The right hook must proceed to ensure that the armour gets across by first light."

It was 0200 hours. Bradburn immediately ordered Lion to advance to the planned start line by Kirsel, a hamlet just north of Üdem. Soon after the column set out, the decision was made to transfer the Algonquin rifle companies from their vehicles onto tanks. Rolling toward Kirsel, the force met scattered pockets of Germans. Some had to be driven off, but most seemed to have been waiting to surrender. Unable to spare any men, the Algonquins disarmed the Germans and sent them westward without escorts. More than three hundred prisoners were sent back this way. Dealing with these Germans delayed the column further. By the time it reached Kirsel, the grey light of dawn touched the eastern sky. It was drizzling and cold. A low mist clung to the ground, making visibility poor.[18]

Confusion reigned. A number of tanks were stuck in the mud, requiring Algonquins to cram together on still mobile Shermans without regard to unit coherence. 'D' Company was missing entirely. Presumably, all its tanks had bogged down. One platoon of 'A' Company and a section from another was missing. 'B' and 'C' Companies were relatively intact.[19]

A heavy artillery barrage involving three field regiments and five medium regiments was already shelling the ground ahead, the medium guns concentrating on the gap. Anticipating what this presaged, the Germans started shelling Kirsel. With 'D' Company still missing, Bradburn quickly reshuffled his plan into a three-company scheme, and the advance began at 0515. Daylight was less than an hour away.[20] Bradburn still hoped to cross the valley floor in the semi-darkness. 'A' Company was on the right and 'B' Company the left. "The attack was to cross over a high ridge, down through a flat valley of ditches and soggy ground and thence uphill for 1,500 yards, passing through a double trench system consisting of mines, wire and pillboxes."[21]

Resistance was surprisingly light, but the mud in the valley was the worst they had ever seen. Only four 'B' Squadron tanks reached the first German defensive line, which extended on a parallel north–south line through Üdemerbruch. The other eleven tanks that had advanced alongside the two infantry companies were mired in mud. German artillery began firing from dead ahead and both flanks. Bradburn retaliated with artillery.[22] 'C' Company arrived right on the heels of the two leading companies. The shelling of Kirsel had grown so intense that Major Clark Robertson had decided his men were safer in the valley than staying there. "After that, it just seemed that we kept going. It was the easiest thing to do," he said.[23]

The force continued on—tanks wallowing and sliding about, infantry wading through knee-deep, watery mud. Resistance intensified as they closed on the defensive line cutting across the front of the gap. But the fire from the remaining tanks eliminated one enemy position after another. Gaining a wide anti-tank ditch, the men of 'B' Company dived into it and spread out. A minefield before them stretched out to a great tangle of barbed wire bordering the actual defence line. On the right, 'A' Company was embroiled in a hard fight amid a group of burning farm buildings. They soon killed most of the Germans there and took the rest prisoner.

Barely pausing to regain their breath, 'B' Company clambered up the steep slope of the anti-tank ditch "to go over the rim in typical 1918 fashion...The minefield was quickly traversed, the few mines which exploded fortunately causing no casualties; and passing through the knee-high wire...the artillery had gapped in numerous places, the men finally reached the trenchworks—the last fixed positions before the Rhine. The few opponents here were either killed or captured, and consolidation began."[24]

It was 0800 hours when the Algonquins started digging in. Two tanks remained. The rest were stuck back in the valley. 'C' Squadron, which was supposed to have been firing in support from the ridge, had been forced to retreat behind the crest to escape the deadly weight of artillery.[25]

Major Robert Stock of 'A' Company had suffered a bad leg wound, but he refused evacuation. Instead, Stock gathered his men into a "tight little defensive knot." Not that evacuation was even possible. The Algonquins and crews of the two remaining tanks realized they were "out on a limb." They were cut off on three sides from friendly support.[26] The attack had caught the Germans somewhat off balance. Having breached the last German prepared positions, the Algonquins now drew their opponents' full ire. They were determined to eliminate this "isolated Canadian spearhead." Successive counterattacks were thrown back, mostly because of accurately directed artillery concentrations that caught the Germans in the open. "From south, east, and north, German guns and mortars concentrated their fire upon the approaches to the gap, and even from north of the Rhine heavy-calibre pieces contributed to the weight of explosive falling on the Canadian positions. Well dug in, the Algonquin companies hung on grimly, suffering casualties whose evacuation across the shell-swept valley became increasingly difficult as the day wore on," the army's official historian wrote.[27]

Stock directed the artillery. He also oversaw the general defence, becoming "the guidance and inspiration of the three company positions," as the Algonquin war diarist put it. His actions would be recognized by a Distinguished Service Order.

Having finally rounded up 'D' Company and other stragglers, Bradburn tried to push through to the embattled force by loading these men on the last 'B' Squadron troop of tanks. "It proved impossible, however, to cross the valley...in daylight and after severe losses in infantry and tanks, the decision to reinforce was postponed until darkness arrived." Kirsel remained unhealthy to be in. It was continually shelled, particularly by many 88-millimetre guns firing out of the Hochwald. At least a dozen headquarters staff were killed or wounded as the day drew on.[28]

Bradburn sent a wireless message to Jefferson reporting that the Algonquins had breached the defensive line "but cannot move."[29] There was no news on how the right hook group fared. The Algonquins facing the gap reported seeing no sign of it. The force should have arrived much earlier. Men glanced back, hoping to see tanks and carriers, and fearing the worst.

SOUTH ALBERTA MAJOR Glen McDougall had ordered 'A' Squadron and the Algonquin carrier platoon to set out at 0600. The mud was terrible. Groping through the dark, the commander of the leading tank failed to see the main anti-tank ditch encircling Üdem until his Sherman plunged head-on into it. The tank had to be abandoned. Then the column found itself negotiating a maze of ditches and trenches. There were so many unmarked farm lanes that McDougall found it impossible to keep on course. It took three hours to pass Üdem and gain the railway leading to the Hochwald Gap. McDougall realized he was several hundred yards farther west than intended and very close to the town. That would not have mattered had it been clear as expected. But holdout Germans still lurked in the southern outskirts, and these started firing Panzerfausts. McDougall had set out with twelve tanks but had lost two. The

Algonquin platoon was down to four of its thirteen carriers. Because of the Germans in the town, McDougall left two Shermans to protect his rear and then led the force eastward along a sunken road adjacent to the railway. It was 0900 hours and broad daylight.[30]

The column was rolling along a partially sunken section of the road and heading for a railroad overpass when "disaster struck with stunning suddenness." The Germans had prepared "an elaborate tank trap of guns and obstacles to cover his withdrawal from the town of Üdem." McDougall's force had driven into the centre of the trap.[31] Trooper Ed Thorn, the gunner in the lead Sherman, saw a Tiger tank squatting about five hundred yards straight ahead. He fired the high-explosive round loaded in the 75-millimetre gun. Following this with two armour-piercing rounds, Thorn knocked the Tiger out. Then a shell whooshed overhead. Thorn spotted more dug-in Tigers about a half-mile to the right. A shell slammed into his Sherman. "It was just like someone hit me on the shoulder with a sledge hammer," Thorn recalled. Tank burning, the crew bailed out. With clever precision the Germans in the Tigers and manning nearby anti-tank guns knocked out the Sherman at the column's rear and the second tank at the front. This left those in the middle helplessly trapped because of the banks on either side of the road. It took only minutes for the slaughter of armour and carriers to be completed. About forty tankers escaped from their tanks. A Wasp carrier exploded in a massive fireball that produced a smokescreen the surviving tankers and Algonquins used to conceal their escape. McDougall led one party of tankers to safety, but another group was taken prisoner.[32] The Algonquin carrier platoon commander, Lieutenant J.J.J. "Jimmy" Sunstrum, led his "wounded and bewildered men" on a long trek back to Kirsel.[33]

While the Algonquins compiled no casualty records, the South Alberta Regiment surprisingly reported losing only one man killed in the ambush—Trooper Frederick Charles Belsey. But fourteen men were taken prisoner, including two officers. The regiment did not divide its tally of men otherwise killed or wounded on February 27 by engagement. Besides Belsey, two other men were reported killed and eight wounded.[34]

LION FORCE HAD not been fighting totally alone in its February 27 attack on the Hochwald. To the left, 2nd Canadian Infantry Division's 5th Brigade had also attacked. Having been in reserve, the Calgary Highlanders carried the charge forward. They were to breach the Hochwald Layback directly in front of the forest and next to a cluster of houses identified on the maps as Schmachdarm. This position lay three thousand yards north of the gap. The distance between the Calgaries and Lion Force to the south was great enough to prevent either advance from supporting the other. But Simonds's decision to launch these two separate and isolated efforts reflected the lack of resources available following the bloody fighting of the previous day.

Brigadier Bill Megill's plan was for the Calgaries, supported by 'C' Squadron of the Fort Garry Horse Regiment, to break through the defensive line with Le Régiment de Maisonneuve close behind. He would then send the Black Watch Regiment through to exploit deep into the forest. The advance involved a long descent down the gentle slope off the Calcar–Üdem ridge into the valley, which narrowed here, and up another slope to gain the fortifications standing before the Hochwald.

Lieutenant Colonel Ross Ellis launched the attack with 'C' Company leading about 750 yards to the left and ahead of 'A' Company. The other two companies and his tactical headquarters followed behind. Lacking any intelligence on German dispositions, Ellis declared that the regiment was playing "an advance to contact role."[35] The advance began at 0400 hours. As Major Bill Lyster's 'C' Company moved through the darkness, they warily eyed nearby farmhouses and outbuildings. All seemed deserted. They saw neither movement nor heard any sounds. The fields were greasy with mud. At 0515, they reached the valley floor. Captain C.L. Keatley's 'A' Company was still descending the slope. Ahead, a deep irrigation canal cut through the centre of the valley, and the fields were delineated into orderly little blocks by smaller ditches. Up the other slope, the forest formed a dense, dark silhouette. Above it, the sky was greying. Daybreak was coming on.

'C' Company had just crossed the main canal when it came under scattered rifle and machine-gun fire from the defensive line fronting the woods. The fire hitched up a notch with every passing minute, as more machine guns sent out rippling bursts of fire. "The enemy threw everything they could at us except shells," 'A' Company Private John Bowron remembered. "They never once threw a shell or a mortar as we went down the hill. We moved on up a road which led across the valley and took two...houses. Then all hell broke loose. They mortared everything that moved."

By this time, 'C' Company was about six hundred yards from the defensive line and the edge of the woods. The fields were crisscrossed by trenches and barbed-wire obstacles. Unable to manoeuvre through the barbed-wire under such a rain of artillery and mortar fire, Lyster's men hit the dirt. Lyster picked his way back to Ellis's battalion headquarters in a farmhouse. With 5th Field Regiment FOO Major William Benjamin Nixon, the officers put together an artillery fire plan to free 'C' Company.

"We were standing in the hallway with our backs to the wall and the door was open," Lyster recalled. "This shell came and dropped outside the door and burst in and I got a chunk of shrapnel in my nose. I grabbed my nose and looked across at Major Nixon and there was a purple hole right smack in his temple...Ross was grabbing his face...he got concussion." Lyster and Nixon were carried back to the Regimental Aid Post, but the artillery officer soon died. Ellis remained at his post.[36]

It was about 1230 hours, and Ellis tried to tee up an attack to get 'B' Company through to the objective with tanks providing fire support. Moments before the attack was to begin, 'C' Squadron's commander reported his tanks were unable to manoeuvre to a position where they could provide effective fire along the line of advance. Ellis got busy substituting artillery fire to cover 'B' Company's advance.[37]

'C' Company was in a bad way. All of its officers were dead or wounded. Company Sergeant Major Harold Omar Larson took command. Deciding that if they stayed put the company would die, he led the survivors forward about two hundred yards to the cover of some buildings. Larson then got on the wireless to arrange artillery fire and ask the supporting Fort Garry Horse tanks to hit the forest with shells. As soon as this fire started, he led 'C' Company in a charge across the remaining four hundred yards to the defensive line. The company plunged in amid the defenders and soon cleared the trench system. Unsure of where 'A' Company was, Larson took three men and set off to contact it. He wanted to tie the two companies together and form an all-round defence. Crawling along a communication trench, Larson encountered a German machine-gun position. He killed two of the crew with a hand grenade and took three prisoners. His little group carried on "until they observed members of the enemy in dugouts, heavily armed with automatic weapons." Realizing his men were badly outnumbered, Larson quietly backed away. He then got on the wireless and gave Ellis details of the enemy position. Ellis sent 'D' Company forward to engage them. Larson's work this day earned a Military Cross—a medal normally not given to anybody under the rank of lieutenant.[38]

'D' Company was closing on the defensive line when Private Red Anderson saw a large German force descending the hill toward them. The company was only forty strong, and its sergeant shouted for the men to dash to the cover of a nearby small farm. "I was with a Bren gunner and told him to spray the shit out of them and run at the same time," Anderson said. "We both took turns on the Bren gun and ran also." From the cover of the farm buildings, 'D' Company beat off the German attack and then started up the slope. They fought their way through trenches and dugouts to a position about three hundred yards south of 'C' Company. Major George Stott pushed the company into the woods a little way and then called for his platoon commanders to join him. Only one showed. The other two platoons had disappeared, and it would be twelve hours before they were located.

To the right, 'A' Company's Captain Keatley had been wounded. Ellis decided to hold this company close to his tactical headquarters, which was now about seven hundred yards southeast of 'D' Company. He ordered Major S.O. Robinson to go forward under cover of artillery concentrations he had teed up, steady 'A' Company, and then pass his 'B' Company through for an advance into the woods. The fighting degenerated into a wild and confused melee that ran until nightfall. In repeated attempts to advance, Robinson and all his platoon commanders were wounded.[39] Robinson refused to leave. At one point, his Company Sergeant Major Harry Baker literally carried

the wounded officer to a new position. By last light, the three forward companies were through the Hochwald Layback, but stuck
either on the edge of the forest or just inside its trees. The men could
hear Germans moving in the woods and were under constant mortar
and artillery fire. But a feared counterattack failed to materialize.[40]
The Calgaries had sent back two hundred German prisoners. Their
losses were eleven killed and forty-four wounded.[41]

The Maisies had dug in back on the ridge overlooking the valley
floor and were to provide covering fire for the Black Watch to cross
over to the Calgaries and then push into the Hochwald. But Brigadier Megill decided it was "too late to follow the original plan...and
the attack was postponed until first light the following morning."[42]

WHILE 2ND DIVISION's forward troops settled in for an uncomfortable night under heavy artillery and mortar fire, 4th Canadian
Armoured Division's 10th Brigade initiated a nighttime effort to
relieve Lion Force and push into the gap. During the day, 10th Brigade's two infantry battalions serving with Tiger Force had returned
to Brigadier Jim Jefferson. He had immediately tried to push the
Argyll and Sutherland Highlanders through to Lion Force in the late
afternoon. Out in the open valley, the battalion drew such intense
artillery and mortar fire it was forced to dig in about five hundred
yards short of the gap. Obviously, a more heavily supported effort
was required.[43]

That evening, Jefferson met with Major General Chris Vokes and
Brigadier Robert Moncel. Vokes ordered Jefferson to push the Argyll
and Sutherland Highlanders, supported by the South Alberta's 'C'
Squadron, through the Algonquins at about 0200 hours on the
morning of February 28. The Argylls were to reach a road running
laterally across the eastern edge of the gap. This entailed an advance
of about 1,500 yards and was to be completed by first light.[44]

Other parts of this operation included securing the railway from
south of Üdem to close to the gap's entrance so the division's engineers could start transforming it into the vital maintenance route for
11 Canadian Corps's advance on Xanten. Once the Argylls won command of the gap, the Lincoln and Welland Regiment were to come

alongside to the south and clear a spur of the Balberger Wald that actually formed the southern boundary of the gap. This spur was called Tüschen Wald. The railway passed through this small forest.[45]

[2 2]

Hunker Down and Pray

THROUGH THE COLD, rainy night of February 27–28, the Argyll and Sutherland Highlanders with South Alberta Regiment's 'C' Squadron alongside struggled to reach even their start line for the attack. There was continual artillery and mortar fire. In addition, snipers had infiltrated the valley. Argyll Major Rupert Fultz, commanding 'A' Company, was shot in the foot. Otherwise, their fire proved more an irritant than a threat. The shellfire took a heavier toll, including wounding Major Bill Whiteside, 'D' Company's commander. Lieutenant Lloyd Grose took over 'A' Company, while Lieutenant Bill Shields assumed control of 'D' Company. Having gained the start line about five hundred yards short of the gap, the battalion found itself completely pinned down by intense fire.[1]

The tanks of 'C' Squadron never got forward. Thirteen set off, following the tracks left earlier by 'B' Squadron. Most were soon "hopelessly bogged."[2] This necessitated a hurried rejigging of the plan whereby a single tank troop from 'B' Squadron, commanded by Lieutenant Leaman Caseley, directly supported the Argylls.[3]

Things were so confused that Argyll Lieutenant Colonel Fred Wigle personally went forward. He radioed back to his headquarters that the companies were under "very heavy mortar and artillery fire. I had to reorganize all three forward companies." To get ahead, he decided, would require an extremely heavy barrage continuing until

0200 hours. The woods on either side of the gap's entrance were singled out for most of this shelling. At 0200, 'A' and 'B' Companies attacking on the right and left, respectively, would push into the gap behind a creeping barrage lifting a hundred yards every three minutes. 'D' Company was to follow 'B' Company closely, while 'C' Company would be farther back behind 'A' Company. If opposition proved light, Wigle planned to push 'C' Company all the way through to a point a few hundred yards east of the gap. Wigle asked for a resupply of batteries for the No. 18 wireless sets, as "wireless communication was in poor shape." He also wanted reinforcement officers so the companies were not being led by lieutenants, but knew this was not going to happen quickly enough to affect the imminent battle. Wigle impressed upon his company officers that this battle would "be a stiff and difficult one."

Because of delays in teeing up the creeping barrage, the attack started forty-five minutes late. To gain the entrance to the gap required climbing a fairly steep hill, which Wigle thought "considerably higher than we had met as yet."[4] Lieutenant Grose, leading 'A' Company on the right, was soon "up by the woods there, and having passed through the Algonquins...we [came] under very heavy fire... The short rounds were landing in the trees and the long ones were just on our left in the open ground...Lieutenant W.J. McArthur was about fifteen to twenty feet from one and it threw him up in the air about six feet and he landed on his back."[5]

Grose found it difficult to prevent his men from going to ground, more from exhaustion than fear. Few Argylls had had more than five hours' sleep since they marched out of Cleve on February 25.[6] 'B' Company under Lieutenant Bill Shields, meanwhile, encountered only sporadic sniper and machine-gun fire. Both companies reported cresting the top of the hill and entering the gap at 0415 hours. By first light, the two companies were past Point 73 and holding on the edge of the woods well inside the gap. About half the men in each company dug in to slit trenches within the trees, with the others in the open. Captain Leonard Perry's 'B' Company concentrated around a house, with some men in slit trenches in the garden fronting the building. The Argylls were under direct German observation from the front and both flanks, with the heaviest artillery fire coming from the Tüschen Wald south of them.[7] The four South Alberta tanks were about two hundred yards below the crest line behind these forward companies and well positioned to provide covering fire.[8]

Back of the leading companies, 'D' Company dug in among the trees on the northern corner of the entrance to the gap to provide a secure base for the other three companies. 'C' Company was a short distance behind 'A' Company on the right. All three leading companies were beyond Point 73 and well out of sight of friendly forces west of them. Wigle had come up to 'D' Company's position but found it impossible to glean what was happening inside the gap. The amount of shell and mortar fire was breathtaking.[9] Many shells were from 88-millimetre guns, but the Germans were also spraying the forward companies at virtually point-blank range with rapid-firing 20-millimetre anti-aircraft guns.[10]

First Fallschirmjäger Army had been steadily building up its gun complement and it now counted 717 mortars and 1,054 artillery pieces, as well as a good many self-propelled guns. A large amount of this firepower was vectoring in on the Argylls. Also heading straight for them was a fresh battalion of 24th Regiment drawn from 8th Fallschirmjäger Division and an armoured battle group of 116th Panzer Division.[11]

Casualties were mounting rapidly when the juggernaut of fresh paratroopers and armour crashed down upon 'B' Company at about 0645 hours.[12] The German armour was a grab bag of about fifteen Mark IVs, SPGs, Panthers, and Tigers. From their hiding positions, the South Albertas opened fire with their 75-millimetre guns.[13] Mixed in among the tanks and trying to infiltrate into 'B' Company through the woods were hundreds of paratroopers. Captain Perry was unable to raise anybody on his wireless to call in artillery fire. Perry saw Corporal Harry Griffin trying to rally his section as a Tiger rolled toward them. A burst of machine-gun fire cut Griffin down.

Lance Sergeant Albert Clare Huffman was in a slit trench in front of the brick farmhouse. The wounded were being nested against an outside wall nearby. There were tanks grinding along the other side of the house, which the German attack was centred on. Huffman was one of the few National Resources Mobilization Act conscripts the Canadian government had sent overseas in late 1944. He had since proven a fine soldier, having recently been promoted to lance sergeant. Huffman ran to where Perry was with a group of men on the edge of the woods. After a quick consultation, Huffman ran back to the house. The entire way, a Tiger tank chased him with its machine gun. Diving into a slit trench, Huffman raised his head and a bullet struck the bridge of his nose and took out an eye. A first-aid man bandaged the wound. Unable to see, Huffman propped himself in a "little kitchen chair" facing the front door with a Sten gun at hand. He guarded the entrance by sound rather than sight.[14]

The firefight's climax came when a Tiger ground up almost on top of Perry's position and the officer commanding it stuck his head out of the turret hatch. He yelled for the men to lay down their arms and surrender. Perry calmly raised his rifle and shot the officer dead. Then a PIAT team knocked out the tank with a well-placed shot.

Lieutenant Colonel Wigle had reached 'A' Company. He had been slightly wounded in one hand and a leg by shrapnel. In the absence of wireless links to 'B' Company, Wigle was being bombarded by "wild stories" that it had been annihilated. At 1400 hours, however, Perry reported that the situation was serious, but that he had a size-able number of men left "and was grimly determined to hold on to his position at all costs."

The German attacks were not continuous. They would put in a fierce attack and then after enough of their men were killed, pull back to regroup. During each lull, 'B' Company would tend its wounded and reorganize the perimeter defence. But the artillery and mortar fire would always start up again. The moment that fire ceased, Perry knew the paratroopers and likely the tanks were coming back.

All day the Germans besieged 'B' Company's perimeter, but by nightfall Perry and a handful of men still held. With all other officers dead and Huffman the last sergeant, Perry left the blinded man in charge and went back to battalion headquarters. Perry said he had fifteen men fighting and five wounded who were in good enough con-dition to be safely evacuated. Wigle, still with 'A' Company, ordered Perry held at headquarters. Captain Bob Pogue and Lieutenant Herb

Maxwell, having arrived as reinforcements, were to bring the survivors home.[15]

Pogue and Maxwell got through to the company, gathered the men, and led them through the night to safety. Among those who came out was Private Tom Sayer. "I was angry and heartbroken," he said. "Some of these guys that were there had been right with me from the beginning in the same companies, and they were...wiped out."[16] At 2330 hours, the Argylls received a welcome message from 10th Brigade that Les Fusiliers Mont-Royal would relieve them at first light on March 1. "Thus the month of February ended on a promising note," the Argyll's intelligence officer, Lieutenant Doug Cruthers, wrote, "with the promise of a few days rest for our badly mauled companies, enabling us to bring them up to strength again with the reinforcements that were already waiting at A-Echelon. The first few days of action in Germany had proved costly to the battalion, but as in the past the Argylls had taken their objectives, killed and captured hundreds of the enemy and had thereby helped to make the operation a success."[17] They also still clung to a thin border of the Hochwald adjacent to the gap, which would be handed to the Fusiliers. It was a thin wedge in the German grip on the forest, but a wedge nonetheless.

LIEUTENANT CRUTHERS WAS likely the only First Canadian Army soldier on February 28 who considered the operation to be proving successful. Every advance had gained little ground and only at great cost in casualties. Right of the Argylls, the Lincoln and Welland Regiment had attacked to clear the northern edge of the Tüschen Wald and secure the section of railway through it. Like the Argylls, the Lincs had struggled to simply reach their start line. Under "spasmodic mortar and rocket fire," they had set off at 0215 hours with British Columbia Dragoon tanks in support. The tanks soon bogged down and were left behind, along with all battalion vehicles. By the time the Lincs reached the start line at 0645 hours, only two tanks carrying FOOS remained alongside. Here the infantry waited under constant shelling. By 1100 hours, a supporting artillery barrage was under way and two troops of tanks had arrived—one from the

British Columbia Regiment and the other the South Albertas. The latter troop was borrowed from the Argylls. At noon, the two forward companies walked toward the woods. Captain W.H. Barkman's 'B' Company was to the left and 'C' Company under Major C.K. Crummer on the right. Once Barkman and Crummer pushed through the woods, the other two companies would advance to secure the railway.[18]

The moment the Lincs reached the woods, they were struck by what even Field Marshal Bernard Montgomery considered the heaviest "volume of fire from enemy weapons...met so far by British troops in the campaign."[19] To Crummer, it was as if the "skies closed in...We were in the middle of it, standing, trying to push forward. Well, we didn't stand long. We went to ground damn fast...You really hunker down and pray to God that you come out of it all right, because you can't do anything for anyone." Crummer was buried twice by earth showering down and had to claw his way to the surface. He crawled under one Sherman, but felt it sinking in the mud and scrabbled out before it crushed him.[20]

Shells burst in the treetops and sprayed down showers of shrapnel and wood splinters. Tree limbs pinwheeled through the air. Artillery, mortars, and Nebelwerfer rocket rounds slammed in. The attack crumbled, and the Lincs fell back to the start line, dragging their wounded. Forty-nine men had been killed or wounded in a few minutes.[21]

IN THE EARLY morning hours of February 28, the Black Watch had advanced through the Calgary Highlanders to push into the Hochwald. Leading companies immediately met intense mortar and shellfire. Moving deeper into the woods, they reached a series of tracks in the woods fifty to a hundred yards apart. Each time men stepped into one of these tracks, the Germans fired 88-millimetre guns straight along it. Across the tracks stood dug-in bunkers and fortresses heavily manned by riflemen and machine-gun crews. The attack quickly ground to a halt.

Trying to reclaim the momentum, twenty-year-old Private John Koropchuk "raced ahead alone for fifty yards, firing his Bren gun from the hip. Close to an enemy post he was finally shot down but not before he had thrown three grenades and killed twenty-three Germans." He was recommended for a posthumous Victoria Cross, but it was denied. The Black Watch were trapped in the dark woods, all further attempts to renew the advance stopped in their tracks.[22]

Grimly, the troops held until nightfall. Finally, 5th Canadian Infantry Brigade sent orders that Le Régiment de Maisonneuve would provide a firm base on the edge of the woods through which the Black Watch could withdraw. Shortly after midnight on March 1, the companies passed through the Maisies.[23] The Black Watch had seven men killed and thirty-five wounded. It was an attack that achieved nothing and only reinforced the Black Watch's hard-luck reputation.

"THE GOOD PROGRESS made during the first two days of the operation by the 2nd Canadian Corps, which seemed to hold promise of a break-through, was held up by stiff resistance in the Hochwald," General Harry Crerar wrote. "The enemy succeeded in stabilizing his line, and still fighting hard, was heavily supported by mortar and artillery fire. On the right of the army front, the xxx British Corps, reinforced by the 3rd British Infantry Division, established three bridgeheads over the tributary [Niers River] northeast of Weeze. I now instructed Lieutenant General Horrocks to develop his main advance on the left along the axis Winnekendonk–Kappellen–Issum, while Lieutenant General Simonds was to continue his thrust along the two axes Sonsbeck–Bönninghardt and the road running southeast from Xanten toward Rheinberg."

The instruction to Simonds to follow these axes failed to reflect that 11 Canadian Corps was nowhere close to breaking through the Hochwald and Balberger Wald. His brigades must do this before the taking of Xanten or Sonsbeck could be considered.

As March opened, Crerar thought the offensive, "entrusted to First Canadian Army, to destroy the enemy west of the Rhine and prepare the way for an envelopment of the Ruhr, was well advanced." This was particularly true when what Crerar described as the "spectacular successes" of U.S. Ninth Army's first six days of Operation Grenade were factored in.[24]

By the last day of February, the Americans had broken German resistance on the plain and were advancing rapidly toward the Rhine and Maas Rivers. The German Fifteenth Army had been virtually destroyed. On March 1, the Americans would be within eighteen miles of First Canadian Army's front lines.

General der Fallschirmtruppen Alfred Schlemm knew his First Fallschirmjäger Army was "in deadly peril." Prior to the American offensive, he had been free to concentrate XLVII Panzer Korps and II Fallschirmjäger Korps on preventing a breakout by the Canadian and British divisions to his west. Now the Americans threatened his line of retreat across the Rhine bridges at Wesel.

Only on February 28 was Schlemm able to get Hitler's permission to begin to shorten his lines and better concentrate his forces. He was also forced to pull some troops facing First Canadian Army away to bolster his XCIV Korps facing the Americans to the south. To organize the forthcoming defence of the Rhine's east bank, Schlemm evacuated the LXXXVI Korps headquarters staff across the river and placed its divisions under command of II Fallschirmjäger Korps.

Although he permitted Schlemm to contract his front, Hitler adamantly refused to concede that the Rhineland was lost. Under pain of death, Schlemm must not allow any of the nine Rhine bridges to fall into Allied hands. At the same time, he was prohibited from destroying any bridge until the last minute. Further, not a man or piece of fighting equipment could pass over the Rhine without Hitler's permission. This left the shrinking bridgehead increasingly "cluttered with damaged tanks, transport, artillery without ammunition and all the other debris of an army fighting a heavy losing action." Equally cluttering the scene were surplus headquarters staff lacking fighting troops to administer and other personnel of no utility to the battle. When the jaws of Blockbuster and Grenade finally came together, many of these men and the equipment would be isolated and captured. [25]

Schlemm's dilemma was clear to the Allies. "The enemy seems to have lost all grip on the battle in this area and his command organisation seems to have broken down," Field Marshal Montgomery said of the American area of operations on March 1. "We have captured static back area units who are quite unaware of the situation and in one area we captured a complete armoured column of tanks moving westwards from Neuss...which was very astonished at being captured."

Since the launch of Veritable, the two armies had taken thirty thousand prisoners. All that remained was to finish the job as quickly as possible. Montgomery was so confident, he had already set a date for the offensive to win a crossing over the Rhine. Code-named Operation Plunder, this offensive was to start on March 24.[26]

THE BIG PICTURE looked bright, but closer to the ground, the morning of March 1 brought continuing dull, rainy weather and the prospect of continued grim fighting in front of the Hochwald. During the night, 2nd Canadian Infantry Division's 6th Brigade had relieved the battered 10th Brigade from its positions within and facing the Hochwald Gap. Patrols sent out by its battalions soon met those sent south through the trees by 5th Brigade's Calgary Highlanders.

Despite the previous day's failures, Lieutenant General Guy Simonds was determined that Blockbuster must continue without pause. With 4th Armoured Division regrouping, it could not return to the attack until the following day. And it would be the evening of March 1 before 3rd Infantry Division was ready to attack the Tüschen Wald on the southern edge of the gap. With 2nd Division's 5th Brigade tied in front of the forest and 6th Brigade still assembling before the gap, Simonds could only call upon 4th Infantry Brigade for a morning operation. Accordingly, 2nd Division's Major General Bruce Matthews ordered the brigade's Essex Scottish Regiment to advance from where the Royal Regiment of Canada was holding on the Calcar–Üdem ridge and push into the northern corner of the Hochwald.[27]

'B' Company's Captain Alf Hodges sent a platoon-sized patrol down the slope at 0240 hours to reconnoitre the German defences. The small unit was quickly driven back by heavy fire. The platoon leader reported that the Germans had set up in a trench system heavily screened by barbed-wire entanglements. Machine guns and mortars covered the open ground between them and the forest. A similar patrol sent by 'A' Company returned the same information, but added that there were Germans just two hundred yards away.[28]

Lieutenant Colonel John Pangman held an Orders Group at 0500 hours. The plan was for Major Fred Tilston's 'C' Company to advance on the left and 'D' Company under Major Paul Cropp the right.[29] A troop of tanks from the Sherbrooke Fusiliers Regiment's

'C' Squadron was in support.[30] The division's three field regiments would put in a barrage.

The thirty-nine-year-old Major Tilston was going into combat for the first time. Considered mild-mannered and affable, Tilston had been a sales manager for a pharmaceutical company in Windsor when the war broke out. Already thirty-four, Tilston was deemed too old by local recruitment officers in 1940. Ultimately, Tilston fudged his age and was accepted by the Essex with the rank of second lieutenant. During training in England he suffered a minor wound that led to his assignment to battalion headquarters. Tilston was still a staff officer when a jeep ran over a mine near Falaise, in Normandy. He suffered superficial burns, and slivers of shrapnel penetrated one eye. Upon returning from hospitalization in England, Tilston became the battalion's adjutant and was promoted to captain. No amount of lobbying, however, could get him the combat command he craved. On February 22, things changed when the battalion was left desperately short of officers. Pangman promoted Tilston to acting major and 'C' Company's command.

Tilston knew his battlefield initiation was going to be rough. Stretching before the company was five hundred yards of open ground that must be crossed in daylight. His company was about a hundred strong, but two-thirds of the men were green reinforcements. It was the same throughout the battalion. 'C' Company had formed in a little cluster of woods next to a farm building, so was well hidden from the Germans across the field. Here the men waited for the barrage to begin and the tanks to arrive.[31]

It proved a long wait, the attack being pushed back a half hour from the planned 0715 start. When the tanks arrived, the troop commander said the mud in the field ahead was too deep for the Shermans to accompany the infantry.[32] As the barrage began, a couple of rounds fell short, landing among the two leading platoons. Several men were badly wounded, and the rest scattered. After a quick reorganization, Tilston led the company through a hedge and into the field.[33]

The two companies slogged through mud, keeping close to the advancing barrage until they reached a ten-foot-wide barbed-wire barrier. As Tilston had been crossing the field, a piece of shrapnel had grazed an ear, and blood trickled steadily down his neck.[34]

Before going into the attack, Tilston had asked Major Cropp where he should be during an attack. Cropp had said behind the two leading platoons.[35] But Tilston was the first man to reach the wire and find a lane through it.

Tilston was shouting encouragement and directions while firing bursts from a Sten gun. Seeing his lead platoon on the left, commanded by veteran Lieutenant Charlie Gatton, pinned down by machine-gun fire, Tilston charged the enemy position. A couple of well-placed grenades killed the crew. Leaving the reserve platoon to mop up this defensive line, Tilston led the other two platoons to the second line in front of the woods. A chunk of shrapnel sliced a four-inch gash in his hip. Tilston fell to the ground, shouting for his men to carry on without him. Struggling to his feet, Tilston followed. He found the platoons had taken the position.[36] But one had only eight of twenty-five men still standing. The company stretched out in a line inside this second defensive position and faced the paratroopers firing out of the forest. The wounded were put in the shelter of an underground compound that also served as a command post. It had a table and several chairs.[37]

German dead were strewn around the position. 'D' Company was to the right and also inside the trenches of the second line. A small road created a hundred-yard gap between the two companies. Cropp's men had not met as heavy fire crossing the field, nor costly fighting at the defensive lines.[38]

The paratroopers started counterattacking from the woods with machine guns and mortars providing flanking fire. Although the Germans were able to get close enough to lob grenades, the Canadians were able to hold them at bay. Tilston limped from platoon to platoon, urging their shrinking numbers to keep fighting. Rain was striking the sandy soil and throwing up grains that kept jamming the Bren guns. Tilston got the wounded in the compound busy wiping the sand out of jammed guns, which were then rotated forward to replace those that were jamming. The wounded stripped off shirts and underwear to use as rags.

With ammunition running low, Tilston half-hobbled, half-dashed to 'D' Company. Not so heavily engaged, Cropp's men could spare bullets. Loaded up with grenades and ammunition, Tilston staggered back to his men. He made several more trips, each requiring crossing the hundred-yard gap of the road. A road swept by machine-gun fire. [39]

'C' Company was down to twenty-seven fit men when a lull settled in. And then 'B' Company arrived, and Captain Alf Hodges led it into the woods ahead of Tilston's position. Half of 'B' Company had been cut down crossing the field. As Hodges passed by, Tilston said, "Keep going, Alf. All they've got is rifles and machine guns."[40]

Tilston decided to make another trip to 'D' Company for ammunition. On the way back, he dodged into a large shell crater. Six feet away, a mortar or artillery round exploded. Shrapnel tore away one of Tilston's legs and mangled the other. Lying in the crater, Tilston wriggled out of his combat webbing and injected himself with morphine. He lay there floating in and out of consciousness, noting that the sounds of fighting were slowly subsiding.[41]

When Major Ken MacIntyre led his 'A' Company through to join 'B' Company, the two went forward into the woods and established a holding position with "comparative ease." This was due to the heavy casualties Tilston and Cropp's companies had inflicted on the Germans.[42] Stretcher-bearers started gathering wounded. Finally, one appeared at the edge of the crater where Tilston lay. He yelled, "There's another one over here!" Three men, Company Sergeant Major Chuck Wold, Private Stanley Carley, and stretcher-bearer Private Paul Bianco, carried Tilston on a stretcher across 150 yards of bullet-swept ground to an ambulance jeep that evacuated him to the Regimental Aid Post.

Tilston's one day of combat was over. He would lose both legs and eventually the sight in the eye that had been wounded in Normandy. His bravery was honoured with a Victoria Cross. As the day ended, the Essex Scottish reported taking more than a hundred prisoners, capturing three 88-millimetre guns, a medium mortar, and many automatic weapons. Scores of Germans lay dead. But the solid base won in the northern edge of the Hochwald cost the Essex thirty-one dead and seventy-seven wounded.[43]

SOUTH OF THE gap, 3rd Division's 8th Brigade had deployed to assist 11th British Armoured Division (still under II Canadian Corps) in its attempt to hook around the southern flank of Balberger Wald and seize Sonsbeck. Simonds had set the Canadian infantry the role of clearing both Tüschen Wald and Balberger Wald. Until the anti-tank guns and artillery in these woods were cleared out, the British tankers could not get forward.[44] If successful, Simonds believed the infantry attack would eliminate the "present bottleneck approach to Xanten."[45] The attack was to be conducted in three phases, with Le Régiment de la Chaudière supported by the 1st Hussars' Regiment's 'A' Squadron clearing Tüschen Wald in a north-to-south drive. Pivoting eastward, the Chauds would then advance into the open ground paralleling the railway and the Hochwald Gap. Second and third phases called for the North Shore (New Brunswick) and Queen's Own Rifles Regiments to attack southward and clean out Balberger Wald. They would be supported by 1st Hussars' 'B' Squadron.[46]

The 1st Hussars were in rough shape, fielding only forty Shermans instead of a normal complement of sixty-one. This was due to a shortage of soldiers, not tanks. Scouring reinforcement depots failed to turn up trained tank crews. Despite heavy casualties and being badly understrength, the Chauds were ready to go. "Our own infantry were still tired after the exhausting battle of the 26th but morale fortunately was very high," a 1st Hussars report noted.[47]

To put in the attack, tanks and infantry had to reach their forming-up position, a north–south-running road facing the woods. Loaded in trucks, the Chauds passed Üdem, crossed the railway, and then followed a narrow secondary road that "finally disappeared, and vehicles and tanks bogged down," Chauds second-in-command Major FJ L'Espérance wrote. The infantry abandoned the trucks and followed the railway to the start line. The tanks trailed along far behind, and Lieutenant Colonel Guy Taschereau decided not to wait for them. It was already dark when the Chauds formed up at 1630, and the attack was set for 1745. Tanks operating in muddy, open fields and then inside thick woods would be useless. The Chauds would do the job alone.

No prior reconnaissance had been possible. Taschereau understood that there were friendly troops holding the most northerly portion of the Tüschen Wald, but he was unable to confirm this.

There were no friendlies at their start line to put them in the picture. The attack was pushed back to 1845 hours.[48] After a mere fifteen-minute barrage of the woods, Major Jacques Castonguay led 'D' Company out on the right, and Major Armand Ross's 'C' Company advanced to the left. Despite artificial moonlight, the moment the platoons entered the dense woods, it became impossible for commanders to maintain contact with them. Castonguay and Ross called a halt and decided they must reform the two companies to advance in single file through to the eastern side of the forest. While the platoon officers reorganized, the two majors went on alone for about a hundred yards. Here they came upon a winding trail and sent back for a section of scouts under Lieutenant J. Dugas to lead the way forward.

The scouts had gone only a short distance when the night erupted with Germans shouting, "*Kamerad, Kamerad.*" Dugas sent word back that he had six prisoners. The Chauds were still badly strung out in single file when the woods on all sides came alive with heavy and light machine-gun fire. Castonguay and Ross dove into nearby holes for cover and stayed put until Dugas, his scouts, and Ross's runner, Private A. Fournier, arrived to extricate them with protective fire. The small force crawled back to where the companies were also pinned down.

Realizing they were going to be surrounded, the majors ordered a withdrawal. The situation was critical, with a dense section of wood about three hundred yards to their rear seeming to be "a breeding ground" for Germans. All wireless communication back to battalion headquarters had been lost, even the set carried by the artillery officer not working. To deceive the Germans into thinking the Chauds were confusedly trying to reorganize, a small rear guard was left behind. While these men made as much noise as possible, the rest of the Chauds fell back section by section to the edge of the woods and established an all-round defensive position. A new effort would have to wait until daybreak, when infantry and tankers could attack together.[49]

Bitter, Close-Range Fighting

WHILE BOTH CANADIAN infantry divisions spent March 1
engaged in bloody battles yielding gains measured in yards,
4th Armoured Division was preparing to break out from the Hochwald Gap. As this was a 4th Armoured Brigade show, Brigadier
Robert Moncel advanced his tactical headquarters to a clearing
northeast of Üdem. There were no tents. Moncel's office was a steel-
roofed half-track. His staff worked out of five tanks, several scout
cars, and two Armoured Command Vehicles—heavy trucks plated
from hood to tail in half-inch armour. The ACVS housed the brigade's
communications equipment. With the clearing under German
observation and subject to sporadic shelling, no jeeps or other unar-
moured vehicles were allowed, and staff was kept to a minimum.[1]

The Algonquin Regiment was under Moncel's command. But the
division's Lake Superior Regiment (Motor), supported by the Canadian Grenadier Guards, would lead. Kicking off from the Canadian
line at the gap's western entrance, three Superior companies carried
in Kangaroos would advance one thousand yards to farm buildings
alongside a road running along the eastern flank of the forest from
Marienbaum to Sonsbeck.

Thereafter, the Governor General's Foot Guards would carry the
Algonquin's 'D' Company another thousand yards to seize a bridge-

head across the Hohe Ley—a narrow, winding stream that emptied into the Kalflach River just east of Marienbaum.[2]

Moncel considered a night attack essential, something various army reports declared a bold, daring undertaking. When Grenadier commander Lieutenant Colonel Ned Amy saw his orders late on February 29, he was "amazed." Amy and British Columbia Regiment commander Lieutenant Colonel Gerry Chubb studied a map. Amy looked at the gap. On one side the Hochwald, Balberger Wald on the other, the slim corridor between. "You'll never make it to Xanten," Chubb warned. Amy pointed to the gap. "Not to worry, Gerry, we'll get stopped here. Then you'll be ordered to pass through."

"Son of a bitch," Chubb replied.[3]

The Grenadiers spent March 1 "licking wounds and reorganizing." They were so shot up, "the remnants" of Nos. 1 and 2 Squadrons were combined to yield a twelve-tank-strong squadron. No. 3 Squadron boasted eight tanks. Regimental headquarters consisted of two more. The attack fell to the composite squadron. Its commander was Captain Pat Grieve. Lieutenants John Oland, A.W. Ferris, and C.E. Chalmers commanded the squadron's three troops. "The only trouble" when the reorganization was complete, wrote regimental intelligence officer Lieutenant John Fergusson, was that "we were still headed toward *that* place."[4]

Lake Superior Lieutenant Colonel Robert Keane had just returned that morning from leave. The battalion's state shocked him. The companies were terribly understrength. 'C' Company was the strongest, with Major Roy Styffe, two other officers, and forty-one other ranks. Major Edmond Gravelle's 'A' Company had another two officers and thirty-one men. 'B' Company under Major George Murray counted just two more officers and twenty-five other ranks. The "men had been fighting steadily since February 26 and were cold, hungry and weary. They had eaten nothing since their last meal near Kirsel in the early morning of the 28th; and few of them had any sleep since that time." The attack was to start at 0200, but only two of sixteen Kangaroos arrived on schedule. Keane suggested delaying the attack until the next night to allow the men to rest, but Moncel scotched that notion. When Keane pleaded with Moncel to "visit the area, talk with the company commanders, and see for himself just what the situation was," the brigadier refused.[5]

Moncel was running a fever. In the morning, the brigade's medical officer would send him to hospital.[6] At this critical moment, the sick man commanded and nobody dared openly defy his orders.

Eventually, the Kangaroos, delayed by muddy roads, arrived and the Superiors mounted up. It was 0300 hours, and the attack was pushed back to 0430. The essential night attack would now occur largely in daylight. Lieutenant Chalmers rolled his tank troop out on the left, and the infantry of 'B' Company tucked behind. Lieutenant Oland's tanks were to the right with 'A' Company following. Captain Grieve's single headquarters tank was just behind the forward group. Lieutenant Ferris's troop and 'C' Company advanced behind him. The leading group was "to bull it through and firm up on the first objective."[7]

Not only had Moncel conceived the attack as a night operation, he had also envisioned Canadian troops inside the woods on either side of the gap providing flank protection. But Le Régiment de la Chaudière's repulse from the Tüschen Wald earlier in the night meant the right flank remained in enemy hands.[8] To the left, Les Fusiliers Mont-Royal of 2nd Division clung to the thin sliver of woods won on the night of February 28–March 1 by the Argyll and Sutherland Highlanders, so at least that flank was safe.

A PRE-DAWN LIGHT brushed the sky to the east, and wind gusts carried icy rain. Watching the attack begin, Grenadier Lieutenant Fergusson thought it resembled "a real old cavalry charge come back into glory again."[9] Tanks and Kangaroos ploughed through mud. Clearing the crest, historical officer Major P.A. Mayer later wrote, a "terrific hail of anti-tank fire met the attacking force...and within a few minutes the whole area became a veritable hell. Tanks went up in smoke as they were struck by 88-millimetre fire, and men were machine gunned as they tried to extricate themselves from the burning hulls. Yet despite this fierce opposition, the leading companies of [the Superiors] gained their first objective by 0715 hours.[10]

'A' and 'B' Companies piled out of Kangaroos that had successfully run the gauntlet of fire. The objective was "some battered houses in a shallow gully midway between the two lateral roads." One road cut through the centre of the Hochwald, and the other hugged its eastern edge. 'C' Company pushed on to the final objective—farm buildings beside the latter road.[11]

Most of the tanks never got through. Six Shermans bogged down early in mud. When the Grenadiers were 150 yards beyond the gap, Lieutenant Chalmers's tank and another plunged into huge shell holes. A Tiger tank firing from the Tüschen Wald knocked out two more. As Lieutenant Howie James bailed out, he was wounded by a sniper. That left just two tanks, including Lieutenant Oland's. They went ahead with 'C' Company. An 88-millimetre shell slammed into Oland's tank. It burst into flame, but the crew escaped. As the remaining tank closed on the farm buildings, a German threw a grenade into the open turret hatch. The explosion killed loader/operator Guardsman Clarence Wilfred Wakegijig.[12]

The three Superior companies were isolated from each other by the intense German fire. Mortars, Nebelwerfers, 88-millimitre anti-tank guns, heavy artillery, and tanks in the woods pounded them all. 'A' and 'B' Companies were dug in four hundred yards apart, the interval between fire-swept. His wireless set malfunctioning, Major Gravelle dashed across to 'B' Company's perimeter inside a copse of trees. But after a brief conference with Major Murray, Gravelle was badly wounded by a machine-gun burst while returning to 'A' Company. Two of his men rescued him from the open field but were each wounded as well.

'B' Company was missing half its men because two of four Kangaroos had been lost. One was wrecked by a mortar bomb, and the other bogged down. That left Murray with just twelve men and a lieutenant under command. Murray decided the little wood was a death trap. Sniper rounds buzzed around his men like swarming bees. If the rifles stopped firing, it presaged an infiltration attempt and an exchange of "frantic rifle and machinegun fire and hurling of grenades." During a brief lull, Murray led his men in a dash to 'A' Company's perimeter around the building cluster. Seeing Gravelle wounded, Murray combined the two companies under his command. He had no sooner finished reorganizing the men than the Germans launched a major counterattack from across the railway to the south. After this was driven off, shellfire drenched the position. Soon all the buildings were smouldering ruins. Deafened by explosions, half-blinded by smoke, mud-covered clothing soaked through and in tatters, the Superiors could only hunker down and hope to survive.

Six hundred yards to the east, 'C' Company's straits were even more desperate. All the officers, including Major Styffe, were wounded. Sergeant Charles Henry Byce took over. Through the smoke, five Kangaroos materialized. They were empty, sent by Murray to rescue the wounded. Styffe, the other officers, and a number of men were put aboard, and the Kangaroos returned through thickening fire to Murray's position. What was left of 'C' Company was then embroiled in "bitter, close-range fighting," the Superiors historian wrote. "Germans and Canadians struggled, shouted and screamed; some filled with loathing for their foe, fought in almost dedicated silence. In the confusion and general disorder the enemy closed in upon 'C' Company's position...the perimeter of their defences becoming smaller and smaller, and their escape corridor to the rear, narrower and narrower."[13]

With the situation growing ever more perilous, the Superiors were amazed when suddenly five tanks bearing two platoons of the Algonquin's 'D' Company materialized out of the smoke. Captain J.M. "Johnny" Jewell had set out at 0500 with thirty-seven men riding on eight Governor General's Foot Guards tanks. The company's third platoon had followed on foot.[14] Three tanks were lost en route, but Jewell and his two platoons rode through on the survivors. Their arrival coincided with that of several Tiger tanks, whose presence convinced the tank commander to withdraw. It was about 0800. Four Shermans were lost during the retreat. The rest set up on a small hill and provided long-range fire support to the infantry east of them.[15]

Despite the ferocity of fire lashing 'C' Company, Jewell decided to attempt seizing the crossing over the Hohe Ley stream. His platoon following on foot had still not appeared. The platoon had, in fact, joined the Superiors of 'A' and 'B' Companies after its lieutenant wisely decided it would be suicide to go farther. Jewell led the rest of his company in a charge, brought abruptly to a halt after three hundred yards by withering fire. The two platoons frantically started digging in. Lashed by unrelenting fire, Jewell realized his men would never reach the stream ahead, nor could they return to 'C' Company. Desperate, he ordered Company Sergeant Major Carl White and Lance Corporal Scotty Cameron to go back to the Algonquin headquarters and bring up tank support and reinforcements.

The two men set off, alternating between crawling and making short dashes. Behind them, the Germans closed in for the kill under cover of intense artillery. A shell burst killed Jewell and wounded several others. As the shellfire lifted, "the little garrison, leaderless, bewildered, and far from assistance, was overrun." Most of the men were taken prisoner.[16]

Three hundred yards away, 'C' Company's situation was critical. Byce, who had won a Military Medal for valour on the Maas in January, was proving a tower of courage. Single-handedly, he knocked out a tank with a PIAT and then used grenades to kill Germans who had seized control of a building. But no amount of courage was enough to win this battle. When another attack began—this time heavily supported by tanks—Byce decided it was time to escape. He guided the men through the narrow, bullet-swept corridor to Murray's perimeter. Only Byce and seven others made it. Undaunted, Byce settled into a sniper position, killing seven Germans with rifle fire and wounding another eleven. His gallantry earned a second decoration, a Distinguished Conduct Medal.[17] All the Superiors were now clustered inside a steadily shrinking perimeter.

IN THE MID-AFTERNOON, Superior's Lieutenant Colonel Keane ordered Captain R.A. Colquhoun to lead some of 'D' Company through to Major Murray's force. With five Canadian Grenadier Guards tanks under command of Captain John Fergusson, just promoted from intelligence officer, this small force surprisingly got through without incident. The tanks helped relieve the situation, but there was no hope of renewing the advance.

Meanwhile, in the late afternoon, Company Sergeant Major White and Lance Corporal Cameron reached the Algonquin Regiment's 'B' Company. Cameron had been wounded. Both men were staggering, exhausted. White explained the situation Jewell's company had been in when they left. Throughout the long day, the other three Algonquin companies had been trying to reinforce the Superiors and Jewell's men. The latter had erroneously been reported as having won the stream crossing. In fact, every attempt was stopped cold and short of the gap's eastern entrance. 'C' Company retired to provide an anchor point at the gap's northwestern corner. 'A' Company, after being cut into three parts by German counterattacks, ended up pinned on the edge of the Tüschen Wald. A little farther back, 'B' Company provided a tenuous link between the other two.

As night fell, word came that 5th Brigade's Black Watch would relieve the embattled 4th Armoured Brigade units in the early morning.[18] At midnight, Fergusson's five tanks withdrew. The relief included the smouldering ruins to which the Superiors still clung and those of each Algonquin company in the gap. Once in position, the Black Watch was to "hold firm on the ground we will occupy," their war diarist wrote. The other two 5th Brigade battalions would then advance through and execute the breakout from the Hochwald Gap. It took all morning on March 3 for the Black Watch to conclude the relief. Reaching the Superiors proved particularly difficult because of heavy mortar and shellfire. The commander of 'D' Company, which had drawn this task, declared it almost impossible during daylight. But slowly the job was completed, and the Superiors withdrew.[19]

"Past the brewed-up tanks and crippled Kangaroos, past the splintered trees and blackened stumps, past the muddy craters," the Superiors "trudged, to food, rest and sleep. Their legs moved as if they were no longer part of their bodies; their faces were taut and drawn and covered with grime; their eyes were heavy. For they had been through something ungodly...so few of them remained unscathed in body—none remained unscathed in mind," their historian wrote.[20]

Algonquin Major George Cassidy was keenly "aware of how important and how vital our thrust was considered by higher command, and how disappointed all must be at our failure to obtain the entering wedge into the Xanten and Rhine-bank area. But anyone who saw the thin trickle of Algonquins who trudged out of the

384 / FORGOTTEN VICTORY

gloom of the forest, who noted their weariness and their wounds, and who could have seen the disappointment on their faces, would have known that no one wanted to get forward and win...more than they did. There was no exultation at being relieved, only a bludgeoned sort of sadness and fatigue. Back in the gap were the bodies of their comrades, the burnout-wrecks of the tanks, and the tragic puzzle of a lost company. Left in them was only, for the moment, an unutterable weariness. It was the morning of the third of March—only a brief five days since 'Blockbuster' had begun. It seemed now like five centuries."[21]

Since the morning of March 2, the Algonquins had suffered eighty-seven casualties, thirty-two (largely men from the overrun 'D' Company platoon) being taken prisoner. Lake Superior losses were fifty-three, including sixteen captured.

The stunning resistance that had stopped the breakout so decisively had been the work of 24th Fallschirmjäger Regiment and the Fallschirmjäger Army Assault Battalion, supported by tanks and artillery of 116th Panzer Division. The paratroopers were fresh and entered battle at full strength. They had outnumbered and outgunned the Canadians—not conditions that give the attacker much chance.[22]

RELIEVING THE 4TH Armoured Brigade force had been made possible largely by efforts of 3rd Division's 8th Brigade in the Tüschen Wald during the previous day, and 2nd Division's continued work at breaking the German grip on the Hochwald. Gains won within these forests decreased the enemy's freedom of movement on the gap's flanks.

Having been once repelled from the Tüschen Wald, Le Régiment de la Chaudière had tried again at 0730. 'A' Company was on the right and 'B' Company the left, with 'A' Squadron, 1st Hussars, in support. Using the narrow forester lanes as objective points, infantry and tankers advanced slowly. There was little direct resistance, but intense mortar and artillery fire forced the Chauds to repeatedly take cover. Lieutenant M.A. Strachan's No. 2 Troop had passed through the gap and then advanced southward along the eastern flank of the woods to provide supporting fire. Meeting little opposition, Strachan led his three tanks right through to the Tüschen Wald's southeastern corner and formed on a cluster of buildings that was actually the attack's final objective. Strachan held there despite heavy shelling and mortar fire. At one point, an 88-millimetre anti-tank gun started firing, and two rounds slammed into one Sherman, prompting the crew to bail out. When the tank failed to brew up, driver Trooper J.E. Jones climbed back in and restarted the engine. Jones drove to where the rest of the crew were hiding; three armour-piercing 88-millimetre rounds struck the tank but failed to penetrate. The crew scrambled in and rejoined the fight. At 1400 hours, the Chauds arrived and declared Tüschen Wald cleared.[23] They had met little resistance and encountered few mines, so casualties were light.[24]

When the other two 8th Brigade battalions pushed through the Chauds and into the northern quadrant of Balberger Wald, things got sticky. The advance began at 1500, and the plan called for clearing half the wood before nightfall, digging in, and then finishing the job the following morning. Both the North Shore (New Brunswick) and Queen's Own Rifles Regiments were badly depleted. Queen's Own Major Ben Dunkelman was the only officer in 'D' Company. He had one sergeant and two corporals as platoon leaders, and they led just forty-five men. The other companies were in similar condition. On the right, 'C' Company led with 'A' trailing. 'B' Company was up front on the left, and Dunkelman's men followed.[25]

The Queen's Own worked through the west side of the forest, while the North Shores advanced straight down the centre, with 'D' Company on the right and 'A' Company the left. Troops from the 1st Hussars 'B' Squadron were in support. Both battalions met stiff resistance, and the woods were heavily sown with mines. Maintaining direction was difficult. North Shore Major Jim Currie led 'D' Company. Nobody had provided a compass bearing to follow. "We simply had to enter a forest that contained many enemy strongpoints and blunder through as best we could. I struck a bearing and we started. The shelling was terrific and...shells were striking trees and bursting. We pushed on and suddenly came upon two German tanks on the move across our front. Luckily, we spotted them and they did not see us. We quickly set up a PIAT and got one tank with a direct hit. Not one of the Jerry crew escaped. The other tank put on speed and we on foot did not try to catch it."[26]

Both North Shore companies were soon halted by a line of dug-in machine-gun crews and riflemen. Lieutenant Owen Kierans's platoon was on the extreme right. Slipping alone through the woods, he worked around behind the Germans. Then he advanced down the line, knocking out one machine gun after another until the surviving Germans took flight. Despite being wounded, Kierans returned to his platoon and refused evacuation until the day's advance concluded. Kierans received a Military Cross.[27]

Queen's Own Rifles commander Lieutenant Colonel Steve Lett considered the "resistance encountered...as determined as any...met in this campaign. Their method is to take advantage of every feature the land offers. They did not always cover [lanes] with heavy small arms fire; but they always placed automatic fire on every rise in the ground, when fighting in woods. Their tactics are based on a heavy volume of small arms fire with automatic weapons and few men, willing to withdraw when attacked, to buildings outside the wood. They invariably counterattacked every advance made, and by dark infiltrated into our positions."[28]

The dense woods blocked wireless communication, and the companies were seldom able to contact their battalion headquarters. It was the same for the tankers, and inter-troop communication was also often impossible. The North Shores resorted to deploying relay teams equipped with wireless sets to pass messages from the leading companies back to battalion headquarters. Results were mixed.[29]

North Shore Major Currie's 'D' Company stumbled into a strongpoint "garrisoned by at least a platoon of paratroopers. It was in a clearing and they could sweep any direct approach with terrific fire. The only hope we had was to get around and try a flank attack. Then the German artillery really opened up and a lot of their stuff began falling around that Jerry post. In a few minutes they all pulled up stakes and beat it, leaving us in sole possession. It was getting dark and cold, so we moved to the edge of the clearing and decided to dig in for the night. To our amazement, we found we were nearly on top of 'A' Company, which was supposed to be over on our left. It was good to have them by us and we arranged a two-company strong-hold. The shelling let up later on but chill awoke me and I found it was snowing and that I had a half-inch blanket of the stuff."[30]

By 2300 hours, the Queen's Own had cleared the western flank of the woods to its southern corner. Here they contacted troops of 11th British Armoured Division. Orders came from brigade to snug down for the night and at first light start working eastward. The North Shores would do the same to their north and left.[31]

ALTHOUGH PROGRESSING SLOWLY, the 8th Brigade advance raised the expectation of imminent victory in these woods. Not so in the Hochwald. On the southern edge of the forest, 2nd Division's 6th Brigade had attempted to pass the Queen's Own Cameron Highland-ers through its Fusiliers Mont-Royal. The Camerons had started out at 1030 hours and immediately met fierce resistance. All day the fighting raged, until the Camerons came to a standstill five hundred yards short of their objective on the forest's southeastern edge. "In this exposed position they came under concentrated artillery and mortar shelling in addition to heavy strafing from machineguns," wrote the regiment's historian. Situation stalemated, the brigade's plan for clearing its sector of the Hochwald was derailed.[32]

In the northern part of the forest, meanwhile, 4th Brigade had met some surprising success. Following the mauling of the Essex Scottish, an advance at 0630 hours by the Royal Hamilton Light Infantry had scarcely been expected to succeed. A former profes-sional football quarterback, Lieutenant Colonel Denis Whitaker decided to fake a frontal assault while swinging out companies to hook behind the enemy—what he called a screen pass. Whitaker anticipated that the Germans had a thin machine-gun line in the woods facing the Essex Scottish and a mobile force farther back ready to meet any threat. He ordered 'B' Company under Major E.L. Smith to attack frontally behind a heavy mortar barrage. At the same time, Major Louis Froggett's 'D' Company would sweep to the left with 'C' Company following on a shorter radius.

The play worked. Froggett's men soon gained the woods, and his biggest challenge was finding the right trail leading behind the German positions. "But we burst right in on the enemy," he recalled. "They didn't have a weapon sited in our direction. They thought they were in a protected position.

"Ken Dugal's platoon headed right for the crossroads, and there was a guy in a slit firing an MG-42...Ken shot him in the shoulder and, without waiting, jumped right into the slit with him. Ken swung the German around. With his Sten at his back, he made him fire on his own counterattack. We didn't have a single casualty—'D' Company didn't—until the counterattack.

"While we held the crossroads, Major Smith pressed down the main axis with 'B' Company and we collected about 60 prisoners. About 80 Germans were killed. There was a fair bit of mortaring and MG fire, but Denny [Whitaker] had really pulled this one off. We made the five hundred yards to our objective with only half the fuss we expected."[33]

It was 1000 hours, but Brigadier Fred Cabeldu was unable to capitalize on the success won because all expectations had been that the battle would be slow and costly. Consequently, it was the next day before the Royal Regiment was ready to advance through the Rileys. "The wood is full of enemy dead, mostly killed by arty and our mortar fire—it may sound ghoulish," the brigade's war diarist recorded, "but the men take heart at seeing the effect of their labours and seeing a little exchange for their pals who have fallen...It was learned today that the Americans are having amazing success. A breakthrough has been effected. Venlo has been captured."[34]

Normally, the Germans would regroup during such a lull and get ready to blunt the next assault. But advancing at 0630 on March 3 on the heels of a short artillery barrage, the Royals met little resistance. Weather was miserable, cold and overcast with intermittent squalls of mixed rain and snow. Opposition consisted entirely of isolated machine-gun positions whose paratrooper crews doggedly fought to the death. By noon, the Royals had reached the Hochwald's northeastern corner. Roving patrols cleaned up machine-gun posts along the northern edge of the woods. As the battalion dug in, the enemy's deadly accurate artillery and mortar fire caused most of the day's casualties. Twelve men killed and one man missing. Lieutenant G.E. Fleury and twenty-nine other ranks were wounded.[35]

Together, 4th Brigade's battalions captured only ten to fifteen prisoners, and the machine-gun crews seemed to be "isolated fanatics." Their resistance had been "badly disorganized." During brigade intelligence staff interrogations, the prisoners generally admitted that "the war is lost for them; they are beaten men—animals more like. The odd few still persist that while they have lost the war we have not won it. Goebbels propaganda certainly gets into them."[36]

EVERYWHERE IN THE woods, March 3 brought a sense that despite continued opposition, the battle for the forests was nearly over. The relief of the Algonquin and Lake Superior Regiments by the Black Watch during the night had secured the Canadian hold there. By mid-morning, Le Régiment de Maisonneuve was providing an anchor point on the northwestern edge of the Tüschen Wald.[37] The 5th Brigade's other battalion—the Calgary Highlanders—was still holding to the north, sending patrols into the Hochwald to link up with the Essex Scottish positions. Heavy shelling, however, prevented any serious penetration into the facing woods, and the battalion was little motivated to push the matter. Lieutenant Colonel Ross Ellis had been told by Brigadier Bill Megill that the Calgaries would move at 0400 the next morning to join the rest of the brigade in the gap for a new operation. By early afternoon, all company commanders were reconnoitering their new areas.[38]

Both the Black Watch and the Maisies recorded being awed by underground dugouts they had captured. "The Jerries really did a job," the Maisies war diarist wrote. "They did not lack comfort at all. They had installations for electricity, stoves, bath and beds. The construction of those underground dugouts had five rows of log covered by earth and grass. It was far better than all the shattered houses we have met." The Maisies only regretted that their tenure would be short-lived. The following morning, they would advance alongside the Black Watch into the open country on either side of the railway.[39]

With two 5th Brigade battalions securing the right flank, 6th Brigade inside the Hochwald made slow but steady progress through the day. The South Saskatchewan Regiment had passed through the Queen's Own Cameron Highlanders at 0730 hours, pushing northeastward through the Hochwald. In support was 'A' Squadron of the

Sherbrooke Fusiliers. Lieutenant Colonel Vern Stott advanced the Sasks along a single axis, leapfrogging one company through the other. When 'D' Company led off, it met only isolated machine-gun positions. These were eliminated easily, with twelve prisoners being taken and six Germans killed.[40]

During the advance, 'B' Company's Private Chic Goodman never saw a single German. But lots of bullets flew through the trees, and shells bursting overhead threw down sprays of shrapnel and wood splinters. He saw two stretcher-bearers coming through the forest carrying a casualty. Suddenly, a shell struck the stretcher dead-on and all three men were torn asunder. It was an image, Goodman said, that "will remain in my memory forever...The Hochwald left no good memories. It was a horror."[41]

The advance proceeded with relative precision. By 1300 hours, the Sasks reached the forest's eastern edge. As the Sasks dug in, 'A' Squadron's No. 4 Troop settled in hull-down position looking out eastward, and its commander spotted two Panthers slipping across the north-south-running road toward the cover of a small wood on the other side. Rather than have the Firefly Sherman mounting the deadly 17-pounder gun expose itself on the crest, the commander went on foot to a point twenty yards in front of it. The gunner fired blind in accordance with the commander's radioed instructions, dropping two ranging shots close to the Panthers. A third armour-piercing round sliced into one Panther, and four more shots struck home. As the tank burned, the crew commander shifted to the other Panther. A similar deluge knocked it out.[42]

Having passed through the Sasks, Les Fusiliers Mont-Royal's company and platoon commanders found the woods they entered so dense that it was difficult to keep track of their men. Fusiliers filtered between trees like Indian warriors might have done hundreds of years before, the regiment's historian noted. Cohesion depended on the "coolness and initiatives of the NCOs." The initial advance by 'C' Company went well despite fairly heavy artillery and mortar fire. By nightfall, the Fusiliers had advanced a half-mile, gaining their objective. As they dug in, the artillery and mortar fire ramped up, and the battalion suffered a number of wounded.[43]

ON THE HOCHWALD GAP's southern flank, 3rd Division's 8th Brigade had continued the slow, dangerous clearing of Balberger Wald. The Queen's Own Rifles advanced eastward along the southern border while the North Shores kept pace to the north. This coordinated two-battalion-wide advance quickly unravelled when the Queen's Own's 'A' Company mired in a thickly sown minefield and came under fire from snipers and mortars.⁴⁴ The North Shore's Lieutenant Colonel John Rowley ordered his battalion to push on alone at 1140. It was a good move. The North Shores made excellent progress. At 1425 hours, 'A' Company had platoons digging in on the forest's eastern boundary. 'D' Company was soon alongside.⁴⁵

The Queen's Own's 'A' Company no sooner got free of the minefield than it came under sniper fire. The company was down to about forty men, and Company Sergeant Major Charlie Martin knew they badly needed rest and reinforcement. Seeing a flash of light, Martin spotted several snipers on a platform high in the trees. Raising his rifle, Martin shot one. That drew a firestorm of rifle and machine-gun fire. Martin knew they had to counter with a charge. When he told the Bren gunner to follow him, the man said, "Charlie, I can't." Martin was growling rebukes when the soldier showed him a shattered right hand. If Martin took the Bren, the soldier said, he would carry the extra magazines in his left hand. The riflemen in the company fixed bayonets and 'A' Company charged, "screaming like Apaches." Suddenly, the Germans broke, dashing through the trees, carrying guns and ammunition boxes. Some surrendered. Others lay dead. Martin looked at the men with him. Of the forty or so, at least a dozen had one or more bandages covering wounds too minor to warrant evacuation. He figured those who survived were under God's protection.⁴⁶

That evening, the Queen's Own dug in among tall, dense tree stands. They were halfway to the forest's eastern border. It would be late afternoon of the following day before the battalion finished clearing its sector. Opposition on March 4 was light, but mines and continual harassing shelling and mortar fire slowed the weary troops.⁴⁷

On the Balberger Wald's northern flank, meanwhile, Le Régiment de la Chaudière had pushed into the open ground between the railroad and the woods on March 3. They met scant resistance and completed the job at 2400. The Chauds dug in behind the road running across their front and tied in with the Black Watch on the right.[48] In clearing the forests south of the gap, 8th Brigade had suffered more than one hundred casualties.[49]

Early on March 4, First Canadian Army declared that the "Hochwald show is over and the enemy has had a sound beating; enemy dead litter the forest." There were still scattered paratroopers in the. Hochwald itself, but Canadian patrols were remorselessly hunting them down.[50]

[2 4]

Nothing Must Delay Us

THE NIGHT OF March 3–4, First Fallschirmjäger Army's General der Fallschirmtruppen Alfred Schlemm decided the Hochwald must be abandoned. He had, in fact, the previous afternoon ordered 116th Panzer Division to withdraw seven miles to Alpen. At midnight, 180th Infanterie-Division replaced the panzer division, forming up adjacent to where 6th Fallschirmjäger Division had established a new line about two miles east of the Hochwald.

The Rhineland battle had entered the endgame phase. Despite orders to hold out, Schlemm knew defeat was imminent. That very afternoon First Canadian Army and U.S. Ninth Army had met when 4th/7th Royal Dragoon Guards of 53rd (Welsh) Division encountered an American XVI Corps cavalry reconnaissance squadron at Berendonk, northwest of Geldern. The same day, advancing alongside the Maas, the fast-moving British 1st Commando Brigade seized Well. Engineers were soon slinging a bridge across the river to give XXX British Corps its long-sought maintenance route. On March 4, the commandos met American troops. By then, the Germans had entirely broken away from XXX British Corps, withdrawing to positions east of Geldern.[1]

With the Americans collapsing the German lines from the southeast, XXX British Corps swung northward after Kapellen fell to 3rd British Infantry Division on March 4. As 3rd Division turned north

393

toward Sonsbeck, the Guards Armoured Division headed due east from Kapellen. The 53rd Division, meanwhile, struck out from Geldern along the road leading through Issum to Alpen.[2]

Alpen was suddenly critically important. The only major highway in front of Wesel that crossed the bridgehead on a southeasterly line ran from Xanten to Rheinberg. To keep this route open, Schlemm must retain Xanten, Veen, and Alpen. Founded by the Romans, Xanten was the legendary birthplace of dragon-slayer Siegfried. It now anchored the bridgehead's northwest corner. Veen, a small village three and a half miles east of Sonsbeck, stood on a small rise that rendered it an effective obstacle.[3] Alpen overlooked where the road descended steeply off the Bönninghardt Ridge to the Rhine, less than three miles distant.[4]

With the Americans closing on Rheinberg and the British on Alpen, seizing Veen and Xanten fell to 11 Canadian Corps. Lieutenant General Guy Simonds planned to carry Veen by advancing a mobile battle group formed by 4th Canadian Armoured Division's 10th Infantry Brigade on a five-mile dash from the Hochwald Gap. Argyll and Sutherland Regiment infantry in Kangaroos would be supported by the British Columbia Regiment.[5]

The Black Watch Regiment inside the gap was to secure the start line. No sooner had the regiment started forward on March 4, however, than the effort was cancelled "owing to the inclemency of the weather, the condition of the ground, and the amount of artillery which the enemy has dug in ahead of us. The ground hereabouts is very soggy, and once more the weather is helping the Hun, enabling him to escape a severe mauling, albeit temporarily," the Black Watch war diarist recorded. Two companies had already moved beyond the gap when the cancellation came. 'A' Company's position was particularly exposed and drew spasmodic artillery and mortar fire. The company would have been even farther along, but Major E.V. Traversy had cautiously held his men back after a prisoner warned there were ninety-six Germans in a building cluster a hundred yards ahead. An eight-man patrol sent to check the buildings was thrown back with six casualties. Traversy called in artillery, but "this proved well-nigh disastrous as many of the rounds fell short. Five men were injured and most of the slit trenches of two platoons caved in, necessitating two hours' work in digging the men out and getting their weapons cleaned. In the meantime the enemy withdrew from the buildings, to all intents none the worse for the bombard. In all, twenty-two casualties were suffered by the company and Major Traversy was left with one sergeant and two corporals as platoon commanders."[6]

Simonds cut new plans. On the northern flank, 43rd (Wessex) Division would push southeast along the Calcar–Xanten road while 2nd Canadian Infantry Division regrouped for a converging attack on Xanten from westward. The 3rd Division's 9th Brigade would clear the Hammerbruch spur, a long ridge extending southeastward from Balberger Wald to a point behind Sonsbeck. Also advancing toward Sonsbeck would be the division's 7th Brigade, from the southwestern corner of Balberger Wald. The 4th Armoured Division was to be ready at Simonds's discretion to advance through 3rd Division toward Veen. On the corps's southern flank, 11th British Armoured Division was to mark time until the Hammerbruch spur was cleared.[7]

As part of its regrouping, 2nd Division was to expand the Canadian frontage east of the Hochwald Gap and win a crossing over the Hohe Ley stream that would enable 5th Brigade to advance north to unite with 43rd Division west of Xanten. The 5th Brigade advance was led by the Calgary Highlanders at 1700 hours on March 4. The battalion advanced on either side of the railway—'B' and 'C' Companies in line to the south, 'D' and 'A' to the north. Moving through the darkness, the Calgaries encountered no enemy and soon deployed in a small wood adjacent to Seelenhof château, about two miles east of the gap.[8]

Extensive patrolling during the morning of March 5 revealed the Germans had a strong force of at least company strength on high ground to the northeast of the Calgary position. When Le Régiment de Maisonneuve attacked on the heels of an artillery barrage, it was brought up short by a deep anti-tank trench behind which the Germans were well dug in. A stalemate ensued. "We now seem to be up against the main Hun outpost defensive line holding the high ground protecting his Wesel bridgehead," 5th Brigade's war diarist reported. Brigadier Bill Megill was ordered to hold in place until 2nd Division's push toward Xanten began.[9]

THE 3RD DIVISION's 9th Brigade effort to clear the Hammerbruch spur had begun at 1900 hours on March 4 with an initial advance from Balberger Wald by the Stormont, Dundas and Glengarry Highlanders. 'A' Company was on the right, 'C' Company in the centre, and 'D' Company on the left. 'B' Company remained in reserve. It was entirely an infantry show, as promised tanks had mired on the road leading to the start line. The first leg was across nine hundred yards of muddy open ground. Several shells caught the Glens on their start line, and Major B.M. Thomson of 'B' Company suffered a leg wound.

A short distance out, 'A' Company's left platoon was pinned by machine-gun fire and volleys of rockets from Panzerschrecks. Half the platoon was killed or wounded.[10] When Lieutenant Alexander Harry Lawson Stephen's platoon moved to assist, it came up against machine-gun fire from four dugouts. Men were cut down like tenpins before the platoon went to ground. Stephen crawled on alone and killed the Germans in one dugout with grenades and bursts of Sten-gun fire. This broke the German resistance, and Stephen led the remnants of the two platoons to the company objective. As 'A' Company dug in, twenty Germans counterattacked and overran the rear section of Stephen's platoon. The Germans set up in an anti-tank ditch and raked 'A' Company with fire. Dashing through the bullets, Stephen scooped up a Bren gun and tackled the German position head-on, killing five Germans, wounding eight, and putting the survivors to flight. His valour earned a Military Cross.[11]

'A' Company remained locked in a hard fight. Corporal Melvin Coulas took over No. 8 Platoon after its officer was wounded. When another counterattack came in, one section was thrown into disarray. Coulas led a desperate charge into the midst of the Germans. Eight enemy were killed, fifteen wounded, and the rest sent running. The company's losses were severe. No. 7 Platoon had just seven men unscathed.[12]

Despite the opposition, the Glens prevailed and in the early morning hours of March 5 declared the start line secure for 9th Brigade's other battalions to pass through. The Highland Light Infantry and North Nova Scotia Highlanders advanced at 0530 hours. Their main objective was a small wood northeast of Sonsbeck.[13] There were three targets for the HLI. 'A' Company on the left went for three wooded knolls, and 'C' Company pushed toward another higher knoll on the right and a nearby group of farm buildings. Once these were taken, 'D' Company would pass through on the other side of the woods.

'A' Company cleared its objective easily, but 'C' Company got tangled in heavy fighting for the fortified buildings. When 'D' Company attempted to turn the flank of this resistance, it was caught on a crossroads by several self-propelled guns that knocked out three supporting Fort Garry Horse Regiment tanks.

The battalion's situation was "an awkward one, with active enemy on three sides and approaches to the position covered by direct enemy fire. On three occasions during the morning, the enemy dropped a smokescreen in behind the forward troops, but on each occasion the anticipated counterattack failed to materialize," the regiment's historian recorded. "Later, he attempted to send a force in an encircling movement to the rear of the battalion but this threat was disposed of with aid from artillery."

A major problem arose when the North Novas ran into heavy opposition that slowed their advance. This lag exposed the HLI's right flank. However, 'A' Company was able to provide enough covering fire to allow 'C' Company to break into the farm building fortifications and clear them. Just after dark, 'D' Company reached its objective. Sporadic fighting continued, but by 0500 hours on March 6, the HLI reported their part of winning the spur complete.[14]

The North Novas' delay had been caused by minefields, which blew up a Bren carrier holding the battalion headquarters wireless sets. At 0615, 'C' and 'D' Companies led the attack. Crossing an open field without difficulty, 'C' Company came up against a long trench filled with Germans, and a short-range gunfight began.[15] Sergeant George Stewart of No. 13 Platoon and a Juno Beach veteran led his men straight into the trench. Capturing a couple of MG-42's, they turned them and gunned down most of the Germans. 'D' Company, meanwhile, had advanced two platoons onto the objective of a small hill and farmhouse to 'C' Company's left. The only occupants proved to be civilians hiding in the cellars. Three hundred yards distant, the Germans were dug into a trench line. An attack was decisively driven back by massed machine-gun, Panzerschreck, and rifle fire. Lieutenant E.N. Lockwood attempted to turn the German flank, but as his No. 16 Platoon moved out, artillery shells hammered down. Lockwood and several men fell wounded. Only seven men from the platoon were unhurt when the shelling lifted. Major Douglas Eastwood moved to rally the rest of the company. Outflanking the trench system, they advanced to a second group of buildings. No sooner had the company cleared these than a Panzerschreck round exploded beside Eastwood. He suffered severe neck wounds and died within minutes.

Back in front of the trench, No. 17 Platoon had kept the German heads down with heavy fire to enable the rest of 'D' Company to gain the buildings. Suddenly, some men dashed from the trench with raised hands and surrendered. When a second group tried to do the same, their comrades shot them down from behind. Finally, a troop of Fort Garry Horse tanks arrived and blasted the rest out of the trench with 75-millimetre-gun and machine-gun fire.

'A' and 'B' Companies passed through at 1515 hours with a full squadron of tanks in support. Pausing by a farmhouse to regroup, 'A' Company's Captain Bill Bean and Lieutenant J.B. Fleury were conferring when a mortar round exploded beside them. Bean fell dead, and Fleury was seriously wounded. This left the company without officers. Despite this calamity, the second phase of the North Novas' attack was soon concluded.[16]

The Glens leapfrogged the other two battalions to finish clearing the spur at midnight.[17] 'C' Company advanced on the right, 'D' Company the left. 'A' Company held in reserve. Hearing some noise ahead, their company's Captain John Palmer crawled forward and came upon "two Germans changing guard in the best parade square style." He killed them with a Sten-gun burst. By first light, the two leading companies had swept their assigned portion of the Hammerbruch spur.[18] Clearing the southern corner was part of 7th Brigade's operation, but for ease of communication and provision of supplies, the Royal Winnipeg Rifle Regiment was put under 9th Brigade command.[19]

Lieutenant Colonel Lochie Fulton was briefed by Brigadier Rocky Rockingham at 0815 on March 6, and the attack started at 1235. There was no resistance except harassing artillery, Nebelwerfer, and mortar fire. The area, however, was "thickly strewn with Schü mines...laid in no particular pattern." Several casualties resulted. Thirteen German deserters were taken prisoner.[20] By 1600 hours, 9th Brigade declared the Hammerbruch secure.

EVEN BEFORE THE Hammerbruch spur fell, 7th Brigade had launched its push toward Sonsbeck in the early morning hours of March 6. The brigade had a new commander, Brigadier Graeme Gibson, brought in on February 27 to replace the fired Jock Spragge. Gibson was a veteran brigadier, having led 3rd Brigade in Italy from October 1943 to April 1944 and then 2nd Brigade in Italy until the September 1944 conclusion of the Gothic Line battle. A series of errors in judgement and inability to win the confidence of a string of battalion commanders had seen him shunted to administrative postings in England. Desperately short of experienced brigadiers, General Harry Crerar had decided Gibson deserved another chance.

Criticism of Gibson's leadership had focused on his sending battalions into hastily and ill-planned attacks that failed to appreciate German resistance. On March 6, Gibson was unusually cautious. Unable to determine whether Sonsbeck was strongly held, he drew up a detailed attack plan "in order to be prepared for the worst." The Canadian Scottish Regiment was to advance to high ground on the outskirts and provide supporting fire as the Regina Rifles entered the town. The Can Scot advance across completely open ground started at 0300 hours behind a creeping barrage.[21]

"The attack was a ghostly affair," the Can Scot war diarist wrote, "as no active enemy appeared to fight for the high ground." A number of German stragglers were captured. The Can Scots secured their objective at 0510 hours, and the battalion's pioneers were sweeping the road for mines with detectors when the Reginas pushed past.[22] Not having been fired on during their advance, the Reginas joined

400 / FORGOTTEN VICTORY

the mine-clearing exercise and by 0700 reported Sonsbeck in hand without a shot fired. They took about twenty prisoners, who reported no organized German forces within five or six miles. In the evening, patrols contacted 3rd British Infantry Division on the edge of a block of forest south of Sonsbeck. [23]

The juncture of the two 3rd Divisions pinched 11th British Armoured Division out of the advance. It was sent into reserve. At this point, xxx British Corps on the Canadian right flank was conducting a northward wheel toward Wesel and the Rhine. [24] During the afternoon, the Reginas were content to watch tank and infantry battalions of 4th Canadian Armoured Division roll through the town on their way into combat. [25] Although the Reginas did not yet know it, 3rd Canadian Infantry Division's role in the Rhineland Campaign was over. There was insufficient shoulder room for three Canadian divisions.

Meanwhile, during the late evening of March 5, 2nd Division's Major General Bruce Matthews decided "a strong infiltration" toward Xanten might throw the Germans off balance so that the town could be easily taken. Accordingly, his 6th Brigade would put in a morning attack. [26] At 2300 hours, Brigadier Holly Keefler convened an Orders Group at his Hochwald headquarters. It was to be a single battalion effort by the Queen's Own Cameron Highlanders, he explained to the newly arrived Lieutenant Colonel A.A. "Bert" Kennedy. Since Lieutenant Colonel Thompson's death on February 26, the battalion had been commanded by Major R.H. Lane. Kennedy, former second-in-command of the Hastings and Prince Edward Regiment in Italy, had taken over that morning.

The Camerons were to pass through the South Saskatchewan Regiment and gain Xanten's northwestern outskirts. If they were successful, the rest of the brigade would exploit the situation. [27] Major David Rodgers would advance 'A' Company on the right while Major H.P. Falloon's 'B' Company went forward on the left behind a heavy artillery barrage. At 0600 hours, the two companies started to cross about seven hundred yards of open ground. Two hundred yards short of the outskirts, machine guns in dugouts to the front and on both flanks of 'A' Company pinned it with heavy fire. 'B' Company had already been forced to ground a short distance back.

Kennedy called in artillery and sent two troops of tanks forward. The tanks found it impossible to manoeuvre through the mud to gain worthwhile firing positions. When Kennedy told Keefler the attack was doomed, the brigadier permitted a withdrawal.[28]

The Camerons, noted their historian, had suffered "one of those periodic episodes wherein an infantry battalion was called upon to do something that later required almost an entire army to accomplish."[29]

Simonds ordered a regrouping for a direct assault by three brigades—2nd Division's 4th and 5th Canadian Infantry Brigades and 43rd (Wessex) Infantry Division's 129th Brigade. The 4th Brigade would capture Xanten's west side, while the 129th approached from the northwest to take the town's centre and the hamlet of Beek beyond. Once these tasks were complete, 5th Brigade would pass on the right and secure high ground between the railway and the oxbow of the Alter Rhein. This was an all-out affair, dubbed Blockbuster II. Because of required preparations, it would not occur until the early morning of March 8.

MEANTIME, SIMONDS ORDERED 4th Armoured Division to capture Veen by dashing a battle group eastward from Sonsbeck. Wigle Force consisted of the Argyll and Sutherland Highlanders (less one company), the South Alberta Regiment (less one squadron), one troop of self-propelled anti-tank guns, one Kangaroo squadron, and one Flail troop. Argyll Lieutenant Colonel Fred Wigle commanded. At 0630 hours on March 6, 10th Brigade's Brigadier Jim Jefferson ordered the advance to commence "as soon as possible."[30]

Spirits ran high. German resistance apparently crumbling, intelligence staff predicted all would go easily. Veen was reportedly held by elderly Volksgrenadiers. Taking it would be "a piece of cake," Argyll Private Donald MacPherson heard one intelligence officer explain.[31] South Alberta Regiment's war diarist declared they were ready "for the mad dash to Veen!" Orders were to "push on as hard as possible. If something was to hinder our advance, that obstacle was to be bypassed...Nothing must delay us."[32]

Wigle Force headed out at 0800 across flat ground dotted with pockets of sparse woods. Numerous stone farm buildings bordered

the road, which ran more or less straight from just north of Sonsbeck to enter Veen from the south.[33] The infantry rode in the
Kangaroos, the entire force stretched out in a long column. Instead
of a dash, the advance became a slow slog. Travelling cross-country
was impossible because fields were virtual sloughs of mud. The road
was heavily mined and blocked by large craters. Three tanks blew up
on mines, and several became stuck. To clear mines, the Flails had
to go around a stuck tank, and all bogged down on the road verge. It
was 1400 and Wigle Force was only about 2,500 yards past the start
line when it came to a huge crater spanning the entire road. The
verges were heavily mined.[34]

To go forward meant first filling the crater. A tank fitted with a
bulldozer blade and other engineering vehicles equipped for road-
clearing work were summoned. The job was predicted to take an
hour. But some of the engineers got lost en route, and the ground
around the crater proved extremely marshy, so the estimate
stretched to three or four hours. Wigle knew such a delay would be
unacceptable to Simonds. He ordered the Argyll's 'C' Company to
dismount and start marching. Eerily, there had so far been no opposition, not even shelling.

At 1600 hours, 'C' Company had marched a mile and was still
unopposed when the engineers finished filling the crater. Wigle
Force caught up to the company and reloaded it in Kangaroos.[35] A
signal from brigade told Wigle "to make haste as it was imperative
for us to be firmed up in Veen by nightfall." No. 3 Troop of 'B' Squadron was leading when, a thousand yards from Veen, an anti-tank
gun fired from a farm south of the road. The lead tank was knocked
out, but the crew escaped and crawled along a ditch to safety. A second shot wrecked a Kangaroo carrying 'C' Company's No. 15 Platoon,
and Lieutenant Gene Boyd Cleroux was killed. The two disabled
vehicles completely blocked the road. The rest of No. 3 Troop took
cover among some buildings opposite the anti-tank gun. 'C' Company disembarked and threw a defensive perimeter around the
tanks. Heavy small-arms fire was coming from the German-held
farm, and the anti-tank gun kept sniping at tanks without scoring
hits. Wigle Force's forward element, consisting of 'B' Squadron and

'C' Company, took refuge in various building clusters running back to the west along the road.[36] Any attempt by tanks to advance off-road ended with Shermans stuck in the "marshy ground."

Wigle returned to his tactical headquarters in Sonsbeck to make a new plan. He had no sooner arrived than Jefferson ordered him to brigade headquarters. Jefferson told Wigle he must "capture Veen before first light." As it was impossible for armour to advance, Wigle could only order the two other Argyll infantry companies forward. 'B' Company under Major Leonard Perry and Captain Sam Chapman's 'D' Company were to advance cross-country on the north side of the road to Veen. The attack was scheduled for 0100 hours on March 7, in order to allow artillery to first fire several concentrations at possible enemy strongpoints.

The two company commanders were to bypass any opposition in front of Veen. Their job was to capture the town. Any bypassed Germans would likely either surrender or withdraw once Veen fell.

Both companies moved off on time and were soon closing on Veen, when they came under heavy machine-gun fire. 'B' Company, on the right, was hit particularly hard. Wigle had good wireless contact with both Perry and Chapman. Because it was so dark and there had been no chance for a preliminary reconnaissance, neither officer had a clue where his company was situated. Wigle had artillery fire phosphorous rounds onto established map references, but this failed to help the two officers.

One 'B' Company platoon became separated and eventually wandered back to Sonsbeck. Perry led what was left of his company toward the southeastern corner of Veen, and Chapman tucked 'D' Company in behind. Wigle lost all wireless contact with 'B' Company at this point.[37]

Perry and Chapman huddled just outside Veen, which was little more than "a dozen loosely scattered houses, farm buildings and that sort of thing." Perry figured it might boast a population of fifty. The two officers decided 'B' Company would go in first and then 'D' Company would leapfrog it. There was a large brick building that looked like a factory on the edge. Perry set that as his objective. Getting to it meant crossing an open field, but a bordering hedge with a deep ditch on the opposite side provided a somewhat covered line of approach. No. 10 Platoon led off, hugging the hedge. As they closed on the building, flares whooshed skyward and bathed the field in a harsh, glaring light. Small arms, machine guns, and Panzerschrecks started firing. Potato-masher grenades bounced down and exploded overhead. Argylls fell dead and wounded. Perry pushed No. 11 Platoon forward. While some men got to within twenty-five yards of the building, more were shot down and crawled wounded into whatever cover they could find. "It soon became evident," an Argyll report stated, "that all who could must get out as best they could. The withdrawal was then started...toward their first starting point." It was impossible to evacuate any wounded because of the intense fire. Perry and many other men were taken prisoner.

Chapman radioed Wigle that 'B' Company had "been wiped out." Unless tanks arrived before daybreak, 'D' Company would suffer the same fate. The company was hidden in a ditch and the only thing saving it was that the Germans were unsure of their location. Dawn would change that. "Can you find your way out?" Wigle asked. Chapman said he could. "All right, come back," Wigle said. Chapman told Company Sergeant Major Tommy Dewell to lead because he was going to be the last man in line. After 'D' Company extricated itself, Chapman realized a third of his men had been lost.[38]

THE FEW PRISONERS taken were identified as paratroopers of the Fallschirmjäger Army Assault Battalion, considered one of the army's most elite reserves. Clearly, the Germans intended to make a determined stand. At 1000 hours on March 7, Jefferson announced a new plan. This time the attack entailed two battle groups going in simultaneously. Chubb Force, constructed similarly to Wigle Force but made up of one British Columbia Dragoon squadron and Lincoln and Welland Regiment infantry, would attack along the south flank of the Sonsbeck–Veen road. This force was commanded by the British Columbia Regiment's Lieutenant Colonel Gerry Chubb. Originally, Chubb Force had been intended to leapfrog past Wigle Force once Veen had fallen and advance due east to Winnenthal.

The second battle group was under command of the South Alberta Regiment and had the Algonquin Regiment for infantry. It would advance north of the road. Teeing up Operation Basher required most of the day, so the attack was set for 1600 hours. Three field and three medium artillery regiments—a total of 144 guns—would support the attack.³⁹

The assault was broken into three phases. In the first phase, the Algonquin's 'A' Company would advance straight alongside the road and secure a group of buildings about two miles from the start line. Here the road angled northward to Veen—about a thousand yards distant. Phase II entailed 'B' Company advancing on a more northerly line to three small clusters of buildings a mile short of Veen and adjacent to a small forest called the Latzh Busch. In Phase III, 'C' Company would pass through 'B' Company and push into Veen from the northwest.⁴⁰ The Lincoln and Welland Regiment was to proceed similarly, except that all three companies would advance in line, with 'D' Company taking the first objective, 'B' Company the second, and 'C' Company the third. 'A' Company, supported by one squadron of tanks, was to swing south and join 'C' Company for the push into Veen.⁴¹

The attack kicked off on time. As soon as the troops moved out, "a terrific mortar and gun concentration struck the extended lines," Algonquin Major George Cassidy wrote. 'A' and 'B' Companies pushed through this storm of fire, leaving a trail of dead and wounded in their wake. Only twenty-five men of 'A' Company reached the objective. A fierce gun battle erupted, and three more men were struck down. The company took nine prisoners. Only one of four South Alberta tanks supporting the company reached the objective. The survivor took up station between two buildings and stayed there, finding that any movement drew 88-millimetre anti-tank gunfire from several positions. 'A' Company dug in, incapable of further action. 'B' Company fared little better. The platoon commanded by Sergeant J.M. Jones had numbered twenty at the beginning but lost eleven getting to the objective. The three platoons were to have cleared separate building clusters. But the one on the right met such intense fire it shrank over to join Jones's platoon in the middle. With its lieutenant wounded, Jones combined the platoon with his. The supporting tanks had followed Lieutenant Donald Howard MacDougall's platoon on the left flank. Having easily secured his assigned building cluster, MacDougall had the tanks shell the buildings that the right platoon had given up on. As the tanks blazed away, MacDougall led two sections along a hedge.[42] Despite the covering fire, snipers and machine guns shredded the little force. Finally, only MacDougall and a corporal remained. Still shy of the buildings, MacDougall told the corporal to cover him. Grabbing a Bren gun and a pouch of grenades, MacDougall ran to the buildings and cleared them one by one. He killed three snipers and a machine gun crew before the rest broke off the engagement by taking flight. MacDougall's bravery earned a Military Cross.[43]

South of the Algonquins, the Lines' 'D' Company under Major Ed Brady had struggled through intense fire and then been heavily engaged by machine-gun positions and mortars. Despite this opposition, at 1745 hours Brady reported the job done. Captain L.H. Hicks passed 'B' Company through. At 1830 hours, Hicks reported his men "running into strong enemy opposition but...advancing slowly." 'C' Company by this time had advanced through 'D' Company and followed Hicks's men. Not until 2035 hours did these two companies win their objectives, and they remained under heavy machine-gun, mortar, Nebelwerfer, and shellfire. The areas were also strewn with mines. 'A' Company had been stopped short of its objective but reported being game to press on.[44]

The Algonquin's 'C' Company had meanwhile attempted to reach 'B' Company's position, intending to continue through to Veen. Advancing a little south of the route 'B' Company had taken, it came under heavy fire from three sides. Lieutenant Gordon Cecil Mowry was killed. His platoon and that commanded by Corporal Ben Hockenstein dug in just south of 'B' Company. The company's headquarters section and third platoon drifted into 'B' Company's perimeter. The Algonquin situation was desperate. Virtually midway between 'A' Company's position and that of the other two companies stood a large farm building that was a German strongpoint. Lieutenant Colonel Bob Bradburn ordered his men to "hang on for dear life until another push could be teed up." The Algonquins created a tight defensive circle around the tanks and sweated out a long, dark night as rain beat down and soaked them.[45]

NOTHING MUST DELAY US / 407

Bradburn had nothing left to help. The Algonquin's 'D' Company had been assigned to support a Canadian Grenadier Guards squadron for a planned end run around Veen to the south to seize Winnenthal. This hamlet was dominated by a large factory and monastery. Intelligence reports indicated it was a vital German control and communications centre. Germans were streaming through it toward the bridges at Wesel—part of what by March 8 was clearly an orderly, general withdrawal from the Rhineland. Seizing Winnenthal might disrupt this orderly flow.[46]

In the end, the only relief on offer for the Algonquins was whatever the Lincs to their south could do to break German resistance in front of Veen. At 0900 on March 8, Lieutenant Colonel Ron Coleman had gone forward to Brady and Hicks's companies to direct the attack. At 1230, Brady's 'D' Company advanced on the left, Hicks's 'B' Company to the right. Thirty minutes later, a hailstorm of fire drove them back to the start line. One of Hicks's platoons remained stranded in a building across from one held by Germans. Four supporting tanks had been knocked out. The Lincs could do no more.[47]

Evening of March 8 yielded the realization at 10th Brigade headquarters "that frontal attack was useless, and the decision was made to complete the encirclement of the place the following morning."[48] The attack was put in by the Argyll's 'C' and 'D' Companies with British Columbia Dragoon tanks in support. Wigle timed it to begin at 0530 hours so that the advance could benefit from darkness during the approach. A heavy artillery program preceded the advance, and the battalion's 3-inch mortars laid down a thick smokescreen. Although the force met opposition, Wigle realized it was "of a very minor character."[49] By 0700 on March 9, early objectives had been reached. At 1030, two tanks and the forward platoons entered Veen and found it abandoned. Although the Argylls fully deployed inside the town, it proved an unhappy location. Artillery and mortar bombardments were constant. Much of the artillery fire came from heavy guns shooting at long range across the Rhine. The Argyll war diarist reported that since Blockbuster had begun, twelve days earlier, the battalion had lost 260 men killed or wounded. Combined with men sick, the total rose to 300, "or almost 75%" of its fighting strength.[50]

With Veen taken, the road was declared open for the Canadian Grenadier Guards and the Algonquin's 'D' Company to take Winnenthal. Recently promoted from lieutenant, Captain Jimmy Sunstrum rode on the tanks with his Algonquins. Closing on the town and meeting little opposition, the tanks found it impossible to accompany the infantry into it. Going it alone, the infantry were drawn into a stiff house-to-house fight. Three men were soon killed and twelve wounded, while only a small corner of the place had been cleared.

Unexpected help arrived at 1715 hours in the form of Lake Superior Regiment's 'C' Company and a squadron of Grenadier tanks. They had been rushed straight along the road from Veen.[51] The Superiors had the regiment's Wasp carriers, and soon many buildings had been set ablaze, but still the Germans refused to quit. Fighting raged through the night inside the "blackened, burning town." By first light, the Germans clung only to the factory and monastery. At 0600 hours, a heavy concentration of fire by the 23rd Field Regiment was called in. As the shelling ceased, two hundred "hard-bitten paratroopers of the 3rd Battalion of the 23rd Para Regiment gave themselves up. They were merely a rearguard force doomed to hold on to the last man. However, they had already suffered severe casualties, and with little hope of ever reaching the Reich, they were disinclined to struggle against the forces that they knew could, and would be brought against them."

As the Superiors' historian concluded, the "engagement at Winnenthal was not a major battle...And yet it was, in some ways, the whole war in microcosm. Here were all the arms and weapons—guns, tanks, flamethrowers, motorized infantry, regular infantry; here were all the problems of approach, investment, assault, house cleaning, mopping up; here were the inevitable mud, mines and determined resistance; here were skill, courage, and death. The little battle at Winnenthal is not to be ignored any more than it should be forgotten."[52]

Take the Company Through

O N MARCH 6, Hitler finally agreed that General der Fallschirmtruppen Alfred Schlemm could entirely evacuate the
bridgehead by March 10. The previous day, Schlemm had ordered
four bridges downstream from Duisburg blown. That left only the
rail and road bridge at Wesel with a vigorous ferry system working
alongside. The Germans anxiously watched for Allied fighter-
bombers, but the continuing poor weather kept tactical air groups
grounded. By the early morning hours of March 7, Schlemm
had withdrawn three corps headquarters and remnants of several
divisions. General der Fallschirmtruppen Eugen Meindl's 11
Fallschirmjäger Korps headquarters controlled the remaining forces,
consisting largely of remains of 6th, 7th, and 8th Fallschirmjäger
Divisions, 116th Panzer Division, a battle group of 346th Infanterie-
Division, and survivors of various anti-tank and anti-aircraft units. At
all costs, Meindl and these troops were to keep the Wesel escape route
open.[1]

The Germans had proven at Veen and Xanten that they still could
fight. On March 5, U.S. 8th Armored Division received a similar les-
son at Rheinberg. While a primarily infantry battle group was to seize
the town, a heavy armoured force was to dash past and win the
bridges at Wesel. Negligible resistance was anticipated. Armoured
task force commander Major John H. Van Houten thought "it was to

be a road march." That illusion was dashed when the infantry got embroiled in a close-quarter shootout on the edge of Rheinberg with swarms of German infantry heavily armed with machine guns and Panzerfausts. An attempt to decide the issue with tanks unsupported by infantry ended in disaster—thirty-nine of fifty-four tanks knocked out. The division had 92 men killed, 31 missing, and 220 wounded by day's end. Although Rheinberg fell by nightfall, the Americans were badly shaken by this "strikingly sharp action when compared with the skirmishing" that U.S. Ninth Army had previously encountered. Two American task forces advanced from Rheinberg the next day toward Wesel, only about eight miles away. It was soon evident that Rheinberg had been "a harbinger of what was to come...the two task forces could do no more than...inch forward."[2] It took the Americans two days to advance the couple of miles separating Rheinberg and Ossenberg. They were shocked to discover every house in the village converted into a strongpoint that had to be hard fought for.

Left of the Americans, 52nd British (Lowland) Division encountered similar resistance in its drive from Issum toward Alpen, which only fell on March 8 after a stiff fight.[3] That evening, Lieutenant General Brian Horrocks transferred his remaining divisions to 11 Canadian Corps and placed xxx Corps headquarters under British Second Army control to prepare for Operation Plunder—the Rhine crossing.[4] With the bridgehead steadily shrinking, 52nd (Lowland) and 43rd (Wessex) were the only British divisions still operational. They were assigned to guard 11 Canadian Corps's flanks.

The 43rd's 129th Brigade was one of three brigades tasked with seizing Xanten. It was to attack in the early morning of March 8 alongside 2nd Canadian Infantry Division's 4th Brigade. While the former took the main part of the town, the 4th would capture Xanten's west side.

"WHEN WILL IT all end? The idiocy and the tension, the dying of young men, the destruction of homes, of cities, starvation, exhaustion, disease, children parentless and lost, cages full of shivering, staring prisoners, long lines of hopeless civilians plodding through mud, the endless pounding of the battle-line," Highland Light Infantry Lieutenant Donald Albert Pearce asked. Although his battalion was finished fighting in the Rhineland, Pearce could hear the guns shelling Xanten and knew other men were going forward to fight and die. "What keeps this war going, now that its end is so clear?"[5]

It was a question many soldiers asked that morning. The fierce repulse of 6th Canadian Infantry Brigade two days earlier left few illusions that Xanten would fall easily. foo Captain George Blackburn of 4th Field Regiment, going forward in a Sherbrooke Fusiliers Regiment tank provided for the artillery officers, knew the Germans were under orders to hold at all costs. They could expect "searing machine-gun fire from slits in fortified barns and thick bunkers and emplacements...while hundreds of German guns and mortars of all calibres [would] pound them with unabated fury from across the Rhine." Like the Hochwald, he expected Xanten to "become synonymous with flaming battle and remorseless killing by men nearing exhaustion from three weeks of almost continuous attacks and counter-attacks."

Blackburn was grateful to be in the tank instead of his regiment's Bren carriers. The tankers had provided a driver and co-driver. There were three gunners in the team. Signaller John Cooper down in the tank's bowels worked the wireless set. Captain Gordon Lucas and Blackburn shared the turret. They supported the Essex Scottish Regiment, which led 4th Brigade's advance on the left. The Royal Hamilton Light Infantry was to the right.[6]

Private Hugh McVicar was on the ground nearby. The thirty-one-year-old had joined the Essex on February 21 and been assigned to 'C' Company. Part of a two-man PIAT team, he had missed the March 1 battle in which Major Fred Tilston won the Victoria Cross. He and his teammate had become separated early in the advance. Left with a PIAT lacking bombs, McVicar had returned to the start line. So he considered this his first battle.

He stood on the start line with stomach churning, but "couldn't be sure whether it was because of fear or something I'd eaten." The platoon had received a new officer the night before, twenty-one-year-old Lieutenant William Lloyd Moore. "He was fair and somewhat short, but...he impressed me as a man who would know how to handle his men and himself in battle." During the Orders Group, Moore said opposition should not be heavy. McVicar doubted this.

With the guns firing a preliminary barrage, McVicar's stomach got the better of him. Stripping off gear and dropping his pants, he entered "a prolonged struggle to rid myself of the cramps. And at any moment would come the signal for the company to move off on its rendezvous with the enemy. What a revolting situation that was!"

Feeling steadier, McVicar returned to his platoon. It was about 0430, and artificial moonlight created a "shimmering light over our heads." The outskirts of Xanten lay 1,500 yards away. A fine rain fell, fogging his glasses.[7]

On the brigade's right flank, the Rileys faced the same "long advance across open ground." Major Louis Froggett's 'D' Company was on the left, Major J.W. "Jimmy" Bostwick's 'A' Company the right. To the right of the Rileys was a small height of ground. Lieutenant Colonel Denis Whitaker understood it was in friendly hands.

At 0530, the signal to advance came. Artillery dropped a smoke-screen, and the infantry followed a creeping barrage. The Rileys immediately came under heavy fire from the right-flank high ground. There was nothing Whitaker could do to quickly stem the fire. All artillery was committed.

Lieutenant Ken Wharton commanded an 'A' Company platoon. Through the boiling smoke, he saw Bostwick guiding the company blindly with a compass. The Germans were dropping artillery and mortar shells into the smoke, knowing there were Canadians there. "That's when Jimmy Bostwick got it. I was running toward him. Then suddenly I saw him go up about eight feet and come down dead...It was a great shock, because he was the kind of guy who gave you so much confidence to be near him. It was hard to believe that suddenly he was dead. The last five words of Bostwick's life were, 'Ken, take the company through!'"

Wharton led the company to a string of buildings on Xanten's southern outskirts. He got there with just twenty-eight men. 'A' Company became entangled in vicious house-to-house fighting that soon stalemated. Wharton had too few men to continue beyond a couple of houses, but the paratroopers seemed to think they were not strong enough to dislodge them. That suited Wharton. Whenever the Germans started to rally, he called in heavy artillery concentrations that took the fight out of them for a while.

Coming in behind 'A' Company, Major Roger Carroll's 'B' Company had also been shredded. Artillery fire killed Carroll halfway to Xanten. Confusion broke out, with two platoons pressing on and the third going to ground. The two platoons captured a house on the outskirts but were then pinned inside it.

On the left flank, Froggett thought this the longest advance ever. It seemed to go on for ninety minutes or more. He and his men waded through "low, wet ground," got into the town, and soon had forty prisoners. Unaware of what was happening on the right flank, he thought things were going well. Following up on the left flank, 'C' Company's Major Ben Bolt reached Xanten having no idea where Froggett's men were. Bolt's company was quickly enmeshed in a desperate hand-to-hand fight. A German pointed a Schmeisser at Bolt, but it jammed. Bolt beat the German to the ground with the butt of his Sten gun. Around him, paratroopers and Rileys had fixed bayonets and slashed at each other or beat in heads with rifle butts. Captain Harry Oliver, meanwhile, had rounded up the third platoon of 'B' Company and reinforced Bolt with these men.

Froggett's initial confidence crumbled as his company was drawn into close-quarters fighting. In the rear, Whitaker had little idea of what was happening. Wireless communication was spotty, and there was no contact with Froggett, 'D' Company's wireless having been destroyed. Hoping to join the companies, Whitaker and 4th Field Regiment's Major Jack Drewery drove toward Xanten in an armoured half-track only to be fired on by a German anti-tank gun. Whitaker jammed the half-track into reverse and backed away at speed, so the Germans only fired a couple of badly aimed shots. Froggett, meanwhile, had decided he and his runner should return to Whitaker. On the way back, the two were jumped by some paratroopers and taken prisoner. Froggett was marched across one of the Wesel bridges with a Luger pistol pressed against his neck to ensure compliance. The runner had been hit by machine-gun fire earlier and left in a cellar, where he was eventually found and rescued by the Rileys.[8]

FROM HIS TANK, Captain Blackburn watched "two or three extended lines of Essex Scottish charging...past...I'd seen our infantry attack before, but in this case they [attacked] across open ground against a very strong position held by German paratroopers armed with many automatic weapons and backed by mortars and artillery. The attacking lines [were] being hit and knocked down by machine-gun fire and well-aimed mortar bombs." He saw one infantryman "hurled at least ten feet in the air. And the same explosion [took] out three or four other men." The infantry went to ground. When the barrage ended, the Essex still lay in the open. Blackburn zeroed artillery on the German positions. But he saw that like the 75-millimetre tank guns firing around him, the shelling was not "all that effective against these deep bunkers." The German artillery began targeting individual tanks with heavy concentrations. The Sherman in front of Blackburn's "was violently rocked by a heavy shell exploding under the front of its hull" but remained in action.[9]

The Essex finally outflanked the bunkers and seized a group of farm buildings just outside Xanten. 'A' Company's manoeuvre brought it up alongside a large château built in the Middle Ages and even surrounded by a water-filled moat. The paratroopers had modernized its defences with many machine guns and Panzerfausts. Essex casualties kept mounting. Private McVicar had been following Private Ernest Andrew Walker, the thirty-two-year-old company runner. McVicar thought that as a veteran, he was a good role model for survival. Mortar rounds splashed down and everyone hit the dirt. When the fire eased, McVicar rose on one elbow. At least a dozen men were dead or wounded. Walker was dead. Lieutenant Moore was down. A stretcher-bearer told McVicar he needed help. The man pressed a white helmet with red crosses into McVicar's hands and said he was drafted.

McVicar went to Moore. The officer had one arm shattered at the elbow. Pointing to a wound in his groin, Moore gasped, "I think I'm hit in the guts." McVicar tore open clothing until the stretcher-bearer took over. McVicar intercepted an ambulance jeep and worked with the driver on shuttling wounded to the Regimental Aid Post. He wanted to get the jeep to where Moore and the others from his platoon were, but they kept encountering wounded farther back that the driver insisted on rescuing first. Finally, the jeep reached McVicar's platoon. Moore and three others had died.[10]

The battle raged on into the early afternoon with the paratroopers in the main bunkers and château aggressively holding out. Blackburn saw a large party of Germans advancing from the rear on foot toward the bunkers. Beside him, Captain Lucas gave Blackburn firing coordinates that he passed by wireless to the regiment's headquarters. Lucas called for a Mike target—all twenty-four of the regiment's guns firing. Barely a minute passed before shells arrived, Germans went down dead or wounded, and the survivors fled back to Xanten.[11]

'A' Company's fight at the château finally ended when Major Ken MacIntyre was able to call in several Crocodile flame-thrower tanks. The tanks fired 75-millimetre shells into the walls to open holes and then squirted jets of flaming liquid through them. That persuaded the Germans inside to surrender.[12] The Crocodiles turned to flaming the bunkers, and after an hour all were silenced. Blackburn watched "batches of prisoners being escorted to the rear, some... laughing and some...crying."[13] By 1500 hours, the Essex Scottish had won all objectives. They suffered 119 casualties, but took more than 250 prisoners.[14]

At midday, Brigadier Fred Cabeldu decided to commit the Royal Regiment. This would support both the 129th Brigade to the north and ease pressure on the embattled Rileys on Xanten's southern outskirts. 'A' and 'C' Companies led. Finding the ground too boggy for Crocodiles, the battalion's Wasps accompanied 'C' Company, and its objective quickly fell. 'A' Company, however, met stiff resistance, with the forward platoon becoming trapped in a building cluster. The weight of fire was so heavy the other platoons were unable to get through to it. Lieutenants M.G. Berry and R.S. Beckley were wounded and evacuated. Despite a leg wound, Major Robert Irving Clarence Wedd soldiered on. Limping toward the factory that was the company objective, Wedd was wounded a second time in the other leg. As he was unable to walk or be evacuated, his men put him in a shell hole. Soon struck by a mortar round, Wedd suffered

devastating shrapnel wounds to chest, neck, and head. He was evacuated to England, where he died on March 16.[15] The surviving Royals
crawled along a ditch until they entered Xanten.[16] Darkness found
them in contact with the 4th Somerset Light Infantry to their left.

The British attack had gone well, with the Somersets advancing
behind a creeping barrage to reach a wide anti-tank ditch easily
crossed on foot. Timely deployment of a tank mounted with a folding light-metal bridge called a scissors bridge enabled Crocodiles to
follow. Hardly a building stood in this part of Xanten. In fact, only 10
per cent of the town's buildings had survived. The Crocodiles
smoked the Germans out of rubble piles. By late afternoon the fight
was over, and the Germans facing the embattled Rileys melted away.
The Rileys had taken the worst mauling of 4th Brigade's battalions,
with 139 casualties. The Royals lost 46 killed or wounded.

Even before the situation in Xanten clarified, Major General
Bruce Matthews ordered Brigadier Bill Megill to launch 5th Brigade
into the operation's second phase. The advance was led by Le Régiment de Maisonneuve in Kangaroos and supported by tanks and
Flails. At 2245 hours, the Maisies charged straight through Xanten
via the Calcar–Xanten road. Two hours later, they reported being
secure on the wooded hills south of Beek and having more than a
hundred prisoners.

The Black Watch passed through on foot, and by 0400 hours
reached its objectives, having met little resistance. It was now the
Calgary Highlanders' turn.[17] They advanced with 'A' Company to the
left of the major railway running southeast from Xanten and 'B'
Company on its right. 'C' and 'D' Companies followed. German
artillery dogged them. Again, little opposition was met, until Major
George Stott's 'D' Company closed on the hamlet of Birten. The
company was picking through a thick minefield when withering
small-arms, machine-gun, and mortar fire lashed out from the hamlet. Unable to advance or withdraw, the company was cut off.

Rescue soon arrived when the Maisies attacked Birten from the
north. At 1630 hours on March 9, the hamlet fell. The Maisies had
taken more than two hundred prisoners. By late evening, the Calgaries had regrouped and crossed a bridge over the Winnenthaler Canal
without meeting opposition.

The battle for Xanten and the Rhineland was hearing an end. At 0700 hours on March 10, a series of great detonations shook Wesel, and the two bridges plunged into the river. Later in the day, 2nd Canadian Infantry Division patrols contacted 52nd British (Lowland) Division at Ginderich, near the bank of the Rhine. The British reported having contact with 35th U.S. Infantry Division to its right and that the Americans were closing on Wesel. On the morning of March 11, two American infantry platoons approached Fort Blücher, an old bastion guarding the crossing point. The few Germans garrisoning it surrendered. From Düsseldorf in the east to Nijmegen in the west, Twenty-First Army Group looked across the Rhine River. The Rhineland Campaign was over.[18]

THOSE CANADIANS WHO fought in the campaign generally considered it the bitterest. The Germans had brought huge numbers of men and weapons to the battle. The initial opposing force of one reinforced infantry division had grown to ten. The U.S. Ninth Army's launch of Operation Grenade on February 23 drew only a little of this strength away. Remaining behind were strong formations of paratroopers who fought with fanatical and skilled determination.

"During the concluding stages," General Harry Crerar wrote, "our...infantry suffered heavy casualties from shelling, mortaring, and rockets. This was consistent with the enemy's tactics throughout the whole of the operation. His fire-power, particularly from machineguns, mortars and cannon had been more heavily and effectively applied than at any other time in the Army's fighting... Not including self-propelled guns, I estimated that at the beginning of March over 700 mortars and more than 1,000 guns of various calibre were available to the First Parachute Army. Only rarely did there appear to be a shortage of ammunition, and on a narrow front, the enemy gunners were able to concentrate their fire on our points of penetration in the natural defiles along the line of advance. The combined effect of guns and going made themselves felt in the loss to us of some 300 tanks. Our material superiority was not without its effect, but the state of the ground and the prevailing wet and overcast weather prevented the full deployment and exploitation of our strength."[19]

With the skies so often socked in, few were the days when tactical air support had been available. Daily reports on air operations "invariably began with the words: 'Due to poor weather...'" When they could, the pilots flew, but they never swarmed the skies. In the period February 26–28, only 753 sorties supported First Canadian Army. From March 1 to 10, a total of 1,407 sorties occurred.[20] All of them took place in the first days of the month. Blockbuster's last week was entirely unsupported.[21]

Throughout the campaign, weather and terrain had combined to present an implacable enemy. In Normandy and even the Scheldt Estuary Campaign, tanks had played a "gigantic part." Not so often in the Rhineland, where the low ground proved generally too soft, and many "high features in the battle area [were] too thickly wooded for satisfactory cooperation with the infantry...Yet casualties in both personnel and armoured vehicles proved beyond doubt that on such occasions as the armoured regiments were committed, they fought brilliantly, regardless of loss," one army report stated. Of the three hundred tanks that were lost, two-thirds belonged to Canadian armoured regiments.[22]

More so than in any other campaign First Canadian Army fought, the Rhineland devolved into a contest of infantrymen supported by artillery and other heavy weapons. It was not just the endless mud and rain that reminded combatants of the Great War, but also the extended and violent attritional battles with their massed artillery fire, infantry advances into drenching machine-gun fire, and close-quarter combat where men resorted to the bayonet.

Not surprisingly, First Canadian Army suffered terrible losses. From February 8 through March 10, altogether 1,049 officers and 14,585 other ranks became casualties. The majority were British soldiers because of the extent of xxx Corps's role in Veritable and its continuing involvement in Blockbuster. Canadian casualties numbered 379 officers and 4,925 other ranks. Most Canadian casualties occurred during Blockbuster—February 26 to March 10. Those thirteen long, bitter days yielded a loss of 243 officers and 3,395 other ranks.

By comparison, during the seventeen days that U.S. Ninth Army was engaged in Operation Grenade, total American casualties were less than 7,300. While the American divisions performed brilliantly in their lightning advance to the Rhine, they faced decidedly less capable German formations, which were often disorganized and unwilling or unable to fight with the determination of those facing First Canadian Army.

The German decision to fight on the Rhine's west bank was ultimately a disastrous folly. From the launch of Veritable to the end of Blockbuster, First Canadian Army captured 22,239 prisoners, and intelligence reports yielded estimates of the number of Germans killed or becoming "long-term wounded" at another 22,000. U.S. Ninth Army returns were 29,739 prisoners and 16,000 other casualties. Tallied together, German losses were approximately 90,000.[23]

Despite the losses, the German withdrawal had been competent. During the night of March 8–9, for example, all remaining artillery west of the river had escaped. Still, about 3,000 Germans were trapped when the last standing bridge—that of the railroad—was destroyed. This remnant force surrendered to the Americans.

Typically, the March 11 Oberkommando der Wehrmacht daily report from Berlin struck an upbeat note: "In order to use the better defensive lines on the east bank of the Rhine, our forces evacuated the left-hand side of the Rhine in the Wesel Bridgehead in a deliberate and disciplined manner."[24] True to a point—no great haul of abandoned armour, artillery, and transport such as had been captured after the Falaise Gap was closed. Most equipment left behind was wrecked or immobilized by mechanical failure.[25]

But the decision to fight in the Rhineland cost the German Army its best divisions in the west. Field Marshal Bernard Montgomery declared this the Germans' "third major blunder." Fighting south of the Seine River in Normandy and launching the Ardennes offensive constituted the other two errors. All these decisions, of course, had been demanded by Hitler.

Had the Germans withdrawn across the Rhine, they would have retained a formidable army that could have offered the Allies a hard fight to win a crossing over that great river. Instead, elite divisions were fed into a meat grinder, often in piecemeal packets. That, of course, had been precisely what Montgomery wanted. First Canadian Army and U.S. Ninth Army had together crushed the Germans as intended. The Rhineland Campaign was the war's last great battle in the west. On March 23, when Twenty-First Army Group launched Operation Plunder to cross the Rhine, they faced "utterly inadequate forces" incapable of stopping it.[26] Thereafter, there was never any question as to the outcome. Although much hard fighting remained to come, it was conducted in the certain knowledge that the Allies would prevail. First Canadian Army's sacrifice in the Rhineland had assured inevitable victory.

THE CRUEL WINTER
IN MEMORY

HERE IS A monument at Driel where the 20th and 23rd Field Companies of the Royal Canadian Engineers and the 260th and 553rd Field Companies of the Royal Engineers carried out their dramatic rescue on the night of September 25–26, 1944. It stands adjacent to the winter dyke over which the engineers dragged their boats to launch onto the Nederrijn and reach the shrinking salient at Arnhem. "They were just whispers and shadows in the night..." reads an inscription. A bronze plaque with raised figures depicts engineers in a boat taking aboard weary paratroopers. Another plaque nearby identifies the squadrons involved and describes the operation on that cold, rainy night. Behind the monument stand four flagpoles. The day I visit, these are empty. But during remembrance ceremonies, the British Union Jack, Canadian Maple Leaf, and Polish and Dutch flags fly.

Except here, in this welcome and excellently designed monument, the fact that Canadian engineers took part in that rescue is largely ignored. In many histories of the Arnhem debacle and Operation

Market Garden, all credit goes to British engineers acting alone. Take Cornelius Ryan's *A Bridge Too Far*, which begat Richard Atten-borough's so-titled epic movie. Neither film nor book mentions Canadian engineers.

Canadians, of course, often share in this failure to recognize or even be aware of what that generation of young Canadian men and women experienced in World War II, let alone a small part of it like the engineers' heroic rescue. Very few films tell their story and not many books either. When a television series about that war airs on Canadian networks, it will be a U.S. production telling American stories. Little surprise, then, that a good many Canadians, as well as Americans, believe World War II began on December 7, 1941, with the Japanese raid on Pearl Harbor.

Thankfully, there is this monument at Driel that sets some of the facts straight, and many more elsewhere in Europe that tell Canada's story. West of Driel, for instance, a large monument stands on Kapel-sche Veer. It honours the bloody struggle there of January 1945. Kapelsche Veer is sobering to visit. Little has changed—flat, feature-less pastures with the Maas flowing past. No cover. A clear death trap for any attacker, as it proved to be for the Polish, British, and Canadian troops who fought a thankless battle for its possession. The monument is set into the base of a low rise of ground, on the summit of which stands a large and much-battered weeping willow. It stood here throughout the battle and continues to hold vigil over the plaques dedicated to those who gave their lives on this muddy patch of ground. Some visitors say they have found slivers of shrap-nel embedded in its rough bark, but I discover none during a fairly careful search.

The battle at Kapelsche Veer was the bitterest action the Cana-dian troops fought during that icy winter of 1944–45 when they faced the Germans across the wide, slow-flowing Maas and in the Nijmegen Salient. Both sides were tired and suffering supply short-ages. A pause was necessary. Fighting was still going on, as the monument attests, but it was mostly patrols and small raids aimed at keeping the enemy off balance, gathering prisoners and intelligence. The stretch from November through January was mainly a test of stoic endurance. There was the constant cold, often accompanied by rain that soaked through uniforms ill-suited to winter conditions. When there was snow, life was even harder. Although those grim months offered some respite from desperate battle, they were not a period of rest. There was also the fear that on any given desultory day, bad luck in the form of a sniper bullet, random shell or mortar round, or poorly placed foot striking a mine could kill you. A common fear of soldiers is to die not in glorious battle but in an incident so minor that it goes unrecorded, possibly even by their friends. As Highland Light Infantry Lieutenant Donald Albert Pearce wrote, by this point in the war, many had become so inured to tragedy that when someone in their platoon was killed, the others tended to simply say, "He got it." Men were buried and, if not forgotten, at least consigned to that place in memory that these soldiers seldom visited—either then or in the years after the war.[1]

Small wonder, then, that when the big buildup for Operation Veritable began, the Canadians were grateful to leave behind the misery of that winter on the Maas—even though they knew that ahead was a battle that would cost many their lives. Together, Veritable and Blockbuster formed the third great campaign First Canadian Army fought in World War II. The first was Normandy and the second the Scheldt Estuary. Each had been uniquely terrible. The Rhineland Campaign, too, unfolded uniquely.

Along a road near Groesbeek Canadian War Cemetery, there is a small monument to Veritable. It is a silver cylinder shaped like an artillery shell, a clever exercise in remembrance minimalism. On the side facing east toward the long expanse of open farmland over which thousands of Canadian and British soldiers advanced on February 8, 1945, a couple of sentences are engraved, first in Dutch and then English. "From this point around three hundred thousand British and Canadian soldiers set off on 8 Feb 1945 for Wesel and the Rhine on Monty's Operation Veritable. Pilgrim, strive with whatever it takes to realise your ideals." On the reverse side, the monument identifies this spot as also where the "Red Devils" of the 82nd Airborne Division's 508th Regiment landed as part of Operation Market Garden on the night of September 17–18, 1944. "Pilgrim, no matter the name or the colour, shield the vulnerable," ends the inscription on this side. While each advice to the pilgrim seems valid, the reason for their presence on the monument is unclear. But the descriptive sentence about Veritable is to the point.

Across the border in Germany, a few small plaques recognizing Veritable and Blockbuster have also been erected. One is attached to a farm building that Sergeant Aubrey Cosens cleared on the night of February 25–26 before a sniper's bullet took his life in the nearby field. The building is unremarkable, a low structure that is poorly maintained. Most exterior walls are overgrown with ivy, but someone cuts the foliage back to keep the plaque visible.

Not far away I find another plaque, beneath an overpass of the railway running by Üdemerbruch. The tracks are mostly gone now. This plaque was installed in 1999 by the South Alberta Regiment. It records that in the battles for the Reichswald and Hochwald, the regiment suffered its heaviest losses "in men, prisoners of war, and equipment. Therefore the veterans of the SAR want to pay their respects to all who paid the supreme sacrifice and hope and pray that this never happens again. May they all rest in peace. We will remember them."

Finally, I am drawn to Groesbeek Canadian War Cemetery. It contains 2,619 graves, 2,590 of which are identified, and all but 9 of those are the graves of fallen members of the Commonwealth. The overwhelming majority of headstones, however, are of soldiers from 11 Canadian Corps's three divisions. The cemetery also includes the Groesbeek Memorial, which commemorates by name more than 1,000 members of Commonwealth land forces who died between the crossing of the Seine and the end of the war and have no known grave. The cemetery is meticulously maintained and regularly visited by many Dutch citizens who live in Groesbeek, Nijmegen, and other nearby communities. Carefully tended roses and other flowers grow between the headstones that extend in long, seemingly countless rows.

It is here that the sombre cost of the great battle that Operations Veritable and Blockbuster constituted is unavoidably recognized. And yet, the Canadian and British troops won a decisive victory. At the end of the Rhineland Campaign, there was no doubt as to the war's outcome. In little more than two months' time, the Allies would win the war. The Rhineland Campaign had paved the way for that speedy end.

The men buried in Groesbeek are part of the price paid. So many young with dreams never realized. So many broken hearts and broken lives that resulted from the necessity of fighting a war they had to win. Looking east from the cemetery, out across the wide fields that typify the Rhineland today, to where that last great battle of the European war was waged by First Canadian Army, I am reconfirmed in my belief that we Canadians of today have a sacred duty to never forget the sacrifice of these young men laid to rest in Dutch soil so far from home.

AMERICAN

Supreme Headquarters, Allied Expeditionary Force (SHAEF), Gen.
Dwight D. Eisenhower

Sixth Army Group, Gen. Jacob L. Devers

Twelfth Army Group, Lt. Gen. Omar Bradley

First Army, Lt. Gen. Courtney H. Hodges

Third Army, Gen. George S. Patton

Ninth Army, Lt. Gen. William H. "Simp" Simpson

BRITISH

Chief of Imperial General Staff, Gen. Sir Alan Brooke

Twenty-First Army Group, Field Marshal Bernard Law Montgomery

Second Army, Lt. Gen. Miles Dempsey

I Corps, Lt. Gen. John Crocker

xxx Corps, Lt. Gen. Brian Horrocks

CANADIAN

First Army, Gen. Harry Crerar

II Corps, Lt. Gen. Guy Simonds

II Corps, Chief of Staff, Brig. Elliot Rodger

II Corps, Corps Royal Engineers, Brig. Geoffrey Walsh

2nd Division, Maj. Gen. Bruce Matthews

3rd Division, Maj. Gen. Dan Spry

4th Division, Maj. Gen. Chris Vokes

4th Armoured Brigade, Brig. Robert Moncel

4th Infantry Brigade, Brig. Fred Cabeldu

5th Infantry Brigade, Brig. W.J. "Bill" Megill
6th Infantry Brigade, Brig. R.H. "Holly" Keefler
7th Infantry Brigade, Brig. J.G. "Jock" Spragge, then Brig. Graeme
    Gibson
8th Infantry Brigade, Brig. James Alan "Jim" Roberts
9th Infantry Brigade, Brig. John "Rocky" Rockingham
10th Infantry Brigade, Brig. Jim Jefferson

GERMAN
Commander in Chief, West, Gen. Gerd von Rundstedt
Heeresgruppe B, Gen. Feld. Walter Model
Heeresgruppe H, Gen. Kurt Student, then Gen. Johannes
    Blaskowitz
I Fallschirmjäger Army, Gen. Fall. Alfred Schlemm
II Fallschirmjäger Korps, Gen. Leut. Eugen Meindl
XLVII Korps, Gen. Heinrich Freiherr von Lüttwitz
LXXXVI Korps, Gen. Erich Straube

APPENDIX B:
THE CANADIAN ARMY IN THE
RHINELAND CAMPAIGN
(COMBAT UNITS ONLY)

FIRST CANADIAN ARMY TROOPS
2ND ARMY GROUP, ROYAL CANADIAN ARTILLERY:
19th Field Regiment
3rd Medium Regiment
4th Medium Regiment
7th Medium Regiment

CORPS OF ROYAL CANADIAN ENGINEERS:
10th Field Park Company
5th Field Company
20th Field Company
23rd Field Company

II CANADIAN CORPS TROOPS
18th Armoured Car Regiment (12th Manitoba Dragoons)
6th Anti-Tank Regiment
2nd Survey Regiment
6th Light Anti-Aircraft Regiment

CORPS OF ROYAL CANADIAN ENGINEERS:
8th Field Park Company
29th Field Company
30th Field Company
31st Field Company

2ND CANADIAN INFANTRY DIVISION
8th Reconnaissance Regiment (14th Canadian Hussars)
Toronto Scottish Regiment (MG)

ROYAL CANADIAN ARTILLERY:
4th Field Regiment
5th Field Regiment
6th Field Regiment
2nd Anti-Tank Regiment
3rd Light Anti-Aircraft Regiment

CORPS OF ROYAL CANADIAN ENGINEERS:
1st Field Park Company
2nd Field Company
7th Field Company
11th Field Company

4TH CANADIAN INFANTRY BRIGADE:
Royal Regiment of Canada
Royal Hamilton Light Infantry
Essex Scottish Regiment

5TH CANADIAN INFANTRY BRIGADE:
Black Watch (Royal Highland Regiment) of Canada
Le Régiment de Maisonneuve
Calgary Highlanders

6TH CANADIAN INFANTRY BRIGADE:
Les Fusiliers Mont-Royal
Queen's Own Cameron Highlanders
South Saskatchewan Regiment

3RD CANADIAN INFANTRY DIVISION

7th Reconnaissance Regiment (17th Duke of York's Royal Canadian Hussars)

Cameron Highlanders of Ottawa (MG Battalion)

ROYAL CANADIAN ARTILLERY:

12th Field Regiment

13th Field Regiment

14th Field Regiment

3rd Anti-Tank Regiment

4th Light Anti-Aircraft Regiment

CORPS OF ROYAL CANADIAN ENGINEERS:

3rd Field Park Company

6th Field Company

16th Field Company

18th Field Company

7TH CANADIAN INFANTRY BRIGADE:

Royal Winnipeg Rifles

Regina Rifle Regiment

1st Battalion, Canadian Scottish Regiment

8TH CANADIAN INFANTRY BRIGADE:

Queen's Own Rifles of Canada

Le Régiment de la Chaudière

North Shore (New Brunswick) Regiment

9TH CANADIAN INFANTRY BRIGADE:

Highland Light Infantry of Canada

Stormont, Dundas and Glengarry Highlanders

North Nova Scotia Highlanders

4TH CANADIAN ARMOURED DIVISION

29th Armoured Reconnaissance Regiment (South Alberta
Regiment)
10th Canadian Independent MG Company (New Brunswick
Rangers)
Lake Superior Regiment (Motor)

ROYAL CANADIAN ARTILLERY:
15th Field Regiment
23rd Field Regiment (Self-Propelled)
5th Anti-Tank Regiment
4th Light Anti-Aircraft Regiment

ROYAL CANADIAN CORPS OF ENGINEERS:
6th Field Park Squadron
8th Field Squadron
9th Field Squadron

4TH CANADIAN ARMOURED BRIGADE:
21st Armoured Regiment (Governor General's Foot Guards)
22nd Armoured Regiment (Canadian Grenadier Guards)
28th Armoured Regiment (British Columbia Regiment)

10TH CANADIAN INFANTRY BRIGADE:
Lincoln and Welland Regiment
Algonquin Regiment
Argyll and Sutherland Highlanders of Canada

2ND CANADIAN ARMOURED BRIGADE:
6th Armoured Regiment (1st Hussars)
10th Armoured Regiment (Fort Garry Horse)
27th Armoured Regiment (Sherbrooke Fusiliers Regiment)

APPENDIX C:
CANADIAN INFANTRY BATTALION
(TYPICAL ORGANIZATION)

HQ COMPANY
No. 1: Signals Platoon
No. 2: Administrative Platoon

SUPPORT COMPANY
No. 3: Mortar Platoon (3-inch)
No. 4: Bren Carrier Platoon
No. 5: Assault Pioneer Platoon
No. 6: Anti-Tank Platoon
    (6-pounder)

'A' COMPANY
No. 7 Platoon
No. 8 Platoon
No. 9 Platoon

'B' COMPANY
No. 10 Platoon
No. 11 Platoon
No. 12 Platoon

'C' COMPANY
No. 13 Platoon
No. 14 Platoon
No. 15 Platoon

'D' COMPANY
No. 16 Platoon
No. 17 Platoon
No. 18 Platoon

APPENDIX D:

CANADIAN ARMY AND GERMAN ARMY
ORDER OF RANKS
(LOWEST TO HIGHEST)

IKE MOST COMMONWEALTH armies, the Canadian Army used the British ranking system. Except for the lower ranks, this system differed little from one service arm to another. The German Army system, however, tended to identify service and rank throughout most of its command chain. The translations are roughly based on the Canadian ranking system, although many German ranks have no Canadian equivalent, and there is some differentiation in the responsibility each rank bestowed on its holder.

CANADIAN ARMY	GERMAN ARMY
Private, infantry	Schütze
Rifleman, rifle regiments	Schütze
Private	Grenadier
Gunner (artillery equivalent of private)	Kanonier
Trooper (armoured equivalent of private)	Panzerschütze
Sapper (engineer equivalent of private)	Pionier
Signaller (signals equivalent of private)	Funker
Lance Corporal	Gefreiter
Corporal	Obergefreiter
Lance Sergeant	Unteroffizier
Sergeant	Unterfeldwebel
Company Sergeant Major	Feldwebel
Battalion Sergeant Major	Oberfeldwebel
Regimental Sergeant Major	Stabsfeldwebel
Second Lieutenant	Leutnant

CANADIAN ARMY	GERMAN ARMY
Lieutenant	Oberleutnant
Captain	Hauptmann
Major	Major
Lieutenant Colonel	Oberstleutnant
Colonel	Oberst
Brigadier	Generalmajor
Major General	Generalleutnant
Lieutenant General	General der (service arm)
(No differentiation)	General der Artillerie
	General der Infanterie
	General der Kavallerie
	General der Pioniere
	General der Panzertruppen
General	Generaloberst
Field Marshal	Generalfeldmarschall
Commander in Chief	Oberbefehlshaber

APPENDIX E:
ARMY DECORATIONS

THE DECORATION SYSTEM that Canada used in World War II, like most other aspects of its military organization and tradition, derived from Britain. Under this class-based system, most military decorations can be awarded either to officers or to "other ranks" but not to both. Canada's army, navy, and air force also have distinct decorations. Only the Victoria Cross—the nation's highest award—can be won by personnel from any arm of the service or of any rank. The decorations and qualifying ranks are as follows.

VICTORIA CROSS (VC): Awarded for gallantry in the presence of the enemy. Instituted in 1856. Open to all ranks. The only award that can be granted for action in which the recipient was killed, other than Mentioned in Despatches—a less formal honour whereby an act of bravery was given specific credit in a formal report.

DISTINGUISHED SERVICE ORDER (DSO): Army officers of all ranks, but more commonly awarded to officers with ranks of major or higher.

MILITARY CROSS (MC): Army officers with a rank normally below major and, rarely, warrant officers.

DISTINGUISHED CONDUCT MEDAL (DCM): Army warrant officers and all lower ranks.

MILITARY MEDAL (MM): Army warrant officers and all lower ranks.

NOTES

Abbreviations: AHQ–Army Headquarters. CMHQ–Canadian Military Headquarters. CWM–Canadian War Museum. DHH–Director of Heritage and History. DND–Department of National Defence. LAC–Library and Archives Canada. NARA–National Archives of the United States. PRO–Public Record Office (U.K.). TNA–The National Archives of the U.K. UVICSC–University of Victoria Libraries Special Collections.

INTRODUCTION

1. L.F. Ellis, *The Defeat of Germany*, vol. 2 of *Victory in the West* (London: Her Majesty's Stationery Office, 1968), 27–29.
2. Ibid., 42–44.
3. 1st Canadian Headquarters Army Group Engineers War Diary, September 1944, Appendix: "20th Field Company Report on Evacuation, 29 Sept. 1944," RG24, LAC, 1.
4. 23rd Field Company War Diary, September 1944, RG24, LAC, 7.
5. 1st Canadian Headquarters Army Group Engineers War Diary, September 1944, Appendix: "23rd Field Company Report on Evacuation, 30 Sept. 1944," RG24, LAC, 1–2.
6. Ibid., 1.
7. John Sliz, *The Storm Boat Kings: The 23rd RCE at Arnhem 1944* (St. Catharines, ON: Vanwell, 2009), 57–58.
8. Appendix: "23rd Field Company," 3.
9. 20th Field Company War Diary, September 1944, Appendix B: "Profile of Nederrijn & Approaches," RG24, LAC, 1.
10. Sliz, 60.
11. Appendix: "23rd Field Company," 2.
12. TNA: PRO WO 171/488, "43 Infantry Division C.R.E. War Diary, Notes by Narrator: Evacuation of 1 Airborne Div. Assault boats and stormboats," 1.
13. Appendix: "23rd Field Company," 2.
14. Appendix: "20th Field Company," 1–2.
15. 43 Infantry Division C.R.E. War Diary, "Notes by Narrator," 1–2, and "Withdrawal of 1 Airborne Div across the R Nederrijn," 1–2.
16. Ibid., 2.
17. Appendix: "20th Field Company," 1–2.
18. Appendix: "23rd Field Company," 2.
19. David Bennett, "A Bridge Too Far: The Canadian Role in the Evacuation of the British 1st Airborne Division from Arnhem–Oosterbeek, September 1944," *Canadian Military Journal* 6, no. 4 (Winter 2005–2006), 98.
20. Sliz, 64.

21. Appendix: "23rd Field Company," 2–4.

22. Sliz, 33–35.

23. 1st Canadian Headquarters Army Group Engineers War Diary, September 1944, Appendix: "3rd Canadian Engine and Maintenance Section (A) Engine and Boat Mtce Party, September 1944," RG24, LAC, 2.

24. Appendix: "23rd Field Company," 2–3.

25. Appendix: "20th Field Company," 1–2.

26. *Canadian Army Overseas Honours and Awards (1939–45)*, DHH, DND, accessed April 17, 2013, www.cmp-cpm.forces.gc.ca/dhh-dhp/gal/cao-aco/details-eng. asp?firstname=Harry Dacker&lastname=Thicks&rec=id1130.

27. Appendix: "20th Field Company," 1–2.

28. Bennett, 99.

29. Appendix: "20th Field Company," 2–3.

30. Elizabeth (Kennedy) Marsh and Russell Kennedy, *Boats, Bridges & Valour: The 23rd Field Company, Royal Canadian Engineers in WWII* (Ottawa: Doculink International, 2008), 2–3.

31. Appendix: "23rd Field Company," 2–5.

32. Marsh and Kennedy, 90–95.

33. Appendix: "23rd Field Company," 4–5.

34. "Withdrawal of 1 Airborne Div across the R Nederrijn," 3.

35. 23rd Field Company War Diary, September 1944, 7.

PART ONE: A CRUEL WINTER

I THE MOST IMPORTANT BIT OF GROUND

1. Brian Horrocks with Eversley Belfield and H. Essame, *Corps Commander* (London: Sidgwick & Jackson, 1977), 127.

2. Johan van Doorn, phone interview by author, February 14, 2014.

3. Charles P. Stacey, *The Victory Campaign: The Operations in North-West Europe, 1944–1945*, vol. 3 of *Official History...War* (Ottawa: Queen's Printer, 1960), 330.

4. Ibid., 424.

5. Johan van Doorn, "German casualties in the Battle of the Scheldt, 14th September–8th November 1944, compiled 22/02/2007," unpublished document in the author's possession.

6. Stacey, 422–23.

7. "Report No. 173, The Watch on the Maas 9 Nov 44–8 Feb 45," CMHQ, DHH, DND, 4–8.

8. Stacey, 430.

9. "Report No. 77, The Campaign in North-West Europe: Information from German Sources, Part IV—Higher Direction of Operations from Falaise Debacle to Ardennes Offensive," AHQ, DHH, DND, 51.

10. Gen. H.D.G. Crerar, "Report by Gen. H.D.G. Crerar, Operations of First Canadian Army from 9th Nov–31st Dec 1944," 215C1.013(D2), vol. 10636, box 125, RG24, LAC, 1.

11. Dominick Graham, *The Price of Command: A Biography of General Guy Simonds* (Toronto: Stoddart, 1993), 183.

12. Paul Douglas Dickson, *A Thoroughly Canadian General: A Biography of General H.D.G. Crerar* (Toronto: University of Toronto Press, 2007), 354.
13. J.L. Granatstein, *The Generals: The Canadian Army's Senior Commanders in the Second World War* (Toronto: Stoddart, 1993), 163.
14. Dickson, 358–59.
15. Douglas E. Delaney, *Corps Commanders: Five British and Canadian Generals at War, 1939–45* (Vancouver: UBC Press, 2011), 123–38.
16. John A. English, *Failure in High Command: The Canadian Army and the Normandy Campaign* (Ottawa: Golden Dog Press, 1995), 192–93.
17. Delaney, 167–68.
18. "Report No. 173," 10.
19. Ibid., 1–2.
20. "Oberst Geyer Account," Record Group 549, B Series, Box 12, B-147, College Park, MD, NARA, 2–3.
21. Ibid., 1.
22. Ibid., 7.
23. Stacey, 428.
24. L.F. Ellis, *The Defeat of Germany*, vol. 2 of *Victory in the West* (London: Her Majesty's Stationery Office, 1968), 164.
25. C.M. MacDonald, *The Battle of Hürtgen Forest* (New York: J.B. Lippincott, 1963), 205.
26. Ellis, 165.

2 BACK TO TRENCH WARFARE

1. 4th Canadian Infantry Brigade War Diary, November 1944, RG24, LAC, 5.
2. Toronto Scottish (MG) Regiment War Diary, November 1944, RG24, LAC, 2.
3. Le Régiment de Maisonneuve War Diary, November 1944, RG24, LAC, 2.
4. Queen's Own Cameron Highlanders War Diary, November 1944, RG24, LAC, 3.
5. Stormont, Dundas and Glengarry Highlanders War Diary, November 1944, RG24, LAC, 10.
6. Canadian Scottish Regiment War Diary, November 1944, RG24, LAC, 10–11.
7. Queen's Own Rifles War Diary, November 1944, RG24, LAC, 6.
8. Will R. Bird, *North Shore (New Brunswick) Regiment* (Fredericton: Brunswick Press, 1963), 479.
9. T.J. Bell, *Into Action with the 12th Field* (Utrecht: J. van Boekhoven, 1945), 98.
10. Will R. Bird, *No Retreating Footsteps: The Story of the North Nova Scotia Highlanders* (Hantsport, NS: Lancelot Press, 1983), 281.
11. Bird, *North Shore (New Brunswick) Regiment*, 479–80.
12. Stewart A.G. Mein, *Up the Johns! The Story of the Royal Regina Rifles* (North Battleford, SK: Turner-Warwick, 1992), 131.
13. James Alan Roberts, *The Canadian Summer: The Memoirs of James Alan Roberts* (Toronto: University of Toronto Press, 1981), 102.
14. "Report on Grave Br. Defences d/19 Dec 44," 235C2.023(D6), vol. 10903, box 267, RG24, LAC, 1.
15. Charles P. Stacey, *The Victory Campaign: The Operations in North-West Europe, 1944–1945*, vol. 3 of *Official History...War* (Ottawa: Queen's Printer, 1960), 430–31.

16. "Oberst Blauensteiner account," Record Group 549, B Series, Box 12, B-262, College Park, MD, NARA, 3–5.
17. "82nd (US) Airborne Div intelligence summaries 13 Oct 44–7 Nov 44," 255U82.023(DI), vol. 10959, box 296, RG24, LAC, 1.
18. South Saskatchewan Regiment War Diary, November 1944, RG24, LAC, 7.
19. Charles Goodman, interview by author, Saanichton, BC, June 2, 2006.
20. George B. Buchanan, *The March of the Prairie Men: A Story of the South Saskatchewan Regiment* (Weyburn, SK: S. Sask. R. Orderly Room, 1958), 44.
21. South Saskatchewan Regiment War Diary, 8.
22. David Bercuson, *Battalion of Heroes: The Calgary Highlanders in World War II* (Calgary: Calgary Highlanders Regimental Funds Fdn., 1994), 196.
23. Royal Regiment of Canada War Diary, November 1944, RG24, LAC, 5.
24. George Blackburn, *The History of the 4th Field Regiment* (n.p., 1945), unpaged.
25. Stacey, 434–35.
26. Donald Pearce, *Journal of a War: North-West Europe 1944–45* (Toronto: Macmillan of Canada, 1965), 97–102.
27. Essex Scottish Regiment War Diary, November 1944, RG24, LAC, 7.
28. William Boss, *Up the Glens: Stormont, Dundas and Glengarry Highlanders, 1783–1994* (Cornwall, ON: Old Book Store, 1995), 135.
29. *Canadian Army Overseas Honours and Awards (1939–45)*, DHH, DND, accessed June 21, 2013, www.cmp-cpm.forces.gc.ca/dhh-dhp/gal/cao-aco/details-eng.asp?firstname=Frank&lastname=Groff&rec=id2337.
30. "Misc interrogation reports Oct/Dec 44, 2 Cdn Inf Div," 235C2.023(D5), vol. 10903, box 267, RG24, LAC, 8.
31. Essex Scottish War Diary, 7.
32. Ibid., 10.

3 DIFFERENCES OF OPINION

1. Chester Wilmot, *The Struggle for Europe* (London: Collins, 1952), 568.
2. L.F. Ellis, *Victory in the West: The Defeat of Germany*, vol. 2 (London: Her Majesty's Stationery Office, 1968), 164.
3. W. Denis Whitaker and Shelagh Whitaker, *Rhineland: The Battle to End the War* (Toronto: Stoddart, 1989), 12.
4. Ellis, 166.
5. R.W. Thompson, *The Battle for the Rhineland* (London: Hutchinson, 1958), 79.
6. Whitaker and Whitaker, 12.
7. Thompson, 88.
8. Whitaker and Whitaker, 12.
9. Ellis, 166–67.
10. Harry C. Butcher, *My Three Years with Eisenhower: The Personal Diary of Captain Harry C. Butcher, USNR, Naval Aide to General Eisenhower, 1942 to 1945* (New York: Simon & Schuster, 1946), 718–20.
11. "Report No. 173, The Watch on the Maas 9 Nov 44–8 Feb 45," CMHQ, DHH, DND, 24–25.
12. Ibid., 22–23.

13. Charles P. Stacey, *The Victory Campaign: The Operations in North-West Europe, 1944–1945*, vol. 3 of *Official History...War* (Ottawa: Queen's Printer, 1960), 433.
14. "Report No. 173," 25.
15. Johan van Doorn, phone interview by author, February 14, 2014.
16. "Report No. 173," 26.
17. Stacey, 434.
18. Gen. H.D.G. Crerar, "Report by Gen. H.D.G. Crerar, C⎯ ⎓⎓ns of First Canadian Army from 9th Nov–31st Dec 1944," 215C1.013(D2), vol. 10636, box 125, RG24, LAC, 4–5.
19. Montgomery, Bernard Law, *The Memoirs of Field-Marshal the Viscount Montgomery of Alamein, K.G.* (London: Collins, 1958), 302.
20. Whitaker and Whitaker, 13.
21. Montgomery, 302–4.
22. Nigel Hamilton, *Monty: The Field-Marshal, 1944–1976* (London: Hamish Hamilton, 1986), 162–63.
23. Ibid., 163.
24. Montgomery, 304–6.
25. Stacey, 438.
26. Brian Horrocks with Eversley Belfield and H. Essame, *Corps Commander* (London: Sidgwick & Jackson, 1977), 152–54.
27. Whitaker and Whitaker, 14.
28. "Operation Veritable, miscellaneous correspondence 13.13.44-20.02.45," 215C1.98(D368), vol. 10710, box 157, RG24, LAC, 59–61.
29. "Report No. 173," 30–31.
30. Ibid., 27–29.
31. George F.G. Stanley, *In the Face of Danger: The History of the Lake Superior Regiment* (Port Arthur, ON: Lake Superior Scottish Regt., 1960), 230–31.
32. Lake Superior Regiment War Diary, December 1944, RG24, LAC, 12.
33. Stanley, 231.

4 ROLL OF THE DICE

1. Charles P. Stacey, *The Victory Campaign: The Operations in North-West Europe, 1944–1945*, vol. 3 of *Official History...War* (Ottawa: Queen's Printer, 1960), 439.
2. Nigel Hamilton, *Monty: The Field-Marshal, 1944–1976* (London: Hamish Hamilton, 1986), 181–84.
3. Brian Horrocks with Eversley Belfield and H. Essame, *Corps Commander* (London: Sidgwick & Jackson, 1977), 164.
4. Richard E. Hayes and Kristi Sugarman, "The State of the Art and the State of the Practice, Battle of the Bulge: The Impact of Information Age Command and Control on Conflict," 2006 Command and Control Research and Technology Symposium, 16–17, accessed November 30, 2013, www.dodccrp.org/events/2006_CCRTS/html/papers/206.pdf.
5. Ralph Bennett, *Ultra in the West: The Normandy Campaign, 1944–45* (New York: Charles Scribner's Sons, 1980), 192–204.
6. Hayes and Sugarman, 16–17.

7. Ibid., 18–19.

8. Hamilton, 183–84.

9. W. Denis Whitaker and Shelagh Whitaker, *Rhineland: The Battle to End the War* (Toronto: Stoddart, 1989), 16.

10. Horrocks, 157–58.

11. Hamilton, 185–86.

12. Chester Wilmot, *The Struggle for Europe* (London: Collins, 1952), 583–89.

13. Donald Pearce, *Journal of a War: North-West Europe 1944-45* (Toronto: Macmillan of Canada, 1965), 119–24.

14. G.L. Cassidy, *Warpath: From Tilly-la-campagne to the Kusten Canal* (Markham, ON: Paperjacks, 1980), 252–53.

15. Gen. H.D.G. Crerar, "Report by Gen. H.D.G. Crerar, Operations of First Canadian Army from 9th Nov–31st Dec 1944," 215C1.013(D2), vol. 10636, box 125, RG24, LAC, 5–7.

16. Hamilton, 201–10.

17. Wilmot, 592–93.

18. Hamilton, 213.

19. Wilmot, 591–92.

20. Bennett, 211.

21. Ibid., 212.

22. Hamilton, 214–17.

23. L.F. Ellis, *Victory in the West: The Defeat of Germany*, vol. 2 (London: Her Majesty's Stationery Office, 1968), 186.

24. Ibid., 195.

5 WAR IS A BITCH

1. Charles P. Stacey, *The Victory Campaign: The Operations in North-West Europe, 1944–1945*, vol. 3 of *Official History...War* (Ottawa: Queen's Printer, 1960), 441.

2. Gen. H.D.G. Crerar, "Report by Gen. H.D.G. Crerar, Operations of First Canadian Army from 9th Nov–31st Dec 1944," 215C1.013(D2), vol. 10636, box 125, RG24, LAC, 7.

3. "Report No. 173, The Watch on the Maas 9 Nov 44–8 Feb 45," CMHQ, DHH, DND, 34–35.

4. Johan van Doorn, phone interview with author, February 14, 2014.

5. Stacey, 443.

6. 4th Canadian Armoured Division War Diary, December 1945, RG24, LAC, 19.

7. Van Doorn interview.

8. Douglas E. Harker, *The Dukes: The Story of the Men Who Have Served in Peace and War with the British Columbia Regiment (D.C.O.), 1883–1973* (Vancouver: B.C. Regt., 1974), n.p.

9. "Anti-Parachute precautions issued by G.H.Q. Royal Engineers, 26 Dec 44," 215A21.013(D14), vol. 10504, box 55, RG24, LAC, 1–2.

10. G.L. Cassidy, *Warpath: From Tilly-la-campagne to the Kusten Canal* (Markham, ON: Paperjacks, 1980), 255–56.

11. Robert L. Fraser, *Black Yesterdays: The Argyll's War* (Hamilton: Argyll Fdn., 1996), 337–38.

12. Alfred James Tedlie, interview by Chris D. Main, June 28 and July 9, 16, and 23, 1979, UVICSC.

13. Bill McAndrew, *Liberation: The Canadians in Europe* (Montreal: Éditions Art Global, 1995), 80.

14. Brig. N.E. Rodger, "Personal Diary of Brig. N.E. Rodger, c of s 2 CDN Corps," Manu 58A 1 114.1, CWM, unpaged.

15. McAndrew, 78.

16. "Report No. 173," 39.

17. Donald Pearce, *Journal of a War: North-West Europe 1944–45* (Toronto: Macmillan of Canada, 1965), 125–26.

18. Stacey, 444.

19. Ibid., 448–49.

20. L.F. Ellis, *Victory in the West: The Defeat of Germany*, vol. 2 (London: Her Majesty's Stationery Office, 1968), 189.

21. Argyll and Sutherland Highlanders War Diary, December 1944, RG24, LAC, 17–18.

22. Fraser, 338.

23. Argyll and Sutherland Highlanders War Diary, January 1945, RG24, LAC, 1.

24. Stacey, 444.

25. Ellis, 189–90.

26. McAndrew, 93.

27. John Manrho and Ron Pütz, *Bodenplatte: The Luftwaffe's Last Hope* (Mechanicsburg, PA: Stackpole Books, 2010), 520–21.

28. Ibid., 223.

29. Ellis, 190.

30. "Report No. 173," 46.

31. Gen. H.D.G. Crerar, "Report by Gen. H.D.G. Crerar, Operations of First Canadian Army 1 Jan–10 Mar 45," 215C1.013(D2), vol. 10636, box 125, RG24, LAC, 1.

32. "Report No. 173," 48.

33. Crerar, "Report, 1 Jan–10 Mar 45," 1–2.

34. Montgomery, Bernard Law, *The Memoirs of Field-Marshal the Viscount Montgomery of Alamein, K.G.* (London: Collins, 1958), 317–22.

35. Nigel Hamilton, *Monty: The Field-Marshal, 1944–1976* (London: Hamish Hamilton, 1986), 303.

36. Chester Wilmot, *The Struggle for Europe* (London: Collins, 1952), 610.

37. Stacey, 450.

38. Hamilton, 303–4.

39. Stacey, 450.

40. Wilmot, 611.

6 THE SMALL-THORN

1. Donald E. Graves, "'If only we had the wisdom of our generals': The Kapelsche Veer, 26–31 January 1945," in *Fighting for Canada, Seven Battles, 1758–1945*, ed. Donald E. Graves (Toronto: Robin Brass Studio, 2000), 322.

2. Charles P. Stacey, *The Victory Campaign: The Operations in North-West Europe, 1944–1945*, vol. 3 of *Official History...War* (Ottawa: Queen's Printer, 1960), 447–48.

3. "Account of the fighting at Kapelsche Veer (Jan 45)," 215C1.013(D33), vol. 10638, box 126, RG24, LAC, 1.
4. Stacey, 450.
5. "Report No. 173, The Watch on the Maas 9 Nov 44–8 Feb 45," CMHQ, DHH, DND, 68.
6. Stacey, 450–52.
7. E.O. Herbert, "Polish Armd Div, 7 Oct 44," Crerar Papers, MG30, vol. 2, LAC, 1.
8. "Report No. 173," 47.
9. Ibid., 49.
10. Stacey, 452.
11. Graves, "If only we had the wisdom," 324.
12. "Report No. 173," 53.
13. Argyll and Sutherland Highlanders War Diary, January 1945, RG24, LAC, 7.
14. "Report No. 173," 53.
15. Stacey, 452.
16. "Report No. 173," 53.
17. Argyll War Diary, Jan. 1945, 7.
18. 4th Canadian Armoured Division (GS Branch) War Diary, January 1945, RG24, LAC, 13.
19. Stacey, 454–55.
20. Chris Vokes, Vokes: My Story (Ottawa: Gallery Books, 1985), 186–91.
21. David Kaufman and Michiel Horn, A Liberation Album: Canadians in the Netherlands, 1944–45 (Toronto: McGraw-Hill Ryerson, 1980), 69–70.
22. 10th Canadian Infantry Brigade War Diary, January 1945, RG24, LAC, 5–6.
23. Lincoln and Welland Regiment War Diary, January 1945, RG24, LAC, 4.
24. Graves, 329.
25. 10th CIB War Diary, Jan. 1945, 6.
26. R.L. Rogers, History of the Lincoln and Welland Regiment (St. Catharines, ON: Lincoln and Welland Regiment, 1954), 220–22.
27. Robert A. Spencer, History of the Fifteenth Field Regiment, Royal Canadian Artillery: 1941 to 1945 (New York: Elsevier, 1945), 201.
28. D.W. Grant, Carry On: The History of the Toronto Scottish Regiment (MG), 1939–1945 (Toronto: 1949), 116.
29. Spencer, 201.
30. Argyll War Diary, Jan. 1945, 10.
31. Robert L. Fraser, Black Yesterdays: The Argyll's War (Hamilton: Argyll Fdn., 1996), 346–47.
32. "Stores & Equipment, Memo re use of moccasins 5 CIB d/30 Jan 45," 265C5.082(D1), vol. 10985, box 310, RG24, LAC, 1.
33. Fraser, 346–47.
34. M.O. Rollerfson, ed., Green Route Up: 4 Canadian Armoured Division (n.p., 1945), 64–65.
35. Canadian Army Overseas Honours and Awards (1939–1945), DHH, DND, accessed October 16, 2013, www.cmp-cpm.forces.gc.ca/dhh-dhp/gal/cao-aco/details-eng.asp?firstname=Mervin George&lastname=Durham&rec=id4687.
36. Rollerfson, 65.

7 NO PROFIT IN IT

1. Jean Bouchery, *From D-Day to VE-Day: The Canadian Soldier in North-West Europe, 1944–1945* (Paris: Histoire & Collections, 2003), 96.
2. John S. Moir, ed., *History of the Royal Canadian Corps of Signals, 1903–1961* (Ottawa: Corps Committee, RCS, 1962), 200.
3. Geoffrey Hayes, *The Lincs: A History of the Lincoln and Welland Regiment at War* (Alma, ON: Maple Leaf Route, 1986), 75.
4. 10th Canadian Infantry Brigade War Diary, January 1945, Appendix 4, RG24, LAC, 1.
5. "Account of the fighting at Kapelsche Veer (Jan 45)," 215C1.013(D33), vol. 10638, box 126, RG24, LAC, 3.
6. Johan van Doorn, phone interview with author, February 14, 2014.
7. "Account of the fighting at Kapelsche Veer (Jan 45)," 215C1.013(D33), vol. 10638, box 126, 3.
8. Hayes, 76.
9. Lincoln and Welland Regiment War Diary, January 1945, RG24, LAC, 7.
10. Hayes, 75.
11. Lincoln and Welland War Diary, Jan. 1945, 7.
12. R.L. Rogers, *History of the Lincoln and Welland Regiment* (St. Catharines, ON: Lincoln and Welland Regt., 1954), 224.
13. "Report No. 173, The Watch on the Maas 9 Nov 44–8 Feb 45," CMHQ, DHH, DND, 68.
14. Hayes, 76.
15. Robert A. Spencer, *History of the Fifteenth Field Regiment, Royal Canadian Artillery: 1941 to 1945* (New York: Elsevier, 1945), 203–4.
16. Hayes, 76.
17. Lincoln and Welland War Diary, Jan. 1945, 7.
18. 10th CIB War Diary, Jan. 1945, 9–10.
19. Hayes, 76.
20. Rogers, 234.
21. *Canadian Army Overseas Honours and Awards (1939–1945)*, DHH, DND, accessed October 17, 2013, www.cmp-cpm.forces.gc.ca/dhh-dhp/gal/cao-aco/details-eng.asp?firstname=Lionel Charles&lastname=Stewart&rec=id1067.
22. Charles P. Stacey, *The Victory Campaign: The Operations in North-West Europe, 1944–1945*, vol. 3 of *Official History...War* (Ottawa: Queen's Printer, 1960), 453.
23. Lincoln and Welland War Diary, Jan. 1945, 7.
24. 10th CIB War Diary, Jan. 1945, 10.
25. Lincoln and Welland War Diary, Jan. 1945, 7–8.
26. 10th CIB War Diary, Jan. 1945, 10.
27. Ibid., 10.
28. Argyll and Sutherland Highlander Regiment War Diary, January 1945, RG24, LAC, 12–13.
29. South Alberta Regiment War Diary, January 1945, RG24, LAC, 13.
30. Donald E. Graves, *South Albertas: A Canadian Regiment at War* (Toronto: Robin Brass Studio, 1998), 252.
31. H.M. Jackson, *The Argyll and Sutherland Highlanders of Canada* (Princess Louise's), *1928–1953*, (Montreal: Industrial Shops for the Deaf, 1953), 163.

32. Argyll War Diary, Jan. 1945, 13.
33. South Alberta War Diary, Jan. 1945, 13.
34. A.J. Kerry and W.A. McDill, *History of the Corps of Royal Canadian Engineers*, vol. 2 (1936–46) (Ottawa: Military Engineers Assoc. of Canada, 1966), 363.
35. Donald E. Graves, "'If only we had the wisdom of our generals': The Kapelsche Veer, 26–31 January 1945," in *Fighting for Canada, Seven Battles, 1758–1945*, ed. Donald E. Graves (Toronto: Robin Brass Studio, 2000), 338–39.
36. Kerry and McDill, 363.
37. Graves, *South Albertas*, 253.
38. Spencer, 204–05.
39. Rogers, 226.
40. "Report No. 173," 69.
41. Jackson, 163.
42. Argyll War Diary, Jan. 1945, 13.
43. Donald E. Graves, *Century of Service: The History of the South Alberta Light Horse* (Toronto: Robin Brass Studio, 2005), 339.
44. Kerry and McDill, 363.
45. Graves, *South Albertas*, 256.
46. Graves, *Century of Service*, 339–40.
47. Rogers, 226–27.
48. Graves, *Century of Service*, 340.
49. Rogers, 226–27.
50. Jackson, 164–65.
51. Spencer, 202–05.
52. "Report No. 173," 70.
53. Rogers, 229.
54. Jackson, 165.
55. "Report No. 173," 70–71.
56. Stacey, 454.
57. Spencer, 207.
58. Stacey, 454.
59. Rogers, 230.
60. Robert L. Fraser, *Black Yesterdays: The Argyll's War* (Hamilton: Argyll Fdn., 1996), 349.

PART TWO: VERITABLE

8 A TERRIFIC PARTY

1. Gen. H.D.G. Crerar, "Report by Gen. H.D.G. Crerar, Operations of First Canadian Army 1 Jan–10 Mar 45," 215C1.013(D2), vol. 10636, box 125, RG24, LAC, 2.
2. H. Essame, *The Battle for Germany* (London: B.T. Batsford, 1969), 141–42.
3. Nigel Hamilton, *Monty: The Field-Marshal, 1944–1976* (London: Hamish Hamilton, 1986), 330–32.
4. L.F. Ellis, *The Defeat of Germany*, vol. 2 of *Victory in the West* (London: Her Majesty's Stationery Office, 1968), 241–47.

5. Paul Douglas Dickson, *A Thoroughly Canadian General: A Biography of General H.D.G. Crerar* (Toronto: University of Toronto Press, 2007), 382.
6. R.W. Thompson, *The Battle for the Rhineland* (London: Hutchinson & Co., 1958), 148–49.
7. Charles P. Stacey, *The Victory Campaign: The Operations in North-West Europe, 1944–1945*, vol. 3 of *Official History...War* (Ottawa: Queen's Printer, 1960), 456.
8. "Report No. 155, Operation Veritable: The Winter Offensive between the Maas and the Rhine, 8–25 Feb 45 (Preliminary Report)," CMHQ, DHH, DND, 10–11.
9. Stacey, 458.
10. Brian Horrocks with Eversley Belfield and H. Essame, *Corps Commander* (London: Sidgwick & Jackson, 1977), 178.
11. W.R. Freasby, ed., *Organization and Campaigns*, vol. 1 of *Official History of the Canadian Medical Services, 1939–1945* (Ottawa: Queen's Printer, 1956), 274.
12. Essame, 145.
13. Stacey, 458.
14. Bill McAndrew, *Liberation: The Canadians in Europe* (Montreal: Éditions Art Global, 1995), 64.
15. "Report No. 155," 23.
16. A.J. Kerry and W.A. McDill, *History of the Corps of Royal Canadian Engineers*, vol. 2 (1936–46) (Ottawa: Military Engineers Assoc. of Canada, 1966), 365–66.
17. Stacey, 457–58.
18. Elizabeth (Kennedy) Marsh and Russell Kennedy, *Boats, Bridges & Valour: The 23rd Field Company, Royal Canadian Engineers in WWII* (Ottawa: Doculink International, 2008), 112.
19. Horrocks, 178.
20. Reginald Ralph, interview by James Murphy, July 26, 1977, UVICSC.
21. "Report No. 155," 22.
22. Brig. N.E. Rodger, "Personal Diary of Brig. N.E. Rodger, C of S 2 CDN Corps," Manu 58A 1 114.1, CWM, unpaged.
23. "Operation Veritable, miscellaneous correspondence 13.13.44-20.02.45," 215C1.98(D368), vol. 10710, box 157, RG24, LAC, 18.
24. Horrocks, 181–82.
25. 4th Canadian Field Regiment War Diary, February 1945, RG24, LAC, 1.
26. George G. Blackburn, *The History of the 4th Field Regiment* (n.p., 1945), unpaged.
27. James Alan Roberts, *The Canadian Summer: The Memoirs of James Alan Roberts* (Toronto: University of Toronto Press, 1981), 106–8.
28. Douglas E. Delaney, *Corps Commanders: Five British and Canadian Generals at War, 1939–45* (Vancouver: UBC Press, 2011), 41.
29. Horrocks, 60–61.
30. Delaney, 41.
31. Horrocks, 182–83.
32. Crerar, "Report, 1 Jan–10 Mar 45," 5–6.

33. Brig. W.J. Megill, "The Role of 5 CDN INF BDE in Operation 'Veritable' (8 Feb. 45), account by Brigadier W.J. Megill, Comd, 5 CDN INF BDE, Given to Historical Officer, 2 CDN INF DIV, 11 Feb 45," 265C5.011(D4), vol. 10985, box 310, RG24, LAC, 1.

9 TO THE LAST MAN

1. GS Int–HQ First Canadian Army War Diary, December 1944, Appendix 4, RG24, LAC, 1.
2. "2 CDN INF DIV INT BRANCH No. 1, Op Veritable," 235C2.023(D3), vol. 10903, box 267, RG24, LAC, 2.
3. GS Int–HQ War Diary, Dec. 1944, Appendix 4, 2.
4. Charles P. Stacey, *The Victory Campaign: The Operations in North-West Europe, 1944–1945*, vol. 3 of *Official History...War* (Ottawa: Queen's Printer, 1960), 460.
5. GS Int–HQ War Diary, Dec. 1944, Appendix 4, 2.
6. "Report No. 155, Operation Veritable: The Winter Offensive between the Maas and the Rhine, 8–25 Feb 45 (Preliminary Report)," CMHQ, DHH, DND, 17.
7. Stacey, 461.
8. R.W. Thompson, *The Battle for the Rhineland* (London: Hutchinson, 1958), 151.
9. Stacey, 461–62.
10. Ibid., 462.
11. "Report No. 155," 18–19.
12. Stacey, 462.
13. "2 CDN INF DIV INT BRANCH No. 1," 2.
14. "Oberst Geyer Account," Record Group 549, B Series, Box 12, B-147, College Park, MD, NARA, 10–13.
15. Franz Kurowski, *Jump into Hell: German Paratroopers in World War II* (Mechanicsburg, PA: Stackpole Books, 2010), 325.
16. "Fallschirmjäger General and Commander General of 11 FS Corps Eugen Meindl: Part III–Rhineland (15 Sep 44 to 21 Mar 45)," Record Group 549, B Series, Box 10, B-093, College Park, MD, NARA, 10.
17. "Oberst Geyer Account," 12.
18. "Report No. 155," 19.
19. W. Denis Whitaker and Shelagh Whitaker, *Rhineland: The Battle to End the War* (Toronto: Stoddart, 1989), 51.
20. "Report No. 155," 19.
21. Whitaker and Whitaker, 69.
22. "Report No. 19, Operation 'Plunder': The Canadian Participation in the Assault Across the Rhine and the Expansion of the Bridgehead by 2 Cdn Corps 23/24 Mar–1 Apr 45," AHQ, DHH, DND, paras. 30–31.
23. GS Int–HQ War Diary, Dec. 1944, Appendix 4, 4–5.
24. Stacey, 463.
25. "Veritable: Planning Intelligence Dossier No. 2, German Defences: Part III—Order of Battle," 215C1.98(D370), vol. 10710, box 157, RG24, LAC, 1–4.
26. "2 CDN INF DIV INT BRANCH No. 1," 8.

27. Gen. H.D.G. Crerar, "Report by Gen. H.D.G. Crerar, Operations of First Canadian Army 1 Jan–10 Mar 45," 215C1.013(D2), vol. 10636, box 125, RG24, LAC, 6.

28. Stacey, 463–64.

29. Crerar, "Report, 1 Jan–10 Mar 45," 6–7.

30. Stacey, 471.

31. William W. Barrett, History of 13th Canadian Field Regiment (n.p., 1945), 104.

32. A.J. Kerry and W.A. McDill, History of the Corps of Royal Canadian Engineers, vol. 2 (1936–46) (Ottawa: Military Engineers Assoc. of Canada, 1966), 367.

33. Barrett, 104–5.

34. Canadian Scottish Regiment War Diary, February 1945, RG24, LAC, 4.

10 OPPORTUNITY IS AT HAND

1. Brian Horrocks with Eversley Belfield and H. Essame, Corps Commander (London: Sidgwick & Jackson, 1977), 183–84.

2. Charles P. Stacey, The Victory Campaign: The Operations in North-West Europe, 1944–1945, vol. 3 of Official History...War (Ottawa: Queen's Printer, 1960), 465.

3. J.L. Moulton, Battle for Antwerp: The Liberation of the City and the Opening of the Scheldt, 1944 (New York: Hippocrene Books, 1978), 95.

4. Gen. H.D.G. Crerar, "Report by Gen. H.D.G. Crerar, Operations of First Canadian Army 1 Jan–10 Mar 45," 215C1.013(D2), vol. 10636, box 125, RG24, LAC, 7.

5. "Air Plan First CDN Army/84 Gp RAF, Operation Veritable," 215C1.98(D369), vol. 10710, box 157, RG24, LAC, 1.

6. "Op Veritable: Pre-Planned Air Support Conference 25 Jan 45," 215C1.98(D369), vol. 10710, box 157, RG24, LAC, 2–3.

7. "Air Plan First CDN Army/84 Gp RAF," 3–30.

8. "Report No. 155, Operation Veritable: The Winter Offensive between the Maas and the Rhine, 8–25 Feb 45 (Preliminary Report)," CMHQ, DHH, DND, 25.

9. "Int Rept on Op 'Veritable' 2 Cdn Inf Div 2 Feb 45, V-Air Appreciation," 235C2.023(D3), vol. 10903, Box 267, RG24, LAC, 1–2.

10. "Op Veritable: Pre-Planned Air Support," 1.

11. Arthur K. Kembar, The Six Years of 6 Canadian Field Regiment, Royal Canadian Regiment (Amsterdam: Town Printing, 1945), 89.

12. Crerar, "Report, 1 Jan–10 Mar 45," 7.

13. Stacey, 467.

14. L.F. Ellis, The Defeat of Germany, vol. 2 of Victory in the West (London: Her Majesty's Stationery Office, 1968), 257.

15. Stacey, 467.

16. Brig. F.D. Lace, "Operation Veritable (8 Feb 45): The Role of 2 CDN INF DIV Artillery: Memo of Account by Brigadier F.D. Lace, OBE, CRA, 2 CDN INF DIV, Given to Historical Officer, 2 CDN INF DIV, 13 Feb 45," 142.32011(D2), DHH, DND, 4.

17. Andrew J. Lucas, "The Land Mattress: Canadian Ingenuity Takes Flight," Gale Force Nine, accessed December 2, 2013, www.galeforcenine.com/Default. aspx?tabid=295&art_id=3779.

18. Lace, "Operation Veritable," 4.

19. David French, *Raising Churchill's Army: The British Army and the War Against Germany, 1919–1945* (London: Oxford University Press, 2000), 268.
20. Lt. Col. E.G. Johnson, "Operation Veritable: Use of the 'Pepper Pot' As a Means of Fire Support: Account by Lt. Col. E.G. Johnson, C.O., Tor Scot R. (MG)," 145.2TI011(2), DHH, DND, 1–2.
21. Lace, "Operaton Veritable," 4.
22. 3rd Canadian Medium Regiment War Diary, February 1945, RG24, LAC, 3–4.
23. Ronald Gill and John Groves, *Club Route in Europe: The Story of 30 Corps in the European Campaign* (Hannover, Germany: Werner Degener, 1948), 131–32.
24. "Report No. 155," 24–25.
25. 3rd Canadian Medium Regiment War Diary, February 1945, 4.
26. Charles B. MacDonald, *United States Army in World War II: European Theater of Operations—The Last Offensive* (Washington, DC: Office of the Chief of Military History, 1973), 70–78.
27. Jörg Friedrich, *The Fire: The Bombing of Germany, 1940–1945* (New York: Columbia University Press, 2008), 115.
28. Ellis, 257.
29. W. Denis Whitaker and Shelagh Whitaker, *Rhineland: The Battle to End the War* (Toronto: Stoddart, 1989), 46.
30. Horrocks, 184.
31. Ellis, 257.
32. George G. Blackburn, *The Guns of Victory: A Soldier's Eye View, Belgium, Holland, and Germany, 1944–45* (Toronto: McClelland and Stewart, 1996), 238–39.
33. Ellis, 257–58.
34. Stacey, 468–71.
35. Le Régiment de Maisonneuve War Diary, February 1945, RG24, LAC, 3.
36. Terry Copp, *The Brigade: The Fifth Canadian Infantry Brigade, 1939–1945* (Stoney Creek, ON: Fortress, 1992), 174.
37. Horrocks, 184.

II NEVER TO BE FORGOTTEN

1. George G. Blackburn, *The Guns of Victory: A Soldier's Eye View, Belgium, Holland, and Germany, 1944–45* (Toronto: McClelland and Stewart, 1996), 240–43.
2. H. Essame, *The Battle for Germany* (London: B.T. Batsford, 1969), 150.
3. Jean E. Portugal, *We Were There: The Navy, the Army and the RCAF—A Record for Canada*, vol. 4 (Shelburne, ON: Battered Silicon Dispatch Box, 1998), 1628.
4. Calgary Highlanders War Diary, February 1945, RG24, LAC, 5.
5. David Bercuson, *Battalion of Heroes: The Calgary Highlanders in World War II* (Calgary: Calgary Highlanders Regimental Fund Fdn., 1994), 202–3.
6. "Report No. 155, Operation Veritable: The Winter Offensive between the Maas and the Rhine, 8–25 Feb 45 (Preliminary Report)," CMHQ, DHH, DND, 26.
7. *History of 2 Canadian Survey Regiment* (n.p., [194?]), 17.
8. "Report No. 155," 26–27.

9. Alex Colville, *Before Zero Hour* (painting), "Exhibition Theme—Battle," *Canadian War Museum*, accessed December 4, 2013, www.warmuseum.ca/cwm/exhibitions/artwar/ artworks/19710261-2031_before-zero-hour_e.shtml.

10. Brian Horrocks with Eversley Belfield and H. Essame, *Corps Commander* (London: Sidgwick & Jackson, 1977), 186.

11. Charles P. Stacey, *The Victory Campaign: The Operations in North-West Europe, 1944–1945*, vol. 3 of *Official History...War* (Ottawa: Queen's Printer, 1960), 468.

12. "Report No. 155," 27.

13. Brig. W.J. Megill, "The Role of 5 CDN INF BDE in Operation 'Veritable' (8 Feb. 45), account by Brigadier W.J. Megill, Comd, 5 CDN INF BDE, Given to Historical Officer, 2 CDN INF DIV, 11 Feb 45," 265C5.011(D4), vol. 10985, box 310, RG24, LAC, 1.

14. Bercuson, 200.

15. Le Régiment de Maisonneuve War Diary, February 1945, RG24, LAC, 3.

16. *Canadian Army Overseas Honours and Awards (1939–45)*, DHH, DND, accessed December 5, 2013, www.cmp-cpm.forces.gc.ca/dhh-dhp/gal/cao-aco/details-eng. asp?firstname=Jean Louis&lastname=Fontaine&rec=id2152.

17. "Role of 5 CDN INF BDE in Operation 'Veritable,'" 1.

18. Roy Farran, *The History of the Calgary Highlanders, 1921–1954* (Calgary: Bryant Press, 1954), 199.

19. "Role of 5 CDN INF BDE in Operation 'Veritable,'" 3.

20. Terry Copp, *The Brigade: The Fifth Canadian Infantry Brigade, 1939–1945* (Stoney Creek, ON: Fortress, 1992), 174.

21. *Canadian Army Overseas Honours and Awards (1939–45)*, DHH, DND, accessed December 5, 2013, www.cmp-cpm.forces.gc.ca/dhh-dhp/gal/cao-aco/details-eng.asp?fi rstname=Joseph&lastname=Lefebvre&rec=id4249.

22. Le Régiment de Maisonneuve War Diary, Feb. 1945, 3.

23. Stacey, 470–71.

24. Essame, 151.

25. Lt. Col. E.G. Johnson, "Operation Veritable: Use of the 'Pepper Pot' as a Means of Fire Support: Account by Lt. Col. E.G. Johnson, C.O., Tor Scot R. (MG)," 145.2T1011(2), DHH, DND, 1.

26. Portugal, vol. 4, 1628.

27. Le Régiment de Maisonneuve War Diary, Feb. 1945, 3.

28. Gérard Marchand, *Le Régiment de Maisonneuve vers la victoire, 1944–1945* (Montreal: Les Presses Libre, 1980), 191–209.

29. *Canadian Army Overseas Honours and Awards (1939–45)*, DHH, DND, accessed December 5, 2013, www.cmp-cpm.forces.gc.ca/dhh-dhp/gal/cao-aco/details-eng.asp?fi rstname=Hector&lastname=Lefebvre&rec=id4248.

30. *Canadian Army Overseas Honours and Awards (1939–45)*, DHH, DND, accessed December 5, 2013, www.cmp-cpm.forces.gc.ca/dhh-dhp/gal/cao-aco/details-eng. asp?firstname=Jean Louis&lastname=Fontaine&rec=id2152.

31. Stacey, 471.

32. Major W.D. Heyland, "Operation 'Veritable' (8 Feb 45): The Capture of Wyler—Memo of account by Major W.D. Heyland, O.C., 'C' Coy, Calg. Highrs. Given to Historical Officer, 2 CDN INF DIV 15 Feb 45," 145.2C1011(D6), DHH, DND, 1.

33. *Canadian Army Overseas Honours and Awards (1939–45)*, DHH, DND, accessed December 9, 2013, www.cmp-cpm.forces.gc.ca/dhh-dhp/gal/cao-aco/details-eng. asp?firstname=Robert Allan&lastname=McMahon&rec=id415.

34. "Operation 'Veritable' (8 Feb 45)," 2.

35. *Canadian Army Overseas Honours and Awards (1939–45)*, DHH, DND, accessed December 9, 2013, www.cmp-cpm.forces.gc.ca/dhh-dhp/gal/cao-aco/details-eng. asp?firstname=Carol Edwin&lastname=Anderson&rec=id30.

36. Bercuson, 204.

37. *Canadian Army Overseas Honours and Awards (1939–45)*, DHH, DND, accessed December 9, 2013, www.cmp-cpm.forces.gc.ca/dhh-dhp/gal/cao-aco/details-eng. asp?firstname=Emile Jean&lastname=Laloge&rec=id4202.

38. "Operation 'Veritable' (8 Feb 45)," 2.

39. Bercuson, 204–6.

40. "Role of 5 CDN INF BDE in Operation 'Veritable,'" 2.

41. Bercuson, 206.

42. "Operation 'Veritable' (8 Feb 45)," 2.

43. Bercuson, 206.

44. *Canadian Army Overseas Honours and Awards (1939–45)*, DHH, DND, accessed December 10, 2013), www.cmp-cpm.forces.gc.ca/dhh-dhp/gal/cao-aco/details-eng.asp? firstname=Michael&lastname=Melnychanko&rec=id446.

45. "Role of 5 CDN INF BDE in Operation 'Veritable,'" 3–4.

46. Bercuson, 206.

47. "Lieutenant Edward Patrick Ford," Regimental Historians and Authors, *The Calgary Highlanders*, accessed December 11, 2013, www.calgaryhighlanders.com/prose-music/authors.htm.

48. Bercuson, 206.

49. Stacey, 471.

50. "Report No. 155," 28.

12 INTO HITLER'S GERMANY

1. Gen. H.D.G. Crerar, "Report by Gen. H.D.G. Crerar, Operations of First Canadian Army 1 Jan–10 Mar 45," 215C1.013(D2), vol. 10636, box 125, RG24, LAC, 7.

2. "Report No. 155, Operation Veritable: The Winter Offensive between the Maas and the Rhine, 8–25 Feb 45 (Preliminary Report)," CMHQ, DHH, DND, 28.

3. L.F. Ellis, *The Defeat of Germany*, vol. 2 of *Victory in the West* (London: Her Majesty's Stationery Office, 1968), 259.

4. Charles P. Stacey, *The Victory Campaign: The Operations in North-West Europe, 1944–1945*, vol. 3 of *Official History...War* (Ottawa: Queen's Printer, 1960), 469.

5. Ellis, 258.

6. Stacey, 472.

7. "Report No. 155," 29.

8. "Major-General D.C. Spry," *Juno Beach Centre*, accessed December 11, 2013, www.junobeach.org/e/3/can-pep-can-spry-e.htm.

9. "Report No. 155," 29.

10. Stacey, 471.

11. Reginald Roy, *Ready for the Fray: The History of the Canadian Scottish Regiment (Princess Mary's), 1920 to 1955* (Vancouver: Evergreen Press, 1958), 363–64.
12. North Shore (New Brunswick) Regiment War Diary, February 1945, RG24, LAC, 4.
13. James Alan Roberts, *The Canadian Summer: The Memoirs of James Alan Roberts* (Toronto: University of Toronto Press, 1981), 111–12.
14. Jean E. Portugal, *We Were There: The Navy, the Army and the RCAF—A Record for Canada*, vol. 5 (Shelburne, ON: Battered Silicon Dispatch Box, 1998), 2329.
15. North Shore War Diary, Feb. 1945, 4.
16. Roberts, 112.
17. Ibid., 113.
18. *Canadian Army Overseas Honours and Awards (1939–45)*, DHH, DND, accessed December 19, 2013, www.cmp-cpm.forces.gc.ca/dhh-dhp/gal/cao-aco/details-eng. asp?firstname=Russell Georald&lastname=Munroe&rec=id545.
19. North Shore War Diary, Feb. 1945, 5.
20. Roberts, 113.
21. Jacques Castonguay and Armand Ross, *Le Régiment de la Chaudière* (Lévis, QC: n.p. 1983), 338.
22. Portugal, vol. 5, 2329–30.
23. North Shore War Diary, Feb. 1945, 6.
24. Queen's Own Rifles War Diary, February 1945, RG24, LAC, 2–3.
25. 8th Canadian Infantry Brigade War Diary, February 1945, RG24, LAC, 3.
26. Roberts, 113.
27. Capt. J.C. Bond, "The use of Smoke support of 3 Cdn Inf Div in op 'Veritable' 7–8 Feb 45, by Capt. J.C. Bond, Tech Offr (CW) 2 Cdn Corps," 225C2.013(D6), vol. 10800, box 215, RG24, LAC, 1.
28. Roy, 365–66.
29. Stacey, 471–72.
30. Stewart A.G. Mein, *Up the Johns! The Story of the Royal Regina Rifles* (North Battleford, SK: Turner-Warwick, 1992), 133.
31. 7th Canadian Infantry Brigade War Diary, February 1945, RG24, LAC, 4.
32. Regina Rifle Regiment War Diary, February 1945, RG24, LAC, 3.
33. 7th Canadian Infantry War Diary, February 1945, 4.
34. "Award Citations, 8/9 Feb 44, Zyfflich," J. Walter Keith file, in the author's possession.
35. Eric Luxton, ed., *1st Battalion, the Regina Rifles Regiment, 1939–1946* (Regina: The Regt., 1946), 56.
36. Roy, 366–67.
37. Canadian Scottish Regiment War Diary, February 1945, RG24, LAC, 6–7.
38. Jean E. Portugal, *We Were There: The Navy, the Army and the RCAF—A Record for Canada*, vol. 4 (Shelburne, ON: Battered Silicon Dispatch Box, 1998), 2076.
39. Roy, 368–69.
40. Canadian Scottish War Diary, Feb. 1945, 7–8.
41. Portugal, vol. 5 , 2220.
42. Canadian Scottish War Diary, Feb. 1945, 7–8.
43. Roy, 370–71.
44. Canadian Scottish War Diary, Feb. 1945, 9.

45. Royal Winnipeg Rifle Regiment War Diary, February 1945, RG24, LAC, 2.
46. Canadian Scottish War Diary, Feb. 1945, 9.
47. Roy, 371–72.

13 THE WATER RATS

1. Gen. H.D.G. Crerar, "Report by Gen. H.D.G. Crerar, Operations of First Canadian Army 1 Jan–10 Mar 45," 215C1.013(D2), vol. 10636, box 125, RG24, LAC, 7.
2. H.G. Martin, *The History of the Fifteenth Scottish Division, 1939–1945* (London: William Blackwood & Sons, 1948), 238.
3. Charles P. Stacey, *The Victory Campaign: The Operations in North-West Europe, 1944–1945*, vol. 3 of *Official History...War* (Ottawa: Queen's Printer, 1960), 474.
4. Martin, 238–40.
5. "Report No. 155, Operation Veritable: The Winter Offensive between the Maas and the Rhine, 8–25 Feb 45 (Preliminary Report)," CMHQ, DHH, DND, 30.
6. Franz Kurowski, *Jump into Hell: German Paratroopers in World War II* (Mechanicsburg, PA: Stackpole Books, 2010), 324.
7. "Oberst Geyer Account," Record Group 549, B Series, Box 12, B-147, College Park, MD, NARA, 13–14.
8. Kurowksi, 324–25.
9. Stacey, 475–76.
10. "Report No. 155," 31.
11. Charles B. MacDonald, *United States Army in World War II: European Theater of Operations—The Last Offensive* (Washington, DC: Office of the Chief of Military History, 1973), 81–82.
12. Stacey, 476–77.
13. Lt. Col. L.G.C. Lilley, "Road to the Rhine: Problems of the Engineers (8 Feb–12 Mar 45), Account Given by Lt. Col. L.G.C. Lilley, CRE 2 CDN INF DIV, to Historical Officer, 2 CDN INF DIV, 15 Mar 45," 143.132011(D1), DHH, DND, 2.
14. Crerar, "Report, 1 Jan–10 Mar 45," 8.
15. Stacey, 476.
16. Brian Horrocks with Eversley Belfield and H. Essame, *Corps Commander* (London: Sidgwick & Jackson, 1977), 186–87.
17. Martin, 243.
18. "Report No. 155," 31.
19. Horrocks, 187.
20. L.F. Ellis, *The Defeat of Germany*, vol. 2 of *Victory in the West* (London: Her Majesty's Stationery Office, 1968), 262.
21. "Report No. 155," 32.
22. L.F. Ellis, 263.
23. 9th Canadian Infantry Brigade War Diary, February 1945, RG24, LAC, 4.
24. Stormont, Dundas and Glengarry Highlanders War Diary, February 1945, RG24, LAC, 4.
25. William Boss, *Up the Glens: Stormont, Dundas and Glengarry Highlanders, 1783–1994* (Cornwall, ON: Old Book Store, 1995), 138.

26. 9th CIB War Diary, Feb. 1945, 4.

27. *1st Battalion, the Highland Light Infantry of Canada: 1940–1945* (Galt, ON: Highland Light Infantry of Canada Assoc., 1951), 88.

28. Capt. J.C. Bond, "The use of Smoke support of 3 Cdn Inf Div in op 'Veritable' 7–8 Feb 45, by Capt. J.C. Bond, Tech Offr (CW) 2 Cdn Corps," 225C2.013(D6), vol. 10800, box 215, RG24, LAC, 2.

29. 17th Duke of York's Royal Canadian Hussars War Diary, February 1945, RG24, LAC, 4–5.

30. Highland Light Infantry War Diary, February 1945, RG24, LAC, 3.

31. *1st Battalion, the HLI*, 88.

32. Capt. R.F. Gray, "Op 'Veritable' Rpt by Hist Offr, 3 Cdn Inf Div, Capt. R.F. Gray, 17 Mar 45," 235C3.011(D4), vol. 10907, box 269, RG24, LAC, 5.

33. Boss, 138–39.

34. *Canadian Army Overseas Honours and Awards (1939–45)*, DHH, DND, accessed December 30, 2013, www.cmp-cpm.forces.gc.ca/dhh-dhp/gal/cao-aco/details-eng.asp?firstname=Ernest William&lastname=Baker&rec=id84.

35. Boss, 139.

36. Stacey, 479.

37. *1st Battalion, the HLI*, 88.

38. Stacey, 480.

39. W. Denis Whitaker and Shelagh Whitaker, *Rhineland: The Battle to End the War* (Toronto: Stoddart, 1989), 57–58.

40. *1st Battalion, the HLI*, 88–89.

41. Boss, 139.

42. *1st Battalion, the HLI*, 89.

43. Will R. Bird, *No Retreating Footsteps: The Story of the North Nova Scotia Highlanders* (Hantsport, NS: Lancelot Press, 1983), 310–12.

44. North Nova Scotia Highlanders War Diary, February 1945, RG24, LAC, 4–5.

45. Whitaker and Whitaker, 59.

14 HEAVY GOING

1. Nigel Hamilton, *Monty: The Field-Marshal, 1944–1976* (London: Hamish Hamilton, 1986), 375–76.

2. Charles P. Stacey, *The Victory Campaign: The Operations in North-West Europe, 1944–1945*, vol. 3 of *Official History...War* (Ottawa: Queen's Printer, 1960), 481.

3. L.F. Ellis, *The Defeat of Germany*, vol. 2 of *Victory in the West* (London: Her Majesty's Stationery Office, 1968), 266–67.

4. Stacey, 481–82.

5. Gen. H.D.G. Crerar, "Report by Gen. H.D.G. Crerar, Operations of First Canadian Army 1 Jan–10 Mar 45," 215C1.013(D2), vol. 10636, box 125, RG24, LAC, 8.

6. Ellis, 264–65.

7. Terry Copp and Robert Vogel, *Maple Leaf Route: Victory* (Alma, ON: Maple Leaf Route, 1988), 37–38.

8. "General der Fallschirmtruppen Alfred Schlemm," Record Group 549, B Series, Box 11, B-084, College Park, MD, NARA, 3–4.

9. Copp and Vogel, 40.

10. Ibid., 40–41.

11. Stacey, 481.

12. Bill McAndrew, *Liberation: The Canadians in Europe* (Montreal: Éditions Art Global, 1995), 132.

13. 16th Canadian Light Anti-Aircraft Battery War Diary, Appendix: "War Diary Summary, 3rd Canadian Light Anti-Aircraft Regiment," RG24, LAC, 1.

14. 9th Canadian Infantry Brigade War Diary, February 1945, RG24, LAC, 6.

15. North Nova Scotia Highlanders War Diary, February 1945, RG24, LAC, 5–6.

16. Will R. Bird, *No Retreating Footsteps: The Story of the North Nova Scotia Highlanders* (Hantsport, NS: Lancelot Press, 1983), 314–15.

17. North Nova War Diary, Feb. 1945, 6.

18. Meaghan Beresford, "My Best Friend," May, 2005, *Canadian Virtual War Memorial*, Veteran Affairs Canada, accessed January 2, 2014, www.veterans.gc.ca/eng/collections/virtualmem/Detail/2663442?Eric%20Greene.

19. Stacey, 482.

20. "The Clearing of Moyland Wood by 7 Cdn Inf Bde: Memorandum of Interview with the Brigade Major and GSO3 (OPS) 7 Cdn Inf Bde, O.C. R Wpg Rif, O.C. Regina Rif, O.C. 1 C Scot R, Given to Historical Offr, 3 Cdn Inf Div," 740.009(DI) DHH, DND, 1.

21. H.G. Martin, *The History of the Fifteenth Scottish Division, 1939–1945* (London: William Blackwood & Sons, 1948), 255–56.

22. Stacey, 482.

23. "Report No. 185, Operation Veritable: The Winter Offensive between the Maas and the Rhine, 8–25 Feb 45 (Final Report)," CMHQ, DHH, DND, para. 133.

24. "Spragge, John Godfrey," Soldiers of the Queen's Own, *The Queen's Own Rifles of Canada Regimental Museum and Archives*, accessed January 3, 2014, qormuseum.org/soldiers-of-the-queens-own/spragge-john-godery/.

25. W. Denis Whitaker and Shelagh Whitaker, *Rhineland: The Battle to End the War* (Toronto: Stoddart, 1989), 146.

26. 9th Canadian Infantry Brigade War Diary, February 1945, 6–7.

27. Reginald Roy, *Ready for the Fray: The History of the Canadian Scottish Regiment (Princess Mary's), 1920 to 1955* (Vancouver: Evergreen Press, 1958), 372.

28. "Report No. 185," paras. 132–33.

29. 9th Canadian Infantry Brigade War Diary, February 1945, 7.

30. Brian A. Reid, *Named by the Enemy: A History of the Royal Winnipeg Rifles* (Winnipeg: Royal Winnipeg Rifle Regt., 2010), 216.

31. Jean E. Portugal, *We Were There: The Navy, the Army and the RCAF—A Record for Canada*, vol. 6 (Shelburne, ON: Battered Silicon Dispatch Box, 1998), 2932.

32. Royal Winnipeg Regiment War Diary, February 1945, RG24, LAC, 5.

33. *Canadian Army Overseas Honours and Awards (1939–45)*, DHH, DND, accessed January 6, 2014, www.cmp-cpm.forces.gc.ca/dhh-dhp/gal/cao-aco/details-eng.asp?firstname=Harry Haultain&lastname=Badger&rec=id1428.

34. D. Gordon Brown, "The Battle of Moyland Wood: The Regina Rifle Regiment, 16–19 February 1945," *Canadian Military History* 6, no. 1 (Spring 1997), 101.

35. "The Clearing of Moyland Wood by 7 Cdn Inf Bde," 740.009(DI), DHH, DND, 1.

36. 7th Canadian Infantry Brigade War Diary, February 1945, RG24, LAC, 7.

37. "The Clearing of Moyland Wood," 1.

38. Stacey, 483.

39. "The Clearing of Moyland Wood," 1–2.

40. Brown, "The Battle of Moyland Wood," 102.

41. Jack Pearson, phone interview by J. Walter Keith, January 2013, transcript in the author's possession.

42. "The Clearing of Moyland Wood," 1.

43. Brown, "The Battle of Moyland Wood," 102.

44. "The Clearing of Moyland Wood," 1.

45. M.D. "Manny" Day, phone interview by J. Walter Keith, January 2013, transcript in the author's possession.

46. *Canadian Army Overseas Honours and Awards (1939–45)*, DHH, DND, accessed January 6, 2014, www.cmp-cpm.forces.gc.ca/dhh-dhp/gal/cao-aco/details-eng.asp?firstname=Edward Stanley&lastname=Tenklei&rec=id1119.

47. Regina Rifle Regiment War Diary, February 1945, RG24, LAC, 6.

48. "The Clearing of Moyland Wood," 1–2.

49. 7th CIB War Diary, Feb. 1945, 8.

50. Canadian Scottish Regiment War Diary, February 1945, RG24, LAC, 15.

51. 7th CIB War Diary, Feb. 1945, 8.

52. Reid, 218.

53. "The Clearing of Moyland Wood," 2.

15 INTO HELL

1. L.F. Ellis, *The Defeat of Germany*, vol. 2 of *Victory in the West* (London: Her Majesty's Stationery Office, 1968), 267–68.

2. "Report No. 185, Operation Veritable: The Winter Offensive between the Maas and the Rhine, 8–25 Feb 45 (Final Report)," CMHQ, DHH, DND, para. 144.

3. "Report No. 185," paras. 148–55.

4. Terry Copp and Robert Vogel, *Maple Leaf Route: Victory* (Alma, ON: Maple Leaf Route, 1988), 42.

5. Regina Rifle Regiment War Diary, February 1945, RG24, LAC, 6.

6. 7th Canadian Infantry Brigade War Diary, February 1945, RG24, LAC, 8.

7. "The Clearing of Moyland Wood by 7 Cdn Inf Bde," 740.009(D1), DHH, DND, 2.

8. D. Gordon Brown, "The Battle of Moyland Wood: The Regina Rifle Regiment, 16–19 February 1945," *Canadian Military History* 6, no. 1 (Spring 1997), 102–4.

9. Royal Winnipeg Rifle Regiment War Diary, February 1945, RG24, LAC, 5.

10. Brian A. Reid, *Named by the Enemy: A History of the Royal Winnipeg Rifles* (Winnipeg: Royal Winnipeg Rifle Regt., 2010), 218.

11. Charles P. Stacey, *The Victory Campaign: The Operations in North-West Europe, 1944–1945*, vol. 3 of *Official History...War* (Ottawa: Queen's Printer, 1960), 483.

12. Reginald Roy, *Ready for the Fray: The History of the Canadian Scottish Regiment (Princess Mary's), 1920 to 1955* (Vancouver: Evergreen Press, 1958), 374–75.

13. Jean E. Portugal, *We Were There: The Navy, the Army and the* RCAF—*A Record for Canada*, vol. 4 (Shelburne, ON: Battered Silicon Dispatch Box, 1998), 2079.

14. Canadian Scottish Regiment War Diary, February 1945, RG24, LAC, 16.

15. Brown, 104–5.

16. "The Clearing of Moyland Wood," 2.

17. Stacey, 484.

18. Jeffrey Williams, *The Long Left Flank: The Hard Fought Way to the Reich, 1944–1945* (Toronto: Stoddart, 1988), 216.

19. Brown, 103.

20. Regina Rifles War Diary, Feb. 1945, 7.

21. *Canadian Army Overseas Honours and Awards (1939–45)*, DHH, DND, accessed January 6, 2014, www.cmp-cpm.forces.gc.ca/dhh-dhp/gal/cao-aco/details-eng. asp?firstname=William James&lastname=Shaw&rec=id938.

22. "Captain Douglas Carrick Howat, Recommendation for Award of Military Cross, Originated 1 Mar 45," photocopy, provided by J. Walter Keith, in the author's possession.

23. C.J. (Chris) Vogt, interview by J. Walter Keith, date unknown, in the author's possession.

24. Brown, 105–7.

25. Dwight Small, "From Armored Corps to Infantry," unpublished memoir annotated by J. Walter Keith, in the author's possession. 1–3.

26. "Captain Howat Recommendation."

27. "The Clearing of Moyland Wood," 2.

28. Eric Luxton, ed. *1st Battalion, The Regina Rifles Regiment, 1939–1946* (Regina: The Regt., 1946), 57.

29. Stacey, 483.

30. Roy, 376.

31. Portugal, vol. 4, 2059–60.

32. Roy, 376–77.

33. Portugal, vol. 4, 2060–61.

34. Roy, 377.

35. Canadian Scottish War Diary, Feb. 1945, Appendix 15: "The Rhine is Our Objective." 1–5.

36. Roy, 380–84.

37. W. Denis Whitaker and Shelagh Whitaker, *Rhineland: The Battle to End the War* (Toronto: Stoddart, 1989), 145.

38. 5th Canadian Infantry Brigade War Diary, February 1945, RG24, LAC, 7.

39. H.G. Martin, *The History of the Fifteenth Scottish Division, 1939–1945* (London: William Blackwood & Sons, 1948), 255–56.

40. Stacey, 486–87.

41. "The Clearing of Moyland Wood," 3.

16 PITCHED BATTLE

1. Dwight Small, "From Armored Corps to Infantry," unpublished memoir annotated by J. Walter Keith, in the author's possession.

2. C.J. (Chris) Vogt, interview by J. Walter Keith, date unknown, in the author's possession.

3. D. Gordon Brown, "The Battle of Moyland Wood: The Regina Rifle Regiment, 16–19 February 1945," *Canadian Military History* 6, no. 1 (Spring 1997), 107.

4. Regina Rifle Regiment War Diary, February 1945, RG24, LAC, 7.

5. Reginald Roy, *Ready for the Fray: The History of the Canadian Scottish Regiment (Princess Mary's), 1920 to 1955* (Vancouver: Evergreen Press, 1958), 380–84.

6. Jean E. Portugal, *We Were There: The Navy, the Army and the RCAF—A Record for Canada*, vol. 4 (Shelburne, ON: Battered Silicon Dispatch Box, 1998), 2068.

7. Roy, 381.

8. Portugal, vol. 4, 2069.

9. Roy, 381.

10. Portugal, vol. 4, 2069.

11. Canadian Scottish Regiment War Diary, February 1945, RG24, LAC, 18.

12. Roy, 384.

13. Portugal, vol. 4, 2080.

14. Canadian Scottish War Diary, Feb. 1945, 18.

15. Roy, 384–85.

16. "Report No. 185, Operation Veritable: The Winter Offensive between the Maas and the Rhine, 8–25 Feb 45 (Final Report)," CMHQ, DHH, DND, paras. 157–59.

17. Fort Garry Horse Regiment War Diary, February 1945, RG24, LAC, 5.

18. "Report No. 185," paras. 157–59.

19. Royal Hamilton Light Infantry War Diary, February 1945, RG24, LAC, 16.

20. Charles P. Stacey, *The Victory Campaign: The Operations in North-West Europe, 1944–1945*, vol. 3 of *Official History...War* (Ottawa: Queen's Printer, 1960), 487.

21. Royal Hamilton War Diary, February 1945, 16.

22. W. Denis Whitaker and Shelagh Whitaker, *Rhineland: The Battle to End the War* (Toronto: Stoddart, 1989), 152–57.

23. "Report No. 185," para. 160.

24. Sandy Antal and Kevin R. Shackleton, *Duty Nobly Done: The Official History of the Essex and Kent Scottish Regiment* (Windsor, ON: Walkerville, 2006), 498–99.

25. "Report No. 185," para. 160.

26. Kingsley Brown Sr., Kingsley Brown Jr., and Brereton Greenhous, *Semper Paratus: The History of the Royal Hamilton Light Infantry (Wentworth Regiment), 1862–1977* (Hamilton: RHLI Historical Assoc., 1977), 310.

27. Whitaker and Whitaker, 157–58.

28. Jean E. Portugal, *We Were There: The Navy, the Army and the RCAF—A Record for Canada*, vol. 3 (Shelburne, ON: Battered Silicon Dispatch Box, 1998), 1485–86.

29. Whitaker and Whitaker, 150–63.

30. Jean Bouchery, *The Canadian Soldier in North-West Europe, 1944–1945* (Paris: Histoire & Collections, 2003), 102.

31. Brown, Brown, and Greenhous, 312.

32. Whitaker and Whitaker, 160–61.

33. Brown, Brown, and Greenhous, 312.

34. Royal Hamilton War Diary, Feb. 1945, 17.

35. Essex Scottish Regiment War Diary, February 1945, RG24, LAC, 7.
36. Antal and Shackleton, 499.
37. Whitaker and Whitaker, 164.
38. Stacey, 490.
39. Antal and Shackleton, 499.
40. Portugal, vol. 3, 1491–92.
41. Stacey, 488.
42. Terry Copp and Robert Vogel, *Maple Leaf Route: Victory* (Alma, ON: Maple Leaf Route, 1988), 46.
43. "Report No. 185," para. 161.
44. Antal and Shackleton, 502–4.
45. George G. Blackburn, *The Guns of Victory: A Soldier's Eye View, Belgium, Holland, and Germany, 1944–45* (Toronto: McClelland & Stewart, 1996), 283.
46. Essex Scottish Regiment War Diary, February 1945, RG24, LAC, 8.
47. Whitaker and Whitaker, 168–69.
48. Stacey, 488.
49. Whitaker and Whitaker, 169.

17 SHEER GUTS AND DETERMINATION

1. Queen's Own Cameron Highlanders of Canada War Diary, February 1945, RG24, LAC, 12.
2. 4th Canadian Infantry Brigade War Diary, February 1945, RG24, LAC, 19.
3. *Canadian Army Overseas Honours and Awards (1939–45)*, DHH, DND, accessed January 13, 2014, www.cmp-cpm.forces.gc.ca/dhh-dhp/gal/cao-aco/details-eng.asp?firstname=Frank Leslie&lastname=Dixon&rec=id5275.
4. Charles P. Stacey, *The Victory Campaign: The Operations in North-West Europe, 1944–1945*, vol. 3 of *Official History...War* (Ottawa: Queen's Printer 1960), 489.
5. *Canadian Army Overseas Honours and Awards (1939–45)*, DHH, DND, accessed January 13, 2014, www.cmp-cpm.forces.gc.ca/dhh-dhp/gal/cao-aco/details-eng.asp?firstname=William Hugh&lastname=Moriarty&rec=id513.
6. 4th CIB War Diary, Feb. 1945, 19.
7. D.J. Goodspeed, *Battle Royal: A History of the Royal Regiment of Canada, 1862–1962* (Toronto: Royal Regt. of Canada Assoc., 1962), 537.
8. Royal Regiment of Canada War Diary, Feb. 1945, RG24, LAC, 7.
9. 4th CIB War Diary, Feb. 1945, 20–21.
10. Stacey, 489.
11. 4th CIB War Diary, Feb. 1945, 21.
12. Essex Scottish Regiment War Diary, February 1945, RG24, LAC, 9.
13. Stacey, 489.
14. 4th CIB War Diary, Feb. 1945, 22.
15. Dwight Small, "From Armored Corps to Infantry," unpublished memoir annotated by J. Walter Keith, in the author's possession.
16. "Report No. 185, Operation Veritable: The Winter Offensive between the Maas and the Rhine, 8–25 Feb 45 (Final Report)," CMHQ, DHH, DND, para. 165.
17. 7th Canadian Infantry Brigade War Diary, February 1945, RG24, LAC, 9.

18. Stacey, 486.
19. "The Clearing of Moyland Wood by 7 Cdn Inf Bde," 740.009(DI), DHH, DND, 3.
20. Brian A. Reid, *Named by the Enemy: A History of the Royal Winnipeg Rifles* (Winnipeg: Royal Winnipeg Rifle Regt., 2010), 219.
21. "The Clearing of Moyland Wood," 3.
22. Jean E. Portugal, *We Were There: The Navy, the Army and the RCAF—A Record for Canada*, vol. 6 (Shelburne, ON: Battered Silicon Dispatch Box, 1998), 2933.
23. Royal Winnipeg Rifle Regiment War Diary, February 1945, RG24, LAC, 7.
24. "The Clearing of Moyland Wood," 3.
25. Royal Winnipeg Rifles War Diary, Feb. 1945, 7.
26. Norman Donogh, "The Battle of Moyland Wood," January 29, 1997, unpublished manuscript prepared for Royal Winnipeg Rifle Regt., in the author's possession, 10.
27. "The Clearing of Moyland Wood," 4.
28. Donogh, 10.
29. "The Clearing of Moyland Wood," 4.
30. H.M. Jackson, *The Sherbrooke Regiment (12th Armoured Regiment)*, (n.p., 1958), 162.
31. "The Clearing of Moyland Wood," 4.
32. Donogh, 11.
33. "The Clearing of Moyland Wood," 4.
34. Donogh, 12.
35. Stacey, 486.
36. Donogh, 12.
37. Portugal, vol. 6, 2934.
38. Stacey, 486.
39. "Report No. 185," para. 166.
40. D. Gordon Brown, "The Battle of Moyland Wood: The Regina Rifle Regiment, 16–19 February 1945," *Canadian Military History* 6, no. 1 (Spring 1997), 108.
41. Reginald Roy, *Ready for the Fray: The History of the Canadian Scottish Regiment (Princess Mary's), 1920 to 1955* (Vancouver: Evergreen Press, 1958), 390–91.
42. Bill McAndrew, *Liberation: The Canadians in Europe* (Montreal: Éditions Art Global, 1995), 136.
43. Stacey, 486.

PART THREE: BLOCKBUSTER

18 ALL THIS IS GOOD

1. Charles P. Stacey, *The Victory Campaign: The Operations in North-West Europe, 1944–1945*, vol. 3 of *Official History...War* (Ottawa: Queen's Printer, 1960), 491.
2. L.F. Ellis, *The Defeat of Germany*, vol. 2 of *Victory in the West* (London: Her Majesty's Stationery Office, 1968), 270.
3. "Report No. 185, Operation Veritable: The Winter Offensive between the Maas and the Rhine, 8–25 Feb 45 (Final Report)," CMHQ, DHH, DND, paras. 206–8.
4. 4th Canadian Armoured Division War Diary, February 1945, RG24, LAC, 10.

5. Gen. H.D.G. Crerar, "Report by Gen. H.D.G. Crerar, Operations of First Canadian Army 1 Jan–10 Mar 45," 215C1.013(D2), vol. 10636, box 125, RG24, LAC, 10.

6. "Conference of Commanders, 2 CDN CORPS, on Operation Blockbuster, held at main HQ 2 CDN CORPS, 221100A Feb. 45," 225C2.016(D16), vol. 10808, box 219, RG24, LAC, 1–2.

7. Stacey, 492.

8. A.J. Kerry and W.A. McDill, History of the Corps of Royal Canadian Engineers, vol. 2 (1936–46) (Ottawa: Military Engineers Assoc. of Canada, 1966), 373–74.

9. "Operation Blockbuster: 3 Canadian Inf Division Engineers," 235C3.013(D17), vol. 10908, box 269, RG24, LAC, 1.

10. Stacey, 492–93.

11. Nigel Hamilton, Monty: The Field-Marshal, 1944–1976 (London: Hamish Hamilton, 1986) 387–88.

12. Charles B. MacDonald, United States Army in World War II: European Theater of Operations—The Last Offensive (Washington, DC: Office of the Chief of Military History, 1973), 143.

13. Ellis, 272.

14. MacDonald, 171.

15. Stacey, 495.

16. "Report No. 171, Operation Blockbuster: The Canadian Offensive West of the Rhine, 26 Feb–23 Mar 45 (Preliminary Report)," CMHQ, DHH, DND, 4.

17. Stacey, 496.

18. Ellis, 271.

19. Stacey, 493.

20. "Report No. 171," 7.

21. Ibid., 10–11.

22. Dominick Graham, The Price of Command: A Biography of General Guy Simonds (Toronto: Stoddart, 1993), 202–3.

23. Roy Whitsed, Canadians: A Battalion at War (Mississauga, ON: Burlington Books, 1996), 139–40.

24. R.M. Hickey, The Scarlet Dawn (Campbelltown, NB: Tribune, 1949), 247.

25. Brig. R.H. Keefler, "Operation Blockbuster, Role of 6 CDN INF BDE (26 Feb 45): Account given by Brigadier R.H. Keefler, Comd 6 CDN INF BDE to Historical Officer, 2 CDN INF DIV, 16 Mar 45," 265C6.011(D3), vol. 10985, box 310, RG24, LAC, 1.

26. Royal Hamilton Light Infantry War Diary, February 1945, RG24, LAC, 25.

27. Stacey, 497.

28. W. Denis Whitaker and Shelagh Whitaker, Rhineland: The Battle to End the War (Toronto: Stoddart, 1989), 192.

19 TOUGHEST SCRAP

1. George B. Buchanan, The March of the Prairie Men: A Story of the South Saskatchewan Regiment (Weyburn, SK: S. Sask. R. Orderly Room, 1958), 49.

2. Brig. R.H. Keefler, "Operation Blockbuster, Role of 6 CDN INF BDE (26 Feb 45): Account given by Brigadier R.H. Keefler, Comd 6 CDN INF BDE to Historical Officer, 2 CDN INF DIV, 16 Mar 45," 265C6.011(D3), vol. 10985, box 310, RG24, LAC, 2.

3. Charles Goodman, interview by author, Saanichton, BC, January 27, 2009.

4. South Saskatchewan Regiment War Diary, February 1945, RG24, LAC, 21.

5. Sherbrooke Fusiliers Regiment War Diary, February 1945, RG24, LAC, 28.

6. South Sask. War Diary, Feb. 1945, 21.

7. Goodman interview.

8. Jack Golding, "Renowned Regiment from Prairies Boosts Boche from Calcar Hills," *The Maple Leaf* (n.p., n.d.), unformatted copy in the author's possession.

9. South Sask. War Diary, Feb. 1945, 22.

10. Goodman interview.

11. South Sask. War Diary, Feb. 1945, 22.

12. *Canadian Army Overseas Honours and Awards (1939–45)*, DHH, DND, accessed January 17, 2014, www.cmp-cpm.forces.gc.ca/dhh-dhp/gal/cao-aco/details-eng. asp?firstname=Lloyd Gordon&lastname=Queen&rec=id3350.

13. Charles P. Stacey, *The Victory Campaign: The Operations in North-West Europe, 1944–1945*, vol. 3 of *Official History...War* (Ottawa: Queen's Printer, 1960), 497.

14. *Cent ans d'histoire d'un régiment Canadien-français: Les Fusiliers Mont-Royal, 1869–1969* (Montreal: Éditions du Jour, 1971), 252.

15. W. Denis Whitaker and Shelagh Whitaker, *Rhineland: The Battle to End the War* (Toronto: Stoddart, 1989), 205.

16. "Operation Blockbuster, Role of 6 CDN INF BDE," 2.

17. Queen's Own Cameron Highlanders War Diary, February 1945, RG24, LAC, 17.

18. "Report No. 186, Operation Blockbuster: The Canadian Offensive West of the Rhine, 26 Feb–23 Mar 45," CMHQ, DHH, DND, para. 38.

19. Stacey, 497.

20. R.W. Queen-Hughes, *Whatever Men Dare: A History of the Queen's Own Cameron Highlanders of Canada, 1935–1960* (Winnipeg: Bulman Bros., 1960), 159.

21. Stacey, 498.

22. "Operation Blockbuster, Role of 6 CDN INF BDE," 3.

23. 5th Canadian Infantry Brigade War Diary, February 1945, RG24, LAC, 11.

24. Brig. W.J. Megill, "Blockbuster and subsequent operations during the advance to the Rhine (26 Feb–11 Mar 45): Role of 5 CDN INF BDE, Account given by Brigadier W.J. Megill to Historical Officer 2 CDN INF DIV, 24 Mar 45," 265C5.011(D3), vol. 10985, box 310, RG24, LAC, 2.

25. Le Régiment de Maisonneuve War Diary, February 1945, RG24, LAC, 7.

26. Black Watch Regiment War Diary, February 1945, RG24, LAC, 13.

27. "6th Canadian Armoured Regiment (First Hussars): Report on Op Blockbuster—Report on Operations Area–Calcar," 141.4A6011(D2), DHH, DND, 1.

28. "Blockbuster and subsequent operations," 1–2.

29. Stacey, 498.

30. "Blockbuster and subsequent operations," 1.

31. Black Watch War Diary, Feb. 1945, 13.

32. Ibid., 16.

33. "Blockbuster and subsequent operations," 1.

34. Black Watch War Diary, Feb. 1945, 13.

35. "6th Canadian Armoured Report," 1–2.
36. *Canadian Army Overseas Honours and Awards (1939–45)*, DHH, DND, accessed January 21, 2014, www.cmp-cpm.forces.gc.ca/dhh-dhp/gal/cao-aco/details-eng.asp?firstname=William Arthur&lastname=Robinson&rec=id3429.
37. "Blockbuster and subsequent operations," 2.
38. *Canadian Army Overseas Honours and Awards (1939–45)*, DHH, DND, accessed January 21,2014,www.cmp-cpm.forces.gc.ca/dhh-dhp/gal/cao-aco/details-eng.asp?firstname=Julien&lastname=Bibeau&rec=id1520.
39. "Blockbuster and subsequent operations," 2.
40. *Canadian Army Overseas Honours and Awards (1939–45)*, Bibeau citation.
41. Gérard Marchand, *Le Régiment de Maisonneuve vers la victoire, 1944–1945* (Montreal: Les Presses Libre, 1980), 197.
42. Le Régiment de Maisonneuve War Diary, Feb. 1945, 7.
43. Terry Copp, *The Brigade: The Fifth Canadian Infantry Brigade, 1939–1945* (Stoney Creek, ON: Fortress, 1992), 179.
44. James Alan Roberts, *The Canadian Summer: The Memoirs of James Alan Roberts* (Toronto: University of Toronto Press, 1981), 116–17.
45. Lt. Col. S.M. Lett, "Account of Operation Blockbuster given by Lt. Col. S.M. Lett to Hist Offr 3 CDN INF DIV, 16 Mar 45," 145.2Q2011(D5), DHH, DND, 1.
46. Lt. Col. J.W.H. Rowley and Maj. O.L. Corbett, "Memorandum of Interview with Lt. Col. J.W.H. Rowley, O.C., N. Shore R. and Maj. O.L. Corbett, O.C. D Coy N. Shore R. Given to Hist Offr 3 CDN INF DIV, 16 Mar, 45," 145.2N3011(D5), DHH, DND, 1.
47. Lett, "Account of Operation Blockbuster," 1.
48. Stacey, 499.
49. Lett, "Account of Operation Blockbuster," 1.
50. W.T. Barnard, *The Queen's Own Rifles of Canada, 1860–1960: One Hundred Years of Canada* (Don Mills, ON: Ontario Publishing Company, 1960), 248.
51. Stacey, 498.
52. Roy Whitsed, *Canadians: A Battalion at War* (Mississauga, ON: Burlington Books, 1996), 141.
53. Barnard, 248–49.
54. Whitsed, 152–53.
55. Michael R. McNorgan, *The Gallant Hussars: A History of the 1st Hussars Regiment, 1856–2004* (Aylmer, ON: 1st Hussars Cavalry Fund, 2004), 202.
56. Whitsed, 152.
57. "In memory of Sergeant Aubrey Cosens, February 26, 1945," *Canadian Virtual War Memorial*, accessed January 22, 2014, www.veterans.gc.ca/eng/collections/virtualmem/Detail/2662995?Aubrey%20Cosens.
58. Whitsed, 153.
59. Lett, "Account of Operation Blockbuster," 2.
60. Whitsed, 141.
61. Charles Cromwell Martin, *Battle Diary: From D-Day and Normandy to the Zuider Zee and VE* (Toronto: Dundurn, 1994), 119–20.

62. "In memory of Lieut. John James Chambers, February 26, 1945," obituary in The Toronto Star, March 7, 1945, *Canadian Virtual War Memorial*, accessed January 22, 2014, www.veterans.gc.ca/eng/collections/virtualmem/Detail/2662902?John%20 James%20Chambers.

63. Martin, 119–20.

64. Whitsed, 141–43.

65. "6th Canadian Armoured Regiment (First Hussars): Report on Op Blockbuster," 141.4A6011(D2), DHH, DND, 2.

66. Martin, 124.

67. Whitsed, 144–45.

68. Martin, 124–25.

69. Barnard, 251.

20 DASH AND SIMPLICITY

1. R.M. Hickey, *The Scarlet Dawn* (Campbelltown, NB: Tribune, 1949), 248.

2. Lt. Col. J.W.H. Rowley and Maj. O.L. Corbett, "Memorandum of Interview with Lt. Col. J.W.H. Rowley, O.C., N. Shore R. and Maj. O.L. Corbett, O.C. D Coy N. Shore R. Given to Hist Offr 3 CDN INF DIV, 16 Mar, 45," 145.2N3011(D5), DHH, DND, 1.

3. Maj. F.J. L'Espérance, "Account of Blockbuster given by Maj. F.J. L'Espérance, 2IC R. de Chaud to Hist Offr. 3 CDN INF DIV, 19 Mar 45," 145.2R2011(DI), DHH, DND, 1.

4. Rowley and Corbett, "Memorandum of Interview," 1.

5. "Attack on 'Keppeln' by N Shore R–26 Feb 45," 145.2N3011(D6), DHH, DND, 1.

6. Will R. Bird, *North Shore (New Brunswick) Regiment* (Fredericton: Brunswick Press, 1963), 508.

7. Jacques Castonguay and Armand Ross, *Le Régiment de la Chaudière* (Lévis, QC: n.p., 1983), 340.

8. J.A. William Whiteacre, "Valour by Day, Audacity by Night," notes of presentation to Arts and Letters Club of Toronto, May 2005, in the author's possession.

9. Castonguay and Ross, 340.

10. L'Espérance, "Account of Blockbuster," 1.

11. Bird, *North Shore*, 514.

12. Rowley and Corbett, "Memorandum of Interview," 2.

13. Bird, *North Shore*, 512–15.

14. Rowley and Corbett, "Memorandum of Interview," 2.

15. Bird, *North Shore*, 513.

16. L'Espérance, "Account of Blockbuster," 1–2.

17. Brandon Conron, *A History of the First Hussars Regiment, 1856–1960* (n.p., 1981), 129.

18. North Shore (New Brunswick) Regiment War Diary, February 1945, RG24, LAC, 17.

19. Rowley and Corbett, "Memorandum of Interview," 2.

20. "6th Canadian Armoured Regiment (First Hussars): Report on Op Blockbuster," 141.4A6011(D2), DHH, DND, 2.

21. North Shore War Diary, Feb. 1945, 18.

22. "6th Canadian Armoured Report," 2.

23. Rowley and Corbett, "Memorandum of Interview," 2.

24. Michael R. McNorgan, *The Gallant Hussars: A History of the 1st Hussars Regiment, 1856–2004* (Aylmer, ON: The 1st Hussars Cavalry Fund, 2004), 202.

25. Bird, *North Shore*, 509.

26. Ibid., 509–10.

27. "6th Canadian Armoured Report," 2.

28. Bird, *North Shore*, 510.

29. McNorgan, 203.

30. "6th Canadian Armoured Report," 2.

31. Bird, *North Shore*, 512–16.

32. L'Espérance, "Account of Blockbuster," 2.

33. Castonguay and Ross, 343.

34. North Shore War Diary, Feb. 1945, 19.

35. Hickey, 249.

36. McNorgan, 204–5.

37. "6th Canadian Armoured Report," 3.

38. Charles P. Stacey, *The Victory Campaign: The Operations in North-West Europe, 1944–1945*, vol. 3 of *Official History...War* (Ottawa: Queen's Printer, 1960), 500–1.

39. "Report No. 186, Operation Blockbuster: The Canadian Offensive West of the Rhine, 26 Feb–23 Mar 45, Appendix 'G,' CMHQ, DHH, DND, 7.

40. Stacey, 500–01.

41. 4th Canadian Armoured Brigade War Diary, February 1945, RG24, LAC, 16.

42. Stacey, 503.

43. Geoffrey Hayes, *The Lincs: A History of the Lincoln and Welland Regiment at War* (Alma, ON: Maple Leaf Route, 1986), 92.

44. A. Fortescue Duguid, *History of the Canadian Grenadier Guards, 1760–1964* (Montreal: Gazette Printing, 1965), 319.

45. "Report No. 186, Operation Blockbuster: The Canadian Offensive West of the Rhine, 26 Feb–23 Mar 45," para. 45.

46. Duguid, 319.

47. Stacey, 501.

48. Stuart Johns, phone interview by author, December 6, 2012.

49. Alfred James Tedlie, interview by Chris D. Main, June 28 and July 9, 16, and 23, 1979, UVICSC.

50. Hayes, 93.

51. Lt-Col F.E. Wigle, "Account of interview with Lt-Col F.E. Wigle, A & SH of C by Historical Officer, 2 CDN Corps, on 24 Mar 45," 145.2A3013(DI), DHH, DND, 2.

52. Johns interview.

53. Hershell Smith, interview by Chris Bell, September 2, 1982, and August 30, 1983, UVICSC.

54. Johns interview.

55. "Report No. 186," para. 55.

56. *Canadian Army Overseas Honours and Awards (1939–45)*, DHH, DND, accessed January 27, 2014, www.cmp-cpm.forces.gc.ca/dhh-dhp/gal/cao-aco/details-eng.asp?firstname=Aloysius James&lastname=Tedlie&rec=id3737.

21 PUSH ON THROUGH

1. Lake Superior Regiment (Motor) War Diary, February 1945, RG24, LAC, 16.
2. Robert L. Foster, et. al., *Steady the Buttons Two by Two: Governor General's Foot Guards Regimental History, 125th Anniversary—1872–1997* (Ottawa: Governor General's Foot Guards, 1999), 215.
3. George F.G. Stanley, *In the Face of Danger: The History of the Lake Superior Regiment* (Port Arthur, ON: Lake Superior Scottish Regt., 1960), 260–62.
4. Foster, 215.
5. Stormont, Dundas and Glengarry Highlanders War Diary, February 1945, RG24, LAC, 12.
6. Glen Tomlin, "I'm Paralysed!" *Heroes Remember,* video of Glen Tomlin interview, March 7, 2005, Veterans Affairs Canada, accessed November 24, 2008, www.veterans.gc.ca/eng/video-gallery/video/7035.
7. William Boss, *Up the Glens: Stormont, Dundas and Glengarry Highlanders, 1783–1994* (Cornwall, ON: Old Book Store, 1995), 140.
8. Charles P. Stacey, *The Victory Campaign: The Operations in North-West Europe, 1944–1945,* vol. 3 of *Official History...War* (Ottawa: Queen's Printer, 1960), 501–2.
9. T. Robert Fowler, *Courage Rewarded: The Valour of Canadian Soldiers Under Fire 1900 to 2007* (Victoria: Trafford, 2009), 214.
10. G.L. Cassidy, *Warpath: From Tilly-la-campagne to the Kusten Canal* (Markham, ON: Paperjacks, 1980), 287.
11. Stacey, 503.
12. Cassidy, 290.
13. Algonquin Regiment War Diary, February 1945, RG24, LAC, 26.
14. Stacey, 503–04.
15. Edgar W.I. Palamountain, *Taurus Pursuant: A History of the 11th Armoured Division* (Germany: Printing and Stationery Service British Army of the Rhine, 1945), 83–84.
16. South Alberta Regiment War Diary, February 1945, RG24, LAC, 11–13.
17. Donald Graves, *Century of Service: The History of the South Alberta Light Horse* (Toronto: Robin Brass Studio, 2005), 346.
18. Algonquin War Diary, Feb. 1945, 26.
19. Cassidy, 294.
20. Stacey, 504.
21. Algonquin War Diary, Feb. 1945, 27.
22. Graves, *Century of Service,* 346.
23. Cassidy, 296.
24. "Report No. 186, Operation Blockbuster: The Canadian Offensive West of the Rhine, 26 Feb–23 Mar 45," DHH, DND, paras. 67–68.
25. Donald Graves, *South Albertas: A Canadian Regiment at War* (Toronto: Robin Brass Studio, 1998), 273.
26. Cassidy, 295.
27. Stacey, 504.
28. Algonquin War Diary, Feb. 1945, 27–28.
29. TNA: PRO WO 171/488, "4th Canadian Armoured Division (G Branch) War Diary, Operation Logs, February 1945," unpaged.

30. Graves, *South Albertas*, 276.

31. Cassidy, 297.

32. Graves, *South Albertas*, 276–77.

33. Cassidy, 298.

34. "Record of Operation Blockbuster, as far as it affects the 29 Cdn Armd Recce Regt–Appendix v, Casualties," 141.4A29011(D2), DHH, DND, 1–2.

35. Calgary Highlanders Regiment War Diary, February 1945, RG24, LAC, 18.

36. David Bercuson, *Battalion of Heroes: The Calgary Highlanders in World War II* (Calgary: Calgary Highlanders Regt. Funds Fdn., 1994), 211–13.

37. Brig. W.J. Megill, "The Role of 5 CDN INF BDE in Operation 'Veritable' (8 Feb. 45), account by Brigadier W.J. Megill, Comd, 5 CDN INF BDE, Given to Historical Officer, 2 CDN INF DIV, 11 Feb 45," 265C5.011(D4), vol. 10985, box 310, RG24, LAC, 2.

38. *Canadian Army Overseas Honours and Awards (1939–45)*, DHH, DND, accessed January 29, 2014, www.cmp-cpm.forces.gc.ca/dhh-dhp/gal/cao-aco/details-eng.asp?firstname=Harold Omar&lastname=Larson&rec=id4224.

39. Bercuson, 212–13.

40. Roy Farran, *The History of the Calgary Highlanders, 1921–1954* (Calgary: Bryant Press, 1954), 203.

41. Terry Copp, *The Brigade: The Fifth Canadian Infantry Brigade, 1939–1945* (Stoney Creek, ON: Fortress, 1992), 179.

42. Brig. W.J. Megill, "The Role of 5 CDN INF BDE," 2.

43. Stacey, 505.

44. "GS Account of Blockbuster 4 CAD forwarded by His Offr," 245C4.013(D12), DHH, DND, 4.

45. Stacey, 505–7.

22 HUNKER DOWN AND PRAY

1. Argyll and Sutherland Highlander Regiment War Diary, February 1945, RG24, LAC, 17–18.

2. "Record of Operation Blockbuster, as far as it affects the 29 Cdn Armd Recce Regt–Appendix v, Casualties," 141.4A29011(D2), DHH, DND, 6.

3. Donald Graves, *South Albertas: A Canadian Regiment at War* (Toronto: Robin Brass Studio, 1998), 280.

4. Argyll and Sutherland Highlander Regiment War Diary, February 1945, 18.

5. Robert L. Fraser, *Black Yesterdays: The Argyll's War* (Hamilton: Argyll Foundation, 1996), 380.

6. Lt-Col F.E. Wigle, "Account of interview with Lt-Col F.E. Wigle, A & SH of C by Historical Officer, 2 CDN Corps, on 24 Mar 45," 145.2A3013(D1), DHH, DND, 6.

7. H.M. Jackson, *The Argyll and Sutherland Highlanders of Canada (Princess Louise's), 1928–1953* (Montreal: Industrial Shops for the Deaf, 1953), 178–79.

8. Graves, *South Albertas*, 281.

9. Wigle, "Account of interview," 6.

10. Argyll War Diary, Feb. 1945, 18.

11. Charles P. Stacey, *The Victory Campaign: The Operations in North-West Europe, 1944–1945*, vol. 3 of *Official History...War* (Ottawa: Queen's Printer, 1960), 507.

12. Argyll War Diary, Feb. 1945, 18.
13. Graves, *South Albertas*, 281.
14. Fraser, 381–84.
15. Argyll War Diary, Feb. 1945, 19.
16. Fraser, 384.
17. Argyll War Diary, Feb. 1945, 20.
18. "Op Blockbuster: Linc & Welld R CA, 22 Feb 45 to 13 Mar 45," 145.2C3011(D1), DHH, DND, 2.
19. Stacey, 507.
20. Geoffrey Hayes, *The Lincs: A History of the Lincoln and Welland Regiment at War* (Alma, ON: Maple Leaf Route, 1986), 96.
21. Stacey, 507.
22. Paul P. Hutchinson, *Canada's Black Watch: The First Hundred Years, 1862–1962* (Montreal: The Royal Highlanders of Canada Armoury Assoc., 1962), 232–33.
23. Black Watch Regiment War Diary, February 1945, RG24, LAC, 15.
24. Gen. H.D.G. Crerar, "Report by Gen. H.D.G. Crerar, Operations of First Canadian Army 1 Jan–10 Mar 45," 215C1.013(D2), vol. 10636, box 125, RG24, LAC, 10–11.
25. Stacey, 508–10.
26. Nigel Hamilton, *Monty: The Field-Marshal, 1944–1976* (London: Hamish Hamilton, 1986), 396–97.
27. Stacey, 510.
28. Sandy Antal and Kevin R. Shackleton, *Duty Nobly Done: The Official History of the Essex and Kent Scottish Regiment* (Windsor, ON: Walkerville, 2006), 507.
29. Essex Scottish Regiment War Diary, March 1945, RG24, LAC, 1.
30. H.M. Jackson, *The Sherbrooke Regiment (12th Armoured Regiment)*, (n.p., 1958), 163.
31. W. Denis Whitaker and Shelagh Whitaker, *Rhineland: The Battle to End the War* (Toronto: Stoddart, 1989), 236–38.
32. G. Kingsley Ward, *Field of Valour*, 100th Anniversary pamphlet (Windsor, ON: Essex and Kent Scottish Regt., 1985), 1.
33. Whitaker and Whitaker, 238.
34. Antal and Shackleton, 508
35. Whitaker and Whitaker, 239.
36. Kingsley Ward, 1.
37. Whitaker and Whitaker, 240–41.
38. Essex Scottish War Diary, March 1945, 1.
39. Kingsley Ward, 1–2.
40. Whitaker and Whitaker, 242.
41. Kingsley Ward, 1–2.
42. Essex Scottish War Diary, March 1945, 1.
43. Stacey, 511.
44. "6th Canadian Armoured Regiment (First Hussars): Report on Op Blockbuster–Pt II," 141.4A6011(D2), DHH, DND, 1.
45. Stacey, 511.

46. "Report No. 186, Operation Blockbuster: The Canadian Offensive West of the Rhine, 26 Feb–23 Mar 45," CMHQ, DHH, DND, para. 95.

47. "6th Canadian Armoured Report," 1.

48. Maj. F.J. L'Espérance, "Account of Blockbuster given by Maj. F.J. L'Espérance, 21C R. de Chaud to Hist Offr. 3 CDN INF DIV, 19 Mar 45," 145.2R2011(DI), DHH, DND, 2.

49. Jacques Castonguay and Armand Ross, Le Régiment de la Chaudière (Lévis, QC: n.p., 1983), 344–46.

23 BITTER, CLOSE-RANGE FIGHTING

1. 4th Canadian Armoured Brigade War Diary, February 1945, RG24, LAC, 21.

2. Charles P. Stacey, The Victory Campaign: The Operations in North-West Europe, 1944–1945, vol. 3 of Official History...War (Ottawa: Queen's Printer, 1960), 511–12.

3. W. Denis Whitaker and Shelagh Whitaker, Rhineland: The Battle to End the War (Toronto: Stoddart, 1989), 225–26.

4. Canadian Grenadier Guards War Diary, March 1945, RG24, LAC, 1.

5. George F.G. Stanley, In the Face of Danger: The History of the Lake Superior Regiment (Port Arthur, ON: Lake Superior Scottish Regt., 1960), 265–66.

6. 4th Canadian Armoured Brigade War Diary, March 1945, RG24, LAC, 1.

7. Canadian Grenadier War Diary, March 1945, 1.

8. Whitaker and Whitaker, 232.

9. Canadian Grenadier War Diary, March 1945, 1.

10. "Report No. 186, Operation Blockbuster: The Canadian Offensive West of the Rhine, 26 Feb–23 Mar 45," CMHQ, DHH, DND, para. 104.

11. Stacey, 512.

12. A. Fortescue Duguid, History of the Canadian Grenadier Guards, 1760–1964 (Montreal: Gazette Printing, 1965), 324–25.

13. Stanley, 267–69.

14. G.L. Cassidy, Warpath: From Tilly-la-campagne to the Kusten Canal (Markham, ON: Paperjacks, 1980), 310–11.

15. Robert L. Foster, et. al., Steady the Buttons Two by Two: Governor General's Foot Guards Regimental History, 125th Anniversary—1872–1997 (Ottawa: Governor General's Foot Guards, 1999), 216.

16. Cassidy, 311.

17. Stacey, 512.

18. Cassidy, 310–12.

19. Black Watch Regiment War Diary, March 1945, RG24, LAC, 2.

20. Stanley, 270.

21. Cassidy, 312.

22. Stacey, 513.

23. Brandon Conron, A History of the First Hussars Regiment, 1856–1960 (n.p., 1981), 131.

24. Maj. F.J. L'Espérance, "Account of Blockbuster given by Maj. F.J. L'Espérance, 21C R. de Chaud to Hist Offr. 3 CDN INF DIV, 19 Mar 45," 145.2R2011(DI), DHH, DND, 3.

25. W.T. Barnard, The Queen's Own Rifles of Canada, 1860–1960: One Hundred Years of Canada (Don Mills, ON: Ontario Publishing Company, 1960), 252.

26. Will R. Bird, *North Shore (New Brunswick) Regiment* (Fredericton: Brunswick Press, 1963), 523.

27. *Canadian Army Overseas Honours and Awards (1939–45)*, DHH, DND, accessed February 5, 2014, www.cmp-cpm.forces.gc.ca/dhh-dhp/gal/cao-aco/details-eng. asp?firstname=Owen Kevin Hugh&lastname=Kierans&rec=id2642.

28. Lt. Col. S.M. Lett, "Account of Operation Blockbuster given by Lt. Col. S.M. Lett to Hist Offr 3 CDN INF DIV, 16 Mar 45," 145.2Q2011(D5), DHH, DND, 3.

29. North Shore (New Brunswick) Regiment War Diary, March 1945, RG24, LAC, 3.

30. Bird, *North Shore*, 524.

31. Lett, "Account of Operation Blockbuster," 3.

32. R.W. Queen-Hughes, *Whatever Men Dare: A History of the Queen's Own Cameron Highlanders of Canada, 1935–1960* (Winnipeg: Bulman Bros., 1960), 161.

33. Kingsley Brown Sr., Kingsley Brown Jr., and Brereton Greenhous, *Semper Paratus: The History of the Royal Hamilton Light Infantry (Wentworth Regiment), 1862–1977* (Hamilton: RHLI Historical Assoc., 1977), 319–20.

34. 4th Canadian Infantry Brigade War Diary, March 1945, RG24, LAC, 2.

35. D.J. Goodspeed, *Battle Royal: A History of the Royal Regiment of Canada, 1862–1962* (Toronto: Royal Regt. of Canada Assoc., 1962), 543.

36. 4th CIB War Diary, March 1945, 3–4.

37. Le Régiment de Maisonneuve War Diary, March 1945, RG24, LAC, 1.

38. Calgary Highlanders War Diary, March 1945, RG24, LAC, 3.

39. Le Régiment de Maisonneuve War Diary, March 1945, 1.

40. South Saskatchewan Regiment War Diary, March 1945, RG24, LAC, 3.

41. Charles Goodman, interview by author, Saanichton, BC, January 27, 2009.

42. Sherbrooke Fusiliers Regiment War Diary, March 1945, RG24, LAC, 3.

43. *Cent ans d'histoire d'un régiment Canadian-français: les Fusiliers Mont-Royal, 1869–1969* (Montreal: Éditions du Jour, 1971), 255.

44. Queen's Own Rifles War Diary, March 1945, RG24, LAC, 1.

45. North Shore War Diary, March 1945, 4.

46. Charles Cromwell Martin, *Battle Diary: From D-Day and Normandy to the Zuider Zee and VE* (Toronto: Dundurn, 1994), 127–29.

47. Queen's Own Rifles War Diary, March 1945, 1–2.

48. "Report No. 186," para. 118.

49. Stacey, 513.

50. 4th CIB War Diary, March 1945, 4.

24 NOTHING MUST DELAY US

1. Charles P. Stacey, *The Victory Campaign: The Operations in North-West Europe, 1944–1945*, vol. 3 of *Official History...War* (Ottawa: Queen's Printer, 1960), 514.

2. "Report No. 186, Operation Blockbuster: The Canadian Offensive West of the Rhine, 26 Feb–23 Mar 45," CMHQ, DHH, DND, para. 121.

3. Stacey, 516.

4. W. Denis Whitaker and Shelagh Whitaker, *Rhineland: The Battle to End the War* (Toronto: Stoddart, 1989), 276.

5. "GS Account of Blockbuster 4 CAD forwarded by His Offr," 245C4.013(D12), DHH, DND, 5.

6. Black Watch Regiment War Diary, March 1945, RG24, LAC, 3.

7. Stacey, 513–15.

8. Calgary Highlanders Regiment War Diary, March 1945, RG24, LAC, 4.

9. 5th Canadian Infantry Brigade War Diary, March 1945, RG24, LAC, 3.

10. William Boss, *Up the Glens: Stormont, Dundas and Glengarry Highlanders, 1783–1994* (Cornwall, ON: Old Book Store, 1995), 141.

11. *Canadian Army Overseas Honours and Awards (1939–45)*, DHH, DND, accessed February 6, 2014, www.cmp-cpm.forces.gc.ca/dhh-dhp/gal/cao-aco/details-eng. asp?firstname=Alexander Hary Lawson&lastname=Stephen&rec=id3643.

12. Boss, 141.

13. "Report No. 186," para. 130.

14. *1st Battalion, The Highland Light Infantry of Canada: 1940–1945* (Galt, ON: Highland Light Infantry of Canada Assoc., 1951), 91–92.

15. North Nova Scotia Highlanders War Diary, March 1945, RG24, LAC, 2.

16. Will R. Bird, *No Retreating Footsteps: The Story of the North Nova Scotia Highlanders* (Hantsport, NS: Lancelot Press, 1983), 327–332.

17. 9th Canadian Infantry Brigade War Diary, March 1945, RG24, LAC, 3.

18. Boss, 142.

19. 9th CIB War Diary, March 1945, 3.

20. Royal Winnipeg Rifle Regiment War Diary, March 1945, RG24, LAC, 2.

21. 7th Canadian Infantry Brigade War Diary, March 1945, RG24, LAC, 2.

22. Canadian Scottish Regiment War Diary, March 1945, RG24, LAC, 2–3.

23. Regina Rifle Regiment War Diary, March 1945, RG24, LAC, 2–3.

24. "Report No. 186," para. 132.

25. Regina Rifles War Diary, March 1945, 2.

26. Stacey, 517.

27. "Report No. 186," para. 136.

28. Queen's Own Cameron Highlanders War Diary, March 1945, RG24, LAC, 3–4.

29. R.W. Queen-Hughes, *Whatever Men Dare: A History of the Queen's Own Cameron Highlanders of Canada, 1935–1960* (Winnipeg: Bulman Bros., 1960), 163.

30. Lt-Col F.E. Wigle, "Account of interview with Lt-Col F.E. Wigle, A & SH of C by Historical Officer, 2 CDN Corps, on 24 Mar 45," 145.2A3013(D1), DHH, DND, 11–12.

31. Robert L. Fraser, *Black Yesterdays: The Argyll's War* (Hamilton: Argyll Fdn., 1996), 393.

32. South Alberta Regiment War Diary, March 1945, RG24, LAC, 9–10.

33. H.M. Jackson, *The Argyll and Sutherland Highlanders of Canada* (Princess Louise's), *1928–1953*, (Montreal: Industrial Shops for the Deaf, 1953), 185.

34. "Record of Operation Blockbuster, as far as it affects the 29 Cdn Armd Recce Regt, Phase II," 141.4A29011(D2), DHH, DND, 3.

35. Wigle, "Account of interview," 13.

36. "Record of Operation Blockbuster, Phase II," 3.

37. Wigle, "Account of interview," 13–14.

38. Fraser, 395–99.

39. Lincoln and Welland Regiment War Diary, March 1945, RG24, LAC, 2.
40. G.L. Cassidy, *Warpath: From Tilly-la-campagne to the Kusten Canal* (Markham, ON: Paperjacks, 1980), 317.
41. "Op 'Blockbuster,' Linc & Welld R CA: 22 Feb 45 to 13 Mar 45," 145.2C3011(DI), DHH, DND, 3.
42. Cassidy, 318–19.
43. *Canadian Army Overseas Honours and Awards (1939–45),* DHH, DND, accessed February 7, 2014, www.cmp-cpm.forces.gc.ca/dhh-dhp/gal/cao-aco/details-eng. asp?firstname=Donald Howard&lastname=MacDougall&rec=id2831.
44. "Op 'Blockbuster,' Linc & Welld," 3.
45. Cassidy, 319–20.
46. Ibid., 323.
47. Geoffrey Hayes, *The Lincs: A History of the Lincoln and Welland Regiment at War* (Alma, ON: Maple Leaf Route, 1986), 100.
48. Jackson, *The Argyll and Sutherland Highlanders,* 186.
49. Wigle, "Account of interview," 16.
50. Argyll War Diary, March 1945, 5–6.
51. Cassidy, 324–25.
52. George F.G. Stanley, *In the Face of Danger: The History of the Lake Superior Regiment* (Port Arthur, ON: Lake Superior Scottish Regt., 1960), 275–76.

25 TAKE THE COMPANY THROUGH

1. Charles P. Stacey, *The Victory Campaign: The Operations in North-West Europe, 1944–1945,* vol. 3 of *Official History...War* (Ottawa: Queen's Printer, 1960), 519–21.
2. Charles B. MacDonald, *United States Army in World War II: European Theater of Operations—The Last Offensive* (Washington, DC: Office of the Chief of Military History, 1973), 181–83.
3. Stacey, 521.
4. Brian Horrocks with Eversley Belfield and H. Essame, *Corps Commander* (London: Sidgwick & Jackson, 1977), 205.
5. Donald Pearce, *Journal of a War: North-West Europe 1944–45* (Toronto: Macmillan of Canada, 1965), 149.
6. George G. Blackburn, *The Guns of Victory: A Soldier's Eye View, Belgium, Holland, and Germany, 1944–45* (Toronto: McClelland & Stewart, 1996), 373–75.
7. Hugh McVicar, "Backdoor to War: A Canadian Infantryman at Hochwald and Xanten, February–March 1945," *Canadian Military History* 4, no. 2 (Autumn 1995), 75–78.
8. Kingsley Brown Sr., Kingsley Brown Jr. and Brereton Greenhous, *Semper Paratus: The History of the Royal Hamilton Light Infantry (Wentworth Regiment), 1862–1977* (Hamilton: RHLI Historical Assoc., 1977), 322–25.
9. Blackburn, 376.
10. McVicar, 78–80.
11. Blackburn, 376.
12. Sandy Antal and Kevin R. Shackleton, *Duty Nobly Done: The Official History of the Essex and Kent Scottish Regiment* (Windsor, ON: Walkerville, 2006), 513–14.
13. Blackburn, 376–77.

14. Antal and Shackleton, 514.
15. D.J. Goodspeed, *Battle Royal: A History of the Royal Regiment of Canada, 1862–1962* (Toronto: Royal Regt. of Canada Assoc., 1962), 545–46.
16. Blackburn, 377.
17. Stacey, 519–20.
18. Ibid., 521–22.
19. Gen. H.D.G. Crerar, "Report by Gen. H.D.G. Crerar, Operations of First Canadian Army 1 Jan–10 Mar 45," 215C1.013(D2), vol. 10636, box 125, RG24, LAC, 12.
20. "Report No. 186, Operation Blockbuster: The Canadian Offensive West of the Rhine, 26 Feb–23 Mar 45," CMHQ, DHH, DND, para. 173.
21. Stacey, 516.
22. "Report No. 186," para. 174.
23. Stacey, 522.
24. Franz Kurowski, *Jump into Hell: German Paratroopers in World War II* (Mechanicsburg, PA: Stackpole Books, 2010), 331.
25. Jeffrey Williams, *The Long Left Flank: The Hard Fought Way to the Reich, 1944–1945* (Toronto: Stoddart, 1988), 252.
26. Stacey, 526.

EPILOGUE

1. Donald Pearce, *Journal of a War: North-West Europe 1944–45* (Toronto: Macmillan of Canada, 1965), 150.

BIBLIOGRAPHY

Abbreviations: AHQ–Army Headquarters. CMHQ–Canadian Military Headquarters. CWM–Canadian War Museum. DHH–Director of Heritage and History. DND–Department of National Defence. LAC–Library and Archives Canada. NARA–National Archives of the United States. PRO–Public Record Office (U.K.). TNA–The National Archives of the U.K. UVICSC–University of Victoria Libraries Special Collections.

BOOKS

Antal, Sandy, and Kevin R. Shackleton. *Duty Nobly Done: The Official History of the Essex and Kent Scottish Regiment.* Windsor, ON: Walkerville, 2006.

Barnard, W.T. *The Queen's Own Rifles of Canada, 1860–1960: One Hundred Years of Canada.* Don Mills, ON: Ontario Publishing Company, 1960.

Barrett, William W. *History of 13th Canadian Field Regiment.* N.p., 1945.

Bell, T.J. *Into Action with the 12th Field.* Utrecht: J. van Boekhoven, 1945.

Bennett, Ralph. *Ultra in the West: The Normandy Campaign, 1944–45.* New York: Charles Scribner's Sons, 1980.

Bercuson, David. *Battalion of Heroes: The Calgary Highlanders in World War II.* Calgary: Calgary Highlanders Regimental Funds Fdn., 1994.

Bird, Will R. *North Shore (New Brunswick) Regiment.* Fredericton: Brunswick Press, 1963.

——— . *No Retreating Footsteps: The Story of the North Nova Scotia Highlanders.* Hantsport, NS: Lancelot Press, 1983.

Blackburn, George. *The Guns of Victory: A Soldier's Eye View, Belgium, Holland, and Germany, 1944–45.* Toronto: McClelland & Stewart, 1997.

Boss, William. *Up the Glens: Stormont, Dundas and Glengarry Highlanders, 1783–1994.* 2nd ed. Cornwall, ON: Old Book Store, 1995.

Bouchery, Jean. *The Canadian Soldier in North-West Europe, 1944–1945.* Paris: Histoire & Collections, 2003.

Brown, Gordon, and Terry Copp. *Look to Your Front...Regina Rifles: A Regiment at War, 1944–45.* Waterloo, ON: Laurier Centre Military Strategic Disarmament Studies, 2001.

Brown, Kingsley Sr., Kingsley Brown Jr., and Brereton Greenhous. *Semper Paratus: The History of The Royal Hamilton Light Infantry (Wentworth Regiment), 1862–1977.* Hamilton: RHLI Historical Assoc., 1977.

Buchanan, G.B. *The March of the Prairie Men: A Story of the South Saskatchewan Regiment.* Weybourne, SK: S. Sask. R. Orderly Room, 1958.

Butcher, Harry C. *My Three Years with Eisenhower: The Personal Diary of Captain Harry C. Butcher, usnr, Naval Aide to General Eisenhower, 1942 to 1945.* New York: Simon & Schuster, 1946.

Cassidy, George L. *Warpath: The Story of the Algonquin Regiment, 1939–1945.* Markham, on: PaperJacks, 1980.

Castonguay, Jacques, and Armand Ross. *Le Régiment de la Chaudière.* Lévis, qc: N.p., 1983.

Cent ans d'histoire d'un régiment canadien-français: Les Fusiliers Mont-Royal, 1869–1969. Montreal: Éditions du Jour, 1971.

Conron, Brandon. *A History of the First Hussars Regiment, 1856–1980.* N.p., 1981.

1st Battalion, the Highland Light Infantry of Canada: 1940–1945. Galt, on: Highland Light Infantry of Canada Assoc., 1951.

Foster, Robert M., et al. *Steady the Buttons Two by Two: Governor General's Foot Guards Regimental History, 125th Anniversary, 1872–1997.* Ottawa: Governor General's Foot Guards, 1999.

Fowler, Robert T. *Courage Rewarded: The Valour of Canadian Soldiers Under Fire, 1900 to 2007.* Victoria: Trafford, 2009.

Fraser, Robert L. *Black Yesterdays: The Argyll's War.* Hamilton: Argyll Fdn., 1996.

Freasby, W.R., ed. *Organization and Campaigns.* Vol. 1 of *Official History of the Canadian Medical Services, 1939–1945.* Ottawa: Queen's Printer, 1956.

French, David. *Raising Churchill's Army: The British Army and the War Against Germany, 1919–1945.* London: Oxford University Press, 2000.

Friedrich, Jörg. *The Fire: The Bombing of Germany, 1940–1945.* New York: Columbia University Press, 2008.

Gill, Ronald, and John Groves. *Club Route in Europe: The Story of 30 Corps in the European Campaign.* Hannover, Germany: Werner Degener, 1948.

Goodspeed, D.J. *Battle Royal: A History of the Royal Regiment of Canada, 1862–1962.* Toronto: Royal Regt. of Canada Assoc., 1962.

Graham, Dominick. *The Price of Command: A Biography of General Guy Simonds.* Toronto: Stoddart, 1993.

Granatstein, J.L. *The Generals: The Canadian Army's Senior Commanders in the Second World War.* Toronto: Stoddart, 1993.

Grant, D.W. *Carry On: The History of the Toronto Scottish Regiment (mg), 1939–1945.* Toronto: N.p., 1949.

Graves, Donald E., *Century of Service: The History of the South Alberta Light Horse.* Toronto: Robin Brass Studio, 2005.

———. "'If only we had the wisdom of our generals': The Kapelsche Veer, 26–31 January 1945." In *Fighting for Canada, Seven Battles, 1758–1945.* Edited by Donald E. Graves. Toronto: Robin Brass Studio, 2000.

———. *South Albertas: A Canadian Regiment at War.* Toronto: Robin Brass Studio, 1998.

Hamilton, Nigel. *Monty: The Field-Marshal, 1944–1976.* London: Hamish Hamilton, 1986.

Harker, Douglas E. *The Dukes: The Story of the Men Who Have Served in Peace and War with the British Columbia Regiment (D.C.O.), 1883–1973.* Vancouver: B.C. Regt., 1974.

Hayes, Geoffrey. *The Lincs: A History of the Lincoln and Welland Regiment at War.* Alma, ON: Maple Leaf Route, 1986.

Hickey, R.M. *The Scarlet Dawn.* Campbelltown, NB: Tribune, 1949.

History of 2 Canadian Survey Regiment. N.p., [194?].

Horrocks, Brian, with Eversley Belfield and H. Essame. *Corps Commander.* London: Sidgwick & Jackson, 1977.

Hutchison, Paul P. *Canada's Black Watch: The First Hundred Years, 1862–1962.* Montreal: Black Watch (RHR) of Canada, 1962.

Jackson, H.M. *The Argyll and Sutherland Highlanders of Canada (Princess Louise's), 1928–1953.* N.p., 1953.

———. *The Sherbrooke Regiment (12th Armoured Regiment).* N.p., 1958.

Kaufman, David, and Michiel Horn. *A Liberation Album: Canadians in the Netherlands, 1944–45.* Toronto: McGraw-Hill Ryerson, 1980.

Kembar, Arthur K. *The Six Years of 6 Canadian Field Regiment Royal Canadian Artillery: September 1939–September 1945.* Amsterdam: Town Printing, 1945.

Kerry, A.J., and W.A. McDill. *History of the Corps of Royal Canadian Engineers.* Vol. 2 (1936–46). Ottawa: Military Engineers Assoc. of Canada, 1966.

Kurowski, Franz. *Jump into Hell: German Paratroopers in World War II.* Mechanicsburg, PA: Stackpole Books, 2010.

Luxton, Eric, ed. *1st Battalion, the Regina Rifles Regiment, 1939–1946.* Regina: The Regt., 1946.

MacDonald, Charles B. *United States Army in World War II: European Theater of Operations—The Last Offensive.* Washington, DC: Office of the Chief of Military History, 1973.

MacDonald, C.M. *The Battle of Hürtgen Forest.* New York: J.B. Lippincott, 1963.

Manrho, John, and Ron Pütz. *Bodenplatte: The Luftwaffe's Last Hope.* Mechanicsburg, PA: Stackpole Books, 2010.

Marchand, Gérard. *Le Régiment de Maisonneuve vers la victoire, 1944–1945.* Montreal: Les Presses Libres, 1980.

Marsh, Elizabeth (Kennedy), and Russell Kennedy. *Boats, Bridges & Valour: The 23rd Field Company, Royal Canadian Engineers in WWII.* Ottawa: Doculink International, 2008.

Martin, Charles Cromwell. *Battle Diary: From D-Day and Normandy to the Zuider Zee and VE.* Toronto: Dundurn, 1994.

Martin, H.G. *The History of the Fifteenth Scottish Division, 1939–1945.* London: William Blackwood & Sons, 1948.

McAndrew, Bill. *Liberation: The Canadians in Europe.* Montreal: Éditions Art Global, 1995.

McNorgan, Michael R. *The Gallant Hussars: A History of the 1st Hussars Regiment.* Aylmer, ON: 1st Hussars Cavalry Fund, 2004.

Mein, Stewart A.G. *Up the Johns! The Story of the Royal Regina Rifles.* North Battleford, SK: Turner-Warwick, 1992.

Moir, John S., ed. *History of the Royal Canadian Corps of Signals, 1903–1961*. Ottawa: Corps Committee, RCCS, 1962.

Montgomery, Bernard Law. *The Memoirs of Field-Marshal the Viscount Montgomery of Alamein, K.G.* London: Collins, 1958.

Moulton, J.L. *Battle for Antwerp: The Liberation of the City and the Opening of the Scheldt, 1944*. New York: Hippocrene Books, 1978.

Palamountain, Edgar W.I. *Taurus Pursuant: A History of the 11th Armoured Division*. Germany: Printing and Stationery Service, British Army of the Rhine, 1945.

Pearce, Donald. *Journal of a War: North-West Europe 1944–45*. Toronto: Macmillan of Canada, 1965.

Portugal, Jean E. *We Were There: The Navy, the Army and the RCAF—A Record for Canada*. 7 vols. Shelburne, ON: Battered Silicon Dispatch Box, 1998.

Queen-Hughes, R.W. *Whatever Men Dare: A History of the Queen's Own Cameron Highlanders of Canada, 1935–1960*. Winnipeg: Bulman Bros., 1960.

Regimental History of the Governor General's Foot Guards, The. Ottawa: Mortimer, 1948.

Reid, Brian A. *Named by the Enemy: A History of the Royal Winnipeg Rifles*. Winnipeg: Royal Winnipeg Rifles, 2010.

Roberts, James Alan. *The Canadian Summer: The Memoirs of James Alan Roberts*. Toronto: University of Toronto Press, 1981.

Rogers, R.L. *History of the Lincoln and Welland Regiment*. Montreal: Industrial Shops for the Deaf, 1954.

Rollerfson, M.O., ed. *Green Route Up: 4 Canadian Armoured Division*. N.p.: 1945.

Roy, Reginald. *Ready for the Fray: The History of the Canadian Scottish Regiment (Princess Mary's), 1920 to 1955*. Vancouver: Evergreen Press, 1958.

Sliz, John. *The Storm Boat Kings: The 23rd RCE at Arnhem 1944*. St. Catharines, ON: Vanwell, 2009.

Spencer, Robert A. *History of the Fifteenth Canadian Field Regiment, Royal Canadian Artillery: 1941 to 1944*. New York: Elsevier, 1944.

Stacey, C.P. *The Victory Campaign: The Operations in North-West Europe, 1944–1945*. Vol. 3 of *Official History of the Canadian Army in the Second World War*. Ottawa: Queen's Printer, 1960.

Stanley, George F.G. *In the Face of Danger: The History of the Lake Superior Regiment*. Port Arthur, ON: Lake Superior Scottish Rgt., 1960.

Thompson, R.W. *The Battle for the Rhineland*. London: Hutchinson, 1958.

Vokes, Chris. *Vokes: My Story*. Ottawa: Gallery Books, 1985.

Ward, Kingsley. *Field of Valour*. 100th Anniversary pamphlet. Windsor, ON: Essex and Kent Scottish Regt., 1985.

Whitaker, W. Denis, and Shelagh Whitaker. *Rhineland: The Battle to End the War*. Toronto: Stoddart, 1989.

Whitsed, Roy. *Canadians: A Battalion at War*. Mississauga, ON: Burlington Books, 1996.

Williams, Jeffrey. *The Long Left Flank: The Hard Fought Way to the Reich, 1944–1945*. Toronto: Stoddart, 1988.

Wilmot, Chester. *The Struggle for Europe*. London: Collins, 1952.

JOURNAL ARTICLES

Bennett, David. "A Bridge Too Far: The Canadian Role in the Evacuation of the British 1st Airborne Division from Arnhem–Oosterbeek, September 1944." *Canadian Military Journal* 6, no. 4 (Winter 2005–2006): 95–101.

Brown, D. Gordon. "The Battle of Moyland Wood: The Regina Rifle Regiment, 16–19 February 1945." *Canadian Military History* 6, no. 1 (Spring 1997): 101–08.

Golding, Jack. "Renowned Regiment from Prairies Boosts Boche from Calcar Hills." *The Maple Leaf.* N.p., n.d. Unformatted copy in the author's possession.

McVicar, Hugh. "Backdoor to War: A Canadian Infantryman at Hochwald and Xanten, February–March 1945." *Canadian Military History* 4, no. 2 (Autumn 1995): 75–81.

WEBSITES

Beresford, Meaghan. "My Best Friend," May 2005. *Canadian Virtual War Memorial.* Veteran Affairs Canada. Accessed January 2, 2014. www.veterans.gc.ca/eng /collections/virtualmem/Detail/2663442?Eric%20Greene.

Canadian Army Overseas Honours and Awards (1939–45). National Defence and the Canadian Forces. DHH, DND. www.cmp-cpm.forces.gc.ca/dhh-dhp/gal/cao-aco /index-eng.asp.

Colville, Alex. *Before Zero Hour* (painting). "Exhibition Theme—Battle." *Canadian War Museum.* Accessed December 4, 2013. www.warmuseum.ca/cwm/exhibitions /artwar/artworks/19710261-2031_before-zero-hour_e.shtml.

"Ford, Lieutenant Edward Patrick." Regimental Historians and Authors. *The Calgary Highlanders.* Accessed December 11, 2013. www.calgaryhighlanders.com /prosemusic/authors.htm.

Hayes, Richard E., and Kristi Sugarman. "The State of the Art and the State of the Practice, Battle of the Bulge: The Impact of Information Age Command and Control on Conflict, Lessons Learned." 2006 Command and Control Research and Technology Symposium. Accessed November 30, 2013. www.dodccrp.org /events/2006_CCRTS/html/papers/206.pdf.

"In memory of Lieut. John James Chambers, February 26, 1945." Obituary in The Toronto Star, March 7, 1945. *Canadian Virtual War Memorial.* Accessed January 22, 2014.www.veterans.gc.ca/eng/collections/virtualmem/Detail/2662902?John%20 James%20Chambers.

"In memory of Sergeant Aubrey Cosens, February 26, 1945." *Canadian Virtual War Memorial.* Accessed January 22, 2014. www.veterans.gc.ca/eng/collections /virtualmem/Detail/2662995?Aubrey%20Cosens.

Lucas, Andrew J. "The Land Mattress: Canadian Ingenuity Takes Flight." *Gale Force Nine.* Accessed December 2, 2013. www.galeforcenine.com/Default .aspx?tabid=295&art_id=3779.

"Major-General D.C. Spry." *Juno Beach Centre.* Accessed December 11, 2013. www.junobeach.org/?s=Major-General+D.C.+Spry.

"Spragge, John Godfrey." Soldiers of the Queen's Own. *The Queen's Own Rifles of Canada Regimental Museum and Archives.* Accessed January 3, 2014. qormuseum.org/soldiers-of-the-queens-own/spragge-john-godery/.

Tomlin, Glen. "I'm Paralysed!" *Heroes Remember.* Video of Glen Tomlin interview, March 7, 2005. Veteran Affairs Canada. Accessed November 24, 2008. www.veterans.gc.ca/eng/video-gallery/video/7035.

UNPUBLISHED MATERIALS

"Account of the fighting at Kapelsche Veer (Jan 45)." 215C1.013(D33), vol. 10638, box 126, RG24, LAC.

"Air Plan First CDN Army/84 Gp RAF, Operation Veritable." 215C1.98(D369), vol. 10710, box 157, RG24, LAC.

Algonquin Regiment War Diary, February–March 1945. RG24, LAC.

"Anti-Parachute precautions issued by G.H.Q. Royal Engineers, 26 Dec 44." 215A21.013(D14), vol. 10504, box 55, RG24, LAC.

Argyll and Sutherland Highlanders War Diary, December 1944, January–March 1945. RG24, LAC.

"Attack on 'Keppeln' by N Shore R–26 Fe 45." 145.2N3011(D6), DHH, DND.

"Award Citations, 8/9 Feb 44, Zyfflich." J. Walter Keith file, in the author's possession.

Black Watch Regiment War Diary, February–March 1945. RG24, LAC.

Bond, Capt. J.C. "The use of Smoke support of 3 Cdn Inf Div in op 'Veritable' 7–8 Feb 45, by Capt. J.C. Bond, Tech Offr (CW) 2 Cdn Corps." 225C2.013(D6), vol. 10800, box 215, RG24, LAC.

Calgary Highlanders War Diary, February–March 1945. RG24, LAC.

Canadian Grenadier Guards War Diary, February–March 1945. RG24, LAC.

Canadian Scottish Regiment War Diary, November 1944, February–March 1945. RG24, LAC.

"Captain Douglas Carrick Howat, Recommendation for Award of Military Cross, Originated 1 Mar 45." Photocopy, provided by J. Walter Keith, in the author's possession.

"Conference of Commanders, 2 CDN CORPS, on Operation Blockbuster, held at main HQ 2 CDN CORPS, 221100A Feb 45." 225C2.016(D16), vol. 10808, box 219, RG24, LAC.

Crerar, Gen. H.D.G. "Report by Gen. H.D.G. Crerar, Operations of First Canadian Army from 9th Nov–31st Dec 1944." 215C1.013(D2), vol. 10636, box 125, RG24, LAC.

———. "Report by Gen. H.D.G. Crerar, Operations of First Canadian Army 1 Jan–10 Mar 45." 215C1.013(D2), vol. 10636, box 125, RG24, LAC.

Donogh, Norman. "The Battle of Moyland Wood," January 29, 1997. Unpublished manuscript prepared for Royal Winnipeg Rifles. In the author's possession.

8th Canadian Infantry Brigade War Diary, February 1945. RG24, LAC.

"82nd (US) Airborne Div intelligence summaries 13 Oct 44–7 Nov 44." 255U82.023(D1), vol. 10959, box 296, RG24, LAC.

Essex Scottish Regiment War Diary, November 1944, February–March, 1945.
RG24, LAC.

"Fallschirmjäger General and Commander General of II FS Corps Eugen Meindl: Part
III–Rhineland (15 Sep 44 to 21 Mar 45)." Record Group 549, B Series, Box 10,
B-093. College Park, MD: NARA.

5th Canadian Infantry Brigade War Diary, February–March 1945. RG24, LAC.

1st Canadian Headquarters Army Group Engineers War Diary, September 1944.
RG24, LAC.

Fort Garry Horse Regiment War Diary, February 1945. RG24, LAC.

4th Canadian Armoured Brigade War Diary, February–March 1945. RG24, LAC.

4th Canadian Armoured Division War Diary, December 1944–February 1945.
RG24, LAC.

4th Canadian Field Regiment War Diary, February 1945. RG24, LAC.

4th Canadian Infantry Brigade War Diary, November 1944, February–March 1945.
RG24, LAC.

"General der Fallschirmtruppen Alfred Schlemm." Record Group 549, B Series, box 11,
B-084. College Park, MD: NARA.

Gray, Capt. R.F. "Op 'Veritable' Rpt by Hist Offr, 3 Cdn Inf Div, Capt. R.F. Gray, 17
Mar 45." 235C3.011(D4), vol. 10907, box 269, RG24, LAC.

"GS Account of Blockbuster 4 CAD forwarded by His Offr." 245C4.013(D12), DHH, DND.

GS Int–HQ First Canadian Army War Diary, December 1944. RG24, LAC.

Herbert, E.O. "Polish Armd Div, 7 Oct 44." Crerar Papers, MG30, vol. 2, LAC.

Heyland, Maj. W.D. "Operation 'Veritable' (8 Feb 45): The Capture of Wyler—Memo of
account by Major W.D. Heyland, O.C., 'C' Coy, Calg. Highrs. Given to Historical
Officer, 2 CDN INF DIV 15 Feb 45." 145.2CI011(D6), DHH, DND.

"Int Rept on Op 'Veritable' 2 Cdn Inf Div 2 Feb 45, V-Air Appreciation." 235C2.023(D3),
vol. 10903, box 267, RG24, LAC.

Johnson, Lt. Col. E.G. "Operation Veritable: Use of the 'Pepper Pot' As a Means of Fire
Support: Account by Lt. Col. E.G. Johnson, C.O., Tor Scot R. (MG)." 145.2TI011(2),
DHH, DND.

Keefler, Brig. R.H. "Operation Blockbuster, Role of 6 CDN INF BDE (26 Feb 45):
Account given by Brigadier R.H. Keefler, Comd 6 CDN INF BDE to Historical
Officer, 2 CDN INF DIV, 16 Mar 45." 265C6.011(D3), vol. 10985, box 310,
RG24, LAC.

Lace, Brig. F.D. "Operation Veritable (8 Feb 45): The Role of 2 CDN INF DIV Artillery:
Memo of Account by Brigadier F.D. Lace, OBE, CRA, 2 CDN INF DIV, Given to
Historical Officer, 2 CDN INF DIV, 13 Feb 45." 142.32011(D2), DHH, DND.

Lake Superior Regiment War Diary, December 1944, February–March 1945.
RG24, LAC.

L'Espérance, Maj. F.J. "Account of Blockbuster given by Maj. F.J. L'Espérance, 21C R. de
Chaud to Hist Offr. 3 CDN INF DIV, 19 Mar 45." 145.2R2011(DI), DHH, DND.

Le Régiment de Maisonneuve War Diary, November 1944, February–March 1945.
RG24, LAC.

Lett, Lt. Col. S.M. "Account of Operation Blockbuster given by Lt. Col. S.M. Lett to Hist Offr 3 CDN INF DIV, 16 Mar 45." 145.2Q2011(D5), DHH, DND.

Lilley, Lt. Col. L.G.C. "Road to the Rhine: Problems of the Engineers (8 Feb–12 Mar 45), Account Given by Lt. Col. L.G.C. Lilley, CRE 2 CDN INF DIV, to Historical Officer, 2 CDN INF DIV, 15 Mar 45." 143.132011(D1), DHH, DND.

Lincoln and Welland Regiment War Diary, January, March 1945. RG24, LAC.

Megill, Brig. W.J. "The Role of 5 CDN INF BDE in Operation 'Veritable' (8 Feb. 45), account by Brigadier W.J. Megill, Comd, 5 CDN INF BDE, Given to Historical Officer, 2 CDN INF DIV, 11 Feb 45." 265C5.011(D4), vol. 10985, box 310, RG24, LAC.

"Misc interrogation reports Oct/Dec 44, 2 Cdn Inf Div." 235C2.023(D5), vol. 10903, box 267, RG24, LAC.

9th Canadian Infantry Brigade War Diary, February–March 1945. RG24, LAC.

North Nova Scotia Highlanders War Diary, February–March 1945. RG24, LAC.

North Shore (New Brunswick) Regiment War Diary, February–March 1945. RG24, LAC.

"Oberst Blauensteiner account." Record Group 549, B Series, Box 12, B-262. College Park, MD: NARA.

"Oberst Geyer Account." Record Group 549, B Series, Box 12, B-147. College Park, MD: NARA.

"Op Blockbuster: Linc & Welld R CA, 22 Feb 45 to 13 Mar 45." 145.2C3011(D1), DHH, DND.

"Op Veritable: Pre-Planned Air Support Conference 25 Jan 45." 215C1.98(D369), vol. 10710, box 157, RG24, LAC.

"Operation Blockbuster: 3 Canadian Inf Division Engineers." 235C3.013(D17), vol. 10908, box 269, RG24, LAC.

"Operation Veritable, miscellaneous correspondence 13.13.44-20.02.45." 215C1.98(D368), vol. 10710, box 157, RG24, LAC.

Queen's Own Cameron Highlanders War Diary, November 1944, February–March 1945. RG24, LAC.

Queen's Own Rifles War Diary, November 1944, February–March 1945. RG24, LAC.

"Record of Operation Blockbuster, as far as it affects the 29 Cdn Armd Recce Regt." 141.4A29011(D2), DHH, DND.

Regina Rifle Regiment War Diary, February–March 1945. RG24, LAC.

"Report No. 19, Operation 'Plunder': The Canadian Participation in the Assault Across the Rhine and the Expansion of the Bridgehead by 2 Cdn Corps 23/24 Mar–1 Apr 45." AHQ, DHH, DND.

"Report No. 77, The Campaign in North-West Europe: Information from German Sources, Part IV—Higher Direction of Operations from Falaise Debacle to Ardennes Offensive." AHQ, DHH, DND.

"Report No. 155, Operation Veritable: The Winter Offensive between the Maas and the Rhine, 8–25 Feb 45 (Preliminary Report)." CMHQ, DHH, DND.

"Report No. 171, Operation Blockbuster: The Canadian Offensive West of the Rhine, 26 Feb–23 Mar 45 (Preliminary Report)." CMHQ, DHH, DND.

"Report No. 173, The Watch on the Maas 9 Nov 44–8 Feb 45." CMHQ, DHH, DND.

"Report No. 185, Operation Veritable: The Winter Offensive between the Maas and the Rhine, 8–25 Feb 45 (Final Report)." CMHQ, DHH, DND.

"Report No. 186, Operation Blockbuster: The Canadian Offensive West of the Rhine, 26 Feb–23 Mar 45." CMHQ, DHH, DND.

"Report on Grave Br. Defences d/19 Dec 44." 235C2.023(D6), vol. 10903, box 267, RG24, LAC.

Rodger, Brig. N.E. "Personal Diary of Brig. N.E. Rodger, C of S 2 CDN Corps." Manu 58A 1 114.1, CWM.

Rowley, Lt. Col. J.W.H., and Maj. O.L. Corbett. "Memorandum of Interview with Lt. Col. J.W.H. Rowley, O.C., N. Shore R. and Maj. O.L. Corbett, O.C. D Coy N. Shore R. Given to Hist Offr 3 CDN INF DIV, 16 Mar, 45." 145.2N3011(D5), DHH, DND.

Royal Hamilton Light Infantry War Diary, February–March 1945. RG24, LAC.

Royal Regiment of Canada War Diary, November 1944, February–March 1945. RG24, LAC.

Royal Winnipeg Rifle Regiment War Diary, February–March 1945. RG24, LAC.

2nd Canadian Infantry Division War GS War Diary, February 1945. RG24, LAC.

7th Canadian Infantry Brigade War Diary, February–March 1945. RG24, LAC.

17th Duke of York's Royal Canadian Hussars War Diary, February 1945. RG24, LAC.

Sherbrooke Fusiliers Regiment War Diary, February–March 1945. RG24, LAC.

"6th Canadian Armoured Regiment (First Hussars): Report on Op Blockbuster—Report on Operations Area–Calcar." 141.4A6011(D2), DHH, DND.

16th Canadian Light Anti-Aircraft Battery War Diary, Feb 1945. RG24, LAC.

Small, Dwight. "From Armored Corps to Infantry." Unpublished memoir annotated by J. Walter Keith. In the author's possession.

South Alberta Regiment War Diary, January–March 1945. RG24, LAC.

South Saskatchewan Regiment War Diary, November 1944, February–March 1945. RG24, LAC.

"Stores & Equipment, Memo re use of moccasins 5 CIB d/30 Jan 45." 265C5.082(D1), vol. 10985, box 310, RG24, LAC.

Stormont, Dundas and Glengarry Highlanders War Diary, November 1944, February–March 1945. RG24, LAC.

10th Canadian Infantry Brigade War Diary, January 1945. RG24, LAC.

"The Clearing of Moyland Wood by 7 Cdn Inf Bde: Memorandum of Interview with the Brigade Major and GSO3 (OPS) 7 Cdn Inf Bde, O.C. R Wpg Rif, O.C. Regina Rif, O.C. 1 C Scot R, Given to Historical Offr, 3 Cdn Inf Div." 740.009(D1) DHH, DND.

3rd Canadian Medium Regiment War Diary, February 1945. RG24, LAC. TNA: PRO WO 171/488.

Toronto Scottish (MG) Regiment War Diary, November 1944. RG24, LAC.

20th Field Company War Diary, September 1944. RG24, LAC.

23rd Field Company War Diary, September 1944. RG24, LAC.

"2 CDN INF DIV INT BRANCH No. 1, Op Veritable." 235C2.023(D3), vol. 10903, box 267, RG24, LAC.

Van Doorn, Johan. "German casualties in the Battle of the Scheldt, 14th September–8th November 1944, compiled 22/02/2007." Unpublished document in the author's possession.

"Veritable: Planning Intelligence Dossier No. 2, German Defences: Part III—Order of Battle." 215C1.98(D370), vol. 10710, box 157, RG24, LAC.

Whiteacre, J.A. William. "Valour by Day, Audacity by Night." Notes of presentation to Arts and Letters Club of Toronto, May 2005. In the author's possession.

Wigle, Lt. Col. F.E. "Account of interview with Lt-Col F.E. Wigle, A & SH of C by Historical Officer, 2 CDN Corps, on 24 Mar 45." 145.2A3013(D1), DHH, DND.

INTERVIEWS AND CORRESPONDENCE

Day, M.D. "Manny." Phone interview by J. Walter Keith. January 2013. Transcript in the author's possession.

Goodman, Charles. Interview by author. Saanichton, BC, June 2, 2006.

Pearson, Jack. Phone interview by J. Walter Keith. January 2013. Transcript in the author's possession.

Tedlie, Alfred James. Interview by Chris D. Main. Victoria, June 28 and July 9, 16, and 23, 1979. UVICSC.

Van Doorn, Johan. Phone interview by author. February 14, 2014.

Vogt, C.J. "Chris." Interview by J. Walter Keith. Date unknown. In the author's possession.

GENERAL INDEX

INDEX OF FORMATIONS, UNITS, AND CORPS

Forgotten Victory is the eleventh volume in Mark Zuehlke's critically acclaimed Canadian Battle Series—the most extensive published account of the battle experiences of Canada's Army in World War II. The series is also the most exhaustive recounting of the battles and campaigns fought by any nation during that war to have been written by a single author. His work has led to many prizes including the 2014 Governor General's History Award for Popular Media, called the Pierre Berton Award. In 2006, *Holding Juno: Canada's Heroic Defence of the D-Day Beaches* won the City of Victoria Butler Book Prize.

He has written six other historical works, including *For Honour's Sake: The War of 1812 and the Brokering of an Uneasy Peace*, which won the 2007 Canadian Author's Association Lela Common Award for Canadian History.

Recently, Zuehlke has turned his hand to graphic novels, working with Renegade Arts on a number of projects based on Canadian history. In 2012, he was the co-author of *The Loxleys and the War of 1812*, and in 2013 wrote the script for a sequel, *The Loxleys and Confederation*, published in the spring of 2015.

Also a novelist, he is the author of the popular Elias McCann series, the first of which—*Hands Like Clouds*—won the 2000 Crime Writers of Canada Arthur Ellis Award for Best First Novel.

Zuehlke lives in Victoria, British Columbia, and is currently working on his next Canadian Battle Series book, which will detail First Canadian Army's advance out of Normandy and through the Channel Ports Campaign. He has recently written *Through Blood and Sweat*, a memoir of his experiences in July 2013, when, over twenty days, he and a small contingent of Canadians retraced the 350-kilometre route through Sicily taken by 1st Canadian Infantry Division soldiers in 1943. On the web, Zuehlke can be found at www.zuehlke.ca and Mark Zuehlke's Canadian Battle Series Facebook site.